NAPOLEON AGAINST HIMSELF

NAPOLEON AGAINST HIMSELF

A Psychobiography

AVNER FALK

PITCHSTONE PUBLISHING
Charlottesville, Virginia 22901

PITCHSTONE PUBLISHING
Charlottesville, Virginia 22901

Printed in the United States of America
First edition, 2007

Library of Congress Cataloging-in-Publication Data

Falk, Avner.
Napoleon against himself : a psychobiography / Avner Falk. – 1st ed.
p. cm.
Includes bibliographical references and index.
ISBN-13: 978-0-9728875-6-4 (hardcover : alk. paper)
1. Napoleon I, Emperor of the French, 1769-1821–Psychology. 2. Emperors–France–Biography. 3. France–History–1789-1815. I. Title.

DC203.F24 2007
944.05092--dc22
[B]

2006031114

Dedication

Leon Pierce Clark (1870–1933), an outstanding if little-known American psychoanalyst and psychiatrist, did pioneering psychobiographical work, published during the last four years of his life, which was way ahead of his time. In the last year of his life, Clark published *Lincoln: A Psycho-biography*, an early masterpiece in this field. His *Napoleon: Self-Destroyed* (1929) is the forerunner of this book, which is both an extension of Clark's work and a tribute to it. It is therefore fitting that this book be dedicated to his memory.

Harold Talbot Parker (1907–2002), a prominent and psychologically minded American historian of eighteenth-century France, made more serious efforts to understand and to explain Napoleon psychologically than any of his colleagues. Among his well-known works are *The Cult of Antiquity and the French Revolutionaries* (1937), *Three Napoleonic Battles* (1944), his two volumes on the French *Bureau of Commerce* (1979 and 1993), and numerous articles on the complex character and career of Napoleon, a subject of enduring fascination for him until the end of his life. As a teacher and writer, Parker developed a lifelong interest in the presentation of history, writing on topics of biography and historiography. He enjoyed an international network of correspondents, to which I had the fortune to belong. He read my original manuscript carefully, encouraged me to write this book, put me in touch with Dorothy Carrington, and spoke highly of this book in an interview in *Napoleon* magazine. He richly deserves the dedication of this book to his memory.

Dame Dorothy Carrington (1910–2002), a British writer who spent most of her adult life in Corsica, was Napoleon's finest scholar. Taking nothing for granted, she left no stone unturned in unearthing documentary evidence and did not hesitate to dispute "well-known facts," such as the purported church wedding of Napoleon's parents and his mother's "beauty and generosity." Her *Napoleon and His Parents* (1988) is the finest book on Napoleon's young life ever written. While not trained as a psychologist, her intuitive grasp of human relations was extraordinary. Dame Carrington read the manuscript of this book, liked it, encouraged me to get it published, and corrected my errors. No one deserves the dedication of this book to his or her memory more than she does.

Contents

Part III: Emperor of the French

Part IV: Self-Inflicted Downfall

NAPOLEON AGAINST HIMSELF

Introduction

The English words "history" and "story" both derive from the same Greek word, *historia*, which originally meant "learning or knowing by inquiry." Indeed, history is nothing more nor less than storytelling. Like beauty, history is in the eye of the beholder. The great French writer François-Marie Arouet de Voltaire thought that "history is little else than a picture of human crimes and misfortunes."[1] More recently, the Japanese film director Akira Kurosawa pointed out in his great film *Rashomon* that there can be as many versions of history as there are people who took part in it and as many historical truths as there are historians. Most of us study history because consciously or unconsciously we wish to understand who we are and how we came to be what we are.[2]

Napoleon Bonaparte probably had more effect on the course of European and world history than any other single leader. Certainly he has fascinated more scholars and writers than any other figure in history. He is so popular that dozens of Napoleonic societies and associations exist all over the world. Napoleon's battles are reenacted by soldiers for mass audiences (without the blood and the horrors of the actual events), Napoleonic meetings, exhibitions, and conferences take place, and Napoleonic uniforms, flags, and mementos are sold. The world is forever fascinated by him. Indeed, there are perhaps as many Napoleon fans as there are detractors of the Emperor of the French.

Any serious scholar must begin, one would think, by reading everything Napoleon wrote and everything written about him. However, the sheer number of works by Napoleon and on him is staggering and impossible to determine.[3] The immense amount of material, both primary and secondary sources, by Napoleon and on him, is only part of the problem. Many scholars have observed that Napoleon was a very complex individual, full of "contradictions" and "strange character traits." Most of his biographers were baffled by his multifaceted personality; many of them confessed that they did not really understand him. One French scholar, Jean Thiry (1899–1980), wrote a twenty-eight-volume history of Napoleon and his time without plumbing his subject's psychological depths.[4] Thiry's countryman Frédéric Masson (1847–1923), who published dozens of works on Napoleon, many of them multivolume, confessed in his preface to the twelfth volume of his thirty-fourth work, *Napoléon et sa famille*: "It may seem hardly credible that after devoting thirty years to the study of one man I have come not to admire him more but to have even less comprehension of this extraordinary being."[5] Napoleon's complex character has exasperated most of his biographers and scholars; this sense of mystery has been shared by many writers.[6]

This book belongs to the field of psychoanalytic biography, a special kind of history. It draws on the insights of psychoanalysis to probe Napoleon's unconscious mind. Sigmund Freud was not the first psychoanalyst to apply his insights to Napoleon. That distinction belongs to Freud's disciple Ludwig Jekels, who in 1914 published the first psychoanalytic study of Napoleon. Ernest Jones, however, another follower of Freud, claimed that Jekels had stolen his own ideas, and that Freud himself was to blame for it. Jones had been psychoanalyzed by Freud, and Jekels was Freud's patient. Jones had told Freud his ideas, and Freud communicated them to Jekels.[7]

Another early follower of Sigmund Freud who wrote about Napoleon was the American psychoanalyst Abraham Arden Brill, a founder of American psychoanalysis. Brill rather simplistically believed that "there is no doubt that Napoleon represents the very acme of primitivity" and that we are fascinated by his embodiment of those primitive qualities we can scarcely acknowledge consciously in "civilized" society.[8] Of Napoleon's psychological scholars, however, only a handful have used psychoanalytic theories, and even fewer were psychoanalysts.

Our emotional life is shaped in our childhood. The seventeenth-century English poet John Milton wrote that "childhood shows the man, as morning shows the day."[9] While no psychoanalyst, Raoul Brice, a French military surgeon with the rank of lieutenant-general, thought that a man's early life was the key to understanding him: "To know a man one must study his infancy: the growth of his personality is a continuous process from the dawn of intelligence onwards. The first impressions made on the virgin brain are never effaced."[10] Brice wrote that most of Napoleon's biographers had ignored his early life. "Corsican writers, such as Marcaggi and Lorenzo [*sic*] di Bradi, declare with pride that the genius of Napoleon was inherited with his blood; but they do not go on to prove it. The rest, even the most recent, such as the nimble Emil Ludwig and the perspicacious Jacques Bainville, pass cursorily over the first part of their subject. It is a mere prelude which seems to them of slight importance. Hence, not one of them has understood Napoleon."[11]

To my knowledge, no full-scale psychobiography of Napoleon has yet been published. The pioneer American psychoanalyst Leon Pierce Clark wrote the closest thing to one back in 1929, yet, in Clark's own words, "no attempt has been made to give a complete life history of Napoleon, which any number of biographers have so excellently and minutely done, but rather to touch upon the high lights of his stupendous career."[12] Many biographical studies of Napoleon are riddled with errors, inaccuracies, exaggerations, myths, legends, and falsehoods, or flawed by poor scholarship. Wherever possible, I have tried to correct the errors of my predecessors. If I have fallen into some inevitable traps, or made some egregious errors, I take full responsibility for my own mistakes.[13]

Part I

Between Two Motherlands

1

A Suffering Motherland

Each of us is born into a particular physical and emotional environment. A person's birthplace is a psychogeographic and cultural entity, with its own special history, language, religion, traditions, customs, morals, myths, and manners. To understand a man's development and character, it is essential to examine both the land of his birth and his family of origin, both his motherland or fatherland and his parents.

Napoleon's motherland was Corsica, an oft-invaded Mediterranean island west of Rome. In the fourth and third centuries BCE., the Greeks, Etruscans, Phoenicians, and Carthaginians fought over Corsica's eastern seaboard. The Romans conquered the island in 259 BCE and turned it into a Roman province. From 450 to 1050 CE, Corsica was occupied by the Vandals, Byzantines, Goths, Lombards, Franks, Roman Catholic Popes, and Moors. Pisa and Genoa fought over Corsica until the Genoese took over the island in 1284. Genoa fought the Spanish kingdom of Aragon over Corsica for one hundred and thirty-seven years, from 1297 to 1434, and retained control of it.

Each of these conquerors put its own cultural stamp on the Corsican island. Dorothy Carrington thought that the Genoese treated the Corsicans as inferior, while the Corsicans, "with few exceptions, detested the Genoese as tyrants and exploiters. With some justification: the Corsicans had little say in the government of their country; all the posts of authority were held by the Genoese. Their magistrates were notoriously corrupt and they imposed trade monopolies that condemned the Corsicans to poverty."[1]

Eighteenth-century European society was stratified, divided into the nobility, the clerics, the bourgeoisie, and the peasants. The Corsican nobles suffered from the ruling Genoese, whose Republic occasionally recognized the nobility of some old Corsican feudal families but did not grant nobility titles. Some families claimed that their nobility had been conferred on them by the Papacy in the Middle Ages in return for an obligation to repel Moorish invaders. As we will see later, only after the French conquest of Corsica did the Corsican nobility regain its former status.[2]

During the first part of the eighteenth century the clannish Corsicans fell into two camps. The majority was nationalist and anti-Genoese, while the minority was pro-Genoese. The patriots were fiercely independent people who stubbornly resisted "foreign" domination. Corsica had a national assembly, the *consulta*, in which major political decisions were taken. The Corsican consulta elected three *generali della nazione* (Generals of the Nation) who ran the island. The consulta did not meet regularly but was convened in exceptional circumstances, infrequent before the great eighteenth-century revolt,[3] when the Corsican patriots rebelled against harsh Genoese rule. Their leader was Giacinto Paoli, a rural notable from Stretta di Morosaglia. In 1730 the "rebels" seized the Corsican interior, while the Genoese held the coastal towns. In 1731 Holy Roman Emperor Charles VI, reigning in Vienna, sent his troops to aid Genoa in suppressing the Corsican nationalists. The first Austrian detachment was decimated by the angry Corsicans. The second beat the Corsicans into submission.

In 1732 Austria forced Genoa to give the Corsican rebels some liberties. The following year, the Corsican revolt against Genoa broke out again. In January 1735 the three *generali della nazione*, Andrea Colonna-Ceccaldi, Giacinto Paoli, and Luigi Giafferi, convened a consulta at Corte which proclaimed Corsican national independence and its new system of government, in effect, adopting a new constitution. The three leaders were proclaimed the Primates of the Realm; the Virgin Mary was proclaimed the Queen of Corsica; and the Corsicans made the Catholic chant "Dio vi salvi Regina" ("God Save You, Queen") their national anthem.[4] In 1736 they crowned as their king Theodor von Neuhof (1694–1756), a bizarre German adventurer and former officer in the French, Swedish, and Spanish armies who had landed in Corsica, perhaps escaping trouble elsewhere. Crowned King Theodore I of Corsica, Neuhof left the island—and his subjects—soon thereafter. In 1738, committing the same error that Austria had committed seven years earlier, Louis XV's France sent troops to Corsica to help Genoa suppress the fiery Corsican nationalists. The first

French detachment was crushed by the Corsicans. In 1739 the marquis de Maillebois led a French expeditionary force to Corsica, and the French Royal Corsican Regiment was created.[5]

In 1745 the Corsican consulta elected three new *generali della nazione*—Gian Pietro Gaffori, Alerio Manta, and Ignazio Venturini. British and Sardinian forces intervened on the Corsican nationalists' side against France and Genoa. The eighteenth-century "Kingdom of Sardinia" was an unusual union of four territories: the Italian island of Sardinia, south of Corsica; the Italian region of the Piedmont; the Franco-Italian duchy of the Savoy; and the French-speaking county of Nice. These four regions were not all contiguous, nor did they all speak the same language. Sardinia-Piedmont-Savoy, fearing French rule in neighboring Corsica, allied itself with Great Britain against France. But it was not until 1751 when the *generale della nazione* Gian Pietro Gaffori convened a consulta at the convent of Orezza and organized a Corsican government along the lines of the 1735 constitution. The Corsican consulta adopted this system of government with Gaffori as its head of state. He was assassinated in 1753. His son, Francesco Gaffori, became prominent in the revolt against France, but in 1769 he surrendered to the French, collaborated with them, became *le colonel* François Gaffori, and commanded the *régiment provincial corse*, a French regiment of Corsican collaborators. He later helped the French forces to supress a bloody Corsican national revolt.[6]

During the six years the French administered Corsica, Giacinto Paoli and his family were banished from Corsica and left for the kingdom of Naples. Giacinto Paoli became a colonel of a Corsican regiment in the Neapolitan army. The war against France went on. Giacinto Paoli's son was the famous Corsican nationalist leader Pasquale Filippo Antonio Paoli, known to the French as Pascal Paoli. He is still revered by most Corsicans as *U babu di a patria* (the father of the fatherland). Pasquale Paoli was born on April 26, 1725, at Stretta di Morosaglia, in the Rostino region of eastern Corsica. He began his studies in Corsica, and after his family's banishment by the French in 1739, Pasquale attended the Naples military academy. In 1741 he joined his father's Corsican regiment in the Neapolitan army. In 1749 he was sent to Sicily. Due to its strategic location, Corsica was a battleground for the ambitions of the European powers. One of these powers was Sardinia-Piedmont-Savoy; another was France. In 1749 and 1751 Pasquale Paoli tried to join the French army but failed. In 1754 he was transferred to the isle of Elba, whence he corresponded with his brother and with the Corsican patriots, who asked him to devise a constitution and invited him to return.

In April 1755, Paoli returned to Corsica and the Corsican nationalists defeated the pro-Genoese faction. On July 14 and 15 the consulta was convened, electing Paoli their *generale della nazione*. This island was independent for fourteen years, the only such period in Corsican history, before being annexed by France in 1769.

Ancien-régime France was divided into civilian *intendances* (superintendencies) and into *gouvernements militaires* (military governments). These divisions roughly corresponded to the old duchies and provinces such as Normandy, Brittany, Provence, Burgundy, and the Franche-Comté. Each French province had its own military governor and civilian superintendent. The two officials had different functions. While the governor lived in the provincial capital, near the people of his province, and commanded the French troops in his area, the superintendent often visited the royal court at Versailles, near Paris.

In 1768 the Treaty of Versilles gave Corsica to France. It took the French another year to take possession of Corsica from Paoli's "rebels." When Louis XVI's France annexed Corsica and made it a French province, a military *gouverneur* and a civilian *intendant* were appointed to the island. The duke of Choiseul passed over Louis-Charles-René *comte* de Marbeuf for the post of governor and appointed General comte de Vaux as commander-in-chief of the French forces on Corsica. Deeply hurt, Marbeuf wanted to plead his case in Paris but had to stay in Corsica to fight the "rebels." A French nobleman named Chardon was appointed superindendent for Corsica. Meanwhile, Paoli governed the Corsican interior while France held the coastal towns. After France annexed Corsica, Paoli issued a defiant proclamation to the Corsican nation and bravely but desperately resisted the French occupation.[7]

In March 1769 General comte de Vaux landed heavy troop reinforcements for his French army at Bastia. He was joined there by his fellow general, Jean-François, comte de Narbonne-Pelet-Fritzlar, a hero of the Seven Years War and a rival of Marbeuf. Narbonne used executions and massacres to subdue the Corsican rebels, yet he was far more popular than Marbeuf. "In view of his scorched-earth tactics, Narbonne's popularity is hard to understand; but his victims were after all humble people who had no voice in public affairs, while his supporters were notables delighted to see order restored. According to a French officer then serving in Corsica, Narbonne's forthright character, combining severity with a sense of justice, endeared him to the army, whereas Marbeuf, never a military figure, failed to earn its respect."[8]

To fight the French, the Corsican consulta at Corte mobilized all Corsican men aged sixteen to sixty. In fact, the Corsicans were by no means united on the issue of the revolt. Most of the common people wanted to fight, while the nobility wanted to join forces with France. On May 8 and 9, 1769, French forces massacred Paoli's rebels at the Battle of Ponte Novo. Paoli fled the island, eventually taking refuge in England.

In August 1769 General comte de Marbeuf, in rivalry with Generals comtes de Vaux and Narbonne, left Corsica for Paris to secure his position as commander-in-chief of the French army in Corsica. He succeeded in securing his appointment and returned to Corsica in May 1770 as commander-in-chief of the French forces and military governor of the island. The comte de Vaux left for France, and Marbeuf ruled Corsica. He now decided who joined the ranks of the nobility and who was appointed to political office. A month earlier the French authorities took a census of the Corsican population and created the *Ordre de la noblesse corse* (Order of the Corsican Nobility). Seventy Corsican families were recognized as noble. Some of them were old feudal nobles, others were descendants of corporals who had toppled the former in the *Au-deça des monts* from the eleventh to the sixteenth century, while still others were members of the foreign nobility which had settled in the island.[9] Governor Marbeuf was the real authority. "All blessings and honours flowed from Marbeuf; he virtually ruled the island, together with the *intendant*. But while the *intendants* came and went . . . Marbeuf, as commander-in-chief, reigned in Corsica from 1770 till his death in 1786."[10]

Marbeuf played a very significant role in Napoleon's life. He had a close relationship with Napoleon's mother Letizia over many years and was rumored to have fathered one or more of her children. During the years of his involvement with Letizia, Marbeuf supported her husband Carlo financially and socially, helping him achieve noble status, obtain legal positions, and finance his economic projects. Marbeuf's nephew, Yves-Alexandre de Marbeuf, was the bishop of Autun and later the archbishop of Lyon. He too helped Napoleon and his family. As we shall see, Napoleon had strong and ambivalent feelings about Marbeuf, which in turn affected his feelings about Corsica and France.

2

A Conflicted Marriage

Many scholars believed that in 1796 Napoleon changed his last name from Buonaparte to Bonaparte, to make it sound more French.[1] In fact, both spellings of the name were used by members of Napoleon's family in official documents. Name-spelling consistency and accuracy did not bother eighteenth-century Europeans as it does us today. Napoleon's ancestors in Italy were called Buonaparte. After they moved to Corsica in the sixteenth century, some of them spelled their name Bonaparte, but Napoleon's father spelled it Buonaparte. The French military hospital of Val-de-Grace in Paris has a letter from Napoleon signed Buonaparte. He used both spellings until 1796, when he took command of the French *armée d'Italie*, and even during his Italian campaign of 1796–97. When Napoleon entered French politics in 1797, he dropped the spelling of Buonaparte and began to spell his name Bonaparte.[2]

The name Buonaparte first appeared in a Tuscan document of 1122, which mentions an officer named Ugo fighting for Friedrich the One-eyed, duke of Swabia and nephew of the German king and Holy Roman Emperor Heinrich V, to conquer Tuscany from the pope. The pope and the Holy Roman Emperor were, as always, struggling for supremacy. Ugo's nephew became a member of the Florentine *signoria* (governing council) and took the name of Ugo della Buonaparte, from the Italian words *della buona parte* (of the good party). To Ugo, the "good party" was that of the emperor; the "bad party" was the papal one. The name Buonaparte was borne by several late-medieval families in Liguria and Tuscany; one of these families had settled near the Tuscan capital of Florence in the eleventh century. In the thirteenth century this family split into two branches. One of them settled in the Tuscan town of San Miniato, southwest of Florence, the other in the Ligurian seaport town of Sarzana, near La Spezia, across the border from Tuscany.[3]

In 1520, shortly after the Genoese had built Ajaccio's ramparts in Corsica, Francesco Buonaparte of Sarzana, a swarthy Tuscan mercenary known as *Il Moro di Sarzana* (the Moor of Sarzana), moved to Ajaccio, where Genoa kept its garrisons. In Corsica the name Buonaparte later became Bonaparte; Napoleon was Francesco's eighth descendant.[4] Because its members were the elders of the town, the Ajaccio City Council was called *il consiglio degli anziani* (the council of the elders). The Bonapartes were elected *anziani* of Ajaccio in every generation from the late sixteenth century to 1764. In the late seventeenth century the Bonapartes began to intermarry with the Bozzi, acquiring their house and annexing it to theirs in the process.

The name Maria was ubiquitous in Corsica. In the Corsican soul, the Virgin Mary had replaced the *magna mater* (Great Mother) goddess of pagan antiquity. Her ubiquity in Corsica attests to the great emotional power of the mother in the Corsican mind. Due to her maternal aspects, the cult of the Virgin Mary was prominent among the Roman Catholic Corsicans. Many Corsican girls were named Maria, and many Corsican boys had Maria as a middle name.[5] Thus, Napoleon's paternal great great great grandfather was named Carlo Maria, as was Napoleon's father; Napoleon's maternal great grandfather was named Giuseppe Maria; Napoleon's maternal grandmother was named Angela Maria; his paternal grandfather was named Giuseppe Maria; and his mother was named Maria Letizia. Napoleon himself would have several lovers named Maria or Marie, and a second wife named Marie-Louise.

The typical Corsican family was fusional. Personal boundaries between parents and children were not clear. Family members shared first or middle names as well as last names. The three commissioners sent to Corsica by the French *Convention nationale* in 1792 to determine its value to France reported: "One is not a Corsican without belonging to a family . . . There reigns in this island a fanaticism of relationship which binds the members of a family together so tightly that the feelings and actions of a single individual become the common and inalienable property of all; whence it follows that as soon as a man is on his feet he forthwith tries every means, undeterred by any scruple, to put all his relations on their feet also."[6] The sharing of Christian names among family members was not the *cause* of the fusional quality of the Corsican family but rather its *symptom*.

Napoleon's father, Carlo Maria Buonaparte, son of Giuseppe Maria and Maria Saveria Bonaparte, was born in Ajaccio on March 27, 1746.[7] Little is known about Carlo's early life. When he was three, the French general who administered Corsica for Genoa, the marquis de Cursay, convened a consulta at Corte. Carlo's father, Giuseppe, represented Ajaccio at this assembly. Giuseppe and his brother-in-law Paravisino welcomed the marquis de Cursay in Ajaccio. In 1759, when Carlo was thirteen, his father Giuseppe and Giuseppe's brother Luciano obtained a formal recognition of kinship from the noble Buonapartes of Tuscany. The original French scholar Joseph Valynseele thought that his was "no more than an adoption, unsupported by any authentic documents linking the Buonaparte of Tuscany with those of Sarzana." Nonetheless, this was a real achievement for these upwardly mobile Corsicans.[8]

Until he was twelve, Carlo attended a Jesuit college in Ajaccio. His father wanted him to study law, the traditional family occupation, but the artistic Carlo preferred poetry. When he was fourteen, he suffered two serious losses: his paternal grandmother, Maria Anna Tusoli Bonaparte, and his only brother, Sebastiano, who was still a child, died in quick succession. The loss of his beloved grandmother especially affected the young Carlo deeply. While he did not name any of his sons after his dead brother, he named at least two of his daughters, perhaps even three, after his dead grandmother.[9]

When Carlo was seventeen, he suffered yet another loss, when his father, Giuseppe, died. Six months earlier his only sister, the twenty-two-year-old Geltruda, had married her cousin, Nicolò Luigi Paravisino. To Carlo, who had already lost his beloved grandmother and kid brother, and who needed his only sister for emotional support, Geltruda's marriage was an emotional abandonment. Geltruda was a combative virago who rode horses and fought battles.[10]

His father's death in late 1763 was a very serious blow to the teenage Carlo. He felt his loss and his abandonment keenly. Orphaned, abandoned by all his loved ones except his mother, and unable to mourn his loss, Carlo sought to restore it. He fell in love with Signorina Forcioli, a young woman who was somewhat older than him and without noble birth or beauty.[11] Deeply concerned with noble birth and reputation, Napoleon's uncles forced him to marry Maria Letizia Ramolina in a church wedding that supposedly took place on June 2, 1764. In fact, it did not (see below). Unfortunately, Carlo's "flame" for the older lady was so bright that he did not love the younger woman he married.[12]

Napoleon's mother Letizia was the chief emotional influence on his young life and has been the subject of numerous studies. Like her husband, she came from an upwardly mobile Corsican family; like him, she was a teenage orphan. As we have seen, in 1770 the French government created the *Ordre de la noblesse corse*. Membership in the order bestowed many privileges. Many Corsican families began actively searching for noble ancestry; many faked old documents to "prove" their relations to noble Italian families. The ambitious Ramolinos looked as far as Milan, Florence, Genoa, and Naples and succeeded in faking their nobility.[13]

Napoleon's maternal great grandfather, Giovann' Agostino Ramolino, had two sons, Giovann' Geronimo Ramolino III and Bernardino Ramolino. Giovann' Geronimo was Letizia's father. In 1743 the twenty-year-old Giovann' Geronimo was made captain of infantry and cavalry and commander of the troops at Ajaccio. Later he became inspector of roads and bridges of Ajaccio province and in 1750 was appointed chancellor of the Genoese jurisdiction at Bocognano, between Ajaccio and Corte.

Like the rest of eighteenth-century Europe, Corsica had a high infant mortality rate. To restore, rather than mourn, their painful losses, *many parents named their children after their dead siblings*, which made these children "living linking objects."[14] to their dead namesakes. In 1743, the year he was named to command the Ajaccio garrison, Captain Giovann' Geronimo Ramolino married Angela Maria Pietrasanta. Their first daughter was born in 1745. Dorothy Carrington believed that this daughter was named Maria Letizia, that she died in her infancy, and that in 1749 her name was given to Napoleon's newborn mother, who was thus a "replacement child" for and a "linking object" to her dead namesake sister. This, however, cannot be ascertained as the baptismal records for the years 1741–60 and the burials records for the years 1739–59 are missing.[15]

Maria Letizia, Napoleon's mother, was born at Ajaccio in August 1749 or 1750. The Italian name Letizia means "joy" or "happiness." *Parents who call their child "joy" are often sad parents who want their child to bring joy to their lives.* Rather than joy, the death of the first Letizia had brought them sorrow. The second would be her replacement. The bereaved husband and wife latched onto their daughter Maria Letizia, who in turn became deeply attached to them. The natural process of separation and individuation, in which a child gradually establishes a "sense of self" separate and distinct from that of its mother, was thwarted, however. She developed a symbiotic and narcissistic mode of attaching herself to others. When Letizia was only five- or six-years-old, she suffered a terrible blow: her father died, leaving the girl feeling abandoned and unable to let go and to separate properly.[16]

Was Letizia beautiful? Many Napoleon biographers believed so.[17] In fact, Maria Letizia Bonaparte was an austere, hard, and severe woman, and by no means a beautiful one: Letizia's portraits "reveal a woman whose mouth was too small, whose nose was too long and whose face was too austere for a claim to real beauty to be advanced."[18] Most likely Letizia's hardness and severity of character were her unconscious defenses against the harsh world of her childhood. She lost her father as a child, and it is not at all certain that her mother could give her the warmth and understanding that she needed. When she was seven or eight, Letizia acquired a stepfather, François Fesch, a Swiss officer. Five years later, when Letizia was twelve or thirteen, her mother gave birth to a son, Joseph Fesch, a future cardinal of the Roman Catholic Church who would play a key role in Napoleon's life. Letizia became stingy and greedy.[19] Her son in turn felt rejected, abandoned, and deprived by her. His rage toward her was denied; as we will see it came through in his lifelong struggle with her, in which money played no less a part than power.[20]

Most of Napoleon's biographers believed that on June 2, 1764, a Catholic church wedding was held at the Ajaccio Cathedral in which Carlo Maria Buonaparte and Maria Letizia Ramolino were solemnly married. In fact, a church wedding never took place. Carlo was concerned with his wife's dowry, so a *dotal act* was signed on May 31. More than seven years later Carlo made a fraudulent entry in the Ajaccio city register of a church wedding that had purportedly taken place on June 1, 1764. In fact, only a day after that fictitious "wedding," on June 2, 1764, did the bishop of Ajaccio grant Carlo *permission* to marry Letizia. Carlo had not gone through with the wedding.

This "non-wedding" indicates the ambivalence with which Carlo agreed to marry Letizia. At the time of their "wedding," Letizia was fourteen or fifteen, Carlo eighteen; the two orphans "married" each other. Maria Letizia "married" Carlo Maria, who did not love her. Letizia was hard, proud, cold, critical, and domineering. She ruled the Casa Bounaparte with an iron hand. Much later an aging Napoleon reportedly told his Saint Helena physician Francesco Antommarchi that his mother was more masculine than feminine; she had "the head of a man and the body of a woman."[21]

In the fall of 1764, when the teenage Letizia was pregnant with their first child, Carlo's profound ambivalence about his difficult wife and his anxiety about his impending fatherhood led him to abandon her and leave Corsica for Italy. He stayed away from Letizia for more than a year. This abandonment also expressed his despair and his rage at his uncles, who had forced him to marry her. Only after he had lost all his money and got into serious trouble in Italy did the pendulum of his feelings swing back; he forgot Letizia's unpleasant qualities, remembered her pleasant ones, missed her, and decided to return.[22]

During Carlo's eighteen-month-long absence, Letizia gave birth to their first child, who died shortly thereafter. In the late nineteenth century, the French scholar Léonce de Brotonne claimed that this child was *a boy* named Napoleone, and that Napoleon was named after him.[23] This scholar gave no evidence for this unsupported assertion, yet many other scholars copied the error.[24] In fact, Carlo Buonaparte said in his memoirs that his first child was *a girl*. Carrington found "no contemporary evidence to support the contention of certain writers that it was a boy called Napoleon, and Carlo would hardly have forgotten so important an event to a Corsican as the birth of his eldest son."[26]

Having lost his own father only two years earlier, the young Carlo found an idealized father in Pasquale Paoli. Returning to Corsica in November 1765, Carlo "resolved to throw in his lot with Paoli."[26] Upon landing in Bastia, however, Carlo approached both Paoli and Paoli's French enemy Marbeuf seeking help. In December 1765 Carlo began to study law at the newly established Università di Corte, once more abandoning his wife Letizia in Ajaccio. The ambitious Carlo knew where his bread was buttered. The next year, he published a Latin-language treatise on the ethics of the law of nature and men, dedicating it to "Paschali de Paoli, Supremo Duci Regno Corsicæ, Publicæ felicitatis, secundum Deum, Authori" (to Pasquale de Paoli, the Supreme Ruler of the Kingdom of Corsica, the Author, after God, of Public Happiness). Carlo signed it "Carolus Bonaparte, Patritius Adjacensis" (Carlo Buonaparte, Patrician of Ajaccio).[27]

Most of Napoleon's biographers believed that his eighteen-year-old father joined the patriotic Corsican struggle against Genoese rule right after his wedding in 1764 and that he was Paoli's personal aide-de-camp. In fact, Carlo was careful not to endanger himself and was busy solving his personal problems. From 1766 to 1768 Carlo was one of Paoli's unofficial secretaries, but, contrary to Napoleonic myth, he was never Paoli's "secretary of state," aide-de-camp, adjutant, or a member of the consulta.[28]

Carlo's marital unhappiness did not prevent him from getting his wife pregnant again after he returned to Ajaccio in late 1765. In the fall of 1766 Letizia probably did give birth to a second baby girl, who also died in infancy. Like the first dead daughter, her name may have been Maria Anna. A third daughter, who was born in 1771 and also died in infancy, and a fourth, who was born in 1777 and survived, were baptized Maria Anna. Did the teenage Letizia grieve? Did she feel sad, sorry, or guilty at the deaths of her baby girls? *With each successive daughter whom she named Maria Anna, Letizia hoped to replace the dead ones that she had lost.* She wished to *restore* her losses, not to mourn them. She also wished to restore her estranged husband. Unable to mourn her losses, Letizia compensated herself by overspending on clothes.[29]

After long and repeated separations beginning soon after their 1764 "wedding," in 1767 the ambivalent Carlo finally decided to "keep house" with Letizia, bringing her to join him at Corte. From 1765 to 1784 Carlo and Letizia had thirteen children; five of them died, two at birth and three in their infancy. Eight children survived.[30]

Carlo and Letizia's third child—and the first surviving one—a son, was born at Corte on January 7, 1768, during the Corsican revolt against France. He was baptized the following day. His given Italian name was Giuseppe (Joseph), after Carlo's father. Letizia became pregnant with Napoleon only ten months later in November 1768. During the nine months of her pregnancy the Corsicans were fighting the French, and Letizia, affected by the fighting, suffered many physical and emotional tribulations, including "trials, anxieties, privations, and sleeplessness."[31] On January 12, 1769, a guilt-ridden Paoli remembered that he had not paid his loyal aide Carlo. Paoli wrote his treasurer in Murato, "I have never given anything to Bonaparte who has served [me] with such punctuality and devotion all through the war," and asked the treasurer to pay Bonaparte two hundred lire for his war services. Carlo received his money and let his pregnant wife enjoy it.[32]

Letizia compensated herself for her hardships by overspending on expensive clothes. On March 13, 1769, "when Corsican independence was threatened by French invasion, and Paoli was calling on every man and boy to hold a gun," she wrote her maternal grandfather, Giuseppe Maria Pietrasanta, in Bastia asking for "a dress of nobility" and a silk dress, which Dorothy Carrington called "a wardrobe of smart clothes."[33]

After Paoli's tragic defeat by the French at Ponte Novo in May 1769, Carlo Bonaparte stayed behind in Corsica. He returned to French-occupied Corte and brought his wife Letizia and his son Joseph back to Ajaccio, where he pondered his future. Carlo quickly tried to ingratiate himself with the new rulers.[34]

Jean-Raymond Frugier, a French neuropsychiatrist, believed that during the nine months of her pregnancy with Napoleon (November 1768 to August 1769), due to the abnormal physical circumstances of the war in Corsica, Maria Letizia Bonaparte was in a state of "violent nervous tension," and that this "in all probability" affected the "vago-sympathetic equilibrium" of the infant before his birth. The traumas that Napoleon had suffered *in utero* may have been the origin of the tremendous nervous energy that he deployed throughout his life.[35] While we do not know enough about intrauterine life, this idea cannot be dismissed. At the same time, as we shall see, Letizia's difficult character and her tormented emotional relationship with Napoleon may have had a much greater effect on her son's development than her tensions during her pregnancy had on his prenatal life.

3

No Milk for Napoleon

Napoleon was born at Ajaccio on the Feast of the Assumption of the Virgin Mary, August 15, 1769. Had he been born a girl, he would almost certainly have been named Anna Maria. Indeed, his mother probably expected and wanted a baby girl, to make up for her previous losses of two baby daughters. For the rest of his life, Napoleon's gender identity was a major psychological issue for him. The name Maria was as ubiquitous in Corsica as it was significant to Napoleon. All the important women in his life bore that name.

Napoleon was born into a warlike environment. He was delivered by *mammuccia* Caterina, a feisty old family retainer. Napoleonic myth has it that "the crusty, quarrelsome old servant . . . laid him, screaming, on a carpet in which were woven [battle] scenes from the *Iliad* and *Odyssey*."[1] Letizia denied the story of the carpet. Letizia recalled that Napoleon's birth was smooth and painless. Had she forgotten her battle with *mammuccia* Caterina, her servant and midwife? The aging Napoleon told his physician Antommarchi on Saint Helena: "I entered the world in the arms of *mammuccia* Caterina. She was stubborn, difficult, continually at war with those around her." The Italian word *mammuccia* is an affectionate diminutive of *mamma*, which comes from the infant's babbling, *ma*, *ma*, and means both "breast" and "mother." Like Letizia herself, Caterina was aggressive and domineering. She fought Letizia tooth and nail for control of the birth and of the newborn child.[2]

Was Napoleon a wanted child? Psychologically, he was born into a war on all fronts: between his nation and France, between his mother and her midwife, between his mother and herself. Letizia had wanted a child, but not a boy. Letizia, who reportedly nursed all of her children, often said that she had breast-fed Napoleon. Yet, a year before she died, Letizia admitted to her companion that she had *not* nursed Napoleon. The conflicting versions of Letizia's story indicate her deep ambivalence about her son Napoleon. Why did she not nurse Napoleon herself? Brice thought that Letizia "was unable" to do so. Parker thought that "her milk failed." Why did Letizia, who apparently had enough milk for all her other children, have no milk for Napoleon? There might have been deep psychological reasons for it. Letizia and her son Napoleon had an uneasy relationship from his birth. Brice thought that Napoleon was a sickly child who was not expected to live. He was also an unappealing baby who repelled his mother and made her unhappy. Letizia feared that he would die just like her first two children. She might have feared investing her feelings in him only to lose him and therefore avoided getting attached to him.[3]

Letizia was most likely disappointed, first and foremost, because her new baby was a boy, rather than the girl she had hoped for, and also because, if not downright ugly, he was less pretty and appealing than his elder brother. On top of that, he was also a sickly child. Did Letizia hate her second son? If she consciously loved her new baby, it is fair to assume that she unconsciously rejected him. She naturally repressed this unpleasant feeling. Her rejection of her son was expressed by her body: it refused to produce milk for Napoleon. She gave her baby to be fed by *mammuccia* Camilla Carbone Ilari, the oft-abandoned wife of a local seaman. Camilla slept with baby Napoleon in a back room, and later took him with her to her home.[4] Camilla, whose husband was often away, became deeply attached to the baby Napoleon; she gave him whatever he wanted; when he cried, she nursed him; she catered to his every whim.[5]

The infant Napoleon was surrounded by many women. Those he remembered with affection were *mammuccia* Camilla and her daughter Giovanna, *minana* (Grandma) Saveria, *zia* (Aunt) Geltruda, *zia* Touta, and *minana* Francesca. Napoleon had less pleasant memories of the cantankerous servant Caterina and his mother Letizia.[6] His nursemaid Camilla was the most important person in his early life. The first words Napoleon understood came from the mouth of his *mammuccia*. He was sung to sleep with folk songs, *nanne*, or *lamenti* (*nanne* were cradle-songs; *lamenti*, laments for the dead); she crooned over him, and his imagination was undoubtedly awakened by the simple traditional tales she told him. He took from her lips the tragic soul of his native land.[7] Camilla was indeed a very special person in Napoleon's early life. Carrington thought that a wet nurse was an unusual luxury in Corsica, where every woman nursed her own children. Camilla loved baby Napoleon much more than did his mother Letizia, and he loved her in return.[8]

On July 14, 1771, shortly before his second birthday, an emotional disaster befell the little boy Napoleon. A baby sister, Maria Anna, was born, taking his place in the family and making him lose his beloved wet nurse. As with Letizia's first two daughters, this baby, too, would ultimately die in her infancy and Letizia would have difficulty mourning her loss normally.[9] But Letizia had plenty of milk for the baby girl. After his baby sister's birth, Napoleon was weaned from Camilla's breast and abandoned by his wet nurse, who left the Bonaparte household. He was also emotionally abandoned by his mother, who nursed her new baby girl and neglected Napoleon.

Meanwhile, Letizia realized that her baby son Napoleon was not going to die after all and decided to have him baptized—along with his baby sister. On July 21, 1771, the nearly two-year-old boy and the newborn baby girl were baptized together. He was christened Napoleone, after his great uncle, who had died in 1767. His baby sister was named Maria Anna, after her dead sisters. Governor Marbeuf, already a close friend of the Bonapartes, had agreed to become Napoleon's godfather, but at the last moment he either could not make it or changed his mind, sending Lorenzo Giubega, the secretary or registrar of the *Assemblée des états de Corse*, in his place. Giubega became Napoleon's godfather.

When Napoleon was in his third year of life, he rebelled, and his mother Letizia made him feel ashamed and humiliated by beating him up when he "misbehaved."[10] She punished him for his "misbehavior" because she could not bear her own feelings of powerlessness and humiliation when she was powerless to control him. Thereafter, throughout his life, Napoleon and his mother struggled for power over each other. Many years after her son's death, the aging Letizia told her companion, Rose Mellini, that Napoleon had displayed an *esprit de principauté* (princely spirit) at an early age. So did Letizia herself. The conflict was inevitable. Napoleon both identified with his aggressive mother and defended himself against her domination of him.[11]

Being formally recognized as noble by the royal French government in Corsica after 1770 carried with it many social privileges and economic advantages. Carlo and his uncle Luciano therefore spent most of 1770 and 1771, during which Napoleon was a toddler, gathering or forging documents that would establish them as noble with the French *Conseil supérieur* in Bastia. Since Carlo's grandfather-in-law, Giuseppe Maria Pietrasanta, was a member of the *Conseil supérieur*, two other councilmen examined Carlo's documents, "it being no doubt considered improper that Pietrasanta, a relation, should participate in the task."[12] While most of Carlo's documents were fake, he curiously failed to submit two genuine ones to the council: the *patente* of nobility issued him by the archbishop of Pisa on November 30, 1769, and an attestation from Ajaccio's "principal nobles" dated August 10, 1771, saying that the Bonapartes had always been considered noble by virtue of their marriages into noble families.

The Corsican *Conseil supérieur* was satisfied and, four weeks after Napoleon's second birthday, pronounced the evidence produced by Carlo "good, sufficient and valid."[13] It was a major event in the life of the family. Nobility carried many vital privileges. On September 18, 1771, a month after Napoleon's second birthday, Carlo proudly wrote his wife's grandfather, Giuseppe Maria, that "Ajaccio is stupefied and filled with jealousy by the news of the nobility conferred on the Bonaparte family."[14] The next month, Napoleon's four-month-old baby sister, Maria Anna, died. For Letizia, this was the third child she had lost. She again had only Joseph and Napoleon. She loved the sweet and pretty Joseph much more than she did the ugly and wilful Napoleon. His mother's preference for Joseph was very painful for Napoleon. At his coronation as Emperor of the French in 1804, he "blackened with rage when his old nurse said that Joseph had been a *joli enfant* while he had not." At age two Napoleon was erupting in violent rage at his elder brother, beating, slapping, biting, scolding, and otherwise venting his fury on Joseph.[15]

Nonetheless, Letizia had special feelings for Napoleon. *She saw herself in him more than she did in any other of her children.* Her feelings for Napoleon were deeply ambivalent. On the one hand, she rejected and abandoned her ugly and difficult son, but at the same time she had a narcissistic and fusional attachment to him. When Napoleon was a "good boy" who did what she wished, remained attached to her, and reflected her idealized image of herself, she loved him; if he disobeyed and sought to become separate from her, she rejected him. Letizia, who lost five of her children and was unloved by her husband, latched on to her surviving children, and to Napoleon in particular, making it very hard for him to break away from her and provoking the unconscious feelings of helplessness that shaped Napoleon's power-hungry character.[16]

In 1773, when Napoleon was four-years-old, Giuseppe Maria Pietrasanta, Letizia's maternal grandfather, died. Losing her grandfather was yet another loss for the repeatedly abandoned Letizia. That year she gave birth to a dead baby girl, the fourth child she had lost. Once more Letizia could not mourn her loss. Soon thereafter she packed Napoleon off to school. Many Napoleon scholars thought that it was a *girls'* school. One thought that the teacher-nuns were Beguines, whose order had been founded in the twelfth century by Lambert Bègue (the Stammerer) in the Belgian town of Liège. The Beguine nuns were less rigid than others. They did not take the perpetual vows of chastity and poverty and retained their private property. They could leave the sisterhood at any time.[17] In fact, it was a coeducational school: both Letizia and Napoleon himself recalled that Napoleon began his formal education "at the age of four or five," when his mother placed him in "a little *mixed* school run by nuns."[18]

At the nuns' school, the five-year-old Napoleon fell in love with a "charming" little girl named Giacomina, holding her hand in rapture. As his socks constantly slid down to his shoes, his rivals teased him about both his socks and his love. Napoleon's memoirs agree with his mother's on the lyrics: "*Napoleone di mezza calzetta fa l'amore a Giacominetta*."[19] This lovely Italian verse can be translated as "Napoleon with stockings at half mast makes love to Giacominetta" or as "Napoleon of the half-socks makes love to Giacominetta."

After a few months, Letizia withdrew Napoleon from the nuns' school and placed him and his elder brother Joseph in a Jesuit school run by the *abbé* Recco. Owen Connelly called it "the best secondary school available" in Ajaccio, which then had a population of only three thousand souls.[20] Napoleon competed fiercely with Joseph for Abbot Recco's love and attention. At one time the *abbé* decided to teach history to his young pupils by having them play the roles of ancient Romans and Carthaginians. He divided the class into two camps. Joseph was made a Roman, while Napoleon was made a Carthaginian. This may have revived in Napoleon's mind the painful feelings of being unwanted and unloved by his mother, while Joseph was loved and wanted. He furiously refused to join the losing side. Joseph was forced to swap sides with Napoleon. When they went home, Napoleon was still agitated, and "it took all the authority of our mother to calm him."[21]

When Napoleon was five years old fresh riots started in Corsica. In March 1774 an obscure Corsican rabble-rouser (or hero, depending on one's viewpoint) named Nicodemo Pasqualini returned from Italy to Corsica, inciting the Corsicans to rebel against France. Sixty rebel leaders met. Pasqualini promised them that the exiled Father of the Nation, Pasquale Paoli, would come to their aid with British and Russian ships. A general revolt broke out in June, which Governor Marbeuf severely repressed. Eleven Corsican leaders were executed in the Niolo region, and many flocks were slaughtered. King Louis XV of France died in May. In August, just as he had done five years before, Marbeuf left for Paris to secure his position with the new king. The French army, led by General Jean-François comte de Narbonne-Pelet-Fritzlar and his colleague General Sionville, mercilessly suppressed the Corsican rebels.[22] Narbonne unsuccessfully tried to replace his rival Marbeuf as commander of the French forces in Corsica by gaining the support of the Corsican political leaders and of their representatives in Paris. In May 1775 Marbeuf returned to Corsica with the new French intendant, Bertrand de Boucheporn, who supported him against Narbonne. Marbeuf was a close friend of the Bonapartes, in love with "the beautiful Letizia."

When Napoleon was not quite six, Letizia gave birth to his kid brother, who was baptized Luciano (Lucien).[23] When Napoleon turned seven, his mother Letizia was pregnant once more. On January 3, 1777, Napoleon's first surviving sister was born and baptized Maria Anna. In later life she called herself Elisa (short for Elisabeth). The arrival of his new siblings was also hard on the boy Napoleon, who had already had to vie with his elder brother for his mother's love. He did this in his unique way. On May 5 the Bonaparte tenant farmer, whom Clark called "the family bailiff," brought two young horses to the Casa Bonaparte. As soon as the tenant farmer was gone, the seven-year-old Napoleon mounted one and galloped off to everyone's utter terror. He reached the farm, astonishing the peasant. "Before he returns he inspects the mill and asks the farmer how much corn it can grind in an hour, and being told, calculates that it can grind so much in a day and so much in a week. When the farmer brings the boy back he tells Letizia that if he lives Napoleon will become the foremost man in the world."[24] Is this yet another Napoleon legend? Did he hope to win his mother's love by such impulsive acts? More likely he made her anxious and she reacted angrily.

Meanwhile the American Revolution was taking place. France signed treaties of alliance with the United States and helped the American revolutionaries against their mutual enemy, Great Britain. In Corsica, Governor Marbeuf, in love with Napoleon's mother Letizia, bestowed his favor on her family. The biannual session of the *Assemblée des états de Corse* took place at Bastia from May 14 to July 13, 1777. With Marbeuf's help, Carlo was reelected to the assembly, which chose him as a member of its three-man delegation (one for each estate) that would go to Versailles to see the king of France. The three were received by King Louis XVI at Versailles two years later. Marbeuf lived in Les Missionaires, a Bastia monastery and the finest house on the island. During the winter of 1777–1778 Marbeuf hosted Letizia all by himself at Les Missionaires. This gave rise to persistent rumors of an adulterous sexual affair between Marbeuf and Letizia, and of Marbeuf's paternity of Napoleon' brother Louis (Luigi), born on September 2, 1778.[25] Carrington, however, thought that it was not necessary to postulate such an affair to explain Marbeuf's rational choice of Carlo Bonaparte as the spokesman for the Corsican nobility at Versailles.[26] What matters, however, is how Napoleon felt about his mother's closeness to Marbeuf. The eight-year-old Napoleon must have seen and heard how his mother was courted by Marbeuf. Moreover, Letizia abandoned him during her stay with Marbeuf in Bastia.

Events in Paris affected Corsica. On January 15, 1778, Claude-Louis, comte de Saint-Germain, the old French war minister, died in Paris. He was succeeded by the Prince of Montbarey, a good friend of Marbeuf, who was given charge of Corsican Affairs. The Prince of Montbarey elevated the comte de Marbeuf to marquis de Cargese. Cargese was a Corsican seaport village some fifty kilometers (thirty miles) up the coast from Ajaccio. Despite the protests of those whose lands had been expropriated, Marbeuf built himself in Cargese "a house such as had never been seen in Corsica before, soberly, imposingly French in its architecture, but Italian in the disposition of its grounds, complete with pavilions and orange groves, fountains and cascades, a pleasure palace where he entertained Carlo and Letizia and their children for weeks on end."[27] Marbeuf's house in Cargese was finer than Les Missionaires in Bastia. From 1778 to 1783, the Bonapartes spent many vacations at Cargese; whether or not Marbeuf made love to Letizia during those stays is another question, but certainly Napoleon may have *thought* he did. Whether or not Marbeuf was Louis's father, Napoleon may have thought that Marbeuf was his brother's father, and this had a profound effect on his entire life.[28]

In early December 1778, Carlo and Letizia again visited Marbeuf in his sumptuous residence at Cargese, along with Count Jean-Victor Colchen, the young secretary of the French intendant, Bertrand de Boucheporn. During the visit, Carlo received his summons to the royal French court at Versailles as the noble member of the three-man delegation from the *Assemblée des états de Corse*. That day Carlo left Ajaccio for Bastia, along with his wife Letizia and his two sons, Joseph and Napoleon. The three-day trip from Ajaccio to Bastia was etched in the eight-year-old Napoleon's memory. Many years later he told General Henri-Gatien Bertrand, his grand marshal of the palace: "I was with Joseph. Madame Letizia was in the carriage of Monsieur de Marbeuf. It was a procession that struck me."[29] Carrington thought that this was "on the last stage of the journey, on the recently built carriage road between Corte and Bastia; the longer distance from Ajaccio to Corte had to be covered by horse or mule."[30] Napoleon, however, made no mention of this crucial detail. The way *he* remembered it, Letizia belonged to Marbeuf during the entire journey. He was profoundly jealous of the governor.

4

A New Motherland

On December 15, 1778, Carlo, Joseph, and Napoleon Bonaparte sailed from Bastia to Marseille, leaving Napoleon's mother Letizia behind with Marbeuf. After the sea voyage from Bastia, Carlo and his two sons landed at Marseille and proceeded to Autun. On New Year's Day 1779, the two Corsican brothers entered the collège d'Autun. Here they were no longer Giuseppe and Napoleone but Joseph and Napoléon.

One of Napoleon's fellow pupils at Autun, Jean-Baptiste de Grandchamp, who was Joseph's friend and a future actor, recalled—at the age of eighty-six—that Joseph was cheerful, gentle, and affectionate, while Napoleon was gruff, taciturn, distant, and irascible—a dreamer. When his fellow pupils taunted him by calling the Corsicans cowards, Napoleon reportedly replied that had the Corsicans been fighting one to four they would never have been defeated; but they had been fighting one to ten. "But you had a good general in Paoli," the school master challenged him. "Yes, sir, and I should very much like to resemble him," Napoleon answered.[1]

The nine-year-old Napoleon acted in a haughty manner, provoking aggression and ridicule from his classmates. He was constantly teased by his teachers and fellow pupils about Corsica's defeat by France, about his small stature, and about his other peculiarities. "Inarticulate with rage, he would hurl himself at his tormentors." His outbursts of violent rage were as severely punished by the schoolmasters as they had been by Letizia at home. The unhappy Napoleon idolized Pasquale Paoli and yearned to emulate him.[2]

The ten-year-old Napoleon withdrew to a world of fantasy. He lived in the ancient past. One scholar wrote: "Shunned by his companions, his only friends were the heroes about whom he read—Caesar, Scipio, Alexander. In time the wounds to his self-esteem healed over. Little by little the sensibility of childhood, which is so impressionable and so defenseless, grew more composed. Under the guidance of the giants of the past he was able to endure the long years of separation from his native land—exile in body, but not in spirit, for in his heart he had never left Corsica. All his aspirations were directed there."[3]

The nine-year-old Napoleon's stay at Autun lasted only four months, but to him it may have seemed like an eternity. He did not develop deep emotional attachments, not because he knew that he had to leave after a short time (he did not), but because of his character: "the essential fault lay in his already established personality rather than in the strictness and unfriendliness of his environment."[4] One of his masters at Autun was the abbé Chardon, who taught Napoleon for three months and twenty days, during which time the boy learned French.[5]

On January 30, 1779, with Carlo Bonaparte still on his way to Versailles, the French war minister, the Prince of Montbarey, wrote the superintendent of Corsica, Bertrand de Boucheporn, that he had accepted Carlo's son Napoleon as a scholar in one of the King's "military colleges." The *collège* system being reserved for noble pupils, Carlo furnished the prince forthwith with proof of his nobility, which the prince forwarded for verification to the royal heraldist in Versailles.

In early March, before being received with his Corsican delegation by Louis XVI, Carlo saw some of the most powerful men in France: the war minister, the Prince of Montbarey; the *contrôleur général*, Jacques Necker; and the former war minister and governor-general of Corsica, the marquis de Monteynard.[6] When he received his certificate of nobility from the royal heraldist at his rented rooms in Versailles, he was overjoyed. The certification of nobility paved the way for his son Napoleon's acceptance to the *collège* de Brienne, in the Champagne region, east of Paris. Two days later, on March 10, Charles-Marie de Bonaparte and his two fellow Corsican deputies were received in audience by King Louis XVI at the palace of Versailles. This must have been the high point of Carlo's life.

Carlo was still arranging Napoleon's affairs when he received the war minister's letter notifying him of Napoleon's acceptance at Brienne-le-

Château. Carlo, whose ancestors had fought the Ajaccio Jesuits over the Odone heritage, had nonetheless also tried to get his son into the large Jesuit military collège at La Flèche (the small fort), in the Pays de la Loire, which had been founded in 1607 by the French king Henri IV and later turned into a military academy. La Flèche was a large military collège with almost five hundred pupils. Carlo had also considered the military collège at Tiron. His plans to have Napoleon admitted to La Flèche fell through, but Brienne was good enough for him. The happy Carlo stayed in Paris until April 25, 1779, when he set out for Brienne "to supervise his son's entry to his new school."[7]

Governor Marbeuf, who had helped get Joseph and Napoleon admitted to the collège d'Autun, had become deeply involved in the Bonapartes' affairs: "It is General Marbeuf who holds Louis Bonaparte at the [baptismal] font; through his influence Joseph and Lucien gain bursaries [scholarships] to Autun, Marianne-Elisa is able to enter [the girls' school at] Saint Cyr and [Joseph] Fesch, Napoleon's half-brother [*sic*], is admitted to the ecclesiastic seminary at Aix [en Provence]. Finally, [Marbeuf] procures Napoleon admission to La Flèche and, when these arrangements are changed, to Brienne. Under the influence of Marbeuf, Napoleon abandons his original plan to enter the Navy in order to join the artillery."[8] In fact, it was not Marbeuf but Napoleon's elder brother, Joseph, who made Napoleon give up his plans for the navy and choose the artillery. Napoleon left Autun on April 21, 1779, bidding farewell to his tearful elder brother. Napoleon was deeply, if ambivalently, attached to his elder brother. The easy-going Joseph remained at Autun without serious trouble for several years, seemingly pursuing a clerical career while secretly aspiring to a military one.

Named after the castle of the archbishop of Toulouse, Etienne-Charles de Loménie de Brienne, and popularly known as the château de Brienne, the school had large white and gold drawing rooms, great halls with parquet or marble-tiled floors, a theater, a library, and a large salon in the center of the main building that looked out on the park and *cour d'honneur*. The French system of *collèges militaires*, of which the collège de Brienne was one, had been founded by the Prince de Montbarey's predecessor, Claude-Louis de Saint-Germain, two years before his death, to prepare poor noble boys for a military career:

> Brienne was one of the ten (later twelve) schools scattered about the [French] provinces to replace the École Royale Militaire in Paris

> in 1776, which was judged to be too costly by the minister. In the new colleges some six hundred king's scholars, sons of the poor nobility, were to mix on equal terms with paying pupils, including sons of foreign nobles living in France. Rich and poor, French and foreign, scholars and paying pupils . . . shared the same Spartan conditions. They were to dress themselves in the prescribed uniform without the help of servants . . . keep their hair short till the age of twelve and afterwards only powder it on Sundays and feast days. Each was to live in a separate, sparsely furnished room (the risk of homosexuality was not forgotten) in an uncurtained bed with one blanket only, even in winter, and wash daily in cold water.[9]

These French military *collèges* were set up in old Catholic monastic schools and entrusted to monks of the Jesuit, Benedictine, Oratorian, and Minim orders. The collège de Brienne had an especially rigid educational system. The monks cherished humility, prayer, study, and scholarship and severely disciplined their pupils for infractions of their rules.

Many biographers thought that Napoleon was unhappy at Brienne. Frank Richardson, however, observed that "the common assumption that his schooldays were unhappy is *not based upon anything he said himself.* Not one word of Napoleon's indicated that his experience at school was traumatic."[10] Yet on the very next page Richardson called Napoleon at Brienne "rather lonely and morose."[11] Napoleon did not say much about his feelings. He, like his mother, was taciturn, acting out his feelings rather than speaking them. Napoleon was not happier at Brienne than he was at Autun. He became isolated and melancholic. Another scholar thought that Napoleon's isolation "turned in a vicious circle. His rejection (by his schoolmates and masters) was particularly humiliating because it was provoked not so much because he was a foreigner . . . but because he belonged to a defeated people."[12]

The boy Napoleon spent five and a half years, from 1779 to 1784, at the collège de Brienne, knowing that, if he succeeded, he had to spend yet at least another year at the royal military school in Paris.

In January 1780 Napoleon's mother became pregnant for the eleventh time. It was to be her sixth surviving child, Napoleon's second surviving sister. On August 15 a lonely Napoleon celebrated his eleventh birthday at Brienne; on October 20 his second sister was born in Ajaccio. She was baptized Maria Paola, a name that recalled those of her mother Maria Letizia, her dead sister Maria Anna, and the Corsican leader Paoli. Her pet name was Paoletta; her French names were Marie-Paule, Marie-Paulette, and Pauline. Napoleon did not see Paoletta until 1786, when she was six years old and he seventeen. When she grew up, the immature and "hysterical" sister loved her brother passionately; she called him *Napoleone caro mio* (Napoleon my dear).[13]

Napoleon had a substitute "mother" at Brienne, but he had to share her with the other schoolboys. They called her *la mère Marguerite* (mother Margaret). She was a peasant woman who sold eggs and milk to the schoolboys. Napoleon loved to see her; she may have reminded him of his beloved wet nurse, Camilla.[14]

Homosexual practices were common at eighteenth-century French military schools and other educational institutions. Richardson thought that during the "normal homosexual phase in boys," some effeminate boys played the passive homosexual role of "nymphs" to the active homosexual role of the more aggressive boys. Napoleon, who deeply feared sexuality of any kind, avoided the "nymphs" like the plague. Napoleon constantly quarreled with his schoolmates, often came to blows, and made many enemies by "the austerity of his morals" among the "dissipated youth."[15] At Brienne, Napoleon's friend Pierre-François Laugier de Bellecour was rumored to be a nymph. Napoleon confronted him about this and advised him to desist from homosexual practices. Laugier denied the allegations; Napoleon apologized to him; he later found that the charge was true. Napoleon said nothing, but he later broke with Laugier when they both moved to the École royale militaire in Paris in 1784.[16]

There were some twenty teachers at Brienne teaching six classes. Among them were Father Patrault, the mathematics teacher, and Father Dupuy, the French teacher. Father Henri Lélue, the principal who initiated Napoleon to Brienne, was dismissed shortly thereafter for his lax discipline and replaced by Father Louis Berton, "a gruff, rather pompous friar in his early thirties."[17] The vice principal was his brother, Jean-Baptiste Berton, "an ex-grenadier known as 'the friar in ique' because he used so many words ending in *-ique*."[18] Father Berton seems to have been an emotionally disturbed individual, hard, rigid, vulgar, pretentious, and incompetent. Napoleonic myth has it that Napoleon and his comrades at Brienne hated Berton and chanted crude songs under his window, at which Berton seized "the little Corsican boy" by the collar and punished him with three days confinement.[19]

Napoleon excelled at mathematics, a highly intellectual science, in which emotions are isolated; and the one man who really liked Napoleon at Brienne was his tall, red-faced mathematics teacher, the good-natured Father Patrault.[20] He was also an avid reader. His readings created for him an inner reality of his own. Deprived of maternal milk, love, and warmth, he devoured books instead. "His boyhood, one may say, was one prolonged reading, and from it he retained a rich harvest of ideas and notions."[21] History became his favorite subject after mathematics. Among other books, Napoleon read Plutarch's *Vies illustres* (*Lives of Famous Men*). Napoleon's immersion in history allowed him to escape into his inner reality, to live in the past. He imagined that he was an ancient hero such as the Macedonian king Alexander the Great, the Roman statesman Marcus Porcius Cato, Julius Caesar's assassin Marcus Junius Brutus, and the Spartan king Leonidas, a hero of the wars against the Persians. These fantasies, however, did not do away with his violent rages, his aggressive defense against his feelings of shame and humiliation.[22]

The child Napoleon had suffered narcissistic injuries—abandonment, rejection, punishment, shame, and humiliation—at the hands of his mother. The proud boy was "an unconscious injustice collector."[23] He unconsciously provoked insults and injuries and then reacted to the perceived wrongs with righteous narcissistic rage. He repeatedly clashed with his schoolmasters and schoolmates; his outbursts were severely punished by the Minim fathers. Cruel physical punishment that induced painful feelings of shame and humiliation was common in an age with little empathy for children.[24]

Napoleon found ways of keeping his sense of mastery and self-respect. When he was nine- or ten-years-old, one "brute of a master"[25] found him reading in bed after lights out and tried to punish him by forcing him to wear a coarse, brown, homespun monk's habit and to eat his lunch kneeling at the refectory door. Suddenly Napoleon had a fit of rage, nausea, and vomiting. When the angry quartermaster tried to force him to kneel, Napoleon rolled over on the floor, his whole body contorted, sobbing and screaming, "In my family we kneel only to God! *N'est-ce pas, Maman!* Only to God! Only to God!" He was at last saved from his predicament by the kindly Father Patrault.[26]

Why did Napoleon throw up? Jekels believed that the vomiting allowed Napoleon to escape the unbearable helplessness of his predicament.[27] In this "psychodrama," Napoleon unconsciously screamed at his absent mother. She, too, had punished him severely for opposing her, and he fought her tooth and nail throughout his life. His fit of "nerves" was Napoleon's defense against losing his sense of mastery and self-esteem. Unconsciously, the punitive "brutish master" stood for his mother, and his vomiting may have been an unconscious attempt to rid himself of her unbearable image within himself. Jekels and Clark thought that this was Napoleon's way of defending himself against his sense of helplessness and worthlessness. Napoleon himself believed that he lost his religious faith when he was eleven-years-old—and again it had to do with his mother:

> The decisive moment came when he was eleven, and once again the operative factor was his sense of justice. Napoleon heard a sermon in which the preacher said that Cato and Caesar were in hell. He was scandalized to learn that "the most virtuous men of antiquity would burn in eternal flames for not having practised a [Christian] religion they knew nothing about." From that moment he decided he could no longer sincerely call himself a believing Christian. *This was a turning-point in Napoleon's life.* But *he had inherited his mother's strong believing instinct*, and he was already a person who needed ideals. The vacuum in his soul did not last long. It was filled by the cult of honour, which he had learned at home, by chivalry, which he had learned about in history classes, and by the notion of heroism, which he learned from Plutarch's *Lives of Famous Men*, and above all from Corneille.[28]

In fact, Napoleon did not read Pierre Corneille (1606–1684), the great French dramatic poet, for another six or seven years. Moreover, his loss of religious faith did not come until two years later, when he was thirteen, after his parents' visit to Brienne.

On December 12, 1780, Carlo and his wife Letizia once more arrived at Marbeuf's "splendid mansion" at Cargese to spend Christmas and the New Year with the governor; they stayed for nearly two months, until the end of January 1781, when they returned to Ajaccio. At that time, the French authorities were trying to stamp out Corsican nationalism. One way to do so was to forbid the use of the word "nation" when referring to Corsica.

On Napoleon's twelfth birthday, Carlo and Letizia returned to Cargese to stay once more with Governor Marbeuf. The lonely Napoleon celebrated his birthday at Brienne all by himself. Carlo and Letizia stayed in Cargese until October. Napoleon did well at Brienne. In 1781 he received his first communion. He won an academic prize.

When Napoleon was twelve-and-a-half years old, his youngest sister was born in Ajaccio. She was baptized Maria Annunziata Carolina (Marie-Annonciade-Caroline).[29] Old Count Marbeuf, having had affairs with Madame Varese, the Cleopatra of Bastia, and Madame Chardon, the wife of the superindendent, was still in love with Letizia. Meanwhile, Napoleon lived under the constant stress of disdain by his schoolmates. Like Parker, Carrington believed that the boy Napoleon rejected both religion and sex. In fact, Napoleon had been brought up a devout Catholic. His masters at Autun and Brienne were monks; until he was thirteen, his religious faith was strong. It was after his thirteenth birthday that he "rejected religion."[30]

Napoleon's parents visited him at Brienne in early August 1782, just before his thirteenth birthday. Napoleon's mother was shocked at his sickly appearance.[31] Years later Letizia told Napoleon's interior minister, Chaptal, that she had found Napoleon "alarmingly thin" and thought that his features had changed.[32] She was not only appalled at his physical condition but also at his choice of the navy as a career. The thirteen-year-old Napoleon briefly considered becoming a sailor. He wanted to be like the French naval heroes, Admiral François-Joseph-Paul de Grasse and Admiral Pierre-André de Suffren de Saint-Tropez, who had distinguished themselves during the American Revolutionary War. Letizia later recalled that "she found the students destined for the navy sleeping in hammocks" and "deplored that in the navy Napoleon would have to fight simultaneously water and fire."[33]

After their brief visit to Napoleon at Brienne, Letizia and Carlo Buonaparte left for Paris. "[Napoleon] kept a vivid memory of his parents' visit to Brienne."[34] He found Letizia "belle comme les amours" (beautiful as the nymphs). In reality Letizia was far from beautiful, but beauty is in the eye of the beholder. Napoleon idealized his critical and rejecting mother, unconsciously denying his mother's rejection of him and his bad feelings for her. Napoleon was disappointed with his father, Carlo, whom the Corsican historian Rossi called "more affable than necessary." The aging Napoleon told General Henri-Gatien Bertrand that his father had "affected too much the ridiculous politeness of the age," being overly solicitous to let a monk pass before him through the door.[35]

Bainville thought that the adult Napoleon did not believe in God because "he was too deeply imbued with the eighteenth-century spirit."

He was "a deist with an involuntary respect and a predilection for Catholicism."[36] Cronin believed that the influence of the Jesuits, of the rationalist philosophers, of Napoleon's fellow "cadets," and of his father's agnosticism made him lose his religious faith.[37] *In fact, it was after his parents' visit to Brienne that Napoleon lost his religious faith.* After all, it was his mother's faith that he lost—or perhaps his faith in her. He believed firmly in God, but considered Christ merely a man. Nevertheless, he retained a sentimental attachment to Catholicism. He was touched by the sound of church bells. Sometimes his mother recalled the lights and singing and incense during High Mass in Ajaccio, and Napoleon would admit to being moved. "If I feel that," he asked "what must believers feel?"

5

A Turbulent Teenager

Napoleon's thirteenth birthday on August 15, 1782, marked the end of his often unhappy childhood and the beginning of his excruciatingly difficult and prolonged adolescence. The teenage boy no longer believed in God. His idea of God had derived from his inner images of his parents. Napoleon had lost his religious faith. In normal human development, the second year of life sees the "psychological birth" of the human infant, the first phase of separation and individuation, while adolescence ushers in "the second phase of separation and individuation." The individual physically and emotionally leaves his family of origin. It is a time when the individual is both a child and an adult.

When Napoleon was an adolescent his father Carlo was at the peak of his career. Carlo was a noble member of the Corsican legislature, close to the great men of France, his sons were in French military schools, and his daughter at the finest girls' school. Five-year-old sister Maria Anna (Marie-Anne Elisa) was admitted to the aristocratic girls' boarding school at Saint-Cyr-l'Ecole, west of Versailles. But after returning to Corsica in September 1782, Carlo became entangled in unhappy lawsuits with his rivals and enemies over the properties of Les Milelli and La Badina. In November his quarrelsome great aunt, Maria Giustina Pozzo di Borgo, who lived in the same house, took Carlo to court over his attempt to block her use of their common entrance and stairs, and humiliated him publicly. In early 1783 Carlo Buonaparte obtained a court ruling against her. When Carlo hung his best suit out to dry, the furious Maria Giustina poured urine on it. Carlo went to court again and she was ordered to pay him the cost of the suit.[1] The affair sullied his reputation, however. Carlo also lost the French government subsidy for his seaside mulberry plantation of Les Salines, whose gardener died and whose trees bore no fruit, and his title to his olive grove at Les Milelli.

Meanwhile, in June 1783 the old *chevalier* de Keralio, the inspector of the French military schools, was replaced by his colleague, the *maréchal de camp* Reynaud des Monts. The new inspector did not accept his predecessor's recommendation to make Napoleon a naval officer. He also found Napoleon too young for promotion to the Royal Military School in Paris. Instead, Napoleon was to stay another year at Brienne and serve in the artillery. Carlo was disappointed.

Napoleon was isolated at Brienne-le-Château. Norwood Young thought that Napoleon's ordeal at Brienne was "burial alive among his nation's enemies."[2] One of his classmates, Élie-Charles Balatier de Bragelonne, later claimed that a few weeks after Napoleon's fourteenth birthday in 1783, his classmates teased Napoleon, calling his mother *la joyeuse Madame Marbeuf* (the joyous Mrs. Marbeuf) and his father, who was in reality *l'assesseur* (assistant judge), *l'huissier* (the doorman). The worst offender was a boy named Pougin des Îlets, who called Napoleon's father "a miserable sergeant." The enraged Napoleon challenged him to a duel, and knocked him unconscious, at which he was incarcerated by the Minim fathers. Napoleon wrote Marbeuf, and the governor of Corsica hurried to Brienne to rescue his protégé.[3]

In October 1783 a disaster occurred to the Bonapartes. Following the death of his wife in mainland France, the seventy-one-year-old Marbeuf married an eighteen-year-old French noblewoman. "Whatever had or had not occurred between Letizia and Marbeuf, it was evident that from now on she would cease to be the centre of his affections and the Bonaparte[s] would play a lesser role in his life."[4] After Marbeuf's second marriage, his hitherto generous support for Carlo dried out. Out of love with Letizia, Marbeuf no longer bestowed his favor on the Bonapartes.

Denying painful reality, the blindly optimistic Carlo had unwisely invested all his money in his mulberry plantation at Les Salines. This blunder led to his financial ruin. His health began to falter. But he tried to do whatever he could to advance his children's careers. His eldest son, Joseph, had had a change of heart, opting for a military career rather than the clerical one that his father and teachers had intended for him. The principal of the collège d'Autun had written a glowing report on Joseph's suitability for an ecclesiastical career. On June 30, 1784, Carlo wrote the

French war minister, the maréchal de Ségur, who was ill at the time, pleading with him as "the father of seven children with an eighth on the way," asking him to grant his son Lucien a scholarship at Brienne and to get Joseph into the artillery or the engineers; Carlo made several other requests of the minister concerning the properties of Les Milelli and La Badina.[5] Lucien joined Napoleon at Brienne.

In September 1784, shortly after his fifteenth birthday and another outburst of violent rage at Brienne, Napoleon received a letter from his ailing father announcing that he was returning home to Corsica from his cure resort in France without stopping again at Brienne to see Napoleon. Napoleon answered his ailing father's letter:

> My dear father, your letter, as you can imagine, has not given me much pleasure, but the reason [for your letter] and the interests of your health and of the family, which are very dear to me, have forced me to approve of your early return to Corsica and have altogether consoled me. Besides, being assured of the continuation of your goodness and of your love and of your eagerness to make me come out and to back me in what can please me, how would I not be glad and content? As for the rest, I hasten to ask you for news of the effect that the waters have had on your health and to assure you of my respectful attachment and of my eternal gratitude.[6]

Napoleon's letter to his father went on to discuss his elder brother Joseph, whose decision to quit Autun and to pursue a military career was troubling the younger brother. Napoleon missed his brother and wanted to have him at Brienne, but he rationalized his own longing in terms of Joseph's own good:

> I am pleased that Joseph has gone to Corsica with you, provided that he is here on the first of November [1785], that is about a year from now. Joseph can come here, because Father Patrault, my mathematics teacher, whom you know, is not leaving. Consequently the principal [Father Berton] has told me to assure you that he will be well received here and can come with confidence. Father Patrault is an excellent teacher and has assured me that he will take charge of [Joseph] with pleasure, and, if my brother is ready to work, we can take the artillery examination together . . . My dear father, for several reasons I hope you will place him at Brienne rather than at Metz:

> 1. Because that will be a consolation for Joseph, Lucien and me . . .
> 2. It is not usual at Metz to learn in six months what Joseph must know for the examination; since my brother knows no mathematics, they would put him with the children. These and many other reasons should decide you to send him here.[7]

Napoleon asked his father to send him Boswell's *Histoire de la Corse* and "other histories and memoirs concerning that kingdom. You need not fear: I will take good care of them and bring them back to Corsica with me when I come, be it even in ten years' time."[8] Napoleon did not express his strong feelings for his father, but he said that his younger brother did: "*Adieu*, my dear father. The *chevalier*—Lucien—embraces you with all his heart. He works well and did very well at the public exercise."[9]

At the end of his letter, an anxious Napoleon wrote his father that the inspector of the royal military schools would be visiting Brienne very soon: "*Monsieur l'inspecteur* will be here on the 15th or 16th of this month at the latest; that is to say in three days' time. As soon as he has left, I shall let you know what he has told me."[10] Napoleon ended his letter in the conventional manner: "Your very humble and very obedient T. C. [*sic*] and son, de Buonaparte, *l'arrière-cadet*." It is not clear what he meant by T. C., which is not a common French abbreviation.[11]

The new inspector of the military schools, the *maréchal de camp* Reynaud des Monts, arrived at Brienne on September 22, 1784, to select the cadets who would be promoted to the *École royale militaire*. The French war minister, the maréchal de Ségur, had authorized Reynaud des Monts to admit to the *École royale militaire* in Paris "all the scholars of the little schools who destined themselves for the artillery, the engineers or the navy, who would have distinguished themselves by their intelligence, their good conduct and their knowledge of mathematics." Several scholars thought that Reynaud des Monts chose *five* cadets for promotion to Paris: Nicolas de Montarby de Dampierre, Henri-Alexandre-Léopold de Castres de Vaux, Pierre-François Laugier de Bellecour, Jean-Joseph de Comminges, and Napoleon de Buonaparte. But Montarby de Dampierre had opted for the cavalry; he did not fit the artillery, navy, or engineering categories specified by the minister. Carrington thought only three cadets in addition to Napoleon were chosen for promotion to the *École royale militaire*.[12]

Napoleon recalled that he left Brienne on October 30, 1784. It was a great triumph for him. After five and a half years at Brienne, the teenage cadet headed for Paris to enroll at the *École royale militaire*. "The fifteen-year-old Corsican boy was flung into the pomp and pride of the century which so far he had only glimpsed faintly . . . from afar." At the same time, Napoleon's departure was an emotional wound for Lucien, who, as we shall see, later disliked his "tyrannical" brother.[13]

Upon Napoleon's arrival in Paris he bought a book titled *Histoire de Gil Blas de Santillane*.[14] This satirical novel was written in the first part of the eighteenth century by the French satirist Alain-René Lesage. Vincent Cronin called *Gil Blas* "a novel about a penniless Spanish boy who rises to become secretary to the Prime Minister." Napoleon's choice of this book was not accidental. He had heard of the book and secretly identified with Lesage's hero.[15]

At the *École royale militaire* in Paris the teenage Napoleon soon gave an ultimatum to the teenage "nymph" Pierre-François Laugier de Bellecour, demanding that Laugier choose between him and his homosexual friends. But Laugier could not resist his homosexual temptations. To avoid losing Napoleon, he told him that he no longer had homosexual relations, which was a lie. Napoleon broke with Laugier for being a "nymph" and for having lied to him about it. This rejection provoked rage on both sides and a violent fight:

> The effeminate Laugier de Bellecour, once in Paris, definitely threw in his lot with the "queers," indeed at one point the school authorities had been so disgusted [with Laugier de Bellecour] that they decided to send him back to Brienne, but were overruled by the [War] Minister. When Laugier tried to renew relations Napoleon replied, "Monsieur, you have scorned my advice, and so you have renounced my friendship. Never speak to me again." Laugier was furious. Later he came on Napoleon from behind and pushed him down. Napoleon got up, ran after him, caught him by the collar and threw him to the floor. In falling Laugier hit his head against a stove, and the captain on duty rushed to administer punishment. "I was insulted," Napoleon explained, "and I took my revenge. There's nothing more to be said." And he calmly walked off.[16]

Was Napoleon's rage at the effeminate Laugier his unconscious way of denying his own homosexual feelings, which made him feel bad about himself? The incident with the "nymph" Laugier so upset the "Spartan"

Napoleon that he drafted "A Memorandum On the Education of Spartan Youth" to the French war minister, Marshal Ségur, suggesting that Spartan education be instituted in all French military academies. He never sent it.[17]

By November 1784, Carlo di Buonaparte was terminally ill in Ajaccio. On November 15 Letizia gave birth to Napoleon's youngest brother, who was christened Geronimo (Jérôme). Napoleon learned of his brother's birth the following month. On December 24 Governor Marbeuf's daughter Alexandrine was born in Bastia, cementing his attachment to his youthful wife and further estranging him from Letizia and the Bonapartes.

This time, at the Royal Military School in Paris, Napoleon shared his room with a fellow cadet. Napoleon's roommate was the sixteen-year-old Alexandre des Mazis, who later, during the Revolution, changed the spelling of his name to Desmazis. Alexandre des Mazis was the same age as Napoleon's elder brother, Joseph. He came from a noble military family in the Alsatian capital of Strasbourg. Des Mazis became Napoleon's best friend at the *École royale militaire.*[18]

Masson believed that Des Mazis was Napoleon's only friend in Paris. Carrington believed that Des Mazis "was one of the few human beings Napoleon ever took to spontaneously, without the prompting of family ties, political contingencies or sexual attraction." Richardson thought that Napoleon's relations with Des Mazis were "latently homosexual." If there *was* a homoerotic *attraction* between Des Mazis and Napoleon, there were no actual homosexual *relations*. Their friendship was close, though: it "withstood political divergenceis, two occasions when Napoleon borrowed money, and a literary reproof from Napoleon when Des Mazis fell in love." The two friends later joined the same artillery regiment.[19]

Life at the *École royale militaire* was hard for Napoleon. He felt despised and looked down upon by the sons of the great French nobility. Thanks to the system of admission and selection, the school's cadets came from noble French families. Raoul Brice thought that Napoleon was "humiliated" by "certain rich and well-connected fellow pupils of the *École Militaire* such as the Rohan-Guéménées or the Montmorency-Lavals." Max Gallo believed that from his very first day at the Royal Military School, Napoleon felt that "a Duke of Fleury, a Laval-Montmorency, a Puységur, a prince de Rohan-Guéménée, cousin of the king, looked at him with contempt and then turned their heads away to show that they were from another race, that this scholar son of a little

Corsican noble was just about French because the royal army had conquered his island."[20]

Napoleon's chief enemy at the *École royale militaire* was neither a Rohan-Guéménée nor a Montmorency-Laval but the eighteen-year-old Louis-Edmond-Antoine le Picard de Phélippeaux. This teenage nobleman had been born in the western French province of Poitou. Phélippeaux had entered the Royal Military School in 1781, three years before Napoleon, and remained there until 1785. Napoleonic myth has it that Phélippeaux and Napoleon hated each other so badly that, when placed side by side, they kicked each other violently under the table. Their *sergent-major*, Henri-René-Marie Picot de Peccaduc, sat between them to keep the peace. He received knocks from both of them.[21]

On New Year's Day 1785 Napoleon's terminally ill father Carlo, who was not yet thirty-nine years old, and his eldest son, Joseph, who had been on extended home leave for several months, left Ajaccio for the northern Corsican port city of Calvi on their way to mainland France, where Carlo hoped to get medical help. From the outset it was a bad trip, mainly due to bad weather. On January 7, 1785, Joseph's seventeenth birthday, the exhausted Joseph and his father Carlo reached Saint-Tropez on the French Mediterranean coast after their terrible crossing, where they celebrated Joseph's birthday. The two moved on to Aix-en-Provence. At Aix, Carlo saw a physician, who advised him to see his colleagues at the nearby university town of Montpellier.[22]

Meanwhile, in Paris, like every cadet at the Royal Military School, Napoleon had to make a formal confession each month to the school chaplain. In January 1785 he went to confession at the school chapel. When he heard the priest, he could not suppress a bellow. The priest admonished him, spoke to him of Corsica and of the need to obey the king, whose grateful scholar and subject he was. The Corsicans, said the chaplain, were too often bandits whose character was too proud. "I have not come here to speak of Corsica," cried the enraged Napoleon, "and a priest does not have the duty to preach to me on this matter!" He then broke with his fist the grille separating him from the father confessor, and the two came to blows.[23] It was psychologically easier for Napoleon to be furious with a clerical father than with his own father, who was about to abandon him by dying.

By February 24, 1785, Napoleon's thirty-nine-year-old father was dying of cancer in Montpellier. His physicians were helpless to save his life. Carlo Buonaparte loved life. He did not want to die. The next day Napoleon's twenty-two-year-old step-uncle, Joseph Fesch, who was at Carlo's deathbed, wrote Napoleon's mother Letizia and Napoleon's great uncle Luciano that in the face of death Carlo had become very religious, calling for the intercession of the Blessed Virgin and for the blessing of priests. In another version of the story—probably invented by Napoleon himself—Carlo became extremely fearful and agitated, screaming for help to all the saints of the Church.[24]

Napoleonic legend has the dying Carlo call for his son Napoleon on his deathbed: "Where is my son, whose sword will make kings tremble, who will change the face of the world? He will protect me from my enemies, he will save my life!" Another version of this myth has Carlo cry out that he was lost and that not even his son's sword, which would conquer Europe, could save him from the Dragon of Death. In any event, the well-meaning ministrations of his physicians did not save Carlo from the ravages of cancer any more than did the intercession of the saints, priests, or the Blessed Virgin Mary. Carlo died at 2:30 a.m. on February 24, 1785. He was buried in a vault of Montpellier's Franciscan church, *L'Eglise des Cordeliers*, as the French nobleman Charles-Marie de Bonaparte.[25]

It took three weeks for Napoleon to learn of his father's death. The fifteen-year-old cadet reportedly refused the headmaster's and the school priest's offer to go to the school infirmary and cry, as was the custom on such occasions, saying, "I have not come to this hour without having thought of death. I accustom my soul to it as to life . . . I am strong enough to bear this pain without anyone taking the trouble to console me."[26] Napoleon feared the soft, emotional, and feminine side of himself. Masson thought that Napoleon's father's death "did not affect him so painfully as to make him express his anguish in cries. That may do for women. He took it like a man, the soldier he already was. As a small child, they were together but little, and in the last six years he had seen him but once, for an hour. He could hardly, therefore, feel that affection for him which, above all, is formed by habit and daily impressions."[27]

On March 23, 1785, the fifteen-year-old cadet Napoleon wrote his sixty-seven-year-old paternal great-uncle Luciano Bonaparte, the archdeacon in Ajaccio. Significantly, that first letter of condolences on his father's death was not addressed to his widowed mother Letizia. The letter to his great uncle expressed Napoleon's grief and his wish for Luciano to replace his father:

My dear uncle, It would be useless to tell you how touched I am by the misfortune which has befallen us. We have lost in him a father, and God knows what a father he was, his tenderness, his attachment to us! Alas! Everything in him spelled the support of our youth to us! You have lost in him an obedient and grateful nephew. You know better than I how much he loved you. *La patrie* [Corsica], I even dare say, has lost by his death an enlightened and disinterested citizen. That dignity with which he has several times been honored shows the confidence that his countrymen had in him; and yet Heaven makes him die, where? A hundred leagues from his land, in a foreign country [*sic*], indifferent to his existence, far away from all he held most dear. *One son, it is true, helped him in that terrible moment*; this must have been a big consolation for him, but surely not comparable with the triple joy that he would have felt had he ended his career in his own house, near his wife and all his family. But the Supreme Being has not allowed it. His will is immutable. He alone can console us. Alas! At least, although he has taken from us that which we held most dear, *he has still left us those who alone can replace him*. Accept therefore to take for us the place of the father whom we have lost. Our love, our gratitude will match so great a service. I end by wishing you a health like my own, Napoleone di Buonaparte.[28]

Dorothy Carrington astutely observed that Napoleon's letter of condolences to his great uncle, rather than express his grief, betrayed his feelings of indifference, even his relief, at his father's death. Although the letter was supervised and edited by the school officials, Carrington found it surprising that so little feeling came through: "The words addressed to Luciano, 'The nation, I even dare say, has lost by his death an enlightened and disinterested citizen,' ring false when one knows that the only nation that then counted for Napoleon was Corsica."[29] In fact, that would not necessarily make it ring false, for Napoleon may well have meant Corsica rather than France.

Five days later, on March 28, 1785, Napoleon finally wrote his mother in Ajaccio. It was not so much a letter of condolences as a son's dutiful and stylized consolations:

My dear mother, Today, when Time has calmed somewhat the first transports of my grief, I hurry to express to you the gratitude which the good deeds that you have done us inspires in me. Console yourself, my dear mother, circumstances demand it. We shall redouble our care and our gratitude, and shall be happy if we can by our obedience somewhat undo the damage of the incalculable loss of this dear husband. I end, my dear mother, my grief commands it, by asking you to calm your own [sorrow]. My health is perfect, and I pray every day that Heaven gratify you with the same. P.S. The queen of France has given birth to a prince named le duc de Normandie on March 27, at seven o'clock in the evening.[30]

Napoleon's post scriptum is no less important than the text of his letter. Just as Napoleon was Letizia's second son, Louis-Charles de France, the prince who Napoleon referred to was the second son of Queen Marie-Antoinette. In his unconscious mind, the queen was his mother, while he was the newborn prince.[31] Rather than a sense of loss, sadness, and mourning, his father's death had brought Napoleon liberation and rebirth.[32]

Three months before Napoleon's sixteenth birthday, the archbishop of Paris, *Monseigneur* Antoine-Eléonor-Léon le Clerc de Juigné, confirmed Napoleone de Buonaparte in the Roman Catholic Church in the chapel of the *École royale militaire*. On September 1, 1785, Napoleon formally graduated from the *École royale militaire*. Before getting his royal artillery officer's commission, however, he had to compete with all the other graduates of France's military schools for promotion to officer's rank, sitting for the school's final examination, whose successful takers were admitted as officers to the royal French artillery. Twenty-five cadets wanted to enter the artillery, but the school's governor, the *marquis* César-Jean-Baptiste de Timbrune-Valence, permitted only eighteen to compete for places. These fortunate eighteen included des Mazis, Picot de Peccaduc, Phélippeaux, Bonaparte, and even the "nymph" Laugier de Bellecour. Excelling in mathematics, the most important subject for artillerymen, Napoleon took the examination after only one year at the school, and at the age of sixteen, whereas most of the other candidates had attended the school for two years and were seventeen years old.

When the results of the entrance examination were published, of one hundred thirty-seven cadets from all over France, fifty-eight were admitted, four of whom were from his own school: Picot de Peccaduc in the thirty-ninth place, Phélippeaux in the forty-first, Bonaparte in the forty-second, and Des Mazis in the fifty-sixth. "This was a handsome success, if one remembers that he had had only one year's preparation, and that most of those placed above him on the list came from the excellent school of artillery at Metz. He became a lieutenant straightway, without being a cadet officer first."[33] In fact, it was an extraordinary achievement. Liberated by his father's death, Napoleon had finished a two-year officer-cadet course in one year. His officer's commission was antedated to September 1, 1785, and Napoleon became an officer of the French king Louis XVI at the tender age of sixteen.[34]

With his friend Alexandre des Mazis and with another cadet named Delmas, who had been accepted as an artillery pupil (rather than as an officer), Napoleon was posted to the royal La Fère artillery regiment. It was garrisoned at Valence, in the Dauphiné province and Rhône-Alpes region of southeastern France.

6

Corsica or France?

Napoleon's emotional relationship with France and with Corsica —his two motherlands—was deeply ambivalent. During his first seven years of military service, from 1786 to 1793, he took no less than five extended home leaves from his regiment in France, totalling more than 36 months. Each time he left mainland France for Corsica and failed to return to his regiment at the appointed time, he placed himself in serious jeopardy as a potential deserter. He stayed away from his regiment—though not from mainland France—for extended periods of twenty-one months (from September 1786 to June 1788) and again fifteen months (from September 1789 to February 1791). At one point Napoleon was actually declared a deserter; yet each time he wound up returning to mainland France and to his regiment. On St. Helena, Napoleon related his childhood and youth to Las Cases, recalling his peregrinations between Corsica and France.[1]

The adolescent Napoleon's fantasy life, fueled by his deepest feelings, was intense, and he expressed it in writing. Intellectualization was his chief unconscious defense against his overpowering inner conflicts. In 1786 he began to write a fragmentary "diary" in his notebook. In fact, it was less a diary than a collection of occasional entries in his notebook concerning various subjects he had read or diverse events he had experienced. Between 1786 and 1793 the youthful Napoleon wrote no less than eleven "literary" works, to which his biographers and scholars later gave posthumous titles.[2]

Lt. Napoleon de Buonaparte spent the winter of 1785–86 with his artillery regiment at Valence, agonizing over whether and when to return to Corsica. During his first three months at Valence he lived like an ordinary soldier and shared his bed with another man. Was it Des Mazis? "Napoleon, as a new officer, served in the ranks and got first-hand experience of the ordinary soldier's duties, including mounting guard. The rank and file were ill-paid and slept two in a bed—until recently it had been three—but at least they were never flogged, whereas soldiers in the English and Prussian armies often were: indeed a sentence of 800 lashes was not unknown."[3] Did the sixteen-year-old Napoleon have homosexual feelings for his bedmate? Did they have homosexual relations? *The teenage Napoleon deeply feared sexuality.* To him, unconsciously, sexual intercourse meant engulfment, fusion, and death.

Some biographers and scholars have spoken of Napoleon's small genitals, and this notion became a popular myth. Whether or not he had small genitalia, the teenage officer Napoleon was worried about his penis and testicles. He feared castration and at times saw himself as a eunuch. At Valence he read the *Essai général de tactique* by the artillery general Jacques-Antoine-Hippolyte de Guibert, and parts of the multivolume *Histoire naturelle* by the prolific eighteenth-century natural scientist Georges-Louis Leclerc, comte de Buffon. Napoleon copied into his notebook a passage from Buffon that cited a castration fantasy of the seventeenth-century French traveler Jean-Baptiste Tavernier:

> "Some men," he noted, "are born with only one testicle, others have three; they are stronger and more vigorous. It is astonishing how much this part of the body contributes to [a man's] strength and courage. What a difference between a bull and an ox, a ram and a sheep, a cock and a capon!" Like many young men, Napoleon seems for a time to have a subconscious fear of castration.[4]

After three months as a common soldier, Lieutenant Napoleon de Bonaparte began to serve as a regular royal officer. He took a keen interest in artillery pieces.[5]

Pierre-Marc Aurel was a Valence bookseller in the 1780s. He operated a library service to which Napoleon subscribed. Among other books, he read the autobiography of Jean-Jacques Rousseau, the revolutionary Genevan philosopher, who became one of the adolescent boy's heroes. Rousseau had lost his mother, who died when he was born, and his father, who fled Geneva after getting in trouble with the authorities when Jean-Jacques was ten-years-old. Jean-Jacques lived for six years as a poor and humiliated relation in his dead mother's family. When he was sixteen, Rousseau fled the home of his dead mother's family and roamed the Swiss, Savoyard, and French countryside, until he met Louise-Eléonore de la Tour du Pil, *baronne* de Warens, who became his protectress. Madame de Warens took the teenage boy into her home in the Savoyard town of Charmettes and made him her steward. He later "confessed" that she had initiated him into love and sexuality. The older Madame de Warens was an obvious mother figure to the teenage philosopher.

The teenage Napoleon soon imagined that he was Rousseau. At Valence, during the winter of 1785–86, he flirted with Madame Grégoire du Colombier, one of the *salon* ladies, and with her young daughter, Caroline. The Colombiers lived at Basseaux, three leagues from Valence, and Napoleon often rode there. He told Madame du Colombier that he wanted to write a history of Corsica. The older lady, who was managerial, not unlike Napoleon's own mother, encouraged him to write the seventy-three-year-old abbé Guillaume-Thomas de Raynal, a well-known French historian and philosopher, head of the Lyon academy, and author of a sixteen-volume history of the European colonies in India and America. Madame du Colombier also advised Napoleon to order books from her Geneva bookseller, Paul Borde. He did so. One of the books she suggested to him was the just-published memoirs of Madame de Warens, who had initiated Rousseau into sexuality.[6]

The youthful Napoleon was a romantic and passionate love-letter writer. At Valence, the teenage artillery officer wrote love letters to a young lady whom he called "Emma." Some scholars thought that "Emma" was Caroline du Colombier. In any event, Napoleon's "Emma" was idealized and embellished with his fantasy. The teenage Napoleon was more in love with himself than with "Emma." There was no sexual affair; their sole delight was eating cherries together. Napoleon idealized her, and, like his mother, "Emma" did not love him.[7]

During his ten months at Valence, from November 1785 to August 1786, Napoleon received many letters from his brother Joseph, who was back home in Corsica trying to take care of his widowed mother and orphaned siblings. Joseph wrote Napoleon that Governor Marbeuf's love for their mother Letizia was diminished and that she needed Napoleon's financial help. Joseph told Napoleon of their mother's financial problems and implored him to return to Corsica. After much soul-searching and inner torment, Napoleon borrowed a small sum of money from his friend Alexandre des Mazis. Napoleon made up his mind to return to Corsica in the spring of 1786, after he learned from Joseph that Governor Marbeuf was very ill, and that his mother badly needed him back home.

Napoleon's impending return to Corsica threw him into an acute inner crisis. On the one hand, he hoped that his homecoming after almost eight years of absence would be joyous. On the other hand, he was obsessed with the sorrows of Mother Corsica and with her oppressors. He had suicidal thoughts and wrote that he felt "forced to praise men that virtue should make me hate."[8] Jekels thought that one of the men Napoleon had in mind was Marbeuf: Napoleon hated the French governor who had seduced his mother and made a "courtesan" out of her, but he had to praise him. In fact, Marbeuf was very ill and died shortly after Napoleon wrote these lines. There was a sadomasochistic streak in Napoleon's suicidal fantasies. The main reason for Napoleon's depression and suicidal ideation in the summer of 1786 was that he was going back to his mother. "The fury that drove him to desire his own destruction" was the unconscious feeling that his individuation from his mother had failed and that he was returning to his fusional relationship with the engulfing Letizia, about which I will tell you more later.

Napoleon had applied for a six-month leave from his regiment. On May 26, 1786, and again two months later, he wrote to his Geneva bookseller, Paul Borde, requesting the just-published memoirs of Rousseau's lover, Madame de Warens, and more books on Corsica. Napoleon, however, made a fascinating slip of the pen, writing "Valens" for "Warens":

> I am writing to you directly, Sir, to ask you to send me the *Mémoires de Madame de Valens* [*sic*] and *Claude Anet* to follow on from the *Confessions* of Jean-Jacques Rousseau. I also beg you to send me the last two volumes of the *Histoire des Révolutions de la Corse* by the abbé de Germanes. I shall be obliged if you will let me have a note of the works on the island of Corsica which you have or could procure for me quickly.[9]

Napoleon's slip of the pen "Madame de Valens" instead of "Madame de Warens" was meaningful. He was living in Valence, and "Valens" is pronounced the same way in French as "Valence." Deep down he was thinking not of Rousseau's lover but of "Madame de Valence"—my lady of Valence. Was that lady Madame du Colombier, who might have initiated

Napoleon into sexuality? What did Napoleon hope to find in Madame de Warens's memoirs?

On August 12, 1786, Napoleon obtained his first leave from his regiment, one of many to come. It was valid for six months beginning on September 1. On September 15 the seventeen-year-old Napoleon returned to Ajaccio. He was welcomed home by Letizia and by his siblings Joseph, Louis, Pauline, Caroline, and Jérôme. Lucien and Elisa were studying in mainland France. Napoleon made the unhappy discovery that he had forgotten the Corsican Italian dialect and that he had to set about learning it again. He was less Corsican than he had imagined, despite his passionate zeal to become so. Governor Marbeuf died in Bastia on September 20, five days after Napoleon's return to Corsica.[10] Napoleon remained in Corsica for an entire year, prolonging his leave by obtaining medical certificates saying that he suffered from "quartan ague." He returned to Paris in September 1787, when he was eighteen-years-old.

When did Napoleon first make sexual love to a woman? One scholar believed that, as the older Madame de Warens had initiated Jean-Jacques Rousseau into sexuality, so Madame du Colombier might have initiated the 16-year-old Napoleon at Valence in late 1785 or in 1786. This view seems to be supported by Napoleon's slip of the pen in writing "Madame de Valens" instead of "Madame de Warens" in his letter of the year before to his Geneva bookseller.[11] Other scholars think that until he was eighteen Napoleon had no sexual relations, either heterosexual or homosexual, and that, unlike Rousseau's affair with Madame de Warens, Napoleon's flirt with Madame du Colombier and her daughter Caroline did not involve sexual relations.[12]

On November 22, 1787, the eighteen-year-old Napoleon met an unnamed Breton prostitute in Paris. Napoleon's description of the encounter is at once touching and cold. To avoid his violent sexual passions, he treated it as a scientific investigation:

> I left the Rue des Italiens and walked quickly down the avenues of the Palais-Royal. With my mind as usual filled with lively thoughts, I was indifferent to the cold; but my imagination cooled, and I began to feel the rigor of the season and entered the gallery. I was nearly at those iron gates when my gaze fell upon a woman. From the time of day, from her figure and from her youth I could not

> doubt that she was a whore. I stared at her; she stopped, not in their usual grenadier manner, but in a way that exactly matched her movement. This harmony struck me. Encouraged by her reticence, I spoke to her—I who am more sensitive of all to the odiousness of a prostitute's trade, who had always felt myself sullied by so much as a single glance from one of them. But her pale complexion, her frail physique, and her soft voice were such that I did hesitate for a moment. Either, I thought, this is a person who will be useful for the inquiry I want to make, or else she is only a half-wit.[13]

Napoleon had considered sexuality a dirty matter and his virginal self pure. At the same time, he thought that his mother had "prostituted" herself to Marbeuf.

Did Napoleon enjoy sexual relations after his encounter with the Breton prostitute in November 1787? Vincent Cronin believed that from the age of eighteen to the age of twenty-five "Napoleon was leading so crowded a life that he had little if any time for girls . . . As his fellow officers noted, he had great self-control and probably continued, as Alexandre des Mazis put it, "clean-living." Only after Toulon, when he was a brigadier, did he have time to see girls."[14]

In mainland France, after a dramatic crisis, King Louis XVI had replaced his *contrôleur général*, Charles-Alexandre de Calonne, with Archbishop Etienne-Charles de Loménie de Brienne. Napoleon and his family in Ajaccio learned about the dramatic events in mainland France in May or June 1787. Letizia, who could not mourn her losses, had not given up her hopes for compensation for the four thousand mulberry trees from her property of Les Salines that she had delivered to the government. She hoped that the new finance minister, Archbishop Loménie de Brienne, would be more favorable to her family than his predecessor had been, and that he would grant her government compensation for the properties she had lost. Letizia wanted Napoleon to leave Corsica, go to Paris, and plead with the new minister for compensation for her lost fortunes—three thousand and five hundred *livres*. Napoleon wavered for many weeks. Did he want to do his mother's bidding? Did he experience his mother's request for him to leave for Paris as yet another rejection?

On August 15, 1787, Napoleon turned eighteen. Shortly thereafter he decided to leave Ajaccio for Paris. Consciously, his aim was to do his mother's bidding and plead with the royal government for compensation for his family's property. Unconsciously, leaving his mother was his only chance for emotional liberation. Rather than join his regiment at Valence, he went to Paris. On December 1, Napoleon's regiment moved from Valence to the royal artillery school at Auxonne-sur-Saône. In mid-December, after three months in Paris, Napoleon left France again for Corsica, having obtained nothing of his mother's hoped-for compensation from the government. It was another failure in a long series that lasted from 1786 to 1793.

On January 1, 1788, Napoleon returned to Ajaccio for the second time, empty-handed. No sooner had Napoleon landed than his unhappy mother filled his ears with her angry complaints of her financial woes, which went on for hours. At home with Letizia were Napoleon's siblings Louis, Pauline, Caroline, and Jérôme, all of them under ten years of age. Napoleon had to take care of all of them. His younger brother, Lucien, was attending the theological seminary at Aix-en-Provence. Napoleon's elder brother Joseph had left for Pisa to obtain a law degree.

After returning to Corsica for the second time on New Year's Day 1788, Napoleon stayed with his mother for five months. On January 7 his elder brother Joseph celebrated his twentieth birthday at Pisa by becoming a doctor of law *in utroque jure*, certified in both civil and religious law. Joseph had been in Pisa for only three months. It is unlikely that he completed his law studies in such a short time. It was Joseph's connections in Pisa, where his father Carlo had obtained his own law degree in a very short time, that made this feat possible.

Napoleon's thrice-extended first leave from his regiment lasted a total of twenty-one months. Did he contemplate abandoning his regiment? He was deeply ambivalent about France, but equally ambivalent about returning to Corsica and his mother again. His back-and-forth shuttle between mainland France and Corsica lasted seven years, from 1786 to 1793, and was a series of failures. One scholar sensed that Napoleon's seven-year battle to break away from Corsica was a desperate struggle to separate and individuate from his mother:

> The adolescent [Napoleon] still looked to Paoli as his hero, imagined his return to Corsica, where he would join [Paoli] as his disciple and right-hand man . . . His education [in France] had not severed him from his emotional dependence on his homeland [Corsica], and on his mother, the focus of his affections. The

> process, *indescribably painful*, took seven years. Officer in the French army, he contrived to spend more than half that time in Corsica. At home he spontaneously assumed the role of head of the family . . . His activities were multiple, undertaken with passionate resolution yet always loaded with disappointment . . . he piled failure on failure until he was finally chased from the island with his family by Paoli's partisans. *All this had to happen before he was free to look beyond Corsica*, to act efficiently, to exploit his gifts, his skills, to love a woman other than Letizia, to become the man known to history.[15]

During the first months of 1789 there were terrible hunger and starvation in France. An unhappy and penniless Napoleon, hoping to escape the dreariness of his life at Auxonne and to visit Paris again, wrote his great-uncle Luciano and his step-uncle Joseph Fesch, the future cardinal, asking them for money to go to Paris and plead the family's case once more with the French authorities. The stingy Luciano made no reply, while Fesch sent his regrets. At the request of his fellow officers, Napoleon drafted the rules of a new association they had founded, *La Calotte* (The Cap), in pompous style, as if he were writing the constitution of a state. "There are constitutive laws," he wrote, "from which one is not allowed to deviate. They must derive from the nature of the Primitive Pact." Napoleon's fellow officers laughed but adopted his regulations.[16]

The French Revolution was beginning. *Ancien-régime* France was still divided into civilian *intendances* and military *gouvernements*. In March of that year food riots broke out in the Burgundian town of Seurre. The commanding general of the royal army in Burgundy ordered the maréchal de camp du Teil, Napoleon's commanding officer, to send his men into Seurre and quell the riots. On April 1 the fifes and drums sounded at the Place d'Auxonne. As the captains and first lieutenants were on Easter holiday leave, Du Teil sent Second Lieutenant Bonaparte with some other officers and one hundred men in three companies of his regiment to restore order. Napoleon and his men took the town. The nineteen-year-old Corsican junior officer reportedly ordered his men to load their guns and shouted to the mob: "Let all honest men go home! I fire only on rascals!" He and his men remained in Seurre through April and May to ensure the peace.[17]

In the spring of 1789 Letizia once more wrote her son asking him to appeal to the French *intendant* of Corsica, François-Nicolas de la Guillaumye, whom Napoleon had met in Bastia, about the condition of the family's mulberry plantation. On April 2, 1789, Napoleon wrote the *intendant*, who was having a good time at the royal palace of Versailles, asking him to take up the matter again:

> Pardon me, Sir, if, even in the center of pleasures, I pursue you with my affairs. It is three years since we were promised indemnity for the cancellation of our contract for the establishment of a plantation of mulberries; it is three years since the deed was drawn up and you were so good as to forward it to the Court, but we have heard nothing further. This delay is seriously harming our situation, which this undertaking has much damaged. You are aware of the justice of our claims and I am now asking your kindness, as the protector of justice, in helping us to obtain it. You know, sir, that last year we delivered four thousand or five thousand trees, although we had ten thousand ready to transplant. This year we have delivered only some hundreds, although the king should still have taken ten thousand. This cultivation is ruining us, and I cannot hide from you that the plantation is now in a very bad state. But something must be done, and it is not just that we should continue to suffer. I await the honour of your reply and will then at once take steps as a result. I am charmed that this circumstance gives me the occasion to recall myself to you. Buonaparte.[18]

Did Napoleon ever receive any reply from the *intendant*? There is no documentary evidence that the royal French government ever paid the Bonapartes the indemnity it had promised them for their property losses —or even answered their plea.

Shortly after his return to Corsica in the fall of 1789, the twenty-year-old Napoleon wrote a short story titled *Nouvelle corse* (Corsican novel) which he ended abruptly after eight pages. In this horror fantasy an old Corsican owns the Isola di Gorgona, an islet in the Tuscan archipelago off northeast Corsica, southwest of Livorno, which Napoleon's father had visited in 1765. Napoleon's *Nouvelle corse* was inspired by General Narbonne-Pelet-Fritzlar's massacres of 1774, which had been blamed on General Sionville, and which Napoleon had heard about as a child. Dorothy Carrington gave us a good summary of this story:

> [*Nouvelle Corse*] begins with the shipwreck of an English traveller on Gorgona, the little island one can see from northern Corsica on

> a clear day, here depicted as *a precipitous rock constantly lashed by furious seas*, a grave of ships and men. Assuming this "sterile" spot to be uninhabited, the Englishman, comparing himself to Robinson Crusoe, pitches his tent in the shelter of some ancient ivy-clad ruins . . . He wakes to see his tent burning and hear the cry "Thus all men perish" above the howling of the waves. His tent has been set on fire by an ancient Corsican and his daughter.[19]

In our unconscious mind, islands often stand for mothers, both good and bad. What did the Isle of Gorgona symbolize in Napoleon's unconscious mind? Why did he choose an Englishman to be shipwrecked on its shores? What did the "old Corsican" and his daughter mean? *Nouvelle corse* goes on to detail the horrors of murder and rape:

> Later, suspecting that his victim may be English and therefore his country's ally, the old Corsican is seized with a paroxysm of remorse and threatens to cast himself into the purifying flames while enjoining his daughter to live on to revenge him on the [French] tyrants of his native land. The Englishman thereupon falls to the feet of the "virtuous old man," who welcomes him to the "cavern" where he lives with his daughter and pours out his fearful tale. Partisan of Paoli, [the old man] kept up the resistance after the [French] conquest, saw forty comrades captured and executed . . . he reaches his village to find *his father lying in his own blood, his mother mutilated and naked "in the most revolting posture" and his wife and seven sons hanging from trees.* His daughter has disappeared . . . [and he settles on the Isle of Gorgona]. French ships are from time to time wrecked on the shore . . . he and his daughter make a point of killing the survivors . . . They burn their bodies on a funeral pyre, the incense of which is pleasing 'to the divinity.[20]

Gorgona, of course, was the mythical Greek female monster with sharp fangs and venomous snakes for hair. She was the symbol of the devouring and petrifying mother. In this fantasy, Napoleon unconsciously displaced his rage at his mother to France, but that did not undo his despair. Pierce Clark thought that "a hatred of France animates the majority of [Napoleon's adolescent] literary productions and the inner projections are hard, cruel and sadistic, and end in dejection and despair."[21]

While most of us associate the French Revolution with the year 1789, some historians believe that the French Revolution began in 1787, and that by 1789 it was in full swing. Before the Revolution, eighteenth-century Europe had consisted of empires, kingdoms, duchies, and principalities. Russia and Austria were empires. France was an absolute monarchy. Germany and Italy were divided into kingdoms, principalities, duchies, and papal states. One of France's chief rivals was the kingdom of Prussia, the most powerful German state. In 1785 the seventy-three-year-old King Friedrich II of Prussia (Frederick the Great) set up the German League of Princes to contain the ambitions of his great rival Joseph II of Austria, whom Friedrich had defeated in the War of the Bavarian Succession (1778–1779). Friedrich died in 1786, Joseph in 1790.

Within twelve years, from 1787 to 1799, the Revolution violently converted France from a monarchy into a people's republic modeled on ancient Greece and Rome. The French revolutionaries worshiped classical antiquity. The German states of Prussia and Saxony were still monarchies. Most of the *Montagnards*, the members of the elevated *Montagne* stands in the national assembly, were members of the *club des Jacobins*, formerly the *Société des amis de la Constitution*, of which Napoleon was a member. It was also called the *Société des amis de la liberté et de l'égalité* (Society of the Friends of Liberty and Equality). The leftist Jacobins were led by the nobleman Jérôme Pétion de Villeneuve and later by Maximilien de Robespierre. The moderate leader of the right-wing Jacobins, Georges-Jacques Danton, led a middle-of-the-road group, *les indulgents*, that sought accommodation with the enemy. From April 7 to July 10, 1793, Danton briefly headed the *comité de Salut public*. After the leftist *conventionnels* ousted Danton, he became the leader of the moderate revolutionary opposition, including the *Club des Cordeliers*.

On October 15, 1791, Luciano Buonaparte, Napoleon's seventy-three-year-old great uncle, died in Ajaccio. Many years later Napoleon recalled that the dying man had called him a "great man" and begged him to deliver him with his "great sword." Carrington rightly observed that Napoleon had not yet shown any military prowess.[22] Napoleon and his siblings, however, inherited the childless Luciano's property, which took a heavy load off their mind.[23] By late 1791 Napoleon was running a grave risk. He was still in Corsica. His leave had expired. In the fall he received a letter from Simon de Sucy, the government's *commissaire des guerres* at Valence, warning him that all army officers absent from their units without leave at the time of the annual review on January 1, 1792, would be struck from the army's rolls and lose their status as officers, unless they had "exceptional reasons" for their absence. In fact, Napoleon was "running a twofold risk: that of being cashiered from the army, and that of being put on the list of *émigrés*." The former would mean the loss of everything he had worked for, while the latter could mean the death sentence.

Napoleon's fears were founded. His commanding officer at Valence, Colonel Campagnol, had not forgotten his humiliation by his subordinate, who had gone over his head to the *maréchal de camp* Du Teil to obtain his leave. On New Year's Day, January 1, 1792, during the regimental review in Valence, with Napoleon having failed to return to his regiment in France, Campagnol took his revenge. His regimental record stated that Napoleone de Buonaparte was absent without leave and a deserter from the French army, and his name was struck from the army list, the list of those soldiers recommended to the *Assemblée nationale* as having legitimate reasons for absence.[24] However, although Napoleon did not know it, owing to the great shortage of officers due to the mass emigration of French noblemen, he could easily have secured his reinstatement.

On February 17, 1792, fearful of losing everything he had worked for, Napoleon wrote Simon de Sucy, the war commissioner at Valence, not forgetting to greet his influential friends:

> Imperious circumstances have forced me, *Monsieur* and dear Sucy, to remain in Corsica longer than the duties of my employment would have allowed. I feel it and yet have nothing to reproach myself with: sacred and dearer duties justify me. Now that I am more free, I would like to come and join you, but first I wish to have your advice: How am I placed as a result of the review of January 1? Has my post been filled and what steps should I take?[25]

Not receiving any reply, Napoleon did not give up. Like a child, being ignored made him redouble his efforts to get attention. He once more wrote War Commissioner Sucy in Valence:

> In difficult circumstances, the post of honor of a good Corsican is to be in his own country. It is with this idea in mind that *les miens* (my people) have asked me to establish myself among them; but since I do not wish to fail in my duty I was planning to offer [you] my resignation [from the army]. Then the general officer of the

département [of Corsica] offered me a *modus vivendi* which has reconciled everything. He has offered me the post of *adjudant-major* in the volunteer battalions.[26]

The elections of *lieutenants-colonels* in the National Guard battalions throughout France, including Corsica, were set for late March 1792. Modern election ethics were unknown. Each candidate tried to buy votes and to coerce his way into office. In mid-March, two weeks before the election, Napoleon bribed his fellow *Gardes nationaux* into voting for him. He invited two hundred fellow guards to stay at the Casa Bonaparte and gave them "lavish board" until the election day. Nor did he neglect the election commissioners. The *directoire* of the *département* of Corsica sent three commissioners from Bastia to supervise the elections. Two of them, a man named Grimaldi and another commissioner, stayed with the Bonapartes. However, a third commissioner, Tiburce Morati, who came from a small town named Murato, stayed with Napoleon's rival, Jean Peraldi. To win the election, Napoleon thought that he needed Morati's support. He had his men kidnap Morati from the Peraldi residence the day before the election and held him captive in the Casa Bonaparte "for his liberty" and "to assure his impartiality." Such an act may seem shocking by today's standards but was fairly common practice in those days.[27]

The elections to the post of *lieutenant-colonel* and *lieutenant-colonel en second* in Napoleon's 2nd *Garde nationale* battalion were held in Ajaccio's Eglise Saint-François on March 28–31, 1792. Five hundred and twenty-one national guards, each with two votes, arrived in the church. Predictably, Napoleon's rival Mathieu Pozzo di Borgo made a rousing speech protesting Morati's kidnaping by Bonaparte. Napoleon's angry followers hissed and booed Pozzo di Borgo, cried "*abasso*!" (down with him!) and pulled him from the platform. Some scholars believed that Pozzo di Borgo might have been murdered had Napoleon and one of his friends not shielded him with their bodies.[28] Yet the Pozzo di Borgos, a powerful Ajaccio clan, considered their rivals, the Bonapartes, criminals. The enmity between the rival clans became murderous.

After a stormy election secured by foul play, surprise and violence, Napoleon's rival Jean-Baptiste Quenza received the most votes and was elected *lieutenant-colonel*. Napoleon, who received 422 out of the 1042 votes, was elected *lieutenant-colonel en second*. Vincent Cronin thought that "by Corsican standards it had been a surprisingly calm election—no one was killed."[29] On April 1, 1792, Napoleon Bonaparte was formally named *lieutenant-colonel en second*. This not only saved him from having to return to his regiment in Valence but was also a promotion. Napoleon had risen from staff officer to deputy commander of his battalion. Moreover, as Quenza had no military experience, Lt.-Col. Bonaparte was the *de facto* commander of his battalion.[30]

The first week of April 1792 was tense in Ajaccio. There were violent fights between Corsican national guardsmen and French sailors. On Monday, April 2, the Quenza-Bonaparte battalion was reviewed on the Place d'Ajaccio by Colonel Louis Maillard, the commander of the régiment du Limousin, the French garrison in the Ajaccio citadel. This regiment, now called the 42nd infantry regiment, had no less than four hundred royalist troops. Colonel Maillard, fearing the Corsican patriots, ordered the guardsmen to leave Ajaccio for Corte. Under Napoleon's influence, however, Lieutenant Colonel Quenza delayed his departure, using various ruses and pretexts. Fearing for their lives, the rich families of Ajaccio left the island for Italy.

It took Napoleon only one week to turn this achievement into failure. On Easter Sunday, April 8, 1792, the pro-Vatican *prêtres non-jureurs* incited the populace against the Civil Constitution of the Clergy. Riots broke out in Ajaccio. The royalist mob attacked Quenza's volunteer guardsmen. Here is one version of the story:

> On Easter, Napoleon got what he expected, and had almost arranged for. While non-juring priests [those who had not taken the oath of allegiance to the Republic] conducted mass at the Capuchin monastery, a fight broke out in the streets. The [National Guard] volunteers got involved, shots were exchanged, and a lieutenant [was] killed. Napoleon barricaded his men in the Capuchin monastery, the town seminary, and fortified houses. Eight days of violence ensued, during which Napoleon defied demands to withdraw from both the municipal authorities and the French commander of the [Ajaccio] citadel, Colonel Maillard. His militiamen, their nerves rubbed raw, fired at anyone in the streets, even killing two women as they emerged from the cathedral.[31]

In fact, the story was more complicated. On April 8, 1792, several *prêtres non-jureurs* celebrated mass in the friary of Ajaccio's Eglise Saint-François where Napoleon's election as *lieutenant-colonel en second* had taken place a week earlier. The priests announced that they would lead a procession the next day. The friary, like many other religious houses in France, had been closed by the French revolutionary government. The Ajaccio Franciscans had protested the closure, as did many devout Corsicans. The celebration of the mass in the friary was a provocation to republican Corsicans, such as the *procureur général syndic*, Antoine-Christophe Saliceti, and Napoleon, who felt that only priests who were loyal to France and its laws should be allowed to celebrate mass. Bloody riots broke out in Ajaccio between nationalist Corsicans who opposed the civil constitution and supported the friars and pro-French Corsicans who favored the new system.

The violent clashes between the Corsican royalists and republicans in Ajaccio lasted through Easter week 1792. At first, Lieutenant-Colonels Quenza and Bonaparte obeyed Colonel Maillard. On the evening of April 8, however, there was a tragic incident near the Ajaccio cathedral. A young *Garde nationale* officer, Lieutenant Rocca della Serra or Roccaserra, was killed in front of Napoleon's eyes. His death shocked the young Napoleon, who may have felt guilty for it. Bonaparte went to see Colonel Maillard and told him that his *gardes* were in mortal danger from the enraged and violent mob and needed to take refuge in the citadel "or at the very least to have access to the ammunition there."[32] Maillard refused and ordered Quenza and Bonaparte to withdraw their volunteers to the *Couvent Saint-François*. Napoleon went to see his friend Saliceti, who gave him a written order overruling the orders of Maillard and of the municipality, and saying that Maillard was duty bound to protect the *Garde nationale* volunteers. Maillard, however, insisted that he would only obey the municipality, which was royalist. While many scholars thought that Bonaparte was the bully in this affair, at least one biographer thought that he clearly had the law on his side.[33]

Napoleon left Ajaccio for Corte, where he still hoped to get a military or civilian job from his hero, Paoli, or to become his aide-de-camp. Colonel Maillard remained in charge of the French troops in Ajaccio. Angry with Napoleon for his "foolish" actions in Ajaccio, however, Paoli appointed someone else as his aide-de-camp. Napoleon was deeply hurt and disappointed: the "great good father" did not love him.

In April 1792 France was plunged into war with Austria and Prussia, a twenty-year-war that later involved Russia and other powers and is now known as the "French Revolutionary and Napoleonic Wars." In mid-May Napoleon left Corsica again for mainland France to take advantage of the new political and military situation. After declaring war on Austria and Prussia, France desperately needed professional officers. Their offenses of absence without leave and even desertion were forgiven, and they were recalled to France to join their units. Napoleon hoped to clear himself of Maillard's accusations before the French war minister.[34] At the same time, his stubborn and greedy mother wanted Napoleon to pursue the matter of her promised French government compensation for her mulberry plantation at Les Salines.

Lucien Bonaparte, who had left the seminary at Aix-en-Provence in 1789, became Paoli's secretary, a post which Napoleon had craved but never got. Lucien had a penchant for politics and power. In 1791 he began to frequent Ajaccio's Jacobin club, in which he became one of its principal and most exalted orators.

An anxious Napoleon Bonaparte waited out the month of June 1792 in Paris to see which way the tide of the Revolution would turn and how the war minister would decide his fate. He wrote frequently to his elder brother Joseph back home in Corsica, demanding immediate replies. War anxiety in France was high and pervasive. It was a time of great political and social instability.

7

Farewell to Bad Mother Corsica

On June 20, 1792, two months before his twenty-third birthday, Napoleon watched the humiliation of King Louis XVI by a Parisian mob. Some five or six thousand frenzied Jacobins led by Antoine Santerre, the commander of the *Garde nationale de Paris*, marched in the streets of Paris, chanting the *Ça ira*, the revolutionary song that later became a rallying cry under the Terror. Marching from Les Halles toward the Seine, the wild, regicidal, and unconsciously patricidal crowd waved a plank to which was nailed the bloody heart of an ox inscribed *Coeur de Louis XVI* (Heart of Louis XVI). At first they forced their way into the *Assemblée législative*, where they angrily filed through the hall, browbeating the legislature. Then they marched on the Tuileries Palace grounds. Entering the *Salon de l'Oeil de Boeuf* (Bull's Eye Hall), the angry mob came upon the king himself. They humiliated him throughout that afternoon. The mob forced the king to listen to their abuse and taunts, to wear a red Jacobin bonnet on his head, and to drink to the health of the people of Paris. After many hours of this royal humiliation, the thirty-six-year-old Jacobin representative Jérôme Pétion de Villeneuve persuaded the mob to leave. The king was deeply traumatized, his self-esteem in tatters.[1]

Meanwhile, Napoleon had learned that the French director of fortifications had written to the National Assembly's military committee that keeping Corsica in France was impossible and useless. Napoleon thought that France would divest itself of Corsica and give it its independence. In his letter to Joseph, he switched from the political to the personal. He could not make up his mind whether to stay in Paris, rejoin his French

Army regiment, or return to his post with the Ajaccio National Guard in Corsica. If he decided to return to Corsica, should he leave his sister Marianne at Saint-Cyr, or take her back home with him? The news he had for his brother was bad. Their claim for compensation for their mulberry plantation at Les Salines was going nowhere.

Mass anxiety triggered collective violence. The humiliation of King Louis XVI on June 20, 1792, was only a beginning. On August 10 the *palais des Tuileries* in Paris, where the king was residing, was seized by a Jacobin mob. The frenzied rioters, joined by excited national guardsmen from Brittany and Marseille, attacked the palace, massacring the courtiers and the Swiss guards. The scene was horrifying. In the palace courtyard, eight hundred men lay dead or dying in a great pool of blood. Frightened to death, King Louis XVI took refuge from the murderous mob in the *Assemblée législative.* He was arrested by the legislature, which took over the Tuileries Palace as its own seat. The king and his family, including his Austrian wife Marie-Antoinette and his seven-year-old son, Louis XVII, were imprisoned in the notorious fortress of Le Temple. Noblemen and clergymen were massacred. It was a time of furious and senseless blood-letting. A few months later the king was guillotined.

Louis-Antoine Fauvelet de Bourrienne, Napoleon's secretary when he was First Consul of France, claimed that he and Napoleon had left their Paris hotel for Bourrienne's brother's pawnshop in the place du Carrousel, where proud French cavalrymen showed off their horsemanship during parades. Napoleon witnessed the bloody scene with horror and disgust. He talked a Marseillais guardsman into sparing the life of a Swiss guard. Napoleon watched the angry and hate-filled faces of the mob and wondered what had become of the great ideals of the Revolution. Bourrienne claimed that Napoleon later told him that he had seen well-dressed women cutting off the sex organs of dead Swiss guards and brandishing them triumphantly. "*Vile canaille*!" (Vile riffraff!), he murmured. Napoleon added that he would have defended the king if he had been called upon to do so. As we have seen, however, Bourrienne's ghostwritten memoirs should be taken cautiously.[2]

The mob's assault on the king shocked Napoleon, as it did the entire French nobility.[3] Like many other French noblemen fearing for their lives, Napoleon concealed his nobility by dropping the "de" from his name and calling himself from now on Napoleon Buonaparte.[4] On August 15, 1792, an anxious Napoleon "celebrated" his twenty-third birthday in Paris. He was grim, unsmiling, and unhappy. The following day, an angry republican government closed down the aristocratic boarding school of Saint-Cyr, where Napoleon's fifteen-year-old sister Maria Anna, the future Elisa, was a pupil. On the evening of September 1, Napoleon took her with him to Paris. There, he took his sister to the opera, where she at first refused to watch the "indecent and devilish" spectacle, but later mellowed. On September 2, 1792, the day of the elections to the new *Convention nationale*, the bells of Paris sounded the alarm. The people of Paris learned that Verdun had fallen to the Prussian enemy. Their anxiety was overwhelming, and violence ensued. From September 2 to September 6 another frenzied mob broke into the Paris prisons, dispensed summary "justice," and massacred over one thousand "suspects and traitors."

Napoleon waited out the "First Terror" of August and September 1792 in Paris. He still wavered on whether to return to Corsica or stay in mainland France. In mid-September the twenty-three-year-old Napoleon and Marie-Anne boarded a stagecoach to Marseille. On September 20 the tide of the war suddenly turned in France's favor and the "First Terror" ended. The French general Dumouriez and his colleague Kellermann had defeated the Austro-Prussian armies. Arriving in Marseille in late September, some local people spotted Elisa's feathered taffeta bonnet, crying "*Mort aux aristocrates*!" (Death to the aristocrats!). Napoleon gamely threw Elisa's bonnet to the crowd, saying, "We are no more aristocrats than you are!" This brazen lie saved their lives. They proceeded to Toulon but could not board a ship to Ajaccio until October 10.[5]

Arriving in Ajaccio on October 15, 1792, Napoleon and Marie-Anne Bonaparte were greeted with bad news. Their elder brother Joseph had failed to get elected to the new *Convention nationale* in Paris. Napoleon's bitter and vengeful rival Charles-André Pozzo di Borgo also returned to Corsica that month after the *Assemblée législative* had expired. Napoleon was still an officer in a *Garde nationale* battalion. On October 18 he wrote Paoli, the commander of all the Corsican National Guards, in Corte, informing him that he was going to take up his post as *lieutenant-colonel en second* of his National Guard battalion in Ajaccio. There was no reply from the ailing Paoli, who did not want Napoleon, whom he considered too French, too ambitious, and too dangerous.

The desperate Napoleon announced to the two companies of his battalion, garrisoned at Corte and Bonifacio, that he would be arriving to take up his post. There was no response to this either. Fearing Paoli, Napoleon contemplated going to India. At the end of October 1792 he went to Corte to see Paoli. But Napoleon's bitter enemy Pozzo di Borgo had become Paoli's intimate adviser. After making Napoleon wait, Paoli refused to give him back his command. This was a narcissistic injury. A furious Napoleon threatened to return to Ajaccio and write to Paris denouncing Paoli's "antinationalist" faction. Paoli calmly told him to leave Corsica if he wanted to. Once more Napoleon was bitterly disappointed. He was on a collision course with Paoli, whom he had loved as a father.[6]

During the night of January 16–17, 1793, the seven hundred and forty-nine members of the French *Convention nationale* voted on whether to condemn their king, Louis XVI, to death. Each deputy made a speech justifying his vote, and the voting lasted all night. On January 17 the votes were tallied. On January 18, when the vote was announced, the patricidal ambivalence of many conventionnels became apparent. Three hundred and eighty-seven conventionnels had voted *la mort du roi* (the death of the king)—including twenty-six in favor of a *debate on the possibility* of staying the execution. Three hundred and thirty-four *conventionnels* had voted against the death sentence, including thirteen who had voted for a *suspended* death sentence. Twenty-eight deputies had been absent or abstained from voting.

Because the vote had been so close, because of the number of votes in favor of a debate on the possibility of staying the execution and of a suspended sentence, and because of the number of absentees and abstentions, on January 19, 1793, the *conventionnels* debated the issue of whether the sentence would be "with or without reprieve and with or without appeal to the people" and took a final vote on the question of a stay of execution. By a vote of 380 to 310, the stay of execution was rejected, and Louis XVI was condemned to death without reprieve and without appeal to the people.

Napoleon's purported reaction to Louis XVI's execution in early 1793 was reported many years later by the French commissioner Charles-Louis Huguet de Sémonville to Etienne-Denis Pasquier, Napoleon's police prefect and last chancellor. Pasquier claimed that on the day Napoleon learned of the king's execution, he became agitated. Pasquier wrote:

> Bonaparte, who, like Pozzo [di Borgo], had originally adhered to Paoli, lost no time in leaving him to defend the rights of the French Government. It was on the news of Louis XVI's condemnation that he reached this decision. I have this fact from Monsieur de

> Sémonville, who was then in Corsica as Commissary of the French Government. Bonaparte came and woke him up in the night. "Monsieur le Commissaire," he said, "I have carefully considered our situation, the people here are ready for any folly. The Convention has no doubt committed a great crime by executing the king and I deplore it more than anyone, but Corsica, whatever happens, must always be joined to France: it can only exist on that one condition: I and my kin, I warn you, will defend the cause of union."[7]

In Napoleon's unconscious mind, Corsica and France may have stood for his mother and himself. In February 1793 Napoleon was in fact at the southern Corsican port city of Bonifacio, preparing the ill-fated French invasion of Sardinia. Sémonville was not in Corsica as a commissioner of his government but as its ambassador-designate to the Ottoman Empire. Napoleon's baptism by fire took place soon thereafter at the Sardinian island of La Maddalena, and it was a disaster that left him wounded in body and soul. The battle began on February 25, the eighth anniversary of Napoleon's father's death, and Maddalena is the Italian version of Mary Magdalen's name. The battle of La Maddalena left Napoleon traumatized, and the sea would always remain his mortal enemy.

In April 1793 things came to a head between Corsica and France—and also between Paoli and the Bonapartes. On April 2 the French *Convention nationale*, fearful that Paoli was plotting with the British against France, issued an ominous decree ordering its three Corsican commissioners—Saliceti, Delcher, and Lacombe Saint-Michel—to arrest Paoli and his lieutenant Pozzo di Borgo and to bring them to justice in Paris. On April 5 the three commissioners arrived in Bastia by sea and proceeded to Corte to see Paoli. Despite Saliceti's actions against Paoli, the latter received him amicably. On April 14 the *Convention*'s arrest decree against Paoli arrived in Corte, and on April 18 Saliceti published it in the official French press. This was a great provocation to the Corsican patriots, who rebelled against France. On April 26—his sixty-eighth birthday—Paoli wrote a conciliatory letter to the *Convention* "which calmly and simply explained the position . . . while assuring it of his attachment to France and redeclaring his readiness to leave the homeland once more should his presence cause disturbances."[8] The old Paoli became embroiled in a bitter conflict with the young Saliceti. Paoli fought his Corsican enemies and the French *Convention nationale* at the same time. Napoleon's hot-headed younger brother, Lucien, made matters worse for his whole family. The fiery Lucien, not yet eighteen, had been manipulated by Saliceti into leading a republican Corsican deputation to mainland France. Napoleon justly feared that Lucien would ruin his family and cause their expulsion from Corsica. He decided to undo the damage by making a public pro-Paoli declaration. In late April 1793, despite being Saliceti's protégé, despite the bitter Paoli-Saliceti conflict, despite his repeated rejection by Paoli, and a few days before Paoli ordered his arrest, Napoleon drafted a passionate resolution for Ajaccio's *Club des amis de la Constitution* urging the *Convention* to rescind its "unjust" decree against Paoli. "Heed my words," it concluded, "silence this calumny and those utterly perverse beings by whom it is used."[9]

Napoleon's fervent defense of Paoli was motivated by fear as much as by love. Napoleon thought that war between Paoli and France was inevitable, that Paoli would win, that he would "proscribe his enemies and confiscate their property," and that "the victorious Paolists would hardly spare the Bonapartes and their possessions."[10] After the *Convention nationale*'s decree against Paoli was published in Corsica on April 18, 1793, the aging Corsican leader "played the cleverest of clever hands" with France.[11] On April 26 he wrote the *Convention* a conciliatory letter saying that his old age and poor health prevented him from traveling to Paris. As the *Convention*'s troops were spread thin in France and in Europe, they could not spare the military forces required to bring Paoli to heel in Corsica. Most of the Corsicans had rallied to Paoli. His angry men, convinced that all the Bonapartes were traitors, refused to discuss the merger. The desperate Napoleon wrote Paoli offering to demonstrate his loyalty to him in any way Paoli chose. *U Babu* ignored him. On May 3 Paoli ordered Napoleon's arrest. Napoleon fled.

A frightened and pursued Napoleon reached Ajaccio on May 6, 1793, three days after he fled Corte. A Jewish friend of the Bonapartes in Ajaccio, the former mayor Jean-Jérôme Lévie, sheltered Napoleon and helped him get away safely. The young fugitive hid in an alcove in Lévie's house, evading Paoli's men. On May 9, after meeting his mother and siblings, Napoleon left Ajaccio by sea for Macinaggio, on the northeastern tip of the Cap Corse, the "finger" of Corsica, from which he went south by land to Bastia, the seat of the French government, to join the anti-Paoli forces.[12] A couple of days later he reached Bastia, where he met his brother Joseph and the *Convention nationale*'s commissioners, Saliceti, Delcher, and Lacombe Saint-Michel, who were fighting the "traitor" Paoli. The three decided to send a naval force to Ajaccio and seize the citadel and the town from Paoli's men. On May 13 the French *Convention* formally dissolved the elected government of Corsica. On May 14 it installed an appointed French administration, infuriating the Corsican nationalists.

On May 16, 1793, events took a dramatic turn. The *Convention nationale* in Paris, having received Paoli's conciliatory letter of April 26, rescinded its arrest order against him. Saliceti, however, who had not received the new decree, still planned to take Ajaccio, then Corte, and to arrest Paoli. From Bastia, an anxious Napoleon, who also did not know of the new turn of events, sent a message to his mother to leave the Casa Bonaparte and hide in the Torre del Capitello (capital tower), a light tower at the eastern end of the Gulf of Ajaccio: "Prepare yourself," Napoleon wrote his mother, "this country is not for us."[13] His mother's house was about to be attacked by Paoli's men.

A week later, on May 23, 1793, Saliceti's "expeditionary force" of four hundred men and a few pieces of artillery sailed from the port of Saint Florent, across the Cap Corse from Bastia, aboard two French ships, the brig *Le Hasard* and the sloop *La Belette*, on their way to Ajaccio. Napoleon sailed his xebec ahead of Saliceti's two-ship "flotilla," hoping to "punish" Paoli and to seize the Ajaccio citadel. It was an ill-fated expedition bound to end in humiliating defeat.

On May 27, Paoli convened an emergency session of the Corsican *consulta* at Corte. On the day Napoleon left Bastia, the Casa Bonaparte was attacked by Paoli's men. The house was looted and partly burned. The Bonapartes' country house at Les Milelli, with its vineyards, olive grove, and herds of livestock were destroyed. Letizia and her children fled their home and hid in the countryside for a week, protected by anti-Paoli Corsicans. When they received Napoleon's message, they proceeded to the Torre del Capitello in the Gulf of Ajaccio.[14] At the Corte *consulta* on May 29, Paoli, citing their actions against Paoli and Corsica, declared the Bonapartes traitors and outlaws and expelled them from Corsica. Their property was confiscated. It was said that their home was burned down. The *consulta*'s order proscribing the Bonapartes used harsh language. It said that they had been corrupted by Marbeuf, born in the filth of despotism, fed and raised "under the eyes and at the expense of a luxurious pasha" who commanded in the island."[15]

After the *consulta*'s drastic action of May 29, 1793, expelling him and his family from Corsica, Napoleon's fury at Paoli erupted in full force. His idealized Father Paoli had cast him out as an outlaw and taken his beloved Mother Corsica away from him. On May 31, 1793, the two-ship French naval "expedition," led by Saliceti, Lacombe Saint-Michel, and Joseph Bonaparte, entered Ajaccio Bay under a hail of fire from Paoli's men in the citadel. When he reached Ajaccio Bay, he found his mother and siblings in the tower. When Napoleon heard that his mother's house had been pillaged and burned, he became "petrified with rage."[16]

Napoleon spent the entire day of June 1, 1793, in the Gulf of Ajaccio vainly trying to take its citadel from Paoli's forces, who were not about to surrender. On June 2, 1793, a frightened, defeated, and furious Napoleon left Ajaccio for Calvi with his family. The following day, June 3, the Bonapartes reached Calvi. Napoleon made sure that his mother and siblings were safe at the Casa Giubega. By now the French controlled only three coastal cities—Calvi, Bastia, and San Fiorentino (Saint-Florent). In view of the Corsican *consulta*'s action against him and his family, his being an outlaw to Paoli's men, and Paoli's growing power on the island, Napoleon's wisest move at that point would probably have been to take his family with him and flee Corsica as fast as he could. Indeed, André Castelot believed that Napoleon left Calvi for Toulon on June 3.[17] In fact, while his mother and siblings stayed with their friends, the Giubega family, Napoleon shuttled between Calvi and Bastia, where he conferred with Saliceti, and only sailed from Calvi with his mother and siblings for Toulon a week later.[18]

On June 10, 1793 Napoleon finally returned from Bastia to the Casa Giubega in Calvi. On June 11, he, his forty-three-year-old mother Letizia, his younger brothers Louis and Jérôme, and their three sisters Marianne, Pauline, and Caroline sailed for Toulon in a French navy xebec. Castelot thought that "this time—and for good—Napoleone had chosen France."[19] But why did Napoleon, a fervent Corsican nationalist and a great admirer of Paoli, have such a profound change of heart over such a short period of time? Let us examine this crucial question from a psychoanalytic viewpoint.

8

Through a Psychological Lens

Napoleon's abandonment of Corsica and his final return to mainland France marked the end of his prolonged adolescence and the beginning of his adulthood. He had achieved a physical separation from his motherland, if not an emotional separation from his mother. Napoleon became a nationalist Frenchman because breaking with his motherland was his only way of breaking away from the image of his childhood mother. For seven years he had shuttled between mainland France and Corsica, his two "motherlands." Now he opted for Mother France once and for all. It can be said that Napoleon then developed a new identity. Therefore, this "turning point in Napoleon's life"[1] is a proper time to examine his early life through a psychological lens and illustrate human factors in the development of his mind and personality until the time when he chose France.

When he was nineteen, Napoleon had written Paoli, whom the younger man was still idealizing at this time, from Auxonne-sur-Saône. Roughly translated, Napoleon's letter, dated June 12, 1789, reads as follows: "General! I was born when the fatherland was dying. Thirty thousand Frenchmen thrown up on our shores, drowning the throne of liberty in torrents of blood, such was the odious sight that first hit my eyes. The cries of the dying, the groans of the oppressed, the tears of despair surrounded my cradle from my birth. You left our island, and with you vanished the hope of happiness: slavery was the price of our submission."[2] From a psychoanalytic viewpoint, this letter can be read as an unconscious personal fantasy of his bloody birth converted into historical and political thought.

Napoleon was not baptized for the first two years of his life. His mother did not expect him to live. Brice believed that "Napoleon was a sickly child. *It was not even thought that he would live.* To save themselves the expense of a public baptism, which seemed to everyone superfluous, *he was merely baptized at home.* When he was still alive two years later he was baptized in Ajaccio Cathedral on the 21st of July, 1771, at the same time as his sister, Marie Anne." Letizia invested neither her money nor her feelings in Napoleon, whom she expected to die like her first two daughters. She did not wish to have to mourn yet another loss. *She rejected Napoleon from his birth.* Napoleon surprised his mother by surviving, which he did under the loving care of his wet nurse Camilla Ilari.[3]

As he grew up, the baby Napoleon had not one but two mothers, psychologically: Letizia Bonaparte and Camilla Ilari. Letizia was less loving and giving to him than Camilla. She had no milk for Napoleon. Under normal circumstances, the infant cannot integrate the good and bad aspects of its imperfect mother, who is at times good and giving but at other times bad and ungiving. The baby splits up its internal image of its mother into an all-good one (the fairy) and an all-bad one (the witch).[4] In Napoleon's case, he had two ready-made maternal objects: the stingy and unloving Letizia and the generous and loving Camilla. He therefore easily imagined Camilla as all-good and Letizia as all-bad. This began the internal *splitting* process, seeing others as all-good or all-bad, which dominated his emotional life.

Joseph was a pretty and likeable baby, with a close and warm relation to his mother. This was not true of Napoleon. At his coronation as Emperor of the French in 1804, *which his own mother Letizia did not attend but his old wet nurse Camilla did,* Camilla Ilari recalled that "Joseph had been a *joli enfant* [pretty child] while he [Napoleon] had not." Napoleon reportedly "blackened with rage" when he heard Camilla say this.[5] Camilla loved him nonetheless. Dorothy Carrington gave us a very astute description of the relationship:

> Camilla Ilari appears as sentimental, bold, and shrewd. She adored Napoleon as a child; years afterwards he remembered the delicacies she gave him in secret when Letizia punished him with a diet of dry bread. In later life she clung to him; her devotion amounted to "a kind of cult," so that she and her family had their share of the

extraordinary experiences that befell almost everyone connected with his career. She was among the first to welcome him when he visited Ajaccio in 1799 on his return from Egypt. She went to Paris for his coronation, amused him and his wife Josephine, amused the Pope, who was present at Napoleon's coronation; she witnessed the fabulous ceremony that his real mother sourly avoided. The Pope gave her holy images and blessings, Josephine diamonds, Napoleon money and land. He would have given her the family home in Ajaccio as well had not Letizia, encouraged by [her half-brother] Joseph Fesch, the future cardinal, insisted it should go to her cousin, André Ramolino; but Napoleon obliged [André] to give [Camilla] his own house in exchange. Even so, faced with Ramolino's opposition, Camilla would never have got possession of it had she not sent her beautiful granddaughter, Faustina, to Paris to plead with the Emperor, who was also her godfather.[6]

William Hudson thought that the adult Napoleon never forgot "those who had helped him in early life" and was deeply grateful to them: "[Camilla's] homely figure might easily have passed out of his recollection amid the stress of politics, the tumult of war, the splendours and responsibilities of a throne. But at her own request, he allowed her to be present at his coronation in 1804; he gave her vineyards and money; and in his will he directed his executors to assure themselves that she was beyond the reach of anxiety and want."[7] Camilla gave the baby Napoleon whatever he wanted and catered to his every whim. This gave Napoleon a feeling of omnipotence, supporting his self-love (narcissism), which he would activate, as we will see, whenever he felt threatened by those "all-bad" objects (persons or things). An aging prisoner of the British on Saint Helena, he told his aide Las Cases, "I have been spoiled, one must admit. I have always commanded. From the moment I entered life, I found myself endowed with power, and the circumstances and my own strength were such that as soon as I was in command I no longer recognized either a master or laws."[8]

The American psychoanalyst Pierce Clark thought that the infant Napoleon's relationship with the mother's nursing breast was extremely delicate and had a profound effect on his personality:

Whence come those emotions that later encourage and protect the growing ego, in infancy so weak? They are drawn essentially from the first associations with the mother—not the mother as a person,

> but as an object present in the act of nursing; in the breast relationship. When the child is weaned it may either experience an insufficiency of living through this epoch, or the period may be too prolonged. As evidenced in Napoleon's infancy, the child may remain bound spiritually to the mother and remain fixed in the nursing relationship. Out of the unrequited longing for this situation of complete self-satisfaction all sorts of character defects arise.[9]

Napoleon's lifelong narcissism and his acting out of his omnipotent fantasies were rooted in this early trauma of weaning and abandonment by his wet nurse, which left the two-year-old boy feeling totally helpless. His unconscious defenses were his omnipotent fantasies and his perfectionism. Napoleon told the poet Antoine-Vincent Arnault that life was a bridge over a fast river and Napoleon himself a traveler "laden with burdens and taking no rest" who tires himself "trying to catch soap bubbles of every color which charlatans blow out into the void from richly decorated platforms. As soon as they are touched these bubbles vanish, sullying the hand that has reached for them."[10]

Like an infant, the adult Napoleon, whose story will appear in the chapters that follow, lived in his illusions, unconsciously denying life's imperfections and seeking the unattainable and imaginary perfection of his archaic life. As Clark put it, "The babe imagines that he has recaptured his former state of perfection and in this imaginary repossession of the foetal situation he lives through a period of magic hallucinatory omnipotence. Napoleon in his adult twilight states and lethargies was repeating this infantile flight from unpleasant reality and thereby relieving [*sic*] his early infancy."[11] Napoleon unconsciously acted out his omnipotent fantasies throughout his life.

Aggression is an unconsciously defensive reaction to painful narcissistic injuries. It converts an unbearable sense of helplessness and worthlessness into a sense of self-esteem, an exaggerated narcissism. Deep down, the little boy Napoleon hated his shaming, humiliating, and rejecting mother. As he grew up, whenever he experienced the painful feelings of shame and humiliation, he had to restore his self-esteem by means of aggressive acts. His numerous wars and "campaigns" were such acts. Raoul Brice believed that Napoleon had an inborn "instinct of domination." In fact, Napoleon's aggressive domination of others was not an instinct, but his unconscious defensive adaptation against his unbearable feelings of shame, humiliation, worthlessness, and helplessness. These feelings came from his mother's rejection of him and began when he was very little, and were reinforced by her physical punishment of him. Bartel believed that during the first months of his life Napoleon had a "sweet and gentle disposition."[12] The child experienced his weaning by his nurse Camilla and her leaving the household as an abandonment. Later on, Camilla may have spoiled the boy Napoleon with sweets because she felt guilty at having weaned and left him.

Napoleon's early feelings of shame and humiliation forged his narcissistic personality. Psychoanalysts have given close attention to shame.[13] Heinz Kohut believed that shame and narcissistic rage were unconscious reactions to the loss of grandiosity and omnipotence in early childhood, while in later stages of life they were reactions to the loss of "narcissistic supplies" such as love, admiration, and praise, which the narcissist gets from "idealized objects" that unconsciously replace real loved ones.[14] Leon Wurmser thought that shame was a narcissistic reaction to the loss of self-esteem: "The more ambitious and peremptory (narcissistic) the ego ideal is, the more painful is the wound about failing and the more pervasive is the narcissistic anxiety about yet more mortifications of such nature—in other words, the more shame-prone is that person."[15] Blema Steinberg, a political scientist and psychoanalyst, has shown the key unconscious importance of shame and humiliation in the decision-making process of political leaders.[16]

The little child Napoleon suffered frequently, if not chronically, from the painful feelings of shame, humiliation, and narcissistic rage, which led to violent aggression. Harold Parker thought that "from at least age two [Napoleon] became irritable, self-assertive, quarrelsome, violent, quick in sizing up human situations and in responding, rivalrous, though also affectionate and remorseful," and that this was a direct reaction to his abandonment by his nurse. "The coincidence of his weaning with the arrival of the third child, Maria-Anna, whom the mother nursed, may have set Napoleon off."[17] Dorothy Carrington, however, thought that it was by no means certain that Napoleon had a "sweet and gentle" disposition during the first months of his life, and that Parker's alleged coincidence of Napoleon's weaning with the birth of his sister "is not proved, not, I think, provable . . . such a coincidence could well have been the lot of any child in a numerous family, and may even have befallen one or other of his brothers and sisters (evidence on the subject is lacking)."[18]

Dorothy Carrington thought that Napoleon's *esprit de principauté* was "a very common Corsican characteristic. It is attributed (by the Corsicans among others) to the long history of foreign conquests and domination of their island. *The reaction of resentment is thought to be passed down from parents to children from infancy* [italics added]. Incidentally, Letizia certainly had leanings of this kind! Napoleon differed from most other Corsicans with such tendencies in that his violent, domineering temperament was allied to a strong practical sense and organisational ability, which are strikingly demonstrated in his career, in civil as well as military affairs."[19] A "princely spirit," however, is not the same as a "reaction of resentment" to foreign rulers. It was precisely because his mother was so domineering, cold, and rejecting that Napoleon acquired his *esprit de principauté*. It was his only way of dealing with the unbearable feelings of helpless panic that she aroused in him. The "reaction of resentment" against "foreign conquerors" is abstract to the little child; the feeling of rage at his mother is very real. If, as Carrington thought, Letizia "passed down" her feelings of resentment against foreign rulers to Napoleon, he may have perceived *her* as the harsh foreign ruler in his family.

The political scientist Harold Lasswell believed that political power is sought by people who have suffered deep emotional injuries in their childhood and who seek to overcome painful feelings of low self-esteem.[20] The historian and psychoanalyst Peter Loewenberg echoed Lasswell: "The avid quest for power . . . is compensatory for the traumas caused to the child by a familial political situation that relentlessly drove home his or her lack of power, impotence, and vulnerability due to smallness and weakness."[21] *Being emotionally abandoned by his mother and wet nurse at age two was the worst blow Napoleon ever suffered.* He reacted with helpless narcissistic rage, and these feelings persisted deep in his soul throughout his life. *Napoleon's lifelong quest for power was unconsciously designed to relieve these painful feelings.* He became a tyrant because this was his only way of relieving his unbearable feelings of helplessness. Fighting became Napoleon's *modus vivendi*. When he was fighting, he did not have to feel the pain of abandonment and nonbeing.

While Napoleon's father often used his French name, spelling it Charles-Marie Bonaparte, the young Napoleon preferred his Italian one, Napoleone Buonaparte. This was no accident. Napoleon's attachment to Mother Corsica was profound and powerful. Carlo was strong, manly, and handsome. Carrington thought that Carlo was an intelligent and capable young man who succeeded in much of what he undertook; his principal aim was to get himself recognized as a noble by the royal French court, which he finally achieved in 1779. Although such recognition conferred many privileges, *Carlo's relentless quest for nobility may have masked a deeper dissatisfaction with himself.* Many biographers portrayed Carlo as a restless, dissatisfied young man never happy with his station, a spendthrift who kept intriguing for other posts and embarking on risky business ventures that resulted in the ruin of his family; Dorothy Carrington has shown this to be untrue.[22] Harold Parker thought that Carlo was "an intriguer and a self-promoter."[23] This father, Carlo, could not help his young son Napoleon free himself from a sticky relationship with his mother. Carlo could not be a role model. This may be an important reason for Napoleon's "belief" that Governor Marbeuf was his brother Louis's father and this had a profound effect on his entire life.

Letizia's profound ambivalence toward her second son from his very birth caused her to send him "double messages" of acceptance and rejection at the same time. As a result, Napoleon himself was tied to his mother with equally ambivalent bonds of love and hate. In public, the emperor "always showered lavish praise on his mother." In private, however, "he allowed himself to express his darker feelings about Letizia."[24] On Saint Helena, for example, Napoleon told Las Cases: "I certainly love my mother, and with all my heart. There is nothing I wouldn't do for her—and yet, if I were informed of her death, I don't think I could express my grief with a single tear."[25] This striking statement betrays Napoleon's unconscious death wish against his mother. She not only deceived him but was also rejecting and mean to him. Sigmund Freud, "the father of psychoanalysis," believed that Napoleon had a "huge Joseph complex" due to his deep ambivalent attachment to his elder brother and that "he had to marry a woman called Josephine."[26] In fact, Napoleon fell in love with his first wife partly because her middle name was Josèphe, the feminine version of Joseph, and it was he who invented her name of "Josephine." One biographer thought that "Napoleon's ambivalence about his mother was part of a general obsession with Letizia" and that Napoleon suffered from a "mother fixation" in addition to his Oedipus complex and Joseph complex.[27] Indeed, Napoleon identified with his mother more than he did with his father. His only way of overcoming his feelings of helpless rage was to "identify with the aggressor."

Did Letizia place her second son Napoleon in the nuns' school because she unconsciously wanted him to replace the daughters she had lost?

Wilhelm Reich, an early psychoanalyst, believed that by placing her son in a nuns' school, and through her overbearing behavior at home, including her corporal punishments, Letizia gave Napoleon an "overfeminized" early socialization, which caused him to develop a "phallic-narcissistic" and "sado-masochistic" character.[28] Frank McLynn, however, thought it "unlikely that [Napoleon's] brief attendance at the nuns' school had any significant role in his [character] formation, and it is surely far-fetched to imagine Letizia's beatings as the genesis of sado-masochistic tendencies. However, [Reich's] general thesis of an unconscious desire for revenge against the opposite sex seems well-grounded in the evidence of his later life. In particular, he always thought of women as being totally without honour, duplicitous, deceivers, liars."[29]

Two French noblemen in Corsica—Count Jean-Victor Colchen, the secretary of the French *intendant*, and Count Alexandre-Louis-Gabriel Roux de Laric, a member of Governor Marbeuf's staff—claimed that Marbeuf was so intimate with Letizia Bonaparte that everyone in Ajaccio thought he had an affair with her and that Marbeuf was the father of Letizia's son Louis.[30] Dorothy Carrington, however, had serious doubts about the reliability of the two noblemen's accounts.[31] Be that as it may, the boy Napoleon very probably *believed* that his mother had had an affair with the governor:

> The small Napoleon, like others, had sufficient grounds to induce a belief in a liaison between Marbeuf and his mother; one that was tolerated, if not encouraged, by his father; and that he had some justification, at least, for forging a phantasy which, as we know, has all the validity of a real occurrence . . . That this indeed was so . . . is clearly shown by something he said at a much later date, when speaking of what he had felt during his first leave in Corsica, after an absence of eight years: "My happiness would have been complete if two loved men had not been absent, my father and Count Marbeuf, whom we lost on 20th September . . . and whom my family long mourned." This juxtaposition of Marbeuf and his father . . . makes it probable that, given this phantasy, Napoleon would feel somewhat unsure which of them was his father.[32]

The young Napoleon also experienced the old Paoli as a father figure. Louis-Antoine Fauvelet de Bourrienne, Napoleon's unreliable onetime secretary and state minister, recalled Napoleon telling him that at age nine, after his schoolmasters had criticized Paoli, he angrily exclaimed to them, "Paoli was a great man: he loved his fatherland, and *I shall never forgive my father, who was his adjutant, for helping to unite Corsica to France!* [italics added] He should have followed his fortunes and succumbed with him."[33] Carlo Bonaparte, however, was never Paoli's "adjutant." General Augustin-Daniel Belliard and Napoleon's elder brother Joseph Bonaparte refuted Bourrienne's statement "as a double calumny, of son and father."[34] Napoleon himself remembered Carlo "as the over-indulgent father rather than the traitor to his country."[35] Despite Bourrienne's unreliability, however, the psychoanalyst Ludwig Jekels made the statement that Bourrienne had attributed to Napoleon (as quoted by François-Gilbert de Coston) the cornerstone of his psychoanalytic study. Jekels concluded that the young Napoleon, before his "turning point" in 1793, passionately loved Corsica, hated France, admired Paoli, and was ashamed of his father's "treason to Corsica."[36]

As we have seen before, Napoleon was a man of many contradictions. The psychoanalyst Pierce Clark thought that "at one time Napoleon was easily moved to tears, at another he was quite insensate; selfish at one moment, lavish at another. He could despise love with its higher connotation of self-sacrifice and yet render himself willingly a slave to passion."[37] He could be both an angel and a devil. When he was enraged and anxious, he became cruel and ruthless; when he was relaxed and happy, he could be kind and generous. "A pinch-penny in personal spending, Napoleon was lavish to friends. On his desk he kept a leather-bound book titled *Dotations*, in which he listed, alphabetically, cash gifts to friends and other public servants. It was a thick book and by the end of the empire almost full."[38] Napoleon himself knew that he could be kind, generous, witty, compassionate, warm, and loving, but also hard, cruel, sadistic, callous, cold, and unfeeling. In 1809 he reportedly said to the political journalist and statesman Pierre-Louis Roederer, "There are two distinct men in me, the man of the head and the man of the heart. In my family circle, I am the feeling man: I play with the children, I chat with my wife, I read aloud to them from novels."[39] The French neuropsychiatrist Raymond Frugier thought that Napoleon himself made his dual nature clearer to us than any of his biographers and scholars.[40]

Napoleon was so complex that his numerous biographers saw in him many different people. Jean-Baptiste Pérès, who seriously believed that Napoleon never existed, wrote that to no one were assigned so many dissimilar characters.[41] Marshal Auguste-Frédéric-Louis Viesse de Marmont,

Napoleon's duke of Ragusa, who knew Napoleon intimately for twenty-two years, said of him: "There are two men in him, physically and morally."[42] One scholar called Napoleon "a living synthesis of good and evil."[43] Madame Permon, Napoleon's mother's friend and the mother of the duchess of Abrantès, who knew Napoleon in his early days in Paris, reportedly said to him: "Napoleon, there are two men in you at this moment. Continue, I entreat you, to be the man I love and esteem, and above all do not let the other get the better of you."[44]

Similarly, the psychoanalyst Pierce Clark thought that "there are two Napoleons . . . One Napoleon was reasoning, cold, and calculating, steely critical—this was the highly talented person of his daily existence, the one the average astute man generally saw. But the other Napoleon was highly unstable, intuitive, motivated at irregular intervals by the fertile genius of his unconscious mind; at these moments he almost excelled human comprehension."[45] And one of Napoleon's best biographers felt that "it was as if there were within him two men, one of whom occasionally, in rare moments of relaxation, found amusement in watching the other."[46]

Narcissistic persons unconsciously split opposing aspects of their selves, such as grandiosity and dependency, or feelings of superiority and inferiority, and keep them separate. Napoleon suffered from extreme up-and-down swings in his self-esteem. His feelings of superiority alternated with feelings of inferiority. Tragically, these two kinds of feelings form a vicious circle in the narcissist's mind. Napoleon's inner splitting was an unconscious defense against his unbearable feelings for his mother. So was his denial. *Napoleon unconsciously denied his murderous rage at his mother.* As we have seen, the aging Napoleon told Las Cases that he loved his mother with all his heart—but added that if she were to die, he would not feel any grief because "my reason has accustomed me in advance to the loss of my mother."[47] This was a rationalization of his unconscious death wishes for her. The French historian Claude Manceron thought that Napoleon and Letizia did not love each other and that "you could put the whole history of their relationship under a magnifying glass and still not find a trace of tenderness."[48] In fact, Napoleon fought a lifelong war against his mother. Dorothy Carrington wrote: "Reading Napoleon's reminiscences of Letizia and hers of him, one has the impression of a constant duel between them."[49]

My interpretation, then, is that the inner splitting in Napoleon's inner life adapted itself to external circumstances. For the first two years of his life, Napoleon's wet nurse, Camilla Ilari, was his nurturing mother. When she left him at age two, and his mother Letizia began to nurse his baby sister Maria Anna, he was enraged at his mother yet depended on her for his survival. He unconsciously split his mother's image inside himself into two. The all-good mother was cast in the image of Camilla, and her image was displaced to Corsica. The all-bad mother was cast in the image of an evil witch. Until 1793 that bad-mother image was displaced to France; afterwards, when Paoli's Corsica rejected Napoleon and took over the role of the all-bad mother, France unconsciously became the all-good mother and "England" the all-bad one.

Children who cannot integrate their mother's good and bad images and their corresponding images of themselves (omnipotent/narcissistic vs. ashamed/helpless) often also cannot integrate the images of their fathers. Ludwig Jekels believed that Napoleon's oft-changing feelings about France and Corsica in 1791–1793 followed the ups and downs in the fate of King Louis XVI, who also unconsciously symbolized his father. The French king's execution in early 1793 symbolically fulfilled Napoleon's unconscious patricidal wishes. Like Oedipus, having "killed" his three father figures—his father Carlo Maria, Governor Marbeuf, and King Louis XVI—Napoleon could identify with Marbeuf (France) and possess his liberated "mother" (Corsica). The psychoanalyst Ludwig Jekels thought that Napoleon attached himself "irrevocably"to France, wished to join Corsica "irrevocably" to her, and turned his Oedipal rage against Paoli, yet another father figure, for preventing Corsica's union with France and for delivering Corsica to the British "foreigners."[50]

While Jekels was right about the power of Napoleon's oedipal conflict, the deeper and more powerful issue in Napoleon's emotions was that of incomplete separation and individuation from his mother. When he was seventeen, in 1786, Napoleon had suicidal ideation and wrote a short piece that scholars have titled *Sur le suicide*. Jacques Bainville, one of Napoleon's best biographers, thought that Napoleon's expulsion from Corsica was a deliverance. "Corsica herself had cured Bonaparte of the sentimental, literary moodiness which pervaded his early youth."[51] In his youth Napoleon had loved Corsica, his idealized motherland, and Paoli, his idealized father. Splitting his inner objects into all-good and all-bad ones, he hated France, unconsciously his denigrated bad mother. Although Corsica unconsciously symbolized his good mother, and France his bad one, the splitting was far from successful.

Napoleon's suicidal wavering before returning to Corsica in 1786 betrayed his profound ambivalence, his yearning for fusion with his early mother as well as his archaic fear of being engulfed by her. Napoleon had returned to Corsica in September 1786, when Governor Marbeuf was dying. Did he wish to see Marbeuf before he died, to take care of his mother and siblings, or to take the place of Letizia's benefactor and lover? Marbeuf's death may have fulfilled Napoleon's oedipal wishes but was also another abandonment for Napoleon. His violent opposition to uniting Corsica with France reverberated in his unconscious mind with his conflict over his own fusion with his mother. When the Corsican *consulta* expelled him and his family, Corsica became the bad mother, and Paoli the bad father, who had to be killed. France, who gave him sustenance, was his new idealized mother, and he wished to unite his old good mother, Corsica, with her.

Napoleon's expulsion from Corsica in 1793 was of his own doing—and he needed it badly. Jacques Bainville wrote, "The interest of Bonaparte's Corsican adventures lies in their showing how petty and pointless were the quarrels and schemes in which he would have spent himself had not his fortunate star expelled him by the hand of Paoli."[52] If we read "his unconscious mind" for "his fortunate star," the statement becomes even truer. As we have seen, Dorothy Carrington thought that Napoleon had "piled failure on failure until he was finally chased from the island with his family by Paoli's partisans. All this had to happen before he was free to look beyond Corsica, to act efficiently, to exploit his gifts, his skills, to love a woman other than Letizia, to become the man known to history."[53] Indeed, Napoleon and Lucien Bonaparte got themselves expelled from Corsica through their own anti-Paoli actions. Napoleon's profound unconscious conflict between the craving for fusion and the need for individuation was never resolved. Throughout his life, this inner conflict shaped his destiny, along with his insatiable need for power and greatness, to combat his deepest feelings of helplessness and nonbeing. In the following chapters, I will examine how Napoleon's personality organization was intertwined with historical events. I shall also explore in-depth Napoleon's lifelong struggle against himself and his self-destructive streak that eventually led to his downfall and death.[54]

Part II

Becoming a Historical Figure

9

The Struggle to Master Inner Helplessness

Psychologically, our life is not a truncated succession of disparate stages. It is a continual process of developing and changing. It is hard to tell when adolescence ends and adulthood begins. In Napoleon's case that milestone was fairly clear: the dramatic events of 1793, which helped him break away from mother Letizia and motherland Corsica. He was rejected at the same time by "father" Paoli and "mother" Corsica. His former love for Paoli turned into hatred. He once and for all abandoned Corsica and embraced France. He was not to see Corsica again until his return from his Egyptian campaign in September 1799, and the main purpose of that visit was to see his old wet nurse, Camilla Ilari. The flight from Corsica in 1793 marked the beginning of his attempted separation and individuation, of his adulthood, and, not surprisingly, of his rapid rise in the French military ranks. He could not, however, succeed in freeing himself from the internal struggles of his developmental years, and his rise in the French ranks were intertwined with the demands of his personality.

Events in mainland France were no less dramatic than in Corsica and in Napoleon's private life. Civil war raged in Corsica and in mainland France. Food became scarce. People went hungry. The *Convention nationale* had its hands full fighting its internal and external enemies. On March 18, 1793, its top general and former war minister, Charles-François du Périer Dumouriez, commanding the *armée du Nord*, lost a decisive battle against the Austrians at the Belgian city of Neerwinden. The Austrian commanders at Neerwinden offered tempting terms to the desperate

Dumouriez, and on April 5 he defected to Austria. The next day the news of his betrayal reached Paris. France was shocked by his treason. Under the stress and anxiety of crisis and war, the French *Convention nationale* created the *comité de Salut public* to watch its ministers and "take emergency measures to defend the French Republic." The *comité de Salut public* was created with good intentions, only to turn into a bloodthirsty monster during the Terror.

The French Revolution was an endless series of military battles and political power struggles. The Reign of Terror in 1793–1794 augmented those struggles and it was very bloody. The anxious republicans executed their real and imaginary enemies. In June 1793 the Montagnards and Jacobins had taken over the French government from the Girondins and instituted dictatorial rule. Popular revolts multiplied. The leftist republicans in the *Convention nationale* were outnumbered by the royalists, moderates, and conservatives; they were afraid of a "rightist' takeover; from September 1793 to July 1794 the *comité de Salut public* arrested, tortured, and executed countless Frenchmen whom it labeled "enemies of the Republic." Many others died or killed themselves after being tortured in prison.

To control its ambitious generals, the *Convention nationale* sent its "people's representatives" to its various armies and kept moving its generals from one army to another. These generals later commanded other armies. The French revolutionaries were violently antinobility and anticlerical. In 1790 the Civil Constitution of the Clergy had placed the Catholic Church under the power of the state. In 1793 the de-christianization of France became virulent. Influenced by the French rationalists, the *Convention nationale* replaced Christianity with "the Religion of Reason." In French, one term for the motherland is *la mère-patrie*. Many French revolutionaries treated their new republic as a human object, an idealized mother. The French *Convention nationale* proclaimed "her birthday" on September 22, 1792, as the first day of the first month of the first year of the French Republic (1 Vendémiaire Year I). The republican calendar lasted thirteen years and three months (1792–1805), isolating France from the rest of the world.

The boat carrying Napoleon, his mother Letizia, and Napoleon's siblings from Corsica to mainland France arrived in Toulon on the night of June 13–14, 1793. They were met on the dock by Napoleon's eighteen-year-old brother Lucien, who had caused their expulsion from Corsica by denouncing Paoli publicly and by writing them the inflammatory letter that Paoli had intercepted. Like many young revolutionaries, Lucien lived in the ancient Greco-Roman past. Identifying with the ancient Roman who had murdered the "tyrant" Julius Caesar, he called himself "Brutus Bonaparte" and had boasted to his elder brother Joseph of being capable of killing any tyrant—while telling him that Napoleon was one. Lucien militated for the Jacobin cause while holding a lowly job as a *garde-magasin des armées* with the army supply department in the south of France. He was too nearsighted to serve in the regular army.[1]

After they landed at Toulon, the Bonapartes were nearly penniless. An obscure lady offered the Bonapartes a run-down house in the citadel of La Valette, a poor village near Toulon. Paolo Casabianca, who had served with Napoleon's late father Carlo on the Corsican delegation to the royal French court at Versailles fourteen years earlier, pleaded their case with the authorities. Napoleon's patron, Saliceti, certified the Bonapartes as "patriotic exiles," making them eligible for a tiny financial assistance and bread rations from the authorities of the villages of Brignoles and Saint-Maximin—the latter renamed "Marathon."[2] The puny relief given to "patriotic" Corsican refugees from Paoli's "persecution" was augmented by Napoleon's meager salary. Saliceti wrote the *Convention nationale* in Paris urging it to compensate the Bonapartes for their Corsican property confiscated or destroyed by "the traitor" Paoli, and the *Convention* voted a grant of six-hundred-thousand francs to the Bonapartes. Joseph Bonaparte, who had gone to Paris to lobby for the compensation, was notified, yet not one sou of compensation was ever paid to the Bonapartes.[3]

The royalist insurrection against the republican *Convention nationale* repeatedly caused the Bonapartes to move in order to escape the rebels' murderous violence. Driven by fear and poverty, Letizia and her children left La Valette for a little village in the Var, near Brignoles, some thirty miles north of Toulon,[4] then moved again to a two-room apartment in a poor neighborhood of Marseille, where life was no less difficult than at Toulon. Letizia had to queue up for food in the local soup kitchen, and Napoleon's sisters had to wash their linen at the public fountain. In early 1794 Napoleon moved his family to a castle-turned-farmhouse near Antibes; a few months later they had to return to Marseille. In 1795 the Bonapartes moved into Marseille's Hôtel de Cypières, which had become a haven for Corsican exiles.

Fortunately for the Bonapartes, Napoleon had good connections in France, and he used them. General Jean de Beaumont du Teil, the brother of Napoleon's former commander at Auxonne, now the commander of the artillery in the French army of Italy, made sure that Napoleon was not treated as a deserter, and had him posted to the 12th company of the 4th artillery regiment at Nice. In mid-June 1793, Napoleon joined his 4th artillery regiment, now garrisoned at Nice, which France had annexed from Sardinia-Piedmont the year before. Napoleon was back in the army of the French Republic. On June 20 Napoleon returned to Toulon, which the Spanish navy was bombarding. The people of Marseille had rebelled against the convention, which sent troops to quell the revolt. The Spaniards were trying to help the rebels. The British Royal Navy was not far away. By August the terrified Toulonnais would deliver the city to them, and by September Napoleon would take part in the republican siege of Toulon.

Napoleon's and Saliceti's report to the *Convention nationale* on the state of Corsica in early June 1793 had reached Paris too late to topple Paoli, but Saliceti's name carried weight with the *Convention*. The report had a dramatic effect on the French revolutionary government. On July 1, at Saliceti's urging, the *Convention* declared all the acts of the Corsican *consulta* null and void and outlawed Paoli, Pozzo di Borgo, and the entire Corsican administration at Corte as "traitors to France."[5] To further weaken Paoli, the *Convention* divided Corsica into two *départements*, the Golo in the north and the Liamone in the south, each named after a Corsican river, and each with its own administration. They correspond to the modern French *départements* of Haute-Corse and Corse-du-Sud.

In late June 1793, at Toulon, Napoleon met his new commander and protector, General Jean de Beaumont du Teil, the commander of the artillery in the *armée d'Italie* and an elder brother of his former commanding officer. On July 3 Napoleon wrote the war minister in Paris, Jean-Baptiste-Noël Bouchotte, proposing the forging of a new model of reverberating furnace, a new invention for casting cannonballs "so that we can build them on our coast and blow up the vessels of the despots."[6] The chief "despot," presumably, was Pasquale Paoli, whom he had so loved and admired just three months earlier. He signed his memo "Bonaparte," rather than the Corsican "Buonaparte," which he had used heretofore. Napoleon no longer wavered about his identity: "He was French, republican, *Montagnard*, a partisan of the *Convention* against the enemies of the republic."[7]

From June to December 1793, while Pasquale Paoli and his Corsican patriots fought France's "occupation forces," the Corsican-born French officer Napoleon Bonaparte fought the royalist rebels in the south of

France, mainly in Toulon. It was the beginning of the Terror in revolutionary France. On July 17 France deployed its land and naval forces in Corsica "to enforce the laws of the French Republic."[8] Napoleon no longer felt powerless, as he had in Corsica. Now he could shoot, kill, and force people to obey him. Within these six months Napoleon was rapidly promoted from captain to brigadier general. In those days there was much rivalry between the various French armies, and the politicians manipulated army generals in their own favor. Castelot thought that Napoleon's patron Saliceti controlled the *armée des Alpes*, deployed north and west of the Alps, while the *armée d'Italie*, which fought south of the Alps in northern Italy, was the fief of the thirty-year-old *commissaire des guerres* Augustin de Robespierre, the younger brother of the "incorruptible" Maxmilien, who ruled in Paris. Serving in these armies, Napoleon fought the federalist rebels of Lyon, Bordeaux, Marseille, and Toulon, who had united in a federation and rebelled against the Terror of the *Convention nationale*. The federalist rebels had joined the royalists and Girondins in fighting the government. Marseille, the largest city of the French south, was the headquarters of the federalists, who wanted a decentralized federal political system for France, vehemently opposing the centralized republican system under which all power flowed from Paris.[9]

André Castelot thought that in July 1793 Napoleon had been assigned to the 12th company of the 4th artillery regiment, which was then stationed at Nice "as part of that *armée des Alpes* which was to make a diversion by attacking the Piedmont."[10] In fact, from mid-June to mid-September, Napoleon served in General Carteaux's army, but in July he went to Avignon, the capital of the Vaucluse *département*, to organize the convoys of the *armée d'Italie*, "a kind of wagoner's job."[11] Avignon, which had belonged to the Roman popes for centuries, and had just become part of France, was occupied by the rebel national guardsmen of the Marseillais federalists, and Brigadier General Jean-François Carteaux was besieging the town with his army. Napoleon joined the siege of Avignon under Carteaux. To Napoleon, Carteaux was an "obstreperous" upstart *sans-culotte*, "a former house painter and former gendarme-turned-dragoon, who had picked up his general's stars in the street one night during a riot."[12] Carteaux "strutted about" his headquarters "covered with gold braid from head to foot."[13] An unhappy Napoleon wrote to the *citoyen ministre de la guerre*, Bouchotte, requesting a transfer to the *armée du Rhin*.[14]

Frank Richardson believed that Napoleon needed constant reassurance in the form of promotions because he felt inferior to other people, being short and ugly.[15] In fact, the young Napoleon was of medium height and rather handsome.[16] The French verb *tondre* means to shear, clip, crop, cut, or trim. Because the older Napoleon's hair was short, some of the French called Napoleon *le petit tondu* (the little cropped one). His troops fondly called him *le petit caporal* (the little corporal). Estimates of his height by the British officers who met him in 1815 ranged from five feet five inches (165 cm) to five feet seven inches (170 cm). At Napoleon's death, he was five feet six and a half inches (169 cm) tall.[17]

The varying estimates of Napoleon's height may have been due to his gradually changing appearance. In his youth Napoleon was thin and handsome, had long hair, and may have looked taller than he was. In his old age he was fat and unattractive, tended to slump, had short hair, and looked stooped and short. But, like beauty, height is in the eye of the beholder. The estimates were due to the state of mind of the observers. André Masséna, Napoleon's future *maréchal* and the hero of many of his battles in central Europe, recalled that when he first met Napoleon in 1796, the latter put on his general's hat, and he "seemed to have grown two feet."[18] In fact, Napoleon's inferiority feelings had less to do with his physical stature and more with his being rejected and put down as a child, and they alternated with superiority feelings.

Toulon has a large, imposing bay. Napoleon had an insatiable thirst for knowledge and an immense need to learn. He observed Toulon's topography and defensive system and drew his conclusions. "Thus it was, not intuitively but by reason, that when Bonaparte took over his post he instantly pointed to the Fort of l'Éguillette, at the southwest entrance to the bay, and declared that Toulon was there."[19] On July 17, 1793, the republicans seized the *fort de l'Éguillette* from the rebels, forcing the British and Spanish man-of-wars to move away from the port of Toulon. Later, however, the *fort de l'Éguillette* was recaptured by the Toulon rebels. At the same time the republican troops fought the federalist rebels at Marseille and Avignon. Napoleon had been posted to the army of Brigadier General Jean-François Carteaux, which was besieging Avignon,[20] and General Jean de Beaumont du Teil, who commanded the artillery in the French Army of Italy, had ordered Napoleon to organize convoys of gunpowder and materiel to Italy.[21] On July 24 Napoleon's artillery company was dispatched to the village of Pontet, near Avignon, and they took part in Carteaux's attack on the rebels in Avignon. Napoleon and his men shot and killed some Marseillais national guardsmen who had "butchered thirty-one civilians in cold blood."[22]

After the fighting at Avignon, Napoleon was so traumatized and felt so guilty for having killed his fellow Frenchmen "on behalf of a terrorist government" that "he fell ill and went to rest at nearby Beaucaire."[23] To the mental-health clinician, this looks like a case of "traumatic war neurosis," a case of "post-traumatic stress disorder" in the current psychiatric textbooks. After some rest at Beaucaire, the traumatized Napoleon returned to Avignon, which had just fallen to General Carteaux's republican troops. He was billeted with Maître Renaudet, a pharmacist living on Avignon's Rue Haute.[24]

In late July 1793, at Maître Renaudet's Avignon home, Napoleon composed twenty pages under the lengthy title: *Le Souper de Beaucaire, ou dialogue entre un militaire de l'armée de Carteaux, un Marseillais, un Nîmois et un fabricant de Montpellier, sur les événements qui sont arrivés dans le ci-devant Comtat B l'arrivée des Marseillais* (The Beaucaire Supper, or a dialogue between a soldier of the Army of Carteaux, a man from Marseille, a man from Nîmes and a manufacturer from Montpellier on the events which have occurred in the former *Comtat* upon the arrival of the Marseillais).[25] This work was an imaginary dialogue between a republican soldier (himself) and a federalist Marseillais rebel.

In Napoleon's fantasy, the republican soldier runs into federalist rebels at a Beaucaire inn. Finding that he is serving under General Carteaux, the angry federalists call Carteaux a murderer. The soldier defends Carteaux. He says that Carteaux has scrupulously observed order and discipline, that at Saint-Esprit and Avignon the republican soldiers "have not taken a pin,"[26] and that Carteaux had imprisoned an officer who had arrested a Marseillais without the authority to do so, as well as a soldier who had been caught stealing. The soldier accuses the federalist rebels of having murdered over thirty innocent people, violated many families's asylum, and filled the prisons with innocent *citoyens*. "Do you not feel that this battle between the patriots and the despots is a mortal combat?"[27] From an angry exhortation to the Marseillais rebels to repent and join the republic, the *Souper de Beaucaire* turns into a violent tirade against the "traitor" Paoli, who had nothing to do with the civil war in France:

> Do not fear the army, it respects Marseille because it knows that no city has made so many sacrifices for the public interest . . . Shake the yoke of the few aristocrats who lead you, take up healthier principles again, and you will have no truer friends than the soldiers . . . You follow, you say, the tricolor flag? Paoli too hoisted it in Corsica, to

> have the time to fool the people, to crush the true friends of liberty, to drag his compatriots into his ambitious and criminal projects; he hoisted the tricolor flag and he shot at the buildings of the Republic, and he chased our troops out of the fortresses, disarmed those who were there, pillaged the stores, *ravaged and confiscated the goods of the wealthiest families because they were attached to the unity of the Republic, and he had himself named generalissimo* . . . and at the same time he had the impudence to call himself the friend of France and a good Republican.[28]

André Castelot and many other biographers mistook Napoleon's *Souper de Beaucaire* for the account of an actual dialogue that took place between Napoleon and four merchants, partisans of the Marseille federalists, at a Beaucaire inn. In fact, it was an imaginary dialogue expressing Napoleon's inner conflict in fantasy form. Napoleon wanted to have his essay printed and distributed as proof of his patriotism. He went to Sabin Tournal, the publisher of *Le Courier d'Avignon*, who was working for the French government, and offered to pay him for the printing of his pamphlet. Tournal agreed to print Napoleon's *Souper de Beaucaire* at Napoleon's expense. Rather than print the lengthy and bombastic title, however, Tournal simply printed the short title, *Le Souper de Beaucaire.*[29] The psychoanalyst Pierce Clark thought that this literary work, written when Napoleon was not quite twenty-four, was much more mature and concise than his previous ones, and that it showed "an almost startlingly brilliant military insight."[30] The astute biographer Jacques Bainville thought that it showed "an unmistakable talent."[31]

Napoleon Bonaparte celebrated his twenty-fourth birthday in Avignon on August 15, 1793, which later became 28 Thermidor Year I of the French Republic. The great inner upheaval that had changed him from nationalist Corsican to proud Frenchman was over, as was his seven-year struggle to separate and individuate from Corsica and his mother and become his own man. Harold Parker doubted that Napoleon ever became "a proud Frenchman." He thought that "after [Napoleon's] expulsion from Corsica and the death of the autonomous Corsican ideal, he became simply a survivor and a climber, loyal to himself and as loyal to members of his family as they permitted him to be."[32] Yet Napoleon identified with France and repeatedly proclaimed his Frenchness to the world.[33] Napoleon now focused his emotional and intellectual energies on fighting and winning battles, sublimating his infantile rage into controlled military activity.

In August 1793 Captain Napoleon Bonaparte turned twenty-four, and Brigadier General Jean-François Carteaux, the commander of the army in which Captain Bonaparte was serving, was promoted to division general. Captain Bonaparte was impatient for a new assignment. The *Convention nationale*'s republicans were fighting the royalist rebels in the gorges of Ollioules, a village west of Toulon, on the road to Marseille. At that battle the commander of an artillery company in General Carteaux's army, *le capitaine* Etienne-Auguste-Charles de Dommartin, who had preceded Napoleon in the French artillery entrance examinations of 1785, was badly wounded, incapacitated, and evacuated to Marseille. This was Napoleon's opportunity for advancement.

On September 16, 1793, the *Convention*'s representative Saliceti named Napoleon to replace the wounded Captain Dommartin. The next day Napoleon took over the command of Dommartin's artillery company in Carteaux's army. The proud twenty-four-year-old Captain Bonaparte now met the blustering forty-two-year-old General Carteaux, in whose defense he had written his *Souper de Beaucaire*. Napoleon later claimed that he was shocked by the general's selfishness at dinner, where Carteaux was served a sumptuous meal while all his guests were served very meagerly.[34] Did the general do what Napoleon himself unconsciously wished to do? In Napoleon's unconscious feelings, Carteaux became his stingy mother. Napoleon found Carteaux's aide-de-camp, Pierre-Louis Dupas, as stupid as Carteaux himself. When the *député-en-mission* Gasparin arrived, Napoleon later claimed, he gave Captain Bonaparte full authority for the siege, displacing General Carteaux. This unlikely story may be an oedipal fantasy, but Carteaux was removed from his command the following month, was transferred to the *armée d'Italie*, then to the *armée des Alpes*, after which he was disgraced and imprisoned.[35] It was the fulfillment of Napoleon's oedipal fantasy.

Napoleon placed his *batterie de la Montagne* above Les Poudières. On September 19, 1793, he bombarded the bay of Toulon and forced a British frigate to turn around. On September 20 Napoleon moved up his *batterie des Sans-Culottes* to Brégaillon and pressed the three-week-old siege of Toulon. The *Convention*'s troops had taken Marseille from the royalist rebels but were stopped at the nearby port of Toulon, where the rebels and their British allies were holding the city.

The sixty-nine-year-old commander of the royal British naval forces at Toulon, Vice Admiral Sir Samuel Hood, supplied the Toulonnais rebels with "not only naval fire for the defense, but also 2000 British, 7000 Neapolitan, and 8000 Spanish troops, which almost doubled the number of defenders."[36] One of Hood's subordinates was the thirty-four-year-old captain Horatio Nelson, master of the sixty-four-gun frigate HMS *Agamemnon*, whom Lord Hood sent to Naples for reinforcements. In Naples, Nelson met the sixty-three-year-old Sir William Hamilton, the "adroit and scholarly" British ambassador who had been living at Naples for thirty years, and Sir William's thirty-two-year-old wife, Emma Hamilton, who was close to Queen Maria Carolina of Naples and Sicily. Hamilton helped Nelson get his reinforcements for Lord Hood's fleet; five years later Nelson repaid Hamilton by taking his wife as his mistress.

The father-son battle between the older General Carteaux and the younger Captain Bonaparte became a life-and-death struggle. Carteaux called his arrogant subordinate *le capitaine Canon*. Napoleon despised his incompetent commander. Bonaparte's artillery barrages on Toulon apparently pleased his patron Saliceti, the powerful representative on mission. On September 29, 1793, the *représentants* Saliceti and Gasparin recommended Napoleon for promotion to *chef de bataillon*. The young officer denounced his commander in chief, Carteaux, to Paul de Barras, Saliceti, and Gasparin. Carteaux's siege of Toulon was faltering; from Napoleon's viewpoint, the general was ripe for shaking.

Napoleon's victory over Carteaux was clinched on October 14, 1793. "For over a month Carteaux [had] blocked the young officer's plan."[37] Thanks to Saliceti and Gasparin, however, Carteaux fell out of favor with the *Convention nationale* and was transferred from his command to the *armée d'Italie*, then to the *armée des Alpes*. He was replaced with General François-Amédée Doppet, the Savoyard physician who had ghostwritten Madame de Warens' "memoirs." The people's representatives called the *Convention nationale*'s attention to Napoleon as the only military officer competent to plan these operations. Max Gallo thought that Napoleon was intoxicated with his newfound power: "This ascendance which one exercises over men, what a joy! What an alcohol! What woman could give such a feeling of drunkenness and of power!"[38] Indeed, Napoleon needed power more than he wanted love or sexual pleasure. It was the antidote to his deepest unconscious feelings of helplessness. General Doppet, however, was an even worse commander than General Carteaux. The angry soldiers reportedly cried, "Shall we always have painters and doctors to command us?"[39]

Like General Carteaux, General Doppet did not last long in his command. On October 19, 1793 Saliceti and his colleagues provisionally promoted Napoleon to *chef de bataillon*, a French military rank equivalent to major. Nine days later, Napoleon's new rank was confirmed. On 26 Brumaire Year II of the French Republic (November 16, 1793) General Doppet left Ollioules, and on the following day he was replaced as the commander of the French republican army at Toulon by the fifty-five-year-old republican general Dugommier, the former aristocrat Jacques-François Coquille du Gommier. After Carteaux and Doppet, he was the third general to command that republican army is as many months. At General Dugommier's war council, Napoleon proposed to his superiors a detailed plan for breaching the fortified city of Toulon. Dugommier's artillery commander, General Du Teil, and the *Convention nationale*'s representatives on mission, Saliceti, Ricord, and Augustin de Robespierre, backed Napoleon's plan for breaching Toulon's defenses. General Dugommier adopted it, even though he knew that its failure would cost him his head.[40]

The battle of Toulon was a great success for General Dugommier, who sent a report to the *Convention nationale* in Paris praising the *citoyen* Bonaparte as the officer who had most distinguished himself. The twenty-four-year-old Napoleon rose fast in the ranks. Dugommier promoted the chef de bataillon Bonaparte to lieutenant colonel.

Napoleon's skin was very sensitive. Expressing its owner's unconscious feelings, it often erupted in blisters and pimples. During the siege of Toulon, Napoleon's skin began to itch. By the accepted account, he had been splashed by the blood of a gunner wounded at his side. Like many scholars, the psychoanalyst Pierce Clark thought that Napoleon had handled "an infected artillery sponge" and contracted "blood poisoning."[41] Napoleon himself recalled that the gunner had been suffering from scabies, that he had been killed by enemy fire, that his ramrod was infected with scabies, and that he, Napoleon, not knowing this, had seized his ramrod and helped recharge the cannon. A few days later he found himself covered with scabies.[42]

The republican troops besieging Toulon hated the royalist Toulonnais with a passion. For three months the rebels had frustrated the republicans' efforts to enter their city. During the night of December 17–18, 1793, General Dugommier's republican troops seized the Fort of Mulgrave, known as *le Petit Gibraltar*. On December 18 the British evacuated Toulon, and on December 19, after twelve exhausting and frustrating weeks, the republican troops breached the walls of Toulon, which they called *la ville infâme* (the infamous city). On December 20 they began the mass executions of the unfortunate souls who had stayed behind. Name-calling was not confined to the republicans. The Toulonnais called their republican enemies *les carmagnoles*, after the short Piedmontese jacket worn during the Revolution as well as of the *rondo* which the French revolutionaries sang and danced in the Provençal *farandole* style. Among the republican troops that entered Toulon was Napoleon's artillery battalion. The frenzied republican soldiers pillaged, raped, and murdered the Toulonnais: 1,100 were massacred and 15,000 others fled the city.[43]

Did Napoleon take part in the Toulon massacre on December 19, 1793? Did he, on the contrary, try to save innocent lives? Or did he stay aloof of the massacre? We have wildly conflicting reports from witnesses and scholars. Louis Viesse de Marmont, the future *maréchal* and Duke of Ragusa, was a nineteen-year-old artillery officer in Dugommier's army at the time of the Toulon massacre. He soon became one of Napoleon's aides-de-camp, along with Andoche Junot, a future general. The old Marmont recalled that Napoleon had tried to save innocent lives amid the horrors at the Place de Toulon.[44] Marmont did not say who had ordered the massacre—the *Comité de salut public* and its representative Joseph Fouché—but he clearly believed that Napoleon had saved some victims from execution and was horrified by the massacre. Arthur Chuquet also believed that Napoleon saved lives at Toulon.[45] André Castelot and Max Gallo believed that Napoleon was horrified and nauseated by the sight of the "strenuous executions by firing squad and the massacre" and that he saved as many lives as he could.[46]

Nonetheless, some scholars have blamed Napoleon for the Toulon massacre. Pierre Bécat wrote that "Bonaparte, having had 800 prisoners executed, made it known in high places that the enemies of the Revolution had perished."[47] Frank Richardson, ignoring all the evidence to the contrary, was convinced that Napoleon personally committed the Toulon massacre.[48] A more accurate assessment was probably given by Frank McLynn, who thought that Napoleon "largely shut his eyes" to the Toulon massacre in order to stay out of trouble with the *Comité de salut public.*[49] Some scholars passed in silence over the massacre that took place at the *place de Toulon* after the capture of the city. Pierce Clark, ignoring the Toulon massacre, believed that Napoleon's "military genius" had found its first expression at Toulon.[50] After the fall of Toulon, the commander of the artillery in Napoleon's army, General Jean de Beaumont du Teil, was so enthusiastic about Bonaparte that he urged the war minister in Paris, Jean-Baptiste-Noël Bouchotte, to promote him.

The British naval base in the Mediterranean moved to Corsica, where Paoli was fighting the French. Captain Horatio Nelson fought the French at the ports of Bastia and Calvi and was gravely wounded in his right eye. On December 22, 1793, four days after he left Toulon, Nelson's boss, Admiral Sir Samuel Hood, anchored his fleet in Corsica, which had broken ranks with France. On that same day Saliceti and the other representatives on mission summoned the twenty-four-year-old Bonaparte and named him provisionally to the rank of brigadier general. Owen Connelly thought that this was nothing special:

> At this stage, Bonaparte was just another of [Lazare] Carnot's fledgling generals. The Organizer of [the] Victory had promoted scores of young officers during the Terror; he made generals of eight of Napoleon's future marshals, out of a total of only twenty-six. Some were raised to higher rank than Napoleon, e.g., [the thirty-one-year-old] Jean-Baptiste Jourdan [who was made a division general]; some brigadiers were even younger than Napoleon, e.g., [the twenty-three-year-old] Louis-Nicolas Davout. Bonaparte knew that he had to continue to prove himself.[51]

In fact, Lazare Carnot, the member of the *Comité de salut public* in charge of the armies, had defeated the Austrians at the northern French town of Wattignies in mid-October 1793, but would only "organize the French victory" at the Belgian town of Fleurus the following June.

Napoleon's liberation from Mother Corsica in 1793 had enabled an unprecedented expression of his aggressive and creative energies. His meteoric rise in the last three months of that year was unparalleled even in the French republican army, which promoted its young officers quickly. Within the next two and half years Brigadier General Bonaparte would be promoted to division general and be given command of the French armée d'Italie at the age of twenty-six.

10

Love, Depression, and Progression

From September 5, 1793, to July 27, 1794, the revolutionary Reign of Terror raged in France, led by the *comité de Salut public*. Its chiefs, Maximilien Robespierre and Antoine-Louis-Léon de Saint-Just, deeply feared their enemies and therefore behaved rigidly and cruelly. The implacable Saint-Just was called "the apostle of the Terror."[1] Noblemen, generals, clergymen, hoarders, and other "enemies of the Revolution" were arrested, imprisoned, summarily tried, and executed. In the spring of 1794, the committee eliminated its enemies to the left (the Hébertists) and to the right (the Indulgents, or followers of Georges Danton). Still uncertain of its position, the committee obtained the Law of 22 Prairial, Year II of the French Republic (June 10, 1794), which suspended a suspect's right to public trial and to legal assistance and left the jury only a choice between acquittal and death. During the Reign of Terror, 300,000 suspects were arrested, 17,000 were officially executed, and many others died in prison or without trial.[2] Estimates of the numbers of people killed vary from 18,000 to 40,000. One of the military men killed by the Terror was the *maréchal de camp* Jean-Pierre du Teil, Napoleon's former commander at Auxonne. Napoleon learned of Du Teil's arrest and tried to save him from execution but failed.[3]

In the midst of the Terror in France, the Corsican civil war ended in Paoli's victory, and the French forces were driven out of the island. Exploiting the French civil war, Great Britain had helped Paoli drive out the French and recover Corsica. On January 19, 1794, Paoli invited the British to take over Corsica. The British Royal Navy landed at San

Fiorentino (Saint-Florent) and the British built up their forces on the island. That summer, twenty-five years after it annexed Corsica, France briefly lost the island.

In early 1794, after a series of successes, things temporarily went wrong for Napoleon due to his own self-destructive actions. Brigadier General Bonaparte, now the inspector general of the coasts from Marseille to Nice, and General Jean-François Cornu de Lapoype feared another bloody revolt by the Marseillais federalists. The two men wanted better control of Marseille. Flanking the entrance to Marseille's old harbor were two forts: the fort Saint-Nicholas and the fort Saint-Jean. The long-neglected fort Saint-Nicholas was in a state of disrepair. On January 4 Napoleon wrote the war minister in Paris, Jean-Baptiste-Noël Bouchotte: "It is indispensable to put the fort Saint-Nicholas in a state of defense, at least against the efforts of some ill-meaning people. We shall have to remove one of the three enclosures. I will have guns placed to control the city."[4] Napoleon's unfortunate letter to Bouchotte reached the *Convention nationale* in Paris, upsetting some of the Jacobin *conventionnels* who suspected him of tyrannical designs. A fiery Marseillais *conventionnel* named François-Omer Granet rose to his feet on the *Convention* floor and roared the accusations: "There is a proposal afoot to rebuild the bastilles [keeps] put up by Louis XIV in order to tyrannize the South. The proposal comes from Buonaparte of the artillery and a former nobleman, General Lapoype . . . I demand that both be summoned before the bar of the *Convention*!"[5]

Alarmed by Granet's warnings, the *comité de Salut public* issued an order for Napoleon's arrest and sent it to Marseille. Napoleon was to be taken to the Conciergerie, the medieval part of the *palais de Justice* in Paris, which had served as a prison since 1392 and was used for incarcerations during the Terror. Being imprisoned in the Conciergerie could easily end up in the prisoner's execution. "To avoid this fatal journey, he had to procure certificates of loyal citizenship, which before long would turn against him and be used to prove his complicity with the men of blood."[6] These "certificates of loyal citizenship" came from Napoleon's protectors, Antoine-Christophe Saliceti and Augustin de Robespierre, both allied with Maximilien Robespierre's Terror regime. Napoleon's future interior minister, Jean-Antoine-Claude Chaptal de Chanteloup, believed that, thanks to Saliceti and Robespierre, Napoleon was briefly placed under house arrest, watched by a single gendarme. Napoleon spent a few days of anxiety while Saliceti, behind the scenes, explained that no offense had been meant and got Granet to drop the matter. Napoleon was released.[7]

Having achieved great military success in a relatively short time, Napoleon was ready to engage in amorous conquest. One of the wealthiest men in Marseille in the 1790s was François Clary (1725–1794), a royalist silk-and-soap merchant with a big house on the upper-class Rue des Phocéens. Jacques Bainville called him a cloth merchant.[8] He and his wife had three sons, Nicolas, Etienne, and a son who killed himself in 1793. They had two daughters, Marie-Julie (1771–1845) and Bernardine-Eugénie-Désirée (1777–1860).[9] Désirée was only sixteen in 1795.[10] One scholar believed that Désirée was born in late 1774 and that when Napoleon met her in 1794 she was nineteen going on twenty.[11]

Désirée was an immature teenager, "a pretty, dark-eyed sprite, scatter-brained, charming, full of laughter and nonsense."[12] In August 1793, when republican troops drowned the federalist revolt in Marseille in rivers of blood, many people fled town. The *Convention nationale*'s representative on mission, Stanislas-Louis-Marie Fréron, nicknamed Don Juan de la Terreur, terrorized the survivors who stayed. Désirée's brothers, Nicolas and Etienne, were arrested as rebels, "and another son, to escape being shot, committed suicide. Four months later [in early 1794] François [Clary] died of worry and grief."[13] The teenage Désirée, who had lost her brother and her father in quick succession, was unable to mourn her losses properly. Instead, she nurtured fantasies of restitution, longing for a man who would make up for her losses and become her father and brother at once. In 1794 Stanislas Fréron was replaced as the *Convention*'s representative on mission to Marseille by Antoine-Louis Albitte (1761–1812), a Jacobin who eagerly executed the rebels in Marseille, and who planned to have the Clary brothers executed.[14]

Désirée Clary met Napoleon's elder brother Joseph in Albitte's office. As with many episodes in Napoleon's life, there are at least two versions of this story. By Désirée's account, she and her brother Etienne's wife had gone to Albitte's office to plead for the life of Etienne. The agitated young wife obtained Etienne's parole from Albitte. She rushed out to get her husband released, leaving Désirée behind, at which point she met Joseph, who had come to see Albitte about supplying the army. Joseph walked Désirée home. On the way they became "*tout à fait* good friends."[15] She invited him to visit the next day, and he accepted. Joseph got to know the Clarys, became their friend and their lawyer, and got all the charges against Nicolas and Etienne Clary dropped. By another version of the story it was

Désirée's mother, Françoise-Rose Clary, who, "while soliciting for Etienne's release, came to know Joseph Bonaparte," and it was Joseph, rather than Etienne's wife, who obtained Etienne's release, probably with Saliceti's help.[16]

The Clarys were grateful to Joseph Bonaparte for the release of their son, but Albitte bore the Bonapartes a grudge for going over his head to Saliceti. The Bonapartes and Clarys became good friends. Joseph fell in love with Désirée, but wound up marrying her elder sister, Julie, the following summer. Max Gallo believed that Napoleon met the "sixteen-year-old" Désirée in the spring of 1795.[17] In fact, Napoleon first met Désirée in 1794, when she was seventeen, and when he first met her he did not fall in love with her. Napoleon was away from Désirée during most of 1794 and the first three months of 1795.[18]

On February 12, 1794, Brigadier General Napoleon Bonaparte moved to Nice, which had been taken by France from the kingdom of Sardinia-Piedmont-Savoy and was now the headquarters of the French *armée d'Italie*. Like most other soldiers, who were billeted with local citizens, Napoleon was billeted in the house of a former nobleman named Joseph Laurenti at 1, Rue de Villefranche (now 6, Rue Bonaparte). Like François Clary in Marseille, Laurenti was a wealthy merchant of Nice. Napoleon unconsciously transferred his feelings for his parents to Monsieur and Madame Laurenti. He fell in love with their teenage daughter, Emilie, and "His memories of Désirée began to fade away."[19]

In March 1794 Napoleon moved his mother and siblings from their poor flat in Marseille's Ruelle du Pavillon to the Château Sallé, a castle-turned-farmhouse near Antibes. After being involved in various relatively minor military activities, including a mission to Genoa, Napoleon returned to Nice on July 27, 1794. It was the very day of the *coup d'état* of 9 Thermidor Year II of the French Republic in Paris, in which the moderate "Thermidorians" ousted the fanatical Maximilien de Robespierre and his *comité de Salut public* from their bloody power.[20]

Naturally, Napoleon had no idea that the Robespierres had just been ousted from power in Paris and were about to be guillotined. It was a time of deep suspicion and fear in France. Napoleon had been sent to Genoa by Jean-François Ricord and Augustin de Robespierre. The Thermidorians who had staged the *coup d'état* suspected Napoleon of Robespierriste sympathies.

News traveled slowly in those days. Napoleon remained ignorant of the grave news for another week. He reported the results of his mission to

Ricord and left with Junot for the Château-Sallé, where he had left his family, but found it empty. Letizia and the children had left for Marseille to attend the wedding of Joseph and Julie Clary at the nearby village of Cuges-les-Pins.[21] A disappointed Napoleon returned his quarters in the Laurenti residence in Nice. Like his brother Maximilien, Augustin de Robespierre had also been executed. In late July, his friend Jean-François Ricord was arrested and replaced by Antoine-Louis Albitte, the former representative on mission to Marseille, whom Joseph Bonaparte had prevented from executing Nicolas and Etienne Clary.

These were very turbulent times in France. After Robespierre's fall in late July 1794, the new "Thermidorian" government purged its armies of all Robespierriste elements. Hundreds of officers were transferred, arrested, imprisoned, or executed. Frenzied mobs broke into the prisons and massacred their inmates. Right-wing gangs calling themselves the *compagnies de Jésus* (Companies of Jesus) and the *compagnies du Soleil* (Companies of the Sun) roamed the land murdering Jacobins and other "traitors." Some scholars thought that Napoleon's younger brother Lucien had been arrested as a Jacobin and thrown into jail at Aix-en-Provence.[22] In fact, Lucien was briefly arrested a year later, was soon released, and served as an aide to Stanislas-Louis-Marie Fréron, on mission to the *armée du Rhin.*[23]

In August 1794, after the *coup d'état* in Paris, Napoleon was briefly arrested by the new rulers. Two weeks later he returned to the *armée d'Italie*, but he no longer commanded its artillery, serving instead as a staff general. Brigadier General Napoleon Bonaparte proposed a detailed action plan to his boss, General Pierre-Jacques Dumerbion,[24] who carried out his subordinate's action plan. In early September Napoleon fought the Austrians in the Mediterranean Alps as a senior gunner. On September 14 General André Masséna resumed his offensive on the Piedmontese and Austrians. He advanced down the Bormida River valley, seizing the towns of Dego and Acqui. His troops were too exposed to enemy fire, so Masséna wisely withdrew them.[25]

The Year II of the French Republic ended on September 16, 1794, followed by the five "complementary days" separating successive republican years. Five days later the French *armée d'Italie* took the Ligurian town of Cairo Montenotte, northwest of Savona, from the Piedmontese and Austrian troops. Brigadier General Bonaparte, again the army's artillery commander, was setting his sights on bigger things. A year and a half later he would command that army himself, and Montenotte would be his first victory. The French word *récompense* means reward, and Montenotte was indeed a reward for the French troops. Masséna quickly moved his men toward Savona, but his advance was halted by bad weather. The *Convention nationale*'s representative to the *armée d'Italie*, Antoine-Louis Albitte, who had wanted to execute Désirée's brothers Nicolas and Etienne Clary, became frightened, recalling the army to Savona and Vado Ligure.[26] Less than two years later, Montenotte became the site of General Bonaparte's first victory as commander in chief of the French *armée d'Italie*.[27]

Napoleon Bonaparte had met Marie-Julie Clary and her teenage sister Désirée-Eugénie in 1794, after his elder brother Joseph had made her acquaintance. At first Napoleon had fallen in love with Marie-Julie, the elder sister, who was more beautiful and appealing than her younger sister; but he quickly became ambivalent about Julie and fell in love with her younger sister, Désirée. Napoleon vacillated between the two sisters. In her memoirs, Désirée recalled that Napoleon finally got her, Julie, and Joseph together and took charge of them all, saying imperiously to Joseph: "In a good household, one of the two yields to the other. You, Joseph, have an indecisive character, and so has Désirée, while Julie and I, we know what we want. You will therefore do better to marry Julie. As for Désirée [he added, taking the young lady on his knees], she shall be my wife."[28]

This mythical scene sounds like Désirée's romanticized version of reality. If we are to believe it, all three of them, Joseph, Julie, and Désirée accepted Napoleon's stunning announcement as a matter of course, and Joseph married Julie that summer.[29] *Napoleon's love for Désirée may have involved unconscious homosexual feelings for his elder brother Joseph*, her first "lover," as well as unconscious incestuous feelings for his sisters, which were transferred to her. Désirée means "desired woman," which may have enhanced her attraction for him, but also frightened him. Napoleon never married Désirée. In early 1795 he may have wanted to marry her, but Madame Clary—or Joseph Bonaparte—reportedly exclaimed, "One Bonaparte in the family is quite enough!"[30] Frank McLynn was convinced that between April 21 and May 7, 1795, Désirée became Napoleon's mistress, but no marriage ensued, because deep down Napoleon feared betrayal by a woman—the main theme of his short story *Clisson et Eugénie* written at that time.[31]

The Napoleon scholar Gertrude Aretz and the psychoanalyst Ludwig Jekels believed that in late 1794 and early 1795, while courting Désirée Clary by mail, Napoleon also had short-lived love affairs with the wives of several prominent military and political men: Madame Carteaux, the wife of his former commanding officer at Toulon, who was in prison; Madame Ricord, the wife of the representative on mission, who was also imprisoned; Madame Saliceti, the wife of Napoleon's former patron, who was busy quelling the revolts in the south of France and drafting a proclamation to the people of Genoa; and Louise-Félicité Turreau de Lignières, the wife of another "people's representative to the armies", who was also in prison.[32] In fact, some of those women met Napoleon but had no love affair with him. Frank Richardson believed that Napoleon's "affair" with Louise Turreau de Lignières did not involve sexual relations.[33] Many years later Napoleon "regretted his abuse of authority" in having sacrificed some of his men to impress Madame Turreau.[34] If any adulterous affairs did occur, Jekels thought, they were oedipal in nature. In Napoleon's unconscious mind, the cuckolded husbands stood for his father, the women for his mother.[35]

In his relations with women Napoleon unconsciously reproduced his early traumatic relationship with his mother. Claude Manceron believed that "no one seduced Napoleon twice."[36] Napoleon had numerous love affairs, most of them brief. He kept changing mistresses because he rapidly went through infatuation-and-disillusionment cycles. He repeatedly fell passionately in love with a woman, only to end up deeply disappointed in her, repeating the tragic cycle of his early relationship with his mother. Napoleon, whose relationship with his mother involved a lifelong power struggle, confused sexuality with power. In Napoleon's relationships with women, the feeling of power mattered more than the feelings of love or sexual pleasure. He could only make love to a woman over whom he felt a sense of mastery.[37]

Needless to say, the French Revolution was turbulent. Fear and anxiety permeated people's daily lives. One never knew how the next day would turn out. Yesterday's heroes became today's martyrs and victims. During the first months of 1795 the poor Brigadier General Napoleon Bonaparte, still suspect in the eyes of the new Thermidorian regime, lived in a succession of cheap hotels in the south of France. In the spring the brigadier-general of the *artillery* received orders to assume the command of an *infantry* brigade in the French *armée de l'Ouest*, fighting the royalist rebels in the Vendée. This was a dangerous demotion, and he decided to go to Paris to fight it. When he arrived in Paris, he rented a seventy-two-livre-a-month apartment. In the next three months he moved at least three more times, each time to save money. For the next eight months Désirée and Napoleon wrote each other love letters like two young people engaged to be married. Napoleon loved Désirée safely, from a distance: she was in Marseille, later in Genoa; he was in Paris.

Like many desperate Frenchman who lost all their savings in the great inflation, Napoleon looked for a way to convert his paper money into real estate before it lost its value. On May 22, 1795, on his way north from Marseille to Paris, he saw a sixteenth-century property in the *département* of Saône-et-Loire, near Dijon, in Burgundy, called *la terre de Ragny*, which belonged to the impoverished Seigneur de Montigny, Marquis de Ragny, a descendant of the Chevaliers du Saint Esprit.[38] The next day Napoleon wrote his elder brother Joseph giving him some financial advice (if not orders) and exhorting him to buy the property in Burgundy and not to leave Marseille for Genoa:

> Yesterday I saw the terre de Ragny belonging to M. de Montigny. If you were a man who likes a good business deal, you would buy this land [of Ragny] with eight million in *assignats*; you could put sixty thousand francs of your wife's dowry into it; this is my wish and my advice. Remember me to your wife, to Désirée, and to the family . . . You will not find France in foreign countries, and to run around the Levant smacks of adventure or at least of the man looking for a fortune. If you are sensible, you have only got to enjoy [your own fortune]. I am sure you can get this place for 80,000 francs in silver; before the Revolution it was worth 250,000. I think it is a unique chance to invest some of your wife's dowry. The *assignats* are losing value daily.[39]

For once, Joseph did not heed his younger brother's exhortations. That summer, Joseph and his brother-in-law Nicolas Clary left Marseille for Genoa. Napoleon stubbornly pursued his scheme. Later, from Paris, he wrote Joseph: "Yesterday I attended the adjudication of the property that I had thought to procure for you, nine leagues from Paris; I had decided to pay one million five hundred francs for it, but, incredibly, it had gone up to three million."[40]

Determined to undo his dangerous demotion to the infantry of the *armée de l'Ouest*, Napoleon reached Paris on May 25, 1795, and checked into an apartment in the Hôtel de la Liberté at 11, Rue des Fossés-Montmartre (now the Rue d'Aboukir). The next day, Bonaparte had an interview with War Minister François Aubry. It was an acrimonious meeting, the two men shouting at each other. Aubry told Bonaparte that he would have to take over an infantry brigade in the *armée de l'Ouest*. Napoleon pleaded with Aubry not to make him do this, but Aubry was adamant.

Most biographers believed that ordering the *artillery* general Bonaparte to command an *infantry* brigade in the *armée de l'Ouest* after summoning him to command the artillery of that army was Aubry's ruse to get rid of him. It was "a form of down-grading, almost an insult, which Aubry had found effective in provoking the resignation of many [other] 'undesirable' officers."[41] Napoleon was furious with Aubry but could not make him change his decision. From his cheap Paris hotel room, a desperate and rancorous Napoleon wrote his elder brother Joseph in Marseille that he could not accept his command of an infantry brigade as an infantry general of the line in the *armée de l'Ouest*. Describing himself as "cold and somber," he declared: "I am beating a retreat, satisfied that the injustice done in return for services rendered is sufficiently realized by those willing to appreciate them."[42]

Rather than openly refuse Aubry's assignment, which would have been dangerous, the resourceful Napoleon obtained a temporary leave from Aubry, and then went to see his powerful patron Paul de Barras, a member of the Thermidorian government, who had known Bonaparte and promoted him at Toulon. Barras obtained for his young protégé a two-month sick leave, retroactive from 27 Floréal to 27 Messidor (May 16 to July 15, 1795).[43] For Napoleon, this was a clever way of dodging Aubry's assignment without formally refusing it. At the same time, Napoleon may really have been sick, if not in body, then in mind.

By June 19, 1795, Napoleon was in dire straits. He quickly lost two of his aides: Louis Viesse de Marmont, the future marshal, and Louis Bonaparte, Napoleon's younger brother and future king. The ambitious Marmont had joined the *armée du Rhin*, fighting in Germany, while Louis Bonaparte left for the artillery school at Châlons-sur-Marne, in the Champagne-Ardenne region east of Paris. Only the loyal Andoche Junot stayed with Napoleon. Hyperinflation was making his money worthless. Indeed, the young ex-brigadier general was sick in mind and body.

Finding life in Paris much too expensive, he moved from his apartment at the Hôtel de la Liberté in the Rue des Fossés-Montmartre to a succession of increasingly smaller, cheaper, and more depressing rooms.[44]

An increasingly depressed Napoleon corresponded with his elder brother Joseph and with his teenage fiancée Désirée. In her letters, the orphaned and immature Désirée latched onto Napoleon as an unconscious father substitute. Napoleon played the father to Désirée, and she the daughter to him. In his later life, an aging prisoner of the British on Saint Helena, Napoleon bragged to his *grand maréchal du palais* that he had made love to Désirée and had told this to her mother, who insisted that they get married at once. In fact, Madame Clary may have opposed her second daughter's marriage to Napoleon.[45]

When he obtained his temporary leave in May 1795, Napoleon was already depressed. He had no job, no income, no occupation. His self-esteem hit rock bottom. Things would become progressively worse for him that summer. On June 22 Napoleon wrote Joseph that he would refuse Aubry's assignment: "I am employed as a brigadier-general in the Army of the West, but not in the artillery. I am sick, which forces me to take leave for two or three months. When my health is restored, I will see what I will do. Today the Constitution is being read in the *Convention*; I will send it to you the moment it is printed and can be had."[46] Napoleon was putting a good face on his own situation, but he was falling into suicidal despair. Unconsciously repeating the rejection trauma of his early life with his mother, Napoleon subtly and unwittingly invited Désirée to reject him. He wrote her, "If you love another man, you should not hesitate to abandon the poor little general without a brigade. You must not hamper your soul. You must not impose obligations upon yourself."[47]

The straw that broke Napoleon's back in August 1795 was his mother's request for money, which he could not fulfill. Letizia, who had moved to Marseille in January 1795, was destitute. She had written Napoleon asking him for money, but he had no money to give her. Her request for money triggered his suicidal despair that summer. Letizia's enemies had spread malicious rumors about her, saying that she had kept a whorehouse in Corsica and that she now had one in Marseille employing her own daughters. These rumors were communicated to her son, and they greatly upset Napoleon. Suffering from a deep sense of insecurity, or a flawed sense of self, he was very sensitive to what people said about him and his family.

The penniless and now powerless Napoleon could neither help his mother financially nor fight the malicious rumors about her. Under the inner stress, Napoleon unconsciously regressed to an infantile mode of feeling and behavior, losing his zest for life and his fighting spirit. Already depressed by his situation with the army, he felt worthless and impotent, and contemplated suicide. Napoleon recalled that his friend Alexandre des Mazis had once more saved him from killing himself by lending him thirty thousand livres to send his mother.[48]

Why did Letizia ask her jobless and penniless second son, Napoleon, for money, when her eldest son, Joseph, enjoyed his wife's dowry of one hundred thousand or one hundred and fifty thousand livres? The fact that Letizia's request drove Napoleon to think of killing himself is significant. *Letizia had unconscious death wishes against Napoleon from his birth, as he did against her*. Carrington thought that Napoleon's mother was the direct cause of his suicidal mood in the summer of 1795.[49] On August 12, 1795, Napoleon was so depressed that he wrote his elder brother Joseph, "if things go on like this, my friend, some day I'll simply fail to get out of the way of a passing carriage."[50]

Did the depressed Napoleon really plan to kill himself in the summer of 1795? Not necessarily. Napoleon was highly narcissistic: the psychoanalyst Pierce Clark thought that "the narcist rarely takes his own life except in outspoken melancholia; suicide is often on his lips but seldom in his heart. The dissolution of the ego into nothingness is hardly conceivable, and voluntary annihilation is rarely thought of."[51] Similarly, Frank Richardson did not think that Napoleon was a suicidal type, "even if he did tell Montholon that he had seriously contemplated suicide in Paris *shortly after the siege of Toulon* [*sic*]. He was stopped, he said, from throwing himself into the river by a chance meeting with Alexandre des Mazis, a former classmate and a brother officer in his regiment."[52] If Napoleon did seriously contemplate suicide in 1795, it was the second time his friend Des Mazis saved him from killing himself. The first had been in 1786, at Valence, when Napoleon had suicidal thoughts before returning to Corsica and his mother.

By his twenty-sixth birthday on August 15, 1795, Napoleon had run out of excuses to give War Minister Aubry. Two days later things came to a head when Bonaparte received an ultimatum from the war minister: if he did not leave for the *armée de l'Ouest* he would be replaced and dismissed from the army. Bonaparte returned to his powerful patron, Paul de Barras, who had met him at Toulon and promoted him rapidly. Barras, now a brigadier general himself and a member of the all-powerful *comité de Salut public*, discussed Napoleon with his colleague François-Antoine Boissy d'Anglas, the *conventionnel* who had courageously faced down the food rioters on May 20 after they had seized a hapless deputy named Jean-Bertrand Féraud, chopped off his head, and paraded it upon a pike. Boissy d'Anglas introduced Napoleon to his friend Louis-Gustave le Doulcet de Pontécoulant, the military operations head of the *comité de Salut public*. Thanks to Boissy d'Anglas, Napoleon secured an interview with Pontécoulant and went to see him at the offices of the *comité de Salut public*, on the sixth floor of the *Pavillon de Flore* at the Tuileries Palace, the seat of the *Convention nationale* and of its powerful executive committees.

Napoleon's meeting with Pontécoulant on August 18, 1795, ended his despair and began his new career. It gave him a sense of self-worth and competence, lifting him out of his suicidal depression. As he had done with General Dumerbion in the *armée d'Italie*, Napoleon announced to Pontécoulant that he had a perfect plan for the French conquest of northern Italy and sketched it on the committee's conference table. Some of the committee staff thought Napoleon mad. Pontécoulant wanted to use the young general to secure an advantage over his rival, War Minister Aubry. Pontécoulant asked Napoleon to put his plans down in writing and submit them to him. Napoleon did so, and Pontécoulant assigned him to the topographic bureau of the *comité de Salut public*. Had Napoleon used Pontécoulant to win his battle with the war minister, or had Pontécoulant used him as a pawn in his power struggle with Aubry?

Like Napoleon's loss of religious faith in 1782 and his expulsion from Corsica in 1793, his new job in August 1795 was a major turning point in his life. He shook off his depression and went back to work. During his first day in the topographic bureau, Napoleon learned that Admiral Laurent-Jean-François Truguet, who, together with General Jacques-Bernard-Modeste d'Anselme, had commanded the disastrous French invasion of Sardinia two years earlier, was on his way to the Ottoman capital of Constantinople to reorganize the Ottoman navy. In 1793 Truguet had been defeated at the Sardinian capital of Cagliari, dismissed from the navy, and imprisoned, but he was set free after the *coup d'état* of 1794, reinstated in the navy, promoted to full admiral, and sent to the Ottoman Empire. His self-confidence restored, Napoleon asked Pontécoulant to reinstate him as an artillery general and to send him to Constantinople with Truguet to reorganize the Ottoman Turkish artillery. He made this request not once but twice.[53] Did Napoleon's idea of leaving France for the Ottoman Empire express his unconscious wish to abandon his "fiancée" Désirée, who had "abandoned" him by leaving France for Genoa and not writing him for two weeks?

On August 20, 1795, a euphoric Napoleon wrote his elder brother Joseph in Genoa boasting of his new position, which he described as no less than a replacement of Lazare Carnot, the "organizer of the victory" at Fleurus in June 1794. The way he saw it, he had only to ask to be sent on a mission to the Ottoman Empire for his wish to be granted.[54] In fact, Napoleon's boss, Pontécoulant, was Carnot's replacement. With his new job at the topographic bureau of the *comité de Salut public*, Napoleon felt secure enough to formally refuse his nomination by War Minister Aubry to command an infantry brigade in the *armée de l'Ouest.*

Political events, however, now threatened Napoleon's chief protector, Paul de Barras. In June 1795 the *Convention nationale* had proposed a new constitution creating a ruling five-man *Directoire exécutif* with a two-chamber legislature consisting of a *Conseil de Cinq-Cents* (council of five hundred) and a *Conseil des anciens* (council of elders). This constitution was adopted by the *Convention* on August 22. Barras was a member of the new *Directoire.* On August 30 the *Directoire exécutif* decreed that two-thirds of the new legislature would consist of former *conventionnels.* This provoked a violent uprising among the French royalists against Barras, which gave General Bonaparte his great opportunity.

In September 1795, however, Bonaparte's fate was still in the hands of Charles-Louis-François-Honoré Letourneur, the member of the *comité de Salut public* in charge of military personnel. As part of the efforts of France's "moderate" Thermidorian rulers to purge their opponents from the armies, Letourneur had been going over the files of Jacobin officers who had been loyal to Robespierre. Letourneur decided to purge seventy-five robespierriste generals from the army. He used Bonaparte's refusal to obey Aubry's order as an excuse to purge him. On September 15, 1795, four members of the *comité de Salut public*—Cambacérès, Merlin de Douai, Boissy d'Anglas, and Berlier—signed a formal order dismissing Napoleon from the army: "Brigadier-General Bonaparte, formerly requisitioned by the *comité de Salut public,* is struck from the list of general officers employed, in view of his refusal to take up the post which had been assigned to him. The Ninth Commission is charged with the execution of this order."[55] The Ninth Commission, headed by Pontécoulant, was the military-affairs commission of the *comité de Salut public.*

The homosexual Jean-Jacques-Régis Cambacérès, a future arch-chancellor of the Empire under Napoleon, may have signed the order dismissing General Bonaparte from the army by mistake. War Minister François Aubry, a member of the *comité de la Guerre*, had slipped the document dismissing Bonaparte from the army onto the desk of Cambacérès, the head of the *comité de Salut public* and of the *comité de Sûreté générale*, who, as a routine part of his functions, signed it without reading it carefully. It may also be that the committee's order dismissing General Bonaparte was based on a misunderstanding.[56]

A few days after Cambacérès had "mistakenly" signed the order dismissing Bonaparte from the French army, the young general went to the politician's private residence and knocked on his door at eight o'clock in the morning. The forty-two-year-old Cambacérès fell in love with the handsome twenty-five-year-old general. Fifteen years later, when he was arch-chancellor of the empire, Cambacérès recalled that Napoleon's first visit to his house reminded him of the Greek myth of Philemon and Baucis, a mythical pious Phrygian couple who received Zeus and Hermes, disguised as paupers, with great hospitality after their wealthier neighbors had turned them away. "He was badly combed . . . Dressed like the devil . . . But through this strange get-up, a slender hand, white, designed to ravish, a charming mouth . . . And then eyes . . . Oh! What Eyes! Sweet, terrible, interrogating, confiding . . . The air of a king under the dress of a shy pauper, or, to put it better, Jupiter ready to visit Philemon and Baucis . . . With that, a full voice, sonorous, caressing, vibrant, moving the heart . . . It was a magical, continual, irresistible fascination."[57] An enchanted Cambacérès reinstated Bonaparte in his military functions.[58]

On 13 Vendémiaire Year IV of the French Republic (October 5, 1795) Brigadier General Napoleon Bonaparte gained national notoriety in France when he mercilessly put down the royalist uprising against the ruling *Directoire exécutif* and saved his patron, Paul de Barras, from being overthrown. Napoleon's artillery massacred hundreds of rebels in the streets of Paris. Barras, the commander of the *armée de l'interieur*, had known Bonaparte since the siege of Toulon in late 1793. Barras had made the young Corsican general his deputy and put him in command of an artillery battery that mowed down the rebels. Bonaparte became known as Général Vendémiaire. It was yet another turning point in Napoleon's amazing career, one that would lead to his appointment as commander of the French *armée d'Italie* within a few months.

After the bloody events of 13 Vendémiaire Year IV, a reassured French government prepared to invade Italy and fight the Austrians. The new French legislature was elected in mid-Vendémiaire. By the "two-thirds" resolution of the outgoing *Convention nationale*, which had been fraudulently approved by the national referendum, two-thirds of the members of the new legislature had come from the outgoing republican *Convention*, preserving a republican majority in the new legislature. The psychoanalyst Pierce Clark believed that France had entrusted her fate to the twenty-six-year-old Bonaparte: "With a mind still highly stored with the keenest of military and national perceptions Napoleon is able to vision [*sic*] all these plans with the shrewdest narcism or self-loving engulfment of his egoistic desires. His genius here as elsewhere is a singular refutation that it is only born of slow maturation and patient years of toil. Thus early is his narcism plumed with fine feathers of predictable desires."[59]

In fact, the idea of invading Italy and fighting Austria had been that of Paul Barras, and was adopted by his new *Directoire exécutif* when it took office in November 1795. As most Frenchmen saw it, General Barras and his deputy Bonaparte had quelled the royalist insurrection in Paris and saved the republic. The expiring *Convention nationale* was grateful. Things now moved rapidly for Napoleon. On October 8, 1795, the *Convention* confirmed him in his function as Barras' deputy, second in command of the *armée de l'interieur*. Napoleon received his pay, and he finally sent money to his mother. Being unable to do so had driven him to suicidal ruminations a couple of months earlier. Napoleon now wrote Joseph: "The family lacks for nothing."[60]

All France was talking about General Bonaparte. On 19 Vendémiaire Year IV (October 11, 1795), before the new *Directoire exécutif* and the new legislature began their political existence, the fiery *conventionnel* Stanislas-Louis-Marie Fréron eulogized General Bonaparte on the floor of the *Convention* as the hero who had saved the republic from its enemies.[61] Agathon-Jean-François Fain, then secretary of the *Convention nationale*'s military committee, wrote: "People wonder where he comes from, what he was, what previous services recommended him. Nobody can answer [this], except his former general, Carteaux, and the Representatives who were at the siege of Toulon or on the line in the Var."[62] On October 12 the outgoing *Convention* promised to reward those who had saved it from the rebels. A few months later Napoleon reaped the benefits of that promise by being named to replace Barras as the commander of the *armée de l'interieur* and then to command the *armée d'Italie*.

11

Inventing Josephine

Napoleon's success in crushing the royalist revolt and in "saving the Republic"—however brutally—on 13 Vendémiaire Year IV of the French Republic boosted his narcissism. Wearing his dashing uniform of the deputy commander of the *armée de l'interieur*, an eager and newly invigorated Brigadier General Bonaparte kept visiting Madame Tallien's literary salon at the Chaumière du Cours-la-Reine, where he met his political patrons, Paul de Barras and Stanislas Fréron. Two years earlier, in late 1793, Barras, whose enemies called him *le roy des pourris* (the king of the rotten ones), had massacred the "rebels" of Toulon along with his colleagues Stanislas Fréron and Joseph Fouché. Ten days after his great military coup, on 23 Vendémiaire (October 15, 1795), in Madame Tallien's salon, the twenty-six-year-old Napoleon met one of Barras's former lovers, a thirty-two-year-old Creole widow named Marie-Josèphe-Rose de Tascher de la Pagerie de Beauharnois. The following day, on 24 Vendémiaire (October 16), Brigadier General Napoleon Bonaparte was promoted to *général de division*, an indispensable step to being given the command of a French army.

The manipulative Creole widow soon seduced the young general. Napoleon invented the name "Josephine" for her and, like the mythical Greek sculptor Pygmalion with his statute Galatea, fell madly in love with his own creation. Napoleon later bitterly recalled that "Josephine" always said "no" to everything he asked her.[1] Did he fall in love with this woman because her coldness and stinginess unconsciously reminded him of his mother? In one of the famous myths that he created about himself,

Napoleon recalled that he fell in love with "Josephine" over a sword. The bloody events of October 1795 had caused the wary *Directoire exécutif*, which was elected on October 31, to order all Parisians to give up their arms. By one version of this myth, the widow Beauharnois had been allowed to keep her dead husband's sword. She had surrendered the sword and then sent her fourteen-year-old son Eugène, who had inherited it from his father, to Napoleon's headquarters in the Rue des Capucines to plead for its return. Napoleon received Eugène warmly and gave him back the sword. A few days later "Josephine" came to thank the young general in person at his headquarters, and the two fell in love. By another version of this myth, Rose did *not* surrender the sword but sent Eugène with the sword to Napoleon to ask him to be allowed to keep it. Eugène, unhappy at the idea of parting from his father's sword, tearfully pleaded with Napoleon to let him keep it. Napoleon granted his wish. The following day Rose herself called on Bonaparte, and a day later Napoleon visited Rose in her new house. The road was short from this to a full-fledged affair.[2]

The Creole widow Rose de Beauharnois was well known in Paris. Though six years older than Napoleon, to him she was a vast improvement over the younger and immature Désirée. "[Rose] was still a fairly young woman, a Creole of dangerous beauty, of outstanding elegance, and combining the nonchalance of the Indies with the manners and bearing of the old régime. The blend had quick appeal for the gentleman cadet who had been touched by the rather mincing charm of the merchant Clary's daughter."[3] The deeper, unconscious sources of Rose's appeal to Napoleon may have been her older age, her motherhood, her widowhood, her resemblance to his mother, and her middle name of Josèphe—the feminine version of his elder brother's name. Some of the stories of Napoleon's relationship with her—which will be reported below—will bear out this assumption.

Napoleon instantly idealized the Creole widow. To him, she was not Rose but "Joséphine." André Castelot thought that Napoleon did not wish to use "this name of Rose pronounced by two many masculine lips."[4] Vincent Cronin believed that Napoleon "did not care for the name Rose. He decided to change it, just as he had changed Désirée to Eugénie. One of Rose's other names was Josèphe. *Napoleon lengthened and softened Josèphe to Josephine* [italics added], and it was by this name that he began to call Rose de Beauharnais."[5] Frank Richardson thought that when Napoleon married Rose, he "decided that she would in future be known as Josephine. Perhaps he wanted to set the seal of his possession upon her, and to make it clear that she was now entering upon a new life." [6]

Rose's social and official name was "the Widow Beauharnois." The deeper reason why Napoleon chose her middle name of Josèphe to call her "Josephine" was his passionate love and unconscious hate for his elder brother, Joseph. Probably unaware that Napoleon himself had invented the name "Josephine" for a woman named Rose, Sigmund Freud thought that Napoleon suffered from a "huge Joseph complex" and therefore "had to marry a woman named Josephine. His overwhelming jealousy of his elder brother had been transformed into warm love under the influence of his father identification, and the obsession was then transferred to his wife."[7] The reason why Napoleon chose Rose's middle name to "lengthen and soften" was that it was the feminine form of his elder brother's name. In fact, Napoleon's unhappy choice of "Josephine" for his first wife had other unconscious determinants as well. Like Letizia, she was a widow and a mother, and "Josephine" was also promiscuous and unfaithful, as Napoleon believed his mother had been with Marbeuf.

Napoleon's love for "Josephine" was narcissistic and fusional. In his unconscious mind, she was a mirror image of himself. Both of them were islanders and, as such, outsiders and foreigners in France. The Corsican-born Napoleon had been nursed by a *nourrice*, while Rose, a Creole from Martinique, had also been nursed by a *nourrice* and brought up by black slaves. Both Napoleon and Rose had been conceived on islands ruled by other nations, and both were born shortly after their islands had been taken over by France. When Napoleon met Rose both Corsica and Martinique were occupied by the British. Most importantly, both of them had been unwanted children, rejected by their mothers. Napoleon's mother had wanted a girl and got a boy; Rose's mother had wanted a boy and got a girl.[8] Napoleon and "Josephine" unconsciously found themselves in each other.

"Josephine" had had a traumatic childhood. In 1766, when she was three years old, a hurricane destroyed her home. The Taschers took refuge in the stone buildings of the sugar plantation. Yéyette, as Rose was called, lived there until she was ten. She entered the school of the *Dames de la Providence* at Fort-Royal but quit school at fourteen, leading the indolent colonial life at La Pagerie.[9] Rose had also been sexually abused as a child and adolescent. The thirty-two-year-old widow Beauharnois had a rich sexual career. As a teenager, Rose had been initiated into sexuality by her paternal aunt, Désirée-Marie-Eugénie de Tascher de Renaudin, a lover of the governor of Martinique, the marquis de la Ferté Beauharnois. The marquis de la Ferté Beauharnois at first wanted his younger son, Alexandre de Beauharnois, to marry Rose's younger sister, Catherine-Désirée, but she died of tuberculosis at age fourteen in 1778. Rose suffered a serious loss, but at the same time she got rid of a serious rival. The marquis then wanted his son to marry Rose's youngest sister Manette, who was only eleven. Madame de Renaudin manipulated her brother, Joseph-Gaspard de Tascher de la Pagerie, into betrothing his eldest daughter, Marie-Josèphe-Rose, to Alexandre de Beauharnois.

During the French spring carnival of Mardi Gras in 1779, a French naval squadron under Admiral Charles-Henri d'Estaing, a future victim of the Terror, anchored for six weeks at Fort-Royal de la Martinique. His officers seduced the local girls. One of them, Scipion du Roure, a nineteen-year-old officer aboard the vessel *Marseillais*, seduced the fifteen-year-old Rose de Tascher de la Pagerie, then engaged to the nineteen-year-old Alexandre de Beauharnois. It is not clear whether she became pregnant, but that summer her formidable aunt, Madame de Renaudin, shipped herself, her niece, her lover the governor, and his son Alexandre to France, where the nineteen-year-old Alexandre married the sixteen-year-old Rose on December 13 at Noisy-le-Grand.

Rose and her aunt Madame Renaudin lived in Paris with Alexandre and his father. In 1781 the eighteen-year-old Rose de Beauharnois bore her first child, Eugène de Beauharnois, the future Prince Eugène-Napoléon and Viceroy of Italy. In 1783 she had her second child, Hortense de Beauharnois, the future wife of Napoleon's younger brother Louis and queen of Holland. Malicious tongues, however, said that Alexandre de Beauharnois was not the father of his wife's children. In 1784 a furious and jealous Alexandre de Beauharnois left his wife Rose and his two children in Paris and went back to Martinique with another woman.

Some scholars considered Rose de Beauharnois promiscuous and unfaithful. Some thought that the sexual arrangements in her family were not altogether normal: Was Napoleon too busy with his own career or with the political and military developments in Paris to discover Rose's sexual history? Jacques Bainville believed that Napoleon did not care about Rose's poverty and promiscuity: "Penniless, yes; a life of adventures and lovers; Bonaparte did not look at that too closely."[10] André Castelot, however, thought that Napoleon had hoped to get a huge fortune from his future wife, who had told him that she had millions of francs in faraway Martinique.[11] In fact, it may have been Rose's very neediness, promiscuity, and unfaithfulness that unconsciously attracted Napoleon. Rose echoed his mother's unfaithfulness with Marbeuf, her neediness, and her abandonment of Napoleon. To him, Rose was "Josephine," and he idealized her beyond all proportion to her real character. Unconsciously, he was setting himself up for a bitter disappointment.

While Napoleon may have had sexual relations with Louise Turreau de Lignières, with Désirée Clary, and with other women before he met "Josephine,"[12] his first love-making session with the sexually experienced widow was of a different nature. "Josephine" made love to Napoleon for the first time in late 1795. It was the first time Napoleon really enjoyed sexual intercourse. He was enthralled. The next morning an adoring Napoleon wrote her a passionate love letter in which he and she were fused into one:

> Seven o'clock in the morning. *I wake up full of you* [italics added]. Your portrait and the memory of the intoxicating last night have given no rest to my senses. Sweet and incomparable Josephine, what a strange effect do you have on my heart? Are you angry? Do I see you sad? Are you worried? My soul is broken with pain and there is no rest for your friend . . . But is there any more of it for me when, giving myself over to the deep feeling which rules me, I draw from your lips, from your heart, a flame that burns me. Ah! It was this night that I realized well that your portrait is not you. You leave at noon, I shall see you in three hours. Meanwhile, *mio dolce amor* [my sweet love], a million kisses, but don't give me any, because they burn my blood.[13]

On 4 Brumaire Year IV of the French Republic (October 26, 1795), General Paul de Barras, about to become one of the five members of the new *Directoire exécutif*, resigned his military rank and his command of the *armée de l'interieur* in favor of General Napoleon Bonaparte.[14] Why had Barras given Napoleon both his command and his mistress? Vincent Cronin thought that Barras was new in power and felt insecure as the only nobleman in the *Directoire*. He needed a friend and ally in the military. By marrying Josephine, Napoleon could prove his political loyalty to the *Directoire*, and Barras would get two useful allies. "So Barras encouraged Napoleon to marry his former mistress, from whom, incidentally, he wished to be disentangled."[15] Frank Richardson believed that Barras had had enough of the unfaithful Rose, but not that Napoleon's command had anything to do with his marrying her: "Barras' memoirs are the main source of the allegation that Napoleon took his discarded mistress off his hands and was rewarded with command of the Army of Italy."[16] Owen Connelly thought that "the ugly rumor went with [Napoleon] that his post was a reward from Barras for making Josephine an honest woman."[17]

The psychoanalyst María Carmen Gear and her colleagues have shown that sadomasochism (a combination of sadism and masochism) is a key psychological component of narcissism.[18] As both partners had significant unresolved emotional conflicts, including unconscious sadism and masochism, it did not take long for "Josephine" to pick her first fight with Napoleon. In late February or early March 1796, a few days before their wedding, Rose tearfully confessed some of her "heavy" past (though by no means all of it) to Napoleon, after which she accused him of seeking her out for his "interests"—her fortune, her title, and the command of the *armée d'Italie*, which he hoped to get from Barras. André Castelot believed that the manipulative Josephine was coy, that she had no real fortune to speak of, that she had lost the noble title of vicomtesse, and that Barras wanted to end their brief affair.[19] In fact, like Napoleon himself, Josephine had a shaky self-esteem. She too had been unwanted and rejected by her mother, and had been sexually abused in her youth. She may have made this scene with her fiancé out of guilt feelings about her sexual promiscuity and feelings of worthlessness, and as an unconscious repetition of the sadomasochistic trauma of her early life.

In accusing Napoleon of marrying her for his interests, Rose may have unconsciously projected her own feelings upon him. The psychoanalyst Pierce Clark thought that Napoleon and "Josephine" both married out of self-interest: "In his pursuit of glory the conqueror [*sic*] pauses long enough to seek and win the hand of the widow de Beauharnais. Though the cable of love has many strands, in a mutuality of tenderness and disinterested affection there is no room for an intensive self-interest. Yet [self-interest] is the factor which singularly brings about the marriage of the ambitious Corsican to the no less ambitious viscountess, and bars the possibility of viewing the relation in the light of a love union."[20] But Napoleon had not yet conquered an inch of foreign soil. Did Clark think of his future conquests? Napoleon was in love, though not with the real Josephine, but with the idealized Josephine of his imagination, who was very unlike his real wife.

Napoleon was deeply hurt by Rose's accusations of his trying to exploit her wealth and her nobility. He could not understand how his "Josephine" could make such a charge against him. As with his mother, he felt weakened by her power over him. When he returned home, he wrote her a tormented letter, swinging between his rage at "Josephine" and his love for her. As with his mother in his childhood, his way of dealing with his conflict was to deny his rage at "Josephine" and to idealize her:

> Nine o'clock in the morning. I left you carrying with me a painful feeling. I went to bed quite angry. It seemed to me that the respect due to my character should have removed from your thoughts the last one which agitated you yesterday in the evening. If it dominated your mind, you would be very unjust, madame, and myself very unhappy! So you thought that I did not love you for yourself!!! For whom then? Ah! Madame, I would have changed very much then! Could such a base feeling have been conceived in such a pure soul? I am still astonished by it, tough less so than by the feeling that, when I woke up, led me without rancor and against my will to you feet. Surely it is impossible to be weaker or to be brought lower. What, then, is your strange power, incomparable Josephine? One of your thoughts poisons my life, rends my heart with the most opposing wishes, but a stronger feeling, a less somber humor binds me again, brings me back and leads me still more guilty [to you]. I feel it well, if we have arguments between us, you should impugn my heart, my conscience: you have seduced them, they are still for you. You, however, mio dolce amor, have you rested well? Have you thought only twice of me? I give you three kisses, one on your heart, one on your mouth, one on your eyes.[21]

Josephine's "strange power" over Napoleon was in his own mind: he unconsciously transferred to her his earliest feelings for his mother, idealized her, and compulsively repeated with her the drama of his early rejection. His repeated use of the Italian phrase *mio dolce amor* (my sweet love) betrayed the unconscious origin of his torment. The Corsican Italian language was his mother tongue. His infatuation with Josephine unconsciously repeated his earlier defensive idealization of his mother. The torments that he and she inflicted upon one another unconsciously repeated their early torments with their own rejecting mothers.

One of the greatest days in the life of General Napoleon Bonaparte came on 12 Ventôse Year IV of the French Republic (March 2, 1796), when the *Directoire exécutif*, in the person of Lazare Carnot, signed his appointment as commander in chief of the *armée d'Italie*, replacing General Schérer.[22] A week later, on March 9, Napoleon married "Josephine."

Marriage was always a complex affair with the ambivalent Bonapartes. Napoleon's father Carlo had never formally married his mother Letizia: they had only signed a dotal act concerning Letizia's dowry. Napoleon himself married "Josephine" in a secret wedding. The thirty-two-year-old "Josephine" manipulated the twenty-six-year-old Napoleon. She took Napoleon to see her notary, Maurice-Jean Raguideau de La Fosse, and sign their marriage contract. Exploiting his idealized love for her, Josephine had been manipulating Napoleon to her ends from the outset. Raguideau, "a tiny man, almost a dwarf,"[23] conferred with Josephine in private, but "inadvertently" left the door ajar. As Josephine and Raguideau had intended, Napoleon, who waited in an antechamber, could hear the notary arguing against the marriage: "This is a great mistake, and you're going to be sorry for it. You're doing something mad, marrying a man who has only his cape and sword, that's the pretty deal that you would be making . . . What does he own, this Bonaparte? A shack? Not even that! Who is he? A little civil-war general, with no future, below all the great generals of the Republic. It would be better to marry a supplier of the armies!."[24] This was obviously a show designed to manipulate Napoleon into signing a contract favorable to Josephine. Napoleon was deeply hurt, but he loved Josephine as an unwanted child loves his rejecting mother.

Josephine's notary Raguideau presented Napoleon with his marriage contract. The young general could not wait to be married. He needed to fuse with "Josephine." The contract, drawn by Raguideau with Josephine's interests in mind, was very unfavorable to Napoleon. There was to be no community of property. Some scholars believed that Napoleon undertook to pay his wife fifteen hundred livres a year for her entire life. Others thought that if Napoleon died, his wife would receive fifteen hundred livres. Napoleon had to declare that he did not own any real estate, nor any property except his wardrobe and his war train. Without informing his mother, and almost without pausing to read the contract, the infatuated twenty-six-year-old Napoleon agreed to all the terms his thirty-two-year-old bride imposed on him and promptly signed his marriage contract with Marie-Josèphe-Rose de Tascher de la Pagerie de Beauharnois in the office of her notary.[25]

On the evening of March 9, 1796, two days before he left Paris for Nice to take over the armée d'Italie, Napoleon married Rose de Beauharnois, in the *salle de mariages* of the *mairie* of the 2nd arrondissement at 3, Rue d'Antin in Paris. Josephine, anxious to establish her property rights under the marriage contract, brought along three heavyweight witnesses: her forty-year-old former lover and Napoleon's patron, Director Paul de Barras; his colleague and friend the twenty-eight-year-old Jean-Lambert Tallien, the cuckold husband of Josephine's friend Thérèse, Notre Dame de Thermidor; and Josephine's adviser and secretary, a lawyer named Jérôme Calmelet, "who approved of her marriage as much as Raguideau disapproved."[26] Josephine had left her children Hortense and Eugène at home.

An ambivalent Napoleon kept his bride, her witnesses, her adviser, and the officials waiting for over two hours. His late arrival might have expressed his deep ambivalence about marrying "Josephine," whom he unconsciously feared and hated—as he did his mother. The mayor of the 2nd *arrondissement*, Charles-François-Théodore Leclercq, became tired. He left and went to bed, leaving in his place the *Directoire*'s commissioner, a Bourbonnais veteran with a wooden leg named Antoine Collin-Lacombe, whom Vincent Cronin called "the acting registrar,"[27] and who had no authority to perform marriages. Arriving late at night, Napoleon brought along only one witness, his aide-de-camp, the capitaine Jean-Léonor-François Lemarois. There were many legal flaws in the civil wedding process. Napoleon and Josephine lied about their age and presented false documents; Lemarois was not yet of age and therefore could not be a witness; and the ceremony was illegally performed by Collin-Lacombe, who had no authority to officiate. André Castelot thought that Leclerq signed the marriage act the next day to legalize it and Max Gallo believed that Leclerq himself performed the marriage ceremony.[28] In short, it would not have been hard for Napoleon or Josephine to obtain an annulment of the marriage if they so wished.

In fact, Napoleon's wedding was a legal farce. Both he and his bride lied, cheated, and used forged documents. The thirty-two-year-old Marie-Josèphe-Rose de Tascher de la Pagerie de Beauharnois officially changed her name to Joséphine and made herself out to be twenty-eight, four years younger than she was. Castelot believed that her lawyer, Jérôme Calmelet, had perjured himself by certifying before a notary that he knew the widow

Beauharnois "perfectly" and that she had been born on June 23, 1767.[29] In fact, Rose had been born in 1763. Had she told Calmelet that she was four years younger, or had he agreed to commit perjury for her? Napoleon made himself eighteen months older than he was. He used his elder brother's baptismal act as his own, making himself out to be twenty-eight years old as well, rather than his real age of twenty-six, and stated that he had been born in Paris, rather than in his birthplace of Ajaccio.[30]

Ignoring Calmelet's perjury, Vincent Cronin thought that Napoleon's use of his elder brother's baptismal act was a practical necessity: "Napoleon did not have a birth certificate and Corsica was occupied by the English. So he did what Lucien had done two years earlier: borrow Joseph's. Josephine did not have a birth certificate either and Martinique also was occupied by the English, so she used the birth certificate of her sister Catherine. This was primarily a practical arrangement, but it had the advantage of making her seem younger than she was."[31] In fact, Napoleon had deeper reasons for using his elder brother's baptismal act as his own and for making himself out to be twenty-eight. This made him and Josephine the same age. In his unconscious mind, Josephine was Joseph, the elder brother that Napoleon wanted to be. In Napoleon's unconscious fantasy, he and Joseph became identical twins. By marrying the "twenty-eight-year-old" Josephine, he unconsciously fused with Joseph as well as with his her. Josephine's sister Catherine-Désirée, born in 1764, was thirty-one, a year younger than Josephine. Josephine could not have used Catherine's birth certificate to make herself out to be twenty-eight. Even her youngest sister, Marie-Françoise (Manette), born in 1766, was only three years younger than Josephine.[32] Had Rose used Manette's birth certificate as her own, that would have made her twenty-nine-years-old, not twenty-eight.

As his elder brother had been baptized Joseph Nabulion, Napoleon cheated at his wedding by using *a copy* of Joseph's baptismal act, made in 1782, as if it were his own. In that copy of the document there were at least two false items: the first name, Joseph, was omitted, leaving only Nabulion, and the date of birth was given as February 5, 1768. Napoleon had been born on August 15, 1769, and baptized two years later, while Joseph was born on January 7, 1768, and baptized the following day.

How could an official copy of Joseph's baptismal act, however, made in 1782, carry a birth date of February 5, 1768, rather than January 7, 1768? Dorothy Carrington thought that on the 1782 copy of the act "the date of the birth was inaccurately copied."[33] It is rather hard to accidentally copy

January 7 as February 5. Could the copy of Joseph's baptismal act have been deliberately falsified? Napoleon also falsely stated at his wedding that he was born in Paris rather than in Ajaccio. Why did he do so? And how could this deception pass unnoticed? Pierce Clark thought that "if the general [Napoleon] were born on February 5, 1768, he cannot state that he was born in Corsica, for the island was not at that date French territory and he would be reckoned an alien; so he claims [that] he was born in Paris. After all, who would see that document?"[34] In fact, Napoleon unconsciously wanted his motherland to be his idealized France and, to get his command of the *armée d'Italie*, he had to be French.

Idealizing his "Josephine," the love-sick Napoleon adored her out of all proportion to her real worth. When he was away from her, she seemed to him a goddess. Like his mother, Josephine did not love him back. He gave her a fine-gold necklace with a gold-and-enamel pendant (or a sapphire ring) on which was inscribed *Au destin* (to destiny). The psychoanalyst Pierce Clark believed that this was a "sinister" message and that there was "no mutual love" in this marriage:

> Napoleon's love life was turned in upon his own ego, hence no spiritual marriage was possible. Only a marriage of convenience could be expected of him. Thus the wedding ring bore no gentle message of mutual love, but the sinister one, "To destiny." What could be the fruition of such a union? Characteristically each thought this passion might ripen into an ideal love with the addition of real tenderness. Each expected it of the other, and both were disappointed. Mutual incriminations [*sic*] followed, and the marriage vows were broken almost before the ink on the certificate was dry.[35]

In fact, as we have seen, Napoleon and Josephine unconsciously repeated with each other their tormented early relationships with their parents, including their early rejections by them. Both were narcissistic. Neither could empathize with the other's feelings. Their ambivalent, seesaw relationship was a torment to them both. Despite his passionate love letters, Josephine felt that Napoleon was selfish, cold and unloving. In many ways, he was. Though he did not know it, his love was narcissistic. She was his narcissistic mirror: he loved himself in her.

When Napoleon's teenage fiancée, Désirée Clary, now living in Genoa, learned that he had married another woman, she was devastated. Still obeying and loving Napoleon like a child, she wrote him a sorrowful letter, calling herself Eugénie—as in his story *Clisson et Eugénie*—rather than Désirée. Her irrational love for the man who had abandoned her and caused her so much pain had a masochistic streak:

> You have made me so unhappy, and I am weak enough to forgive you. So you are married. Poor Eugénie must no longer love you, or think of you, and you said that you loved me, and a delay in a letter makes you break irrevocably with her whom you called your dear Eugénie and makes you marry another woman. You, married! I cannot get used to this idea, it kills me. I cannot stand it . . . My one consolation is that you will know how steadfast I am . . . I will show you that I am more faithful to my commitments [than you are], and even though you have broken the ties that united us, never shall I belong to another, never shall I marry. My misfortunes teach me to know men and to be wary of my heart. I have asked you through your brother to return my portrait, I renew my request; it must be indifferent to you, especially now that you own one of a woman, no doubt dear to you. The comparison that you make must be to my disadvantage, your wife being superior in everything to the poor Eugénie, who probably only surpassed her in her extreme attachment to you. After a year of absence, I who believed that I had touched happiness, who hoped to see you again soon and become the happiest of women by marrying you . . . Your marriage has shattered my happiness . . . I desire nothing but death. Life is a terrible torment to me, since I may no longer dedicate it to you . . . All the same I wish you the greatest joy and blessing in your marriage. May the woman you have chosen make you as happy as I had intended to make you, and as happy as you deserve to be. In the midst of your present happiness *do not quite forget poor Eugénie, and be sorry for her fate.*[36]

Did Désirée know "Remember me, but, ah! forget my fate," the heart-rendering aria of the dying Dido, abandoned by her lover Aeneas, at the end of Henry Purcell's seventeenth-century opera *Dido and Aeneas*? Désirée, however, was no Dido. Soon after her abandonment by Napoleon, Désirée became engaged to General Mathurin-Léonard Duphot (1769–1797), who was the same age as General Bonaparte. Duphot was killed in a street fight the following year, and in 1798 Désirée married Napoleon's thirty-five-year-old rival, his elder brother's friend,

General Jean-Baptiste-Jules Bernadotte. In 1810 Bernadotte became crown prince of Sweden and Norway.[37]

Two days after Napoleon wed Josephine, he kissed her goodbye and left Paris for Nice to take over the *armée d'Italie*. Why did Napoleon not take his wife along with him, as some of his fellow generals did? Max Gallo believed that Napoleon first had to accomplish "a difficult task."[38] His army was poorest and least equipped of all the French armies, while the French armies of the Rhine were well provided for. The job of Napoleon's *armée d'Italie* was to hold down the Austrian army in Italy, while his rivals, Jean-Victor-Marie Moreau and Jean-Charles Pichegru, fought the Austrians in Belgium and in Germany at the head of the *armée du Nord*, the *armée du Rhin* and the *armée de Moselle*. A year earlier Moreau had replaced Pichegru at the head of the *armée du Nord*, while Pichegru had taken over the *armée du Rhin*. Bonaparte had to defeat the Austrians with only thirty thousand men at his command. In fact, this was an unconscious excuse. Leaving Josephine behind had two aims in Napoleon's unconscious mind: it enabled him to idealize her from afar and it enabled her to have an affair with another man, Louis-Hippolyte Charles, as we will see, repeating Napoleon's childhood experience of his mother's affair with Marbeuf, whether real or not.[39]

The love-sick Napoleon wrote Josephine almost daily. On March 13, 1796 he wrote her from Châtillon, and on March 14 from Chanceaux:

> I wrote you yesterday from Châtillon . . . Every instant is taking me farther away from you, adorable friend, and with every instant I have less strength to endure being so far from you. You are the perpetual object of my thought; my imagination exhausts itself trying to guess what you are doing. If I see you sad, my heart is torn and my pain grows; if you are gay, playful with your friends, I reproach you with having so soon forgotten the painful three-day separation; you are then light, and henceforward you are no longer affected by any deep feeling. As you see I am not easy to satisfy; but, my good friend, it is quite another thing if I fear that your health has changed, or that you have reasons to be upset that I cannot divine. Then I rue the speed with which they are taking me away from your heart . . . May my genius, which has always protected me amid the greatest dangers, surround you, cover you, and I will give myself up uncovered. Ah, do not be gay, but a little melancholic . . . Write me,

my tender friend, and at length, and receive the thousand and one kisses of the tenderest truest love.[40]

Napoleon addressed this letter to "*la citoyenne Beauharnois*, 6, Rue Chantereine, Paris," rather than to the *citoyenne Bonaparte*, his wife's official name since their recent wedding. André Castelot wondered whether Napoleon was afraid that the mailman would not find his wife under her new name.[41] Perhaps, in Napoleon's unconscious mind, the *citoyenne Bonaparte* was his mother rather than his wife.

Events during the French Revolution moved rapidly and dramatically. Following internal power struggles, the *Directoire exécutif* merged the *armée du Rhin* with the *armée de Moselle*, and on March 14, 1796, named Napoleon's rival General Moreau to command the new *armée de Rhin-et-Moselle*. Moreau prepared his army for an invasion of Germany and a campaign against Austria. On March 20 Napoleon reached Marseille and at once went to see his mother, whose demand for money had almost caused him to kill himself the previous summer. Thanks to the money that the newly rich Napoleon had sent her the previous November, Letizia had left the Hôtel des Cypières, the haven for Corsican exiles, where she had lived for thirteen months, for one of Marseille's best apartments at 17, Rue de Rome. Napoleon felt that she owed him a debt of gratitude. Instead, Letizia fixed him with her suspicious, critical gaze, as if he had hurt, compromised, or betrayed her. Napoleon told his mother of his marriage to Josephine. Many biographers and scholars believed that Letizia was shocked when she learned about Napoleon's marriage: her new daughter-in-law was a viscountess, a woman of fashion, a widow six-years older than Napoleon, a woman of many lovers, known for her loose sexual morals, and with two children to support, who would eat up Napoleon's salary. In fact, Letizia had heard about Josephine's history and reputation from her other sons, and she resented Josephine for stealing her son from her. Trying to make peace between his mother and his wife, Napoleon gave his mother a friendly letter that he had made Josephine write to her and drafted a polite reply for Letizia to write to Josephine.[42]

An anxious Napoleon bombarded his wife with passionate love letters, which were more accurately love-hate letters. Josephine, who hated letter writing, wrote him much less frequently, and almost stopped writing her husband altogether. By now she was madly in love with Louis-Hippolyte Charles and thought little of Napoleon. The unhappy Napoleon idealized Josephine, missed her terribly. In one of his love letters he wrote: "I do not pass an hour without loving you; I do not drink a cup of tea without damning the glory and ambition that made me separate from my soul and my life . . . My soul is sad; my heart is enslaved."[43] Frédéric Masson thought that these letters were "a constant cry from a hungry heart, from a man who had lived chastely, to the mistress older, more worldly, more sophisticated than himself, who satisfied his heart and senses."[44] Several scholars have noted the strange, pathetic, infantile, and fantastic quality of these love letters.[45]

Napoleon's Josephine was not the real Rose. She was more an idealized mother than a flesh-and-blood wife. He did not address her as "my dear wife" or "my dear love" but as "my good friend." In one letter he called her "my incomparable little mother."[46] The word "incomparable" was Napoleon's favorite term of endearment, and Josephine was his idealized mother. When she did not answer him, his love letters to her often became letters of rage. Jacques Bainville noted the pathetic quality of Napoleon's letters to Josephine:

> There was something a little ludicrous about Bonaparte's passion for his faithless spouse, and the "old mustachios" thought him too free in displaying the portrait of his beloved whilst disdaining the beauties of Milan who offered themselves to the liberator. But what matter? Beautified by time, the romance of Bonaparte and Josephine provides the Italian campaign with an accompaniment of love. Already the picture of a woman, of sensibility, *a core of sorrow within the gleam of fame*, were beginning: to shape the cloud of legend around his face and accoutrements. Those love letters of his, ablaze with passion, often with rage, and haunted by the idea of death, make a strange contrast with the jubilation of victory which he raised into poetry by a romantic backward glance after action; and a still stranger contrast that "transcendent faculty of geometry" which he applied to the arts of war.[47]

Indeed, in his love life, Napoleon was living in fantasy. He imagined his wife as the ideal "goddess" that she never was. He cast her in his infantile image of his mother and living with her the very painful and traumatic relationship all over again.

12

In War and in Love

Napoleon's appointment as commander-in-chief of the French *armée d'Italie* in early March 1796 gave him an exhilarating sense of power. He vanquished his feelings of powerlessness by establishing his absolute authority over his subordinates. It is hard to tell the exact size of Napoleon's *armée d'Italie*. It numbered anywhere from thirty thousand to forty-five thousand men, depending on which scholar you trust. A likely figure is thirty-eight thousand.[1] In an initial meeting with his division commanders, Bonaparte reportedly stared them down and emerged triumphant. On 7 Germinal Year IV of the French Republic (March 27, 1796), drunk with his power after his initial meeting with his generals, Napoleon reportedly issued his first proclamation to his *armée d'Italie*. By any measure, it was a grandiose proclamation:

> Soldiers! You are naked, starving; the government owes you much, it can give you nothing. Your patience, the courage that you show in the midst of these rocks are admirable. But they get you no glory, no shining light reflects on you. I want to lead you into the world's most fertile plains. Rich provinces, great cities will be in your power. There you shall find honor, glory, and riches. Soldiers of Italy, will you lack for courage and constancy?[2]

In fact, this famous proclamation, cited in every book on Napoleon, was made up by Napoleon himself when he was an aging prisoner of the British on St. Helena.[3]

In late March 1796 Napoleon marched his *armée d'Italie* eastward along the Mediterranean coast into Italy. It was a big gamble. The British Royal Navy was patrolling the French coasts and its gunboats could fire on Napoleon's army. Gallo thought that Napoleon wanted to prove that he did not fear to march under enemy fire. His army crossed the border into Liguria and occupied the Riviera di Ponente, between San Remo and Genoa. Meanwhile Napoleon kept thinking and dreaming of Josephine. In one of this early letters from Italy, he wrote her, "Whether I am in the midst of business matters, leading the troops, or dashing through the camps, my adorable Josephine, and she alone, is in my heart, and occupies my mind and my thoughts."[4] Unconsciously, Napoleon took a small step away from his mother, addressing this letter to "*la citoyenne Bonaparte, chez la citoyenne Beauharnois.*"

In early April 1796, Napoleon began to sign his last name "Bonaparte" rather than "Buonaparte." He was taking psychological leave of his father, who had spelled his name "Buonaparte," and becoming "his own man." But as he was becoming happy in war, he was becoming unhappy in love. When fierce fighting erupted all over northwestern Italy, an unhappy Napoleon wrote his wife:

> I have not taken a cup of tea withgout cursing the glory and the ambition that keep me away from the soul of my life . . . One day you will no longer love me; tell me. I will know at least to deserve the unhappiness. Truth, frankness without limits . . . Josephine! Josephine! Do you remember what I have told you several times: nature has made my soul strong and decided; she has made you of lace and gauze. Have you stopped loving me? . . . Adieu, adieu, I shall go to sleep without you. I beg you, let me sleep. For several nights I have felt you in my arms. Happy dream, but it is not you![5]

In fact, Napoleon's wife Josephine never really loved him. The ambivalent relationship between Josephine and Napoleon had a neurotic seesaw character: when he loved her passionately, she became cool to him; when he had another lover, or grew cool to her, she became passionate and jealous. When Napoleon wrote Josephine passionate love letters from Italy, she ignored his mail or wrote him cold letters. When Napoleon complained of her coldness, sending her "a thousand kisses as burning as you are cold,"[6] Josephine wrote him back "a few ardent, erotic lines . . . in her own blood."[7] As we have seen, both of them unconsciously repeated with their spouse the tormented relationships of their early lives.

General Napoleon Bonaparte was a strict disciplinarian. The lack of discipline among his men made him anxious and enraged him. Fearing his deep sense of helplessness, he needed total control of everything and everybody around him. On April 5–6, 1796, he moved his headquarters to the conquered Ligurian town of Albenga, some fifty-five miles east of Nice on the Mediterranean coast. When two royalist officers in his army shouted "*Vive le roi!*" (Long live the king!), Napoleon had them court-martialed. Two days later he informed the *Directoire exécutif* of this incident. Napoleon issued an order of the day stating that "discipline is the nerve of the armies."[8] In another proclamation on Christmas Day 1799, General Bonaparte said that "constancy and discipline" were the soldier's chief virtues.[9]

At the same time Napoleon practiced the nepotism and favoritism that were common in his time. He invited his elder brother Joseph, who was living in the Ligurian capital of Genoa and had gone into business with his brother-in-law Nicolas Clary, to supply his "ragged" army. In cooperation with Antoine-Christophe Saliceti, the *Directoire*'s commissioner to the *armée d'Italie*, Joseph did so "with speed and energy."[10] He came to Albenga and conferred with Napoleon. Joseph seems to have stayed with Napoleon until late April. When he learned how badly his younger brother was hurt by Josephine's coldness toward him, Joseph wrote Josephine begging her to join her husband in Italy.[11]

A hyperactive "control freak," General Bonaparte barely slept during his initial battles in northwestern Italy. He was feverish with excitement and anxiety as he drove his men relentlessly for four days and nights, from April 14 to April 18, 1796, from the Riviera up to the Alps. Napoleon's strategy of dividing the Piedmontese army from its Austrian allies was working. His generals gave the enemy no rest. On April 17 the French reached the heights of the Montezzemolo, looking down upon the plains. Napoleon reportedly told his soldiers that "Hannibal crossed the Alps, but we have outflanked them."[12] Napoleon was in a euphoric frenzy. "For ninety-six hours almost non-stop Napoleon had marched his army up and down the steep foothills of the Alps, across passes, and through defiles, and he had thrown them into four major battles."[13]

In April 1796, shortly after she married Napoleon, his unfaithful wife Josephine took a lover nine years her junior. He was Louis-Hippolyte Charles, a cavalry lieutenant in the First Hussar regiment who had just been attached to the *armée de l'interieur* in Paris. Hippolyte Charles was five-feet-six-inches tall, had jet-black hair, brown skin, and blue eyes, dressed with great taste, and had a pretty face and a hairdresser's assistant's elegance. Owen Connelly called Hippolyte Charles "a perfumed lieutenant" and claimed that he may have been "a homosexual friend [of Josephine's] who passed for [her lover]."[14] In fact, Josephine had a very passionate love affair with Charles, and he was her only great love.[15] Frank Richardson called it a "passionate and dangerous liaison."[16] Denying reality, Napoleon only discovered his wife's betrayal three years later, and his rage was terrible.[17] The cuckolded Napoleon had Hippolyte Charles's file removed from the archives of the French War Ministry. The often ruthless Napoleon could have done Charles much worse harm, such as sending him to fight and get killed at a dangerous front, but he did not. This was not because Napoleon was kind (although he could be very kind, as well as very cruel); it was part of his tragic sadomasochistic relationship with Josephine, which fed on pain and suffering.

Napoleon was happy in war but unhappy in love. He was winning his battles, but his beloved and idealized wife was ignoring his letters. His victories could not satisfy the impossible demands of his inner mother and his idealized self, or ego ideal, nor heal his deep sense of worthlessness. After capturing Mondovi on April 21, 1796, Napoleon, who badly missed his wife, denying her unfaithfulness, asked the *Directoire exécutif*'s permission to let her join him in Italy. He wrote Director Barras in Paris—Josephine's former lover—asking him to send Josephine to join him in Italy as a reward for his victories: "I want my wife very much to come and join me."[18] By April 23 Napoleon's army had fought six battles, taken twelve thousand prisoners, killed six thousand Piedmontese, and taken twenty-one enemy flags and forty cannon. Yet he was unhappy. His army marched on the Piedmontese capital of Turin.[19] Two divisions had taken the Tenda Pass from the Austrians, while another division marched through the high Tanaro River valley toward Turin.

On April 24, 1796, from his Piedmontese headquarters at the hilltop town of Carrù, near Cuneo, Napoleon sent his elder brother Joseph to the *Directoire exécutif* with several dispatches. But Joseph's real mission, to Napoleon, was to carry a letter to Josephine begging her to leave Paris at once and join him:

> My brother will bring you this letter. *I have the greatest love for him* and I hope he will gain yours; he deserves it. Nature has given him

> a sweet and utterly good character; he is full of good qualities. I am writing to Barras to get him appointed consul in some Italian port. He wants to live with his little wife far away from the hurly-burly and political affairs; *I commend him to you.*[20]

This was almost an unconscious invitation for Josephine to have an affair with Joseph. Not content with sending his brother into his wife's arms, Napoleon sent her yet another handsome young man, his dashing young aide-de-camp, Major Andoche Junot, along with him, carrying the captured enemy flags. Ostensibly Joseph and Junot were sent to fetch Josephine to him but, unconsciously, Napoleon may have wanted them to have an affair with his wife. If Josephine did not seduce Joseph, would she not tempt Junot? Napoleon's letter to his wife practically invited her to seduce his young aide:

> Junot is bringing twenty-two [enemy] flags to Paris. You must come back with him, do you hear? If this is not done at once, let him not come back. Unhappiness without remedy, pain without consolation, continual suffering, if I had the misfortune of seeing him return alone. *Adorable friend, he will see you and breathe in your temple! Perhaps you will even grant him the unique and priceless favor of kissing your cheek?* And I, I shall be alone, and far, far away! But you are going to come, aren't you? You are going to be here at my side, in my arms, on my heart, on my mouth! Take wings, come, come! But travel gently. The road is long, bad, tiring. Suppose you had an accident, or fell ill; suppose fatigue—come gently, my adorable love, but think of me often.[21]

Napoleon's military achievements at the outset of his Italian campaign were stunning and unprecedented. In fifteen hectic days (April 12–27, 1796) he won six victories over two enemy armies outnumbering his own and had put one of them out of the war. Jacques Bainville thought that Napoleon had taken over "a decrepit and grudging an army, Republican and Jacobin" of thirty thousand sans-culottes and turned them into an outstanding fighting force. "From the very start he showed himself a master mind, sizing up situations at a glance, and controlling them."[22] Vincent Cronin believed that Napoleon had "four exceptional qualities" that helped him defeat the enemy and conquer northern Italy: his broad chest and big lungs, which gave him "an unusually quick rate of metabolism"and helped him act with great speed; his need for very little sleep; his keen eye for topography; and his artillery skills.[23] In fact, Napoleon slept little because of his anxiety and insatiable ambition, his narcissistic need for perfection to maintain his grandiose self, and his obsessional need to control everything in order not to feel his unbearable sense of helplessness.

On April 26, 1796, a month after his first grandiose proclamation to his troops, Napoleon issued yet another high-minded proclamation to his army. Having promised them "great cities and rich provinces," he now preached as an antipillage moralist.

> Soldiers! You have won six victories in fifteen days, taken twenty-one flags, fifty-five pieces of cannon, several fortified places, conquered the richest part of the Piedmont . . . Soldiers! Up till now you have fought for barren rocks, made famous by your courage but useless to the *patrie* . . . Deprived of everything, you have made up for everything; you have won battles without guns, crossed rivers without bridges, made forced marches without shoes, bivouacked without brandy and often without bread. The republican phalanxes, the soldiers of liberty alone were able to suffer what you have suffered. Thanks are due to you, soldiers! . . . Soldiers! I demand that you respect the peoples you have delivered and stop the pillage . . . Soldiers! The patrie has the right to expect great things of you! Will you justify that expectation? . . . You still have battles to fight, cities to take, rivers to cross . . . But, soldiers, you have done nothing, because you still have things to do.[24]

André Castelot wryly observed that pillage was forbidden to the French soldiers because it was reserved for their government.[25] From a psychological point of view, however, Napoleon unconsciously projected his problem with himself upon his soldiers. No achievement could satisfy him for long. However great his achievements, his internal conflicts were not resolved. He repeatedly felt that he had achieved nothing, even when he had conquered vast territories and done great things. Whatever he achieved, his insatiable "ambition" demanded ever greater "glory."

The armistice between France and Sardinia-Piedmont-Savoy was signed at the Piedmontese town of Cherasco during the night of April 27–28, 1796, and bore the date of April 27. General Bonaparte signed for

France and the Savoyard general Salier de la Tour for Sardinia-Piedmont-Savoy. King Vittorio Amedeo gave Napoleon the key cities of Coni, Tortona and Alessandria, and the right to cross the River Po at Valenza without a fight. Napoleon had obtained from Piedmont-Sardinia in less than three weeks that which his predecessors had not done in four years of warfare. Three months earlier the *Directoire exécutif* had appointed Antoine-Christophe Saliceti, Napoleon's former ally, patron, and sometime enemy, who was twelve years Napoleon's senior, its wars commissioner to Napoleon's *armée d'Italie*. Saliceti arrived in Cherasco on April 28, where he met Napoleon just after the signing of the armistice. For seven months Saliceti stayed with the *armée d'Italie* and "revolutionized northern Italy," but he could not complete his ambitious project of uniting Italy and making it over in France's image.[26]

Not content with having dispatched Junot and Joseph to fetch Josephine to him—or, unconsciously, to seduce her—on April 29, 1796, from Cherasco, Napoleon sent yet another dashing young man to Paris to bring his wife to him in Italy: his first aide-de-camp, Colonel Joachim Murat. Napoleon knew that the promiscuous Josephine had had love affairs with several men, including his patron Barras and perhaps even Murat himself. As with Junot and Joseph, this was an unconscious invitation for Josephine to have a sexual affair with his dashing young aide-de-camp. Although he did not yet know it—he only guessed at it—she had also taken up with Hippolyte Charles. Josephine had reportedly seduced both Murat and Junot, and would have seduced Joseph if she could.[27]

The desperate Napoleon wrote an ambivalent letter to Josephine, full of entreaties and accusations, which he gave to Murat to deliver to her:

> How happy Murat is to kiss your little hand . . . Ah! If you do not come!!! It will be a happy day when you cross the Alps. It is the prettiest compensation for my pains and for the victories that I have won . . . Bring your chambermaid with you, your cook, your coachman. I have horses here at your service, and a pretty carriage. Do not carry anything but that which is personally necessary. I have here silverware and porcelain which will be at your service . . . Never has woman been loved with more devotion, fire and tenderness . . . How do you want, me, my life, not to be sad?! No letter from you. I only receive one every four days. Instead of which, had you loved me, you would have written me twice a day. But one must chatter with the little gentlemen visitors, from ten o'clock in the morning,

> and then listen to the frivolities and inanities of a hundred puppies until one o'clock after midnight. In countries with morals, from ten o'clock in the evening everyone is at home. But in those countries one writes to one's husband, one thinks of him, one lives for him. *Adieu, Josephine, you are to me a monster that I cannot explain* . . . I love you more each day. Absence cures the little passions, it increases the big ones. A kiss on your mouth, or on your heart. There is no one but me, is there? And then, one on your breast.[28]

The word "monster" was neither humorous nor accidental. This was how Napoleon had imagined his motherland, and unconsciously his mother, in his adolescent *Nouvelle Corse*, set on the Isle of the Gorgon. Deep down, Napoleon knew that his wife had a lover. He denied this unbearable idea while doing everything he could to make it true. Josephine was in no hurry to join him. She was happy with her new lover in Paris.

Having "pacified" the Piedmont and driven a wedge between it and its Austrian allies, Napoleon prepared to fight Austria. He also continued to write deeply ambivalent letters to Josephine, full of entreaties and accusations, love and hate. In one poignant letter he correctly guessed that his wife had taken a lover, and hinted at suicide and murder:

> Do you have a lover? Have you taken up with some stripling of nineteen? You know that I shall never endure to see you with a lover, still less suffer you to have one: tearing out his heart and seeing him would be the same thing to me; and then if I could raise my hand against your sacred person . . . No, I would never dare, but I would leave a life in which that which is most virtuous would have betrayed me. I am sure and proud of your love . . . A thousand kisses on your eyes, your lips! . . . If it were true, though! Fear Othello's dagger![29]

This was the first written indication that Napoleon consciously thought that his wife had a lover. Naturally, he denied this unbearable thought as long as he could. Unconsciously, however, Napoleon wished to preserve a situation in which his wife was unfaithful, just as he thought his mother had done. But why did Napoleon imagine his wife's lover to be nineteen years old rather than any other age? Had Josephine teased him about taking a nineteen-year-old lover? Nineteen was the age of her first husband when she married him. In any event, Napoleon was only four years off the mark: Hippolyte Charles was twenty-three-years-old.

An ambitious, tenacious, and stubborn Napoleon relentlessly pursued his war against the Austrians in Italy. On May 10, 1796, General Bonaparte and his army reached Lodi. Across the River Adda were the Austrians. At the battle of Lodi, three hundred and fifty of Napoleon's men were killed or wounded. Of the nine thousand Austrian soldiers at this battle, his men had killed one hundred and fifty-three and taken seventeen hundred prisoner, many of them wounded. Napoleon, however, wrote the *Directoire exécutif* in Paris that the Austrians had numbered *eighteen thousand* and that the enemy had *three thousand* casualties. Why did Napoleon need to exaggerate his exploits? Connelly thought that "this sort of fiction became habitual in later bulletins."[30] Consciously aimed at pleasing his bosses in Paris, the gross exaggeration was unconsciously aimed at bolstering Napoleon's self-esteem. His victory at Lodi, and the adulation of his troops, made Napoleon feel great and powerful.

The battle of Lodi was another turning point in Napoleon's career. After his victory at Lodi, he had an unprecedented authority over his men, who idealized Napoleon and considered him out of the ordinary. The real heroes at Lodi were Napoleon's subordinates. The troops nonetheless glorified their commander in chief, General Bonaparte, over and above his subordinates, and Napoleon's official bulletins described him as the great victor. Pierce Clark thought that "perhaps at the bridge of Lodi, or on the night thereafter when General Bonaparte sees himself as 'an exceptional man,' he crystallizes his image of a legend worthy of the heroes of antiquity. He certainly lives more and more into this heroic mold when he is not otherwise engaged in an intense subjective projection of his immediate will and purpose."[31] Napoleon's veterans affectionately called him *le petit caporal* (the little corporal)[32] but the French people, somewhat less affectionately, later called him *le petit tondu* (the little shorn one). Napoleon's grandiose self, however, was given a big boost at Lodi.[33]

Josephine, Napoleon's unfaithful wife, ignored his passionate love letters. Every few days, after receiving several frantic letters from Napoleon, she had her teenage daughter, Hortense, answer the letters of her "funny little general" for her.[34] Napoleon wrote Josephine, "I shall be frantic if I do not have a letter from you tonight."[35] Happy with her lover Hippolyte, she took her sweet time answering him and did everything to avoid leaving Paris.

Despite Napoleon's entreaties and threats, the *Directoire exécutif* had done nothing to get Josephine join him. In fact, they had tried to keep her in Paris, fearing that her presence in Italy would distract their young general from his warlike pursuits. On May 14, 1796, Napoleon received a letter from his wife telling him that she was ill and leaving Paris for a cure in the country in a hurry. So ill, in fact, and in such a hurry, that she had cut short her letter and left . . . Napoleon consciously suspected, and unconsciously knew, that his wife had a lover. Indeed, the thirty-two-year-old Josephine had been sleeping with her twenty-three-year-old lover Hippolyte Charles for a whole month. For some reason, however, Napoleon still thought that her lover was only nineteen years old:

> I receive a letter that you interrupt to go to the country. And after that, you take on the tone of being jealous of me, who am here overwhelmed with business and with fatigue. Ah! My good friend . . . It is true that I am wrong. In the spring the country is beautiful. And then the lover of nineteen years was there no doubt?[36]

Denying what he intuitively knew, Napoleon swallowed Josephine's lies hook, line, and sinker. He then panicked. Unconsciously, Josephine was his mother. His wife's "illness" made him regress to an infant's fear of losing his mother:

> My heart feels an indescribable anxiety. You are ill, and far away from me. Be gay, and take good care of yourself, you who, in my heart, I value more than the universe. Alas! The idea that you are ill make me very sad . . . Ah! Do not stay in the country. Be in the city. Try to have fun. And believe that there are no torments more real for my soul than to think that you are ill and upset. I thought that I was jealous, but I swear to you that there is nothing to it. Rather than see you unhappy, I think I would give you a lover myself.[37]

As yet another ruse, Josephine informed Napoleon via his aide-de-camp Joachim Murat that she was pregnant. It was another lie. In response, Napoleon wrote her touching, heartrending letters about their future child.[38]

While Napoleon was preoccupied with Josephine, historical events took their course. For three years, from Bonaparte's conquests in 1796 until the French were driven out of Italy by the Austrians and Russians in

1799, the northern part of the country was organized into French-style republics under French control. First Genoa and all of Liguria became the *Reppublica ligure*. In late 1796 the duchies of Reggio and Modena and the papal states of Bologna and Ferrara, which had been taken from "the Holy Father," were joined into the *Repubblica cispadana*, which was created at the Congress of Modena and adopted an anticlerical republican constitution. In June 1797 the *Repubblica cispadana* was incorporated into the new *Repubblica cisalpina*, based in Milan and including all of Lombardy, which had a strong executive branch and president in the person of Prince Gian Galeazzo Serbelloni, and a weak bicameral legislature consisting of a *Consiglio dei Juniori* and a *Consiglio dei Seniori*. These short-lived republics were run by Italian noblemen who professed to embrace the new French republican ideas.[39]

Napoleon was leading a double life: the glorious warrior to the world, the unhappy cuckold inside. On June 11, 1796, having temporarily faced the painful truth about his wife, he wrote her former lover, Paul de Barras, in Paris: "I am in despair, my wife is not coming, she has some lover who keeps her in Paris! . . . I curse all women, but I embrace my good friends."[40] It was like saying, "I hate my mother, but I love my father." André Castelot wondered, "Has he guessed the truth?"[41] Of course he had. In fact, Napoleon had been told that Josephine had *several lovers* and that she had also seduced his aides Murat and Junot, but Murat had returned to Italy and joined Napoleon. The misogynist tone, which goes back to Napoleon's mother, is unmistakable. Deep down Napoleon knew the unbearable truth, but had been denying it to himself, just as he had his deep disappointment with and rage at his mother.

On the same day, a deeply unhappy Napoleon wrote his unfaithful wife again. This time he did not blame his unhappiness on her, nor on himself, nor on *la fortune*, who he still thought loved him, but on *le sort* (fate), who he felt crushed him, and on Josephine's *destin* (destiny). After a one-week encounter with his painful reality, Napoleon denied it again. He referred to a letter Josephine had written him "with her blood":[42]

> Josephine, where shall one deliver this letter to you? If it is in Paris, my misfortune is then certain, and you no longer love me! I have only one thing left: to die . . . Oh! You! . . . My tears flow. No more rest nor hope. I respect the will of the immutable law of fate. It

> overwhelms me with glory to make me feel my unhappiness more bitterly. I would get used to everything in this new state of things, but I cannot get used to no longer esteeming you . . . It is not possible! My Josephine is on her way, she loves me at least a little. So much love promised cannot have vanished in two months . . . I hate Paris, women and love . . . This state is terrible . . . and your behavior . . . But should I accuse you? No. Your behavior is that of your destiny. So lovable, so beautiful, so sweet, should you have to be the instrument of my despair? Despite destinies and honor, I will love you all my life. I have re-read, tonight, all your letters, even that written with your blood. What feelings they have made me experience![43]

André Castelot thought that "perhaps nothing was lost" because Josephine's letter "written with her own blood" was one in which she reminded him graphically of the sexual pleasures that she had had in his arms, or he in hers.[44] In fact, everything had been lost. Napoleon's narcissistic relationship to Josephine was sadomasochistic: for each unconscious ounce of pleasure he paid with many conscious pounds of pain.

There was a hidden but important connection between Napoleon's state of feeling for wife and his orders to his army. He felt helpless and impotent with his wife. There was nothing he could do to force her to join him. Without her, he felt empty and worthless. To relieve this unbearable feeling, he sought a feeling of power in war. Fighting made him feel that he existed and was worthwhile. General Bonaparte was ruthless in imposing his will on others. On June 13, 1796, his troops occupied the papal city of Bologna, a prelude to the French conquest of all the papal states. On June 14 General Bonaparte learned from Director Barras that Josephine had once more declared herself too ill to travel. Once more denying reality, imagining again that she loved him, Napoleon wrote her plaintively:

> Murat wants to convince me that your illness is light; but you are not writing me; for a month I have not received any letters from you. You are tender, sensitive, and you love me. You struggle between the illness and the physicians . . . If your illness continues, obtain for me permission [from the *Directoire exécutif*] to come and see you for an hour. In five days, I am in Paris, and on the twelfth, at my army. Without you, I cannot be useful here. Let he who wishes love glory, let he who wishes serve the *patrie*, my soul is suffocating in this exile; and when my good friend suffers, is ill, I

> cannot coldly calculate victory . . . My tears flood your portrait; it alone does not leave me.[45]

On that same day, June 14, 1796, Napoleon ordered his chief of staff, General Louis-Alexandre Berthier, to court-martial the Italian rebel prisoners taken the previous night; they would be accused of murdering Frenchmen; before noon the following day their affair had to be concluded. Berthier was to imprison the entire city council of Bosco; if they did not hand over a list of at least twelve assassins, they were all to be executed immediately. Like an alcoholic or a drug addict, Napoleon desperately tried to fight his feeling of helplessness with his wife by intoxicating himself with his sense of power over the rebels. Terrorizing others into doing his will was Napoleon's way of surmounting his feelings of helplessness from his childhood.

The unconscious defenses of denial and displacement did not work. Napoleon was depressed and anxious. He realized that while externally brilliant, he was inwardly unhappy. He confided his unhappiness in a letter to his elder brother Joseph:

> My friend, I am in despair. My wife, all that I love in the world, is ill. I can no longer think straight . . . Reassure me, speak to me true, you know my heart, you know how ardent it is, you know that I have never loved anyone but Josephine, that Josephine is the first woman I adore . . . I love her furiously, and I can no longer stay away from her. If she did not love me, I would have nothing left on this earth . . . Adieu, my friend, you shall be happy. I am destined by nature to have only shining appearances.[46]

Ironically, and tragically, among his other unconscious motives for his unhappy marital relationship, it was Napoleon's deep and ambivalent feelings for Joseph that had made him fall in love with his wife Rose-Josèphe and to rename her "Josephine." What he wrote Joseph in this letter was, to say the least, inaccurate. Napoleon had been in love with his sister-in-law Désirée Clary. Did he intend this pained and private letter for Joseph's eyes only? Joseph was concerned about his younger brother, and Napoleon's letter found its way to Barras, who shared it with the entire *Directoire exécutif*. They too were concerned about their young general's well-being.

To gain time, Josephine falsely wrote Napoleon again that she was ill, and Barras confirmed it to him. Once more, Napoleon was taken in. To escape his unbearable pain, he denied reality. Turning his rage upon himself, he felt guilty and asked his wife's forgiveness:

> I have been wrong about you so many times that I do not know how to make up for it. I accuse you of staying in Paris; you were ill there! Forgive me, my good friend: the love that you inspired in me has taken away my reason; I shall never find it again. One does not recover from this illness. My presentiments are so deadly that I shall keep myself to seeing you, pressing you to my breast for two hours and then dying together. Who is taking care of you? I guess you have called Hortense . . . What is your illness today? If it is dangerous, I warn you, I shall leave for Paris at once![47]

At the same time Napoleon asked the *Directoire exécutif*'s permission to return to Paris and tend to his ailing wife. He gave both his letters to his courier, ordering him—pathetically—to hand Josephine's letter to her and not to leave her until she has written at least ten pages in reply. An exasperated *Directoire* decided that if it wished to keep northern Italy, it had better send Josephine to Napoleon without further delay.

On June 24, 1796 Josephine finally left Paris for Milan in her horse-drawn carriage, which she shared with Napoleon's elder brother Joseph, his aide-de-camp Junot, her pug Fortuné—and her lover Hippolyte Charles, who, incredibly, came along and rode in her own carriage. In another carriage behind them were Josephine's chambermaid, Louise Compoint, who had become Junot's lover, and her two servants, Antoine Labesse and Jean Laurent. In a third carriage were Prince Gian Galeazzo Serbelloni, future head of the *direttorio* of the French-created Cisalpine Republic, and Nicolas Clary, Joseph's brother-in-law. The convoy made a stop at Fontainebleau, at the home of Josephine's aunt, Madame de Renaudin, where the party was joined by Antoine Hamelin, the husband of Josephine's friend Fortunée.[48]

Monsieur Hamelin brought along his friend, Monsieur Monglas, and Josephine's two guests rode in a post chaise, a four-wheeled eighteenth-century carriage for the rapid transportation of persons and mail. Hamelin and Monglas came to Italy with Josephine because they hoped to obtain a lucrative business through her husband. The manipulative Josephine knew how to make her connections pay. She had already received ten thousand francs for arranging the furnishing of twenty thousand blankets to the army. Napoleon had written Josephine, "If you have someone to place, you can send him to me, I shall place him."[49] Hamelin had lost his fortune and badly needed to be "placed." At Josephine's request, he and Monglas had lent her two hundred louis and given her an expensive English scarf worth thirty louis. In return, she had promised them to get Napoleon to give them a letter of recommendation to the *Directoire exécutif* in Paris to make them the official suppliers of the French Army of Italy. She gave them an appointment at Fontainebleau, whence they would proceed to Italy together. At the same time, Josephine had promised the same thing to the fiftyish financier Joseph Robbé de Lagrange, an old admirer of hers, who had advanced her another five hundred louis. He, too, had been invited to Fontainebleau.[50]

As General Bonaparte's wife, Josephine was officially called *la générale Bonaparte* (Madame General Bonaparte). Napoleon's courier Moustache preceded her convoy and took care of the horses at each relay. Wherever they stayed, Josephine and Hippolyte occupied adjoining rooms, as did Andoche Junot and Louise Compoint, the chambermaid.[51] Vincent Cronin thought that "during the journey [from Paris] to Milan, the situation which Napoleon had described in 'Clisson et Eugénie' was enacted in real life: an aide-de-camp slept with his wife."[52] Hippolyte Charles, a former officer of the *armée de l'interieur*, was never Napoleon's aide-de-camp; Andoche Junot, however, was.[53]

On June 30, 1796, Napoleon reached the Tuscan capital of Florence, where a courier handed him a letter from Joseph announcing Josephine's arrival in a fortnight. Napoleon was ecstatic. July 13 was a dramatic day for Napoleon. His Austrian enemies were retreating. He had "marched 300 miles in under six weeks, cowed all central Italy, and seized, in booty and indemnities, forty million francs, mainly gold."[54] Now a courier told him that his wife was going to arrive in Milan in one hour's time. Napoleon, terribly excited, left the battlefield and rushed back to Milan to welcome Josephine, who finally arrived from Paris. Joseph and his aide Junot knew that Hippolyte Charles had been sleeping with Josephine for three months but feared to upset Napoleon by telling him. Vincent Cronin believed that "Napoleon, of course, did not know this."[55] Deep down, he knew it well: Napoleon had written Barras—and Josephine herself—that he thought his wife had a lover, Yet he denied what was happening before his very eyes: "He was so consumed with desire that he did not even notice the presence, at his wife's side, of Hippolyte Charles. Not only that, but during the first two days that he spent with her in Milan, he entertained her lover at dinner and in his salon"[56]

After four months of excruciating separation, Napoleon spent only two days with his wife in Milan before leaving her again and heading for the battlefield. On July 17, 1796, a once-again-unhappy Napoleon wrote Josephine from Mantua. As he had done with his rejecting mother, he defensively idealized his wife out of all proportion to reality. He even wanted to kiss her mean dog Fortuné, who had viciously bitten him. Napoleon wanted to die fused with his idealized Josephine:

> Since I left you, I have always been sad. My happiness is to be beside you. All the time I recall your kisses, your tears, your nice jealousy; and the charms of the incomparable Josephine ceaselessly light a lively and burning flame in my heart and in my senses . . . A few days ago, I thought I loved you; but since I saw you [again], I feel that I love you a thousand times more. Since I have known you, I adore you more every day. This proves how false is La BruyPre's maxim that *l'amour vient tout d'un coup* [love comes suddenly]. Everything in nature has its own course and different degrees of growth. Ah! I beg of you, let me see some of your defects; be less beautiful, less gracious, less tender, less kind above all. Above all, never be jealous and never weep; your tears take away my reason and set my blood on fire . . . Get plenty of rest. Regain your health quickly. *Come and join me; and at least, before we die, we can say: We were happy for so many days!!!* Millions of kisses, and even to Fortuné, despite his meanness.[57]

Needless to say, Napoleon's supplications could not change the manipulative Josephine: she would continue to weep and make jealous scenes, even though it was she who was two-timing her husband, not the reverse.

A few days after leaving Milan, Napoleon received a bag of mail for himself and for Josephine from Paris. Unable to check his curiosity, and his suspicion, he opened not only his own mail, but also his wife's. Napoleon had asked Josephine for permission to open her mail, and his ambivalent wife had given him a limited, conditional permission, while at the same time asking him not do it. Did he open her mail due to his jealousy, his wish to find out whether she was unfaithful, or his feeling that he and she were one? Napoleon wrote his wife another letter, still denying her unfaithfulness. The letter betrayed his profound ambivalence:

> I have received some mail from Paris. There were two letters for you; I read them. Yet, even though this act seems to me quite simple and you had given me permission to do it, I fear it will make you angry, and this thought afflicts me much. I would have wished to reseal them: Fie! That would have been a horror. If I am guilty, I ask your forgiveness; I swear to you that it is not out of jealousy; no, indeed, I have too high an opinion of my adorable friend for this. I would like you to give me full permission to read your letters: with that there would be no remorse or fear. Achille has just arrived with the Milan mail; no letters from my adorable friend! *Adieu mon unique bien* [my only possession]. When can you come join me? I will come and fetch you to Milan myself. A thousand kisses as burning as my heart, as pure as you.[58]

Napoleon could not stand his separation from the woman who had replaced the fusional mother in his unconscious feelings. While on the one hand he idealized Josephine, his unconscious image of the monstrous mother was also displaced to his wife:

> For two days now I have had no letter from you. This is the thirtieth time today that I made this observation to myself. I have my men call the courier; he tells me that he has been to see you, and that you told him that you had no order to give him. *Fie! Mean, ugly, cruel, tyrannical, pretty little monster!* [italics added] You laugh at my threats, at my foolishness; ah! If I could, you know it well, shut you up in my heart, I would imprison you there . . . Tell me that you are gay, well, and quite tender.[59]

If Josephine was "tyrannical," so was Napoleon himself. It was easier for him to see his faults in her. Napoleon's inner conflict was excruciating: deeply enraged at his wife while loving her just as deeply, the unhappy Napoleon suffered from severe tension headaches, which almost incapacitated him. He repeatedly swung between idealization and denigration of his internal mother. On July 21, 1796, in his mind, Josephine was no longer a dreadful monster but once more a bountiful goddess:

> What are you doing at this hour? You are sleeping, aren't you? And I am not there to take in your breath, contemplate your graces and overwhelm you with my caresses. Away from you, the nights are

> long, stale and sad. Near you one is sorry it is not eternal night. Adieu, beautiful and good, quite incomparable, quite divine. A thousand loving kisses, everywhere, everywhere . . . I hope that you will be able to accompany me to my headquarters, never to leave me again. Are you not the soul of my life and the feeling of my heart?[60]

The tragic inner conflict within Napoleon' soul about Josephine in particular and women in general could never be solved: due to his tormented early relationship with his mother, he longed for total fusion yet he dreaded it; he unconsciously split women into all-good goddesses and wicked monsters, and his feelings kept alternating between the two poles. He rarely saw a woman he loved as she really was.

13

War as a Cure for Depression

While the conservative Austrians placed their armies in the hands of aging noblemen, the revolutionary French gave their command to bright and daring young generals. Napoleon was only twenty-seven years old on August 15, 1796. By now the young general had become the fearsome "liberator" of Italy. Napoleon's army had inflicted numerous defeats on the Austrians. There was no peace to be had with him. His reckless gambling was taken for courage, his impulsiveness for flexibility. On the battlefield, he seemed fearless and reckless for his life. Harold Parker wrote, "I do not think that we can deny Bonaparte the qualities of courage and bravery; he has been accused of many faults but to my knowledge never of cowardice."[1] Yet Owen Connolly found that Napoleon, "a military genius . . . began almost every military campaign with a strategic blunder—almost deliberately."[2] Was Napoleon's physical courage a "counterphobic" defense against unconscious feelings of fear and helplessness? He often acted on the battlefield as if he were immortal or suicidal, exposing himself to unnecessary danger.

The details of Napoleon's battles with the Austrians under the old Austrian field-marshal Dagobert-Sigismond von Wurmser, who commanded the Austrian forces in northern Italy, are beyond the scope of this book. In the summer and fall of 1796 Napoleon's *armée d'Italie* defeated Wurmser's Austrian armies at Milan, Modena, Bologna, Ferrara and Verona. In three weeks of fighting, the Austrians lost twenty-seven thousand men, killed or wounded, and twenty-two banners. But Wurmser rallied his forces and staged a daring counterattack on Napoleon's forces at

Mantua. On September 9, 1796 Wurmser's decimated army almost defeated Napoleon's. "Bonaparte woke up to what Wurmser was doing and responded by adopting an almost suicidal plan."[3]

For a week the tide of war turned against Napoleon. There were many ups and downs and several more battles at Caldiero and Arcola before Bonaparte achieved his final victory over the Austrians at Rivoli. At Arcola he lost his twenty-two-year-old aide-de-camp, Colonel Jean-Baptiste de Muiron, who had been Napoleon's deputy at Toulon, as well as Elliot Clarke, a nephew of General Clarke. Muiron gave his life for Bonaparte at the outset of the battle, shielding his general with his body on the Arcola bridge and getting himself killed. Deep down Napoleon felt guilty for this and never got over his loss. He repeatedly evoked Muiron's name and named a battleship after him.

The unhealthy, sadomasochistic, and neurotic pattern of Napoleon's relationship with Josephine had been set by now. Alternating between ardent idealized love and jealous murderous rage at her, Napoleon wrote Josephine passionate but deeply ambivalent love letters which expressed both extremes of his feelings. She ignored him, or wrote him cold, detached letters. On September 17, 1796, when Napoleon had a brief respite from his battles with Wurmser, he wrote another bitter letter to his wife, hinting at his wish to die. The "incomparable mother" and "stunningly beautiful" Josephine had become an ugly witch:

> You are a mean and ugly woman, as ugly as you are light. It is perfidy to betray a poor husband, a tender lover! Must he lose his rights because he is far away, overwhelmed with work, fatigue and pain? Without his Josephine, without the assurance of her love, who remains for him on the earth? What would he do there? . . . We had a very bloody affair yesterday, the enemy lost many men and was totally beaten. We took the suburbs of Mantua from him.[4]

While bombarding his wife with letters, Napoleon also wrote the *Directoire exécutif* in Paris very often. In his unconscious mind, the five Directors were a set of bad fathers—or a bad mother—that he constantly struggled with. Although he was unaware of it, Napoleon had repeatedly tried to provoke the *Directoire* into dismissing him by threatening to resign. He was unconsciously turning his passive rejection by his mother into an active provocation of rejection by the *Directoire*. On October 8, 1796, a defiant Napoleon wrote the *Directoire* that the political system it had prescribed for Italy was "very bad"—and once more threatened to resign: "Whenever your general in Italy is not the center of everything, you will be running great risks . . . This manner of speaking will surely not be attributed to ambition . . . I have more honors than I need, and my health is so broken that I am going to find it necessary to ask you to appoint a successor."[5] But Napoleon had also wisely sent the *Directoire exécutif* forty million francs in "enemy contributions" and looted treasure. They let him keep his job.

Meanwhile, Corsica became "French" again. By the fall of 1796, the French expedition to Corsica, led by a Corsican-French general named Gentili, had succeeded in driving out the British and taking the citadel of Ajaccio.[6] Gentili asked the *Directoire exécutif* in Paris to send Napoleon's elder brother, Joseph, and their former patron, Saliceti, back to Corsica, to organize the government pending the arrival of the *Directoire*'s own envoy, André-François Miot, the future comte de Melito. Joseph Bonaparte and Antoine-Christophe Saliceti landed in Bastia in October 1796, redivided the island into two French *départements*, with Ajaccio and Bastia as their capitals, and ran their affairs.

After various victorious battles with Austrians, on November 19, 1796, a victorious Napoleon entered Verona through the Porta di Venezia to cries of "*Evviva il liberatore!*" (Long live the liberator!) Napoleon had hoped to find some mail from Josephine in Verona. There was none. Two days later, he wrote her another plaintive letter, "Don't you know that without you, without your heart, without your love, there is neither happiness nor love for your husband," while making a flippant allusion to her pubic hair as "the little black forest."[7] Josephine ignored Napoleon. Feeling unloved, rejected, and betrayed, and filled with narcissistic rage, the unhappy Napoleon convinced himself that it was he who was rejecting her. Two days later, he wrote her yet another deeply ambivalent letter, in which he clearly suspects her of having a lover:

> I don't love you any more, on the contrary, I detest you. You are ugly, quite gauche, quite stupid, quite a Cinderella. You don't write me at all, you don't love your husband; you know the pleasure that your letters give him, and you do not write him six lines jotted down by chance! What do you do all day, then, Madame? What affair is so important as to deprive you of the time to write to your very good lover? What affection stifles and puts aside the love, the tender and constant love that you have promised him? What can be

> this marvelous, this new lover who absorbs all your moments, tyrannizes your days and keeps you from taking care of your husband? Josephine, take heed, a beautiful night, the doors broken in, and there I am![8]

Napoleon was obsessed with Josephine's pubic hair. In his letters to her he repeatedly alluded to her "little black forest."[9] Had he seen his mother's "little black forest" as a child? Unconsciously recreating his tragic early relationship with his mother, the more Josephine rejected him, the more Napoleon loved her. On November 24, 1796, he wrote her again: "I love you madly. I am writing to Paris by this post. All is well. Wurmser was defeated yesterday at Mantua. Your husband lacks for nothing to be happy but the love of Josephine."[10] How sad it was that she could not give him that love.

What the French called *l'Angleterre* (England) was really the United Kingdom of Great Britain and Ireland, with its worldwide empire, which I shall loosely refer to as Great Britain. By the fall of 1796, the British had begun to take note of General Bonaparte, who was not only driving the Austrians out of Italy but also driving the British out of Corsica. The British prime minister William Pitt the Younger sent his friend James Harris, the earl of Malmesbury, who had been to France and met Bonaparte, as his ambassador to Paris, seeking peace with France. The proud republic, however, "would not bow its head to England."[11] In the very presence of Lord Malmesbury, "to force the British government to sincere negotiation,"[12] the French Legislative Corps enacted a law forbidding the sale and use of British goods throughout the republic. The furious Pitt instituted a hardline anti-French foreign policy. In November the earl of Malmesbury published an official thumbnail sketch of "General Buonaparte" describing him as "a clever, desperate Jacobin, even terrorist."[13] No one knew Napoleon's true heart and deep pain.

In early December 1796 the *Directoire exécutif*'s thirty-one-year-old commissioner to the *armée d'Italie*, Henri-Jacques-Guillaume Clarke, who had initially clashed with Napoleon over the *Directoire*'s intention to sign an armistice with Austria, sent a very favorable report on General Bonaparte to the *Directoire exécutif* in Paris, while denigrating the two commissioners sent by Director Lazare Carnot to supervise him:

> Everyone here regards him as a man of genius... He is feared, loved and respected in Italy. I believe that he is attached to the republic and *without any ambition save to retain the reputation he has won* [italics added] . . . His sang-froid in the most lively affairs is as remarkable as his extreme promptness in changing his plans when unforeseen circumstances require it. His manner of execution is knowledgeable and well-calculated. It would be a mistake to think that he is a party man. He belongs neither to the royalists who slander him nor to the anarchists whom he dislikes. The Constitution is his guide. Rallied to it and to the *Directoire* which wants it, I believe that he will always be useful and never dangerous to his country . . . But General Bonaparte is not without defects. He does not spare his men sufficiently... Sometimes he is hard, impatient, abrupt or imperious. Often he demands difficult things in too hasty a manner. He has not been respectful enough towards the Government commissioners. When I reproved him for this, he replied that he could not possibly treat otherwise men who were universally scorned for their immorality and incapacity . . . Saliceti has the reputation of being the most shameless rogue in the army and Garrau is inefficient: neither is suitable for the *armée d'Italie*... Bonaparte will be placed by posterity in the ranks of the greatest men.[14]

Clarke assured the *Directoire exécutif* that he was not writing out of wild enthusiasm, and that he was in a calm state of mind when appraising Napoleon. In fact, Napoleon was boundlessly ambitious and was to prove Clarke wrong by staging a *coup d'état* against the *Directoire* only three years later.

Emotionally and sexually abandoned by his wife, unable to mourn his losses, the unhappy Napoleon "acted out" his unconscious conflicts by waging war, which the Italian psychoanalyst Franco Fornari has called "the paranoid elaboration of mourning."[15] From May 1796 to January 1797 General Bonaparte lived in Milan's *palazzo Serbelloni*, often leaving the palace to wage his battles with the Austrians. Burning with revolutionary fervor, Bonaparte, who thought of himself as an ancient Roman proconsul, set about creating his new republics in northern Italy. These republics, however, "were so only in name. Everything passed through him."[16] On New Year's Day 1797, Bonaparte wrote the Italian deputies meeting at Ferrara to found the *Repubblica Cispadana*, urging them to ratify the constitution of the new republic, so that they might achieve freedom without revolutions and crimes. Jacques Bainville thought that as time went by, Bonaparte rose "step by step to a rôle greater than that of Proconsul, influencing the progress of events, modeling them himself, and forming from them his resolve really to become the man of whom it was being said that he obtained everything that was wanted, and was a universal conciliator."[17]

Pope Pius VI had been on good terms with Austria against France and felt that he could rely on her, but his territory was invaded after the last Austrian defeat by Napoleon. After Napoleon's seizure of the papal states, France's brief armistice with Pius VI lasted all of seven months before the former broke it on January 31, 1797. The *Directoire exécutif* in Paris ordered General Bonaparte to march south and punish the pope for his support of Austria and of the French *émigrés* against the French Republic. On February 1 Napoleon set out for Rome with his army. The following day, after withstanding two French sieges lasting a total of eight months that decimated his forces, the Austrian field-marshal Wurmser surrendered Mantua to Napoleon. The victorious Bonaparte entered Mantua in triumph. The *Directoire* had ordered Napoleon to execute the Alsatian-born Wurmser, whom they regarded as traitor to France. Once more defying their orders, however, Napoleon magnanimously gave Wurmser the honors of war and refused to take his sword. "For many the sight of Wurmser and his dejected, half-starved staff, stripped of flags, guns and men, setting wearily out on the road to Vienna, was an image of Austria's defeat in Italy."[18] An old, humiliated, and heartsick Wurmser died in Vienna a few months later. Bonaparte, on the other hand, was triumphant. "In less than ten months Napoleon has vanquished the fifth army which Austria has sent against him."[19] Napoleon had defeated yet another father figure—not to mention the Pope.

Owen Connelly thought that Napoleon had won thanks not only to his subordinates but also to his own bulldog tenacity and persistence:

> These victories made Napoleon a national hero in France and *stupor mundi*—the wonder of the world—elsewhere. In one year he had defeated five armies, each larger than his own. He had captured 160,000 prisoners. He had sent millions of francs in precious metals to Paris, together with priceless works of art. Since he had kept the Directory solvent and even sent Augereau (September 1797) to support a *coup d'état* which preserved a moderate government, he had political clout as well as fame . . . *He won because he never*

> *stopped going after the enemy*. He did not brood over his mistakes and failures; he developed new plans to win or, as at Arcola, doggedly made a bad plan work. *He never quit* . . . He also had exceptional subordinates, especially Masséna and Augereau . . . There was also, of course, the ineptitude of Napoleon's enemies.[20]

For three months, from late May to late August 1797, General Bonaparte held court like an ancient Roman proconsul at the castle of Mombello outside Milan. His unprecedented victories over mighty Austria had made him a hero in France and famous throughout Europe. While in Germany the Austrian archduke Carl Ludwig (1771–1847) had defeated Napoleon's colleagues Jean-Baptiste Jourdan and Jean-Victor Moreau and forced them to beat a humiliating retreat across the River Rhine into France, in Italy the same Austrian general was roundly defeated by Napoleon and had to sign the armistice of Leoben in April. Archduke Carl was a young military genius, a son of the future Holy Roman Emperor Leopold II (1747–1792). He had grown up in Austrian-ruled Tuscany, and had taken over the Austrian army of the Alps in early 1797, soon after Field-Marshal Wurmser's surrender.

Soon after Napoleon set up his headquarters at Mombello castle, his attractive and seductive sixteen-year-old sister Pauline came to Mombello, and lost no time in "ravaging" the castle.[21] Napoleon had summoned her there to cut short her affair with Stanislas-Louis-Marie Fréron, *Don Juan de la Terreur*, and to marry her to the general of his choice, the twenty-five-year-old Brigadier General Charles-Victor-Emmanuel Leclerc. On June 1 Napoleon's mother Letizia and her children Jérôme, Caroline, and Elisa (Maria Anna) arrived at Mombello to pay him a visit. When Letizia saw Napoleon, she found him thin and pale. She became anxious and, as usual, criticized him. Pierce Clark aptly described their verbal duel:

> When Napoleon's mother meets him after his battles she embraces him saying, "You are thinner than ever; you are wearing yourself out." "Not a bit of it," Napoleon rejoins, "I am really living now." "Yes, for posterity," says Letizia. "Well, do you call that dying?" As he leaves her he says, "Do take good care of yourself, mother. *If you die*, there will be no one left with any authority over me."[22]

Napoleon may actually have said this to his mother a year earlier, when he visited Letizia in Marseille before leaving for Italy, and his original words were, "if you died, I would have only inferior people left in the world."[23] The phrase "if you died" is very striking—in both senses of the word. The psychoanalyst observed that "[the] only sort of immortality such narcistic [*sic*] characters desire is the symbolic preservation of their own ego."[24] While this may be true, Napoleon's phrase "if you die" also expressed his unconscious death wish for his mother.

Unhappily married himself, Napoleon became a compulsive matchmaker. He ordered his officers to marry the women he thought were good for them. On June 14, 1797, Pauline and Maria Anna, who had also arrived at Mombello castle, celebrated their double wedding in the chapel of Mombello's Oratory of Saint Francis. The sixteen-year-old Pauline married the 25-year-old brigadier-general Charles-Victor-Emmanuel Leclerc, Napoleon's deputy chief of staff, while her twenty-year-old sister Maria Anna, who called herself Elisa, and her thirty-five-year-old husband Félix-Pascal Baciocchi, who had married in a civil ceremony in Marseille six weeks earlier, had a church wedding as well. From Mombello, Letizia went back home to Corsica with her daughter Marianne Elisa and son-in-law Felix Bacciocchi. There she received a large French government indemnity to restore their Casa Bonaparte in Ajaccio.

While he was concerned with the members of his family Napoleon also thought about his old motherland Corsica. During his Italian campaign of 1797 Napoleon wrote the *Directoire exécutif* in Paris:

> *In order to tie Corsica irrevocably to the Republic*, the following must be done: (1) the island must always be divided into two départements; (2) not a single Corsican must be employed in a [French] government position; (3) about fifty [Corsican] children should be selected and distributed among the various educational institutions of Paris. This last method, which is very inexpensive, must be regarded as essential . . . [In Paris, the children] will receive a better education than at home, and, above all, will be taught to love France to the exclusion of all else.[25]

Raoul Brice believed that Corsican family culture had forged Napoleon's secret soul: "When years of solitary existence, devoted chiefly to reading, had broken down his prejudices, he recognized the barbarity [sic] of his [Corsican] countrymen. He criticized their beliefs and their conduct. He decided that the time had come to put his childhood behind him. After the failure of all his enterprises in the island he maintained in all sincerity that there was nothing of the Corsican in him."[26] Brice was referring to the general influences of the Corsican family culture rather than to Napoleon's particular family relationships. Nonetheless, his basic idea was correct. The role of the unconscious mind in Napoleon's life cannot be overestimated. Napoleon's just-quoted letter to the *Directoire* may have expressed his deepest wish to repair his "bad mother" Corsica so as to make her part of his "good mother" France. His statement in that letter that "not a single Corsican must be employed in a [French] government position" is revealing: Napoleon's father, Carlo Buonaparte, had been a French government official. This letter thus expressed not only Napoleon's idealized transference love for France, which had unconsciously become the good mother for him, and his denigration of Corsica, which had become the bad mother, but also his ambivalent feelings about his dead father. Also, "to tie Corsica irrevocably to the Republic" may have unconsciously meant "to tie myself irrevocably to my mother."

In Paris, meanwhile, the power struggles between the republicans and the royalists intensified. On 14 Messidor Year V of the French Republic (July 1, 1797), the forty-three-year-old clubfooted liberal diplomat, statesman, and "bishop of the revolution," Charles-Maurice de Talleyrand, read a famous paper to the *Institut national de France*, of which he was a member, saying that France could not reconquer its former American colonies and should therefore seek to establish African ones. Egypt, Talleyrand said, was a country that France would greatly profit from conquering. At the same time, Talleyrand opposed further conquest and expansion. Three days later the *Directoire exécutif* dismissed France's forty-eight-year-old war minister, Claude Petiet, who had been suspected of royalist sympathies. A couple of weeks later Director Barras, impressed with Talleyrand, made him France's foreign minister.

While Napoleon was conquering Italy, the wily Talleyrand sought to stop France's expansionist wars and to flatter Bonaparte at the same time. On July 24, 1797, he wrote General Bonaparte, "Justly frightened by the functions whose perilous importance I feel, I need to reassure myself with the feeling that your glory shall bring means and facilities in the negotiations. The name Bonaparte alone is an auxiliary which must remove all obstacles."[27] One narcissist was skillfully manipulating the other with flattery. Napoleon responded to Talleyrand's flattery in kind. On August 5, 1797, he wrote the new foreign minister: "The choice made by the *Directoire* in naming you Minister of External Relations makes honor for its discernment. It proves you are a man of great talents, with a purified civic sense, a stranger to the aberrations which have dishonored the Revolution." The more he thought about it, the more Napoleon liked Talleyrand's idea of invading Egypt. The fantasy of conquering the Orient greatly excited him. In 1798 it would lead to one of the great self-destructive adventures of his life—the Egyptian campaign.

14

Facing the Ottomans and the British

Through his Italian campaign, the twenty-eight-year-old Napoleon had expanded his adoptive mother, France, and restored her to her "natural and historic" borders. In October 1797, as France's envoy plenipotentiary to the Austrians, he had signed the Campo Formio Treaty with Austria on his own initiative, ignoring the *Directoire exécutif*'s instructions. The French foreign minister, Talleyrand, gave his approval *post factum*. Napoleon, who had angrily told his forty-four-year-old Austrian counterpart, Johann Ludwig Joseph von Cobenzl, that Austria's "Holy Roman Empire of the German Nation" was "an old cook accustomed to be raped by all and sundry" was so euphoric after signing the treaty that he apologized to Count Cobenzl for his rudeness during the negotiations: "I am a soldier accustomed every day to risking my life. I am in all the fire of my youth and I cannot show the restraint of a trained diplomat."[1] France and Austria were temporarily at peace, but Talleyrand warned the *Directoire* that a peace treaty did not erase the old enmities, and that "all the powers with which we have treaties powers continue to be our secret enemies and remain in a secret coalition against us."[2]

The power struggles in Paris led to the *coup d'état* of 17–18 Fructidor Year V of the French Republic (September 3–4, 1797), in which Barras and his allies ousted their leftist rivals, exiled them to French Guyana, "the dry guillotine," and consolidated their power. One of Barras's allies declared euphorically that "not a drop of blood had been spilled" but, as André Castelot dryly observed, "the 160 persons who had been shot by a firing squad on the plain of Grenelle did not entirely share that estimate of the situation"[3] After the *coup d'état* General Bonaparte wrote Foreign Minister Talleyrand from Italy: "What a tragedy it is for a nation of thirty million inhabitants living in the eighteenth century to have to use bayonets to save the fatherland!"[4]

Ironically, however, Napoleon had sent those very bayonets to Paris with his deputy, General Augereau. Jacques Bainville thought that "Bonaparte would have preferred to dispense entirely with bayonets. His future power would only be the stronger for it. There his vision was accurate, but in practice he went beyond moderation. His desire, as a true son of his century, would have been to triumph by the pure force of Reason."[5] By sending Augereau's division to support the *coup d'état*, Napoleon helped oust Lazare Carnot—the man who had launched his career, made him a general, and given him a job that saved him from suicide only two years earlier, but also the man who had opposed Napoleon's appointment to command the *armée de l'interieur*, and who had tried to control Bonaparte through his commissioners, Saliceti and Garrau.

The two ousted directors, Carnot and Barthélemy—one had fled while the other had been arrested—were replaced by the forty-three-year-old justice minister, Philippe-Antoine Merlin de Douai, and the forty-seven-year-old interior minister, Nicolas-Louis François de Neufchâteau. The *coup d'état* made the already prominent count Barras the virtual head of the *Directoire exécutif* and the most powerful man in France. Two days after the *coup d'état*, Foreign Minister Talleyrand announced the news by courier to General Bonaparte. Talleyrand's letter reached Napoleon at Udine on September 12, 1797. The general replied to the foreign minister: "Let us but have energy without fanaticism, principles without demagoguery, severity without cruelty, let us but stop being weak and trembling, let us but not be ashamed, so to speak, to be republican; let us but sweep away from France this horde of slaves sworn against us; let but the government, the ministers, the first agents of the Republic not listen to any voice but that of posterity, and the fate of Europe is decided."[6] The "horde of slaves" were obviously the royalists and the politicians who had just been ousted.

On that very day, the new rulers of France removed the forty-eight-year-old General Jean-François-Aimé Dejean, who had commanded the French troops in Holland, from his post for having refused to associate himself with Bonaparte's complaints against the legislative councils. The Netherlands and Belgium were a major concern of France. Over the centuries, the low countries had been governed by a succession of foreign powers: France had taken decisive action in the low countries. Two years earlier the *Convention nationale* had voted to annex the *Pays-bas autrichiens*—the formerly Austrian provinces of Belgium—and the principality of Liège and of Stavelot-Malmédy—to France. This meant the annexation to France of the left bank of the Rhine, which was sure to provoke Great Britain. Jacques Bainville thought that France's annexation of Belgium was a decision "of supreme gravity, and a redoubtable pledge for the future . . . [It] made England the Revolution's enemy"[7]

In late 1797 the Austrian Holy Roman Emperor and the French *Directoire exécutif* ratified Napoleon's treaty of Campo Formio. This treaty concluded the first phase of the French Revolutionary and Napoleonic Wars. As a result of Napoleon's successful Italian campaigns, the Austrians had been forced to sign the preliminary peace treaty of Leoben on April 18 and the final peace of Campo Formio on October 17. After the signing of the treaty of Campo Formio, Great Britain remained France's only official enemy. The victorious Napoleon had grandiose fantasies of conquering England. He wrote Talleyrand that France should now conquer *l'Angleterre*: "Let us concentrate all our energies on the navy and destroy England. That done, Europe is at our feet."[8] Talleyrand, however, had other ideas: he wanted France to stop expanding in Europe and conquer the British outpost in Egypt instead. Napoleon was deeply ambivalent about Britain. As a youth he had greatly admired the British. Now he hated *l'Angleterre* with a passion. England had taken the place of the bad mother in Napoleon's unconscious feelings.

Nine days after General Bonaparte and Count Cobenzl signed the Treaty of Campo Formio the *Directoire exécutif* created a new *armée d'Angleterre* to fight and invade England—that is, Great Britain. Its provisional commander in chief was not General Bonaparte but the twenty-nine-year-old general Louis-Charles-Antoine Desaix de Veygoux, who had distinguished himself in all the French wars in Germany during the past four years. Shortly thereafter, however, the *Directoire* named Bonaparte the permanent commander in chief of the *armée d'Angleterre*, with Desaix as his chief of staff and with some of France's best-known generals as his subordinates. Three months later it named General Berthier, who had been Napoleon's chief of staff for two years, the new commander of the *armée d'Italie*.

Did Napoleon owe his new command to his crucial help in staging Barras's *coup d'état*? More likely Bonaparte's rivals in Paris, the *Directoire exécutif* and Talleyrand, used it as a pretext for removing him from Paris.

The five directors and their foreign minister feared the ambitious young Corsican general. They exploited his passionate hatred for England to keep him away from Paris. "The Directory was in no hurry to see him again. They appointed him to the command of the army which was to invade England and dictate the final peace in London—a chimera which returned periodically, and would return again . . . Above all, the Directory did not wish see the Proconsul appearing too soon in Paris, straight from his conquests and with all the glory of his pacific victories about him."[9] To make sure he stayed away from Paris, on October 27, 1797, the *Directoire* named General Bonaparte its envoy plenipotentiary to the Congress of Rastatt, in the margravate of Baden, which was to fix the political status of Germany—and which would last many months.[10]

Bonaparte, who had been a virtual sovereign in Italy, received his new appointments and orders in late October or early November 1797. He obeyed his Paris bosses, leaving Italy for Rastatt, but he took his sweet time getting there. On his way to Rastatt, in the Piedmontese capital of Turin, Bonaparte met the French diplomat André-François Miot, who later claimed that Bonaparte told him that he was no longer capable of obedience: "I have tasted supremacy, and I can no longer renounce it."[11] Power had always been Napoleon's antidote to his deep feelings of helplessness. Nonetheless, Napoleon did obey the *Directoire exécutif*, biding his time until he could topple them from power and take their place.

During the winter of Year VI of the French Republic (1797–1798) General Bonaparte was idle and unhappy. His *armée d'Angleterre* had nothing to do, as France was not ready for an invasion of England. The French royalists and *émigrés* hated the republican Bonaparte, who had massacred them in Paris two and a half years earlier. The turning point for Napoleon came on February 14, 1798, while he was on an inspection tour of his new army: Talleyrand presented the *Directoire exécutif* with a report on the "Egyptian Question" in which he recommended a French expedition to Egypt. On February 20 Napoleon returned to Paris. Three days later he penned a lengthy letter to the *Directoire exécutif* in which he argued that a French invasion of England was unrealistic. He had realized the futility of his planned invasion of England. France lacked a navy to match the mighty Royal Navy. Giving up his illusions of conquering *l'Angleterre*, Bonaparte told the *Directoire* that an invasion of Great Britain was impossible, and that peace should be made with her. "What Napoleon did not say in his letter of 23 February was that his own future prospects precluded a descent on England. This was a venture fit for a political gambler betting on a rank outsider, and Bonaparte was too well ensconced to need to take such risks."[12]

At the meeting of the *Directoire exécutif* on February 24, 1798, General Napoleon Bonaparte had a dramatic showdown with the fifty-year-old Alsatian-born director Jean-François Reubell over the invasion of England. Reubell had disapproved of Bonaparte's peace treaty with Austria and was eager for war with *l'Angleterre*. The director insisted that the general carry out France's invasion of England, while Bonaparte was dead set against it. Bonaparte offered to deputize his forty-one-year-old Corsican protégé, General Louis-Marie-Joseph-Maximilien Caffarelli du Falga, to command the *armée d'Angleterre*, but Reubell proposed an "independent" general of his own. Bonaparte became furious and shouted, "Do what you will, but I am [not] commanding any descent on England!" Just as agitated, Reubell demanded Bonaparte's resignation. Director Paul de Barras mediated a compromise by which Bonaparte would deliver a memorandum to the *Directoire* on the subject.[13]

The idea of an expedition to Egypt was nothing new in France, and it had to do with the French colonies in southeastern India. Long before the French Revolution, French generals wanted to strike at "the English tyrants of the seas" by seizing the keys of Suez in Egypt. France sought native allies in both lands to help it drive away the British. After several weeks of deliberations, on March 5, 1798, the *Directoire exécutif*, led by Barras, informally authorized General Bonaparte to lead the French expedition to Egypt, and on April 12 it published a directorial decree creating a new *armée d'Orient* and naming Bonaparte its commander in chief. The decree gave Bonaparte the authority to assemble 25,000 troops at Toulon and to create a new fleet for the transport and security of the expedition.[14] The following month Bonaparte sailed for Egypt with anywhere from 38,000 to 54,000 men.[15]

On March 12, 1798, Foreign Minister Talleyrand invited General Bonaparte to dinner along with Pierre-Louis Roederer, a French political journalist. Roederer was an independent-minded person. He repeatedly disagreed with Napoleon, contradicted him, objected to his plans, and, in general, made life difficult for the man who always wanted to have his own way. Yet Napoleon cultivated his friendship and later made Roederer his aide. Napoleon's relationship with Roederer was not unique: his relationship with his elder brother Joseph also "flourished on constant difference." Napoleon always needed an "intimate enemy" with whom he could repeat the painful relationships of his early life and an *alter ego* who would say to him the things that he could not say to himself.

While the unhappily married Napoleon had been denying the unbearable fact of his wife's infidelities, his denial was repeatedly shattered by those close to Josephine. In the winter of 1797–1798, after an especially unpleasant argument, Josephine dismissed her young chambermaid, Louise Compoint, who had become Andoche Junot's lover. The hurt and vengeful Louise sought out Napoleon and told him of her former mistress's affair with Captain Hippolyte Charles on their way from Paris to Milan two years earlier. "I could well have done without this revelation,"[16] a bitter Napoleon later admitted. He angrily confronted his wife with her chambermaid's story. Playing the injured party, Josephine became angry, sobbed heavily, and vehemently denied that she had ever spent a night under the same roof with Charles. Napoleon tried to extract a confession from his wife: "Come on, admit it, it's not so bad, and then, you could have slept in the same inn and traveled together without making love to him."[17] Josephine heatedly denied it, and Napoleon accepted her denial. The truth was much too painful for him to face.

On March 21, 1798, Napoleon's elder brother "opened Napoleon's eyes" again. Joseph Bonaparte told his younger brother that not only was Louise Compoint's story true, but that Josephine was *still* meeting her lover Hippolyte daily at 100 rue Saint-Honoré in Paris, where the captain's friend, Louis Bodin, a shady supplier of Bonaparte's *armée d'Italie* who billeted the officer, had his bachelor pad. A furious Napoleon once more confronted his wife about her affair, but she again denied it, breaking into sobs. An agitated Napoleon again denied his painful reality and apologized to Josephine, convincing himself that the persistent rumors about his wife's infidelity were false. Josephine wrote her lover: "I abhor those two brothers . . . What have I done to those monsters? But they can do what they like, I shall not be the victim of their atrocities . . . Please tell Bodin to deny that he knows me; that it is not through me that he got the business of the armée d'Italie; that he tell the doorman at No. 100 that if one asks him whether Bodin lives there, that he say he does not know him . . . Ah! They can torment me as much as they like, they will never tear me away from my Hippolyte; my last breath will be for him."[18]

General Bonaparte's *armée d'Orient* had six divisions: five infantry divisions under Generals Jean-Baptiste Kléber, Jean-Louis Reynier, Louis-

Charles-Antoine Desaix, Louis-Andrée Bon, and Jacques-François de Boussay de Menou, and a cavalry division under General Thomas-Alexandre Davy de la Pailletterie Dumas. Napoleon did not like the French navy, but he needed it to transport his army to Egypt. For his Egyptian expedition he chose the forty-five-year-old admiral Francis-Paul de Brueys d'Aigailliers to command the fleet. Brueys's chief of staff was the forty-three-year-old rear admiral Honoré-Joseph Ganteaume, who would play a key role in Bonaparte's future naval wars. Brueys's one-hundred-twenty-gun flagship, *L'Orient*, was captained by the thirty-six-year-old Captain Luc-Julien-Joseph de Casabianca, a Corsican friend of the Bonaparte family. Some experts have thought that *L'Orient* was "the most heavily armed ship in the world."[19]

Napoleon had an obsession with "the Orient," which to him included grandiose fantasies of conquering the Ottoman Empire and becoming the ruler of the Orient, like Alexander the Great or Tamerlane. Without knowing it, he acted out his fantasies. The American psychoanalyst Pierce Clark put it poetically:

> The East forever fascinates the occidental mind. Not only does it exercise a charm on Napoleon but it inspires in him a passion that never leaves him. Back of his interest in the Orient is his ever present craving for a splendour and majesty beyond anything that sober Europe can bestow. *The craving in fact is beyond appeasement* [italics added] even in his oriental dreams. But it is a characteristic of this narcistic [*sic*] dreamer to undertake a realization of his dreams. So he turns from idle watching to an active plan which in the end is to prove just as fruitless. *If he cannot strike at the heart of his redoubtable adversary* [Great Britain], *he may, perhaps, strike a vital blow at some of her exposed members* [italics added].[20]

Clark's striking depiction of Great Britain as a redoubtable woman solves the psychological riddle: to Napoleon, England was the bad mother who choked off France's lifeline, just as the infant Napoleon felt that his mother had done to him. Napoleon's "redoubtable adversary" can be no other than his mother. His craving for vengeance on England was unconsciously a longing to revenge himself on his mother, who had withheld her milk and rejected him emotionally. Napoleon unconsciously wanted to kill his mother for doing this to him. As Clark put it, Napoleon wanted to "strike a vital blow at some of her exposed members."

Imitating the young Alexander the Great, who had taken along the best minds of Greece on his "Oriental" campaign, the twenty-eight-year-old General Bonaparte invited many well-known French scientists and artists to join him on his expedition to "the Orient," to study its treasures and to write the history of his conquests. Most of them accepted his invitation. They ranged in age from young men in their twenties to "old men" in their fifties.[21] One biographer was deeply impressed: "In ten weeks Napoleon [had] recruited 150 civilians, including almost every talented young scientist in France. It was a far cry from 1794, when Coffinhal had sent Lavoisier to the guillotine with the remark, 'The Republic has no need of scientists.'"[22] Several French artists and scientists, however, turned down Napoleon's invitation to Egypt.[23]

General Bonaparte's Egyptian campaign had been kept secret, the official story being that the troops gathering at Toulon were "the left wing of the *armée d'Angleterre*." Within ten weeks, twenty-one brigades were detached from French army divisions in France, Corsica, Italy, and Switzerland.[24] On May 19, 1798, at 7 a.m., Bonaparte's huge fleet, carrying some 38,000 to 54,000 men aboard 280 to 400 ships, sailed out of Toulon, Marseille, Genoa, Ajaccio, and Civitavecchia, heading eastward to Egypt. Napoleon's adulterous wife, Josephine, saw him off at Toulon. Pierce Clark wishfully imagined that Josephine had given up her lover and was in love with her husband: "This man of small stature has a face of saffron hue; his eyes are piercing; there lurks about his mouth an expression strangely cruel, covert, treacherous. Josephine, now fully enamoured of her Napoleon who so magically traverses the broad heavens of political romance, bids this fulminant wonder an affectionate farewell at Toulon."[25] In fact, Josephine was still in love with Hippolyte Charles and not with her husband, and was greatly relieved at Napoleon's departure, for now she could see her lover Hippolyte all the time.[26]

Despite the French secrecy, the British were aware of Bonaparte's preparations. The British Mediterranean fleet was now commanded by the sixty-three-year-old admiral Lord John Jervis, Earl of Saint Vincent. His deputy was the thirty-nine-year-old rear admiral Sir Horatio Nelson, whom Jervis had sent to spy on the great French fleet gathering at Toulon. Nelson's naval squadron was back at Toulon, trying to find out the purpose of the French fleet gathering there. Luckily for Napoleon, the sea was tempestuous. Nelson's spy ships were scattered by a storm, and before Nelson could resume his position, the French fleet sailed away. Nelson soon discovered, however, that the French fleet had gone east, carrying

Bonaparte's troops for an invasion of Egypt. Jervis at once sent Nelson after Bonaparte with a naval squadron comprising fourteen ships-of-the-line and seven frigates.

Nelson deployed his naval squadron in the eastern Mediterranean, but a violent northwesterly gale blew his squadron off station. The French navy eluded the British again. The French biographer Jacques Bainville engaged in some "counterfactual" historiography: "Nelson sought them feverishly, but missed them everywhere. He reached Malta too late, and the French escaped him by chance at Candia. He spread all sail for Alexandria, and that haste was again unfortunate for him. He could not find the French squadron, supposed it was heading for Syria, left port to intercept it, and crossed its course within a few miles during the night. If dawn had come, or if Nelson had held a slightly different course, the later disaster off Aboukir, the Battle of the Nile, would have occurred before the army had landed."[27] Bainville thought that while Napoleon's countrymen believed in his "lucky star" and infallibility, Napoleon himself "made good use of that belief, though he hardly shared it . . . this fantastic expedition, which, against all reason, he turned to his advantage, gave new force to that impression among Frenchmen that to this hero of past exploits all things were possible."[28] In fact, Napoleon had a grandiose sense of his own omnipotence and often spoke of his lucky star and of his being favored by Fortune.[29]

The Mediterranean island of Malta was held by the Knights of the Order of the Hospital of Saint John of Jerusalem, also known as the Knights Hospitaller, the Knights of Malta, or the Knights of Saint John. Their order had been founded during the medieval crusades, and they had ruled Malta since it was given to them by "Holy Roman Emperor" Charles V—who was also King Carlos I of Spain—in 1530, having been driven from Rhodes by the Ottomans under their sultan Süleyman the Magnificent in 1522. After an unsuccessful siege of Malta by the Ottomans in 1565, the traumatized Knights of Malta fortified their capital of Valletta so strongly that it became one of the greatest strongholds in the whole Mediterranean Sea.

On June 10, 1798, General Bonaparte's fleet reached the Maltese port of Valletta. Bonaparte dispatched his aide-de-camp Colonel Marmont as an emissary to the Maltese government to seek their permission to enter their port for water supplies. It was a ruse. Bonaparte's real intention was to take Malta for France, either by guile or by force. The fearful Maltese knights placed many conditions on their permission to enter their port. A furious General Bonaparte came out in the open with brute force, invading Valletta. The Knights of Malta briefly put up a resistance. Colonel Marmont took the flags of the Knights of Saint John and Bonaparte promoted him to brigadier general. On June 18, 1798, General Bonaparte left Malta with his huge fleet, heading for Alexandria.

Eighteenth-century Egypt was an Arab land under Ottoman rule. Its languages were Arabic and Turkish. Nine years earlier, in 1789, during the Ottomans' five-year war with Russia and Austria (1787–1792), Selim III had succeeded Abdülhamit I as Sultan of the Ottomans and Caliph of the Muslims. Sultan Selim had a favorite French-born concubine, Nakshidil, who later became *valide sultan*, the most powerful woman in the empire. She had been baptized Aimée-Rose du Buc de Rivery in Martinique in 1776 and was a distant cousin of Napoleon's wife Josephine.[30] Ottoman Egypt was administered by pashas (generals) and beys (governors). A pasha was the military governor while a bey was the civilian ruler. In Egypt, the Ottoman pasha was an Egyptian Arab general named Abu Bakr or Aboubaker, and most of the beys were Egyptian Arabs. Abu Bakr Pasha nominally governed Egypt, but the beys held real power, and the Mamelukes were their soldiery.[31]

The Egyptian Mediterranean port city of Alexandria had a special meaning for Napoleon: it had been founded by his great hero of antiquity, Alexander the Great. Taking Alexandria made Napoleon imagine himself in Alexander's shoes (or sandals). Fortunately for Napoleon, the British fleet, commanded by Rear Admiral Horatio Nelson, had sailed to Sicily, in the Kingdom of Naples, for supplies, and was not in his way. Aboukir is a small peninsula northeast of Alexandria. Nelson was away from Egypt when Napoleon reached Aboukir Bay. On July 2, 1798, General Bonaparte's *armée d'Orient* took Alexandria from the Ottoman garrison there. A euphoric Napoleon set foot in Egypt. He issued a grandiose proclamation to the Egyptians saying that he had come to Egypt as a friend of Islam and of the Ottoman sultan, its caliph, to punish the "usurping Mamelukes" and their "impious Beys" and liberate the people of Egypt.

Napoleon's great dream soon became his great nightmare. The invading Frenchmen were heavily dressed and unprepared for desert warfare, oppressive heat, sand, poverty, squalor, illiteracy, ignorance, and hostility. As they had done in Italy, the French armies financed themselves by pillaging the conquered lands, only here there was not as much to plunder. As Napoleon marched from Alexandria to Cairo, he had to fight the Egyptian beys and their Mamelukes. Bonaparte used the classic French square formation, and the charging Mamelukes, who were "hampered by the medieval style of their weapons," were massacred by Napoleon's artillery and rifle fire.[32]

Bonaparte's victory was short lived. During the battle for Cairo, Napoleon, who had been denying his wife's infidelity for over two years, received a rude shock. On July 19, 1798, at a place called Wardan, Napoleon's aide-de-camp Andoche Junot, who had just been promoted to brigadier general, received a letter from France saying that Napoleon's wife, Josephine, had returned to Paris from the resort of Plombières-les-Bains with Hippolyte Charles in her carriage. All Paris said that Josephine and Hippolyte were lovers. In the presence of Bourrienne and Berthier, Junot informed Napoleon of the letter.[33]

Predictably, Napoleon reacted to the news of his wife's betrayal—which deep down he had known all along—with narcissistic disillusion, rage, and depression. He lashed out at Bourrienne and Berthier for not having informed him earlier, then wrote his elder brother Joseph bemoaning his tragic fate:

> My friend, I hope to return to France soon. I received your letter via Tunis. Prepare the procedure so that my divorce will be prepared upon my arrival. I give you power of attorney to that effect. My decision is irrevocable. I know that you will approve it . . . I am sometimes very unhappy. But I am twenty-nine years old. Forgetfulness will come . . . I may be in France in two months. I commend my interests to you. *I have much bitter grief in my domestic life; the veil has been entirely torn away* [italics added]. You alone remain to me in the world. Your friendship is very dear to me. It only remains for me to lose it and to see you betray me for me to become a misanthrope . . . It is a sad position to have at once all the feelings for the same person in the same heart . . . You hear me . . . Arrange for me to have a country house upon my arrival, near Paris or in Burgundy. I plan to pass the winter and to closet myself there. I am weary of human nature. I need solitude and isolation. Great deeds leave me cold, feeling is dried up, glory has faded. At twenty-nine years, I have drained the entire cup, and nothing is left for me but to become totally selfish. I plan to keep my house. Never will I give

it to anyone. I no longer have anything to live on. Adieu, my only friend, I have never been unjust toward you. You owe me that justice, despite my heart's desire to be so! . . . You hear me! Kiss your wife.[34]

Vincent Cronin understood that Napoleon's narcissistic perfectionism was one of the sources of his personal tragedy.[35] With most of his lovers and mistresses, except the Polish Maria Walewska, Napoleon was at first very excited and then deeply disillusioned. Pierce Clark thought that "a longing for 'something better' ever harasses the narcist," while Arnold Rothstein saw perfectionism as a key feature of the narcissistic personality, and María Carmen Gear thought that another key aspect of narcissism was sadomasochism.[36] Despite Napoleon's promise to his elder brother to return to France quickly and divorce his unfaithful wife upon his arrival in Paris, he would stay in the "Orient" for another fifteen months and, upon his return to France, allow himself to be appeased by her. It would take him another ten years to divorce Josephine.

Soon after "discovering" Josephine's infidelity Napoleon became the master of Lower Egypt, yet he was deeply unhappy, overwhelmed by disillusion, rage, and despair. His victory in Egypt did not heal his narcissistic injury. Ultimately, he was the author of his own problems, having chosen the promiscuous and unfaithful Josephine for a wife, and alienating her with his "monstrous" personality (as she saw it). As we have seen, Napoleon's unhappy choice was unconsciously caused by his traumatic early life relationship with his mother, by his narcissism, perfectionism, and sadomasochism.

Alarmed by the French conquest of Egypt, the British Royal Navy had followed Bonaparte to Aboukir Bay, northeast of Alexandria. A month after his landing at Aboukir, on August 1–2, 1798, Rear Admiral Nelson inflicted a deep humiliation on Napoleon, destroying his fleet at Aboukir Bay, and killing the French admiral François-Paul de Brueys, who had committed the capital error of fighting while his ships were at anchor. Brueys was cut in half by a British cannonball before dying aboard his exploding flagship, *L'Orient*. His humiliation by Nelson cemented Napoleon's passionate and irrational hatred for England. Napoleon, who was in Cairo, did not witness this battle. On August 15, two weeks after his naval defeat at Aboukir Bay, an unhappy Napoleon celebrated his twenty-ninth birthday in Cairo, seeking to repair his damaged self-esteem. His defeat at Aboukir Bay was the worst birthday present Napoleon could have received. His grandiose fantasies had once more been dashed against the hard rock of reality. Back home in Paris, on August 17, two days after Napoleon's birthday, his former fiancée Désirée-Eugénie Clary married the thirty-five-year-old general Jean-Baptiste-Jules Bernadotte, a future king of Sweden. In Naples, back from his victory over the French at Aboukir, Napoleon's enemy, the married, one-armed Horatio Nelson received a hero's welcome from his lover Lady Emma Hamilton, wife of the British ambassador Sir William Hamilton.

After his twenty-ninth birthday, Napoleon became Egypt's magnanimous ruler and its terrible executioner at the same time. Following an ancient Egyptian tradition, the Egyptian Arabs treated the Nile as a god and each year, at the time of its flooding, celebrated his sexual union with his bride by drowning a statue of a female virgin in the river.[37] At dawn on August 18, 1798, Napoleon presided over the traditional feast celebrating this event. General Bonaparte showed up at 6 a.m. at the junction of the Nile and the Khalidj Canal, with all his generals in tow. The Egyptian Arab delegation included the *kiaya* of the pasha, the aga of the janissaries, and several Muslim notables. The statue of the Bride of the Nile was thrown into the water; the huge Arab crowd plunged into the river for the ritual bathing; and the local Arab poets chanted an ode calling Napoleon *Sultan al-kebir* (the Great Ruler). Emulating Alexander the Great in Persia, Napoleon wore an Arab turban and robe, but became embarrassed and doffed them when his general staff could not help laughing.

As we have seen, Napoleon needed absolute power because less than that made him feel helpless—just as any imperfection made him feel disillusioned. Suffering from deep-seated feelings of insecurity, he was very sensitive to what people said about him, reacting to criticism with narcissistic rage. In Egypt, however, he learned that absolute power was unattainable, and that he could not stop people from speaking ill of him. Years later, an aging prisoner of the British on Saint Helena, he told his memorialist, Count Las Cases:

> When I was in Egypt, conqueror, lord, and absolute master though I was, laying down the law to the population by simple decrees, I should not have dared to order the houses to be searched, and it would have been beyond my power to prevent the population from speaking freely in the coffeehouses. They were freer and more independent in their speech than the Parisians. Though they submitted to slavery in everything else, they meant

to be free in that respect. The coffeehouses were the castles of their opinions. [38]

After his twenty-ninth birthday Napoleon seems to have been in a constant mood of depression and rage. The onset of his thirtieth year, his wife's unfaithfulness, his defeat at Aboukir Bay, and his helplessness in the face of the Egyptians' free speech made him furious. On September 6, 1798, Napoleon executed Mohammed al-Koraim, an Egyptian Arab who had been convicted of having betrayed the French Republic after having sworn loyalty to her—just as Josephine had betrayed Napoleon after swearing eternal love to him. The traitor's severed head was paraded in the streets of Cairo. This killing may not only have been an unconscious outlet for Napoleon's murderous rage against his wife but may also have relieved Napoleon of whatever sense of disloyalty to France that he may have had himself.

By the fall of 1798 Napoleon had yet another cause for depression and rage. He had not only "discovered" his wife's betrayal but also that of his "friend and ally" Talleyrand, the double-dealing French foreign minister. The Ottomans had been planning to drive the French out of Egypt, and Talleyrand had promised Napoleon to go to Constantinople and negotiate a peace treaty with them, removing the Ottoman threat from Syria and taking the pressure off Napoleon in Egypt. Napoleon finally learned that Talleyrand had broken his word and had no intention of going to Constantinople. Before declaring war on France, an Ottoman army gathered in Syria in order to invade Egypt. The Ottomans were known for their war atrocities and Bonaparte feared a catastrophe if they entered Egypt. Talleyrand's betrayal forced him to undertake his disastrous "Syrian" expedition. It was only the first in a long series of betrayals that Talleyrand was to perpetrate on Napoleon.[39]

Not content with taking Egypt from England, republican France fought royalist Great Britain everywhere. While Bonaparte chopped off "rebel" Arab heads in Egypt, his *Directoire exécutif* bosses in France once more mounted futile naval expeditions to British Ireland, hoping to help the Irish revolt against British rule which had broken out in the summer of 1798 and had been bloodily suppressed. From August to November the French mounted four naval operations against the British in Ireland, with increasingly bigger flotillas, larger forces, and Irish generals, but all failed miserably.[40]

Many Egyptian Muslim Arabs did not love General Bonaparte. They saw him as a foreign invader who looted their country and debased their religion. As with the Arabs and Americans in present-day Iraq, there were anti-French plots, violence and terror. Money was Napoleon's unconscious antidote for being unloved. In Cairo, on September 16, 1797, Bonaparte ordered all diamonds, jewels, gold pieces, and precious cloth taken from the Egyptians sold at auction. He ordered all property left by people dying without heirs and all goods seized by his army sold and the money used by his paymaster. Nelson's spectacular victory over Napoleon at Aboukir Bay in early August 1798 had emboldened the Ottoman sultan Selim III, the caliph of Islam, to declare a *jihad* against the French Christian "infidel."

Ironically, however, the Sultan ordered his envoys to Saint Petersburg and London to negotiate a military alliance with Christian Russia and Great Britain, who were equally "infidel." On December 5, allied with Russia and Great Britain, the Ottoman Sultan and Caliph of Islam declared holy war on France. The French ambassador to the Sublime Porte at Istanbul was arrested along with his fellow citizens, and all French assets in the Ottoman Empire were seized. Ahmet Cezzâr Pasha, the sixty-three-year-old military governor of Syria, was named pasha of Egypt as well. The Turkish name Cezzâr or Djazzar meant "the butcher."[41]

The Sultan's declaration of *jihad* on France provoked a fresh Egyptian Muslim Arab revolt against French rule. There were riots in the streets of Cairo. French soldiers were brutally attacked and killed, and French hospitals were set afire. Any Arabs caught fighting in the open were summarily executed. Legions of Arab informers spied on their neighbors for the French. Anyone caught with arms or suspected of being a rebel, was summarily shot. These killings may have subdued the revolt, but they did not make Napoleon happy. The best defense, he knew, was offense. Anticipating an Ottoman offensive against his army in Egypt, Napoleon preempted it by launching a counteroffensive in Syria. On December 7, 1798, General Louis-André Bon's division took the town of Suez from the Ottoman garrison in a prelude to Bonaparte's Syrian campaign, which was really an ill-fated military excursion into Palestine.

A few months after he "discovered" his wife's infidelity in the summer of 1798, Napoleon took his first mistress in Egypt. She was the twenty-year-old Marguerite-Pauline Bellisle Fourès, the attractive wife of Lieutenant Jean-Noël Fourès of Napoleon's 22nd *chasseurs-à-cheval* regiment. Madame Fourès had the singular advantage of bearing the first names of

Napoleon's "adoptive mother" at Brienne, la mère Marguerite, and of his sister, Pauline. Madame Fourès was a ravishing blonde. Her maiden name, Bellisle, meant "beautiful isle," and she was nicknamed "Bellilote" (beautiful islet). Smitten with the dashing young lieutenant, her employer's nephew in Carcassonne, the young Marguerite-Pauline had married him and followed him to Egypt disguised as a man and wearing her husband's uniform. This created a sensation and drew Napoleon's attention. Pauline, however, was only one of three hundred women who had accompanied Bonaparte's army as seamstresses and laundresses, and many officers' wives, mistresses, and girlfriends had defied General Bonapartes proscription on women in his army by disguising themselves as male soldiers.[42] Was it the masculine-feminine combination in Pauline Fourès that drew Napoleon to her? Was it her names? One biographer believed that while Napoleon thought that he was suffering from Josephine's betrayal, "he was only vexed. In fact, Josephine's faithlessness gave him freedom. He took a mistress, the wife of one of his officers. In his misanthropy he became something of a Pasha."[43]

André Castleot thought that during Napoleon's first meeting with Pauline Fourès on December 1, 1798, he intentionally spilled a carafe of water over her white dress, "which made it possible for him to repair the damage in his private apartments."[44] Frank Richardson believed that Napoleon had spilled *a cup of coffee* on Pauline's dress.[45] Frank McLynn placed the incident at General Dupuy's headquarters on December 19,[46] and Gertrude Aretz wrote that it was Napoleon's aide Andoche Junot who spilled the coffee on Pauline's dress.[47] Junot had already embarrassed Napoleon by announcing Josephine's infidelity to him in the presence of Berthier and Bourrienne, and had also messed up his embassy from Napoleon to Pauline by presenting Napoleon's suit in crude sexual terms.[48] If it was Napoleon who spilled the coffee on Pauline's dress, it was an act of unconscious aggression: "the latent hostility a misogynist like Bonaparte would have felt because Pauline [had] kept him waiting before succumbing to his overtures may well have found expression in just this way."[49]

Napoleon also expressed his narcissistic sadism as he "plumbed the depth of bad taste by taking [Pauline] on his knee and kissing her repeatedly in [his stepson] Eugène's presence."[50] He wanted Eugène to inform his mother, Josephine, so as to hurt her back for her betrayal of him. To repair his narcissistic injury, and to revenge himself on his wife for humiliating him, Napoleon imagined divorcing Josephine and marrying Pauline.

Napoleon had one of his army's officials who had the legal power to do so perform a legal divorce between Jean-Noël Fourès and his wife Pauline. The young lovers spent New Year's Day 1799 in the general's plush Cairo residence. Napoleon proposed marriage to Madame Fourès—if she gave him a child. This, however, did not come about. Napoleon reportedly lamented, "The little fool cannot make one!" Pauline reportedly replied with a laugh, "By God, it's not my fault!" When she lived with Napoleon, Pauline Fourès was called "*la souveraine de l'Orient*," "*Notre Dame de l'Orient*," and "Bonaparte's Cleopatra." After Napoleon's return to France she became General Kléber's mistress. She was an accomplished and gifted lady who later became a countess and wrote three novels.[51]

Napoleon said goodbye to his mistress Pauline Fourès on February 10, 1799, when he left Cairo for his Syrian expedition. He would only see her again when he returned from his disastrous "Syrian campaign" the following summer. Bonaparte's plan was to march his army along the Mediterranean coast, lay siege to the Ottoman port city of Acre, capture it from the Ottomans, and then proceed to Damascus. He made a serious blunder in sending his siege train by sea, which allowed the British navy to capture it.

At the end of the eighteenth century, the Mediterranean town of Jaffa (now part of Tel Aviv, Israel) was an Ottoman port city, inhabited by Arabs, Turks, and Albanian soldiers, all of whom were Muslims. On March 3, after being held up at El Arish for eleven days and then capturing the port city of Gaza from the Ottomans, Bonaparte's *armée de Syrie*, with thirteen thousand infantrymen and nine hundred cavalrymen, reached Jaffa and laid siege to the city.

The capture of Jaffa by General Bonaparte led to a tragic massacre. The frenzied French soldiers, having encountered Ottoman atrocities on their way, fell upon Jaffa's civilians—men, women, children, and old people—slaughtering everyone in sight. Several thousand Ottoman soldiers, mostly Albanians, were taken prisoner by the French. Napoleon had to decide their fate. Apparently, he had many of them executed. How many exactly were killed, and why, has been a source of bitter controversy among Napoleon's biographers. Did Napoleon personally commit a massacre at Jaffa? If he did, why? How many men did he execute? As in Akutagawa's and Kurosawa's *Rashomon*, there is no absolute truth but widely differing versions.[52]

Incredibly, Napoleon convinced himself that he would take the heavily fortified Ottoman coastal city of Acre just as easily as he had taken the lightly fortified Jaffa. From March 19 to May 20, 1799, his *armée de Syrie* laid siege to Acre, "the key to Palestine," and fought its Ottoman and British defenders, vainly trying to breach the walls of Acre's medieval castle. The Ottoman garrison at Acre under Ahmet Cezzâr Pasha was helped by the British naval squadron in the eastern Mediterranean, commanded by Commodore Sir William Sidney Smith, who had captured Napoleon's siege train. After the siege of Jaffa and the long march from Egypt, Napoleon had only twelve guns left and very little ammunition. At Acre, he had his men pick up spent enemy cannonballs and with this ammunition "he succeeded three times in breaching the Acre castle walls; three times his men charged into the forecourt; three times they were driven out by slashing scimitars."[53]

Napoleon's Syrian campaign, which had aimed to capture Acre and then Jerusalem and Damascus, was disastrous. The French flotilla that had sailed from the Egyptian port of Demietta with the siege train and cannon under Rear Admiral Jean-Baptiste-Emmanuel Perrée and headed for Acre was intercepted and seized by the British. The Ottomans sent reinforcements to Acre from Rhodes. It was no accident that the commander of the British naval force that defeated Napoleon, Commodore Sir William Sidney Smith, had escaped from the notorious *Le Temple* prison in Paris, assisted by Antoine le Picard de Phélippeaux, Napoleon's boyhood rival at the *École royale militaire* in Paris and his lifelong enemy. Bonaparte's fleet vainly besieged Acre for two months, attacking it no less than forty-two times, but was repeatedly pushed back. Finally the defeated Napoleon gave up and lifted the siege of Acre, ordering his army to march back south toward Egypt. Napoleon believed that Sidney Smith had made him "miss his destiny."[54]

On the way back to Egypt, in Jaffa, a terrible bubonic plague ravaged Napoleon's army, and Napoleon ordered his military physicians to "expedite the end" of the dying soldiers for whom there was no hope of recovery. When Bonaparte's chief army physician, René-Nicolas Desgenettes, who had inoculated himself against the "bubonic fever" with pus from plague sufferers, refused to carry out the order, Bonaparte ordered his pharmacists to administer laudanum to the dying men. How many *pestiférés* did Napoleon's pharmacists kill at Jaffa? The numbers cited by various sources range from Napoleon's seven—whom he said he did not kill—to Wilson's five hundred and eighty. The British hate press of the time put the number of sick men killed at three hundred and fifty.[55]

The remnants of General Bonaparte's *armée de Syrie* had sadly retreated from Acre along the Mediterranean coast and through the Sinai desert all the way back to Cairo. By early June 1799, the unhappy survivors of the *armée de Syrie* were back in Egypt, where Mustafa Pasha, the Ottoman commanding general, had an army of anywhere from ten thousand to twenty thousand troops ready for them. On June 14 Napoleon returned to Cairo after a five-month absence, badly defeated and humiliated. He regained his mistress, Pauline Fourès, to whom he had written many love letters from Syria, but his heart was heavy. The cautious Mustafa Pasha deployed his forces defensively. Owen Connelly thought that if Mustafa Pasha had been more aggressive, he could have taken Cairo form the French garrison before Napoleon's army returned "and picked up local support and French hostages."[56]

On July 11, 1799, Commodore Sidney Smith's British flotilla disgorged Mustafa Pasha's Ottoman army at Aboukir Bay, northeast of Alexandria, the site of Nelson's victory over Napoleon the previous August. The British admiral Horatio Nelson had inflicted a humiliating defeat on Napoleon at Aboukir Bay, which had temporarily made Napoleon feel worthless. He projected the painful feeling on his dead admiral, François-Paul de Brueys, whom he blamed for the defeat, but the humiliation rankled him. Napoleon sought to heal his narcissistic injuries by defeating the Ottomans and the British at the very site of his defeat, Aboukir, as if to undo his earlier defeat. The Ottomans, eager to recapture Egypt from France, had sent more than ten thousand men to Egypt under Mustafa Pasha, carried and reinforced by the British naval squadron of Commodore William Sidney Smith.

The French garrison at Fort Aboukir, at the tip of the narrow Aboukir Peninsula, under Brigadier General Marmont, held out against vastly superior Ottoman numbers for an entire week, from July 11 to July 18, 1799, giving Bonaparte precious time to move against Mustafa Pasha. After the Ottomans had massacred most of them, however, the French were forced to surrender. Rather than thank them, Napoleon railed against their cowardice and perfidy.[57] Things were going badly for Bonaparte, and, back in Europe, things were going baldy for France. The formerly victorious France was losing its wars in Germany, Switzerland, and Italy. During the spring and summer of 1799 the Russians defeated the French in Switzerland—but not the revolutionary ardor of the Swiss masses.

In Egypt, Bonaparte prepared for a decisive battle. Mustafa Pasha deployed his forces in Fort Aboukir and in two defensive lines about a mile apart, stretching to about two kilometers before the fort; there were some nine thousand Ottoman men in the front line and a total of twenty thousand men in the fort and in the two defensive lines. Napoleon wanted to meet the Ottomans with an army of equal size, but he could muster only seventy-seven hundred men and seventeen guns. He arrived in Alexandria during the night of July 21–22, 1799, with five thousand infantrymen and one thousand camel-riding troops. With unequal forces, the outcome depended almost entirely on Napoleon's strategy and tactics.[58]

The battle of Fort Aboukir between the Ottomans and the French lasted from July 25 to August 2, 1799. It was a bloodbath, but Bonaparte's vastly outnumbered forces won it on the first day of the battle, and Mustafa Pasha himself was captured, even though the Ottomans held on to the fort for another week.[59] Brigadier General Marmont was freed and returned to Bonaparte. Napoleon's victory at Fort Aboukir temporarily helped him heal his narcissistic injuries. "It wiped out the stain of Acre."[60] But his deeper sense of worthlessness continued to plague him, and he needed to find new, heroic deeds to heal his *amour-propre*.

During his Syrian campaign Napoleon had forbidden his officers to communicate with the hated British naval commander assisting the Ottomans, Commodore Sidney Smith, who had captured Napoleon's siege-train flotilla. After his victory at Fort Aboukir, anxious for information about the state of affairs in France, from which he was isolated, Napoleon ordered his aide Marmont to negotiate with Sidney Smith and to obtain some news from him on events in Europe. In early August 1799 the two men negotiated the exchange of Napoleon's Ottoman and British prisoners, including Mustafa Pasha, against the French prisoners held by the British and the Ottomans.

Marmont sent one of his naval officers to Sidney Smith, who received him warmly and told him that his boss, Admiral Nelson, had intercepted a French vessel carrying messages from the French *Directoire exécutif* to Napoleon, that the *Directoire* had ordered Bonaparte back to France with his army, and that he, Sidney Smith, had been ordered to prevent that return. Sidney Smith deliberately gave the young French officer some recent British and French newspapers, including *The Times* and the *Gazette française de Francfort*. His aim was to demoralize Bonaparte by apprising him of his country's defeats in Europe. The young naval officer delivered Sidney Smith's news and newspapers to his boss, Marmont, who rightly thought them important enough to wake up his commander, General Bonaparte.[61]

Napoleon reacted quickly. "Roused at midnight, Bonaparte immediately read through the gazettes. He learned that the general war had broken out again, that the armies of the republic were everywhere withdrawing, that Scherer [the commander of the French *armée d'Italie*] had been beaten on the Adige and that Italy was lost, that [Jean-Baptiste] Jourdan [the commander of the French *armée de Rhin-et-Moselle*], likewise defeated in the Black Forest, had recrossed the Rhine."[62] The issue of the *Gazette française de Francfort* published on June 10, 1799, reported all the French defeats in the preceding months, including the loss of northern Italy and the dismantling of the French-created Cisalpine Republic. Austria, Naples, Russia, Great Britain, Ottoman Turkey, and the other European powers had been dealing France military defeats. The Austrians had recaptured all of Italy, except Genoa; the British and Russians had taken the Netherlands; Russian troops had invaded Switzerland.[63]

Commodore Sir William Sidney Smith had succeeded in his "newspaper offensive." Napoleon was devastated. He did not know whether Sidney Smith was telling the truth, nor whether the *Directoire exécutif* had ordered him back to France. Sidney Smith had not sent him the orders that he claimed to have been intercepted by Nelson. One scholar thought that it was impossible for Napoleon to bring his army back to France. "All Napoleon's constructive work in Italy was for the moment undone. Worse even than this, France was in a state of economic collapse. According to the newspapers, it would be only a question of time before Louis XVIII sat on the throne."[64]

In Cairo, on August 14, 1799, Napoleon agonized over his course of action. For a whole year he had received no word from his *Directoire exécutif* bosses in Paris.[65] Should he wait for his orders from Paris, which might never make it through the British naval blockade, or try to run it and return to France? The next morning, an unhappy Napoleon celebrated his thirtieth birthday. The thirty-year mark made the narcissist assess his own worth: "What have I done? What have I achieved? Shall I remain in Egypt for the rest of my life? Is there no greatness in store for me?"

To answer the demands of his grandiose self, Napoleon plotted to return to France, seize power, take revenge on his enemies—and restore Mother France to her former glory. In this way he would repair the injuries to his self-esteem. Napoleon huddled with his chief of staff,

General Berthier, for four hours. Then he summoned Admiral Ganteaume, who had replaced the dead Brueys as the commander of his fleet, for a meeting that lasted two hours. Ganteaume reported that four French ships were available for the voyage, including the ex-Venetian frigate *La Muiron*, named after Napoleon's aide-de-camp who had died at Arcola shielding him with his body. Bonaparte decided to run the British blockade. "His decision was taken. He would return [to France]."[66] Napoleon would sail aboard *La Muiron*, the other three ships serving as an escort. To reduce the chances of being captured by the British Royal Navy, Napoleon decided to return to France secretly, without informing his army in advance. The "secret," however, soon became known.

While Napoleon painted his Egyptian-Syrian campaign to his army and to all France as a great victory, deep down he knew that it had been a humiliating defeat. Raoul Brice considered it a total failure: "The Egyptian expedition, which brought him so much renown, ended, to tell the truth, in a disaster. Admiral Ganteaume, sent to bring home what was left of the expeditionary force, was unable to make a landing. Napoleon's army, besieged in Alexandria and Cairo, had to capitulate; Malta had already fallen into the hands of the English, who henceforward were in control of the whole of the Mediterranean. The failure was complete."[67] Connelly thought that the entire Egyptian campaign had been "a blunder, a waste, and accomplished nothing, militarily or in terms of the power balance."[68]

In the summer of 1799, Napoleon's elder brother Joseph Bonaparte sent him a confidential letter advising him to return to France. The letter was hand-carried to Egypt by a secret agent in a hollowed-out cane. Some scholars thought that Joseph's letter clinched Napoleon's decision. In fact, he may have received the letter before deciding to leave Egypt. Bonaparte deceived the Egyptian *divan* by writing them on August 17: "I leave tomorrow for Menouf, whence I shall make different rounds of the Delta, to see the injustices that might have been committed with my own eyes."[69]

Instead, he left Cairo for Alexandria. On August 22 Bonaparte wrote General Menou in Cairo: "I leave for France this evening."[70] On the night of August 22–23, a week after his thirtieth birthday, without receiving the *Directoire exécutif*'s orders or permission to leave Egypt, Napoleon left his *armée d'Orient*—and his mistress, Pauline Fourès—in care of his deputy, General Kléber, who later claimed that Bonaparte had deserted him like a thief in the night.

Napoleon's secret and unauthorized abandonment of his army in Egypt has provoked many interpretations. Napoleon's narcissism had been badly hurt by his Syrian debacle. The psychoanalyst Pierce Clark thought that Napoleon admired himself for daring to leave for France, and that he hoped to convince his countrymen that he had won the battle.[71] Frank Richardson thought that Captain Hippolyte Charles, with whom Napoleon's wife Josephine was having her passionate and scandalous affair in France, was "one factor determining his unauthorised desertion of his army in Egypt."[72] There were other, less conscious factors, however. Like one's country, one's university, and one's church, the officer's army is his alma mater. In French *l'armée* is a feminine word. Unconsciously, while he was cut off from France, *l'armée d'Orient* had been Napoleon's mother. Now he was abandoning her. By abandoning his army, Napoleon unconsciously reenacted—in reverse—his own early abandonment by his wet nurse and his mother.

General Kléber was furious with General Bonaparte for deserting him and leaving him holding the miserable Egyptian bag. He reportedly told his fellow officers that Bonaparte had "left us with his breeches full of shit. We'll go back to France and rub it in his face."[73] But Kléber was more rational than Napoleon. He understood the unhappy situation of his army in Egypt, realizing that it would continue to suffer indefinitely from assassinations, revolts, and endless casualties. Kléber began peace negotiations with the Ottomans and British. This led to the signing of the El-Arish convention on January 13, 1800, by which the French would leave Cairo for Alexandria within forty days and would be given safe conduct to France. But the hardline British prime minister, William Pitt the Younger, rejected the convention, demanding an unconditional French surrender. The Ottomans re-occupied most of Egypt. Feeling cheated and betrayed, the furious General Kléber refused to surrender his Ottoman and British prisoners, and renewed the war on the Ottomans, defeating them on March 20 at Heliopolis, near Cairo. On June 14, however, after three months of bloody war, Kléber was assassinated by a Syrian Muslim Arab fanatic.

By the rules of the French army, the dead Kléber was to be provisionally replaced by the oldest general in the *armée d'Egypte*. This happened to be the French general Jacques de Menou—who had converted to Islam. "Abdallah" Menou continued to govern Egypt, more or less well, until March 1, 1801, when a British fleet arrived off Alexandria. The outcome was not in doubt. Six months later Menou capitulated and signed an agreement to evacuate all of Egypt. The British took over from the French. Napoleon's megalomanic expedition had come to its foreseeable tragic end. By that time, however, Bonaparte had become the ruler of France.

15

France's Ruler

General Bonaparte evaded the British naval blockade and made it to France. On October 9, 1799, he landed at the French Mediterranean port of Saint-Raphaël, from which he proceeded to Fréjus on his way to Paris. On October 16 he arrived in Paris, where he found his house devoid of his wife Josephine. But Napoleon discovered that "his popularity had grown beyond all his hopes." The Provençal people literally threw themselves upon the man they saw as the liberator and hero of the *patrie*.[1] Normally, all persons arriving in France, whatever their rank, were quarantined by the French naval health officers for at least one month. Landing in Fréjus somehow exempted Bonaparte from the quarantine that the *Directoire exécutif* had clamped on all arrivals from lands where the plague and other violent diseases were raging. As he traveled from Fréjus to Paris, Napoleon could feel the anarchy in France.

The dramatic news of General Bonaparte's return to France reached Paris before he did. After four years of corrupt government, the French people were pining for a new leader. On October 10, 1799, when his wife Josephine received her son Eugène's telegraphed dispatch from Fréjus at the Luxembourg palace, she went to the castle of Malmaison, took her daughter Hortense with her, jumped into a carriage, and, as her son had advised her to do, ordered the driver to head for Lyon via the Burgundy road, which ran through Sens, Joigny, Auxerre, Chalon, and Mâcon. She did not know that Napoleon was heading for Paris on the Bourbonnais road, which ran through Cosne, Nevers, and Moulins. Josephine was terrified of divorce: after buying the castle of Malmaison and furnishing it, she owed a million francs to the seller and to her suppliers. She was thirty-seven-years-old. Had her daughter Hortense married when they returned to Paris from Plombières-les-Bains a year earlier, she might have been a grandmother. The two women drove frantically on their way to Lyon. Hortense later claimed that in each town on their way, triumphal arches had been erected to Bonaparte, and the people asked her and her mother whether it was true that their savior had arrived.[2]

Why was the autocratic General Bonaparte so eagerly awaited by the French and hailed as their savior? Jacques Bainville thought that he had a reputation for achieving "victories that brought with them peace."[3] Bonaparte, wrote the biographer, was untainted with reaction or royalism, he "used grapeshot if necessary" to restore order, he had no streak of feudalism, did not hurt people's feelings, "and persecuted neither persons nor interests."[4] Above all, as a Corsican, he was unmoved by the revolutionary or counter-revolutionary feelings "which sundered true-born Frenchmen."[5] In fact, it was the unconscious charisma of the foreigner. As Bainville put it, "By the very fact of his remoteness, away in Egypt, Bonaparte had made himself desired, and nobody had come forward to play the rôle of savior. Besides, how could the fact be overlooked that victory, in Bonaparte's absence, [had] deserted the French camp?"[6]

In fact, while General Bonaparte had been defeated in Egypt, his rivals, Generals Masséna and Brune, both future marshals, had just won stunning victories for France: Masséna beat the Austrians and Russians in Switzerland and Brune defeated the Russians and British in Norway. It was Bonaparte's incomplete Frenchness that played a key role. The charisma of the foreigner springs from infantile feelings in our unconscious mind that date from an early phase of our development, when the mother's body seems at once familiar and foreign to us.[7]

People's capacity to deceive themselves is endless. In 1799 France was in dire straits. Inflation and unemployment were rampant, food scarce, and life unsafe. Longing for a savior to redeem them from their sufferings, the French people deluded themselves about the autocratic General Bonaparte. Remembering his victories in Italy, they considered his defeat in Egypt and Syria another victory and thought that the tyrant would be their savior:

> The news, which the Directory had announced to the council by a messenger preceded by a band, spread with the speed of electricity . . . The bands from the garrisons of the capital were already

> marching through Paris, showing how joyous they felt. They were followed by a host of citizens and soldiers. When night fell, fireworks were improvised in all parts of the city, and Bonaparte's return—as longed for as it was unexpected—was announced in all the theaters with shouts of "*Vive la République! Vive Bonaparte!*"[8]

The last five-man *Directoire exécutif* consisted of Louis-Jérôme Gohier, Paul de Barras, Jean-François Moulin, Pierre-Roger Ducos, and Emmanuel-Joseph Sieyès, a former Catholic abbot whom Napoleon personally detested. The *coup d'état* had been brewing for months. Talleyrand secretly hoped to restore the Bourbon monarchy and return to his former post of foreign minister. Napoleon wanted allies within the *Directoire*, while they wanted their "sword." Although Gohier was the president, Barras was the key figure. He had decided the outcome of three previous *coups d'état*.

The once-powerful Barras was thoroughly corrupt and was now on a binge of self-destruction. Vincent Cronin thought that Barras was following in the dangerous footsteps of the dissolute Donatien-Alphonse-François, marquis de Sade, the author of "sadistic" novels. "Paul Barras had gone downhill. He neglected his work for loose women and gambling parties; leading the life described by his cousin the Marquis de Sade, he would sell any job to pay for his pleasures. Government was virtually nonexistent and thus had led to inflation."[9] Napoleon secretly offered Barras to help him drive his rivals out of the *Directoire exécutif*. Barras, whom Napoleon soon thereafter toppled from power and humiliated, later claimed that he had told Napoleon all about Josephine's infidelities, fanning the flames of his jealousy and rage. The madly jealous Napoleon reportedly heaped abuse on Josephine: "There was scarcely any limits to his foul statements about his wife."[10] Moving cautiously, however, neither Gohier nor Barras made any political commitment to Bonaparte.

Unbeknownst to Napoleon, his exhausted wife Josephine and her daughter Hortense were on their way back from Lyon to Paris after vainly trying to catch up with him. During the night of October 16–17, 1799, after his meetings with Directors Barras and Gohier, an unhappy Napoleon returned home to 6, Rue de la Victoire. Josephine was nowhere to be seen. The following day Napoleon was to appear for his crucial hearing before the *Directoire exécutif*. He anxiously prepared for this fateful hearing. General Bonaparte had deserted his army in Egypt without the *Directoire*'s orders or permission, and his furious successor, General

Kléber, had vehemently denounced Bonaparte to the *Directoire*. At least one director, Moulin, wanted Bonaparte court-martialed for desertion and insubordination.[11] Bonaparte's excuse was his wish to save France from political, military, and economic collapse. Fortunately for him, Moulin and his colleague Ducos were "nonentities," while the real powers were Bonaparte's patron Barras, Sieyès, and Gohier.[12]

The corrupt *Directoire exécutif* was highly unpopular, and most Frenchman wanted it replaced with a better government. When Napoleon showed up for his public hearing before the *Directoire* on October 17, 1799, he wore a a bizarre mixture of military and civilian, European and Oriental garb.[13] The fifty-two-year-old war minister, Edmond-Louis-Alexis Dubois de Crancé, known as Dubois-Crancé, had warned Director Barras that Bonaparte was preparing a *coup d'état* against the *Directoire*. Incredibly, Barras did nothing. Did he fear Bonaparte, who knew about his treacherous conniving with the royalists to restore the Bourbons to the throne, and believe he might expose it publicly, which could have cost Barras his life—or was Barras hell-bent on destroying his own career? Barras spoke up for Bonaparte, reminding his fellow directors of the general's great victories in Italy. Rather than court-martial Bonaparte for illegally deserting his army in Egypt, as Director Moulin had demanded, the frightened directors offered Bonaparte the command of any army of his choice, hoping to get him away from Paris. Plotting to topple them, Bonaparte asked the directors for time to think it over and to recover his health. Three weeks later, he overthrew them.

Incredibly, Josephine and her daughter Hortense, who had taken only two days to travel from Paris to Lyon on the Burgundy road, and had missed Napoleon, took five or six more days to return to Paris. Two days after Napoleon's return, Josephine, who, thanks to her son Eugène, had taken the wrong road to Lyon and missed her husband, finally returned home. The enraged Napoleon had cleared the house of Josephine's enormous wardrobe and sent it down to the concierge, with instructions not to admit Josephine into the house. The manipulative Josephine, however, "softened [the concierge] with tears or browbeat her way to her husband's door (the account varies)."[14] An enraged Napoleon would not open his locked door. Fearing a divorce, the alarmed Josephine enlisted her two children, Eugène and Hortense, to disarm her husband. Through the locked bedroom door, Josephine sobbed violently, while Eugène pleaded with his stepfather, taking the blame upon himself. Unable to stand his wife's sobbing, however, Napoleon broke down, forgave Josephine, and made up with her. Jacques Bainville thought that Josephine had close ties to Directors Barras, Gohier, and Moulin, which Napoleon considered crucial in his plan to expel and exile them.[15] Unconsciously, however, Napoleon was compulsively repeating the pattern of love for the rejecting woman that had characterized his early relationship with his mother.

Was Josephine chastened by this dramatic incident? She had panicked at the thought of being divorced by Napoleon, not having the money to pay her debts, and being thrown back into poverty and obscurity. Raoul Brice thought that "from this moment Josephine was a changed woman. She devoted herself without reserve to the husband who had pardoned her faults. Napoleon became her god."[16] This is an idealized version of the Napoleon-Josephine relationship. Outwardly, it looked stable. From now on, it seems, Josephine was faithful to Napoleon and jealous of him. When he was away from home, however, he no longer wrote her passionate love letters. It became a marriage of convenience. She helped him socially and politically. Her closeness to Gohier, the *Directoire exécutif* president, briefly brought the latter on Napoleon's side in his *coup d'état* the following month. Inwardly, however, the ambivalent feelings on both sides, the unhappy, fusional, and sadomasochistic relationship persisted, and the two were only divorced ten years later, when Emperor Napoleon wanted a son and heir.

Napoleon had brought with him to France as his personal servants the two teenage Mamelukes whom he had received from the Egyptian Sheikh al-Bekri: Roustam Raza and Ali. Like most Mamelukes, Roustam Raza had been kidnaped in his native Georgia at the age of thirteen and bought by a Cairo bey who died soon thereafter. Roustam then passed into the service —and ownership—of Sheikh al-Bekri. Three days before Napoleon's thirtieth birthday, al-Bekri gave the seventeen-year-old Roustam to Napoleon, along with Ali. Roustam was Napoleon's favorite bodyguard; Napoleon gave Roustam a sword and two pistols, took him along on his horseback trips, and made him sleep before his bedroom door. One scholar described the big Mameluke as "Roustan [*sic*], a giant sinister figure always behind his master, on foot or on horseback, turbaned and scowling, scimitar at the ready."[17]

By 1801 the retreating French troops had brought to France more than one hundred Mamelukes from Egypt.[18] The married Roustam was

Bonaparte's First Mameluke and his friend Ali was Second Mameluke. Roustam's physical closeness to Napoleon gave rise to widespread rumors of a homosexual relationship. The scurrilous British Jewish pamphleteer Lewis Goldsmith charged Roustam with being both Josephine's lover and Napoleon's, and Napoleon himself with being dissolute with women and addicted to homosexuality.[19] Goldsmith's smears may have been the result of unconscious externalization and projection of his own faults and feelings. Ostensibly because he was "brutal and dangerous," Ali was dismissed by Napoleon and sent to Fontainebleau, giving rise to rumors of a soured homosexual relationship. In 1811 Napoleon filled the position of Second Mameluke with the Frenchman Louis-Etienne Saint-Denis, who was called "*le Mameluck Aly*." In 1814, after Napoleon's desertion by Roustam, "Aly" became Napoleon's only "Mameluke."[20]

Did Napoleon have a homosexual relationship with Roustam, with Ali —or with anyone else, for that matter? It is true that Napoleon liked to think of himself as a new Alexander the Great, who had homosexual affairs—a practice common in ancient Greece. Roustam was a Georgian, and the Georgians provided the Arabs with both male and female prostitutes. Napoleon's soldiers suspected him of sexual relations with Roustam. Vincent Cronin, however, believed that "Napoleon was never accused of homosexual relations, save perhaps in the English press. Indeed, he disliked homosexuality, as most Frenchmen did then, and still do."[21] Frank Richardson thought that the only people who ever accused Napoleon of "sodomy" were Lewis Goldsmith and the French royalists.[22] The big Roustam, however, became the subject of legends and novels.[23]

On November 1, 1799, General Bonaparte's ally, Director Emmanuel-Joseph Sieyès, formally proposed setting up a new, provisional, three-man consulate to replace the five-man *Directoire exécutif*, pending the creation of a new government. Bonaparte demanded a seat on the consulate, and Sieyès, whom Napoleon hated, accepted his demand. Napoleon deftly divided the *Directoire* against itself. Sieyès and Ducos became Napoleon's allies and fellow plotters against their colleagues Gohier, Moulin, and Barras. Jacques Bainville thought that everything favored the *coup d'état* against the *Directoire*. Two of the directors, Sieyès and Ducos, were planning it from within. The *conseil des Anciens* was for it, as were most of the French people. Napoleon's brother Lucien was the president of the *conseil des Cinq-Cents*. Even the aristocratic *faubourg Saint-Germain* wanted the *coup*. Yet it almost failed due to Bonaparte's refusal to arrest the handful of deputies who opposed his *coup d'état*.[24]

Like most narcissists, Napoleon was a natural manipulator. He and his fellow plotters planned to deceive the Legislative Corps into believing that the Parisians were preparing an uprising, which would make them entrust their security to General Bonaparte. Josephine exercised her charms on Gohier. Talleyrand and Fouché played their double-dealing roles. Lucien was to manipulate the legislators. Castelot thought that "in a pinch it was hoped that Gohier, thanks to Josephine, would enter into the plot. No one particularly cared for the insignificant General Moulins. As for Barras, a large amount of money would certainly quiet his scruples."[25]

On November 6, 1799, General Bonaparte and General Moreau (who now commanded the French *armée du Rhin*) were the guests of honor at a solemn banquet given by the two chambers of the Legislative Corps in their honor. The banquet was thrown by Napoleon's younger brother, Lucien Bonaparte. Lucien's thirty-franc-a-plate banquet was held at the icy *Temple de la victoire*, formerly the church of Saint-Sulpice. It was presided over by the *Directoire exécutif* president, Gohier, and attended by all five directors. Seven hundred people attended the banquet. It was not a happy feast. The coming *coup d'état* was on everyone's mind. Fear was in the air. Everybody feared and suspected everybody else. Lucien proposed a toast "to the French armies on land and sea."[26] Napoleon, who knew classical Roman history, toasted "the union of all Frenchmen" but did not touch his food, fearing that it might be poisoned. Instead, he consumed a loaf of bread and half a bottle of wine that were brought to him by his own servant.[27] By inspiring fear among his enemies, Napoleon had won his *coup d'état* before he even staged it, yet, ironically, he was already the victim of his own terror, always fearful of being poisoned.

On November 9, 1799, 18 Brumaire Year VIII of the French Republic, the people of Paris woke up to see white posters covering the walls of their city. They had been put up by two of Napoleon's fellow plotters, the political journalist Roederer and the political leader Michel-Louis-Etienne Regnaud de Saint-Jean-d'Angély, who had been with Napoleon in Egypt and now ran the *département de la Seine*. The posters denounced the directors who had twice surrounded the legislators with troops and forced to them to annul the elections, saying that they had acted in such a way that meant there was no longer a constitution.

General Bonaparte, who had risen at 5 a.m. that morning, had summoned France's top generals and was on his way to the Tuileries Palace, seat of the *Directoire exécutif*. The plotters met and agreed that the following day the *conseil des Cinq-Cents* and the *conseil des Anciens* would meet at the castle of Saint-Cloud and appoint Bonaparte, Sieyès, and Ducos as the provisional consuls of the new consulate government. The *conseil des Anciens* assembled at the Tuileries Palace at 7:30 a.m. One of Napoleon's fellow plotters, Claude-Ambroise Régnier, sounded the alarm: "The Republic is threatened by the anarchists and by the foreign party; we must take measures of public safety; we are assured of General Bonaparte's support; under the shade of his protecting arm the councils will be able to deliberate the changes required by the public interest." [28] Régnier pointed out that under Article 102 of the Constitution of the Year III of the French Republic they could move their seat from Paris to Saint-Cloud, where they could deliberate in peace and quiet, without fear of the Parisian Jacobins.

Mathieu-Augustin Cornet, head of the inspectors commission of the *conseil des Anciens*, who presided over their morning session, made a rousing speech referring to the republic as a mother:

> The most alarming symptoms have appeared for several days . . . the motherland is aflame and those who will escape the fire will shed bitter but useless tears upon the ashes it will have left behind. You, the representatives of the people, can still prvent it; a moment will suffice, but if you do not seize it, the Republic will have existed and its skeleton will be in the hands of the vultures that are fighting over its unfleshed members.[29]

In this charged atmosphere, the *Anciens* committed political suicide. Citing as their pretext the Jacobin plot to overthrow them, they accepted Cornet's suggestion of moving to the castle of Saint-Cloud, west of Paris, by noon the next day. In effect, the *Anciens* gave Napoleon command of their own legislative guard, of the Paris garrison, and of the *Garde nationale de Paris*. They placed themselves under the protection of the man who sought to dissolve them. The *Anciens* adopted the following four-article decree:

> Article 1.—The Legislative Corps is transferred to the commune of Saint-Cloud. The two councils shall sit in the two wings of the palace.

Article 2.—They will report there tomorrow 19 Brumaire at noon. All continuation of the functions and of the deliberations is forbidden elsewhere and before that time.

Article 3.—General Bonaparte is charged with the execution of this decree; he will take all measures necessary for the safety of the national representation.

Article 4.—General Bonaparte is called to the bosom of the council to receive this decree and to take an oath. [30]

Castelot wryly observed that Napoleon "was supposed to swear his loyalty to a system he was preparing to overthrow."[31] Fouché, who at this time was the police minister, rushed from the Tuileries Palace to Napoleon's home informing him of the *Anciens*' decrees and adding that he had closed the Paris city barriers and stopped all traffic. Napoleon told him that it was unnecessary: he was acting with the support of the nation, and would make sure the *Anciens*' decrees were respected. At the same time, Napoleon exceeded his authority by ordering a grand parade of the *Garde nationale de Paris*. Directors Sieyès and Ducos, in cahoots with Napoleon, joined the inspectors commission of the *conseil des Anciens*, headed by Cornet, which arrived at Napoleon's home to present him with their solemn decrees; "they found him on the steps of his house haranguing his officers on the perilous condition of the country."[32]

Upon receiving his new appointment from Cornet, Napoleon "changed into his general's uniform: white breeches, blue frock-coat with wide gold-embroidered lapels, at his waist a red, white and blue sash."[33] Admiral Eustache Bruix, the commander of the French naval squadron that had failed to come to Napoleon's assistance in Egypt, had lent Napoleon a big white-headed black Spanish horse, which he now mounted. Napoleon shouted "follow me!" to all those around him and rushed out on his way to the Tuileries Palace, followed by his generals and staff officers. At 10 a.m. Napoleon appeared before the *conseil des Anciens*, presided over by his fellow conspirator, Louis-Nicolas Lemercier. As the new commander of the *Garde nationale de Paris*, Napoleon took an oath of loyalty to the régime he was about to overthrow.

Like his fellow directors, Paul de Barras had resigned his *Directoire exécutif* seat and left Paris for his castle of Grosbois. After the deaths of Napoleon's father Carlo, of Governor Marbeuf, and of King Louis XVI, and after defeating Paoli, toppling his former protector Barras was yet another unconscious patricide for Napoleon. Three other directors beside Barras had also resigned, and one was under surveillance. The *conseil des Anciens*, under the leadership of Napoleon's allies Lemercier and Cornet, invoked Article 94 of the Constitution of the Year III of the French Republic, declared that the republic's situation was urgent and grave, and decreed that the *Directoire exécutif* no longer existed and that an interim executive commission be set up to govern the republic.

Under the current constitution, the *conseil des Cinq-Cents* had to vote on the resolutions of the *Anciens* before they became law. Most of the five hundred, however, driven out of their hall by their own grenadiers, had fled the castle of Saint-Cloud for their lives. A handful of legislators (thirty, fifty, or eighty, depending on whose version of the story one credits)—those who felt they could count on General Bonaparte's protection—had remained behind. On 19 Brumaire Year VIII of the French Republic (November 10, 1799), Lucien Bonaparte rounded up the deputies who were still at Saint-Cloud in the *Orangerie* and made them vote by candlelight to adjourn their session until December 22. To govern France during the forty-two days in the interim, the frightened legislators created a provisional three-man consulate. The three provisional consuls later agreed to take daily turns in their presidency: each of them would preside over the consulate for one day at a time.[34] To perform France's legislative functions in the interim, the cowed legislators set up a provisional fifty-man body, the *commission intérimaire législative*.

Why had the French legislators set up a three-man consulate to run their country? The idea was Napoleon's.[35] The title of consul harked back to the ancient Roman Republic, which was ruled by two consuls, who served one-year terms. Why did Napoleon want *three* consuls? Was it only the necessity of paying his political debts, or were there also deeper, unconscious motives? Sieyès and Ducos, the other two consuls, were both born in 1748, the same year as Napoleon's dead father, Carlo Bonaparte. Did Napoleon unconsciously repeat with the other two consuls his earlier relationship with his father and with his elder brother Joseph, both of whom were his rivals and both of whom he had displaced?

The provisional consul Roger Ducos was "a mere cipher"[36] who let his colleagues Sieyès and Bonaparte run the show. A few years later, when

Napoleon was Emperor and Ducos asked him for power, a furious Napoleon reportedly yelled at him, "You're not asking me anything, Monsieur Ducos!" He then reportedly exclaimed to his aides, "This midget Ducos, this legless cripple Ducos, a limited and facile man!"[37]

On November 11, 1799, at the Luxembourg palace, where the *Directoire exécutif* had resided, Bonaparte and Sieyès met to draft the new Constitution of the Year VIII. On the same day, Napoleon and Josephine Bonaparte left their modest Paris residence on the Rue de la Victoire and moved to the suburban castle of Malmaison, Josephine's "dream house."[38] On the same day, too, Bonaparte named his loyal aide and chief of staff, General Louis-Alexandre Berthier, as France's new war minister.[39]

In the power struggle that ensued between Bonaparte and Sieyès in the new provisional consulate, General Bonaparte sidelined Abbot Sieyès, whom he intensely disliked. The outcome of the five-week duel between the general and the cleric over the new constitution was a foregone conclusion. On December 1, 1799, there was a dramatic showdown between the two men. Sieyès angrily accused Bonaparte of wanting to be king and left the meeting in a huff. The following day he tendered his resignation from the provisional consulate. "In this contest the thirty-year-old Napoleon had all the cards: he had physical magnetism and presence, he could concentrate on detail for hours on end without tiring, and he impressed everyone with his pithy commonsense and exceptional intelligence."[40]

Predicably, Abbot Sieyès had lost his battle with General Bonaparte, who became France's virtual sole ruler. To Bonaparte, the *coup d'état* quickly brought its material and emotional rewards. On November 15, 1799, Napoleon moved into the Petit Luxembourg palace, the former residence of the five directors. Bonaparte gave up his uniform in favor of mufti. The psychoanalyst Pierce Clark thought that "the balance of his mind restored, Napoleon, as a concession to win public favour, always appears in civilian garb. As he jokes about the scenes at Saint Cloud, his face is pale and his cheeks are hollow, but there is withal an irresistible vigour and magnetism about him."[41]

Napoleon went about repairing his damaged mother, France. "Everything, everywhere, had to be refashioned, from roads to law courts."[42] During the first four months of his rule as First Consul of France, he compulsively reformed each and every institution of French society. Napoleon needed absolute power. Less than that made him feel hampered, frustrated, and powerless. He wanted to be the sole ruler of France, not to share his powers with his older and ambitious colleagues,

Sieyès and Ducos. Napoleon sought to replace his two colleagues with less ambitious and more docile men. On December 12, 1799, Bonaparte staged yet another *coup*, this time inside the *commission législative interimaire*. In the presence of its fifty members, Pierre-Claude-François Daunou, who hoped to be third consul, read his draft Constitution of the Year VIII to Bonaparte in the consul's private hall at the *palais du petit Luxembourg*. One scholar thought that the fifty commissioners adopted the new constitution "on the spot,"[43] but most other scholars thought that it was adopted on the following day. This constitution gave vast powers to the *premier consul*, the other two consuls having limited functions. Napoleon, who was going to be First Consul, had obtained near-absolute power. Popular elections were abolished. The people would choose "eligibles," while the senate would choose the members of the other two assemblies from the "national list."[44]

By mid-December Bonaparte had worn down Sieyès and his party. The Constitution of the Year VIII of the French Republic was presented to the interim legislative commission on the evening of December 13, 1799. The fifty commissioners ratified and signed it then and there. Less than two weeks later it became the law of the land and made General Napoleon Bonaparte the sole ruler of France.

16

Boundless Power

As General Bonaparte had expected, the two provisional consuls Sieyès and Ducos lost their jobs after forty days in office, while Bonaparte kept his. The new Constitution of 22 Frimaire of the Year VIII created the consulate and made Napoleon Bonaparte France's First Consul, Jean-Jacques-Régis Cambacérès its second consul, and Charles-François Lebrun the third consul. Incredibly, by our modern standards, it went into effect on 4 Nivôse Year VIII of the French Republic (Christmas Day, December 25, 1799)—six weeks *before* the official results of the French plebiscite on it were tallied and published. On December 26, 1799, the day after he took office, Bonaparte decreed his State Council's first regulation. It gave his ministers the right to enter the council and "direct" or "guide" it,[1] thus robbing the State Council of its independence. Henceforth it did not take very long for the State Council to become a rubber stamp for Napoleon's wishes. He became a dictator in all but name.[2]

Jacques Bainville thought that Bonaparte's most urgent task was "to put on its feet a stricken country which, once the winter was past, would have to sustain a war again."[3] France needed every one of her citizens in the forthcoming war against the European monarchies, which would resume in the spring. Many thousands of former *chouans* (royalist and Catholic rebels in the Vendée and other rebellious regions) and *émigrés* (royalists and antirepublicans who left France to fight the republic from abroad) opposed the republic. Napoleon wanted them on his side. On December 26, 1799, he offered a conditional amnesty to the "victims of Fructidor" (the *coup d'état* of 18 Fructidor Year V of the French Republic) if they laid down their arms and swore allegiance to the Republic. Bonaparte gave the insurgents only ten days to accept his peace terms.

Ironically, Napoleon himself had made "Fructidor" possible by sending General Augereau's division of his *armée d'Italie* to Paris to help Barras and the other the republican members of the *Directoire exécutif* unseat their royalist enemies. Consciously, it was an adroit political move. Unconsciously, Napoleon may have felt guilty for his role in that bloody coup and sought to assuage his painful feelings through this amnesty. His amnesty to the "victims of Fructidor" applied to the rebel *chouans* but not to the royalist *émigrés*. Many *émigrés*, however, returned to France clandestinely, passing themselves off as *chouans* to benefit from the amnesty. Bonaparte used the *émigrés*' plight to increase his own power.[4]

The royalist leaders were a tough nut to crack. On the day he issued the amnesty to the "victims of Fructidor," Napoleon received Baron Jean-Guillaume Hyde de Neuville, the young head of the Bourbon royalist agency in Paris, who had come to speak for the *vendéen* rebels, and on the following day he saw General Louis-Marie-Auguste-Fortuné d'Andigné de la Blanchaye, commander of the royalist troops of Anjou.[5] Jacques Bainville believed that Bonaparte flattered the rebel leaders' courage and character, "giving them to believe if need be, that he would not be opposed to a return of the Bourbons."[6] That same day the new *Sénat conservateur de la constitution* was inaugurated. Like the tribunate and the State Council, the new senate was a mere adjunct to the First Consul's wishes. In the new regime, he alone had any real power. And he was convinced that everything he did was for the good of Mother France.

If the other consuls and organs of government did Bonaparte's bidding, the rebel leaders did not. Baron Hyde de Neuville and General d'Andigné de la Blanchaye proposed to mediate the return of Louis XVIII to the throne of France. Napoleon angrily rejected their proposals. On January 11, 1800, he wrote of the two royalist leaders: "The security of the State and of the citizen demand that such men perish by fire and fall under the blade of the national force."[7] In the future, he would lock up his royalist foes in the notorious *Le Temple* prison or in the infamous *maison de santé*, a psychiatric clinic for political prisoners run by Dr. Claude-Henry Jacquelin-Dubuisson at 303 rue du faubourg Saint-Antoine in Paris.

On December 28, 1799, three days after he formally took office, First Consul Bonaparte officially proclaimed the end of the French Revolution.

His first months in office were devoted to ending France's internal wars, "rifts, religious persecutions, class conflicts."[8] Only after achieving this could he turn his mind to France's external wars with Austria, Russia, England, and its other enemies. However, Bonaparte's foreign minister, Talleyrand, sought to end France's disastrous wars in Europe, which First Consul Bonaparte was equally determined to pursue until France's enemies were crushed and her "natural borders" were recognized. As soon as Bonaparte took office as France's First Consul, Talleyrand tried to get him to end the state of war between France and her chief enemy, Great Britain. On Christmas Day 1799, the day he formally took office, at Talleyrand's urging, Napoleon wrote a letter to King George III of the United Kingdom of Great Britain and Ireland, who also styled himself "King of France," and whom Napoleon called *le roi d'Angleterre* (the king of England). Napoleon appealed to the king's reason and love of peace. He wrote George III:

> Your Majesty will see in this overture only my sincere desire to contribute by a prompt step taken in confidence, and freed from those forms which, however necessary to disguise the feeble apprehensions of feeble states, only serve to discover in the powerful a mutual wish to deceive. France and England, abusing their strength, may long defer the period of its exhaustion; but I will venture to say that the fate of the civilized nations is concerned in the termination of a war, the flames of which are raging throughout the whole world . . . Why should the two most enlightened nations of Europe . . . go on sacrificing their trade, their prosperity, and their domestic happiness to false ideas of grandeur?[9]

Talleyrand sent Napoleon's letter to his British counterpart, the forty-year-old British foreign secretary and future prime minister, William Wyndham Grenville. Lord Grenville forwarded it to his king, who suffered from mental illness, possibly due to porphyria, and who had already had some psychotic episodes. On New Year's Day 1800, the first day of the new century, an ill-humored George III wrote Lord Grenville complaining about "the Corsican tyrant's letter."[10] It was impossible, the king wrote, "to treat with a new, impious, self-created aristocracy."[11] The king would not deign to answer Bonaparte's letter. Lord Grenville must write Talleyrand demanding that the Bourbons be restored to the throne of France and that France withdraw to its 1789 borders. A furious Bonaparte would once more prepare an invasion of England that never took place.

During his three and a half years as First Consul, Napoleon ruled France as he saw fit. He made peace—however temporary and illusory—with Austria, the Papacy, and Great Britain, ended the Revolution, restored the Roman Catholic religion, abolished the republican calendar, and undid many social and political changes made by the Revolution. His ambition and greed were insatiable, his need for power unquenchable, his wars interminable. He invaded the western and central European lands, including the low countries (Belgium and the Netherlands), Switzerland, Austria, and parts of Germany and Italy, annexing many of them to France. Other lands were made French dependencies. Napoleon feared and hated his enemies. As his fears grew, Napoleon's rule became increasingly tyrannical and oppressive, giving rise to a vicious circle of fear and violence.

The high-level narcissistic Napoleon was a rare mixture of ego strength and psychopathology. He could not share his glory with others. The psychoanalyst Pierce Clark thought that, although Napoleon became cautious as First Consul, "within his mental prison his ideal is still as grandiose as ever. His ability to endure adversity is always extraordinary. Before Napoleon gained a commanding position in the world, he failed no less than six times, yet he ever had the courage to climb anew. Though the hardiness of his youth makes him resilient to disasters, it is mainly the surety of his self-convictions that renders him so impervious to failure. This virtue so very necessary for his ascent is the chief cause of his final debacle."[12]

Talleyrand's wish to end France's disastrous wars was understandable. By early 1800 France was losing its war against Austria in Italy. Genoa was the only French outpost left in Italy, and the Austrians sought to drive the French out of Genoa. Napoleon was eager to return to Italy and fight the Austrians again. They had robbed him of his Italian victories. He hoped to restore his self-esteem by taking Italy back from them. Bonaparte planned to cross the Alps from Switzerland into Italy's Val d'Aosta, then launch his attack on the Austrians.

Napoleon organized a new French *armée de la reserve*, which he headed personally, and named his former subordinate General Masséna to command the forty-four thousand troops of the French *armée d'Italie* holed up in Genoa. Masséna's job was to hold down the Austrians at Genoa, making it possible for Napoleon to defeat them elsewhere. In February Masséna left for Genoa to take command of the *armée d'Italie.* From February to June 1800 the outnumbered Frenchmen under Masséna fought the Austrian armies under the seventy-year-old Field Marshal Michael Friedrich Benedict Melas. On April 20 the Austrians began their siege of Genoa, which lasted forty-five days. Melas defeated Masséna and forced him to capitulate honorably on June 4.[13] Meanwhile the brave but unfortunate General Kléber fought the British and Ottomans in Egypt against overwhelming odds.[14]

In France's internal affairs, First Consul Bonaparte moved on the political front as fast as he did on the financial. On February 17, 1800, the new Legislative Corps adopted the new administrative organization of France, including Bonaparte's departmental prefects. To sustain his grandiose self, Napoleon needed ever more titles, offices, and victories. Not content with being First Consul, he wanted to be the supreme commander of all the French armies. The Constitution of the Year VIII of the French Republic, however, limited his power to "organizing and distributing" the armies. The French armies had enjoyed many victories, but had also suffered reverses, mainly against the Austrians, in Italy, Switzerland, and Germany. Saddled with bureaucratic chores, Napoleon, who could "organize and distribute" the French armies but not command them, deeply missed his military life. On March 15 an unhappy First Consul Bonaparte wrote his chief rival, General Jean-Victor Moreau, who had watched Directors Gohier and Moulin during the *coup d'état* and was rewarded with the command of the united French *armée du Rhin et d'Helvétie*:

> Today I am a kind of puppet who has lost his freedom and his happiness. Great honors are fine, but only when one imagines or remembers them. I envy your happy lot. Together with brave men, you are going to do admirable things. I would gladly trade my consular purple for the epaulets of a brigade commander under your orders. I very much hope that circumstances will permit me to come and give you some help.[15]

Did the power-hungry Napoleon really want to trade his near-absolute power for the command of a brigade in Moreau's army? Napoleon envied Moreau's fame and popularity. To weaken General Moreau, First Consul Bonaparte tried to truncate his army. He ordered his former war minister, the loyal General Berthier, to set up the new *armée de réserve* at Dijon, near the Alpine passes into Italy, that would absorb half of Moreau's army. Defying the First Consul, a proud and angry Moreau refused to give up any part of his army to Berthier, or to Bonaparte, for that matter.

Napoleon was furious. He had his new war minister, Lazare Carnot, reprimand Moreau for his disobedience. Ignoring Carnot's reprimand, Moreau crossed the Rhine with his *armée du Rhin et d'Helvétie* to attack the Austrians, whom he defeated at Hohenlinden in late 1800. Curiously, Napoleon did not attempt to force his will on Moreau. As First Consul, he had the authority to remove Moreau from his command. Did Napoleon fear that Moreau's popularity would make the people rebel? Was there an unconscious motive involved in his lack of firmness? Leaving Moreau in his post was a self-destructive act on Bonaparte's part: four years later Moreau was implicated in a plot to overthrow Napoleon.

In the spring of 1800 the republican French armies had fought the imperial Austrians on two fronts: north of the Alps in Germany and south of the Alps in Italy. The French general Moreau, commanding the joint *armée du Rhin et d'Helvétie*, led the French campaign in Germany, while his chief rival, First Consul Bonaparte, commanded the French campaign in Italy. In his grandiose imagination, Napoleon was Hannibal himself, once more invading Rome by crossing the Alps. Bonaparte marched his forty thousand men through the Great Saint Bernard Pass, one of the highest of the Alpine frontier passes, lying at an altitude of 8,100 feet (2,469 meters), which lies on the Italian-Swiss border, east of the Mont Blanc group in the southwestern Pennine Alps. In Napoleon's unconscious fantasy the Great Saint Bernard Pass was a mighty old man, a father or grandfather whom he had to vanquish. He wrote his fellow consuls, Cambacérès and Lebrun: "We are fighting against ice, snow, torrents and avalanches. The Great Saint Bernard, astonished at seeing so many men crossing it so abruptly, is putting up a few obstacles against us."[16]

Twice Bonaparte almost lost his new Italian campaign, yet he was ultimately successful. After a bloody campaign in northern Italy, on June 2, 1800, one of Napoleon's generals, General Joachim Murat, entered Milan and took its citadel from the defending Austrians. This victory facilitated Napoleon's subsequent conquests in Italy, culminating in his victory at Marengo on June 14. Murat had sent word to Napoleon at Turbingo that Milan's citadel had surrendered to him. Napoleon headed for Milan at once to make a grand appearance as France's head of state. On the evening of June 2, wading through a horrendous rainstorm, his drenched consular escort looking like "muddy water spaniels,"[17] Napoleon reached Milan, which he had left three years earlier. Murat's troops kept the curious spectators at bay. When the crowd proved less than enthusiastic about his arrival, Napoleon flew into a rage.[18] For actors and politicians, the crowd often plays the unconscious role of the early mother: they thrive on its love and become enraged or depressed when they do not get it.

The key battle between the thirty-year-old First Consul Bonaparte's Frenchmen and the seventy-year-old Field Marshal Melas's Austrians took place twelve days later, on June 14, 1800, at Marengo, in northwestern Italy, across the Bormida River from Alessandria. The Austrian commander Melas had thirty-four thousand troops at Marengo. Napoleon, who had dispersed his army across northwestern Italy, had only fifteen thousand men left at the battlefield. The carnage at Marengo was horrific. The psychoanalyst Pierce Clark believed that Napoleon was either catatonic or suicidal: "The air is filled with whirling branches of trees and debris of every sort, but . . . [Napoleon] himself sits in the midst of this carnage, quite unmoved. He seems to court death; bullets repeatedly tear up the ground even beneath his horse's feet. He refuses to take cover from the terrific fire."[19] Napoleon may have unconsciously believed in his own immortality, as many narcissistic people do.

The Austrians fought fiercely at Marengo, but the tide of battle finally turned in the Frenchmen's favor. In terms of men killed and wounded, the battle of Marengo was one of the worst in the history of Napoleon's wars. The Austrians had ninety-five hundred casualties: one thousand men killed, fifty-five hundred wounded, and three thousand taken prisoners. The French had "only" fifty-six hundred casualties: eleven hundred killed, thirty-six hundred wounded, and nine hundred men captured.[20] It was a "glorious victory" for Napoleon, but an unmitigated disaster for everyone else. One of the fallen Frenchmen was General Louis-Charles-Antoine Desaix, who had served Bonaparte in Egypt—and who had saved his from defeat at Marengo by arriving with his division in time to push back the Austrians.

Over the years, Napoleon kept changing his views of what had happened at Marengo on June 14, 1800. He could not get over the fact that he had been saved by his subordinate, and that this subordinate had given his life for him. He was never happy with one version of the story for long. Napoleon wrote no less than three different accounts of the battle of Marengo, and gave a fourth account verbally. The first account was the military bulletin he published after the battle and it "told the story much as it had transpired."[21] Napoleon's second account of the Battle of Marengo was written three years later, in 1803, during his preparations for an invasion of Great Britain, and it painted his own role in a better light, yet "The result was not altogether pleasing to the First Consul, although it expanded his role in the victory."[22]

Five years after Marengo, in 1805, Napoleon, now Emperor of the French and King of Italy, ordered a third account of the battle of Marengo written and published. Napoleon now believed that his own planning, rather than Desaix's action, had saved the day.[23] This new account was a gross distortion of reality. It was designed to paint Napoleon as a hero who had planned his victory at Marengo and had never doubted it.[24] It was really Desaix who had saved Napoleon from defeat at Marengo, yet Napoleon convinced himself of his own victory. It was his way of dealing with his painful feelings of shame, humiliation, and guilt, and of salvaging his self-esteem.

Yet even this third account did not put Napoleon's mind at rest. In 1814, after he was toppled from power by the allies, Napoleon told Colonel Sir Neil Campbell, the British commissioner on the isle of Elba, that he had personally saved the battle of Marengo.[25] In 1815 Napoleon produced yet another fantasy version of the battle of Marengo in which his role and Desaix's were reversed. By this version, it was a heroic Napoleon who had encouraged a desperate Desaix to fight on rather than a heroic Desaix who had saved a desperate Napoleon from certain defeat.[26] This was a wishful-thinking fantasy. Napoleon could not forgive Desaix for having saved him—and for making him feel a failure.

By the spring of 1800, before Napoleon began fighting the Austrians in Italy, his archrival, General Moreau, had led his *armée du Rhin et d'Helvétie* against Austria in Germany, and defeated the Austrians at Stockach, north of Lake Constance. Seeking glory for France—and for themselves—Bonaparte and Moreau competed with each other in Italy and Germany, like two brothers vying for the love of their mother. This violent "sibling" rivalry was to lead Moreau to join the plot on Napoleon's life four years later.

Napoleon savored his threadbare victory at Marengo by forcing the "liberated" Italians to honor him and Mother France. On June 18, 1800, Milan's city fathers celebrated the "liberation of the Cisalpine Republic from the Austrian yoke" by singing a solmen *Te deum* in their cathedral in Bonaparte's honor—and in his presence.[27] On June 22 the news of the Marengo victory reached Paris, just in time for the bimonthly reception given by the two other consuls for the diplomatic corps. The official *Gazette nationale ou le Moniteur universel*, commonly known as *Le Moniteur*, trumpeted the victory of "Maringo."[28]

On June 23, 1800, Napoleon ordered his army to collect a special war tax of two million livres in the entire Cisalpine Republic, "to be paid by the individuals who had occupied posts with the Austrian government, or who have shown themselves to be notorious partisans of that government."[29] In his own unconscious mind, Napoleon was Hannibal, Alexander, and the other great conquerors of antiquity rolled into one. Throughout his life, however, whatever victories he won, whatever lands he conquered, he was never satisfied. There were always more lands to conquer. His "internal mother," his grandiose self and his narcissistic perfectionism never gave him peace.

While the young First Consul Bonaparte was fighting the Austrians in Italy, his older rivals in Paris schemed to take his place. The chief plotters were Napoleon's double-dealing foreign minister, Charles-Maurice de Talleyrand, and his wily police minister, Joseph Fouché. Their plot was called the "Marengo Conspiracy." In late June 1800 false news had reached Paris of General Desaix's death and of a "lost battle" at Marengo. General Desaix had indeed been killed, but his arrival had turned the tide for Napoleon, who had won the battle. Some thought that Napoleon would not return from the battlefield. Joseph Bonaparte even proposed himself as his younger brother's successor. The forty-one-year-old Fouché and the forty-six-year-old Talleyrand plotted with a prominent fifty-year-old senator, Dominique Clément de Ris, to set up a ruling "triumvirate." When Napoleon returned to Paris on the night of July 2, 1800, he was bitterly disappointed and angry to learn of the plots of those who wanted to take his place. Henceforth, he later said, he never trusted anyone.[30] Yet, despite clear and repeated evidence of their plots against him, Napoleon kept Talleyrand and Fouché in their jobs and ultimately let them dethrone him. It was yet another in a series of self-destructive actions and inactions that ran through Napoleon's life.[31]

As Shakespeare put it, "Uneasy lies the head that wears a crown."[32] To control his powerful rivals and make them beholden to himself, Napoleon distributed honors, titles, ranks and dignities to France's politicians and generals. Before creating the *Ordre de la Légion d'honneur* in 1802, he gave some of them "swords of honor" inscribed with the phrase "Battle Commanded by the First Consul in Person."[33] At the same time the wary Napoleon constantly watched out for plots against him.

Several plots against Bonaparte were indeed hatched in Paris. Both the extreme-left Jacobins and the extreme-right royalist and Catholic rebels hated Napoleon and sought to kill him. Not only did his own ministers, Talleyrand and Fouché, plot against him in the "Marengo Conspiracy," France's most prominent generals also wanted their piece of the pie. In the so-called "Rueil Conspiracy" several generals met at General Masséna's residence in the Paris suburb of Rueil and planned to present their First Consul with an ultimatum: if he did not want them to depose him, he would have to carve up France into several parts, "each of the great military leaders being given appanages like his own."[34] The last thing Bonaparte would do, however, was to cut up his symbolic mother into pieces.

As Bonaparte personified the Revolution, its enemies hoped to kill it by murdering him. As the royalist leader Baron Jean-Guillaume Hyde de Neuville put it, "Power became incorporated in himself."[35] The increasingly controlled French press, which First Consul Bonaparte had reduced from seventy-three newspapers to thirteen, all of them republican, was still defiant. On July 10, 1800, a leftist French newspaper called *Le Journal des Hommes Libres*, which suspected Bonaparte of royalist leanings, criticized him for using the words *France* and *français* in his official pronouncements, rather than *patrie* and *citoyens*. An angry Napoleon sought new ways to weaken and muzzle the press. Vincent Cronin thought that as Napoleon saw it, freedom to publish was a minor freedom "and had to be sacrificed in order to preserve greater freedoms. All but a handful of Frenchmen agreed."[36]

Unable to change his internalized bad mother, Napoleon needed to repair and reform her good substitute, Mother France. One area of French life that badly needed reform and codification was the law. In northern France a customary law based on medieval Frankish institutions prevailed, while in the south Roman law was prevalent. Royal decrees and ordinances and a case law developed by the *parlements* (courts) governed many legal matters. The Roman Catholic church controlled marriage, sexuality and family life. Each area had its own customs. Efforts at unification and streamlining of the law were blocked by vested interests who stood to lose their privileges. The French Revolution had brought matters to a head. Napoleon wanted a new Civil Code to strengthen the family against society and the state. Napoleon, whose mother did not breast-feed him, wanted the code to force parents to feed their impoverished children "even when grown up."[37] He, whose sisters were forced to marry against their will, wanted to oblige parents to provide their daughters with dowries. He, whose mother had abused him physically and emotionally, wanted to give grandparents the right to protect their grandchildren from parental abuse.[38] He did not always get his way with the jurists, but his legislative wishes sprang from his own emotional wounds.

On September 1, 1800, two weeks after Napoleon's thirty-first birthday, the Austrians broke their armistice with the French and resumed their hostilities against them in Italy. Great Britain seized the island of Malta, which Napoleon had taken two years earlier. This was a *casus belli* for Bonaparte. In November, the first anniversary of his *coup d'état*, First Consul Bonaparte ordered his armies to resume their war on Austria. He dispatched General Brune's *armée d'Italie* to fight the Austrians again in northern Italy.

Thanks to Bonaparte's greedy foreign minister, Talleyrand, who had also served under the *Directoire exécutif*, France had also become embroiled in a war with its former ally, the United States. In late 1796 the sixty-one-year-old John Adams had been elected the second president of the United States, succeeding George Washington. Shortly thereafter President Adams sent three American envoys to Paris to negotiate an agreement with France for the protection of United States shipping from French naval raids. Once in Paris, these three Americans were approached by three French secret agents, code-named X, Y, and Z in the Americans' dispatches home. X, Y, and Z demanded a bribe of two hundred and fifty thousand dollars for Talleyrand and a loan of ten million dollars to France if they wanted the agreement to be discussed by the *Directoire*. From 1797 to 1800 the United States and France fought an undeclared but furious naval war in the Caribbean, known in American history as the "Quasi-War with France." Some historians think this war had begun in 1791, when George Washington had sent messages to the Senate about the Treaty of Amity and Commerce with France. The United States was divided. The American Federalists wanted to pursue the war, while the American Republicans wished to create a military and political alliance with Republican France.

On September 30, 1800, after three years of "Quasi War" and months of arduous negotiations, Napoleon's France signed a new "convention" with the United States at Joseph Bonaparte's castle of Mortefontaine, outside Paris. This "Convention of 1800" or "Convention of Mortefontaine" did not resolve the thorny issues in Franco-American relations.[39] Worse still, on the following day, behind America's back, France signed a secret treaty with Spain at San Ildefonso, by which Spain gave France the Spanish-owned Louisiana Territory in North America, extending all the way from the Mississippi river to the Rocky Mountains. The sixty-five-year-old U.S. president John Adams lost that year's presidential race to his fifty-seven-year-old rival, Thomas Jefferson. The Treaty of San Ildefonso was confirmed by Franec and Spain on March 21, 1801. Two years later, in what is known in American history as the "Louisiana Purchase," First Consul Bonaparte sold the entire Louisiana Territory to the United States, which agreed to pay France $11,250,000 outright and assumed claims of its citizens against France in the amount of $3,750,000. Interest payments incidental to the final settlement made the total price $27,267,622. The French reckoned the value of the sale at eighty million francs.[40]

17

Imperial Ambitions and Infernal Machines

In Paris, plots and conspiracies against First Consul Bonaparte were being hatched both inside and outside his own government. Most of these plots were aborted, failed, or foiled by Fouché's spies. Some of the aides of General François Hanriot, who had commanded the Paris Revolutionary Guard and was guillotined with Robespierre in 1794, plotted to assassinate Bonaparte, but their plan was aborted by Fouché. On October 10, 1800, some rebels plotted to stab Bonaparte with daggers at the Opera. They were led by the forty-five-year-old Italian-French sculptor Joseph Céracchi, the thirty-one-year-old painter François-Jean-Baptiste Topino-Lebrun, and the twenty-nine-year-old adjudant-général Joseph Aréna, a younger brother of the deputy Barthélemy Aréna, Bonaparte's Corsican enemy. They were seized and executed before they could touch their daggers.

In late 1800, however, an assassination plot called *la machine infernale* almost took Napoleon's life. On December 17 three royalist *chouans* named François-Joseph Carbon, Pierre Picot de Limoëlan, and Pierre Robinault de Saint-Régeant entered the shop of a grain dealer named Lamballe. Carbon said he was a pedlar who had bought a supply of brown sugar that he needed to convey to Laval in Brittany to barter for cloth and wished to buy Lamballe's cart and old mare for that purpose. Lamballe sold him the cart and mare for two hundred francs. Carbon and his friends drove it to 19, Rue Paradis, near Saint-Lazare, where they had rented a shed. There they spent five days hooping a large wine cask to the cart with ten strong iron rings. The idea was to fill the cask with gunpowder, make an "infernal machine" bomb and explode it near Napoleon as he drove to a public place like the Opera.

On December 22, 1800 Saint-Régeant drove to the place du Carrousel looking for a placement for the "infernal machine." He chose a spot in the Rue Saint-Nicaise, north of the Tuileries Palace, toward the Rue du Faubourg Saint-Honoré, where Napoleon had massacred the royalist rebels with his guns in 1795, "more or less abreast of what is now the Place du Théâtre Français. The Rue de la Loi (today the Rue de Richelieu), which led to the Opera, was almost a continuation of it."[1] Saint-Régeant decided that this was the perfect spot. "They would position the cart carrying the barrel in the Rue St.-Nicaise, toward the Rue St.-Honoré, some 20 meters from the Place du Carrousel . . . One of them would stand watch before the Hôtel de Longueville, at the far side of the square. Thus he would see the carriage when it left the Tuileries, and would be able to signal to the person, who, with a long fuse, would ignite the bomb."[2]

On Christmas Eve, December 24, 1800, the plotter Carbon, who had made the "infernal machine," harnessed the mare to the cart with the big win cask and with Limoëlan drove it to the Porte Saint-Denis, on the northern outskirts of Paris. In a deserted building, they loaded the cask with gunpowder. Then they drove it to the Rue Saint-Nicaise, north of the palace. Limoëlan crossed over to the place du Carrousel, whence he could signal his two fellow plotters to light the fuse. Saint-Régeant saw a teenage girl named Marie-Jeanne Pensol, whose mother sold fresh-baked rolls and vegetables in the nearby Rue du Bac. He paid Pensol twelve sous to hold the mare for a few minutes. At 8 p.m., thinking his police had caught the plotters against him, a relaxed but tired Napoleon reluctantly drove to the Opéra to attend a performance of Joseph Haydn's majestic oratorio *Die Schöpfung* (The Creation), performed in France for the first time.

First Consul Bonaparte's carriage was preceded by a resplendent cavalry escort from the *Garde consulaire*. Bonaparte's military aides General Louis-Alexandre Berthier, General Jean Lannes, and Colonel Jacques-Alexandre-Bernard Law de Lauriston rode with the First Consul. From their memoirs, the nineteenth-century French psychologist Adolphe Garnier deduced that the exhausted Napoleon fell asleep in his carriage, and that he had a bad dream reviving his traumatic Tagliamento River battle against the Austrians in Italy three years earlier.[3] Sigmund Freud believed that Napoleon was "an extremely sound sleeper."[4] Freud explained: "When we decide to go to sleep, we may succeed in temporarily bringing to an end the cathexes of energy attaching to our waking thoughts. Anyone who can do this easily is a good sleeper; the first Napoleon seems to have been a model of this class."[5] In fact, Napoleon slept heavily at times, but at other times he slept very poorly.

Bonaparte's carriage was followed by another carriage carrying his wife Josephine, her daughter Hortense, and Napoleon's sister Caroline, who had married General Murat early that year and was nine months pregnant. While he had been dreaming, Napoleon's carriage, tragically driven by a drunken coachman named César, passed the Rue Saint-Nicaise and entered the Rue du Faubourg Saint-Honoré. Limoëlan, standing in the place du Carrousel, panicked and failed to signal Saint-Régeant in the Rue Saint-Nicaise, who thus lost a precious minute or two. When the leading grenadiers in Napoleon's guard rode past him, Saint-Régeant finally lit the fuse and fled. The drunken César "raced through the narrow street [Rue Saint-Nicaise] at full speed and whirled into the next street, Rue de la Loi."[6]

At that moment the "infernal machine" exploded in the gap between Bonaparte's carriage and that of the three ladies following him at some distance in the Rue Saint-Nicaise, demolishing the entire street, killing the teenage girl Marie-Jeanne Pensol, who was holding the mare, and some innocent bystanders. Freud thought that Napoleon had harbored a traumatic memory of the Tagliamento River battle, which was revived by the explosion, and that to deal with this intruding physical stimulus, the sleeping Napoleon "wove" the sound of the explosion into his dream before waking up.[7] Still dreaming that he was being bombarded by the Austrians, Napoleon woke up crying, *Nous sommes minés!* (We have been mined!).[8]

Freud believed that Napoleon's dream was an "alarm-clock dream" that weaves external stimuli into its structure in order to maintain the dreamer's sleep and prevent him from being disturbed by external noises. "Napoleon could sleep on—with a conviction that what was trying to disturb him was only a dream-memory of the thunder of the guns at Arcole [*sic*]."[9] In fact, Napoleon had been dreaming of his Tagliamento River battle in March 1797 rather than of his Arcola battle in November 1796, but Freud had read two different versions of this dream.[10] The river may have unconsciously symbolized Napoleon's feelings and the horses his ambitions. But Napoleon did not sleep after the explosion: "Bonaparte decided to go ahead immediately, without losing one minute in which the enemy could take advantage to kill him."[11]

If Napoleon was traumatized by the "infernal machine" explosion, he had escaped the assassination attempt physically unscathed, which reinforced his narcissistic illusion of omnipotence and immortality. When he reached the Opéra he received a standing ovation from the audience. The explosion, however, had killed several innocent bystanders. How many is unclear. André Castelot believed that "*a dozen persons were killed*, and twenty-eight were wounded"[12] in the blast. Vincent Cronin thought that "*nine innocent people died* and twenty-six were injured."[13] Jean Tulard, however, wrote that the bomb *killed only two people*, including a very young girl, and injured six people gravely (and others lightly).[14] Frank McLynn put the number of people killed or maimed at "fifty-two bystanders and some of the consul's escort." [15]

The mare hitched to the cart carrying the bomb was killed along with the teenage girl who held her. "A woman standing at her shop door to cheer Napoleon had her breasts ripped off; another was blinded."[16] As in all such cases, there were also psychic wounds, now called post-traumatic stress disorders. The three ladies that followed Bonaparte in the second carriage were all hurt. Napoleon's wife, Josephine, fainted. Her daughter Hortense's hand was lacerated. Napoleon's sister, Caroline Murat, who was in her ninth month of pregnancy, and whose emotional health was less than robust, was severely traumatized. She became anxious and depressed. The son she bore the following month, Achille Murat, was born an epileptic.[17]

Napoleon had convinced himself that the attempt on his life had been made by the extreme-left Jacobin *exclusifs*. Police Minister Fouché accused the *chouans*, but First Consul Bonaparte would not listen to him. He was "deeply shocked and very angry."[18] He believed that he had done wonders for France and that his would-be assassins were ungrateful. Seeking to restore his self-esteem through narcissistic vengeance, an enraged Napoleon told his *Conseil d'état*, "For such an atrocious crime we must have vengeance like a thunder-bolt; blood must flow; we must shoot as many guilty men as there have been victims."[19] Napoleon wanted his leftist "Jacobin enemies" removed from Mother France. Even after the real culprits—all right-wing royalists—were apprehended by Focuhé's police, Napoleon refused to pardon the innocent ones, insisting that they be deported from France:

> A Royalist attempt would upset his policy of fusion. He refused to believe in that; a Jacobin attempt suited him, as conforming to his

system of the moment. It was a good pretext for annihilating the last remains of the violent factions, but a "purging" like that of Robespierre when he sent the "*exagérés*" to the guillotine, that of the Convention when they condemned the accomplices of the 1st of Prairial, that of the Directory when they shot Babeuf. At bottom, it was the progressive obliteration of the active Republicans which had made possible the return to order; and there too Bonaparte was carrying on rather than innovating. When their small number had disappeared, no counter-attack from the extreme Jacobins need be feared. There would be Royalist plots, military plots, domestic palace plots. There would be no further Republican conspiracies. [20]

Napoleon's "policy of fusion" was designed to fuse his moderate republican followers with the royalist followers of the old regime and to create a nonrevolutionary, peaceful, united France. In his unconscious mind, was he longing for his archaic infantile fusion with his mother? The innocent "Jacobins" whom he purged paid the price for this "policy of fusion":

One hundred and thirty suspects, hardly any of whom reappeared, were the ransom of the infernal machine. When Fouché held the real culprits . . . it was too late. There was no pardon for the proscribed Jacobins because their proscription had been really desired. By a subtle precaution they had not been condemned for participation in the affair of the Rue Saint-Nicaise, but dealt with under a measure of public safety. The First Consul turned everything to his advantage: public anger, the annihilation of the intransigent Revolutionaries, and the indication that he had implacable enemies among the Royalists. Nor was that all. The very difficulty of making a law to meet special circumstances placed in his hands a ruler's instrument of incomparable convenience.[21]

Bonaparte's revenge for the "infernal machine," though it fell on innocent victims, was equal to the injury he had suffered. The one hundred and thirty unfortunate Jacobin suspects were deported from France to infernal places like French Guyana and Devil's Island without trial and without the right of appeal. Napoleon increasingly felt that he had the power to do anything he wished. On January 7, 1801—Joseph Bonaparte's thirty-third birthday—he named his loyal aide André-François Miot, the future *comte de Melito*, the administrator of the two Corsican *départements* of the Golo and the Liamone, where *antibonapartiste* sentiment was strong, and where First Consul Bonaparte had suspended constitutional rule.[22]

Police Minister Fouché had wanted to prove to First Consul Bonaparte that it was the royalist *chouans*, not the republican *exclusifs*, as Napoleon had thought, who had tried to murder his boss. But Bonaparte would not listen to Fouché. He was seething with vengeance against the "violent" Jacobins. On January 9, 1801 the four "daggers conspirators"— the Jacobins Ceracchi, Aréna, Topino-Lebrun and Demerville—were found guilty of plotting to murder the First Consul and condemned to death. Their desperate protestations of innocence and of being tortured into confessing went unheeded. A fearful, furious, and vengeful Napoleon — who had once been a fervent Jacobin himself—could not admit that he was wrong. He still believed that the Jacobin *exclusifs* had tried to kill him. Napoleon turned a deaf ear to Fouché. His fear, his rage, and his inability to accept his own shortcomings and to admit his mistakes, got the better of him. He would get rid of all those that wished to harm him.

When Napoleon was anxious and furious, he could be monstrous. On January 11, 1801, an unfortunate Jacobin chemist named Chevalier, who had not made the "infernal machine," was executed by order of First Consul Bonaparte after being found guilty of treason. On January 18, the *chouan* bomb maker Carbon was arrested by the police. Under torture he gave the names of his fellow plotters, Limoëlan and Saint-Régeant. But Napoleon's fear was as deep as his vengeful rage. On January 19, four weeks after the explosion of the "infernal machine" that missed him, Bonaparte executed the *exclusif* pamphleteer Metge and two of his *exclusif* friends, even though there was no proof that any of them had been involved in the plot against him. On January 25 Carbon's fellow *chouan* plotter, Saint-Régeant, was arrested by Napoleon's police. Vincent Cronin thought that "the courts [not Napoleon] judged and sentenced to death Limoëlan and Carbon. Saint-Réjant escaped to the United States and—the least the would-be assassin could do—became a priest."[23] In fact, Saint-Régeant and Carbon were guillotined on April 20 at the place de Grève in Paris, while Limoëlan escaped Fouché's police and wound up in the United States, where he became a priest out of guilt feelings at the death of the girl Marie-Jeanne Pensol.[24]

Even after he had punished the plotters, Napoleon could not understand why anyone would wish to kill a man as generous and kind as he was, and he burned with vengeance against his enemies. The political journalist Roederer claimed that Napoleon had told him, "If I die in four or five years, the clock will be wound up and will run. If I die before then, I don't know what will happen."[25] Three years later he reportedly once more harangued Roederer: "These fanatics will end by killing me and putting angry Jacobins in power. It is I who embody the French revolution."[26] Indeed, in his unconscious mind, Napoleon was fused with Mother France and with her Revolution.

In February 1801 the winds of peace briefly blew in Europe. After six weeks of arduous negotiations, the envoys of France and Austria signed a peace treaty at the French Lorraine town of Lunéville, in the Meurthe-et-Moselle départerment, near Nancy. Napoleon's chief diplomat and elder brother, Joseph, a state councillor and Legislative Corps member, signed for France. It was a major victory for First Consul Bonaparte. The treaty gave France the entire German-speaking left bank of the Rhine, including the Ruhr, Saarland, Mosel, and Rheinland-Pfalz.

By the treaty of Lunéville, Austria recognized the French-created Batavian (Dutch), Helvetic (Swiss), Cisalpine (Lombard), and Ligurian (Genoese) republics, all of them French puppets. Austria also accepted France's occupation of the Piedmont and let France arbitrate the fate of the German states. [27] The treaty's terms were highly favorable to France. "It was vast—intoxicating —too beautiful. Too beautiful, because Austria could not sign such a peace in full sincerity, leaving part of Germany and part of Italy under French domination or influence."[28] Indeed, Austria secretly intended to take those lands back from France as soon as she was militarily strong enough to do so.

Bonaparte was not one to lose precious time. On March 8, 1801, under the provisions of the treaty of Lunéville, France annexed the German lands along the left bank of the Rhine. The German Ruhr became the "French" *département* of the Roer, with its capital at Hamm. The German Saar became the French *département* of the Sarre and its capital Saarbrücken the French city of Sarrebruck. The German Mosel became the French *département* of Rhin-et-Moselle with its capital at Metz. The German Rheinland-Pfalz, with its Hardt mountain range and Donnersberg peak, became the French *département* of Mont-Tonnerre, and its capital Mainz became the French city of Mayence. On March 16 the new French prefects of those new *départements* were installed in their new capitals. Napoleon now ruled not only France but also large parts of Germany, Italy, and the Netherlands.

The United Kingdom of Great Britain and Ireland had just gone through a political crisis. The "mad" King George III and his stubborn prime minister William Pitt the Younger had been fighting over rebellious Ireland. On February 10, 1801, King George III replaced Pitt with his more flexible and pragmatic friend Henry Addington. The peace-loving Addington sought to end the war with France. It would take almost a year for a peace treaty to become a reality in the Treaty of Amiens, and even then it was short lived.[29]

The Russian empire, too, was undergoing a political upheaval. On the night of March 23–24, 1801, the Russian plotters moved against their hated and "mentally unbalanced" tsar Pavel Petrovich.[30] They penetrated Saint Petersburg's Mikhailovsky Palace, went to the tsar's apartments, and tried to force Pavel to abdicate in favor of his son, Aleksandr Pavlovich. In the tragic scene that unfolded in Pavel's bedroom, the tsar refused to abdicate, became agitated, and physically resisted the plotters. A violent struggle ensued, and during the *melée* the plotters murdered Tsar Pavel Petrovich in his bedroom. The orphaned twenty-three-year-old Aleksandr Pavlovich became tsar of all the Russias. He was to become Napoleon's best friend and worst enemy.

Aleksandr was emotionally excitable and unstable. He was ambivalently attached to his engulfing mother. After his father's death, Aleksandr suffered from lifelong feelings of patricidal guilt. Rod Usher believed that Aleksandr had suffered a "nervous breakdown,"[31] a common euphemism for a psychotic episode, following his father's assassination, while Frank Richardson thought that the new tsar was "mentally unstable, a case of schizophrenia in all probability."[32] Pierce Clark thought that Aleksandr may also have been an epileptic.[33] The assassination of the tsar of Russia had brought to the Russian throne the man whom Napoleon would fall in love with six years later and consider his best friend—and who would later invade Napoleon's France and drive Napoleon from the throne.

The King of France had signed a *Concordat* with the Vatican in 1515, but the French Revolutionaries had repudiated it in 1790, at the peak of their anticlerical fervor. First Consul Bonaparte was eager to revise this *Concordat* in France's favor. His oedipal battle with Pope Pius VII lasted several years. The negotiations began in Paris in late 1800 and lasted many months. The pope sent the forty-five-year-old archbishop Giuseppe Spina, whom he elevated to cardinal in February 1801, as his envoy, while

Bonaparte chose as his delegate the thirty-eight-year-old priest Etienne-Alexandre-Jean-Baptiste-Marie Bernier, a former *vendéen* rebel who had fled to Switzerland and returned to Paris under Bonaparte's amnesty. Napoleon instructed Bernier to insist on two key issues: France must keep all its nationalized Church properties, and the pope must force all the French bishops to resign so that France can choose its own bishops.[34]

The pope and Cardinal Spina were stubborn, but so was First Consul Bonaparte. The negotiations were very tough, and the new *Concordat* went through several drafts, the fifth of which was personally dictated by Bonaparte. He sent it directly to Pope Pius VII with a fifty-eight-year-old envoy named François Cacault, a seasoned French diplomat, and with an ultimatum: if the pope did not sign it within five days, Bonaparte would withdraw his envoy (and, presumably, march on Rome). The five days went by without a signature, but Cacault left Rome for Paris with a new envoy from the pope—his forty-three-year-old secretary of state, Ercole Cardinal Consalvi—who was more flexible.

The signing of the Concordat on July 15, 1801, by the French and Papal envoys finally ended the French Revolution and defined Napoleon's consular regime. The First Consul of France was given the right to nominate French bishops, the bishoprics and parishes were redistributed, and the erection of seminaries was allowed. The pope condoned the actions of those who had acquired church property, and by way of compensation the French government would give the bishops and priests suitable salaries. The French government, however, unilaterally added to the Concordat provisions of "Gallican" tendencies, called the Organic Articles, which harked back to the seventeenth century, when *le roy Soleil* King Louis XIV had disputed the authority of the Holy See. In 1682, when Innocent XI was pope, a conclave of French bishops, led by Jacques-Bénigne Bossuet, had issued a defiant declaration with four "Gallican" Articles which asserted the independence of the French Catholic Church from Rome. France reasserted its "Gallican" freedom. The Concordat was officially promulgated at Easter 1802.[35]

Incredibly, Napoleon used his Concordat with the pope to make himself a saint by proxy. During the reign of Louis XVI, the king's birthday, August 25, had been celebrated as the national feast, the *fête de la Saint-Louis*. Napoleon replaced this Bourbon feast with a *fête de la Saint-Napoléon* on his own birthday, August 15. To please Napoleon, Pope Pius VII ordered his legate in France, Giovanni Battista Cardinal Caprara, to search the Roman Catholic Church's Book of Martyrs for a saint named

Napoleon, so that the First Consul's birthday could be celebrated on that day. Caprara found an ancient Egyptian Greek saint whose name was Neapolus. The pope formally declared that this Neapolus had been "martyred" in Alexandria by the Roman emperor Diocletian and fixed his feast on August 15, which was also the Feast of the Assumption of the Holy Virgin Mary and Napoleon's birthday. Saint Napoleon was pronounced the patron of warriors and bonapartistes. In 1805, when Napoleon was Emperor of the French, August 15 was proclaimed *la fête de la Saint-Napoléon* and made the French national holiday.[36]

Frank Richardson, however, thought that the feast of Saint Napoleon was fixed on the following day, August 16, because Catholics could not celebrate the feasts of two saints on the same day, and the Pope would not give up the Feast of the Assumption. Napoleon therefore settled on changing the *fête de la Saint-Roch* on August 16 into the *fête de la Saint-Napoléon*, "thus killing two birds with one stone, conveying a mark of Imperial displeasure to the curé of the parish of Saint Roch, who had refused a Christian burial to Mademoiselle Chameroy, a dancer at the Opera."[37] In fact, Napoleon's unconscious fear of being identified with Mary and of being a woman may have led him to force the pope to make this gesture. After the *Concordat* was signed in 1801, a month before his thirty-second birthday, Napoleon's chronic psychosomatic symptoms alleviated. He felt better. Still, it took no less than nine months for the Concordat to be ratified by the hostile tribunate and formally promulgated at Notre-Dame cathedral at Easter 1802.

Napoleon was still anxious. Fearing his own people, and especially their newspapers, he muzzled the French press. On September 29, 1801, First Consul Bonaparte signed a peace treaty with Portugal. Meanwhile, in Corsica, Napoleon's numerous enemies fought his *bonapartiste* supporters. Wishing to stamp out the Corsican cult of vendetta, on which he had been brought up, and fearing revenge from his Corsican enemies, on October 1 First Consul Bonaparte decreed the enrollment of three corps of scouts in the Corsican Golo and Liamone *départements*, complete with courts-martial and summary executions for "any brigand taken arms in hand, and any person presumed guilty of assassination from motives of revenge or in pursuance of inveterate family hatred." [38] When these drastic measures failed to suppress the Corsican *antibonapartistes*, Napoleon placed Corsica under the direct control of his police minister, Fouché.

After six months of talks between Lord Cornwallis for the United Kingdom of Great Britain and Ireland and Joseph Bonaparte for the

Republic of France, the Franco-British peace negotiations were successful. On March 25, 1802, Joseph Bonaparte and Lord Cornwallis signed the Treaty of Amiens. This short-lived peace treaty was guaranteed by Russia, Austria, and Prussia. It was cosigned by the Spanish ambassador, Señor Azzara, for the Kingdom of Spain, and by Rutger Jan Schimmelpenninck, the Dutch ambassador, for the "Batavian Republic." The treaty pointedly avoided the thorny questions of the French Belgian territories, the Savoy, Switzerland, and British-European trade. Great Britain was to return all its colonial conquests to France and her allies, except for Ceylon (Sri Lanka), taken from the Dutch, and Trinidad, taken from Spain. Within six months, Great Britain was to restore Alexandria to the Ottomans, Elba to France, and Malta to the Knights of St. John (the Knights Hospitaler). In return, France was to return Taranto to the Kingdom of Naples and Sicily, recognize the Republic of the Seven Ionian Islands off Greece, and respect the independence and territorial integrity of the Kingdom of Naples, Portugal, the "Batavian" Republic, and the papal states.

Despite the efforts of the treaty's British opponents like Charles Grey, William Eliott, and William Windham, who cried in Parliament that France had abolished marriage and had become "one universal brothel," the Treaty of Amiens was ratified in the British parliament—276 to 20 in the House of Commons and 122 to 16 in the House of Lords.[39] But the treaty was illusory. It was favorable to France, but neither side intended to honor its obligations. Raoul Brice called the Treaty of Amiens "a delusive peace."[40] Napoleon had not renounced his ambition of invading England, and King George III did not want peace with the "upstart Buonaparte."

On the surface, Josephine's feelings for Napoleon seemed to have changed since he had returned from Egypt and became First Consul of France. To please Napoleon, she gave up her lover, Hippolyte Charles, and some of her unsavory lady friends. On October 18, 1801, she wrote her mother: "Bonaparte . . . makes your daughter very happy. He is kind, amiable, in a word a charming man."[41] Napoleon, for one, began to take an interest in his wife's clothes. Vincent Cronin thought that "if he had done so earlier, there might have been no Hippolyte Charles."[42] Deeper below, however, the unhappy and ambivalent marital relationship was unchanged. One sign of trouble was that Napoleon consistently misspelled his wife's maiden name of Tascher, writing Tachère instead.[43] The error was not accidental. The French word *tache* means "stain," and *tacher* means "to stain." The word *tachère* thus means "a woman who stains."

Napoleon felt that Josephine had stained his reputation with her adultery. The error unconsciously expressed his bad feelings.

Sexual matters preoccupied First Consul Bonaparte. He decreed that unmarried French mothers would receive no help from the state because their behavior was contrary to good morals. Was he thinking of his mother's affair with Count Marbeuf when he was a child? He also created special criminal courts to try seditious organizations, rebellions, and plunder of all kinds without juries, without the right of appeal, and without recourse to annulment. As we have seen, Napoleon had a sadomasochistic side to his narcissistic personality. His sadomasochism was not sexual but emotional, and it was part and parcel of his narcissism.

Napoleon's imperial ambitions came out in the open in the winter of 1802. An obscure French colonel named Guillaume-Marie Ayral de Bonneville had published a pamphlet titled *Mon opinion sur la récompense due à Bonaparte* (My Opinion on the Reward due to Bonaparte), urging his people to proclaim Napoleon *premier empereur des Gaullois* (First Emperor of the Gauls) and to make the office hereditary in his family. Whether or not Ayral ever existed is unclear, but the French press began publishing articles expressing the same view. Public speeches were made glorifying the First Consul, letters written to the press and to the government asking that Napoleon be created *Empereur des François* (Emperor of the French). Vincent Cronin believed that "the wish to make Napoleon emperor originated in the French people's desire to acclaim the man they considered a hero, to raise him higher and higher. The feeling increased with each plot discovered."[44] In fact, that wish was no less Napoleon's own, and his minions got the press and the legislature to promote the idea.

Unhappy in his marriage, the thirty-two-year-old First Consul of France compulsively arranged other people's lives. He was already acting like an absolute monarch. He forced his twenty-three-year-old brother Louis Bonaparte to marry his adoptive stepdaughter, Hortense. Napoleon replaced his thirty-three-year-old embezzling personal secretary, Bourrienne, with the twenty-four-year-old nobleman Claude-François de Méneval, who had served Napoleon's brother, Joseph, during the negotiations for the treaty of Lunéville, the Concordat and the treaty of Amiens. Being Napoleon's personal secretary was a crushing job. Méneval had to work day and night, taking dictations by shorthand, writing Napoleon's letters, and filing his correspondence. For eleven years (1802–1813), Méneval was Napoleon's closest aide.

Having restored the Roman Catholic religion to France in the Concordat, Napoleon wanted to win over the former rebels and "enemies of the republic"—*vendéens*, *chouans*, and *émigrés*. On April 26, 1802, he issued a new amnesty to all the French *émigrés*—except those who had borne arms against Mother France in the service of her enemies—if they returned to France by September 23, 1802, and swore allegiance to his government. Having one's name on the list of *émigrés* was very dangerous for a Frenchman. If he returned to France, he could be tried for treason and executed. Forty thousand expatriate Frenchmen accepted Napoleon's amnesty, returned to France, were struck off the list of *émigrés*, and "swelled the ranks of the officer and professional classes."[45] One of them was Napoleon's old friend Alexandre des Mazis, who had lent Napoleon money in his hour of need and saved him from suicide. Des Mazis had emigrated from France in 1792 and had served in the *émigré* army of the Prince of Condé. Napoleon sent Des Mazis ten thousand francs and a handwritten note saying, "Des Mazis, you lent me money once; now it is my turn."[46] In fact, Des Mazis had lent Bonaparte money *twice*.[47]

While on the surface he had rational reasons for wanting to unify France and bring about a "fusion" between its warring political factions, Napoleon's treatment of the French *émigrés* and *vendéen* rebels was highly conflicted and ambivalent. Although he had granted an amnesty to the *vendéen* rebels and to the émigrés, his police arrested hundreds of expatriate noblemen who came back, including Louis-Alexandre de Launay d'Antraigues, and Joseph-Hilarion de Gautier du Vernègues, a secret agent of Louis XVIII, even though these two noblemen were attached to a foreign diplomatic mission. In 1800 General Gabriel-Marie-Théodore d'Hédouville, commanding the French republican forces in the Vendée, signed an armistice with the *vendéen* leaders Georges Cadoudal and Louis de Frotté. Napoleon broke General Hédouville's word of honor to the rebels by executing the forty-five-year-old count of Frotté. General Hédouville was furious with the First Consul. One Bourbon royalist leader, the forty-eight-year-old Louis-Guérin de Bruslart, wrote Napoleon a venomous letter: "Hail to you, who came out of the dust of the king's military schools."[48]

After the "infernal machine" attempt on his life in late 1801, an enraged Napoleon, believing that the royalist *émigrés* had betrayed his trust, had some one hundred former *émigrés* who lived peacefully in Paris arrested, including the young Louis-Auguste-Victor de Ghaisnes, *comte* de Bourmont, who had fought with the *vendéens* and had been in touch with the rebel general Pichegru, but who had honorably surrendered to Napoleon's government. Most of these noblemen were incarcerated in the notorious *Temple* prison. In 1804 Napoleon had the thirty-one-year-old Louis-Antoine-Henri de Bourbon-Condé, duke of Enghien, an *émigré* nobleman kidnaped from the German electorate of Baden, tried by a special military commission stacked with Napoleon's men, found guilty, condemned to death, and executed. Napoleon may have unconsciously projected his matricidal-guilt feelings and externalized his own "treacherous self" upon the *émigrés*, who had left "the motherland"[49]

In March 1802 Lucien Bonaparte took his place in the tribunate, where he helped push forward his elder brother's projects: the Concordat and the *ordre de la Légion d'honneur*. Lucien, a former interior minister, was elected president of the tribunate's interior section. He got the two projects passed for his brother. In July Lucien was elected an "organic" member of the Great Council of the Order of the Legion of Honor. At the urging of First Consul Bonaparte, on August 4 the Senate passed a *sénatus-consulte* which, among other things, made Lucien a Grand Officer of the Order of the Legion of Honor as well as a member of the senate. This *sénatus-consulte* became known as "the Constitution of the Year X."[50] Among other things, it gave First Consul Bonaparte the right to choose his own successor. Lucien's Mediterranean missions enriched his collection of famous paintings, while he led the good life at his château du Plessis and at his hôtel in the rue Saint-Dominique in Paris, where a court of artists, scholars, and writers assembled around him.[51]

The formerly hostile hundred-seat tribunate now had at least twenty members friendly to First Consul Bonaparte, including his own brother Lucien, who worked tirelessly on his behalf. On May 6, 1802, the tribunate extended the tenure of the First Consul to ten years. Its forty-four-year-old president, Georges-Antoine Chabot de l'Allier, invited the senate "to give the consuls a token of the national gratitude."[52] This, however, enraged the narcissistic Napoleon, who could not abide having to share his glory with his two colleagues. When a delegation of tribunes came to inform him of their decision, he warned them that if he personally were no longer in office, the republic would perish. In his unconscious mind, he and Mother France were one. On

May 8, by a vote of 61 to 2, the adoring—or fearful—senate ratified the tribunate's decision and elected Napoleon First Consul for another ten years—on top of the ten for which he had already been named. On May 10 the consulate decreed a plebiscite to decide whether to elect him consul for life.[53]

Bonaparte's police minister, Fouché, and other politicians secretly opposed the life consulship for the power-hungry Bonaparte. Nonetheless, Napoleon won this plebiscite hands down, with a more impressive landslide than that he had received two years earlier. Over three and half million Frenchmen voted "oui" while less than nine thousand voted "non." Obviously, the figures had been rigged—thanks to Lucien Bonaparte, the great manipulator. The fractious Corsicans, however, were not so enthusiastic about a life consulship for their native son, and there were more Coriscan *antibonapartistes* than *bonapartistes*. The governor of Corsica at the time of this plebiscite, André-François Miot de Melito, later observed that "if all the departments of France had been animated by the same spirit as those of Golo or Liamone, Bonaparte's rapid rise would perhaps have met with more obstacles"[54]

By making himself consul for life, however, and by identifying his own fate with that of France, Napoleon had put his own life in mortal danger: "the very phrase was an incitement to murder, as the regime still depended on the existence of Bonaparte."[55] As soon as Bonaparte became consul for life, the question of his succession began to haunt France. The narcissistic Napoleon hated this question and became very angry every time it was raised. For one thing, he unconsciously imagined that he was immortal, and the question of the succession threatened this fantasy. For another, he felt that he was unique, that nobody could be like him, that no one deserved to succeed him. The French legislators discussed whether Bonaparte should have the right to name his own successor. Napoleon "constantly brushed the question aside, but it was forever being presented to him to the pitch of an obsession."[56]

Since Josephine could not give him a son, however, Napoleon's brothers Joseph, Lucien and Louis were naturally among those most interested in succeeding him. He, however, would not hear of it: "if there was one thing that Napoleon detested in was the idea of bequeathing his power to his brothers. Why should he? What claim had they?"[57] In late 1800 an angry Napoleon "exiled" Lucien to Spain as France's ambassador for raising the taboo subject in public. He would later exile Lucien from France seriously and permanently for having defied his will in his personal life. In

1804 Napoleon's mother Letizia did not attend his coronation as emperor, preferring to be at Lucien's side in Italy.

Unhappy in his personal life, Napoleon did not know how to conquer his own suffering and melancholy brought on by his tormented love for Josephine. He often wished to die, and several times to kill himself; but he never did. Instead, he kept suffering. On May 12, 1802, Napoleon learned that one of his consular guards had killed himself. This must have evoked painful memories of his own depressions and suicidal wishes in 1786 and in 1795. The anxious Napoleon tried to delegalize suicide: "The grenadier Grobain has killed himself for love. Otherwise he was a very good citizen. This is the second time in a month that such an event has occurred in the Guards. On command of the First Consul the following is put into the order of the day: that a soldier must know how to conquer the suffering and the melancholy brought on by the passions."[58]

Napoleon's tyrannical personality never ceased to provoke some of his countrymen. During the winter of 1801–1802, after First Consul Bonaparte had stacked the tribunate with his own men, yet another plot to assassinate him was hatched, this time by some Jacobin officers of General Bernadotte's *armée de l'Ouest*, led by General Edouard-François Simon, Bernadotte's chief of staff. The Jacobins had the support of at least six generals—Bernadotte, Moreau, Augereau, Lecourbe, Delmas, and Simon. [59] Bonaparte's police arrested a group of republican officers who had distributed anti-Bonaparte pamphlets at the Breton capital of Rennes calling First Consul Bonaparte a tyrant and exhorting the soldiers to rise up against him. Bernadotte and Joseph Bonaparte, who were brothers-in-law, may have been involved in that plot. [60]

The Rennes plotters planned to act on Easter Sunday, April 18, 1802, when First Consul Bonaparte was to celebrate republican France's first religious holiday, its reunion with the Roman Catholic Church, at Notre Dame cathedral in Paris with a *Te Deum* by his favorite composer, the sixty-two-year-old Giovanni Paisiello. The sixty-nine-year-old Cardinal Caprara officiated at this Solemn Restoration of Public Worship. The assassination plot fell through when Bonaparte's consular guards overpowered the conspirators. The rebel officers were arrested and charged with plotting to overthrow the legitimate government. Their leader was General Simon, chief of staff of the *armée de l'Ouest*, who may have taken the fall for his boss. The Rennes Plot was derisively called *la conspiration des libelles* (the lampoons plot) or *le complot des pots-de-beurre* (the butter-pot conspiracy). Some scholars believed that all that the plotters had done in reality was to send anti-Napoleon pamphlets from Rennes to Paris in butter pots. In fact, the plot had been much more serious.[61] Jacques Garnier believed that General Bernadotte was the real culprit in the Rennes plot, but that his friend, Police Minister Fouché, who was himself among the plotters, covered up his involvement.[62] Certain it is that both Bernadotte and Fouché later joined Napoleon's enemies.

Napoleon gradually annexed or took over the lands adjacent to France. In the summer of 1802 First Consul Bonaparte, the *de facto* ruler of the "independent" Helvetic Republic, detached the Valais, a key passage from France into Italy, from that republic, and made it into a separate republic. He called it the *République du Valais* or *République Rhodanique* (after the Latin name of the River Rhone which flows through it) and forced it to give his armies permanent right of passage in the Rhone valley. On September 11 the French Senate issued a *sénatus-consulte* annexing the Piedmont to France, which already occupied it. Jacques Bainville believed that this annexation was "an idea and outcome of the Revolution,"[63] as were the creation of the "Italian Republic," the occupation of Holland and Belgium, and the creation of the Germanic Confederation of the Rhine. In fact, the annexation of the Piedmont was a unilateral act, in the midst of peace, and without negotiations with any other state. It was an act of aggression, violating the principles of international politics such as natural frontiers and the rights of peoples to rule themselves. This annexation led to the resumption of the Franco-British war the following spring.

Jacques Bainville thought that Napoleon's annexations and manipulations of France's neighboring lands made his countrymen glorify and deify him: "from all sides, by the natural plays of forces, the First Consul was brought to heights of greatness which lacked nothing now but the supreme consecration. An apotheosis was beginning from which he reaped the good grain of his sowing before he reaped the bad."[64] This astute biographer, however, was troubled by whether Bonaparte was a great peacemaker or a great warmonger: "And with that, a doubt, an enigma, rises to the mind. Had Bonaparte shared the illusion of other Frenchmen? Did he believe that the Revolution was completed, abroad as at home? Did he believe in a definitive peace? Did he wish for a resumption [of the war with Great Britain] because his authority and renown were linked up with war? It would be in vain to try to fathom his intentions and his conscience."[65] While Napoleon's conscious intention was to magnify and glorify France, his unconscious purpose was to magnify and glorify himself, to feel immortal and omnipotent—so as not to feel little, fearful, mortal, and impotent.

In the fall of 1802 the thirty-three-year-old First Consul Bonaparte removed the forty-three-year-old Police Minister Joseph Fouché from his post. Bonaparte's police prefect, Louis-Nicolas Dubois, who had arrested the Rennes conspirators, and his police minister, Fouché, were archrivals. Fouché had secretly opposed and worked against the life consulate for Bonaparte. This angered Napoleon, who felt that he fully deserved this consulate, and that Fouché, whom he had given his job, was ungrateful and disloyal. Dubois told Bonaparte that General Bernadotte had been in on the Rennes plot and that Fouché had covered up for him. Bonaparte relieved Bernadotte of his command of the *armée de l'Ouest*, but, ostensibly because he was the husband of Napoleon's former love, Désirée, did not put him on trial, and two years later elevated him to marshal. It was another self-destructive act on Napoleon's part. Bernadotte would repeatedly fail him in battle and ultimately topple him from his throne.

Dubois' intrigues against Fouché finally succeeded. One of Fouché's enemies, beside Joseph, Lucien and Talleyrand, was Pierre-Louis Roederer, the political journalist and Bonaparte's state councillor. Roederer, who often disagreed with Bonaparte, had upset him by opposing his wish to name his own successor, by his close ties to Napoleon's brothers, and by refusing to work with Napoleon's interior minister, Jean-Antoine-Claude Chaptal de Chanteloup. An angry Napoleon decided to to rid himself of Fouché and Roederer at the same time. On September 13, 1802, using the pretext of the Treaty of Amiens, the three consuls formally abolished Fouché's police ministry. Fouché and Roederer were kicked upstairs to the senate. Police functions came under the *grand juge*, the French justice minister. The fifty-two-year-old Grand Juge André-Joseph Abrial, who had served since the beginning of the consulate in 1799, was replaced by the fifty-six-year-old Claude-Ambroise Regnier, whom Bonaparte considered better suited and more loyal.[66]

18

Taking on England

Around the time of his 33rd birthday Napoleon, who had already had several mistresses, began a new affair with the fifteen-year-old actress Mademoiselle George. Her real name was Marguerite-Joseph Weymer (or Marguerite-Joséphine Weimer), but she had adopted the anglicized form of her father's Christian name as her stage name.[1] She was apparently bisexual and emotionally disturbed, the daughter of a traveling-theater director and a singer. Marguerite-Joseph had been noticed and promoted by a prominent, masculine and lesbian actress, Mademoiselle Raucourt, whose real name was Françoise-Marie-Antoinette Saucerotte, and who picked her up and became her protectress. Following the popular theatrical custom of adopting stage names, the teenage actress took the name of Mademoiselle George.[2] Mademoiselle George had made her theatrical debut as Clytemnestra in Racine's tragedy *Iphigénie en Aulide*. She was "a big, strapping girl with burning dark eyes. Napoleon considered her the best actress in Paris."[3] The next day Napoleon sent his valet Constant Wairy to invite Mademoiselle George to his castle at Saint-Cloud. She accepted on condition that Napoleon's valet pick her up at the theater, "so that no one would fail to see what was happening."[4]

Frank Richardson thought that "Mademoiselle George's outstanding quality was her ability to make the First Consul laugh."[5] In fact, the teenage actress had several other *unconscious* attractions for Napoleon. First, she had begun her sexual career at the age of fourteen with the twenty-eight-year-old actor Pierre Lafon, who was also one of Pauline Bonaparte's lovers, and she had also had affairs with Napoleon's younger brother Lucien Bonaparte and with the twenty-nine-year-old Polish price Aleksander Antoni Leon Konstanty Sapieha, her current lover. Through her, Napoleon could unconsciously have an incestuous affair with his own sister. Second, her first name, Marguerite-Joseph, combined those of Napoleon's adoptive "mother" at Brienne, *la mère Marguerite*, and that of his elder brother, Joseph. Third, she was a pubescent girl who did not threaten him as an engulfing mother. Fourth, Mademoiselle George had another lover, Prince Sapieha, which made it possible for him to act out his oedipal conflict with her. Mademoiselle George's sexual ties with Napoleon's younger brother Lucien and with the young Polish prince may have excited Napoleon's unconscious fantasies: he was going to take his young "sister" away from his rival brothers.

In her old age Mademoiselle George claimed that Napoleon invited her to his castle at Saint-Cloud and kept her there for four nights, and that "nothing happened" during the first two nights,[6] and that when Napoleon learned that her veil was a gift from her lover, Prince Sapieha, he became madly jealous and "tore it into a thousand little pieces."[7] She told him that her name was Marguerite-Joséphine. As he had done with Désirée, Josephine and other women, Napoleon invented his own name for her: Giorgina. This way she was not the big, masculine and threatening "George" but the little "Giorgina." She had dainty hands but big feet. Napoleon hated fat women with "crude extremities."[8] They unconsciously reminded him of his mother's big body when he was an infant. "With his genius for making hurtful remarks," she claimed that he said to her: "You must have hideous feet for you keep your stockings on."[9]

On the third night of their meetings Napoleon finally made love to his teenage mistress, but he treated her like a mother rather than like a wife or a daughter. The sadomasochistic Mademoiselle George, who may have been used to physical violence in her sexual relations, was disappointed: "He played the little boy and the child to please me. He was no longer the Consul. He was a man in love, perhaps, but it was a love in which violence and roughness had no part."[10] Napoleon reportedly invented an elastic garter for "Giorgina" because her buckle garter was hard for him to open.[11] Before leaving for his *Camp de Boulogne* on the English channel, whence he wanted to direct his invasion of England in 1803, he gave her forty thousand francs, "slipping the packet of bank notes between her breasts."[12] They sat on the carpet of the library and played like the little children that, emotionally, they were.[13]

During one of Napoleon's nocturnal assignations with Mademoiselle George in his Saint-Cloud apartments, the teenage actress saw him have what she called an "epileptic-like seizure."[14] Napoleon's "epilepsy," however, may have been a pituitary-gland disorder, a symptom of venereal disease, a temporary loss of consciousness due to heart blockage, his physical expression of his sexual excitement, or his body's twitching during an orgasm. Mademoiselle George, who was undressed, became "terrified that her lover was dead and that she would be accused of murdering him."[15] Rather than get dressed and try to waken Napoleon, she panicked and began to scream. This caused Josephine and Napoleon's valets to rush upstairs, where they witnessed the embarrassing scene. "When Napoleon came to and realized the situation he fell into such a rage that onlookers thought he was going to have a second fit."[16] Frank Richardson thought that Napoleon "never quite forgave [Mademoiselle George] for arousing the Palace in her alarm, for he hated to be made to look ridiculous, and on this occasion he most certainly was."[17] After this incident the First Consul avoided Mademoiselle George.

By early 1803 France's relations with Great Britain began deteriorating. The Treaty of Amiens was illusory. The British press began the war on France before its government did. On January 18 *The Times* published a favorable review of a defamatory book by the twenty-five-year-old British officer Robert Thomas Wilson about the Egyptian campaign, which accused Bonaparte of having massacred the Ottoman soldiers at Jaffa and of having killed his own plague-stricken men.[18] On February 1 *The Morning Post* vilified Napoleon as "an unclassifiable being, half-African, half-European, a Mediterranean mulatto."[19] When these newspapers reached Napoleon, his unjust criticism by England echoed in his unconscious mind with his unjust punishments by his mother when he was a child.

Enraged with England for her unjust attack on him, Napoleon wanted to make his Good Mother France strong enough to take on Bad Mother England. Great Britain's continued occupation of Malta, coupled with its hold on Gibraltar, gave him a *casus belli*. On February 15, 1803, he said, "Of all the calamities that could happen to the French people, none is comparable to that one."[20] In mid-February the thirty-three-year-old First Consul Bonaparte summoned the fifty-year-old British ambassador, Charles, Lord Whitworth, to the Tuileries Palace and presented him with an ultimatum. Unless the British evacuated Malta and Alexandria forthwith, France would go to war with England.

On March 8, 1803, King George III sat on his throne in London and made a speech to his parliament, preparing it for war with France. The news quickly reached Paris. A few days later, First Consul Bonaparte invited Lord Whitworth to a reception attended by the entire Paris diplomatic corps at the Tuileries Palace. When Napoleon saw Whitworth at the reception, he was overwhelmed by his narcissistic rage. In totally undiplomatic fashion, Bonaparte accosted the British ambassador, dressed him down, and upbraided him for England's perfidy.[21] Screaming and threatening in gross language, and shaking with rage, the First Consul of France attacked King George's speech from the throne and shouted, "If the English are the first to draw the sword, I shall be last to return it to the scabbard! Treaties must be respected. Woe to those who violate them!"[22] Napoleon gave Whitworth a public dressing-down in front of the entire diplomatic corps, which watched the scene "mute with astonishment and fear." [23]

It was an embarrassing and frightening scene. Lord Whitworth himself, who remained silent during Bonaparte's *algarade*, later recalled it with disdain.[24] Some scholars thought that this outburst of rage was conscious playacting designed to bully the British, and that the scene had been planned and carefully controlled by Napoleon. Frank Richardson thought that Napoleon "gave a performance worthy of Hitler" and deliberately tried "to provoke Lord Whitworth into appearing to play the part of the aggressor."[25] It was more likely an uncontrollable outburst of rage. Whitworth himself had written his government that Bonaparte used expressions "too trivial and vulgar to find a place in a dispatch, or anywhere but in the mouth of a hackney coachman."[26]

Nevertheless, Napoleon still hoped that England would opt for peace. He still believed that France's illusory peace with England would last. His profound ambivalence for his mother was unconsciously displaced to England. Jacques Bainville thought that "never did Bonaparte show more vacillation."[27] On March 13, 1803, after his public outburst at Lord Whitworth, Napoleon told his elder brother Joseph that he had been in a bad mood when he came to the reception, had not felt like attending, and had been wrong to treat Whitworth as he did.[28] Napoleon's ambivalence about Great Britain was as profound as his mixed feelings for his mother. During his outburst of rage at the British ambassador, Lord Whitworth, he felt guilty and "softened, as if he were still anxious to preserve peace, and then broke out afresh when he perceived that soft words were useless."[29] Bonaparte later even tried to be civil to Whitworth. On March 17 the British ambassador wrote home confidently: "I can say with absolute certainty that no armaments of any consequence are carrying on in the French ports . . . the First Consul has no desire to go to war."[30]

In the Treaty of Amiens, the British had undertaken to restore France's Indian territories to her. Trusting in this, Bonaparte sent a naval squadron bearing the thirty-three-year-old general Charles-Mathieu-Isidore Decaen, the *capitaine général* of the French establishments in India, and a division to recover the French Indian trading ports, such as Pondicherry on the Coromandel Coast in southeastern India, the former capital of French India, which the British had taken from France. Decaen reached Pondicherry in July but was met with a barrage of British gunfire: the war between France and Great Britain had resumed two months earlier.[31]

The war party in London had won the battle. A new French war with England had become inevitable. The issue of Malta was the pretext. Unconsciously, both sides needed war to avoid mourning their losses and to heal their narcissistic injuries. On May 1, 1803, Lord Whitworth gave an "offer of agreement" to Talleyrand: Great Britain would keep Malta for another ten years and keep the nearby island of Lampedusa forever. France was to evacuate Holland at once. Lord Whitworth gave Talleyrand seven days to deliver his reply, or else Whitworth would leave France.[32]

The British "offer of agreement" was a humiliating ultimatum. Napoleon could not allow himself to lose face—or to feel helpless—by accepting it. His reaction was twofold: to make a counteroffer to the British—and to sell the Louisiana Territory to the United States. Bonaparte told Talleyrand, "I don't want the conference to turn into a sharing of the spoils. Be chilly, aloof, and even a bit proud. If the note contains the word 'ultimatum,' make him understand that the word implies war—that his manner of negotiating is that of a superior with an inferior. If the note does not contain that word, see that he puts it in. Tell him we have to know how things stand—that we have had enough of this state of anxiety."[33] On Napoleon's instructions, Talleyrand made a "counteroffer" to Whitworth: France would let England keep Malta "for three or four years" after which it would pass to one of the powers guaranteeing the Treaty of Amiens—Russia, Austria, or Prussia.

The sale of the Louisiana Territory in North America to the United States, known as the Louisiana Purchase, was Napoleon's second reaction to the British ultimatum. He did not believe that "England" would accept his counteroffer. France's war with Britain had become a certainty. The

British Royal Navy had grown by leaps and bounds since 1789. Preparing for war with France, it patrolled the coast of New Orleans. Fearing an imminent British invasion of the Louisiana Territory, Bonaparte sold it to the United States.[34]

By May 1803 Napoleon's conflict with England had escalated beyond repair. The diplomatic "conference" between Whitworth and Talleyrand led to nought. On May 2 Lord Whitworth asked for his passports. On May 12 Great Britain repudiated the Treaty of Amiens and withdrew its ambassador, Lord Whitworth, from Paris. The final rupture came on May 16, when First Consul Bonaparte formally broke France's diplomatic relations with Great Britain. To the Prussian ambassador to France, the fifty-one-year-old Luccan nobleman Geronimo Lucchesini, Napoleon boasted grandly of his imminent conquest of *l'Angleterre*. "I am going to risk the most difficult but most fruitful undertaking in terrifying results ever conceived by politics. In three days' time, some foggy weather and somewhat favorable circumstances can make me the master of London, of Parliament, of the Bank."[35]

On May 20, 1803, First Consul Bonaparte, in a message to the senate, Legislative Corps, and tribunate, made war with *l'Angleterre* official. On May 23 Great Britain declared war on France. [36] On June 14 Bonaparte created his *grande armée d'Angleterre*, with its headquarters at Boulogne-sur-Mer on the English Channel, also known as the *armée de Boulogne*. He was seriously planning an invasion of England. Vincent Cronin wrote, "For the next twelve years Europe was to reek with the acrid smell of gunpowder"[37] He forgot to mention the sickening smell of rotting corpses.

Napoleon's compulsive need to dominate others repeatedly set them against him, especially those who could not stand to be dominated because to them—as to him—it meant feeling unbearably helpless. These people included some of France's generals, such as Moreau and Bernadotte, who never ceased to hate Bonaparte in their hearts and to plot against him. In August 1803 their vague designs against the First Consul coincided with a real conspiracy to assassinate him. The chief plotters were two Breton generals, the forty-two-year-old Jean-Charles Pichegru and by the thirty-two-year-old Georges Cadoudal. This plot ended with the deaths of both Pichegru and Cadoudal the following year.

The unending plots against him caused a wary Napoleon to increasingly censor the French press. On September 27, 1803, he issued a consular decree that was pure Orwellian Newspeak: "To ensure the liberty of the press [*sic*], no bookseller can sell a work before presenting it to a commission of revision."[38] Unhappy in love, pursued by his plotting enemies, and fighting his unconscious feelings of worthlessness, Napoleon sought solace in grandiose fantasies. He wanted to build a monument to Charlemagne, his idealized self. On October 5, the eighth anniversary of his Vendémiaire triumph, he decreed: "There shall be raised in Paris, in the middle of the Place Vendôme, a column on the scale of the one erected in Rome in honor of Trajan . . . The column will be capped by a pedestal bearing the pedestrian statue of Charlemagne."[39] Did the great column symbolize an erect penis in Napoleon's unconscious mind, calming his profound fears of impotence and inferiority?

As he could have foreseen, Napoleon's preparations for an invasion of England in 1803 were fruitless. Just as it had been five years earlier, his invasion plan was irrational vengeful fantasy. At sea, the French admirals were repeatedly defeated by British ones. The French navy progressively lost its self-confidence. The British Royal Navy patrolled the French coasts. Napoleon blamed all his naval defeats on his rigid and conservative admirals, who repeatedly rejected his innovations, telling him that he did not understand the navy. In fact, First Consul Bonaparte was in charge of his navy as well as of his army. He named its chiefs; he was responsible for its actions. But, unable to stand his painful feelings of shame and humiliation, he unconsciously sought scapegoats for his own failures. Like many narcissistic people, when under stress Napoleon boosted his own self-esteem by putting down others.

Napoleon's vendetta against *l'Angleterre* was so personal and irrational that even his admirer Raoul Brice asked rhetorically "what could he hope from war with England but the appeasement of his soul?"[40] When he inevitably failed, he conceived the irrational "Continental System," which lasted from 1806 to 1814, hoping to strangle "England" through a "continental blockade" that ultimately failed as well. Harold Parker thought that "at one point the blockade of England nearly succeeded until Napoleon himself relaxed it."[41] If this is so, the relaxation indicated his profound ambivalence about England.

Napoleon's narcissistic perfectionism never let him enjoy himself for long. He was never happy with his achievements and was consumed with the fire of his own ambition, his grandiose self demanding ever greater "glory," that is, defeating the "enemy" and conquering his lands; but Napoleon had signed a peace treaty with Great Britain, his chief enemy; he provoked the British into war by humiliating the British ambassador and by making impossible demands. Many Frenchmen were unenthusiastic about Napoleon's wars. In 1803 there were 108 *départements* in France, with a total population of 33 million people. Many young Frenchmen failed to show up for military service. An anticonscription revolt broke out in the Maine-et-Loire, the Vendée and the Deux-Sèvres. As Napoleon became more frightened and angry, his rule became harsher. On October 12, 1803, Napoleon decreed the creation of eleven "military depots" to detain the conscripts who would be condemned as "refractory."[42]

Six years earlier, Napoleon's sister Pauline Bonaparte had married General Charles-Victor-Emmanuel Leclerc. Five years after her wedding, however, she lost her husband. The young general, who was with his wife at the French Caribbean island of Saint-Domingue (now Haiti), died of the yellow fever on November 2, 1802. The "hysterical" Pauline, unable to mourn her loss, reacted theatrically: she cut off her hair and placed it in her dead husband's coffin, had the physicians excise her husband's heart and embalm it, then placed it in a sealed urn and took it with her back to France for burial.[43]

Pauline's grief did not last very long, however. On August 31, 1803, before the end of the one-year period of widowhood mandated by her brother's Civil Code, the twenty-two-year-old Pauline married the twenty-eight-year-old Roman prince Camillo Borghese, who had been "more scared than astonished" to receive the marriage proposal.[44] Napoleon had wanted his sister to wait until her obligatory widowhood was over, but she did not. Pauline and Camillo were married at Joseph Bonaparte's castle of Mortefontaine. The First Consul, from his *camp de Boulogne* on the English Channel, wrote Pauline: "Love your husband, make your home happy and above all do not be light and capricious. You are twenty-four years old, you should be ripe and sensible."[45] In fact, Pauline was not yet twenty-three, and, far from being "ripe and sensible," she was immature and impulsive, if not promiscuous.

Whether the Borghese marriage was "consummated" is uncertain: when she left her husband in Rome some time later, Pauline said that Camillo was impotent. On November 14, 1803, the newlyweds left Paris for Rome. Napoleon once more offered unsolicited advice to Pauline:

"Conform to the customs of the country; never run down anything; find everything splendid; and don't say, 'We do this better in Paris.'"[46] In Rome, Camillo and Pauline lived in the magnificent Villa Borghese. Pauline, however, did not like Rome and wanted to return to Paris. She loved her brother Napoleon much more than she did her husband. Like an infant, she was narcissistic and sexually perverse. Pauline had a "foot fetish," and also adored other women's breasts. "Inordinately proud of her small feet she spent hours caring for and perfuming them, and her pedicure was often performed in public with the help of a page. She loved to caress the breasts of her ladies-in-waiting, with her feet. This sent them in to squeals of sensuous ecstasy; and it presumably 'did something' for Pauline."[47]

Pauline's blind adoration for Napoleon did not repair his self-esteem. Less than absolute power made him feel powerless. Napoleon's rule grew increasingly oppressive. His police ministry had a special secret-police division. Afraid of assassination plots, he governed France with a repressive regime of fear. The press was muzzled and censored, plays banned, individual liberties curtailed. In 1810 Emperor Napoleon began to censor books as well. Vincent Cronin thought that Napoleon's censorship was "part of a general attempt to safeguard first principles."[48] In late 1811 Napoleon ordered his censors to ban only "positively libelous works" and to "let writers speak freely on everything else."[49]

When he did not feel threatened, however, Napoleon was generous and permissive. The French theater, which did not threaten him as did books and newspapers, flourished under Napoleon, who had several actresses as mistresses. As Emperor of the French, he revoked the ban on his favorite plays—Molière's *Tartuffe*, Corneille's *Polyeucte*, Racine's *Athalie*, and Corneille's *Cinna*, which he saw at least twelve times. The *Directoire exécutif* had banned *Cinna* because it contained the line "the worst of states is the popular one," which it considered offensive, seditious and antirepublican.[50]

19

Kidnapping and Executing a Young Duke

Napoleon's obsession with invading *l'Angleterre* kept him at his English Channel headquarters, the *camp de Boulogne*, until early 1804. It was perhaps a good unconscious excuse to leave the unloving Josephine. When he returned to Paris, he had no peace either. In May 1804 King George III replaced his prime minister, Henry Addington, with his predecessor, William Pitt the Younger. The new British cabinet, presided over by Pitt, put all its hopes, not only in the English coastal batteries, but also in the conspiracy under way in Paris. With British help, the *chouan* generals Georges Cadoudal and Jean-Charles Pichegru were plotting to assassinate First Consul Bonaparte. Cadoudal was a big man of Napoleon's age. On August 20, 1803, five days after Bonaparte's thirty-fourth birthday, a Spanish brig deposed him and some fellow plotters at the Norman coastal town of Biville.[1] The plotters moved on to Paris and prepared to murder First Consul Bonaparte.

On January 16, 1804, thirty-five French *émigrés* in the pay of the British government secretly disembarked in France and soon joined Cadoudal in Paris. They included General Pichegru, Armand-Jules-Marie-Heraclitus, Duke of Polignac, his younger brother Auguste-Jules-Armand-Marie, Prince of Polignac, Charles-François Riffardeau de Rivière, and some thirty lesser accomplices. Soon thereafter the police apprehended several *chouans*, who were quickly tried, found guilty, and sentenced to death. Among them was a health officer who, under torture and threat of execution, confessed to being a secret agent for the French *émigrés* in London.[2] The desperate captive offered information on his accomplices in exchange for his life. He revealed that Pichegru, Moreau, and Cadoudal had been plotting to assassinate Bonaparte, and that Cadoudal was in Paris with sixty men determined to carry out the assassination. He gave a precise description of Cadoudal: "Height 5 *pieds*, 3 to 4 *pouces* (173–176 cm), very powerful, big-bellied, handsome fresh color, white and colored, grey eyes, clear chestnut hair combed Titus style, broken nose scarred at the top, rather wide below, large ears, very white teeth (he is missing one on the side but that is not apparent), disheveled beard. He marches while balancing himself, his arms extended."[3]

Thanks to the tortured men's confessions, the police quickly arrested Cadoudal's second in command, Athanase-Hyacinthe Bouvet de Lozier, who, under torture, unsuccessfully tried to kill himself. Under the shock of his own suicide attempt, he admitted that Cadoudal and Pichegru were in Paris. After the dramatic confessions of the captured plotters, First Consul Bonaparte's police desperately sought their ringleader, Georges Cadoudal, in Paris. Fouché's police ministry had been abolished in 1802, and all police functions were under the justice ministry, headed by the fifty-four-year-old Grand Juge Claude-Ambroise Regnier. The acting police chief, the forty-seven-year-old Pierre-François Réal, who had failed to succeed Fouché two years earlier, told First Consul Bonaparte that he had only uncovered a quarter of this affair.[4] Réal's police had no qualms about using torture to obtain information. The confessions brought up false accusations against a thirty-two-year-old *émigré* nobleman named Louis-Antoine-Henri de Bourbon-Condé, Duke of Enghien, the only son and heir of the ninth Prince of Condé.[5]

The names Enghien, Condé, and Bourbon had been linked since the sixteenth century. Condé was the name of a major branch of the House of Bourbon, as well as of no less than five French towns. The ancestral castle of the princes of Condé was at the Walloon town of Enghien (Edingen), southwest of Brussels, in the French-speaking Belgian province of Hainaut, which belonged to the Franco-Belgian Duke of Arenberg. Just as the Prince of Wales is the hereditary title of the firstborn son of the king or queen of the United Kingdom, so the Duke of Enghien was the hereditary title of the firstborn son of the Prince of Condé. When the Prince of Condé died, the Duke of Enghien became the next Prince of Condé. Even after the ancestral castle of the Condés was sold to the House of Arenberg in the early seventeenth century, the princes of Condé still bore the title of Duke of Enghien.

The Duke of Enghien had actually been born in the castle of the princes of Condés at Chantilly, north of Paris, on August 2, 1772. He had been raised as a French nobleman. Like many other royalist noblemen, he had emigrated with his father and grandfather in 1789, at the height of the revolution, and had then followed his grandfather to various cities which were successively taken by the armies of France, including the Belgian cities of Mons and Brussels, the Piedmontese capital of Turin, the Rhenish German city of Worms, which was annexed to France in 1797, and the Austrian city of Graz , before settling in the Baden town of Ettenheim, east of the Rhine, forty kilometers south of Strasbourg.

Napoleon was very upset about the plot by Cadoudal, Moreau, and Pichegru, in which Bernadotte might have been involved. He considered the plotters ungrateful "brigands" and "assassins." On February 14, 1804, First Consul Bonaparte called a special session of his inner circle, the restricted State Council, to discuss the plot against him and the role in it of the Duke of Enghien. Tragically, this meeting was attended by Napoleon's former police minister, Joseph Fouché, whose knowledge and power Napoleon irrationally feared. Fouché accused not only Moreau, Cadoudal, and Pichegru, but also the innocent Duke of Enghien of complicity in the plot against Napoleon. The council decided to arrest Cadoudal, Moreau, and Pichegru and the Duke of Enghien on charges of plotting to assassinate the first consul.

On February 15, 1804, Réal's police arrested General Moreau. He admitted only that he had been told about the plot, not that he had taken any part in it. General Pichegru, whom Bonaparte's police sought all over Paris, was apprehended ten days later. On March 9 the chief plotter, Georges Cadoudal, was arrested by the police. The "terrible" Georges had left his hiding place in the back of a Paris fruit shop, disguised as a market porter and accompanied by an accomplice. A sharp-eyed policemen had noticed the porter's resemblance to Cadoudal's description and given the alert.

While First Consul Bonaparte lived in the castle of Saint-Cloud near Paris, the Duke of Enghien lived quietly in Ettenheim, in the electorate and grand duchy of Baden, a part of the Holy Roman Empire of the German nation. Like his father, the Prince of Condé, the duke did not like Napoleon's regime, but neither had he been plotting to kill the first consul. The duke was a handsome man and, unlike Napoleon, he bore himself gracefully. The duplicitous—and envious—Fouché and Talleyrand both manipulated Bonaparte in this affair, hoping that it would bring about his downfall. After Fouché had falsely pointed the finger at the Duke of Enghien, Talleyrand urged Napoleon to have the Duke kidnaped in Baden, tried in Paris, condemned to death, and guillotined.[6]

Siding with the *bonapartistes*, Vincent Cronin believed that Napoleon had the legal right to kidnap the Duke of Enghien: "The Duc d'Enghien was a Frenchman born and bred. He happened to be living in Germany, but as a Frenchman he was subject to French law. Already sufficient evidence had come in to show a *prima facie* case against him; his private papers and questioning might reveal more."[7] In fact, abducting the duke from Baden violated the sovereignty of the sixty-six-year-old Carl Friedrich, Grand Duke and Elector of Baden, whose government, before giving the Duke of Enghien political asylum, had formally asked for and received the consent of the French government.[8]

In March 1804, as Napoleon secretly prepared to kidnap the Duke of Enghien, his mother Letizia left him and Paris and headed for Rome. Letizia had sided with her younger son Lucien in his quarrel with Napoleon. On May 24, 1803, Lucien's lover, the widow Alexandrine Jacob de Bleschamp Jouberthon, had given birth to a baby boy fathered by Lucien. The next day, Lucien, who three years earlier had lost his first wife, Christine Boyer, secretly married Madame Jouberthon, one of the most beautiful women in France who had reportedly resisted Napoleon's own advances. Lucien had assumed his paternal responsibility by marrying the mother of his child. But Napoleon was furious. The woman who had rejected him had made love to his younger brother, born him a son, and become his wife. This revived Napoleon's painful early feelings about his rejection by his mother.

Lucien Bonaparte, who by now had a child by Alexandrine, and who rightly felt that he had been instrumental in his elder brother's accession to power, angrily refused Napoleon's demand that he divorce his second wife and marry the widowed queen of Etruria. The furious Napoleon banished Lucien from France and refused him the title of a prince. An equally furious Lucien cursed Napoleon's coming "dynastic monarchy" and left in a huff. In Rome, Letizia Bonaparte was warmly received by Napoleon's antagonist, Pope Pius VII, and was soon joined by her younger son Lucien and his wife Alexandrine. In May 1804 Letizia and Lucien learned of the proclamation of the empire in France and of Napoleon becoming Emperor. Letizia "kept a cool head."[9] She supported Lucien against Napoleon, who was deeply hurt by his mother taking his brother's side. Letizia stayed away from Napoleon's coronation, inflicting on him another deep emotional wound that Dorothy Carrington called "the crowning injury" of Napoleon's life.[10]

Despite his apparent firmness with his advisers, the ambivalent First Consul Bonaparte vacillated for four days before making up his mind to arrest the Duke of Enghien. While he rationally knew that abducting the young duke would violate the sovereignty of Grand Duke Carl Friedrich, the elector of Baden, provoking an outcry across Europe, his narcissistic rage got the better of him. On the night of March 14–15, 1804, the Duke of Enghien was kidnaped and taken to the castle of Vincennes. On the night of March 20–21 he was tried by a special French military tribunal, headed by the ruthless thirty-year-old General Anne-Jean-Marie-René Savary and stacked with Bonaparte's henchmen. The duke was found guilty of treason and immediately executed, having been denied the right to appeal his verdict or sentence.[11] It was one of the most fateful and self-destructive decisions of Napoleon's life, and the one for which he has been attacked and criticized most often over the past two centuries.

In his memoirs, Napoleon's elder brother Joseph Bonaparte claimed that he had tried to save the Duke of Enghien from execution. On March 20, 1804, Joseph later recalled, after he learned that Napoleon had ordered the duke tried for treason, he hurried to his younger brother, and tried to talk him out of his mad scheme:

> Joseph found Napoleon at [the castle of] Malmaison. "I reminded him of his political principles, which put him above all factions . . . I recalled to him the circumstances under which he entered the artillery after the encouragement given me by the Prince of Condé . . . in 1783, at the collège d'Autun." [Joseph] reminded [Napoleon] of their teacher's poem: "Condé! such a name! The universe reveres it." Napoleon was taken aback. He sat silent, making nervous movements, avoiding Joseph's eyes. The Duke is no leader of a movement, Joseph told him; his father and grandfather are alive! Napoleon showed impatience. "His pardon is in my heart," he said, "since I have the power to pardon. But that is not enough for me; I want the grandson of the Great Condé to serve in our armies; I feel strongly about that."[12]

It is hard to tell whether Joseph's memory was accurate, whether his memoirs were self-serving, or whether they were an unconscious attempt to relieve his own guilt feelings about the duke's execution. Napoleon, for his part, reportedly told his aide Pierre-Louis Roederer five years after the duke's execution that Joseph himself had told him the duke's whereabouts and advised him to execute the duke.[13]

The Duke of Enghien's kidnaping and execution shocked all Europe and were traumatic for Napoleon himself. Many Frenchmen feared First Consul Bonaparte as a new Robespierre who could execute them at his whim.[14] The duke's murder also left Napoleon with profound guilt feelings for the rest of his life. He repeatedly felt the need to exonerate himself. Many years later, a prisoner of the British on Saint Helena, Napoleon read British newspapers accusing him of having murdered the Duke of Enghien. He angrily rejected this accusation, protesting that he had had the right to defend himself. Ten days before his death, he entered a paragraph in his will saying that the Count of Artois, the brother of King Louis XVI and King Louis XVIII and the future King Charles X, had kept sixty murderers in Paris at the time planning to assassinate him, and that, under similar circumstances, he would still do the same thing.[15] Napoleon might not have made any statement at all about the Duke of Enghien before dying had he not felt guilty about his murder.

Part III

Emperor of the French

20

Of Cocks and Bees

Being First Consul of France was not enough for the grandiose, narcissistic, perfectionist, and power-hungry Napoleon. For a long time he had longed to turn France into an empire and to become *Empereur des François*. There was no inherent contradiction in the minds of most Frenchmen between the notions of republic and empire. In the ancient Roman republic, on which the French republic was modeled, the *imperator* (emperor) exercised *imperium* (command) on behalf of the people of the *res publica* (republic), the institutions of the republic continued to exist, and coins displayed the emperor's head on one side and the word *res publica* on the other. Napoleon's idea of the empire, however, like his idea of his consulate, was that of an absolute monarchy. His consulate had been a military dictatorship. His minions told him what he wanted to hear: that he must become emperor for the good of France.[1]

The creation of the French empire was now only a matter of time. In mid-April 1804 Napoleon's police, which had sounded out the French people, told him that the people considered the title of emperor "a sure means of establishing peace and quiet in France."[2] Napoleon's generals, eager to be promoted to marshals by the new emperor, approved the idea, as did the senior members of his state council. Napoleon's wife Josephine opposed the idea, saying "No one will understand the necessity behind it; everyone will attribute it to ambition or pride."[3] Vincent Cronin thought that "as a prediction of later sentiment this was remarkably accurate" but that Josephine's real motive was her fear of Napoleon using the fact that she had not born him a child as a pretext to divorce her.[4] In fact, perfectionism, power-hunger, ambition, and pride, all integral parts of Napoleon's narcissism, were no less behind the idea than his concern for France.

Two weeks after the execution of the Duke of Enghien, things moved rapidly toward the creation of Napoleon's empire. Under the Constitution of the Year VIII, the tribunate had to approve this empire. Even though First Consul Bonaparte had packed the tribunate with his own men and had reduced its membership from one hundred to fifty, it was still a bastion of revolution and republicanism. Napoleon's chief henchman in the tribunate was its forty-eight-year-old secretary and former president, Jean-François Curée, whom Napoleon had wisely made a member of the *ordre de la Légion d'honneur*. On April 3, 1804, Curée formally moved in the tribunate that France be proclaimed an empire. Few tribunes had doubts about whom Curée had in mind for emperor. The tribunate adopted the motion on the spot.[5]

From here on events moved swiftly. On April 30, 1804, Curée moved in the tribunate that Napoleon Bonaparte be proclaimed emperor of the French and that the imperial dignity be hereditary in his family. After only three days of debate on Curée's motion, the tribunate voted 49 to 1 for the following resolution: "1. That Napoleon Bonaparte be named Emperor, and that in this capacity he be made responsible for governing the French Republic. 2. That the title of Emperor and the imperial power be made hereditary in his family, from male to male, by primogeniture. 3. That in effecting the modifications of the organization of constituted authorities demanded by the establishment of hereditary power, equality, liberty and the rights of the people be preserved in full."[6] Only one tribune, Lazare Carnot, an old rival and opponent of Bonaparte who had resigned as his war secretary, dared to vote *non*. On May 4 a tribunate delegation presented its resolution to the senate, whose president congratulated the tribunes for "exercising for the first time that republican and popular initiative which the basic laws have delegated to you."[7] The tribunes were deceiving themselves. Three years later, Emperor Napoleon the First dissolved the tribunate.

The following day, May 5, 1804, saw a serious naval engagement between the British and French navies off Lorient, a maritime town of western France, in the *département* of Morbihan. Their renewed fear of military defeat made the French legislators eager to inaugurate their new emperor. On May 11, after a week of debate, lobbying and intrigue, the senate almost unanimously approved the tribunate's resolution, proclaiming an imperial government headed by Napoleon "since this is important for the interests of the French people."[8] Only three senators dared to oppose the motion. The senators were as good at self-deception as the tribunes. The rubber-stamp Legislative Corps had easily approved the motion to make Napoleon emperor.[9]

On May 18, 1804, the senators arrived at the castle of Saint-Cloud to proclaim Napoleon Emperor of the French. The homosexual second consul and president of the senate, Jean-Jacques-Régis Cambacérès, who hoped to keep his titles and positions under the new empire, concluded his solemn speech: "For the glory and happiness of the Republic, the Senate proclaims, from this moment, Napoleon Emperor of the French."[10] Surrounded by his state councillor and generals, Napoleon made a dramatic acceptance speech:

> Everything that can contribute to the good of the *patrie* is essentially tied to my happiness. I accept the title that you deem useful to the glory of the nation. I submit to the sanction of the people the law of heredity. I hope that France will never regret the honors that she will bestow upon my family. In any case, my spirit will no longer be with my posterity the day they cease to deserve the love and confidence of the great nation.[11]

The assembled dignitaries cried "Long live the Emperor!" The thirty-two-year-old general Géraud-Christophe-Michel Duroc, Napoleon's aide, friend, and confidant, now his new palace chief, announced the names of the "princes high dignitaries of the empire." Napoleon's elder brother, "Imperial Prince" Joseph, was proclaimed grand elector of the empire. His younger brother, Louis, was named grand constable of the empire. The second consul, Jean-Jacques-Régis Cambacérès, was made the archchancellor of the empire, while the third consul, Charles-François Lebrun, became the archtreasurer of the empire. Fourteen generals were elevated to marshal of the empire.[12]

General Duroc announced that the two former consuls and the other high dignitaries of the empire would henceforth be addressed as *monseigneur*, Napoleon's ministers as *excellence*, and his marshals, whose maximum future number was fixed at sixteen, as *monsieur le maréchal*. Napoleon's younger brothers, Lucien and Jérôme, who had disobeyed Napoleon (Lucien by refusing to divorce his second wife and marry the queen of Etruria, Jérôme by marrying a young woman in America), were excluded from any imperial dignity. The following year Duroc was named *grand maréchal du palais*, a title that harked back to Charlemagne's times and that made one think of its bearer as having a higher military rank than the marshals of the empire, which, of course, he did not.[13]

France was now both a republic and an empire. The republican calendar, which set France off from the rest of the world, was kept in force as France's official calendar for another five years. On May 28, 1804, the show trial of the chief plotters on Napoleon's life—Moreau, Cadoudal, Rivière, the Polignac brothers, Bouvet de Lozier—and their accomplices opened at the Criminal Court of the Seine. (General Pichegru, one of the chief plotters, had been found strangled to death in his *Le Temple* jail cell two months earlier). There was no jury. Napoleon's case against Moreau was shaky and fabricated; the witnesses lined up against him by Napoleon's police repeatedly contradicted themselves, retracted their depositions, and even perjured themselves. Nonetheless, Emperor Napoleon forced the judges to convict Moreau. As we have seen, his tyranny was his defense against his profound sense of helplessness in the face of plots against him that he failed to comprehend. Moreau was found guilty but condemned to only two years in prison—a light sentence that expressed the judges' disapproval of their emperor's tactics.

When Emperor Napoleon heard Moreau's verdict at the castle of Saint-Cloud, he flew into a holy rage, swore at his *grand juge*, Regnier, who had promised him that Moreau would be condemned to death, and dismissed Judge Lecourbe, the brother of the Jacobin general who supported Moreau during his trial. Napoleon reportedly roamed the corridors of the castle yelling, "These animals tell me that [Moreau] cannot avoid capital punishment, that his complicity is evident, and here they go punishing him like a petty thief. What do you want me to do? Keep him? It would yet be a rallying point. Let him sell his goods and leave France. What will I do with him at *Le Temple?* I have had enough of him."[14]

The irrationality of this statement indicates that it was an unconscious rationalization. Releasing this dangerous enemy was yet another self-destructive act on Napoleon's part. As he had done with most of his other enemies, Napoleon could have kept Moreau in prison, and could even have had him tortured or killed. Instead, General Moreau formally asked the emperor's pardon, and Napoleon commuted Moreau's sentence from two years in prison to exile from France. Moreau left France for the United States, where he lived for nine years planning his revenge. In 1813 he returned to Europe to join Napoleon's enemies in their struggle to topple him. Fortunately for Napoleon, however, Moreau was killed at the Battle of Dresden fighting his hated rival and sovereign.[15]

During the months that led to Napoleon's coronation in late 1804, the simmering lifelong rivalries between Napoleon and his siblings came to a head. The issue that ostensibly sparked the conflict, which raged on until the senate proclaimed the empire, was that of the imperial succession. The firstborn Joseph passionately believed in the traditional rule of primogeniture, which held in all European monarchies: the firstborn son was the heir to the throne. Napoleon's status as the second-born son and his rejection by his mother made him deeply jealous of Joseph; he just as passionately rejected primogeniture. Owen Connelly explained that under primogeniture Napoleon would be succeeded by Joseph:

> A great reason for creating the [French] Empire was to provide for hereditary succession, thus securing the permanence of government. The senate, initially, favored primogeniture—the standard European rule. Unless Napoleon fathered a legitimate male child, Joseph would have succeeded him, then, unless Joseph had a son, Lucien, and so on. Napoleon, however, announced that he wanted to adopt an heir, for which there was no precedent later than Roman times. Joseph was furious. "I am fed up with his tyranny!" He can appoint a successor now! Why create an Empire? "No heredity, no family, no intermediary caste! No obstacle to the ambitions of military chiefs . . . who can hope to [replace Napoleon] . . . No resistance in the legislative bodies!" Was *no one*, not even his family, to share power with Napoleon? He angrily threatened to join with "patriots and friends of liberty to destroy such tyranny!"[16]

Was it only envy of his younger brother that drove Joseph to such fury? Joseph's adviser when he was king of Spain, André-François Miot, *comte* de Melito, thought that Joseph was not aware of the vast ambition that motivated him.[17] Joseph's biographer thought that "pride of family was more in evidence. Napoleon's position, [Joseph] felt, was an insult to them all. Were they not good enough to be a real imperial family? Whom would he adopt? What if it were Eugène de Beauharnais, son of that slut Josephine[?]"[18]

The thirty-six-year-old Joseph had good reason to envy the twenty-three-year-old Eugène, his younger brother's stepson and his chief rival for the imperial succession. Napoleon adored Eugène. After the creation of the empire, Napoleon made Eugène a colonel of the cavalry, president of the electoral college of the Loie-et-Cher *département*, a brigadier general, a prince, and a state archchancellor. In 1805 Napoleon named Eugène his Viceroy of Italy and placed him in command of the *armée d'Italie* in place of Marshal Masséna. In 1806, two days before the twenty-four-year-old Eugène married the seventeen-year-old Princess Auguste Amalie of Bavaria, Napoleon formally adopted Eugène as his son, renamed him Eugène-Napoléon, recognized his right to the crown of Italy if Napoleon had no direct heirs, and made him Prince of Venice.[19]

Joseph Bonaparte, now the grand elector of the empire, tried to have the senate write primogeniture into the new constitution of the empire. Napoleon offered Joseph the title of imperial prince if he renounced primogeniture. Pierre-Louis Roederer, Napoleon's gadfly, claimed that Joseph consulted him on Napoleon's offer, and that he advised Joseph to decline it. When Napoleon learned of this, he became furious. He summoned Roederer and yelled at him, "I thought that you were my friend. You ought to be, but you're nothing but a troublemaker!"[20] Losing control of his rage, Napoleon slapped Roederer on the face. Napoleon told the stunned Roederer that it was as if Joseph had made love to his mistress, whose name was Power.[21] Vincent Cronin thought that Roederer "was big enough to forget the incident" and that he and Napoleon soon made up.[22] In fact, Roederer had been humiliated by Napoleon and secretly bore him a grudge. Joseph himself relented and accepted Napoleon's offer of the imperial prince title. The fraternal fight was finished—until the next one.

As we have seen, while Napoleon fought his elder brother Joseph on the succession issue, he also had a nasty showdown with his ambitious younger brother, Lucien, on the same issue. Lucien had left for Rome, where he joined his mother. On the evening of May 18, 1804, after he was formally proclaimed Emperor of the French, Napoleon held a festive dinner for France's dignitaries and his family. At this dinner he sadistically humiliated his sisters, Elisa Baciocchi and Caroline Murat, who had no imperial dignities or titles, by addressing their two sisters-in-law, Joseph's wife Julie and Louis's wife Hortense, as "Princess" and "Imperial Highness." Josephine's twenty-four-year-old lady-in-waiting, Claire-Elisabeth-Jeanne Gravier de Vergennes de Rémusat, later recalled that Caroline, the wife of Marshal Joachim Murat, became so hurt, envious, and angry that she openly cried at the dinner table and "drank glass after big glass of water, trying to get hold of herself" and drown her rage.[23] Madame Rémusat thought that Napoleon hated and despised women.[24]

The next morning Caroline and Elisa came to see Napoleon and made a theatrical scene, sobbing, "screeching," and moaning that they, too, deserved an imperial title.[25] The often-humorless Napoleon became uncharacteristically witty, saying "To hear you talk, my ladies, one would think that I have just robbed you of the heritage of our late father, the king."[26] Caroline, who had no sense of humor, fainted. The shocked Napoleon caved in and made both his sisters imperial highness. He withheld this dignity from their husbands, though. Four years later Napoleon made Caroline's husband, Joachim Murat, king of Naples. The bitter and vengeful Caroline, however, plotted against him with his ministers, seeking to topple her brother and replace him with her husband.

Manipulating and exploiting other people is a hallmark of the narcissistic personality. Napoleon used other people's vanity to control them even as he conferred titles and honors upon them. But behind the manipulation lay loneliness and anxiety. Jacques Bainville believed that Napoleon conferred so many titles and honors on those around him because he felt anxious as a new emperor and feared that his shaky dynasty would flounder.[27] Years later he said to Las Cases: "I felt my isolation. So I cast anchors of safety all round into deep water."[28] Bainville thought that Napoleon's feelings of loneliness accounted for his self-destructive acts more than did his "vainglory" and that "there is something even tragic in that unavowed anxiety of spirit."[29]

When Napoleon became Emperor of the French, several prominent French composers wrote musical works in his honor. As in other things, Napoleon was a musical dictator. He kept telling the musical institutions how to conduct their business and personally ran their affairs. In 1802 the music lover First Consul Bonaparte had wooed his favorite composer, Giovanni Paisiello, from the court of King Ferdinand IV of Naples to Paris to direct the new chapel that he had created at the Tuileries Palace. But in 1803 the Parisian public received Paisiello's French opera, *Proserpine*, unenthusiastically, and a deeply disappointed Paisiello returned to Naples. Napoleon turned the old *Théâtre des Arts* into his new *Académie impériale de musique*, which included the Paris Opera, and chose its directors. On July 13, 1804, the thirty-four-year-old Emperor Napoleon went to the

Paris Opera to attend a performance of *Ossian, ou Les bardes*, a new opera by his 44-year-old choirmaster, Jean-François Le Sueur, who had succeeded Paisiello as the Director of Music of the Tuileries. Le Sueur wrote a highly flattering dedication to the new emperor, which is almost too embarrassing to read:

> Sire, your glorious name at the head of the opera of *Ossian* recommends it to posterity. The glory of this hero of the third century filled a part of our continent: if my voice has sometimes been raised in the attempt to sing his praise, it is because my heart had before it constantly as a model the living picture of a hero, the pride of our age, whose name and glory fill the globe upon which we live I might almost say, the universe; is this presuming too far? He fulfills the designs of the Author of all things; he occupies the thoughts of the Mover of the world; his destiny is as conspicuous as the stars which shine upon us. But how could I rise to the level of this model, the object of my songs? He is bound to be that of centuries to come. I see in him the heroes of future races, inflamed by the thought that they may deserve comparison with him. Tears rise to their eyes as they follow his history. One day they in their turn will receive the tribute of these tears of sublime emulation; they will receive it from the traveler who reads upon their tombs: "They had something of Napoleon in them." Yours respectfully, Le Sueur[30]

Martial Teneo, a modern librarian to the Paris Opera, wrote, "In spite of its inflated style, which is almost worthy of a madman, this dedication flattered Napoleon. And so for the whole evening he insisted on keeping the musician at his side in his box."[31]

In July 1804, as Napoleon was inspecting his army and navy at Boulogne-sur-Mer, he had a public confrontation with Admiral Eustache Bruix, the commander of the French Atlantic fleet at Boulogne and inspector general of the ocean coasts. Napoleon told Bruix that he wished to inspect the ships of the Boulogne naval base at sea. The sea, however, was becoming ominously stormy, and Bruix, reluctant to order his men and his ships into the storm, did not give the order. With his Mameluke Roustam in tow, Napoleon went on his horseback promenade around Boulogne. When he returned, he was furious to see that none of the ships had moved. Overwhelmed by his narcissistic rage and "humiliation" of his will being thwarted, he said to Bruix, "Monsieur, I gave my orders, why did you not carry them out? The consequences are my affair alone. Obey!" The courageous Bruix, however, who knew that his men would drown in the stormy sea, bravely answered: "Sire, I shall not." The furious Napoleon cried, "Monsieur, you are insolent!" Riding-whip in hand, an enraged Napoleon advanced on Bruix, meaning to strike him. Bruix paled, stepped back, put his hand on his sword and cried, "Sire! Watch out!" There was a terrible moment as the enraged emperor and the shaken admiral, both pale, faced each other. The incident ended with over 200 sailors drowning in the storm, while Admiral Bruix was banished to Holland.[32]

When Napoleon was away from his wife Josephine, he idealized and missed her. On August 6, 1804, Empress Josephine was at Charlemagne's ancient capital of Aachen, which the French call Aix-la-Chapelle, where the new emperor planned to present himself as Charlemagne's successor. Napoleon wrote Josephine from Calais, "I have a great wish to see you. You are always necessary to my happiness."[33] At the same time, however, Napoleon was entertaining the beautiful nineteen-year-old actress Marie-Thérèse-Etiennette Bourgoin, whom the French called "the goddess of joy and pleasure," and whom Napoleon had made his mistress. The teenage Mademoiselle Bourgoin had been the lover of Napoleon's forty-eight-year-old interior minister, Jean-Antoine-Claude Chaptal de Chanteloup, on whose knees she reportedly sat in his Paris Opera box. Once more Napoleon had triumphed over a father figure. A furious Chaptal resigned his ministry in protest.[34]

In August 1804, while inspecting his *armée de Boulogne*, with which he still intended to invade "England," the new emperor was preoccupied with his forthcoming coronation. On August 14 Napoleon wrote his wife from the Belgian seaport of Ostend that he was "very well satisfied with the army and with the flotillas."[35] Napoleon celebrated his thirty-fifth birthday on August 15 with the generals of his *armée de Boulogne*. The real celebration came the next day, August 16, at the Pas-de-Calais village of Terlincthun, near the Atlantic coast. In the middle of a carpeted platform, he had his aides place a golden throne which had supposedly seated the ancient Frankish king Dagobert some twelve centuries earlier. It looked like an ancient Roman curule chair, and is now in the Cabinet of Medals at the *Bibliothèque nationale de France*. Hidden under a canopy, Napoleon's men had placed a trophy of enemy flags, colors, and standards taken from the Austrians and Ottomans in Italy and Egypt. Seated on his imperial throne, the new emperor awarded the Cross of the Legion of Honor to 2,000 soldiers of his *armée de Boulogne*—which never left France's shores.[36]

In the unconsciously sadomasochistic relationship between Napoleon and his wife Josephine, the tables had been turned. Five years earlier Napoleon had "discovered" Josephine's infidelity. Now he was repeatedly unfaithful to her, and she kept "discovering" his affairs. As we have seen, Napoleon often fell in love with women who bore the names of his sisters. His best-known love affair in Egypt had been with Pauline Fourès, who had the same first name as his sister Pauline. One of Napoleon's sisters, Maria Anna Baciocchi, called herself Elisa (short for Elisabeth). Napoleon's attraction to Marie-Antoinette-Elisabeth Barberot de Vaudey de Vellexon, a young lady in waiting to his wife Josephine who briefly became his mistress, may also have had to do with her name. But the young beauty was "capricious, exacting and extravagant" as well as an inveterate gambler.[37] After repeatedly paying her gambling debts, Napoleon refused to go on doing so. When the manipulative Elisabeth threatened suicide, he gave her the last handout but forced her to resign as Josephine's lady in waiting.

Napoleon's brief affair with Elisabeth de Vaudey in the fall of 1804, shortly before his coronation as emperor, reportedly caused a terrible fight between him and his wife. As Napoleon may have unconsciously wished, he and Elisabeth were discovered by the jealous Josephine, who had spied on her husband, caught him *in flagrante delicto*, and made a dramatic scene. Napoleon in his turn exploded with uncontrollable rage at his wife and told her to prepare to leave the castle of Saint-Cloud as he would divorce her.[38] The scene, however, greatly resembles another one with Madame Duchâtel, related in the following paragraph, and Napoleon scholars may have confused the two incidents.[39] Psychologically, however, Napoleon could not leave Josephine, to whom he was tied with the deepest emotional bond, unconsciously repeating with her his earliest love-hate relationship to his mother.

While he was still first consul of France, Napoleon had begun a passionate love affair with another one of Josephine's ladies in waiting, Marie-Antoinette-Adèle Papin Duchâtel. She was a beautiful married brunette with dark-blue eyes and long, silky eyelashes. In the eighteenth century, European women often married in order to survive. Two years earlier this gorgeous young woman had married the fifty-one-year-old State Councillor Charles-Jacques-Nicolas Duchâtel, director general of the French registry of properties. The jealous Josephine kept spying on her husband, just as his mother Letizia had done when he was a boy. One night Josephine surprised Napoleon on his way to Madame Duchâtel "and immediately broke into tears and complaints."[40] By another account Josephine "wept, she pleaded, she got her children to beg Napoleon to give up the younger woman."[41] A terrible scene followed. A furious Napoleon threatened to divorce Josephine, who was beside herself with hurt and despair.[42] Then the couple made up and went back to their sadomasochistic business as usual.

Ever since Napoleon became emperor with the imperial title hereditary in his family, Josephine feared that he would divorce her, using the powerful pretext of her not having given him a son and heir. In September 1804, however, in Charlemagne's ancient capital of Aachen, Napoleon and Josephine played the loving imperial couple. The local cathedral chapter gave Napoleon a talisman which Charlemagne had worn in his battles. The Aachen priests gave Josephine an ancient casket telling her that whoever could open it would meet with great good fortune. She had scarcely touched the lid when it opened, and the superstitious Josephine believed in this omen.[43] Napoleon ordered Charlemagne's regalia brought from Aachen to Paris for his forthcoming coronation. Two men turned up with two swords, each swearing that his was Charlemagne's coronation sword, and "Napoleon chose the one with better credentials."[44]

In Aachen, Napoleon's minions claimed to have found Charlemagne's scepter, inscribed *Sanctus Carolus Magnus, Italia, Roma, Germania*. Charlemagne's crown was not found, so Napoleon ordered a copy made, as well as another crown with which he would be crowned, an open gold laurel-wreath crown, "just such a crown as the Roman people had awarded to victors, but in gold."[45] France's "Gallican Articles" of 1682 and the *Concordat* required that the pope respect the customs of the French Catholic church, and Napoleon could have been consecrated by a French archbishop. Napoleon, however, would not have any lesser clergyman than the pope consecrate him, and Napoleon himself would place the gold laurel crown on his own head. Cronin believed that Napoleon did this not out of arrogance but "in order to avoid disputes between dignitaries as to who is to give the crown."[46]

Napoleon was deeply ambivalent about inviting Pope Pius VII to consecrate him Emperor of the French. The pope was an unconscious father figure to him. Although he had been proclaimed emperor by the senate, Napoleon, who had lost his father at the age of fifteen, and who felt that he had never had the father he really wanted, longed for the recognition and blessing of the Holy Father. At the same time, he wanted to be his own man, not that of the Holy Father. Napoleon had made his step uncle, Joseph Fesch, archbishop of Lyon and primate of the Gauls, and in 1803 Fesch became a cardinal. In the spring of 1803 the forty-year-old Fesch had left Paris for Rome with the thirty-five-year-old French diplomat François-Auguste-René de Chateaubriand, who later became one of Napoleon's chief critics. Fesch, who replaced the diplomat François Cacault as the emperor's legate to Rome, now negotiated Napoleon's proposal with the pope. The pope was not in position to refuse the French emperor's invitation. After an initial hesitation, the pope accepted and prepared to leave Rome for Paris.

For his consecration and coronation, Napoleon had to select an imperial emblem for his new dynasty. The first suggestion in his state council was the French symbol of the cock as his imperial emblem. The *gallus* or cock was the source of the ancient Roman name Gallia for France because the ancient *Gaullois*, who fought the Romans, had worn cock feathers. Napoleon, however, refused to adopt the cock as his imperial symbol, saying, "The cock belongs in the farmyard. It is too weak . . . The cock has no strength: it cannot be the emblem of an empire such as France."[47] In fact, as English slang usage suggests, and as the prominent anthropologist Alan Dundes has found in cock fights, the cock is an unconscious symbol of the penis.[48] Napoleon's idea of the cock as "weak" and his refusal to accept it as his imperial emblem may have had to do with his unconscious doubts about his virility.

With the cock out of the race for the new imperial emblem, Napoleon's fifty-one-year-old State Councillor Louis-Philippe de Ségur suggested the lion, who could "conquer the leopard of England."[49] Another councillor opined that the lion is man's enemy, and yet another proposed the elephant. Emperor Napoleon said, "We must choose between the eagle, the elephant and the lion."[50] He finally chose the eagle. When it came time to choose his own personal emblem, Napoleon significantly picked the metal bees found in the tomb of the sixth-century Frankish king Chilperic in the Belgian town of Tournai. Those bees were thought to have come from Chilepric's royal robe, but had actually come from his wife's. Chilperic was "a brutal, sexually perverted, and emotionally disturbed warrior whom the Frankish historian Saint Gregory of Tours compared to Nero and Herod the Great."[51] Napoleon's rationalization for this choice was that "he wanted something ancient. He was trying to build up a future, but to do so he had to find roots in the past: if possible before 987, when the Capetian kings began to rule."[52] In fact, Napoleon may have unconsciously identified with the brutal Chilperic.

In the midst of his stormy scenes with his jealous wife and his assignations with her ladies in waiting, Emperor Napoleon ran his affairs of state. On October 30, 1804, he spoke to his state council against a proposed measure to suppress the French jury system: "We have to entrust decisions concerning property to civil judges because such matters demand technical knowledge; but in order to pronounce judgment about a deed, the only thing needed is a sixth sense, namely conscience. So for criminal cases one can call on individuals drawn from the crowd. The citizens then have a guarantee that their honour and life are not being abandoned to the judges who already decide about their property."[53] Napoleon's father had fought legal battles to hold his property, and the judges had not always been favorable to him.[54] Did Napoleon have his father's struggles over his property in mind, or was he moved by his feelings about the judges?

On November 2, 1804, a month before the date set for Napoleon's consecration and coronation, the sixty-two-year-old Pope Pius VII left Rome with a retinue of 108 cardinals, archbishops, and bishops. The pontiff traveled slowly toward Paris, with many stops on the way. Pius VII reached Paris on November 28 and stayed over four months. In Paris, Napoleon gave Pius a room at the Tuileries Palace which looked exactly like his room at Rome's Quirinale Palace. Napoleon's old wet nurse, Camilla Ilari, arrived from Corsica with her daughter to attend the coronation. An elated Napoleon, who loved Camilla much more than he did his mother Letizia, gave her an audience with the pope. Letizia herself, meanwhile, remained in Italy with her favorite son, Lucien, his wife Alexandrine, and their child.

Some Frenchmen groused about their alliance with the Vatican, but most were euphoric. Behind the scenes, however, things were less rosy. Pope Pius VII wanted Emperor Napoleon to modify the Organic Articles of 1802 which had been appended to the *Concordat* by the French Legislative Corps. Napoleon refused. The pope wanted to place the crown upon Napoleon's head, just as his predecessors had done with "Holy Roman Emperors" Pepin and Charlemagne. Jacques Bainville thought that "Pius VII had come to Paris only after receiving the assurance that there would be no innovations in the traditional rite contrary to the honor and dignity of the Supreme Pontiff."[55] Napoleon, however, informed Pius that while the pope would consecrate him, he, Napoleon, would crown himself. Some scholars thought that Pius protested this, others that he did not. Napoleon told the pope that he would be swearing an imperial oath promising to preserve the freedom of religious worship. The Catholic pope would not lend his presence to such an oath. The two men agreed that when Napoleon took the oath, the pope would retire to the Notre-Dame sacristy and unvest.[56]

Josephine and Napoleon were still unmarried in the eyes of the church. On the night of December 1, 1804, just before Napoleon's and Josephine's coronation, Napoleon's step uncle, Joseph Cardinal Fesch, who had returned from Rome with the Pope, secretly gave the sacrament of holy matrimony to Napoleon and Josephine in the private chapel of the Tuileries Palace in the presence of Foreign Minister Charles-Maurice de Talleyrand and War Minister Louis-Alexandre Berthier. Five years later, Napoleon would use the secrecy of the ceremony and the fact that no parish priest had attended it as a pretext to have his marriage to Josephine annulled by the Paris ecclesiastical court.[57]

On the day of his consecration and coronation, Sunday, December 2, 1804, Emperor Napoleon dressed up in his finest clothes, white silk and gold with a black felt hat adorned with soaring white plumes. His elder brother Joseph Bonaparte, the grand elector of the empire, arrived dressed almost as dazzlingly. On their way to the coronation at Notre-Dame cathedral in Paris, the proud Napoleon reportedly said to his brother "Joseph! If only our father could see us now!"[58] Deep down Napoleon imagined, and hoped, that their dead father would love him, now that he was Emperor, more than he did Joseph. At the consecration, however, his beloved old wet nurse, Camilla Ilari, came forward to greet Napoleon. He was overjoyed, but when Camilla reminded him that Joseph had been a handsome child, while he, Napoleon, had not. Napoleon's face reportedly "blackened with rage."[59]

Eight thousand noblemen, marshals, generals, ministers, prefects, and other important people, relatives and friends of Napoleon from all over

Europe had gathered at Notre-Dame cathedral in Paris to see their thirty-five-year-old emperor consecrated and crowned. After reciting the Catholic prayer litanies, Pope Pius VII anointed Napoleon and Josephine, then said the *Kyrie*, the first part of the Latin Mass. Not surprisingly, in view of his profound attachment to his idealized mother in the person of the Virgin Mary, Napoleon had chosen a votive Mass of Our Lady rather than the customary Mass for the First Sunday in Advent. After the Gradual, the pope blessed Charlemagne's regalia—his orb, justice hand, sword, scepter, and crown—which had been brought in from Aachen, and handed them to Napoleon. The imperial orchestra played solemn church music by Giovanni Paisiello, Napoleon's favorite composer and former music director. The pope and his entourage performed various rituals—removing and replacing of mitres, placing incense in censers, hand washing, kissing rings, books and garment hems—which Napoleon "found merely boring."[60]

After Pope Pius VII had anointed and consecrated Napoleon, it was time for him and his wife to be crowned Emperor and Empress of the French. Napoleon climbed the steps to the Notre-Dame altar, "a lone figure under the soaring columns,"[61] took the gold laurel-wreath crown in both his hands and—as he had told the pope he would do—placed it upon his own head. He crowned himself "in the name of the French people and army."[62] At the conclusion of the Mass of Our Lady, the choir chanted *Vivat imperator in aeternum* (May the Emperor Live Forever). Josephine came up and knelt at the foot of the altar steps, "tears of emotion dropping on her clasped hands."[63] Napoleon took Josephine's crown, lifted it up, approached her and placed it on her head. The emperor and empress mounted their imperial thrones.

At this point, as had been agreed, the pope retired to the sacristy and unvested, while Emperor Napoleon the First took an oath of loyalty to Mother France:

> I swear to uphold the integrity of the Republic's territory, to respect and cause to be respected the laws of the Concordat and religious freedom, to respect and cause to be respected equality of rights, political and civil liberties, and the irrevocability of the sale of national property, to raise no duties and to establish no tax except through the law, to uphold the institution of the Legion of Honour, and to rule solely with a view to the interests, happiness and glory of the French people.[64]

Significantly, Napoleon had referred to France in his oath as "the Republic" rather than "the Empire" that she had been for the past seven months. Just as significantly, his imperial coins bore his likeness on one face and the words *La République* on the other. *La République*, a feminine noun in French, had a deep maternal meaning for him. *L'Empire*, a French masculine noun, was nowhere as maternal. Even though he had founded an empire to boost his grandiose self, it was the republic that he really cherished.

When Napoleon had finished his oath, the herald at arms announced in a loud voice: "The most glorious and most August Napoleon, Emperor of the French, is consecrated, crowned and enthroned!" But did Napoleon mean what he said in his oath? The key part of the oath was Napoleon's promise never to revoke the sale of national properties and his implication that he and the Republic were "one and indivisible."[65] Napoleon would keep all of France, Belgium, the Savoy, the lands east of the Rhine, and the Piedmont in the Republic. Napoleon's vow not to levy taxes or duties "except under the law" was hollow, as he could make whatever laws he liked.[66] He alluded to some old basic laws and swore to preserve the conquests of the Revolution. This was make-believe: France was no longer a democratic republic, or a revolutionary society, but an autocratic empire. Napoleon's unresolved fusional relationship with his mother had unconsciously been transferred to the Republic.

Why did Napoleon's mother Letizia stay away from him on the most important day of his life? Jean Tulard thought that she was loth to see her hated daughter-in-law, Josephine, crowned.[67] In fact, it was an act of aggression, an expression of Letizia's long-standing rejection of Napoleon, and a declaration of her preference for his younger brother Lucien. Indeed, Napoleon was deeply hurt by his mother's absence from his coronation. He had made himself Emperor of the French to show his mother who he was, to make her love him after all. She did not come to see him in his glory. Napoleon could not bear this maternal rejection. He ordered the painter Jacques-Louis David to include Letizia in the official coronation picture—a measure of how painful it was for him not to have his mother there. David did Napoleon's bidding, and Letizia appears in his coronation picture, which hangs in the *Musée du Louvre*, as if she had attended the coronation.[68] As we have seen, Dorothy Carrington thought that Napoleon's mother's absence from his coronation was "the crowning injury" of his whole life.[69]

Napoleon's narcissistic and perfectionistic need for greater glory, his grandiose self, never let him rest. Being Emperor of the French was not enough. It did not win him his mother's love, nor satisfy his grandiosity. One day after his consecration and coronation, Napoleon was already unhappy with himself. After all, Alexander the Great had been deified, while he, Napoleon, was a mere mortal. He imagined being Jesus Christ. Here is what Napoleon reportedly said to his forty-three-year-old navy minister, Admiral Denis Decrès, the day after his coronation:

> I have come too late, nothing great remains to be done! Yes, I have a fine career, I admit, I have gone far; but what a difference with antiquity! See Alexander: when he had conquered Asia and announced himself to the nations as the son of Jupiter, except for [Alexander's mother] Olympias, who knew better, except for Aristotle and a few Athenian pedants, all the Orient believed him. Well, myself, if I were to proclaim myself today the son of the Eternal Father and if I announced that I would give grace to Him in that capacity, every fishwife would hiss me on my way. The masses are too enlightened today, there is nothing great left to be done.[70]

After Napoleon's consecration and coronation, his mother Letizia left her son Lucien in Rome and returned to Paris. On December 19, 1804, she settled into the Hôtel de Brienne in the rue Saint-Dominique, which she had bought from her son Lucien. Napoleon received her coolly. The tables had been turned. It was now Letizia who was trying to win back her son's love. At Napoleon's demand, she persuaded Lucien to obey his elder brother—if not to to give up his wife, Alexandrine Jouberthon. Letizia also asked her youngest son, Jérôme, to have his marriage to the American heiress Elizabeth Patterson annulled. Three months later a grateful Napoleon conferred upon his mother the imperial title of *Madame, Mère de l'Empereur* (Madam, Mother of the Emperor) with an income from the Imperial Treasury of three hundred thousand francs and a household complete with chaplains, ladies in waiting, readers, chamberlains, order secretaries, and many other employees.[71] She was henceforth known as *Madame Mère.* Napoleon might as well have titled himself *Monsieur Fils*

(Master Son): his entire unconscious life revolved around his tormented relationship with his mother, which had shaped his narcissistic character, and all his achievements were unconsciously designed to win the love that she could never give him.

21

Trafalgar and Beyond

Even though First Consul Bonaparte had proclaimed the end of the French Revolution and republican France had now become an empire under Napoleon, it still officially called itself *La république française* and kept its republican calendar, which in September 1804 was the beginning of the Year XIII of the French Republic. The British Royal Navy blockaded all of France's and Spain's naval ports. One hundred and thirty-five British ships blockaded forty-five French vessels at Toulon, Rochefort, and Brest, and thirty Spanish ships at Cadíz and El Ferrol. Emperor Napoleon of France still imagined that he could invade *l'Angleterre*. His navy, based at Brest, Rochefort, and Toulon, and his *grande armée d'Angleterre*, headquartered at Boulogne-sur-Mer on the English Channel, were the key to his imagined success against the English. His chief admirals were Pierre-Charles-Jean-Baptiste-Silvestre de Villeneuve, commander of the French Mediterranean fleet at Toulon, Honoré-Joseph Ganteaume, commander of the French Atlantic fleet at Brest, and Edouard-Thomas de Burgues, comte de Missiessy, who commanded the French fleet at Rochefort.

Napoleon wishfully thought that he could easily deceive the British. Admiral Villeneuve and his "magnificent" Mediterranean fleet, the Emperor said, would again evade the British siege of Toulon, lure Admiral Nelson and his British Mediterranean fleet to the West Indies, lose them there, race to the English Channel, and, in combination with the French fleets from Brest and Rochefort, join Napoleon's invasion of England. In fact, Villeneuve's "magnificent" fleet was in a state of disrepair, disorganized, and run down by the Revolution. The French naval scholar Etienne

Taillemite thought that Napoleon's plan was an excellent strategic idea but that, to succeed, it required a powerful navy in good shape that was well trained and commanded by daring and enterprising chiefs.[1]

The sea was Napoleon's mortal enemy. He had lost his first real battle at the isle of La Maddalena, off Sardinia, in 1793, and the battle of the Nile in 1798. His fantastic naval invasion of England would crumble before it began. Predictably, his admirals kept losing their battles against the British Royal Navy. In the French naval campaign of 1805, Napoleon was repeatedly humiliated by the British. One of Napoleon's ablest naval officers, Admiral Eustache Bruix, the inspector general of the ocean coasts, who had confronted Napoleon the year before at Boulogne, died of tuberculosis in March. The unfortunate Admiral Villeneuve had endless trouble. His colleagues from Brest and Rochefort, Ganteaume and Missiessy, never met him as planned. Villeneuve's Mediterranean fleet sailed from Toulon, evaded the British navy, and headed for the West Indies, trying to lure the British into a chase. But Ganteaume's Atlantic fleet remained blocked by the British Royal Navy at Brest. Missiessy's fleet broke away from the British blockade at Rochefort but, after a long voyage across the Atlantic, missed Villeneuve's fleet at Martinique and returned to port at Rochefort. On its way back home, on July 22, Villeneuve's fleet blundered into a British naval squadron commanded by Admiral Sir Robert Calder off Cape Finisterre in northwest Spain. The ambivalent Villeneuve, who knew the British naval superioirty, fought indecisively and "was mauled in a confused battle in deep fog. He was not beaten, but he considered it impossible to reach the [English] Channel, much less control it."[2]

In August 1805 Emperor Napoleon returned to Boulogne-sur-Mer on the English Channel to prepare his fantastic two-tide naval invasion of *l'Angleterre*. For two years the Emperor had been preparing his *grande armée d'Angleterre* at Boulogne to invade "England." To divert the British Royal Navy, he had ordered Villeneuve to sail all the way across the Atlantic to the West Indies, entice the British Royal Navy to pursue it, then sail back for the English Channel at top speed and join the French invasion force before the British Royal Navy could return to defend it shores. Napoleon did not yet know what had happened to Admiral Villeneuve. The narcissistic and perfectionist emperor really believed that his admirals would carry out his plans to perfection and that he could really invade and conquer England.

After the unhappy battle at Cape Finisterre, Admiral Villeneuve had succeeded again in eluding the British Royal Navy. Instead of sailing to

Brest and safety, however, Villeneuve tragically decided to join his miserable Spanish allies. He anchored his fleet at the Spanish port of El Ferrol and sent word of his arrival to Emperor Napoleon. On August 17, 1805, word reached Napoleon that Villeneuve had reached El Ferrol, and that he had not left it for the English Channel, as Napoleon had ordered him. Predictably, Napoleon had a fit of narcissistic rage. He reportedly summoned the thirty-eight-year-old Pierre-Antoine-Noël-Bruno Daru, his just-named state councillor and civil-list director, and dictated to him a dramatic shift in France's military plans:

> The news brought on one of his most violent outbursts of passion. He was seen with "a ferocious look," his hat rammed down on his eyes, his eyes like lightning: "What a navy! What an admiral!" he cried. Then immediately the scene was shifted, and he became a man of realities and action, with the gift of driving away one thought at will, and putting another in its place. He dictated to Daru, as if spontaneously, the plan of campaign against Austria which he had been pondering. But he was still so uncertain of what decision to take that he held on to the supreme chance that Villeneuve might have only touched at [El] Ferrol and might be heading north towards Brest. Napoleon did not know that "the scoundrel Villeneuve," finding [El] Ferrol unsafe, was already off Cadiz when, ten days later, having waited to the last possible moment, he began to turn his Army towards the heart of Germany.[3]

While many Napoleon biographers have cited this "dictation of Boulogne" as the turning point in Napoleon's plans, when he decided to give up his invasion of England and to send his *grande armée d'Angleterre* to the heart of Europe, the French scholar Bernard Bergerot thought that the "dictation of Boulogne" was a legend.[4]

When Emperor Napoleon learned that Admiral Villeneuve was at the southern Spanish port of Cádiz rather than on his way to the English Channel, as Napoleon had ordered him, he became enraged again and "hurled cruel and furious insults at him."[5] A furious Napoleon ordered his navy minister, Denis Decrès, "to expel Villeneuve from the navy with ignominy."[6] Instead, on September 14, 1805, Villeneuve was ordered "to make a powerful diversion" with his squadron in the Mediterranean.[7]

The Third Coalition against France consisted of Great Britain, Austria, Naples, and Russia. Jacques Bainville wrote that Villeneuve "was to appear off Naples, which was an enemy ally, but, above all else, he was to keep the landlocked ocean from falling into English dominance. Villeneuve wasted a few days longer in hesitations. Was he now, under the worst conditions, to face the battle he had always dreaded? But his honor had to be cleansed. The luckless admiral rounded off his unhappy career by staking the fate of the French Navy, in one day, in one desperate fling, against the English fleet under the command of its greatest captain."[8] Villeneuve would soon face Nelson at Trafalgar, with tragic results for both admirals.

While struggling with the British Royal Navy and preparing for war with Austria, Emperor Napoleon did not forget France's internal affairs. Having virtually ended the French Revolution by turning France into a consulate and informally ended the French Republic by turning it into an empire, Napoleon abolished the Republican calendar as well by having his Senate issue a *sénatus-consulte* on September 9, 1805, which made the current year of the French Republic the last official year of the republican calendar—and its shortest as well, to end with the Gregorian year less than three months later. The Republican calendar would expire on 11 Nivôse Year XIV–December 31, 1805.

By the fall of 1805 the Franco-Austrian war was in full swing. On September 10 the Austrian army marched into Bavaria again. Napoleon was determined to drive them out again, just as he had done five years earlier, but this time he would go after them all the way to Vienna. Having made up his mind to attack and invade Austria, Napoleon moved swiftly. During late September and early October he moved his *Grande Armée*, which included Bavarian and Dutch divisions, across the Rhine into Germany. After some initial blunders, the French pushed forward, crossed the Danube River and defeated the Austrians at Haslach and Elchingen. For Napoleon, these battles were a mere prelude to the "glorious" battle of Ulm on October 15–20. On October 17 the commander of the Austrian army of Bavaria, the fifty-three-year-old Austrian general Carl Mack von Leiberich surrendered to the French at Ulm with his twenty-six thousand soldiers.

On the same day, October 17, 1805, Napoleon's former foreign minister, Talleyrand, wrote him an "insolent" letter warning him that his conquests were too far gone and that he should now seek to make peace with France's enemies. When he received Talleyrand's letter, Napoleon was incensed. His entire self-esteem was built on continual expansion and conquest. On October 19, after Mack had surrendered to him in person and signed the transfer of Ulm to the French the following day, Napoleon boasted to Josephine of his victories: "I have accomplished my design; I have destroyed the Austrian army by simple marches; I have taken 60,000 prisoners, taken 120 artillery pieces, over 90 flags, and over 30 generals. I am going to move against the Russians; they are lost. I am happy with the army. I have not lost over 1,500 men. Adieu, my Josephine."[9] Obviously, he was better at making war than at making love. To the narcissistic emperor, the lives of 1,500 of his own men were nothing compared to his "glory."

In September 1805, after the forty-seven-year-old British admiral Horatio Nelson returned from his fruitless transatlantic pursuit of the Franco-Spanish fleet of the forty-two-year-old French admiral Pierre-Charles de Villeneuve, rather than engage that fleet at sea, he went back home to England, where he spent twenty-five days sorting out his official affairs and his "scandalous" personal life. Soon thereafter, however, Villeneuve faced Nelson's British fleet at Cape Trafalgar, a Spanish Atlantic cape south of Cádiz and west of Gibraltar. On October 20 the unsuspecting Villeneuve sailed from Cádiz with his thirty-three-vessel fleet, of which almost half were antiquated Spanish ships. On October 21 Villeneuve's no-longer-magnificent fleet ran into the superior British fleet of 27 ships under Admiral Nelson and his second-in-command, the fifty-seven-year-old admiral Cuthbert Collingwood, west of Cape Trafalgar. Nelson's flagship was named the HMS *Victory*, while Collingwood's was the HMS *Royal Sovereign*.

Nelson's *Victory* was very big and had seen a lot of action in its forty years of service. It was a hundred-gun ship with a length of 186 feet (fifty-seven meters), a displacement of 2,162 tons, and a crew of more than eight hundred. An unorthodox, aggressive, imaginative, and flexible commander, Admiral Nelson overwhelmed Admiral Villeneuve and destroyed his fleet: At 11:50 a.m. Nelson signaled his famous message: "England expects that every man will do his duty." Then he attacked. Vincent Cronin thought that Nelson won because he "broke all the rules, much as Napoleon had done on the first Italian campaign: he attacked in two columns and cut Villeneuve's fleet into three. Nelson's last signaled message from the *Victory* was 'Engage the enemy more closely,' and for this kind of in-fighting the French big guns proved useless. Seventeen of Villeneuve's ships were captured, one blew up and Villeneuve, in an agony of remorse, later took his own life."[10]

Indeed, the end was tragic for both Villeneuve and Nelson. As for Nelson's personal role in the Battle of Trafalgar, the accepted legend is that he thought of nothing but Mother England. In fact, he all but committed suicide. It was almost as if Nelson was happy to die:

> The Battle of Trafalgar raged at its fiercest around the *Victory*, and a French sniper, firing from the mast of the *Redoutable*, shot Nelson through the shoulder and chest. He was carried below to the surgeon, and it was soon clear that he was dying. When told that 15 enemy ships had been taken, he replied, "That is well, but I had bargained for 20." Thomas Hardy, his flag captain, kissed his forehead in farewell and Nelson spoke his last words, "Now I am satisfied. Thank God, I have done my duty."[11]

Admiral Villeneuve was taken prisoner by the British, released after six months, after giving his word of honor not to fight them again, and returned to France. Humiliated, ashamed, depressed, his self-esteem in tatters, on April 22, 1806, after learning the extent of the emperor's displeasure with him, the desperate forty-two-year-old Villeneuve stabbed himself to death at a Rennes inn.[12] Such was the price that Napoleon's admirals and generals paid for his unconscious wish to punish his bad mother, *l'Angleterre*.

Napoleon, who had defeated the Austrians at Ulm, was advancing on Vienna when he learned of Villeneuve's tragic defeat at Trafalgar on November 16, 1805. His defense against the perceived humiliation was denial. He wanted to forget Villeneuve and Trafalgar and to think only of his victories against Austria.[13] But his naval defeat at Trafalgar meant that Napoleon's fantastic, persistent, and stubborn plans for the invasion of England from 1803 to 1805 had failed miserably and definitively. This was yet another humiliation that Napoleon dealt with by forever trying to shore up his self-esteem through ever more military conquests and victories, whatever the tragic cost in other people's lives.

Napoleon's strategy for total control of Europe called for as many of his relatives as possible to marry the heirs of its most important rulers. He had fallen out with his younger brothers Lucien and Jérôme over this issue. By the end of 1805, he would defeat Austria and make some German grand duchies into kingdoms. Napoleon's adopted stepson Eugène would marry the princess of Bavaria, Josephine's niece Stéphanie de Beauharnois would marry the Prince of Baden, his youngest brother Jérôme would marry the Princess of Württemberg, Antoinette Murat would marry the Prince of Hohenzollern-Sigmaringen, and Josephine's other niece, Stéphanie de la Pagerie, would marry the Prince of Arenberg. For the time being, however, Jérôme upset Napoleon's plans. In the United States, Jérôme had married a young American woman, Elizabeth Patterson, and had stayed with her in Baltimore until Napoleon became Emperor of the French, was consecrated by Pope Pius VII, and crowned himself, by which time Elizabeth was pregnant with Jérôme's child.

In early 1805 the twenty-year-old Jérôme, who loved his American wife, took her along with him on the Atlantic crossing to Europe. But Napoleon had issued strict orders not to let "the woman in the company of M. Jérôme Bonaparte"—without naming her—into any part of his empire: "It is essential that she not be allowed to disembark at Bordeaux, and that she be instructed to return to America. She must be called 'Mademoiselle Patterson' with a meaning that will be made plain to her. You understand how much interest I take in this matter."[14] The French *chargé d'affaires* in Lisbon informed Jérôme that His Imperial Majesty had sent a passport for him, but that "the woman in his company" could not enter the territory of the French empire.[15] Jérôme sent his unhappy wife to Amsterdam, while he proceeded to Alessandria, in northwestern Italy, to face his imperious brother.

Napoleon had to have his own way, or else he felt unbearably helpless. He promised Jérôme the world if he only gave up his wife.[16] Compared with his defiant older brother Lucien, the young Jérôme was rather docile. Vincent Cronin thought that Jérôme "had a healthy fear of his older brother" and "did as he was told."[17] After ten days of long-distance written negotiations Jérôme caved in and informed Napoleon that he was ready to give up his beloved wife. Napoleon received Jérôme for an hour-long interview in Alessandria and forced him to formally request the annulment of his marriage. A shaken Jérôme emerged from this meeting "visibly agitated."[18] The marriage was annulled by imperial decree and Jérôme married the woman Napoleon had dictated to him, Princess Catherine of Württemberg, and later became King of Westphalia.

With his younger brother in total capitulation, a triumphant Napoleon left Alessandria for Milan. On May 26, 1805, he was consecrated and crowned King of Italy at Milan's cathedral in front of Leonardo's *Last Supper*, with the ancient Lombard motto in Latin, *Rex Totius Italiae* (King of All Italy). Napoleon crowned himself with the Iron Crown of the kings of Lombardy, which had been brought from Monza, taking the terrible oath of the ancient Lombard kings: "God gave her to me. Woe to him who touches her!" The "she" in this oath was both the crown (a feminine word in Italian and French) and Italy herself. The poetical psychoanalyst Pierce Clark described the dramatic scene: "A year after his Paris coronation he crowns himself in Milan with the iron crown of the Lombards, for the border states are to become monarchies like France itself. His voice reverberates through the cathedral as he thunders the traditional formula of the Carlovingian [*sic*] kings."[19]

The pope was upset by the new developments. Napoleon's new title of *Rex Totius Italiae* "greatly alarmed Pius VII, who was the ruler of central Italy . . . and the Bourbon king and queen of Naples."[20] Nonetheless the pope had allowed Napoleon to be consecrated and his crown to be blessed by his seventy-two-year-old former legate to France, Giovanni Battista Cardinal Caprara, now the archbishop of Milan. Napoleon had his treasury mint commemorative medals bearing the inscription *Napoleo Rex Totius Italiae.* He felt as great as Charlemagne: "Like Charlemagne, I unite the crown of France to that of the Lombards, and my empire marches with the east," he said.

All this was before Napoleon's defeat at Trafalgar, which undid his plans for the invasion of England. The bad mother had to be seized by the throat and strangled. While Napoleon was in Italy in the spring of 1805, he never forgot his fantasy of invading *l'Angleterre.* It preoccupied him during the Milan festivities. He thought of it every night. His correspondence from Italy often dealt with England. But Napoleon was aware of his navy's inferiority to the British Royal Navy, so he ordered his admirals to engage the British Royal Navy whenever possible and "to sacrifice everything, provided that enough vessels remained to master the Channel, were it only for the space of one day. Everything rested on the schemes planned to allow passage for the splendid army of 132,000 men which was impatiently awaiting the moment for cutting the knotted coalitions in the heart of London, and 'avenging six centuries of insult and shame.' Because the plan failed, it has been believed to be impossible . . . But there is ample proof that he applied his mind to it with passion."[21]

Napoleon felt compelled to continually expand his empire, which, in his unconscious mind, was an extension of his own self. Otherwise, he felt small, inadequate and worthless. This perfectionistic compulsion caused him to repeatedly annex territories to France. On June 4, 1805, he annexed the Ligurian Republic—the former Republic of Genoa—to his

French empire. Napoleon's annexation of Genoa to his Empire was used by Russia and Austria as *a casus belli* to join Great Britain in a new alliance against France.

Meanwhile, with the kingdom of Italy part of his empire, Emperor Napoleon brought several other prominent Italians into his government. While he was king of Italy, Napoleon could not govern it in person, being the emperor of France in Paris. He needed a viceroy to govern Italy for him. On June 7, 1805, Napoleon named his twenty-four-year-old stepson, Eugène de Beauharnois, *vice-roi d'Italie*. Eugène's duties included presiding over the Italian council of ministers and council of state and governing Italy in Napoleon's absence. Napoleon bought his mother Letizia a magnificent seventeenth-century castle at Pont-sur-Seine in the Aube *département*, giving her another sixty thousand francs just for the purchase of furniture. But the greedy Letizia, who had already received three hundred thousand for her household, found her son's allotment too small. She drew another one hundred sixty thousand francs from the French Imperial Treasury. Letizia made long stays at Pont-sur-Seine, to the chagrin of her ladies in waiting, who complained of the lack of entertainment at the old and isolated castle.[22]

Napoleon's unquenchable thirst for power, territority, and domination repeatedly caused the European powers to unite in military alliances aganist France. One of the battles aganist France took place at the Czech town of Austerlitz on December 2, 1805, and is often called "the battle of the three emperors," because the emperors of France, Austria, and Russia fought in it. In fact, there were only two emperors present at Austerlitz, Napoleon of France and Aleksandr of Russia. The thirty-seven-year-old Emperor Franz of Austria, who was also Holy Roman Emperor Francis II, had elevated his kingdom of Austria to the status of a *Reich* or empire the previous year, soon after Napoleon had made himself Emperor of the French. Franz was in Hungary, far away from the battlefield, even though it was in his own country. While the Frenchmen mauled the Russians, the stubborn Aleksandr "stuck doggedly to his plan, ignoring the cost and the fact that he was weakening his right (north) flank."[23] The cost was horrific. Ten thousand Russians were killed at Austerlitz. Fifteen thousand others were wounded, scattered or taken prisoner. Tsar Aleksandr sat among the Russian dead and wept.

Napoleon had won a "spectacular" victory at Austerlitz against the combined Austrian and Russian armies, but the slaughter at Austerlitz was unspeakable. On December 3, 1805, the day after the battle of Austerlitz, Napoleon issued his 30th Bulletin of the *Grande Armée*, telling the story of previous day's battle and detailing its course. Napoleon glorified the battle: he and his army, he wrote, had broken and dispersed one hundred thousand enemy soldiers within four hours. "Soldiers! I am well pleased with you," he told his men. "Those who escaped your steel were drowned in the lakes."[24] Napoleon ended his bulletin with the famous phrase: "It will be enough for you to say 'I was at the battle of Austerlitz!" for the answer to come, 'There is a hero!'"[25]

When he was twenty years old, Napoleon had written a horror story titled *Nouvelle corse* (Corsican Novel). In his 30th Bulletin, the thirty-six-year-old Napoleon told a new horror story:

> At one o'clock in the afternoon the victory was decided. It had never been in doubt. Not a single soldier of the reserve had been needed, and none had been used. The cannonade continued only on our right. The enemy corps which had been surrounded and dislodged from all the heights was now in a depression, with its back against a lake. The Emperor attacked it with twenty artillery pieces. This corps was hunted from position to position, and a horrible spectacle could be seen . . . twenty thousand men throwing themselves into the water and drowning in the lake! . . . Never did a battlefield look more horrible. From the middle of the immense lake, the screams of thousands of men could be heard, but there was no way of coming to their aid. It will take three days before all the enemy wounded can be evacuated to Brünn. The heart bleeds! May all this bloodshed, may all these woes be avenged at last on the perfidious islanders who are their cause. May the cowardly oligarchs of London be visited with punishment for so much suffering![26]

Napoleon's horror imagery is striking, the more so since this "horrible spectacle" on the icy lake was mostly a figment of his own imagination. Friedrich Kircheisen stated that the entire incident was "pure invention"[27] while Christopher Herold believed that the number of Russians killed at Austerlitz and the "immensity" of the lake were exaggerated: "The Russians may have tried to escape across a frozen pond and drowned when Napoleon directed his guns to fire on the ice."[28]

Why did Napoleon exaggerate the horrors of Austerlitz to make it seem like the most horrible battle in human history? The unconscious meaning of his icy-lake fantasy can be deciphered from the end of his official bulletin above: Napoleon blamed these horrors not on himself but on "the perfidious islanders" of England. In his unconscious mind, one bad mother, Corsica, had been replaced by another, England. She was his Bad Mother Letizia, who caused all his miseries and suffering. She, Napoleon's mother, was "the perfidious enemy." So, for now, were the Russians and Austrians. What he did to them was an unconscious repetition of—and revenge for—what his mother had done to him. When he was a screaming infant in pain, she had not come to his aid. Letizia had not heard him. She had rejected him. She had stayed away from his consecration and his coronation, a year to the day before Austerlitz. His heart had bled at this "crowning injury."[29] The "immense frozen lake" of his Austerlitz fantasy was an unconscious symbol of the cold mother of his infancy. The painful memories of his early life had produced this horror fantasy.

Emperor Franz of Austria learned of his defeat at Austerlitz on the night of December 2–3, 1805. To cut his losses and save face, the defeated *Kaiser* sought an interview with Emperor Napoleon. Their meeting took place two days later, at the Austrian city of Pressburg (now the Slovak capital of Bratislava). The two emperors signed an armistice allowing the Russian army to withdraw from Austria by stages while the Austrians undertook peace negotiations with France. The talks were complicated. Napoleon did not want to wipe out the Habsburg monarchy, for do so "would mean the continuance of a war whose main goal lay elsewhere"—in England.[30]

Napoleon did, however, intend to show that he, not Austria's Franz, was Charlemagne's successor as "Holy Roman Emperor." The Treaty of Pressburg that he dictated to Franz, which was signed by the Austrian general Joseph Johann von Liechtenstein in December 1805, was a humiliation for the latter: Austria had to cede all her Italian territories, including Istria and Dalmatia on the eastern Adriatic coast, to Napoleon's French empire and his kingdom of Italy. She had to cede Swabia to France's ally Württemberg, cede the Tyrol to France's ally Bavaria, and pay France a war indemnity of 40 million francs. In 1806 Napoleon abolished Austria's "Holy Roman Empire of the German Nation." By humiliating his enemy so badly, Napoleon sowed the seeds of his own destruction. He made sure that Austria would once again join a coalition to topple him just as soon as she and her allies, Britain and Russia, felt strong enough militarily to do so.

During the year 1806, after his victory over Austria, Napoleon was busy consolidating his French empire, which now consisted of three parts: France—including Belgium, the Savoy, the left bank of the Rhine, Corsica, and the northwestern parts of Italy; the Kingdom of Italy; and the French vassal states in Germany.[31] After Austria had taken the field against Napoleon for the third time in 1805, and was again defeated, Napoleon dictated the dissolution of the Holy Roman Empire, and Emperor Franz of Austria abdicated as Holy Roman Emperor.

That year was dramatic in Napoleon's life, and in that of Europe. Unlike Austria, Germany was still divided into numerous states—kingdoms, duchies, principalities, and electorates. Napoleon, who had ended the "Holy Roman Empire of the German Nation," wanted to get as many German princes as he could on France's side against Austria, Prussia, Russia, and Great Britain. Napoleon and his advisers conceived the idea of a new confederation of German states allied with France.

In mid-July 1806, after lengthy negotiations, Napoleon's France and fifteen German states signed a treaty setting up a new Confederation of the Rhine, a union of German states excluding Austria and Prussia, free in theory but in reality subservient to France. The head of the new confederation was the sixty-two-year-old Carl Theodor von Dalberg, the former archbishop and elector of Mainz, elector of Regensburg, primate of Germany, and archchancellor of the "Holy Roman Empire of the German Nation." In Dalberg, the French emperor had a man he could trust to obey him. Dalberg presided over the first federal assembly of the Rhenish Confederation in Frankfurt, which created its constitution. Frankfurt became the capital of the new confederation, and Emperor Napoleon of France was proclaimed its protector.[32] While Dalberg wanted to unify Germany, however, Napoleon sought to divide and rule it by setting its Rhenish states against Austria and Prussia.

By the summer of 1806 the entire continental part of the kingdom of Naples, including Calabria, had been conquered by France. Napoleon made his elder brother, Joseph Bonaparte, king of Naples. Sicily and its neighboring islands such as Lampedusa, however, remained under the rule of the Bourbon king Ferdinando and his Austrian wife Maria Carolina, protected by the British Royal Navy. While Joseph promoted liberty and uprooted feudalism in Naples, Sicily remained under autocratic feudal rule. On August 2 Joseph abolished all baronial jurisdiction, all rights to personal services, and all special water rights in Naples. Two days later Archbishop Dalberg, the Prince Primate of the Confederation of the Rhine, presented Emperor Napoleon with the constitutional act of the new federation of which Napoleon was the protector. Napoleon's grandiosity received another boost.

In the spring of 1806 Napoleon had issued his imperial catechism, which the papal legate Giovanni Battista Cardinal Caprara had approved as "conforming to the doctrine of the Catholic Church," but which revolved around Emperor Napoleon rather than around Jesus Christ.[33] The imperial catechism required all true Christian believers to revere their emperor. Those who opposed him would suffer eternal damnation. The psychoanalyst Pierce Clark believed that Napoleon truly thought of himself as God's anointed son:

> When Napoleon causes this to be taught, there is in him no hypocrisy; it is his one conviction. He is opposed to the shedding of blood unnecessarily, but is absolutely unscrupulous in shedding any amount of it to carry out his own purposes, for he looks upon them as divine, sanctioned from on high. He believes himself to be the prophet of God as certainly as did Mahomet. He treats those who resist his will with outrage, and covers them with insult, because they oppose the will of Heaven, operating through him. He keeps no faith with his enemies, and breaks treaties as soon as made, considering himself justified because he is swept forward by the breath of God; force is a manifestation of God, and he who has the power is the minister of God to use what is given to him. With Napoleon religion is a conviction that he is the anointed of God. Apart from himself, he cannot conceive of God acting.[34]

Predictably, Napoleon's omnipotent fantasies led to disaster whenever they clashed with the hard rock of reality, or when his enemies did not accept him as God's anointed son. His disastrous defeat at Trafalgar in October 1805 had led to the tragic suicide of Admiral Villeneuve. It was bad news for Napoleon, who may have felt guilty over appointing Villeneuve in the first place, but Napoleon unconsciously defended himself by projecting his guilt feelings on his subordinate. He continued to think that it was Villeneuve, not himself, who had caused his humiliating failure to invade and conquer *l'Angleterre*.

22

The Jews as a Projection of Napoleon's Self

The Jews had been the hated minority of Christian Europe since the earliest times. They had been persecuted by the Christians, who believed that the Jews were the murderers of Jesus Christ, children of the Devil and of the evil Sow, his wife.[1] Napoleon, who liked to think that he was enlightened and had no racial prejudices, had met some Jews during his Italian campaign of 1796–1797, in which he liberated the Jews of Ancona and other towns from medieval discrimination. In early 1806 Napoleon met organized Jewry for the first time during his visit to Strasbourg on the way back from Vienna to Paris. How did he treat them? Was he a liberal or a bigot, a racist or an enlightened ruler?

The true answer is both. The *bonapartistes* and some of the post-revolutionary French socialist philosophers, such as Claude Henri de Saint-Simon and his follower Pierre Leroux, considered Emperor Napoleon an enlightened and liberal ruler: "Wherever he ruled or placed his rulers, the Inquisition, feudal rights, all exclusive principles, were abolished, the number of monasteries was reduced, customs barriers between provinces thrown down . . . social prejudices which divided humanity into castes, all sorts of inequalities."[2] The Dutch scholar Pieter Geyl thought that "The worst that our generation has had to witness, the persecution of the Jews, had no parallel in Napoleon's system" and that Napoleon never discriminated against the Jews.[3]

Dorothy Carrington agreed that "Napoleon cut through a mass of prejudice and injustice inherited from feudal and ecclesiastical authority."[4] Norman Dixon thought that "Napoleon's policy, that all members of a society should have equal opportunities for education, may be taken as further evidence ... for his lack of ethnocentric tendencies."[5] One Jewish "scholar" even believed that Napoleon was the most enlightened and generous ruler the Jews ever had.[6] In fact, Napoleon's feelings about the Jews were deeply ambivalent and often changing. While in certain cases he was enlightened and liberal, at other times he was no less racist and prejudiced than most of his contemporaries. There were times when he hated the Jews with a passion. In 1808 Napoleon wrote his younger brother Jérôme, the king of Westphalia, calling the Jews "the most despicable of men."[7]

Napoleon may have met some Jews in his youth, but his first serious encounter with the Jews came in early 1806. Since the beginning of the French Revolution, German Jews had been immigrating to France, most of them settling in France's German-speaking provinces, Alsace and Lorraine. Many central-European Jews became French when Napoleon's conquests and annexations made their provinces part of France.[8] Of these, many became money lenders because this was one of the few occupations open to Jews. Money-lending was a perilous occupation. Debts were often not repaid. Many lenders were violently attacked, some were murdered. The high interest rates imposed by lenders were commensurate with the high risk involved in money-lending. They could be as high as 50 percent or even 100 percent of the loan. To the Christians, this meant outrageous usury. They hated the Jews for doing that which the Christians themselves had forced them to do.

In Strasbourg, on his way home to Paris from his victories in Austria, Emperor Napoleon heard bitter complaints about the usurious Jews from the angry Alsatian Christians, who falsely accused the "usurious" Jewish money-lenders of having "taken over" Alsace and said they would soon take over all of France.[9] Napoleon's lifelong rage at his greedy and controlling mother was now unconsciously displaced to the Jews. After his visit to Alsace, the Jews were very much on his mind. The racist, Jew-hating French political right wing was growing vocal. To Napoleon, the Jews were defying his control, they were "a state within a state."[10] This was a situation he could not tolerate. In such cases he was always decisive—or impulsive. Vowing to settle "the Jewish Question" once and for all, Napoleon charged his state council with settling the legal status of the French Jews. He later attended a meeting of his state council that discussed the complaints of the Alsatian authorities against their "usurious" Jews and argued that the Jews were not ordinary French citizens but "a nation within a nation" who must be treated as a separate political entity.[11]

Napoleon's state council had an interior section as well as an external-affairs section. The head of the interior section was the forty-four-year-old Michel-Louis-Etienne Regnaud de Saint-Jean-d'Angély, a high court official. In this interior section, which had to debate the Jewish question, an internal struggle arose between the hard-core Jew haters and the liberal members of the state council led by Regnaud. In early 1806 Emperor Napoleon named the liberal legal scholar Jean-Claude Beugnot, a forty-five-five-year-old former prefect of the Seine-Inférieure department, to his state council and attached him to its interior section. At about the same time, however, Napoleon named the twenty-five-year-old Louis-Mathieu Molé, a racist political writer and rabid Jew hater, to the interior section.

On April 30, 1806, Beugnot presented his liberal, favorable, and balanced report on the Jews to the state council in the emperor's presence. Napoleon, who wanted to punish the "usurious" Jews for their "usurpation" of Alsace, expressed his displeasure with Beugnot's report and angrily called the Jews "a contemptible and degraded nation which is capable of the lowest deeds."[12] Unfortunately for the Jews, Beugnot was intimidated by Napoleon, became anxious, and did not make an effective presentation of his pro-Jewish report to the council. To allay his anxiety, he rigidly defended his report. Overruling both Regnaud and Beugnot, a furious Napoleon forced his state council to adopt the lengthy, fulminating, and virulently anti-Jewish report written by the racist Molé. Like other anti-Jewish hate tracts, Molé's report on the Jews was severely flawed as a scholarly work.[13]

After the official anti-Jewish report of his state council, however, Napoleon had second thoughts. A week later, at the next meeting of his state council, he rejected both Molé's hostile report on the Jews and Beugnot's favorable one, announcing to the state council that he wanted nothing less than a total regeneration of the Jews. On May 30, 1806, Napoleon issued an imperial decree whose purpose was to fight "Jewish usury." Using the "royal we," the emperor put forth his grand project for reforming the Jews:

> These circumstances have also acquainted Us with the urgent need to revive, among those of Our subjects who profess the Jewish religion, that sense of civic morality which unfortunately has been blunted in too many of them by the degraded status in which they have always been kept. To maintain or restore that status does not

> enter into Our intention. In order to accomplish this purpose, We have resolved to call an assembly of the foremost Jews and to communicate Our intention to them through commissioners whom We shall nominate to that end. These commissioners will at the same time receive the Jews' proposals concerning the most expedient methods of reviving the exercise of useful acts and professions among their brethren, so that the shameful practices by which many of them have earned their livelihood through the generations may be replaced by honorable industriousness.[14]

Napoleon's imperial decree of May 30, 1806, imposed a one-year moratorium on all debts owed to Jews by farmers in the four French *départements* on the left bank of the River Rhine: the two Alsatian *départements* of Bas-Rhin and Haut-Rhin, as well as the two Vosges *départements* between Alsace and Lorraine. The section of the decree that dealt with usury was clearly racist and discriminatory as it only applied to Jews. The liberal fifty-six-year-old senator and Catholic cleric Henri-Baptiste Grégoire, who had fought for equality and Jewish rights, and against slavery, oppression, and discrimination, and who had become the bishop of Blois, protested the discriminatory nature of the decree. Napoleon ignored Grégoire's objections and the following year extended his anti-Jewish measures for another year.[15]

Napoleon now became obsessed with reforming the "degenerate" Jews. In his unconscious mind they stood for the parts of himself that he could not accept. On June 11, 1806, Emperor Napoleon appointed three of his petitions masters to his newly created Imperial Commission for Jewish Affairs. One of them was the thirty-nine-year-old Etienne-Denis Pasquier, a son of the former president of the Chamber of Inquiries at the *parlement de Paris* who had been executed during the Terror in 1794, and a future police prefect. Another commissioner for Jewish affairs was the twenty-eight-year-old Joseph-Marie Portalis, son of Jean-Etienne-Marie Portalis, the religions minister who had drafted Napoleon's Civil Code. The third member of Napoleon's Imperial Commission for Jewish Affairs was his twenty-five-year-old favorite, the racist Jew-hater Louis-Mathieu Molé. The liberal Beugnot and his open-minded boss Regnaud were left out of the commission.

To reform the "degenerate" Jews, Emperor Napoleon called a meeting of all the representatives of French Jewry for July 15, 1806, in Paris. Napoleon's state council created a new Assembly of Jewish Notables, to serve as a rubber stamp for Napoleon's imperial decrees. There were 111 Jewish delegates to the *Assemblée des notables juifs*, all chosen by the prefects of the *départements* rather than by their own Jewish constituencies. The leading ones were the sixty-two-year-old Berr-Isaac Berr of Nancy, the sixty-one-year-old Joseph-David Sinzheim of Strasbourg and the fifty-year-old Abraham Furtado of Bordeaux. Napoleon would use these men to lead a Grand Sanhedrin of French Jews that would carry out his reforms. Unconsciously it was his own defects that he was trying to repair, having projected them upon the Jews.

While Emperor Napoleon subjected the "degenerate" Jews, whom he hated for the very "defects" that he could not stand in himself, to various humiliations and "reforms," he elevated his brothers to royalty. The Emperor of the French decided to make his younger brother Louis king of Holland. Under threat of annexing the Dutch provinces to France, Napoleon forced the Dutch "Batavians" to elect Louis their king. Louis's wife and step-niece, Hortense de Beauharnois, became queen of Holland. The new royal couple had severe marital problems, including infidelities, rows, separations and depressions. A few years later Napoleon would remove Louis from his throne.

Napoleon had not forgotten "the Jewish Question," however. On Saturday, July 26, 1806, the Jewish Sabbath, on which Jews are not allowed to work, the Assembly of Jewish Notables met in the *Salle Saint-Jean* behind the Paris city hall. The fifty-year-old Jewish leader Abraham Furtado of Bordeaux was elected president of the Jewish assembly, whose deliberations lasted nine months. It was a fake show of freedom. Publicly, Napoleon's commissioners presented the assembly with twelve questions concerning the status of the Jews; privately, they dictated the answers that the emperor wished to receive.[16]

Calling themselves "*les Israélites de France*," the French Jewish notables affirmed that the French Jews were not a separate nation but loyal Frenchmen of the "Israelite" faith, ready to die for France, and not affiliated with the British Jews or any other Jews outside France. It declared that Jewish religious law had no political force. It sanctioned Jewish-Christian intermarriage and voted thanks to the Holy See of Rome for its protection of the Jews. The Jewish historians Max Margolis and Alexander Marx thought that the Jews "rose fully to the occasion"[17] and that their vote of gratitude to the Roman Catholic Church was not an act of servility. "The Assembly voted to forgive and forget the harsh measures of some popes . . . It was a gesture of reconciliation."[18] In fact, the French Jews had been forced to bow to a superior power.

Napoleon, however, was still dissatisfied. The Jewish assembly's acts did not have the doctrinal force of established religious councils. The Emperor wanted to give its acts the doctrinal force of ancient Jewish law. On August 23, 1806, he wrote his fifty-year-old interior minister, Jean-Baptiste de Nompère de Champagny, that the *Assemblée des notables juifs* must be augmented by a new *Grand Sanhédrin*. No one knew where Napoleon had got the idea. His mind often merged history with fantasy. The Hebrew word *sanhderin* was a corruption of the Greek *synhedrion* (joint seat or council), which had entered Hebrew during the Hellenistic period in Jewish history. The Great Sanhedrin of the Jews had gone out of existence after the fall of Jerusalem to the Romans in 70 CE. Some thought that it was Abraham Furtado's idea to create the new Great Sanhedrin, others that it was the idea of Israel Jacobsohn, a German Jewish leader and financial agent to Napoleon's younger brother, King Jérôme of Westphalia; more probably it was Napoleon's own idea.[19] Unconsciously, it was the acting out of a personal fantasy, a projection of Napoleon's wish to repair his own self.

Napoleon's obsession with reforming the Jews did not let up. On September 3, 1806, the Emperor of the French ordered his interior minister, Champagny, to set up a Great Sanhedrin of French Jews representing the "Organization of the Mosaic Religion in France." This grandiose act betrayed Napoleon's unconscious identification with the Jews, and his externalization of his inner conflicts on them. They, like him, had been mistreated, rejected, and oppressed since time immemorial. They, like him, were greedy, usurious, and degenerate. They, like him, would become "great" again. As usual, Napoleon's wishes and fantasies were carried out to the letter. Like its ancient namesake, the Great Sanhedrin had seventy-one members (seventy plus the president), of whom forty-six were rabbis and twenty-five Jewish laymen. This gave its acts of the Great Sanhedrin the doctrinal force sought by Napoleon.[20]

On January 31,1807, while Napoleon entertained his new lover, Maria Walewska, in Poland, and his armies fought the Russians in East Prussia, the sixty-one-year-old Rabbi Joseph-David Sinzheim of Strasbourg presided over the opening session of the Great Sanhedrin of French Jews in the *chapelle Saint-Jean* behind the Paris city hall, in which the Assembly of Jewish Notables also met. Rabbi Sinzheim made a euphoric speech and chanted a special prayer in honor of Emperor Napoleon: "Thanks be given, Israel, to the liberator of your people, to the hero who has harnessed human passions, as he has confounded the pride of nations."[21] On February 5 the Great Sanhedrin of the French Jews that Napoleon had decreed into existence unanimously thanked the Holy See of Rome "for the protection that the Catholic Church had never ceased to give to the persecuted Israelites."[22]

On February 9, 1807, the Great Sanhedrin met again in Paris to carry out Napoleon's extraordinary wishes. The Great Sanhedrin had two Italian rabbis as its assessors. In contrast to the Assembly of Jewish Notables, which had deliberated for many months and would go on doing so for two more, the Great Sanhedrin debated for one month only. On March 9 it gave its formal answers to Napoleon's questions. Some Frenchmen thought that Napoleon's tyranny over the Jews was due to the scheming of a sixty-six-year-old Jesuit priest named Augustin Barruel, who fervently believed that the Jews, the medieval Knights Templar, the Bavarian illuminati, the French Jacobins, and other "secret societies" had conspired to overthrow Christianity, and that the French Revolution was of their doing.[23] As Napoleon had wished, the Great Sanhedrin acts gave doctrinal force to the answers of the Assembly of Jewish Notables. Frank McLynn thought that "Napoleon was personally anti-semitic" and that he had ordained a number of discriminatory anti-Jewish measures.[24]

In mid-March 1806, while Emperor Napoleon was preoccupied by the Jews, his new, eighteen-year-old lover, Eléonore Denuelle de la Plaigne, a reader to Napoleon's sister, Caroline Murat, became pregnant—probably by Napoleon. This was the first time Napoleon knew that he might become a father. It is not clear what effect, if any, this happy news may have had on his dealings with the "degenerate and usurious" Jews. The Great Sanhedrin's answers to his questions—which he had dictated—led Emperor Napoleon to issue two imperial decrees on the organization of the Jewish religion in March 1808. The first decree, promulgated by the French ministry of religions on March 17, set up Jewish consistories in every French *département* with a Jewish population of two thousand or more. Each consistory consisted of both rabbis and laymen, who received no salary from the French state, as well as the *Consistoire central des juifs de France* in Paris, with authority over all the French Jews, whose main task was to conscript the French Jews into Napoleon's *Grande Armée*.[25]

To weed out "Jewish usury," however, Napoleon's interior minister, Jean-Baptiste de Nompère de Champagny, and the three imperial commissioners attached to the March 17 decree a second one, whose goal was "the social reform of the Jews" and which the Jews called "the infamous decree."[26] This decree humiliated the Jews by restricting Jewish loans, requiring Jews to obtain permits from their departmental prefects to engage in trade, excluding all Jews except farmers from the new *départements* of northeastern France, and prohibiting Jewish substitutions for military service, which were allowed to Christians. Some Jewish historians thought that "these hardships ruined the economic life of thousands of Jews; but the injury to Jewish feeling was immeasurably greater."[27] The very act of making special laws for the Jews was a "grave deviation from the principle of emancipation."[28]

Like most other Jews, most French Jews did not have family names, using patronymics and class designations instead. This made it hard for the authorities to classify and control them. In 1792, during the French Revolution, at the same time that the reforms of Emperor Joseph II in Austria had done the same thing, a French law had already required the Jews to take last names, but it had not been enforced. On July 20, 1808, Napoleon issued another imperial decree which required the Jews to take family names. Napoleon meant it. All French Jews had to report to their local authorities and declare their last names. Jacques Godechot thought that "despite its discriminatory, and at times harassing, character the Empire's legislation on the Jews completed the work of Revolution, and unquestionably accelerated their integration and their assimilation" into French society.[29]

What did the Jews mean to Napoleon? Why did he at times liberate them and at other times hate them so much? Napoleon's unconscious displacement of his rage at his greedy and stingy mother to the "usurious" and "degenerate" Jews was only part of the story. Considering Napoleon's lifelong struggle to maintain his self-esteem, and his unconscious dissociation of those aspects of his self that were too painful for him, it is likely that he unconsciously externalized upon the Jews, as he did upon women and others, those traits that he could not accept in himself: strangeness, dishonesty, disloyalty, effeminacy, passivity, and weakness. Being himself different from others, he sought to reform the Jews and to assimilate them into the French state because he could not bear their being different. His feelings for the Jews were as complicated, mixed and ambivalent as those he had for himself. The Jews were a mirror in which he unconsciously saw the unhappy aspects of his own self.

23

The Polish Lover

By the fall of 1806 most of the European monarchs feared and hated Emperor Napoleon of France, and sought to join in an alliance to topple him. The Franco-Prussian peace talks had broken down, and a Fourth Coalition against France, including Great Britain, Prussia, Sweden, Saxony, and Russia, was fast becoming a reality. While Austria waited anxiously in the wings to see how things would turn out, Great Britain prepared for naval war, and King Friedrich Wilhelm III of Prussia, secretly allied with Tsar Aleksandr Pavlovich of Russia, mobilized 250,000 soldiers, of whom 145,000 were battlefield-ready. The dukes of Saxony, Brunswick, and Hessen-Cassel joined Prussia's anti-French alliance.

Napoleon had brought this trouble upon himself. He "believed in humiliating those he had defeated, not conciliating them."[1] Rather than make peace with Prussia, whose king had been less hostile to him than the other European sovereigns, Napoleon had repeatedly provoked Friedrich Wilhelm: he demanded that Prussia give up territories to France, insisted that Prussia join his Continental Blockade of England, lashed out militarily at signs of German nationalism, and offered the former Prussian duchy of Hanover to Great Britain in exchange for peace. The furious Friedrich Wilhelm was now eager for war with France.

On September 6, 1806, King Friedrich Wilhelm announced to Tsar Aleksandr of Russia that his army was ready to attack "the perturber of the peace of the universe"[2] as soon as the Russian armies marched westward and the British war subsidies reached Prussia. Russia sent her Prussian ally an army of 120,000 men, but they would take several weeks to arrive on the battlefield. On September 12, 1806, Prussian troops moved into Saxony, joined their Saxon allies, and marched toward Bavaria, which was allied with France. An alarmed and self-righteous Napoleon at once wrote to *Sa majesté Frédéric-Guillaume de Prusse*, calling the new war a "sacrilege" and a "disaster"[3] and blaming the Prussian king for starting it:

> I must say this to Your Majesty: war shall never be of my doing, for if it were, I should look upon myself as a criminal. Criminal is what I call a sovereign who, for a whim, undertakes a war which the policy of his country does not justify . . . If I am compelled to take up arms in my own defense, I would employ them against Your Majesty's troops only with the greatest regret. So intertwined are the interests of our two states that I would regard it as a civil war. I want no part of it; I have demanded nothing of it.[4]

Egged on by his allies and by his wife, however, King Friedrich Wilhelm of Prussia gave Emperor Napoleon of France an ultimatum: take your army out of the Confederation of the Rhine, cross the Rhine into France and get out of all of Germany by October 8, 1806—or face war with Prussia. But the imperious Napoleon could not accept any ultimatum. He had already made his war plans. If he meant to defeat Prussia, Napoleon had to attack her quickly, before the large Russian army came to her aid. By the day on which the Prussian ultimatum to Napoleon expired, his forces were deployed across the Saale River valley in Thuringia. King Friedrich Wilhelm had named the seventy-one-year-old Duke of Brunswick the commander-in-chief of the Prussian armies. Under the duke were two other Prussian generals, both veterans of the Prussian wars with France: the sixty-year-old Friedrich Ludwig, Prince of Hohenlohe-Ingelfingen, and the fifty-two-year-old Ernst Friedrich von Rüchel. Hohenlohe's army was east of Gotha, along the Saale River, while Rüchel's army was farther west, at Eisenach.

On October 9, 1806, the new Franco-Prussian war began near the Thuringian village of Schleiz, north of the Franconian Forest, across the Saale river from Saalburg. Emperor Napoleon and his marshals beat back the Prussians under Carl Wilhelm Ferdinand, the Duke of Brunswick. The second battle took place on October 10 at the Thuringian town of Saalfeld, on the Saale River southwest of Jena. Prince Ludwig of Prussia was killed, and a happy Napoleon wrote in the Second Bulletin of the *Grande Armée* that "the first blows of the war have killed one of its instigators."[5] Napoleon believed that the Prussians would regroup at the Saxon town of Gera on the Elster River, southwest of Leipzig. In fact, the old and hesitant Duke of Brunswick, who commanded the Prussian armies, gathered his forces near Jena and on the plain of Weimar to its west.

The battle of Jena on October 14, 1806, provoked a series of tragic errors on both the French and Prussian sides. At dawn Napoleon's forces gathered around Jena. His Imperial Guard and Marshal Lannes's 5th Corps were atop the Landgrafenberg, Marshal Augereau's 7th Corps was on the nearby Galgenberg on their left, Marshal Soult's 4th Corps was in the Saale valley on their right, Marshal Ney's 6th Corps was on its way in from Roda, and Marshal Davout's 3rd Corps was on its way in from Naumburg. Marshal Bernadotte's 1st Corps was near Dornburg, where Napoleon, in his orders to Davout, had "hoped" it would be. Due to Napoleon's ambiguous orders, however, Bernadotte's 1st Corps circled Dornburg during the entire battle of Jena and nearby Auerstädt, awaiting Napoleon's further orders, which never came, and taking no active part in the battle. Napoleon was furious at Bernadotte, but several scholars believed that it was his own fault for not telling Bernadotte what he wanted him to do.[6]

An anxious Napoleon sent Lannes' 5th Corps down toward the Prussians while he and his Imperial Guard remained entrenched on the Landgrafenberg. Due to the massive fog and poor visibility, Lannes's corps went off course. One of its divisions took the village of Closewitz, while the other two blundered toward the village of Vierzehn-Heiligen. When the fog began to clear the Prussians attacked Lannes's flank, marching in straight drill-field lines. Augereau's and Ney's corps came to Lannes' rescue. Ney was bloodied and almost cut off, but finally linked up with the others. At 10 a.m. the French took Vierzehn-Heiligen. The Prussian generals' bickering and their commander in chief's indecisiveness badly damaged their coordination. Prince Hohenlohe awaited reinforcements from his colleague General Rüchel, whose corps inexplicably took four hours to march the six miles (ten kilometers) from Weimar to Vierzehn-Heiligen. This gave Napoleon badly needed time to gather his forces. Soult's corps reinforced Lannes's on its right flank, and Murat's reserve cavalry also arrived. At the end Napoleon and his marshals defeated the outnumbered Prussians at Jena.

On the same day of October 14, 1806, the unfortunate Marshal Davout was in the reverse situation at the town of Auerstädt, ten miles north of Jena. Davout's 26,000-man 3rd Corps was vastly outnumbered by the

64,000 men of Brunswick's army. Davout fought a desperate and bitter battle. The Austrian troops at Auerstädt were led by the sixty-four-year-old Prussian general Gebhard Leberecht von Blücher, an old and resolute adversary of Napoleon. Blücher fought well, but at the end Marshal Davout's brilliant tactics at Auerstädt defeated the vastly superior Prussians. Davout's corps, however, suffered eight thousand casualties. By the early afternoon the Prussian army was in full flight from Auerstädt, pursued by Davout's infantry and cavalry. Davout's victory was complete.[7]

Owen Connelly thought that Napoleon had "blundered to glory" at Jena and Auerstädt.[8] He had misjudged the Prussian forces. His subordinates, not he, were the real victors, and the Prussian errors had handed him his victory. The battle "preyed on Napoleon's mind" and he kept reinterpreting its events.[9] To sustain his grandiose self, Napoleon convinced himself that he, rather than Marshal Davout, had defeated the Prussians, and that the victory had been won at Jena rather than at Auerstädt. The battle of Jena-Auerstädt sealed the fate of Prussia. The Prussian army had been decimated. The defeated and unhappy King Friedrich Wilhelm ordered the remnants of his army to retreat and sought an armistice with Napoleon. The French emperor imperiously turned him down. He marched his army on Berlin, or rather on nearby Potsdam and its Sans-Souci Palace, forcing the king to flee to Memel in East Prussia, in the Prussian Baltic provinces.[10]

On October 24, 1806, fifteen days after the beginning of their Prussian campaign, Marshal Davout's 3rd Corps entered Berlin. Emperor Napoleon, with his imperial guard, went to Potsdam, southwest of Berlin, the site of Sans-Souci, Frederick the Great's palace, now owned by Friedrich Wilhelm III. Napoleon reached Potsdam, "in a rather heightened state of emotion."[11] Napoleon had long admired *Frédéric le grand* as one of the great military leaders and rulers in human history. Occupying Sans-Souci, Napoleon found many documents left behind by the fleeing Prussian king. One of them was a letter from King Carlos IV of Spain saying that he would "attack the French from the rear while Napoleon was still on the banks of the Elbe!"[12] If this "treacherous" letter confirmed Napoleon's fear of Spain and his resolve to invade it, his intentions of conquering Spain had been of long duration. Napoleon toured Frederick the Great's apartments, examined his field glass and his books, and took Friedrich's waistband, grands cordons, and sword as war trophies.

Treating Prussia like an unfaithful wife or mother, the angry Emperor of the French forced his "treacherous" enemy to pay heavy reparations to France and to cede to France all its western territories, between the Rhine and the Elbe.[13]

Emperor Napoleon of France stayed at Potsdam's Sans-Souci palace for three days. On October 25, 1806, he reviewed his imperial guard at Sans-Souci, visited Frederick the Great's tomb, and declared that the latter's sword would be taken with the other Prussian spoils to Paris and placed in the *Hôtel des Invalides*: "I would rather have these trophies than all King Frederick's treasures. I will send them to my old soldiers of Hanover; I will give them to the superintendent of Les Invalides who will keep them as a token of the Grand Army's victories and the vengeance it took for the disasters of Rossbach."[14] The "disasters of Rossbach," however, had occurred in 1757, twelve years before Napoleon was born, during the Seven Years' War of 1756–1763, when the forty-two-year-old French marshal Charles de Rohan, Prince of Soubise, was defeated by Frederick the Great at the Saxon town of Rossbach, near Halle. The following year Marshal Soubise defeated the Prussians at Sonderhausen and Lützelburg, continuing to serve King Louis XIV until the general peace of 1763.

Jacques Bainville thought that Napoleon's stay at Sans-Souci "was one of Bonaparte's [*sic*] most glorious hours: to a man of the eighteenth century the King of Prussia, soldier, legislator, philosopher, had seemed the perfect hero. But in the imagination of the peoples, it was he [Napoleon] who should take the place of that Frederick whose sword was his most glorious trophy, whose alarm clock he would take to St. Helena. He sent that famed and symbolic sword to the Invalides."[15] In fact, taking Frederick the Great's sword was an unconscious oedipal act. Napoleon incorporated the dead king's manliness and felt as potent as the king he idealized and admired via the unconscious process of "projective identification."[16]

After their defeat at Jena and Auerstädt, the Prussian troops were traumatized and demoralized, and their remaining strongholds fell like dominoes before Napoleon's advancing army. On October 27, 1806, after leaving the palace of Sans-Souci, Napoleon entered the French-occupied Prussian capital of Berlin, whose king had fled to East Prussia. King Friedrich Wilhelm sued for peace, and on November 16 an ephemeral Franco-Prussian armistice was concluded at Berlin's Charlottenburg castle. The king of Prussia refused to ratify it, however, and no peace treaty was signed. Prussia was still at war with France. Worse still for Napoleon, the fake Franco-Prussian armistice provoked Great Britain into declaring war on France.[17] On November 21 in Berlin a furious Emperor Napoleon decreed a continental blockade of the British Isles.[18]

Despite his defeat at Auerstädt, the indomitable Prussian general Gebhard Leberecht von Blücher, whose by-name was "March Forward," was undeterred, saying "Our misfortune should only strengthen our courage and our will." Blücher was taken prisoner by Marshal Bernadotte and conducted to Hamburg, where he stirred local sympathies in his favor. He was soon set free in a prisoner exchange against the forty-two-year-old French general Claude-Victor Perrin, the future marshal and duc de Bellune, better known as General Victor. During the rest of the Prussian campaign of 1806–1807 Napoleon defeated Prussia and shore it of its eastern lands and one half of its population. Blücher, however, lived to deliver the ultimate defeat to Napoleon at Waterloo in 1815.

For many years, Napoleon had been desperate to become a father, not only to ensure his narcissistic "immortality" by having a son and heir, but also to calm his lifelong doubts and fears about his manliness. As far as he knew, none of his mistresses had become pregnant by him. On December 13, 1806, however, while Napoleon prepared to fight the Russian army in Poland, his nineteen-year-old former mistress Louise-Catherine-Eléonore Denuelle de la Plaigne gave birth to a baby boy, whom she baptized Charles Léon. At her lawyer's advice, Eléonore publicly claimed her son to be Emperor Napoleon's child. Raoul Brice called this date "the date of Josephine's divorce sentence"[19]—a long-overdue "sentence" which, however, due to Napoleon's profound ambivalence about his wife, took another three years to carry out.

On December 26, 1806, Emperor Napoleon's *Grande armée* fought its first battle with Tsar Aleksandr's Russian army at the Polish town of Pultusk. The French beat back the Russians but Marshal Lannes wrote that he had never seen such fierce combat.[20] Napoleon was overjoyed when her learned of the birth of Eléonore's son in Pultusk on New Year's Eve, December 31.[21] He was convinced that he was the father of her child. Eléonore's "outraged" ex-husband, however, later claimed that she had also been "abducted" by Napoleon's brother-in-law, Marshal Joachim Murat, her employer's husband.[22] Could Napoleon be sure that he was the father of her child?

On the cold, wintry, icy New Year's Day 1807, Napoleon met Maria Walewska, the woman who would become his new lover, at a horse-relay station outside Warsaw. Three years later she was to bear him another illegitimate son. The twenty-year-old countess Maria Leszczynska Walewska, whom Napoleon within a short time made his mistress, was "the least pretty but the most sensitive, loyal and passionate of Napoleon's mistresses."[23] Coming from the royal Polish family of Leszczynski, and born in late 1786, Maria had lost her beloved father as a child. The father had "disappeared when she was still a very young girl,"[24] perhaps because he could not abide his domineering wife. Maria's mother, however, told her that her heroic father had died from wounds received at the battle of Maciejowice, where his commander, the Polish leader Tadeusz Kosciuszko, had suffered his greatest defeat against the occupying Russians.[25]

The loss of her beloved father had marked Maria for life. It was a major trauma for her. She could not mourn her loss of him, and she idealized him into a great hero. She remained immature, forever looking for a father figure, whom she unconsciously longed to seduce, but at the same time feared her incestuous wishes. As an orphan girl she lived with her mother, brothers and sisters at Kiernozia, "a dreary manor house full of bats" set amid mortgaged estates.[26] As a teenager, Maria was brought up on the Bonaparte legend, and in her fantasies the heroic Napoleon took the place of her heroic dead father. She attended a Catholic convent school, but her "mania for politics"—or her rebellious personality—soon got her kicked out of that school.[27]

When Maria was expelled from the convent school, before she was sixteen-years-old, her aggressive and domineering mother forced her to choose between marrying a handsome young Russian nobleman and a very old twice-widowed Polish one. Maria "would have preferred death to marrying the son of one of those generals of the czar who were oppressing her country"[28] and who, she believed, had killed her beloved father. In early 1804, the seventeen-year-old Maria married the wealthy sixty-nine-year-old, twice-widowed Polish nobleman Count Athanasius Colonna Walewski, who governed a Polish province and lived on his estate of Walewice, at Plock, on the Vistula River, outside Warsaw.[29] In 1805, during her nineteenth year of life, Maria had given birth to Count Walewski's son, Antoni Walewski.

In the last three decades of the eighteenth century, Poland had been partitioned three times—in 1772, 1793, and 1795. Its size had been progressively cut until its whole territory was completely partitioned among Prussia, Austria, and Russia, and Poland disappeared as a political entity. Many Poles felt deep pain and rage, as if their mother's body had been truncated. Napoleon's "Grand Duchy of Warsaw" only comprised a small area of central Poland, yet, in Maria's unconscious fantasies, Poland was the good mother that her mother could never be, and Emperor Napoleon of France the good father who would come and liberate Mother Poland from her oppression by the bad father, Tsar Aleksandr of Russia. Even after she was married, Maria kept Napoleon's pictures on her walls, "for he was fighting Poland's destroyers: Russia and Prussia."[30] The wide-eyed Maria had ridden out to the horse-relay station to meet the great father, Napoleon. She had disguised herself as a Polish peasant girl to greet her idol, the Emperor of the French. Napoleon, who thought that he had fathered a child by Eléonore Denuelle de la Plaigne, had lost interest in her as a love object. When he met Maria, he fell for her at once. Her glowing admiration for him fed his narcissism.

Consciously, Maria had no intention of seducing Napoleon; her ardent desire was to rescue her motherland and restore the united kingdom of Poland and Lithuania, which may have represented her family in her unconscious mind. She reportedly said to the Emperor, "Welcome, Sire, a thousand times welcome to our land . . . Nothing we can do will be a sufficiently strong expression, either of our feelings of admiration for you or of our pleasure at seeing you tread the ground of our fatherland, which had awaited your arrival to rise up . . . All Poland is overwhelmed to feel your step upon her soil."[31] Napoleon made no answer, and his coachman drove away, but Maria had already seduced him with her childish mien and passionate, admiring, expression.

For Napoleon, it was a *coup de foudre*; he fell in love with the young Maria at first sight. Not knowing her helped him idealize her. Vincent Cronin thought that Napoleon's love for Maria was narcissistic: "Napoleon seems to have glimpsed his own youthful Corsican self in this twenty-year-old girl who dreamed of Polish freedom."[32] The psychoanalyst Pierce Clark believed that all of Napoleon's love affairs were "on this autoerotic and passionful level and in their wake came disillusionment and bitterness" except for his love for Maria, which "has about it a touch of sacrifice and tenderness."[33] Yet he later "ruthlessly" discarded her in favor of marrying the Austrian princess Marie-Louise.[34]

Three men helped Napoleon make Maria his mistress: his loyal aide General Duroc, his foreign minister Talleyrand, and the forty-four-year-old head of the Polish government, Prince Jozef Antoni Poniatowski. In mid-January 1807 Prince Poniatowski threw a grand ball at Warsaw's Blacha Palace in honor of Napoleon, who, the Poles believed, had come to liberate Poland from the Russian yoke. Maria was invited to this ball without her husband. She came. In typical hysterical fashion, unconscious of her inner conflicts, the adolescent mother Maria unintentionally seduced her unconscious and idealized father figure, Napoleon. When Napoleon tried to make sexual advances to her, Maria was overcome with incestuous anxiety. The "proud" young woman feared Napoleon and resisted his efforts to "conquer" her. After the ball, an infatuated Napoleon sent a bouquet of flowers to Maria with a note saying, "I saw only you. I admired only you. I desire only you. Please favor me with a quick reply to assuage the impatient ardor of N."[35] The anxious, proud, and indignant Maria made no response. What did the Emperor take her for? Had the head of the Polish government become a procurer of women for Napoleon?

Napoleon planned his conquest of his new mistress like a military campaign. He followed up Prince Poniatowksi's ball with a great banquet thrown by Napoleon himself at Warsaw's royal castle on January 26, 1807, to which Maria and her husband Count Walewski were invited. When she demurred, Poniatowski sent his mistress, Henriette de Vauban, to soften her. The French-born Madame de Vauban had lived in Versailles, Brussels, and Vienna, whence Poniatowski had brought her to Warsaw during the French Revolution. She ran Poniatowki's life. Madame de Vauban came to Madame Walewska to initiate her into the "the secrets of court etiquette."[36] Napoleon wrote Maria a passionate love letter, which Madame de Vauban "slipped into her hands."[37] The proud Maria resisted, but she finally caved into the enormous pressure of Madame Vauban and accepted the invitation to Napoleon's banquet. One biographer thought that "the nerves of the nineteen-year-old girl must have been completely frayed."[38] Napoleon, who hated domineering women who were like his mother, would later advise Marshal Davout to ignore the vain Madame de Vauban.

The devoutly Catholic Maria, in the throes of her unconscious conflict between the amorous longing for her father and the horror of incest, with the French emperor playing the role of her father, sobbed bitterly when she was left alone with Napoleon. He spoke to her tenderly; she calmed down, and let him kiss her, but not make love to her, which to her unconscious mind was incest. Later the infatuated Napoleon wrote Maria more passionate love letters. She answered them. They met twice during the last week of January 1807, "that week when he was doing everything possible to make her yield."[39] As part of his ardent wooing Napoleon sent Maria a spray of diamonds with a note asking her to wear it and to squeeze it when she was in his company and he put his hand upon his heart; Maria showed up for dinner without it. Napoleon was furious. The somewhat hysterical Maria later dramatized the scene in her memoirs:

> He took off my coat and hat, and seated me in an armchair. Then he said: "Come, now! How can you clear yourself of the crimes I have charged you with? Why did you make a point of inspiring in me a feeling that you do not share? Why have you rejected even my laurels? What have you done with them? I associated so many interesting moments with them, and you have deprived me of them. My hand has not left my heart, but yours has not moved. Once only did you answer my signal. Oh, Marie! You don't love me! And yet I love you passionately. How can this be?" And he struck his forehead in a gesture of rage.[40]

If this account, published by one of Maria's descendants 127 years later, is accurate, Napoleon was not aware that his love for Maria unconsciously repeated his tormented early relationship with his rejecting mother, Maria Letizia. His rage at Maria repeated his early narcissistic rage at his rejecting mother. The dramatic scene unfolded:

> After a moment of silence that I dared not interrupt [Napoleon said]: "There's a Polish girl for you! You have confirmed the opinion that I have of that nation!" At this point I found my tongue and exclaimed: "Ah! Please, Sire, tell me what it is!"[41]

Maria seemed more interested in what the Emperor of the French thought of her nation than in his love for her. Her nation was her idealized mother.

> [Napoleon replied] "Well, Marie, I consider the Poles to be passionate and frivolous. I believe that they do everything out of fantasy and nothing by way of system. Their enthusiasm is impetuous, tumultuous, and instantaneous. They have no notion how to regulate it and perpetuate it. And isn't that your portrait, too? *Belle Polonaise!* Didn't you come running like a madwoman—at the risk of being stifled by the crowd—to see me and flatter me? I let myself be taken in by that melting look, by your passionate expression. And then you vanished. I tried in vain to seek you out; I could not

> find you. And when you finally did appear, all I found in you was ice, while I myself was burning![42]

Without being aware of it, both Napoleon and Maria were acting out their unconscious conflicts. Napoleon unconsciously repeated his earliest relationship with his rejecting mother, whose first name—before Letizia—was also Maria, in which he sought to make her love him and she kept rejecting him. Maria repeated her childish relationship to her dead father, desiring him yet fearing incest with him. Like the medieval knights seeking their Holy Grail, Napoleon had no idea that his obsessive pursuit of those things that he could not get had to do with his interminable quest for his mother's love:

> [Napoleon said] "Listen, Marie! I want you to know that every time I have believed something was impossible or difficult to achieve, I have desired it ardently. Nothing discourages me. The phrase 'It can't be done!' merely spurs me on, and I continue to advance. Since I am used to seeing people yield eagerly to my wishes, your resistance subjugates me. The idea of seducing you has gone to my head, and I am set upon it. I want—and you must understand this word well—I want to force you to love me."[43]

To win her love, the frenzied Napoleon swung between promises and threats. At first he made promises to Maria concerning the liberation and independence of her motherland. When she still resisted his demands for sexual love, he became enraged and "with a wild look" flung his gold watch to the floor and broke it with his heel, crying "If you persist in refusing me your love, I shall grind your people into dust, like this watch under my heel!"[44] This is how Maria described the scene in her memoirs:

> [Napoleon said] "Marie, I have revived the name of your country. It still exists, thanks to me. And I will do more than this! But just remember that, like this watch that I hold in my hands, which will shatter at your feet"—and he did throw it at my feet—"its name will perish. And so will all your hopes perish if you drive me to extremes by rejecting my heart and refusing me yours." I fell lifeless at his feet. He was in an indescribable state of violence.[45]

Maria fainted because her inner conflict and anxiety had overwhelmed her. While she was unconscious, she later wrote, Napoleon took advantage of her fainting to "abuse her,"[46] presumably by making love to her while she was unconscious, which is unlikely. When she came to, "There he was on his knees, swearing that he loved her to the point of madness—that madness which was his only excuse. He said things that touched the heart of the unfortunate young woman, and Marie did not run away."[47] André Castelot quoted from Maria's memoirs as published by her descendant:

> "The man who had the whole world at his feet," she continues, "was at my feet, drying my tears. He raised me up gently. 'You can be sure, Marie, that the promise I gave you will be kept.'" She saw so much passion in Napoleon's eyes that, stirred by the violence of his love (and perhaps a bit dazzled also), she forgave him. Not only that, but she began to love him, to judge by the letter that, evidently, he sent her the next morning at five o'clock, in which he laid bare all his love.[48]

Maria seems to have enjoyed the infantile fantasy that she was more powerful than the most powerful man in the world. The idealizing love letter that Napoleon sent to Marie the morning after he first made love to her was strongly reminiscent of his love letters to Josephine, whom he had similarly idealized; and, in true oedipal fashion, he was already imagining of Maria having an affair with another man:

> Madame, I am very eager to hear from you that you have not been put out of sorts, and how you slept. At no time during the night did you cease to occupy the same place in my thoughts . . . I feel a need to tell you how dear you are to me. If you have any doubts of it, you will give me great pain . . . Remember that I love you, Marie, and that you gave me reason to hope that you share my feelings. You will be faithful, won't you? A thousand kisses on your hands, and one on your heart, whose tranquillity I would like to disturb just a bit. As you can see, that was said in a spirit of vengeance. *Adieu, mon amie.*[49]

In an echo of his childhood trauma of his mother's unfaithfulness to his father with Count Marbeuf, Napoleon was already fearful of Maria being unfaithful to him. Maria's reaction to her new sexual "conquest" was to write a "Dear John" letter to her old husband, Count Walewski. The unhappy and helpless count withdrew to his estate of Walewice at Plock, near Warsaw, while Madame Walewska was chaperoned by his two sisters to Napoleon's bedroom.

On February 5, 1807, Napoleon's nemesis, the eighty-two-year-old Corsican leader Pasquale Paoli, died in London. Two days later, on February 7–8, Napoleon's *Grande armée* fought the Russians and Prussian armies at the East Prussian town of Eylau (now the Russian city of Bagrationovsk). The battle of Eylau exacted a horrible price in human blood. Tens of thousands of French, Russian, and Prussian corpses lay dead on the battlefield. The dead included five of Napoleon's generals: Jean-Joseph-Ange d'Hautpoul, who had commanded a cavalry division; Jacques Jardin, also known as Desjardins, who had commanded one of Marshal Augereau's hapless divisions; Nicolas Dahlmann, who had only become a general six weeks earlier; Joseph-Alexandre Bonnet d'Honnières, who had been wounded at Auerstädt; and Louis Varé, who had fought for Napoleon at Austerlitz.

Worst of all, the bloodbath at Eylau was a useless massacre. Owen Connelly thought that Napoleon had failed at Eylau: "He thought his corps were close enough together to be united for a major battle, but they were not. He had failed to consider the condition of the roads, the [Russian] Cossacks' ability to interdict communications, and the poor morale of his commanders and men. He was lucky that he was not defeated at Eylau and captured in the bargain. [Marshal] Davout saved him and almost won the battle for him late in the day."[50] The acerbic Talleyrand would say caustically, "Eylau was a slightly-won battle."[51]

To recover from the trauma of Eylau, Napoleon resumed his contact with his married young Polish lover, Maria Walewska. During the winter campaign of 1806–1807 Napoleon seized western Poland from Prussia and parts of eastern Poland from Russia. The battles took place in East Prussia (now northern Poland and western Russia). On April 1, 1807, during the siege of Danzig (now the Polish city of Gdansk), Napoleon moved his headquarters north from the East Prussian city of Osterode (now the Polish town of Ostróda) to Finckenstein castle, near the shores of the Baltic Sea. By the end of April 1807 Napoleon's young Polish lover had joined him at Finckenstein castle. Their relationship was both sexual and tender. Owen Connelly thought that "she was his comfort during the terrible winter campaign."[52] André Castelot thought that Maria "now loved the great man of whom she had been so afraid: she loved him, and understood that despite his promises, he could not yet establish the Kingdom of Poland."[53]

Maria Walewska wanted to sacrifice herself for her beloved and idealized motherland. The psychoanalyst Pierce Clark believed that the narcissistic Napoleon could not love any woman maturely, but that Maria "offered herself as a national sacrifice, for was not the possible rehabilitation of Poland dependent upon the good will or whim of Napoleon? How else could he be induced to take a keener interest in [Poland's] resurrection than through the pleadings of one capable of stirring his affections? The so-called love affair thus had its rationalization. Nevertheless Walewska proved a gentle and sympathetic companion; secretly visiting Elba [after Napoleon's downfall and exile in 1814], she would willingly have shared the dethroned emperor's exile."[54] Many biographers and scholars have considered Napoleon's love for Maria to have been his only true love. Freud, however, believed that every love, however "true," is based on unconscious transference, projection, and identification.

After his ambiguous "victory" at Eylau in February 1807, the traumatized Napoleon needed a real victory to restore his military reputation and his sagging self-esteem. Four months after Eylau, on June 14, 1807, at the East Prussian city of Friedland (now the Russian city of Pravdinsk), the old and incompetent Russian commander, General Leonty Leontyevich Bennigsen, who had already been beaten at Eylau, handed Napoleon the victory that he so badly craved. It was a victory that many compared with Austerlitz. After his "glorious" but very bloody victory at Friedland, Napoleon conquered all of Prussia, including its eastern provinces. He was now the master of most of Europe.

In the East Prussian port city of Danzig (now the Polish city of Gdansk), Napoleon's foreign minister, Talleyrand, was alarmed by his emperor's insatiable ambitions—which unconsciously echoed his own. On June 18, 1807, Talleyrand wrote Napoleon that his victory at Friedland was a harbinger of peace and that he should not pursue any further wars: "That is why I value it so much. For, fine as it is, I must admit that in my view it would be diminished more than I can say, if your Majesty were to go on to new battles."[55] This piece of "insolence," which repeated Talleyrand's previous provocation of 1805, infuriated Napoleon and cost Talleyrand his job. When Emperor Napoleon returned to Paris in late July, Napoleon forced the clubfooted bishop to resign from the French foreign office, which Talleyrand did in early August. He was succeeded by his deputy, d'Hauterive, and then by Napoleon's interior minister, Jean-Baptiste de Nompère de Champagny, who moved into the External Relations Ministry. Napoleon had "kicked Talleyrand upstairs" by making him Vice Grand Elector of the Empire. Police Minister Fouché dryly observed, "This was the only vice that he had lacked." His dismissal, in turn, was a severe narcissistic injury for Talleyrand which made the clergyman deeply bitter and vengeful. He began to plot against Napoleon, ultimately bringing about his downfall.

After France had won the battle of Friedland, Tsar Aleksandr of Russia realized that he had to talk peace with Emperor Napoleon of France, the ruler of Europe. The thirty-seven-year-old Napoleon prepared to meet the twenty-nine-year-old Aleksandr for the first time. On June 25, 1807, after twelve days of preliminary talks, a theatrical meeting took place between the Emperor of the French and the Tsar of all the Russias at the East Prussian town of Tilsit on the River Niemen, on the Prussian-Russian border (now the Russian city of Sovietsk, on the Lithuanian border). With their two armies ranged on the two opposite banks of the Niemen, Napoleon was rowed to a raft in the middle of the river, where he met Aleksandr. Napoleon, who had vowed to charm his Russian counterpart, came away enchanted by "this very handsome, fine, youthful emperor."[56] He was soon calling Aleksandr "a Greek of the Late Empire."[57] Unconsciously, Napoleon saw himself in Aleksandr as in a narcissistic mirror.[58]

Napoleon had spent ten months in Berlin, Poland, and East Prussia, completing his conquests and waiting for a peace deal with Russia. On July 7 he signed a peace treaty with Prussia at Tilsit, in which the Prussian king Friedrich Wilhelm had to cede almost everything, including his eastern territories in Poland, to France. On July 9 a triumphant Emperor Napoleon of France and a jubilant Tsar Aleksandr of all the Russias signed the second Treaty of Tilsit, which in effect partitioned Europe between France and Russia. Western Europe, including Prussia, was now ruled by Napoleon and Eastern Europe, including parts of Poland, by Aleksandr. In the secret provisions of the Treaty of Tilsit, Napoleon agreed to help Russia "liberate" most of European Turkey if Ottoman Turkey rejected French mediation in its conflict with Russia, while Aleksandr promised to join Napoleon's Continental System against British trade if Britain rejected Russian mediation in its conflict with France. Russia was given a free hand to conquer Finland from Sweden. Prussia was forced to join the Continental System and close all its ports to British trade.[59]

By mid-July 1807, with the Treaty of Tilsit in his pocket, the victorious Napoleon was ready to return to Paris. But his great victories over Russia and Prussia did not satisfy him; his grandiose self demanded ever more. As Pierce Clark put it, "A longing for 'something better' ever harasses the narcist. Napoleon is always possessed by an insatiable desire for more power than he already possesses."[60] As the secret provisions of the Treaty of Tilsit indicate, Napoleon now wanted to conquer the Ottoman Empire and make Constantinople a base for conquering all of Asia. When one of Napoleon's ministers flattered him on his great achievements in the Treaty of Tilsit, he answered gruffly, "You are just like all the rest of them. I shall not be master until I have signed the peace of Constantinople."[61]

By July 27, 1807 Emperor Napoleon of France was back in Paris from his Prussian conquests. Rather than return to his imperial residence in the Tuileries Palace or at Saint-Cloud castle, the emperor moved to the palace of Fontainebleau, south of Paris, where he had met the pope. From now on he ruled Europe from Fontainebleau.[62] In August he forced his foreign minister, Talleyrand, to resign and replaced him with his deputy, the fifty-three-year-old nobleman Alexandre-Maurice Blanc de la Nautte d'Hauterive and then with Champagny. The French statesman Maurice Schumann believed that Talleyrand had been preparing his "voluntary disgrace" since 1805.[63] In fact, Talleyrand suffered a deep narcissistic injury, was enraged, and nursed fantasies of vengeance against Napoleon, which he would realize seven years later.

24

Midlife Crisis

Napoleon's middle age began in his mid-thirties. At the age of thirty-four he began to eat richer food and put on weight. By the time he was forty the formerly lean and lanky fighter was stout and fat. The change expressed his mid-life crisis. It was dramatic, and was accompanied by similar psychological changes.[1] The emperor's transformation was noted by one of Napoleon's astute observers, Auguste-Frédéric-Louis Viesse de Marmont, whom Napoleon made a marshal in 1809. Marmont described the younger and older Napoleon as two different men. While not knowing the psychological meaning of "ego splitting," Marmont described it well, and his account is worth quoting in full:

> There were two men in him, physically as well as mentally. The first, lean, sober, a man of prodigious activity, insensible to privations, thinking nothing of his well-being and material pleasures; preoccupied only with the success of his undertakings, foreseeing and cautious, except when carried away by passion; knowing how to give things to chance, but taking from chance all that prudence allowed him to foresee; resolute and tenacious in his resolution, knowing men and the morale which plays such a big role in war; good, just, capable of true affection and generous toward his enemies. The second, stout and heavy, sensual and preoccupied by his comforts to the point of making them his first consideration, careless and fearful of fatigue; bored by everything, indifferent to everything, disbelieving truth except when it was in accordance with his passions, his

> interests and his caprices; of a Satanic pride and of great contempt for other men; thinking nothing of humanity's interests; neglecting in his conduct of war the simplest rules of caution; counting on his fortune, on what he called his *star*, that is to say, on a wholly divine protection; his sensibility had been blunted, without making him mean; but his goodness was no longer active, it was quite passive. His spirit was still the same, the vastest, broadest, deepest, the most productive that ever was; but his will and resolution were gone and in their place was a restlessness that had an air of weakness ... [2]

It is hard to pinpoint the turning point in Napoleon's physical and mental state. In his early thirties Napoleon still had the "lean and hungry look" of Shakespeare's Cassius, but in his mid-thirties he began to overeat and put on weight. Frank Richardson thought that "in about 1805 or 1808" Napoleon became passive, lethargic, mentally decadent, puerile, peevish, boring and untidy, and that he spent most of his time lying on a couch.[3] Richardson believed that Napoleon dreaded the age of forty and said that "forty would be his dangerous age, when he expected to become very fat. He said that at forty a man is too old to make war."[4] Raoul Brice believed that the profound changes in Napoleon's body and mind began when Napoleon was about thirty-eight:

> The turn for the worse began with the beginning of the year 1808. Those who were in the Emperor's company day by day observed a change in his person and habits. His features coarsened, his body grew heavier, his stomach [*sic*] protruded. At the same time his look grew less alert and his voice less commanding. He was not unwell; he was becoming lethargic. His fat was beginning to tell on him. There was an opposition of body and mind like a thundery sky that never breaks into a storm. "Forty years are forty years," he wrote to Josephine on the 9th of October from Erfurt.[5]

The psychoanalyst Pierce Clark, however, thought that Napoleon had become not only physically fat but also emotionally obese. Clark found a striking parallel between Napoleon's physical and emotional plumpness:

> One who reads more deeply . . . will discern but a natural unfoldment of egoistic traits that were his from birth. Physically he keeps pace with the mental change; indeed, the two are counterparts . . .

> The desire to dominate, so unconsciously fashioned from childhood, masters its possessor, and *while Napoleon masters others, he is powerless to master himself* . . . As his secret forebodings of uncertainty are stilled, his figure becomes overlaid with stealthily creeping fat . . . Soon the fiery spirit of this supremely exhilarating young man will lie deep buried, a slumbering volcano.[6]

Writing in the late 1920s, this unusual and penetrating psychoanalyst believed that the primary change in Napoleon was psychological rather than physical. His astute analysis is worth quoting in full:

> As the disfocus of Napoleon's mind grows and he becomes truly mystic he is careless at the same time of affairs of greatest moment, delays and procrastinates where once he was prompt and vigorous . . . the libido, withdrawn from the already tenuous thread of objectivity, is reclaimed to its parent stem—the ego—once more, and this augments the narcism. Self-love grows apace without requiring nurture from actual deeds accomplished; deeds proposed or dreamed suffice. Phantasies and wished-for things replace reality, and the latter's zestfulness is lost, hence we see strange silences and lethargies becoming more frequent, and the simple lucidity of Napoleon's powerful mind has shorter sunbursts, so that writer after writer notes his growing inelasticity, as though a man ordinarily wore out or became senile before middle-age.[7]

Clark understood that the deterioration of Napoleon's body were expressions of the change for the worse in his state of mind:

> Napoleon scarcely reaches the height of his power before senility sets in. The insidious emotional deterioration becomes more and more obvious. His habits and attitudes are hardening. He is more peremptory . . . External problems seem to gather to thwart Napoleon's will and purpose, but not so insistently as do the phantasies of grandeur that generate within his forceful mind . . . The essential defect is that the core of his desire is the infantile wish for universal dominance.[8]

Ignoring Clark's psychological insights, other medical scholars still embrace the dubious theory put forward by their colleague Leonard

George Guthrie in 1913 that Napoleon suffered from hypopituitarism and hypogonadism, and that this was the cause of his later-life obesity and "lethargy."[9] Some physicians had more psychological sensitivity. Raoul Brice understood that Napoleon caused his own physical decline,[10] while Boris Sokoloff sensed that Napoleon suffered from "the malady of power . . . in which abuse of power leads to destruction of the physical balance with endocrine changes and altered personality. Julius Caesar and Alexander the Great . . . shared Napoleon's irritability, peculiar paroxysms of fury, convulsions, nervous spasmodic movements and involuntary twitchings."[11] This is yet another example of how the search for physical causes can obscure our psychological vision.

Part IV

Self-Inflicted Downfall

25

Wars, Narcissism, and Oedipal Struggles

After his victories over Prussia and Russia and the Treaty of Tilsit in July 1807, which gave him control over half of Europe, Napoleon could have rested on his laurels and enjoyed peace and tranquility. His empire was larger than Charlemagne's.[1] But his grandiose self, ever hungry for more conquest and power, demanded new lands to conquer, new power to possess, and new glory to cover himself with. Napoleon now longed to annex Spain, the one country in Western Europe that he did not yet control, and that was an ally of his great foe, *l'Angleterre*. On July 29 Napoleon ordered the immediate gathering in the French Basque city of Bayonne, on the Spanish border, near the Bidassoa River, of a French army of twenty thousand men. This force comprised two army corps—the *1er corps d'observation de la Gironde* under the thirty-six-year-old General Andoche Junot and the *2^e^ corps d'observation de la Gironde* under the forty-two-year-old General Pierre Dupont de l'Etang. The official aim of this army was Portugal, formally neutral but heavily influenced by Great Britain. Napoleon's real aim, however, was Spain. He wanted to remove Spanish Prime Minister Manuel de Godoy, the Spanish queen's lover, dethrone the entire Spanish royal family, place his elder brother Joseph on the throne of Spain, and make the kingdom of Spain as part of his empire.

Napoleon's "Spanish adventure" was one of the most self-destructive of his life, barring perhaps his later decision in 1812 to invade Russia. Owen Connelly thought that in retrospect "His decision to seize Iberia was probably the most disastrous of his career because of the 300,000 casualties his armies sustained in the five-year war which ensued, the enormous costs in money and materiel, and the effect on French morale."[2] In fact, the tragic "Peninsular War" in Iberia lasted seven years, from 1807 to 1814. Connelly thought that Napoleon misperceived Iberia's political reality; he treated the Spaniards and Portuguese like unhappy children and acted like a well-meaning but narcissistic father who thinks he knows best what is good for his children: "As he saw it, Spain and Portugal belonged in his empire and the Continental System for their own good. Their governments were medieval, their dynasties degenerate (especially the Spanish Bourbons), their peoples under the twin tyrannies of feudalism and the Church. Napoleon was certain that the [Spanish and Portuguese] people would be grateful to him if he intervened."[3]

Threatened with France's invasion of the Iberian Peninsula, Napoleon's enemies formed yet another "coalition." War was imminent. On August 11, 1807, Great Britain called upon Denmark (which also included Norway) to join the Fourth Coalition against France. Caught between France and Great Britain, King Frederik VI of Denmark and Norway hesitated. On August 15 Napoleon turned thirty-eight. During the next few months, from the various corps he had assembled on the western and eastern ends of the Pyrenees, he formed his *armée du Portugal* and *armée d'Espagne* and sent them marching into Portugal and Spain, where they encountered fierce fighting and got deep into the Iberian mire. During the next seven years Spain would become his chief concern, his major headache—and the cause of his downfall.

In January 1808 Napoleon named his thirty-nine-year-old marshal Jean-Baptiste Bessières to command the 2nd Corps of his *armée d'Espagne*, which had been occupying the western Spanish province of Salamanca.[4] Bessières, a cavalryman whom Marshal Marmont and others considered incompetent and unworthy, but whose Imperial Guard cavalry had helped save Napoleon's army at Eylau, marched into Spain with his corps and with part of Napoleon's Imperial Guard and set up his headquarters at the northern city of Burgos, where he joined his fifty-three-year-old colleague Marshal Bon-Adrien Jeannot de Moncey and his *corps des Côtes de l'Océan*. In February, Napoleon's *armée d'Espagne* grew further when General Philibert-Guillaume Duhesme took the Spanish fort at the Catalan city of Figueras and marched into the Catalan capital of Barcelona with his *corps d'observation des Pyrénées-Occidentales*.[5]

On February 20, 1808, Napoleon named his brother-in-law Marshal Joachim Murat his lieutenant-general in Spain. With the expansion of his army in Spain, and with the military reverses he suffered there, Napoleon needed fresh recruits each year. The year 1808 brought fresh signs of this when Napoleon's war minister, General Henri-Jacques-Guillaume Clarke, formally announced that eighty thousand young Frenchmen would be drafted that year. Napoleon was anxious about his Spanish adventure, "as if filled with presentiment of danger, he remained hesitant and perplexed, torn between several plans. He was far from having a formulated decision."[6] To leave himself all the options, Napoleon gradually increased the number of his troops in Spain. By March his *armée d'Espagne* had five army corps numbering almost one hundred thousand men in Spain as well as large forces in France waiting to cross the border.[7] Vincent Cronin thought that Napoleon did not have to invade Spain, that he ignored the lesson of history, which he knew so well, about the two centuries it had taken Rome to conquer Spain, that he went into Spain "in a quixotic mood," and that he seriously miscalculated Catholic Spain's violent opposition to France's anti-religious revolutionary ideas.[8]

On top of his unrealistic Continental System, which was meant to strangle *l'Angleterre* with a worldwide blockade on its seaports, Napoleon had evolved a fantastic scheme for driving England out of its overseas possessions into its island home: a joint French and Russian army would take Constantinople from the Ottomans "and cut the British lifeline to India while a French fleet carried the war to the cape of Good Hope and the East Indies."[9] As for Sicily, which was part of Joseph's kingdom of Naples, and where the Neapolitan Bourbons had taken refuge under the protection of the British Royal Navy, on January 24, 1808, Napoleon wrote his brother Joseph, the king of Naples, sending him a detailed plan for the invasion of Sicily. Needless to say, it was not to be realized.

Napoleon sought to win the love of his brothers—and to strengthen his empire—by making them kings. Three of Napoleon's brothers were already kings: Joseph in Naples, Louis in Holland, Jérôme in Westphalia. The independent and rebellious Lucien, who had refused to divorce his beloved second wife, was estranged from Napoleon, exiled, and living in Rome. Napoleon's brother-in-law Marshal Joachim Murat, Grand Duke of Berg and Clèves, who was now lieutenant general of the emperor in Spain, was hoping to become King of Spain, but Napoleon planned to move his brother Joseph from Naples to Spain, and put Murat on the throne of Naples. In March 1808 King Carlos IV of Spain abdicated in favor of his son, Fernando VII. Promising Carlos the world, Murat lured Carlos, his wife Maria Luisa, and her lover Prime Minister Godoy to the castle of Marracq, near the French Basque city of Bayonne, which they reached on April 30, 1808. Napoleon came to Bayonne to play the king and his son off against one another and dethrone both.

The month of May 1808 was dramatic in Spain. On May 2, just before King Carlos of Spain signed his final abdication at Bayonne, the Spanish *infantas* left Madrid for Bayonne to join their father and mother. On that day, with their king in France, the Spaniards rose up against their French occupiers. At Murat's orders, the Spanish rebels were brutally massacred. The horrors were painted from memory years later by the great Spanish painter Francisco Lucientes de Goya. Two days after the insurrection of the *dos de Mayo*, King Carlos named Napoleon's brother-in-law, Marshal Joachim Murat, lieutenant general of the Kingdom of Spain. The following day Carlos ceded his states to Napoleon and abdicated in favor of his own son, Fernando, who had taken his father's place. At Napoleon's behest, Murat manipulated the ambivalent and unhappy former king into writing to Napoleon retracting his abdication and reclaiming the throne for himself.[10]

The Spanish king's abdication and his subsequent retraction left Spain with two kings, father and son. Napoleon decided to dethrone both kings, annex Spain to France, and make his brother Louis, the king of Holland, king of Spain. It was a bad decision for both brothers. Louis was indignant at being transferred like a pawn from one throne to another. He wanted to stay in Holland, where he was liked by the people and where he felt at home. Louis angrily turned down Napoleon's offer. Although he did not yet have the Spanish crown, Napoleon now offered it to his elder brother Joseph, the king of Naples, and the throne of Naples to Murat.

As he had done with his stepson Eugène, Napoleon formally adopted Joachim Murat as his son. He added his name to Murat's, making him *le roi Joachim-Napoléon de Naples*, and he moved Joseph to Spain, like a pawn on a chess board. Both men complied with Napoleon's wishes. The Neapolitans called Murat Gioacchino Napoleone. The diplomat-writer François-Auguste-René de Chateaubriand, whom Napoleon later removed from his post, bitterly wrote that "with one move of the hand, the Emperor stuck these bonnets on the heads of the new kings, and they went marching off, each in his own direction, like two recruits who had just traded shakos."[11]

Napoleon had convinced himself that the Spanish people would welcome his occupation of their country. "When my banner bears the words *Liberty, Emancipation from Superstition, Destruction of the Nobility*, I shall be received as I was in Italy, and all the truly national classes will be with me. You will see that I shall be regarded as the liberator of Spain."[12] This dangerous delusion would lead to Napoleon's downfall six years later. Jacques Bainville thought that "never yet had Napoleon so gravely deceived himself."[13] While the Spanish *afrancesados*, those who loved French culture and wanted to make Spain more French, wanted the French to stay and to continue their rule of Spain, most other Spaniards felt that their French occupiers were not their saviors but their oppressors, and rose up in arms against them. Napoleon knew that he was prone to making mistakes but felt that he was entitled to be. He said to Talleyrand, "I have so often made mistakes that I do not blush for them."[14] Napoleon may have felt that his superiority allowed him to make such an avowal, but, as Bainville put it, "here the error was all-embracing, and was thereby bound to make everything conspire to his hurt." [15] What looked like an "error" to Bainville, however, was an unconscious act of self-destruction due to Napoleon's grandiose self.

As we have seen, the Spanish revolt against Napoleon began on May 2, 1808, when a Spanish mob gathered at the Puerta del Sol, the central plaza near the royal palace in Madrid, to catch a glimpse of their royal family, who were actually in the French city of Bayonne. The mob became agitated and surged forward against Murat's eighty-six Mameluke guards, who furiously fired upon the rebels, pursued them into their homes and beheaded them, rolling their heads down the stairs. Their cannon fire and cavalry charges brutally quelled the revolt. The Christian Spaniards, who had driven the Muslim Moors out of Spain after seven centuries if warfare, thought of the Mamelukes as their hated successors. "During the evening and the next morning a [French military] tribunal under General Grouchy sat in the Hotel la Post. By noon of 3 May some two thousand Spaniards had died in the fighting or before Grouchy's firing squads. Murat boasted to Napoleon that the Mamelukes had taken one hundred heads. This was literally true. Fired on from houses, they had entered, decapitated men, women, and children, and tossed their heads into the streets."[16] The next day Murat's soldiers caught and executed all Spaniards believed to have been involved with the uprising on the Monte Principe Pio. The massacre was complete.

To many Spaniards, their *dos de Mayo* massacre by the Mamelukes evoked their centuries-long wars against the Muslim Moors. The

Mamelukes had horrifying connotations in Spanish minds: "*Mamelukes!* For the Spanish the word would always mean *Dos de Mayo*, blood, and horror. Napoleon had sent *Moslems* to slaughter Christians! It was forgotten that there were only *eighty-six* Egyptian warriors in Murat's army of 40,000. Napoleon had set *Moors* on Spanish women and children, the rebel propagandists would say. Could he but be the servant of the Devil?"[17] In reality, however, Napoleon's Mamelukes were not the North African Moors. "The Mamelukes were of European stock. The Egyptian ruling caste replenished itself with boy-slaves, who were reared as Moslems. So barbaric and difficult to discipline were they that the entire French army never had over 150."[18]

Emperor Napoleon of France threatened Spain's new king, Fernando, that if he did not at once recognize his father Carlos as king of Spain, he would be treated as a rebel and executed. Scared to death, Fernando abdicated, leaving behind a provisional *junta nacional* in Madrid to govern Spain. Napoleon sent Fernando to the French castle of Valençay, where Fernando was his prisoner. Some of the members of this *junta* vigorously represented the king's rights to Marshal Murat, but the Emperor's lieutenant had no power to change the emperor's decisions. On May 5, 1808, King Carlos abdicated again, this time in favor of Joseph Bonaparte. Napoleon's elder brother became the new king of Spain. On May 23 Joseph left Naples for Bayonne, whence he would proceed to Madrid. Anti-French riots broke out all over Spain, encouraged by the Spanish Catholic clergy. Like Eugène and Murat, Joseph had to take on his younger brother's name. He would be known as King José Napoleón the First of Spain, and his turbulent reign would last less than five years.

Napoleon fought his interminable wars on many fronts at the same time. While mired in his disastrous war in Spain, he also revived his simmering conflict with the pope, a new version of the age-old conflict between the popes and the "Holy Roman Emperors." It was yet another self-destructive act. Jacques Bainville asked the obvious psychological question: "Why did Napoleon, who had so well understood the importance of the Catholic Church, allow himself to be drawn into violences against the Pontiff which would destroy the moral effect of his coronation at the Pope's hand?"[19] The reason, the biographer thought, was the same as that for Napoleon's Spanish "adventure"—his obsession with destroying England. Since Pope Pius VII had refused to join Napoleon's Continental System, and the papal states continued to trade with Great Britain, the French biographer thought, if Napoleon wished to enforce his blockade, he had no choice but to make war on Pius.[20]

Napoleon's obsession with "strangling England," however, was itself self-destructive. His continental "system" was as irrational as his battle with the Holy Father. While his struggle with England was unconsciously matricidal, his conflict with the pope was unconsciously patricidal. The pope was an older man, the emperor much younger. Like father and son, Laios and Oedipus, they vied with one another for supremacy and for possession of their symbolic mothers, the Church and Europe. Napoleon unconsciously displaced his unresolved oedipal conflict to the "holy father." Napoleon imagined himself as Charlemagne's successor.[21] In one of his grandiose moments, in September 1804, before his coronation, he told his step-uncle, Cardinal Fesch, "I am Charlemagne," and in early 1806, he wrote Fesch, "for the Pope I am Charlemagne because like Charlemagne I unite the crown of France with that of the Lombards, and my empire borders on the Orient."[22]

Charlemagne was a medieval king, son of the eighth-century king Pippin the Short, the first Frankish king to be anointed by a pope, first by St. Boniface and later, in 754, by Pope Stephen II. In 800 Pope Leo III crowned Charlemagne Emperor of the Romans; in 962 Charlemagne's successor, King Otto of the Germans, founded the "Holy Roman Empire of the German Nation." As Voltaire reportedly observed, however, it was neither holy, nor Roman, nor an empire. In fact, it was a psychogeographical fantasy, not German, not even a nation. It was a loose confederation of some three hundred independent principalities and some fifteen hundred semi-sovereign states in central Europe and northern Italy. Nonetheless the Holy Roman Empire had great psychological power. Christian Europe had two great fathers: the Roman Catholic pope and the "Holy Roman Emperor." The pope of the Roman Catholic Church has many titles: His Holiness, the Holy Father, the Bishop of Rome, the Sovereign Pontiff. His throne is called the Holy See. He was also a temporal prince, ruler of the papal states. Naturally, there were perennial power struggles between popes and emperors.

Napoleon's France had conquered some of the papal states in northern Italy. The conflict between the young Emperor and the old Holy Father was as inexorable as a Greek tragedy. In March 1806, when Napoleon named his elder brother Joseph Bonaparte king of Naples and Sicily, Pope Pius VII insisted that the king of Naples had to be invested by him and refused to recognize Joseph as king of "the Two Sicilies."[23] A furious Napoleon seized the papal principalities of Ponte Corvo and Benevento, fiefs of the Holy See as well as parts of the Kingdom of Naples, made them "duchies great fiefs of the Empire," and gave them to his marshals as their personal fiefs. When Napoleon set up his irrational Continental System to blockade Great Britain, he included the papal states in it. When Pius VII refused to become Napoleon's customs officer, an enraged Napoleon told Monsignor Tommaso Arezzo, the pope's nuncio in Paris, that he would take away the pope's temporal domains.

From 1806 to 1808 Napoleon's France nibbled at the Holy Father's papal states in Italy, slowly reducing them back to the small Patrimony of Saint Peter. In the summer of 1807 the simmering oedipal conflict between the young emperor and the old pope reached the boiling point. On July 22, 1807, from Dresden, a frustrated and angry Napoleon addressed a letter to his twenty-six-year-old stepson, Prince Eugène-Napoléon, the viceroy of Italy.

> My son, I have seen in the letter of His Holiness . . . that he is threatening me. Would he think that the rights of the throne are less sacred in the eyes of God than those of the tiara? There were kings before there were popes . . . They want to denounce me to Christianity! This ridiculous thought can only come from a profound ignorance of the century in which we live; there is an error of one thousand years in the date. The pope who would lend himself to such a move would cease to be a pope in my eyes. I would only consider him an Anti-Christ sent to confuse the world . . . What does Pius VII wish to do? . . . Interdict my thrones? Excommunicate me?[24]

Excommunicate Napoleon was precisely what the proud and stubborn old pope would do. In fact, Pius VII excommunicated Napoleon twice—in 1808 and again in 1809.[25] André Castelot thought it "rather strange" that by early 1808 only two people dared defy Napoleon: "the new, frail and very young Princess of Arenberg" (actually the Duchess of Arenberg, wife of the fifty-eight-year old Louis-Engelbert-Marie-Joseph-Augustin, Duke of Arenberg), and "a feeble priest, adorned, it is true, with a prestigious title: His Holiness the Pope."[26] Napoleon, however, like the mythical Greek king Oedipus, could not help fighting the Holy Father. He railed on to his stepson Eugène:

> Does he believe that our century has returned to the ignorance and mindlessness of the ninth century? . . . Surely, I begin to blush and to feel myself humiliated by all the follies that the Court of Rome makes me endure; and perhaps the time is not far, if one wishes to continue to trouble the affairs of my States, when I shall only recognize the Pope as Bishop of Rome . . . I will not fear to reunite the Gallic, Italian, German and Polish churches in a Council to conduct my affairs without a pope, and protect my peoples from the pretensions of the priests of Rome . . . This is the last time I shall enter into discussions with that priestly gang.[27]

On March 27, 1808, the drama between the young emperor and the elderly pope reached a climax when Pius excommunicated Napoleon. The emperor's oedipal war on the Holy Father took another dramatic turn on May 22, when the Emperor of the French and King of Italy annexed the papal states of Urbino and Ancona to his Kingdom of Italy.[28] Napoleon's relations with Pius VII went from bad to worse. In Rome itself, Napoleon's forty-nine-year-old general Sextus-Alexandre-François de Miollis, who had invaded and taken over the city, ruled with an iron fist. The papal legate in Paris, Giovanni Battista Cardinal Caprara, had warned his boss that it would be folly to resist Napoleon, urging him to fall in with the emperor's Continental System against Great Britain. The old pontiff, however, could not yield to the young emperor in this father-son struggle. Pope Pius declared publicly that he could "no more yield to Napoleon than Christ could ally himself with Belial," a biblical Hebrew word meaning evil or the devil.

The "sovereign pontiff" forbade his Catholic subjects everywhere to take an oath of allegiance to the king of Italy or to France, or to serve, aid, or support that "interloping government." Napoleon ordered General Miollis to arrest the pope's sixty-year-old secretary of state and close aide, Giulio Cardinal Gabrielli, which Miollis did on July 17. At Napoleon's insistence, the fifty-two-year-old Bartolomeo Cardinal Pacca replaced Cardinal Gabrielli as the Vatican's secretary of state. The "sovereign pontiff" and his tiny Swiss Guard were helpless against the mighty army of the French emperor. Another climax was reached the following year when Napoleon arrested Pius VII himself and brought him to France as his prisoner. Napoleon's oedipal triumph—however short-lived —was complete, but its tragic consequence was Napoleon's downfall in 1814.

While getting his men killed in Spain, Napoleon reformed Mother France and kept replacing his women, with whom he underwent an endless succession of *coups de foudre* and disappointment. One of his mistresses in 1804 had been the beautiful teenage actress Marie-Thérèse-Etiennette Bourgoin, who was known in Paris as "the goddess of joy and pleasure."[29] One of her unconscious attractions for Napoleon may have been that she had been the lover of his older interior minister, Jean-Antoine-Claude Chaptal de Chanteloup, who had replaced Lucien Bonaparte in 1800 and had run France's public education system. Mademoiselle Bourgoin's sexual link with Chaptal may have fired Napoleon's oedipal flames. Chaptal was a scientist, an industrialist, and a man of letters. In 1802 he had bought the Duke of Choiseul's old estate at Chanteloup. Chaptal had planned to reform the French schools.

In 1804, after the nineteen-year-old Mademoiselle Bourgoin became Napoleon's mistress, Chaptal de Chanteloup angrily resigned his ministerial post. Some scholars thought that the rivalry between Napoleon and Chaptal caused the latter to resign "amicably."[30] In fact, Chaptal was deeply hurt and incensed, as was the lady. Napoleon had humiliated Chaptal by having Mademoiselle Bourgoin brought to him late at night, while he and Chaptal were conferring. "Realizing what such a visit meant at this late hour, the minister picked up his portfolio and left. The next day he sent in his resignation—final this time."[31] André Castelot wondered about Napoleon's motives. "Had the Emperor done this on purpose—to get rid of Chaptal, whom he called Papa Enema? In any case, Mlle. Bourgoin conceived a deadly rancor toward the master because of it."[32] Napoleon's lack of empathy for other people's feelings was part and parcel of his narcissism, and his need to humiliate older people was both part of his Oedipus complex and of his narcissistic sadomasochism. Napoleon paid a high price for his unconscious oedipal victory: he made lifelong enemies of both his minister and his mistress.

At the same time, Napoleon's narcissism also had creative, constructive and reparative aspects, which found their expression in his educational reforms. Since 1795 every French *département* had a "central school," a public school which taught the conventional subjects of secondary education in the spirit of Antoine-Louis-Claude Destutt de Tracy's *idéologie*. After the signature of the *Concordat* with the Holy See in 1801, the French Catholic Church set up ecclesiastical high schools and small seminaries to train their clergy. Napoleon did not like the *idéologues*. In 1802 First

Consul Bonaparte closed down the "ideological" central schools and replaced them with rationalist *lycées* and with secondary schools which, like many of Napoleon's creations, exist to this day.

Napoleon, who had suffered the rigors of "classical" French education as a child, reformed all levels of French education. He ordered the creation of a *lycée* in every French town with more than ten thousand inhabitants. Napoleon's France had a national cultural and scientific center, *L'Institut national*, of which Bonaparte had been a member, and which incorporated the *Académie française*, but did not have a national university. In 1808 Napoleon became serious about creating an imperial university. On March 17, 1808, the Emperor issued an imperial decree creating his *Université impériale*, headed by a *grand-maître* appointed by the Emperor.

As in other things, there were many different sides to Napoleon's character. On the one hand, he was an intellectual conservative who feared innovation and revolution. Napoleon's university was an illiberal institution designed to make educated citizens conform to his laws. He made Latin and mathematics the bases of secondary education. He failed to encourage the teaching of observational and experimental science and instituted a spirit of intellectual conformity. On the other hand, on his Egyptian expedition, Napoleon had collected a large group of scientists and scholars and encouraged scientific investigation and discovery. He spent large sums of money, even out of his own pocket, rewarding scientists for their discoveries and inventions. Napoleon offered a million francs to whomever invented a linen-making machine, gave Joseph-Marie Jacquard, the inventor of the mechanical loom that bears his name, an annual pension of three thousand francs, and gave the engineer Louis-Benoit Fouques-Duparc, who made sugar from grapes, a reward of forty thousand francs.[33]

Some biographers and scholars found these contradictions in Napoleon's behavior "strange" or "curious." In fact, they were aspects of his split self. Napoleon's Jekyll-and-Hyde personality was evident in his social relations. When he was relaxed and happy, he could be kind, warm, gentle, liberal, generous, charming, and graceful. The prefect of the Tuileries Palace, Louis-François-Joseph de Bausset, had rosy recollections of his boss: "Nothing could equal the grace and amiability of Napoleon. Endowed with a lively wit, a superior intelligence, and extraordinary tact, he surprised and enchanted people the most in his moments of abandon and chatting."[34] But when he was tense, angry, or unhappy, Napoleon could be rude, abusive, cruel, and sadistic. Because he was so absorbed with himself, he kept forgetting other people's names and repeatedly asked people he knew, "What's your name?" The composer André-Ernest-Modeste Grétry, author of several comic operas and the serious opera *Richard Coeur-de-Lion*, claimed to have been asked this question at least twenty times. In reply, Grétry sighed, "It is still Grétry, Sire."[35]

Napoleon's violent feelings of rage for his narcissistic, domineering, and aggressive mother were unconsciously displaced to other women, to whom he was rude and even sadistic. In 1804, after he became emperor, Napoleon had granted an amnesty to all French *émigrés* who returned to France. Among those who accepted the emperor's amnesty was Anne Françoise-Aimée de Franquetot de Coigny, Duchess of Fleury, a twice-divorced noblewoman of Napoleon's age. The Duchess of Fleury had been married to André Hercule de Rosset, marquis de Rocozel, Duke of Fleury, and to Claude-Philibert Hippolyte de Mouret, count of Montrond. Napoleon considered her "a fast woman." At a Tuileries Palace reception, Napoleon asked the Duchess of Fleury publicly, "Well, Madame, are you still so fond of men?" She put him in his place acerbically, "Yes, Sire, when they are polite."[36]

Raoul Brice believed that Napoleon's rudeness to women was intentional, meant to show them that he was the master. "He was abrupt, sometimes even offensive, but always aware of what he said. The intriguing woman, the coquette whose one preoccupation was to subdue the stronger sex, was in his view an enemy who had to be made to capitulate. He upbraided one for her red arms, another for a headdress awry, a third for the bad taste of her dress. He amused himself by affecting ill-breeding in order to deprive these seductresses of all illusion about their power."[37] While this may be true of Napoleon's conscious intentions, unconsciously his rudeness expressed his profound rage at women, beginning with his mother, and his fear of them. Napoleon often let his lovers use him, deceiving himself into believing that they loved him, until his fantasies were shattered by reality and he was sorely disillusioned. His women in turn often complained of his rudeness, impotence and misogyny.

26

More Self-Destructive Moves

On July 7, 1808, in the French Basque city of Bayonne, where Emperor Napoleon of France had forced King Carlos of Spain to abdicate in favor of Napoleon's elder brother Joseph, the new Spanish Constitution was signed by Spaniards of the highest distinction. Among them were dukes, counts, marquises, and heads of the Spanish religious orders. Joseph Bonaparte swore allegiance to the new Spanish constitution before by Monsignor Manuel Cid Monroy, the archbishop of Burgos. This was Joseph's "coronation" as king of Spain. Many members of the Spanish *junta nacional* (of whom three fourths had been appointed by the French) stayed away from Bayonne. Those who came attended the official "coronation" of Don José Napoleón I, king of Spain. As Joseph was being "crowned," Napoleon had one of his uncontrolled outbursts of rage: "Suddenly he was on his feet, hurling threats, standing silent for awful minutes between outbursts. When he sat down, after an hour, he had really said only one thing: *Those who oppose me will be destroyed*."[1] Owen Connelly thought that this outburst was another deliberate theatrical performance by Napoleon:

> He had greeted the delegates with smiles and promises; he wanted to leave them with a taste of fear. Joseph would never show strength; he would. Then, too, he was angered by news of scattered revolts in Spain. Far from being grateful that the Spanish, so far, had made his task easy, he had developed a great disdain for them. His opinion that they were spineless and benighted had been con-

firmed. If, he said in so many words, they were so stupid as to reject the benefits he offered, he could whip them into line—and easily.[2]

In fact, there were deeper, unconscious reasons for Napoleon's outburst of narcissistic rage. Although the slightest threat to his authority made Napoleon feel powerless, flooding him with anxiety and rage, this particular outburst was unconsciously directed at his elder brother, of whom he had been jealous since his early life. *If you oppose me you will be destroyed*, he was warning Joseph, with whom he had been unhappy as king of Naples. Although Napoleon himself had "elevated" Joseph—whom he deeply loved and envied at the same time—to the throne of Spain, he had also removed him from the throne of Naples. Napoleon reacted with panic and rage to Joseph's enthronement, which threw Napoleon back to their early-life rivalry and power struggle. Their mother had had plenty of milk for Joseph, but none for Napoleon. She loved Joseph, but rejected Napoleon. Joseph had sat on their mother's throne. His "coronation," such as it was, revived Napoleon's death wishes for his elder brother. Joseph's "coronation" as king of Naples two years earlier had provoked similar feelings in Napoleon, but had taken place in Napoleon's absence. He had mocked his elder brother for being too soft on his new subjects. *This* coronation was too close for comfort.

On July 21, 1808, having made his elder brother king of Spain, Emperor Napoleon left the castle of Marracq, near Bayonne, with his wife Josephine, heading for Paris. Napoleon himself did not set foot in Spain until November of that year, when the war against the Spanish rebels went badly for him. On their way back to Paris, the emperor and empress were euphoric, playing with each other like youthful newlyweds. At the same time Napoleon was eyeing the eighteen-year-old Viriginie Guillebeau or Guillebaut, his wife's new reader. She read little, but played the harp prettily and had a rare freshness. As Napoleon's Polish lover, Maria Walewska, had returned to Paris, Frank Richardson believed that Josephine "threw the attractive young Mademoiselle Guillebeau in his way in an attempt to detach him from Walewska."[3] In fact, Josephine repeatedly "threw" her pretty young readers or ladies-in-waiting in Napoleon's way—only to stage scenes of violent jealousy when he had affairs with them.

While the Spanish *afrancesados* welcomed Joseph Bonaparte as their king, the angry Spanish rebels called him "the intruder king," while they affectionately called their exiled king *Fernando el deseado* (Ferdinand the Desired). Little did they know how tyrannical Fernando's rule would be after he returned to the throne in 1814. The rebels did not accept Joseph as their king and fought Joseph and Napoleon's France. Joseph realized that the Spaniards considered him an intruder. On July 21, 1808, he wrote his first letter from the Spanish royal palace of El Escorial, northwest of Madrid, to his younger brother Napoleon: "You must be persuaded that the feelings of the [Spanish] nation are unanimous against all that has been done at Bayonne."[4] This gloomy message was a prelude to the six years of heartbreak that Joseph Bonaparte was to endure in Spain. Joseph's brother-in-law, Marshal Joachim Murat, had left Madrid for Naples to take up Joseph's former throne. As Joseph began to realize what a bad gift his younger brother had given him, he became increasingly depressed and angry.

When King Joseph met the unsavory general Anne-Jean-Marie-René Savary, who had replaced Marshal Murat at the head of Napoleon's *armée d'Espagne*, he became even more upset. General Savary defied Joseph's orders and did what he liked in Spain—or rather, what Napoleon told him to. The king of Spain protested Savary's insubordination to his younger brother: "Is it I or he who has the right to command? That right cannot be shared."[5] Napoleon replied, "My brother, you are in command. I told you that. I make it an order."[6] Nevertheless, Napoleon constantly interfered with Joseph's actions in Spain through his personal envoys.

Napoleon did not fully trust his elder brother and did not let him rule freely. Despite Napoleon's letter to Joseph saying "You are in command," General Savary did not obey Joseph, and it was not clear which of the two men had the supreme authority over the French forces in Spain. Savary wanted to punish the Madrileños for their "outrageous" reception of their new king: some had closed their shutters and hung rags from their windows to protest his arrival. Joseph angrily refused: Murat's Mamelukes had done enough savagery to give the French a bad name already. Savary told Joseph that he had recalled the division of General Jacques-Nicolas Gobert, which was part of Dupont's army fighting the rebels, to Madrid. Joseph told Savary to order it back to the battlefield. Savary protested that Marshal Berthier, Napoleon's war minister, had ordered him to cover Madrid with its forces. An angry Joseph told Savary again to order Gobert's division back to Dupont's army. On July 23 the sad news of General Gobert's death on the battlefield reached Madrid.[7]

In July 1808 the *2e corps d'observation de la Gironde* of the French *armée d'Espagne*, under the greatly reputed forty-three-year-old General Pierre-Antoine Dupont de l'Etang, battled the Spanish *armada de*

Andalucia commanded by the fifty-five-year-old rebel general Francisco Xavier Castaños. Two days later, on July 19, came the French military disaster at the Andalusian town of Baylén, in which Dupont's "picked" French corps lost to Castaños's "inferior Spanish troops aided by peasant bands."[8] This military catastrophe was a prelude to five years of war in which Napoleon had three hundred thousand casualties and lost 3 billion francs in gold, and "Many times that in arms, materiel, and horses."[9] While most of the damage to the French was done by the British, rather than by the Spaniards, it was still a disastrous war without any rational motive.

For a week after the French surrender at Baylén, King Joseph Napoleon of Spain did not know that on July 19, 1808 General Dupont's entire corps, comprising seventeen thousand to twenty thousand men, had been defeated by the Spanish rebels, and that on July 22 Dupont had surrendered to the Spanish rebel generals commanding the *armada de Andalucia* (as Dupont himself had been wounded, the surrender was signed the day before by his chief of staff, General François-Marie-Guillaume Legendre d'Harvesse, whom a furious Napoleon later humiliated in public). After the surrender, the French survivors of the battle were taken to the Spanish prison fort of Cabrera, where they were kept prisoner under very harsh conditions for five years. Many were tortured and killed. The French *grognards* filed many petitions with their jailers asking them to improve the harsh terms of their imprisonment. They had their own commander, General Savary, to thank for their bitter fate.

In late July 1808, at El Escorial palace outside Madrid, King Joseph Napoleon of Spain received the bad news of the French defeat and surrender at Baylén. Emperor Napoleon was at Bordeaux, on his way to Paris, when he too learned of the disaster at Baylen. He exploded with narcissistic rage at his "incompetent" generals, calling their "shameful" action — which had been meant to save French lives—an "ignominy."[10] Jacques Bainville thought that "the Emperor instantly saw the dire consequences that would come from Baylen. They exceeded his fears. The loss of twenty thousand men was nothing . . . But such a prodigy of success over the finest army in the world had roused enthusiasm among the Spaniards. The moral effect was immense, and it unleashed the strength of the insurrection, to the humiliation and disheartening of the French."[11] Napoleon wrote his elder brother Joseph: "Events of such a kind compel my presence in Paris. Germany, Poland, Italy, etc., are all linked. It is truly painful to me that I cannot be with you at this moment, and amid my soldiers."[12] After he left Bordeaux, Napoleon learned that his "invincible" forces were being trounced all over Iberia. He became so enraged that he smashed a large earthenware footbath that he had just been given as a present.[13]

In the summer of 1808, at Joseph's request, Napoleon sent him reinforcements. They were too little and too late. In the face of his elder brother's troubles, Napoleon wrote to Joseph: "You will have to conquer your subjects before you can be their father. Good kings have passed through that school."[14] The Emperor warned Joseph not to retreat beyond the line of the Douro River, the third longest river of the Iberian Peninsula, which runs across northern Spain between Valladolid and Zaragoza. Crossing the Douro would symbolically mean the French defeat in Spain. Napoleon sent Joseph reinforcements, but asking Joseph not to cross the Douro was an unconscious fratricidal act: the Spanish rebels would have executed their "intruder king" had they caught him alive.

As Shakespeare's Falstaff says, discretion is the better part of valor.[15] If Joseph wanted to stay alive, he had no choice but to seek refuge beyond the Douro. On August 16, 1808, the day after his thirty-ninth birthday, an unhappy Napoleon learned that Joseph had left Madrid and retreated not only beyond the Douro but also beyond the Ebro, the longest river in Spain, which rises in springs of the Cantabrian Mountains in northern Spain and flows southeastward to the Mediterranean Sea, between Barcelona and Valencia. Napoleon was incensed at what he saw as his brother's cowardice. He wrote Joseph: "The army would appear to be commanded not by generals but by postal inspectors. How can you evacuate Spain without reason—without even knowing what the enemy is doing?"[16]

Napoleon's reference to postal inspectors was not accidental. He had just created a "black cabinet" under his thirty-nine-year-old postmaster general, Antoine-Marie-Chamans de Lavalette, whose task was to open all mail sent to Spain and read his subjects' private letters. Napoleon's evergrowing fear and suspiciousness of others fueled his ever-greater need to control others, his ever-increasing censorship of the press, literature and mail. Agathon-Jean-François Fain, who replaced Méneval as Napoleon's personal secretary in 1813, recalled that Napoleon's political police bureau was totally independent of his general police ministry, and that it had a concealed door leading to the *hôtel des postes*. Its employees were well-traveled, highly trained, and knew all the tricks of the trade. Not lacking a sense of humor, they sent their discoveries to the emperor in a red Morocco-leather folder marked "Foreign Newspapers." Jean Tulard thought that "Napoleon did not invent the violation of private mail, but he carried it to a new level of perfection."[17]

The Peninsular War of 1808–1814 in Spain and Portugal had its ups and downs, but it mostly went badly for France. The British joined the Spanish and the Portuguese to defeat the French. On August 21, 1808, Napoleon's *armée du Portugal* under General Andoche Junot, Napoleon's lieutenant in Portugal, fought the British army of General Sir Arthur Wellesley, the future Duke of Wellington, and his Portuguese allies at Vimeiro, north of Lisbon. The French were defeated. Napoleon's Spanish "adventure" was disastrous. Atrocities and horrors abounded on both sides. The Iberian "rebels" fought their occupiers fiercely. Like most other wars in human history, it was bloody, tragic, and unnecessary.

In late September 1808, oblivious to his military reverses in Spain, Napoleon dragged most of the crowned heads of Europe, including three kings—Maximilian of Bavaria, Friedrich August of Saxony, and Friedrich of Württemberg—and thirty-five princes, including the German princes of the Rhenish Confederation, to the Thuringian capital of Erfurt for his summit conference with Tsar Aleksandr of Russia. Erfurt was a French-held German town not attributed to any German prince and thus formally French. The conscious purpose of the Erfurt meeting was "to make plain to Europe the unalterable friendship of the two Emperors, to declare it with compelling brilliancy."[18] Unconsciously, however, Napoleon needed to convince *himself* of Aleksandr's friendship and love, which he feared to lose. There were other unconscious motives at play. Napoleon intuitively sensed that the thirty-year-old Aleksandr had something in common with him. The two emperors shared a narcissistic character, domineering mother (or grandmother), and oedipal guilt.

From that point on, Napoleon made more and more disastrous decisions that would seal his fate. In yet another self-destructive move, he sent none other than the two-faced Talleyrand, whom Napoleon had disgraced the previous year by removing him from the Foreign Ministry, to Erfurt to prepare his meeting with Tsar Aleksandr of Russia. Napoleon wrote the double-crossing Talleyrand, who was conniving with Aleksandr behind his back: "We are going to Erfurt, and I want to return from there free to do in Spain whatever I wish; I want to make sure Austria is worried and contained, and I do not want to commit myself in a precise manner to Russia in the affairs of the Levant. Draft an accord for me that would please Emperor Alexander, that would above all be directed against England, and in which I shall be well at ease about the rest; I will help you:

there will be no lack of prestige . . . My dear Talleyrand, I want you to be at Erfurt a day or two before us . . . You know the Emperor Alexander well, and can talk the right kind of language to him."[19]

The vengeful and double-dealing Talleyrand betrayed Napoleon at Erfurt. He urged Tsar Aleksandr of Russia to stand up to Napoleon and save Europe from his tyranny. Talleyrand told Aleksandr that France did not want the territories that Napoleon had conquered in central Europe. Why did Napoleon invite the scheming, double-talking Talleyrand, whom he had lost faith in and removed from office, to deal with Tsar Aleksandr of Russia, making it possible for Talleyrand to betray him? Jacques Bainville believed that "the Emperor, always inclined to be variable when he felt insecure in the saddle, required for this task of diplomatic consolidation a subtle and tactful man, a diplomat of the old school and of wide renown."[20] Bainville also rationalized Talleyrand's betrayal of Napoleon as an attempt to save him from disaster: "Talleyrand was accused of treachery at Erfurt . . . Actually, he was playing a very complex game. Talleyrand fancied that, being more perspicacious and reasoning than Napoleon, he was really serving him . . . Unable to convince him, Talleyrand took the perilous path of constraining him . . . Talleyrand's penetrating eye saw that the Emperor was blinding himself with regard to the Russian alliance, and he feared that he might go even farther astray and let a partition of Turkey lead him into Oriental adventures . . . But Talleyrand was the blinder of the two men in imagining that the conquests could be preserved by limiting their extent."[21]

Bainville's rationalizations notwithstanding, Talleyrand did betray Napoleon at Erfurt, and Napoleon dangerously deluded himself about him. André Castelot thought that "Talleyrand's interests no longer coincided with those of his master."[22] Behind Napoleon's back, Talleyrand incited the tsar against him: "Sire, what have you come to do here? It is up to you to save Europe, and you can only do that by standing up to Napoleon. The French people are civilized, their sovereign is not. The sovereign of Russia is civilized, but his people are not. It is thus for the sovereign of Russia to be the ally of the French people . . . The Rhine, the Alps, the Pyrenees are the conquest of France; the rest is the conquest of the Emperor. France does not insist on them."[23] This was not what Napoleon wanted him to say to Aleksandr. As Bainville admitted, "Napoleon was to be the dupe of Erfurt."[24]

Napoleon had committed several other self-destructive "errors" during the past year, among them arresting the pope, toppling the Spanish monarchy, and moving Joseph from the throne of Naples to that of Madrid. Castelot listed the other errors: "Of all the irreparable errors of the past year—the creation of the Kingdom of Westphalia, to be ruled by Jérôme, that charming and amusing buffoon of a king; the appointment of the incompetent and morbidly hot-headed Junot to the Lisbon command; the occupation of Rome; and the ambush of Bayonne, followed by the ridiculous game of kings' musical chairs played at Madrid and Naples —sending Talleyrand to Erfurt on a diplomatic mission was certainly the one error that would weigh most heavily on the future of the Empire." [25] While on the surface these were "errors," deeper down in Napoleon's unconscious they were self-destructive acts fueled by his insatiable grandiose self and incurable narcissism.

The summit meeting between Emperor Napoleon of France and Tsar Aleksandr of Russia at Erfurt lasted from September 27 to October 14, 1808. Its prime motivation was Napoleon's narcissism. Consciously, to him, Aleksandr was an adversary, but unconsciously the Russian emperor was a mirror image of his own grandiose self. The psychoanalyst Pierce Clark described their psychological fusion with a poetic touch:

> And now the two emperors who like two colossi bestride Europe, are really one, for one is but the shadow of the other . . . As host at Erfurt, Napoleon is to drink deep from the nectary [*sic*] of his own self-love. For eighteen days this mirage dazzles and bewilders all Europe . . . Erfurt is Napoleon's, and as he offers unparalleled luxuries and barbaric entertainments to Alexander, the latter's heart is softened, made receptive to the finer touches of mental adulation by the presence of Germany's greatest scholars and men of letters, who grace the occasion.[26]

Napoleon had brought the *Comédie-Française* with him to Erfurt, and later to Weimar. They performed famous French plays every night. The dramatic highlight of the summit came on the sixth evening, October 2, 1808, at the Erfurt Opera House, where the *Comédie-Française* staged Voltaire's play *Oedipe*. The play includes the verse "*L'amitié d'un grand homme est un bienfait des dieux*" (a great man's friendship is a gift of the gods). When the forty-five-year-old French actor François-Joseph Talma spoke this famous verse, the two emperors staged their own show from their opera box. Pierce Clark dramatized the scene: "Alexander rises, grasps Napoleon's hand, and in this moment of high exaltation a renewed alliance is born. The packed house, whose humblest seat is filled by a princeling or noble, rises in tremendous applause. It is a Napoleonic moment, timed and planned to a nicety even as a perfected battle—an Austerlitz or a Friedland."[27]

Indeed, one of the chief motives for the Erfurt summit was Napoleon's need to reassure himself that despite his serious military reverses in Spain and Portugal, he was still great, omnipotent and omniscient. But in reality Napoleon was weary. His negotiations with "the sweet" Aleksandr did not go as he had expected. Knowing of Napoleon's defeats in Spain and Portugal, the Russian tsar, whom Talleyrand had secretly encouraged to resist Napoleon, drove a hard bargain. He wanted to annex to his empire the formerly Ottoman Danubian provinces of Walachia and Moldavia (now in Romania and Moldova), and above all wanted Napoleon to take his army out of Central Europe.

Napoleon had no intention of giving up his hard-won conquests. Aleksandr, whom Napoleon had thought warm and loving became cool, reserved, impatient and angry, until he threatened Bonaparte: "You are violent; I am stubborn. With me, anger avails nothing. Either we talk reasonably, or I shall leave."[28] Napoleon was deeply disappointed. Unaware that the double-crossing Talleyrand had incited Aleksandr against him, Napoleon complained to Talleyrand that the hard-of-hearing Aleksandr was narrow-minded and stubborn, playing deaf when he heard things that did not please him. Castelot thought that Talleyrand "must surely have laughed up his sleeve."[29]

After protracted negotiations, Napoleon and Aleksandr did reach a partial agreement. Russia took Finland and the Danubian provinces of Moldavia and Wallachia, giving France the freedom to take Spain. If Austria attacked France, the Tsar promised, Russia would come to France's aid. Aleksandr confided to Talleyrand that he had only just realized how good Napoleon was . . . On October 9, 1808, three days after a great court ball at Weimar, a weary Napoleon wrote Josephine from Erfurt: "Everything is going well. I am satisfied with Alexander, and I think he is with me. If he were a woman, I think I would make him my mistress. I will be with you soon. Keep well. I want to see you plump and fresh."[30] But Napoleon himself felt old and weary. He wrote Josephine that he had attended the great ball at Weimar with the tsar but, unlike Aleksandr, had not danced: "Forty years are forty years."[31] In fact, he was thirty-nine.

Frank McLynn pointed out that Napoleon made self-destructive errors at Erfurt. One of them was to refuse Aleksandr a free hand in Poland and not to let him take Turkey. This refusal made an enemy of Aleksandr and eventually led to Napoleon's downfall and untimely death. "For mysterious and unexplained reasons, Napoleon could not bring himself to do so; almost certainly the explanation is the 'Oriental complex', for such obstinacy has no rational basis."[32] Napoleon's "Oriental complex" was only part of his psychological problem. The other part was his need for an "intimate enemy," a compulsion to repeat his impossible early-life fusion with his mother, and to be forever locked in a fatal life-and-death embrace with a mother substitute. It was no accident that he imagined Aleksandr as a woman.

On October 14, 1808, a weary, unhappy, and disappointed Napoleon left Erfurt for Paris. Deceived and betrayed by Talleyrand, he had failed to secure a dynastic marriage with Tsar Aleksandr's sister, Grand Duchess Yekaterina. Four days later he was back at St. Cloud, and on October 29 he set out again for Spain, where he would continue to enact his own destruction while convincing himself that he was liberating the Spaniards. While he was away, Talleyrand and Fouché, despite their rivalry and enmity, conspired against him in tandem. In early November Napoleon and his *armée d'Espagne* reached the French Basque city of Bayonne and crossed into the Spanish Basque country. When a deputation of Spanish Capuchin monks met him at Tolosa, after he had crossed the Spanish border, an angry Napoleon told them to stay out of politics and wars, warning them that if they had the effrontery to meddle in military affairs, he would hack off their ears.[33]

On December 2, 1808, a month after Emperor Napoleon left France, he reached Madrid, which formally capitulated to him on December 3. Jacques Bainville thought that Napoleon came to Spain as a "chastiser" of the Spanish "rebels" while assigning his elder brother Joseph that of "intercessor and protector" of the Spaniards.[34] The emperor forbade his elder brother to return to Madrid and take up residence there until the Madrileños formally asked him to so, and did not let Joseph be at his side when Napoleon's forces "mercilessly cut down"[35] the Spanish rebel bands. Considering Joseph incompetent, [36] Napoleon gave him no military command and pursued the war with his marshals. Needless to say, Joseph felt this as yet another humiliation by his imperious brother.

27

More Plots and Conspiracies

Emperor Napoleon of France had come to Spain in November 1808 to "chastise" the Spanish rebels, rescue his brother Joseph, and drive the British out if Iberia. In December the emperor had furiously pursued the retreating British army of Lieutenant General Sir John Moore, which was making for La Coruña in northwest Spain. Like his entire "Spanish adventure," it was a wasteful and self-destructive act that led to no real gains for Napoleon. General Moore and his British army reached La Coruña safely. On December 31, Napoleon wrote his wife Josephine from Benavente in Zamora province that Marshal Lefebvre had been captured by the "cowardly English" and asked her to console his wife.[1]

An angry and anxious Napoleon celebrated New Year's Day 1809 mostly on horseback. That night he joined Marshal Bessières, the commander of his 2nd Corps, at Astorga, in the León mountains of northwestern Spain, on the Santiago pilgrims' route. Bessières gave Napoleon dispatches and letters bearing bad news. His homosexual archchancellor, Jean-Jacques-Régis Cambacérès, had written Napoleon that Austria was rearming and preparing for war with France. In early January Napoleon reached the town of Astorga.[2] Napoleon's wife, Josephine, warned him that a plot was being hatched by Napoleon's police minister Fouché and his former foreign minister Talleyrand to topple him from his throne. Josephine wrote Napoleon that Fouché and Talleyrand had been reconciled to one another and were plotting with Napoleon's sister Caroline Murat, who was upset at not becoming queen of Spain, to put her husband, King Joachim-Napoléon of Naples, on the throne of France, should Napoleon be killed in Spain.[3]

Napoleon was alarmed by the bad news. One of the plotters against him was the fifty-five-year-old liberal senator Jean-Denis Lanjuinais, who five years later would sign Napoleon's dethronement by the French senate. "This information, reminding Napoleon of the frailty of his monarchy, made him the more anxious because, six months earlier, a plot had been revealed to him regarding which he had not been able to discover precise details. It was a Republican conspiracy, in which were mentioned the names of General Malet, an adherent of Moreau, La Fayette, Lanjuinais, the liberals in the Senate, the former Girondin minister Servan. In all, something rather obscure: Fouché had minimized the affair to nothing, although the rumor ran that he himself was compromised. This vagueness made the Emperor anxious. And this vexation pursued him. The dispatches he had received renewed [Napoleon's] suspicion and alarm. Instantly he decided to return [to Paris]."[4]

Not quite so instantly, though. Napoleon was anxious. Not only did he have to face the plotters in Paris, he also had to prepare for a new war with Austria. Napoleon stayed in Spain until mid-January 1809 still trying to drive the "English" into the sea, awaiting further news from Paris, and trying to make up his mind about Talleyrand and Fouché. On January 3 he was still "pursuing the English, sword to back."[5] On January 5 he signed an imperial decree ordering another mass conscription of young Frenchmen.[6] When he received his elder brother Joseph's New Year's greetings, Napoleon replied, "I have no hopes of Europe being pacified during this year. I have so little hope that I have just issued a decree for raising one hundred thousand men . . . The hour of repose and tranquillity has not yet struck." Indeed, for the unquiet Napoleon, it never would.

On January 9, 1809, Napoleon tried to comfort his anxious wife: "I see, my friend [*sic*], that you are sad and that you are worried stiff. Austria will not make war on me. If she does, I have one hundred and fifty thousand men in Germany and as many on the Rhine, and four hundred thousand Germans to answer her with. Russia will not separate herself from me. They are mad in Paris. All is well. I shall be in Paris, as soon as I think it useful. I advise you to watch out for ghosts. A beautiful day, at two o'clock in the morning . . . But adieu, my love, I am well and all thine."[7] Was Napoleon deceiving himself? General Paul-Charles-François-Adrien-Henri-Dieudonné Thiébault recalled that four days later, at Valladolid, while awaiting further news that would help him make up his mind whether to return to Paris forthwith, an anxious Napoleon had another uncontrollable public outburst of narcissistic rage, this time against General François-Marie-Guillaume Legendre d'Harvesse, the officer who had signed the French surrender to the British at Baylén. Napoleon humiliated Legendre in public, just as he had done to Admiral Bruix in 1804.[8]

On January 17, 1809, the wavering Napoleon finally made up his mind. He left Valladolid for Paris at full gallop, leaving his *armée d'Espagne* under Marshal Soult. The emperor was hurrying back to Paris to deal with the plotters against him—Talleyrand, Fouché, and his sister Caroline. Riding furiously, Napoleon was in such a state of rage, anxiety, and impatience that he rode the 115 kilometers from Valladolid to Burgos in less than five hours. General Thiébault, "the worst tongue of the army,"[9] recalled that Napoleon passed him near Burgos, "galloping hell-for-leather, whacking Savary's horse, ahead of him, with his crop, far ahead of his guards, aides, and Mameluke attendant."[10]

On January 23–24, 1809, the anxious and furious emperor finally "hit Paris like a bomb."[11] It took that "bomb" a few days to explode, however. For four days Napoleon held feverish meetings with his counselors, closest aides, and allies. On January 27 he summoned Police Minister Joseph Fouché and gave him a private tongue-lashing. Yet, amazingly, Napoleon did not try, execute, or even fire his treacherous police minister. André Castelot explained that Napoleon "had too much need of Fouché," and therefore did not apply his own maxim, "Those whom one can no longer reward should be dismissed."[12] In fact, Napoleon yet again unconsciously sowed the seeds of his own destruction.

On January 28, 1809, the emperor finally summoned the principal traitor, Talleyrand, to a Council of Ministers meeting at the Tuileries Palace. After making Talleyrand wait for three hours while standing, Napoleon faced his former foreign minister and lashed out at the traitor in the presence of Arch-Chancellor Cambacérès, Arch-Treasurer Lebrun, Senator Montesquiou-Fezensac, Navy Minister Decrès—and Police Minister Fouché, Talleyrand's fellow conspirator. Napoleon delivered a verbal thunderstorm to Talleyrand, who "leaned against a console, pale as death."[13] The furious Napoleon reportedly yelled at the traitor: "You are a thief, a coward, a man without faith; you do not believe in God; all your life you have failed at your duties, you have cheated, betrayed everyone; there is nothing sacred to you; you would sell your own father . . . you are a piece of shit in a silk stocking!"[14] The enraged Napoleon said to both Talleyrand and Fouché, "Remember that if a fresh revolution should come, it would break both of you the first, whatever part you took in it."[15]

Incredibly, however, Napoleon did not follow his verbal thunderbolts with any serious disciplinary action against either Talleyrand or Fouché. As Jacques Bainville correctly noted, "The great scene of January 28, 1809, calculated for public notice, was chiefly remarkable for the absence of any subsequent punishment."[16] True, on January 29, Napoleon stripped Talleyrand of his title of grand chamberlain, but the emperor nonetheless let the traitor remain one of the great dignitaries of the French empire and Prince of Bénévent, and he left Fouché in his post of police minister. Napoleon's striking lack of action against Talleyrand and Fouché, the two men who had plotted to topple him from his throne, was obviously self-destructive: a few years later it led to his downfall. Napoleon's contemporaries were puzzled by his lack of force and indecision. General Savary attributed Napoleon's lack of firmness to "the misfortune of his position."[17] Lazare Carnot, the former military chief of the *Directoire exécutif*, was amazed by Napoleon's "inconceivable weakness" in not punishing his aides, [18] adding that Napoleon was "forever repeating his fault of threatening without striking, and of leaving the power to do harm in the hands of those whom he had injured, great or small."[19]

As we have seen, André Castelot thought that Napoleon needed Fouché too much and therefore did not apply his own formula to his treacherous minister.[20] Jacques Bainville believed that Napoleon did not yet know of Talleyrand's treachery at Erfurt nor of his treasonous advice to Russia and Austria.[21] The psychoanalyst Pierce Clark, however, thought that Napoleon did not punish Fouché and Talleyrand because he had a "Jehovah complex": he felt omnipotent, divine, and immortal, and did not fear anyone.[22] Another psychoanalyst, Edmund Bergler, believed that Napoleon unconsciously used Fouché to punish himself masochistically for his imagined oedipal crimes.[23] In fact, by keeping the treacherous Fouché in his post, Napoleon unconsciously repeated his archaic relationship with his rejecting mother: emotionally, she too had wanted to get rid of him. Keeping Fouché in his post was a grossly self-destructive act. The fact that Fouché's first name, Joseph, was the same as that of Napoleon's elder brother, whom Napoleon both loved and hated, may also have contributed to Napoleon's ambivalence and passivity toward him.

Talleyrand lost no time in avenging himself for his public humiliation by Napoleon. On the following day, January 29, Talleyrand secretly went to the Austrian embassy in Paris and met Count Clemens Wenzel

Nepomuk Lothar von Metternich-Winneburg-Beilstein—better know as Metternich —the Austrian ambassador, negotiating with Austria behind Napoleon's back. The former foreign minister sought to heal his narcissistic injury with his greed for money. Austria paid Talleyrand four hundred thousand francs—some scholars say one million francs—for his treason. Fouché also saw Metternich, but was not paid for his treason. Talleyrand remained a secret agent of Austria and of Russia, although the tsar turned down his greedy request for one and a half million francs. [24]

In late 1808 and early 1809 Napoleon's self-created problems were multiplying.. His worst problem was not the treacherous Talleyrand and Fouché but his elder brother Joseph. Napoleon had returned Joseph to the Spanish throne but robbed him of his authority and power. His "rescue" of Joseph was more of a humiliation, showing King Joseph to be impotent without his Emperor brother. Spain was now part of Napoleon's empire, and by 1809 Napoleon had at least five agents in Madrid spying on Joseph and restricting his power. King Joseph of Spain was exasperated with his younger brother's attempts to control him and begged Napoleon to take his personal agents off his back: "I pray you to believe that I have more pains and embarrassment than I deserve, and that I should receive from you fraternal consolation and advice."[25]

While Joseph tried to liberalize Spain's government and give freedom to its people, Napoleon wanted strong and authoritarian rule. On February 6, 1809, Emperor Napoleon, unhappy with what he considered King Joseph's weak and misguided actions in Spain, wrote his elder brother: "I am angry that the system is changing in Madrid and that they have become too complacent there."[26] The French emperor added that he, Napoleon, not Joseph, had conquered Spain, that Spain must remain French, that its government must be French, and that no liberties must be given to its people. [27] In fact, it was Napoleon himself who was misguided. His harsh rule in Spain was driving the rebels to extremes and was going to lose him all of Iberia.

The bitter exchange of letters between Napoleon and his elder brother in continued during the spring of 1809. The hypersensitive Napoleon interpreted everything Joseph wrote about himself as an insult to him. By April the conflict between Napoleon and his elder brother was far from resolved. Joseph once more vented his frustration and anger in a letter to Napoleon:

> Sire ... the minister of war complains that there is no instantaneous central impulsion which directs the movement of the armies. He ought to know that such *instantaneous and central impulsion* cannot exist . . . when every day various generals receive . . . orders which I cannot change without running the risk of seeing my orders disobeyed because they contradict those which come from Paris . . . If . . . the minister . . . will correspond only with Marshal Jourdan . . . if Your Majesty would give me his advice . . . it would be possible to have central and instantaneous impulsion. [28]

Marshal Jean-Baptiste Jourdan, chief of staff of King Joseph's French army in Spain, however, was the man that Napoleon most distrusted. He considered Jourdan a dangerous left-wing "Jacobin" who wore the red Spanish cockade on his hat.[29] Napoleon did not formally remove Jourdan from his post, but he omitted Jourdan's name from his Table of Marshals for 1809. Nothing was resolved in the conflict between Napoleon and his elder brother. Napoleon kept Joseph where he was but robbed him of his power. Joseph resumed his reign in Spain but lost his battles against the Spanish rebels and their British allies. His forces let the British general Sir Arthur Wellesley, the future Duke of Wellington, escape with his army at the battle of Talavera de la Reyna, in the central Spanish province of Toledo, which took place on July 27–29, 1809, and move his army back to Portugal. Napoleon constantly interfered with Joseph's rule by issuing direct orders to his marshals, generals, ambassadors and agents. Another man might have abdicated his throne in protest against his younger brother, but Joseph's ambition, his Spanish mistresses, and his greed—or his own unconscious masochism and repetition of early-life trauma—may have kept him from taking this drastic measure.

28

New War with Austria

The war in Spain was not the only one on Napoleon's mind. After returning to Paris from Spain in January 1809, he also mobilized his *Grande Armée* against Austria. Napoleon's war minister, General Clarke, had already called up the French conscript classes of 1809 and 1810. In February 1809 Napoleon called his former chief of staff, Marshal Louis-Alexandre Berthier, to Germany to reorganize the ninety thousand-man French *armée du Rhin* into a new *armée d'Allemagne* and integrate the German troops from the Rhenish Confederation into his *Grande Armée.* The emperor named Berthier the commander-in-chief of the *Grande Armée*, subordinating to him the able marshals Louis-Nicolas Davout, André Masséna and Charles-Nicolas-Victor Oudinot, while Napoleon himself remained in Paris. Frank McLynn thought that this was a major blunder, because Berthier was a disastrous commander who "could not even keep abreast of the flow of orders from the Emperor."[1] Like Napoleon's other "errors" and "blunders," his choice of Berthier was yet another unconsciously self-destructive act.

As part of his self-destructive acting out of his unconscious conflicts, Napoleon made two other grave mistakes: he assumed that the Austrians would make their main military effort in Italy, and he did not take the weather into account. These errors were to cost him heavily during the Austrian campaign of 1809. Napoleon put five of his army corps, some of which he had pulled out of Spain, under Marshals Davout, Oudinot, Masséna, Lannes, and Lefebvre. Marshal Bessières was given command of the cavalry reserve. Most of Napoleon's Imperial Guard were brought from Spain to Germany. Napoleon prepared to take command of his army in Bavaria. His three best corps, however—Marshal Soult's 2nd Corps, Marshal Ney's 6th Corps and Marshal Mortier's 5th Corps—remained tied down in Spain.

The Austrians, who hated Napoleon, called him *der Krampus*, "the Austrian word for a horned devil."[2] By other versions of this myth, Krampus is a companion of Santa Claus who rewards good children and punishes bad ones, a good-natured imp fused with the pious slave Ruprecht. The Austrian emperor Franz had an eighteen-year-old daughter with the short name of Maria Louise Leopoldine Carolina Francisca Theresia Josepha Luzia von Habsburg-Lothringen, whom the French called Marie-Louise. She reportedly hated Napoleon, to whom she may have unconsciously displaced her bad feelings for her father and mother. After the Austrian defeat at Austerlitz in late 1805, the furious Maria Louise had burned her dolls and imagined that she was "roasting the Corsican."[3] She called the French "Huns" and Napoleon "Antichrist."[4] Ironically, within less than two years, Marie-Louise would become Napoleon's second wife.

To undo the narcissistic injuries of his defeats at Ulm and Austerlitz, Emperor Franz of Austria now prepared a new war on France. The Austrian war party included the Emperor's beautiful twenty-two-year-old third wife Maria Ludovica, the forty-five-year-old chancellor, Johann Philipp Carl von Stadion-Warthausen, and the *Kaiser*'s brothers, Archdukes Johann and Ferdinand. Napoleon prepared his *Grande Armée* for this new war. In March 1809, hoping to rally the Rhenish Confederation princes to Austria's side, Archduke Carl, the Austrian war minister, proclaimed a "war of German liberation" against France after having raised a regular Austrian army of three hundred thousand men and a national guard of about one hundred fifty thousand.[5] Archduke Carl took command of the Austrian *Deutschlandsarmee* and gave command of the Austrian *Alpenarmee* to his younger brother, Archduke Johann.

In response, Napoleon ordered the German Rhenish Confederation princes to assemble their troops for battle against Austria and join his army by March 20, 1809. Marshal André Masséna, the Duke of Rivoli, rallied the German troops from Baden, Hessen, and Saxony to the *Grande Armée* and left for Vienna with a corps of forty thousand men. General Henri-Gatien Bertrand assumed the command of the *Grande Armée*'s corps of engineers. Napoleon raised the annual quota of draftees from eighty thousand to one hundred thousand men. The French emperor now had an *armée d'Allemagne* of two hundred thousand men. But the deep resentment and vengeance stirring within the hearts of his enemies would keep simmering. No amount of men and no additional victories would save him from his downfall five years later.

Meanwhile, the Russian Tsar's spies in Paris endeavored to find out everything that Napoleon was doing. Emperor Napoleon's alliance with Tsar Aleksandr was sorely tested by Austria's war preparations. The Tsar of all the Russias had written Emperor Franz of Austria enjoining him not to fight his ally, France. Napoleon was not satisfied, however. He instructed his thirty-six-year-old ambassador to Russia, General Armand-Augustin-Louis de Caulaincourt, "to remind the Russian Government that notes to Vienna were not enough, that words should be supported by threatening forces, and to make it plain, in fine, that the peace would not have been disturbed if the pledges of Erfurt had been firmer and more definite, more in accordance with Napoleon's desires."[6] The tsar, however, took no action against Austria, and Napoleon finally realized—too late—that his "alliance" with Russia was a chimera.

The humiliating Schönbrunn treaty that Napoleon had imposed on Austria four years earlier had torn the Tyrol from Austria and annexed it to Bavaria, which was upgraded from a grand duchy and electorate to a kingdom and joined to Napoleon's Confederation of the Rhine. To repair his narcissistic injury, the Austrian emperor wanted the Tyrol back. On April 7, 1809, his younger brother, Archduke Johann, left the Carinthian town of Villach in southern Austria with the seventy-two thousand men of his Austrian *Südarmee*, heading south for the Tyrol. On April 8, feeling militarily powerful enough to withstand a French assault, Austria declared war on France. On April 9 Archduke Johann's army crossed the River Inn and reentered—or "invaded," as Napoleon saw it—the formerly Austrian Tyrol, in Napoleon's Rhenish Confederation. Johann temporally liberated the Tyrol from French-Bavarian rule, installing a young Austrian nobleman, Count Josef Ignaz von Hormayr-Hortenburg, as its governor. Hormayer lasted only thirteen days in this job—from May 1 to May 13, when the French reoccupied Vienna.

The ambitious thirty-six-year-old Austrian ambassador to Paris, Count Metternich, had provoked his country into a disastrous war on France, for which he briefly paid a personal price. In his diplomatic dispatches to Vienna, Count Metternich had portrayed Napoleon's France as bent on liquidating the Austrian empire. When Austria declared war on him, a furious Napoleon detained Count Metternich in Paris. Fearing for

Metternich's fate, Emperor Franz's government arrested Napoleon's *chargé d'affaires* in Vienna, Sieur Dodun, took him away to Hungary and kept him prisoner. Napoleon retaliated by arresting Count Metternich and keeping him hostage in Paris. The crisis was resolved in June 1809 when Napoleon agreed to exchange Metternich against Dodun.[7]

As Napoleon might have known, had he taken the trouble to study political developments inside Russia, the ambivalent Tsar Aleksandr, who had pledged at Tilsit two years earlier to aid Napoleon militarily if Austria attacked France, did not keep his word. The Russian troops the tsar had pledged to attack Austrian Galicia (formerly part of Poland, now in the Ukraine) did not turn up, and those who took part in the later campaign did so half-heartedly. Napoleon, who had loved "Alexandre," was bitterly disappointed. "Napoleon, for whom friendship was all or nothing, could not understand why Alexander had let him down."[8] Vincent Cronin explained the motives behind the tsar's change of heart:

> Ever since Tilsit, Alexander had been under pressure from family, court and nobles to abandon his alliance with Napoleon. After Tilsit one Russian wrote in his diary: "Love for the Tsar has changed to something worse than hatred, to a kind of disgust." His influential mother had warned Alexander against going to Erfurt, fortress of "a blood-stained tyrant"; his generals urged him to grab Poland on his own account. Too straight to go back on his word, not strong enough to carry informed opinion with him, Alexander had taken a weak middle course. But this kind of behavior was incomprehensible to Napoleon. Any ruler worth his salt stood by [his] friends and principles. What then was Alexander? A schemer, "a Byzantine Greek." Napoleon felt keen personal disappointment as well as political frustration.[9]

During the spring of 1809 a frustrated, bitter, and angry Napoleon fought the Austrians in Italy and in Germany at the same time. Several bloody battles were won and lost, and many more men lost their lives and limbs, before Napoleon's troops occupied Vienna on May 13 and Napoleon once more settled into Schönbrunn palace, where he received his young Polish lover, Maria Walewska. The Austrians had destroyed the permanent Danube River bridges and withdrawn to Bohemia, Moravia, Hungary, and other Austrian lands to fight the French outside the capital. By the summer,

Napoleon's victories over Austrians and the pope made him feel so omnipotent that he likened himself to God. By early July he had built up a huge army on Lobau Island in the Danube, near Vienna, and felt strong enough to renew the battle of the Danube against Austria.

The decisive Franco-Austrian battle of 1809 took place on July 4–6 at Wagram, northeast of Vienna. The battle had begun on May 22 at the Austrian villages of Aspern, Essling, and Enzersdorf, which lie in a row from west to east across the Danube River from Lobau Island. Owen Connelly thought that Napoleon had one hundred ninty thousand men and 480 guns, while the Austrian war minister, Archduke Carl, had one hundred forty thousand men and 450 guns.[10] Jacques Garnier believed that Carl had two hundred seventy thousand troops but that he could only bring one hundred thirty-six thousand to Wagram while preparing for Napoleon's army to cross the Danube from Lobau Island to the north bank between Aspern and Essling. [11]

A brilliant military leader, Archduke Carl withdrew his Austrian army behind the River Russbach, running parallel to the Danube some six miles to the northeast, leaving some twenty-five thousand men along the lightly fortified Aspern-Essling-Enzersdorf line to delay the French army, while the mass of Carl's army advanced to fight them. Owen Connelly, however, believed that Carl had made a tactical mistake: "This was a good plan, except that he should have left either fewer or more troops on the Aspern-Essling-Enzersdorf line, where the fortifications were very weak, especially near Enzersdorf. Fewer might have observed the French, briefly delayed them, and then moved back; a greater number was needed to hold them. As it was, [Carl's] advance detachment quickly was overrun and lost."[12]

Prince Eugène, General Macdonald, and General Marmont, whose French troops had been tied down by the Austrians in Italy, Slovenia, and elsewhere, managed to get their forces to Wagram in time to join Napoleon's *Grande Armée* before the decisive battle began on July 4, 1809. During the next two days a horrible battle, perhaps the bloodiest of Napoleon's career, was fought by three hundred thousand to four hundred thousand men at Wagram, near Vienna. The young French captain Maurice-Charles-Marie de Tascher, a cousin of Napoleon's wife Josephine, felt the tragic absurdity of war: "Three hundred thousand men who did not hate each other—who might have become friends if they had known each other—were crowded into the narrow space of three square leagues, ready to kill one another the moment the signal was given."[13] No less than fifty thousand men were killed, wounded, or disabled during those two days.

The thirty-nine-year-old Emperor Napoleon of France had not forgotten his struggle with the sixty-seven-year-old Holy Father in Rome. On the night of July 5–6, 1809, during the battle of Wagram, a dramatic event occurred in faraway Rome. The old Pope Pius VII spent that night at Rome's Quirinale Palace. At Napoleon's orders, the forty-seven-year-old French General Etienne Radet entered the Quirinale with his men and arrested the old pope, along with several of his cardinals. One of Napoleon's generals decided to bring the pope to the southeastern French city of Grenoble, which only caused everyone to venerate him along the route. Napoleon ordered General Radet to go back and take Pius VII to Savona in northwestern Italy. Radet's gendarmes took the pope to Savona, where they held him in the local bishop's palace. The previous year, at Napoleon's insistence, Bartolomeo Cardinal Pacca had replaced Giulio Cardinal Gabrielli, whom Napoleon had arrested and removed from his post, as the Vatican's secretary of state. Now Cardinal Pacca himself was locked up at the Piedmontese state prison at Fenestrella. Napoleon did not publicly admit to ordering the pope's arrest, but he made General Radet a baron and said: "A thing should be accomplished if you are to admit to having thought of it."[14]

Napoleon had symbolically "castrated" the Holy Father by taking away the icons of his power—his archives, tiara, and Fisherman's ring, and, as Frank Richardson observed, "all this without a single French official resigning his office in a country still nominally Catholic."[15] The psychological self-punishment for father-castration, however, is severe. The Roman Catholic faithful all over the world denounced Napoleon as the Anti-Christ, and five years later, in 1814, his aggression against the pope would be "one of the elements in the catastrophe" that led to his downfall.[16]

Napoleon got his peace treaty with Austria by guile. On October 8, 1809, Emperor Franz of Austria named his former ambassador to France, Count Metternich, his new foreign minister, replacing the older Prince Johann-Philipp von Stadion, who had become the scapegoat for Austria's defeat. Metternich, who, like La Fontaine's fox, understood Napoleon's narcissistic vanity and exploited it, gained a respite for Austria by seeking a peace treaty and offering Napoleon the hand of Austria's imperial princess, Marie-Louise, in marriage.

Metternich dispatched Prince Johann Joseph von Liechtenstein, who had signed the humiliating Treaty of Pressburg in 1805, to negotiate with

Napoleon. On October 14 Napoleon talked Prince Liechtenstein into signing a provisional treaty with him at Schönbrunn Palace. The prince, however, had yet to seek the approval of his emperor. No sooner had the prince left Schönbrunn for Holitsch than Napoleon publicly announced the Peace Treaty of Vienna and had one hundred cannon rounds fired. The emperor had no choice but to approve the treaty if he did not want to renew the war and destroy his country by publicly calling Napoleon a liar. The oppressive treaty of Schönbrunn was another humiliation for Austria, which agreed to pay France 196 million livres in war indemnities. But the Austrian people wanted peace at any price. Emperor Franz and Count Metternich could not repudiate the accord. Metternich sent the thirty-eight-year-old general Prince Carl Philipp zu Schwarzenberg, the former Austrian ambassador to Russia who had led the Austrian cavalry corps at Wagram, to take his former post as the Austrian ambassador to Paris. At Metternich's urging, the Austrian emperor would soon give his teenage daughter Maria Louise in marriage to Napoleon.

29

Divorce and Second Marriage

The worst news from Paris that Napoleon received at Vienna's Schönbrunn Palace in the summer of 1809 was the action of his police minister Joseph Fouché, who had "spread alarm through the country."[1] In yet another self-destructive act, on June 29 the French emperor had named the treacherous Fouché his acting interior minister as well as keeping him as minister of police. Napoleon had even made Fouché the Duke of Otranto. The scheming Fouché had regained Napoleon's trust by compiling a daily "bulletin of the ministry of the general police" which presented to the emperor the police's most important discoveries on his enemies.[2] Now, Napoleon learned, Fouché had raised the French national guard in the fifteen *départements* of northern France as if an invasion by foreign forces was imminent, called up republicans soldiers, and "armed the malcontents."[3] In fact, Fouché had raised a military force capable of overthrowing Napoleon's government. Complaints against Fouché kept flowing into Schönbrunn. Napoleon was alarmed and furious. After several years of growing evidence and unconscious denial, he finally understood that Fouché had betrayed him and had plotted to topple him from power. On October 7, 1809, Napoleon dismissed Fouché as his acting interior minister, relieved Marshal Bernadotte of his command of the new army raised by Fouché, and discharged the national guards. Yet, incredibly, despite Fouché's open plot against him with Talleyrand only ten months earlier, Napoleon left Fouché in his post as police minister for another eight months.

While Great Britain's war with France in the Low Countries in the summer of 1809 ended in Napoleon's victory, the Emperor of the French was busier fighting Austria. He was also facing a crisis in his personal life: his fortieth birthday on August 15, 1809, and his impending divorce from his first wife, Josephine, which came soon thereafter—and not by accident. Letting go of people to whom he was attached was one of Napoleon's greatest emotional difficulties. Raoul Brice rightly wondered why Napoleon was so loyal to his treasonous or incompetent aides—the archchancellor Jean-Jacques-Régis Cambacérès, the archtreasurer Charles-François Lebrun, the police minister Joseph Fouché, the former foreign minister Charles-Maurice de Talleyrand, the chief justice Claude-Ambroise Régnier, the finance minister Martin-Michel-Charles Gaudin, the former treasury minister François-Nicolas Mollien, the war minister Jean-Gérard Lacuée, and the state councillor Pierre-François Réal:

> He never, on principle, dismissed anyone except for a grave offense. The names that stand in the Imperial gazette of 1814 are the names of those who were by his side during the Consulate: Cambacérès, Lebrun, Fouché, Talleyrand, Régnier, Gaudin, Mollien, Lacuée, Réal etc . . . down to the chiropodist, Tobias Coen, who was in his service from 1801 at Malmaison right on to the Hundred Days. *Why did he not in the cases of many of them apply his own maxim: 'One ought to disgrace those one can no longer reward'?*[4]

The unconscious reasons why Napoleon could not dismiss his treacherous and useless aides lay in his traumatic early life. His ambivalent fusional attachment to his rejecting mother was repeated in every intimate and close relationship he had with others. He had great trouble separating from those he was close to, even when—or especially when—they were bad for him, beginning with his mother and ending with Josephine. In the end, Napoleon's "repetition compulsion" joined with his self-destructive sadomasochism to cause his own undoing.

Napoleon's Polish lover, Countess Maria Walewska, who already had a son by her elderly husband, arrived in Schönbrunn Palace in July 1809. The Emperor of the French put her up in the picturesque nearby village of Mödling, and they spent almost every afternoon together.[5] By early August Maria was pregnant. On August 15, when Napoleon turned forty, he had a "mid-life crisis." Deeply anxious about his health, he left Schönbrunn for Vienna to consult his thirty-nine-year-old French physician, Jean-Baptiste Lanefranque, a *protégé* of the great Jean-Nicolas Corvisart and a member of the *Maison de l'Empereur*, whom Napoleon greatly appreciated and whom he had made a *Chevalier de l'Empire*. Perhaps thanks to Lanefranque's advice, Napoleon fought his middle-age depression through sexual activity. While in Vienna, he reportedly took up with a nineteen-year-old Viennese lady named Eva Kraus, who became pregnant and was later said to have born him a son.[6]

In October 1809 Maria Walewska announced to Napoleon that she was two months pregnant by him. Two years earlier Napoleon's former mistress Eléonore Denuelle de la Plaigne had born a son, Count Léon, but that child's parentage was far from certain. In Maria's case, Napoleon clearly believed that he was the father. The news that he could father a child filled him with joy. He resolved to divorce his wife Josephine by having their marriage annulled, and to marry another woman, who would give him a son, thus fulfilling his narcissistic fantasies of immortality.

After signing the Treaty of Vienna on October 14, 1809, Napoleon could have returned home at once. Yet he lingered at Vienna's Schönbrunn Palace for two more days before leaving for France. One of the reasons was his ambivalence about his wife Josephine. He wanted to return home only after making up his mind to divorce her and to marry a Russian or Austrian princes. Napoleon feared that being near Josephine would make him change his mind again. After thirteen years of marital strife and no children, he was still unable to bring himself to divorce Josephine. When his fifty-five-year-old aide Pierre-Louis Roederer urged him to repudiate Josephine, Napoleon replied, "It is from a sense of justice that I have refrained from a divorce. My interest and the interest of the State demand, perhaps, that I should marry again. But, as I have said, how can I send this good woman away just because I have become great? I have the heart of a man, I was not whelped by a tigress."[7]

Napoleon left Austria for Paris on October 16, 1809, and Maria Walewska returned to her husband's estate of Walewice, in the Polish province of Lodz. On May 4, 1810, she bore Napoleon a son, whom she named Alexandre Walewski. Napoleon's son once more bore another man's last name. Was he really the father of that son?

On October 26, 1809, the victorious Napoleon returned from Vienna to Fontainebleau. This time, knowing that he could father a son, he was determined to divorce his wife Josephine and marry a child-bearing princess upon his arrival. Ten years earlier, when General Bonaparte had returned home from Egypt, he had locked his door against his unfaithful wife, but her tearful pleas and heartrending sobs quickly moved him to forgive her and open his door to her. This time Napoleon kept his doors firmly shut and sealed up against Josephine—both the physical door and the emotional one. Through the unconscious process of projection, one of his principal emotional defenses, he could see all blame in her:

> For three weeks she never managed to get a minute alone with him, for he insisted on inviting members of his family to all his meals. Every evening the vindictive Pauline held parties for her brother and threw Italian beauties at him, while pointedly not inviting Josephine. Projecting the guilt he felt about the intended divorce on to her, and therefore holding her in some sense to blame for the awkward position he was in, he declined to tell her what was on his mind but reacted to her presence with cold rage. He spent all his spare time hunting—an activity Josephine was known to detest—and visited numerous fantasies on the dumb beasts; on one occasion he and his fellow Nimrods slaughtered eighty wild boar in a Roman-style arena.[8]

On October 26, 1809, upon his return to Fontainebleau, Napoleon summoned his archchancellor, Jean-Jacques-Régis Cambacérès, to his palace, and told him that he wanted to marry *un ventre* (a belly).[9] Was Napoleon's coarse language his unconscious defense against his ambivalence, anxiety and despair? It took the unhappy Napoleon another many sleepless nights to make up his mind. He could not let go of his "beloved" Josephine even though—or because—she had hurt him so much. Jacques Bainville thought that "his attachment to her was habit and, it had been said, a superstition. He might lose in her a lucky charm. But really he felt the need for a surer talisman. Policy now demanded divorce, just as, on his return from Egypt, it had counseled forgiveness. Napoleon did not feel that fortune would desert him when he had repudiated Josephine. He repudiated her because he felt that fortune was going to desert him."[10] In Napoleon's unconscious mind, the goddess of Fortune—and Josephine—were his mother in disguise. The reasons of policy that he gave were rationalizations used by his unconscious mind to explain his irrational behavior to himself.

Josephine's chamberlain at that time was the twenty-six-year-old French nobleman Charles-François-Tristan de Montholon-Sémonville, a future general and Napoleon's future chamberlain on Saint Helena.

Montholon, a favorite of Napoleon, desperately tried to intercede with the emperor in favor of his empress, but Napoleon's affection for him did not help Josephine. The emperor was looking for a new wife who would give him a son and heir. Nothing else mattered to him at this point. His powerful fantasies of greatness and immortality were at stake. To make himself even greater, he wanted to join France to Russia. On November 4, 1809, Napoleon sent a formal proposal to Tsar Aleksandr of Russia in St. Petersburg, offering to marry Aleksandr's teen-age sister, Grand Duchess Anna Pavlovna. [11]

Unable to personally tell Josephine his decision to divorce her, fearing her heartrending sobs, Napoleon successively asked his stepdaughter Hortense, his stepson Eugène, and his archchancellor Cambacérès, to break the bad news to her. They all refused, each for his own reasons. Napoleon then moved from Fontainebleau back to the Tuileries Palace in Paris, where on November 30, 1809—more than a month after his return to France—he held a formal dinner with Josephine to pronounce his "sentence" on her. Josephine, who knew what was coming, had wept all day. She was pale and withdrawn, in a kind of catatonic stupor,[12] unconsciously denying her grief and her rage at Napoleon for abandoning her. After dinner, a still ambivalent Napoleon announced to his wife his intention of divorcing her. He told her that he wanted a legitimate son and heir. "I still love you," Napoleon reportedly said to Josephine, "but in politics there is no heart, only head."[13] The devastated Josephine fainted (or pretended to), then wept and pleaded with her husband. An anxious Napoleon summoned his prefect of his palace, Louis-François-Joseph de Bausset, and the two men carried the "unconscious" empress downstairs to her apartment. When Bausset tripped on the staircase, however, a very conscious Josephine reportedly whispered to him, "Watch out—you are squeezing me too tight!"[14] Jacques Bainville was full of admiration: "How well she could play the woman's part!"[15]

During the first two weeks of December 1809, after he announced to his wife his decision to divorce her, Napoleon's ambivalence about Josephine was at its height. He pined for her and felt sorry for himself. After Josephine's children Eugène and Hortense—manipulated by their mother—threatened to give up their crowns and follow their mother into her internal exile, the unhappy Napoleon blamed the divorce on his cruel fate and was often found by his intimates "in tears of regretful expostulation."[16] While Josephine attended official receptions and dinners as if she was his eternal wife, Napoleon promised to let her keep her title of

Empress, her castle at Malmaison, her jewels, and her annual income of three million francs in gold, and gave her the new title of Duchess of Navarre. After she moved to Malmaison, his love for her rekindled. Out of sight, he once more idealized her, as he had his difficult mother when he was a child.

On December 14, 1809, Napoleon convened his imperial family and state council, consisting of the Bonapartes, the Beauharnois, and the emperor's closest aides, in the Throne Room of the Tuileries Palace to announce his divorce. As had been agreed by the couple—or decreed by the husband—Napoleon and Josephine jointly announced their "divorce by mutual consent."[17] In fact, it was a unilateral annulment of their marriage by Napoleon. Jacques Bainville thought that Josephine's unhappiness was real: "She stopped with consummate art in the middle of her statement, choking with sobs. Not that her tears were forced: after all her struggles to keep her husband, she might well be nervously exhausted. Nor need one rule out her sensibility, her regrets, and even the humiliations arising from a failure, nor yet the memories of her youth and her former love."[18] André Castelot, more sympathetic to the repudiated wife, called Napoleon's divorce of Josephine an unfair judicial process involving an arrest, trial, verdict, sentence, and execution, with Napoleon as gendarme, prosecutor, judge, jury, and executioner.[19]

By all accounts, the scene of the "trial" was heartrending. A tearful Josephine read out a prepared statement to the imperial family and state council: "We are both glorious by the sacrifice that we make to the good of our fatherland."[20] At this point she broke down in sobs and could not proceed. The secretary of state for Napoleon's imperial family, Regnault de Saint-Jean-d'Angély, read out the remainder of her statement for her. Napoleonic myth has it that "the Emperor bent the knee to his victim and wept for three days after."[21] Josephine's son Eugène, the viceroy of Italy, fainted as he left the room with his mother, while Josephine "burst like a crazy woman into Napoleon's apartments that night and began kissing him wildly. Sobbing and tears followed."[22] Napoleon's only way of escaping his impossible emotional predicament was to make sure he was not left alone with Josephine the next day when she packed her belonging and left the palace for Malmaison.

Even divorced from his wife, Napoleon could not let go of Josephine. The physical separation was short-lived. Napoleon's treasury minister,

François-Nicolas Mollien, recalled that right after the divorce announcement, Napoleon left the Tuileries Palace for the Trianon at Versailles, where he stayed for three days, deeply depressed.[23] Raoul Brice thought that Napoleon "was completely prostrated and refused to see any one on any pretext whatever; his official life was entirely suspended—his correspondence, audiences and even the Council of Ministers."[24] On December 16, 1809, the day his imperial senate formalized the divorce, Napoleon went to see Josephine at Malmaison. He kept seeing her for a whole week, but avoided physical intimacy and being alone with her. Nine days later, on Christmas Day, Josephine and her daughter Hortense dined with Napoleon at the Trianon. A lady of the imperial court later reported that "their majesties were so happy together that one might have fancied they had never separated."[25] Puzzled by this happiness, William Henry Hudson thought that Napoleon's "attitude towards his divorced wife and his feelings for her present a curious study in psychology."[26] Unconsciously, Napoleon was repeating with Josephine his deeply ambivalent love-hate relationship with his mother.

Back in Napoleon's "Grand Duchy of Warsaw," his young and married Polish lover, Maria Walewska, still loved him, and was four months pregnant, probably by him. He loved her too, as far he could love at all. But she was still married to the old Count Walewski, and Napoleon wanted a wife and an heir. Napoleon never gave Poland the liberty he had promised Maria Walewska in exchange for her love. He feared to relax his control. Napoleon did create the "Grand Duchy of Warsaw," but it was a truncated Poland, a French puppet state. Napoleon looked elsewhere—to the great powers of Russia and Austria—for a new wife.

A "control freak," Napoleon left nothing to chance. After having his imperial senate dissolve his civil marriage to Josephine, he had his religious marriage annulled by the Roman Catholic Church. On January 9, 1810, at the emperor's command, the Diocesan Ecclesiastical Court of Paris annulled the marriage on the flimsy formal pretext that when Cardinal Fesch had secretly married the couple in the Tuileries Palace chapel on December 1, 1804, the day before Napoleon was crowned and consecrated Emperor of the French, no parish priest had attended the ceremony, and that Napoleon had not given his formal consent to it. As usual, Napoleon's wishes were carried out. The Metropolitan Ecclesiastical Court of Paris confirmed the annulment ruling, and Napoleon was a "free man"—but not free of his inner conflicts.

In late 1809 and early 1810 Napoleon was preoccupied with his forthcoming remarriage and with his alliance with Russia. After he announced to Josephine his intention of divorcing her, he first opted for the Russian option, promoted by his aide Camabacérès. Already in early November 1809 Napoleon had instructed his ambassador to Russia, General Caulaincourt, the Duke of Vicenza, to ask Tsar Aleksandr to give him the hand of his teen-age sister, Grand Duchess Anna Pavlovna, in marriage. Napoleon wanted Aleksandr to come in person to Paris and to bring his sister Anna with him, and even the "blasé Parisians became excited about the coming union of Rome and Byzantium, of Charlemagne and Irene." [27] The emperor instructed General Caulaincourt to tell the tsar that "no importance was attached to the conditions, not even the religious ones." [28] A generous—or desperate—Napoleon offered to grant Aleksandr a huge loan in advance of the union and to give Russia back its Polish territories in the "Grand Duchy of Warsaw."

Tsar Aleksandr vacillated, not only because of Napoleon's rumored impotence but also for several other personal and political reasons—Aleksandr's domineering mother, the Russian military situation, Great Britain's pressures, Aleksandr's feeling of having been humiliated by Napoleon at Tilsit and at Erfurt, and the pressure of his nobles. Despite his public show of affection for Napoleon at Erfurt, Aleksandr privately disliked him, and secretly plotted with the former French foreign minister, Talleyrand, with Emperor Franz of Austria, and with King Friedrich Wilhelm of Prussia to overthrow Napoleon. The tsar's family and court hated Napoleon. Aleksandr feared the marriage of his teen-age sister Anna Pavlovna to Napoleon. He ducked the issue by referring it to his mother, Maria Fyodorovna, who in turn consulted her daughter, the *tsaritsa* Yekaterina Pavlovna, the Duchess of Oldenburg. The duchess approved the marriage, but her mother hesitated, asking for time to think it over.

General Caulaincourt's letters to Emperor Napoleon in late 1809 and early 1810 informed Napoleon of the Russian tsar's vacillations and of his inability to stand up to his mother. At the end the tsar and his mother foiled Napoleon's plans. On February 6, 1810, when Napoleon finally received Aleksandr's refusal to let him marry his sister, however couched in diplomatic niceties, he was deeply hurt, enraged, and disappointed. "Alexander's lack of zeal, his everlasting plea that everything depended on his mother, the slowness and questionings of the old Empress, notoriously hostile to the Corsican usurper, kept things dragging on, and brought doubts of Russia's good faith."[29] In Napoleon's feelings, Russia was like his mother, who pretended to love him but in her heart rejected him. The war with perfidious Russia, which was to break out in 1812, began in Napoleon's heart in early 1810. His homosexual archchancellor, Cambacérès, who favored the Russian alliance, warned that within two years Napoleon would have to fight either the Russian or the Austrian imperial house, "the one whose daughter the Emperor did not marry."[30]

Napoleon's wish to marry Princess Marie-Louise of Austria did not only derive from his unconscious wish for immortality and conscious considerations of political expediency. It was also his irrational way of taking vengeance on rejecting Russia. On the evening of February 6, 1810, after he received the Russian refusal, an enraged and vengeful Napoleon convened his "great family and state council"[31] to seek the advice of the great dignitaries of his empire regarding his match with Princess Marie-Louise of Austria. The war minister, Jean-Gérard Lacuée, who opposed the Austrian marriage, suggested that Austria was no longer a great power. Napoleon answered him sharply, "It is clear, sir, that you were not present at Wagram."[32] Napoleon's brother-in-law Joachim Murat, the king of Naples, also opposed the Austrian marriage, but Napoleon couldn't care less. Jacques Bainville thought that Napoleon had made up his mind to marry the Habsburg princes because he imagined that such a marriage would pull the rug from under his enemies' attempts to portray him as a Jacobin revolutionary seeking to topple all the thrones of Europe. "The mingling of his blood with that of the most conservative of dynasties would legitimate him in the eyes of all; he would join up their preservation with his own; and this would be, as he thought, the definitive stabilization that he sought for himself."[33] The perceptive Jacques Bainville, however, noted that all these thoughts "were so many illusions."[34]

One of Napoleon's wishes in marrying an Austrian princess was to emulate King Louis XVI, who had married Princess Marie-Antoinette of Austria, a great aunt of Princess Marie-Louise. After repudiating Josephine, a depressed Napoleon fled the Tuileries Palace to the Trianon, Louis XIV's refuge at Versailles. From November 1809 to February 1810 Napoleon waited for Tsar Aleksandr's reply to his offer of a political marriage with the tsar's teenage sister. Before receiving Aleksandr's refusal, Napoleon had prepared a backup plan. He had asked Prince Carl Philipp zu Schwarzenberg, the Austrian ambassador to Paris, to mediate his marriage to Marie-Louise. Jacques Bainville thought that Napoleon's "well-trumpeted" marriage to Marie-Louise, which would bring another "Austrian woman" to Paris, was "a bold stroke" on his part.[35] In fact, it was the self-destructive act of a desperate man.

On February 7, 1810, Napoleon signed a provisional contract of marriage with the eighteen-year-old Archduchess Marie-Louise of Austria. On the surface, it was a political marriage designed to cement his control of Austria and to produce a son and heir who would keep his "dynasty" alive. Above all, it was Napoleon's desperate way out of a personal crisis of depression, ambivalence and indecision following his "divorce" from Josephine (who stood for his mother in his unconscious mind), and his inability to separate from her emotionally. It was his way of restoring his shaky self-esteem and expressing his narcissistic hopes for immortality. Unconsciously, as well, the Austrian marriage was a self-destructive act on Napoleon's part: he knew too well that it was the Austrian queen Marie-Antoinette who had brought about her husband King Louis XVI's downfall and his execution seventeen years earlier. Moreover, Princess Marie-Louise was too young, did not speak French, and did not love Napoleon. Her most important skill was cardplaying. After being deposed by her father and betrayed by Marie-Louise herself four years later, Napoleon noted ruefully that when Marie-Louise arrived in Paris, she played whist with "two regicides," Cambacérès and Fouché, both of whom had voted for King Louis XVI's execution. [36]

Marie-Louise did not know Napoleon and did not love him. In fact, she feared him. Raoul Brice believed that "her inborn apathy made her accept her marriage with Napoleon, though his very name caused her to tremble."[37] Frank Richardson spoke of "the strange character of Marie Louise" whom some detractors called "neither wife nor mother."[38] Why did *Kaiser* Franz give his daughter to that *Krampus* Napoleon? The Austrian emperor set the stage for the union—or appeased his guilty conscience—by formally declaring Napoleon to be a direct descendant of the dukes of Tuscany, worthy of marrying into the House of Habsburg. Invoking the Greek myth of Ariadne and the man-eating bull of Minos, Brice thought that "the Court of Vienna delivered up a daughter of the Emperor Francis I, the Archduchess Marie Louise, as a tribute to the French Minotaur."[39]

Metternich later said that the emperor had sacrificed his daughter to "the ogre" Napoleon in exchange for a halt in the war with France that would give him three or four years to rebuild his army.[40] In fact, it was

Metternich's own idea to "sacrifice" Marie-Louise to Napoleon. Raoul Brice compared this "sacrifice" to Agamemnon's sacrifice of Iphigenia during the Trojan War. "The most ancient monarchy in Europe, the most pedantic in the enumeration of its quarterings and the most enslaved by etiquette, declared itself honored by the choice of its conqueror."[41] In fact, Napoleon was neither a Minotaur nor an ogre, except in the imagination of those who feared him. In person, when not under stress, he could be charming and loving. Brice himself pointed out that Marie-Louise was initially happy with Napoleon.[42]

Napoleon could not wait for his bride to arrive in order to wed her. On March 11, 1810, in the Augustine chapel near the palace, the Very Powerful Napoleon the First, Emperor of the French, King of Italy, Protector of the Confederation of the Rhine, Mediator of the Helvetic Confederation, formally married Marie-Louise, Imperial Princess of Austria, Royal Princess of Hungary and Bohemia. The bride, however, was absent: she was represented by her paternal uncle, Archduke Carl. Napoleon would not see Marie-Louise in the flesh until late March. Unable to wait, he would ride out to the little village of Courcelles-sur-Vesle, on the Soissons-Reims road, and get drenched by the rain for his impatience.[43] While the revolutionary young Napoleon had upset the established royal houses and the old nobility of Europe and created his own empire and nobility, after the age of forty Napoleon became increasingly conservative. Owen Connelly thought that in marrying Archduchess Marie-Louise of Austria, Napoleon compromised with the *ancien régime*.[44] At the age of forty, Napoleon made his peace with the old royalty and nobility of Europe.

Napoleon's brothers, however, were another matter. After two years of brewing trouble, Napoleon's simmering conflict with his elder brother Joseph came to a head on February 8, 1810—two days after he learned of his humiliation by the tsar of Russia and a day after he contracted to marry Marie-Louise of Austria. On that day Napoleon tore off from Joseph's kingdom the Spanish provinces adjacent to France—Catalonia, Aragon, Navarre, and the Basque provinces—and turned them into imperial French military governments ruled by generals directly answerable to Napoleon.[45] In May 1810 Napoleon turned two more Spanish provinces into French military governments: Burgos and Old Castile, including Valladolid, Salamanca, Palencia, and Toro, to which León and Zamora were added in July.[46] Joseph sent his sixty-four-year-old ecclesiastic-affairs minister, Don Miguel José de Azanza, the Duke of Santa Fé, to intercede with Napoleon to revoke his decrees, but to no avail.[47]

Unconsciously, Napoleon had taken revenge on Joseph for being their mother's favorite son. Joseph became a king without a kingdom, reduced to governing Central Spain—and even there Napoleon created his own army.[48] His tearing off large sections of Joseph's kingdom and annexing them to his empire was an act of aggression against his elder brother, a deep humiliation for Joseph, and a blatant violation of the constitution of Bayonne which he had proudly given the Spanish people. Naturally, Joseph was furious. He wrote Napoleon that he was deeply hurt by his actions and proposed to abdicate. Napoleon in turn saw this proposal as a desertion by his elder brother and was hurt and angry himself. There was bitterness and acrimony between the two brothers for three years.[49] On August 15, 1810, Napoleon's forty-first birthday and the Feast of the Emperor in France, Joseph lost his cool, cursed his younger brother "for treating him like a perfect," and sent Napoleon another angry proposal of abdication, which the Emperor of the French ignored.[50]

When not upset with his elder brother Joseph, Napoleon was obsessed with his new Austrian bride, Marie-Louise, with whom he was smitten form afar. What was it about the teenage Marie-Louise that so pleased and attracted the forty-one-year-old French emperor? For one thing, Marie-Louise was sexually attractive: "Her eyes were too prominent, but they were a pretty light blue; her nose was too long, but it gave her features a touch of nobility; her chin was a bit too heavy. Her breasts were high and full, as the fashion demanded. All this combined to give an impression, if not of grace, at any rate of pink and blond freshness."[51] Vincent Cronin believed that Marie-Louise was "more sensual than Josephine" and that on her first night with Napoleon, at the castle of Compiègne, in late March 1810, she was so delighted with his love-making, she invited him "to do it again."[52] Napoleon's pleasure in Marie-Louise was even greater, for the following morning, he reportedly told one of his intimates, "Marry a German girl, my dear." [53]

Several psychological questions arise from these glowing descriptions of Napoleon's sexual bliss with his second wife. Was it for real? Were Marie-Louise's sexual skills greater than Josephine's? Did she provoke less unconscious conflict in Napoleon than his previous wife did? A much younger wife is more likely to two-time her husband than one who is her husband's contemporary. Was the middle-aged Napoleon attracted to the teen-age Marie-Louise because deep down he knew that she would be unfaithful to him? Did he unconsciously seek to reenact his early trauma of his mother's unfaithfulness to his father?

For the time being, a happy Napoleon postponed his war on Russia. Although the Emperor of the French, unable to get the hand of the Russian tsar's sister, had decided to marry the daughter of Austria's emperor, he wanted to keep Russia's friendship as well. The emperor instructed his ambassador to Russia, General Caulaincourt, to exercise "gentleness, discretion, [and] prudence [and] avoid anything that might wound [Russia]."[54] Those, however, were "Caulaincourt's instructions for the moment."[55] Two years later, Napoleon would invade Russia in the most self-destructive act of his entire life.

Napoleon's double-dealing police minister, Joseph Fouché, had repeatedly plotted against his emperor. Fouché truly believed that Napoleon had made too many enemies and that his career had no future. Behind Napoleon's back, he negotiated France's future after Napoleon with Austria and Great Britain. The emperor treated Fouché with suspicion and had his secret police spy on him. The reactionaries at the Tuileries Palace hated the "Jacobin" Fouché. Finally, after years of plots and betrayals by his police minister, Napoleon made up his mind about Fouché. On July 3, 1810, Napoleon wrote Fouché a confidential letter of dismissal: "The place of police minister requires a complete and absolute trust; this trust can no longer exist."[56] Napoleon replaced Fouché with the ruthless younger General Jean-Marie-René Savary, whom he felt he could trust.

Fouché stalled his emperor while hiding and destroying compromising documents; Napoleon became furious; Fouché feared being arrested. He fled France for Italy, where he wandered from one city to another with his elder son, thinking of leaving Europe for America. Fouché finally went to the southern French city of Aix-en-Provence, where he was given a residence by the emperor. In August 1811 Napoleon allowed Fouché to return to his castle of Ferrières in the Seine-et-Marne département, near Paris, but he kept Fouché under close surveillance. In May 1813 Napoleon sent Fouché away to the Saxon capital of Dresden, and later he sent him farther away, to the Slovenian capital of Laibach (Ljubljana), as governor of the French "Illyrian Provinces."[57]

From 1808 to 1813 Napoleon fought the British, Spanish, and Portuguese in the Iberian Peninsula. The Peninsular War grew worse and worse for France, until Napoleon withdrew from Spain in 1813 and lost his own throne in 1814. Why did Napoleon let his "Spanish adventure" destroy his career? Owen Connelly thought that Napoleon would have won the Peninsular War had he personally commanded his armies in Iberia in 1810 or 1811.[58] Napoleon, however, made light of the Spanish war and deluded himself into thinking that he could win it at any time. "He did not appreciate the importance of the Peninsular War until too late, perhaps not fully until he could take a long view of it from St. Helena."[59]

Napoleon had rational explanations—or unconscious rationalizations—for his fatal personal absence from Spain and Portugal during the Peninsular War: in 1809 he was busy fighting Austria; in 1810 he was "absorbed with his marriage to Marie-Louise"; in 1811 he was engrossed with his newborn son; in 1812 he was busy fighting Russia; in 1813 he was "fighting for his life in Germany."[60] In fact, in denying the gravity of the war in Iberia, and in making it impossible for his elder brother to govern Spain, Napoleon was moved by an unconscious self-destructive compulsion to repeat his painful early-life trauma—his rejection by his mother, her preference for Joseph, and his murderous jealousy of his elder brother. He unconsciously set up a large-scale psychodrama in which he and his elder brother acted out their tragic parts until both were driven out of Spain by the British.

In 1809 Great Britain had assembled the Fifth Coalition against France with its European allies. Fearful of Napoleon, Russia, Prussia, Naples, and Sweden stayed away. Count Metternich, the Austrian ambassador to Paris, had provoked his emperor into making a disastrous war on France. Under Metternich's influence, Emperor Franz of Austria, who had been humiliated by Napoleon, accepted the British offer, provided Great Britain pay Austria's vast military expenses. The Fifth Coalition, set up in the spring, consisted of Great Britain and Austria; it ended in July with Napoleon's "miraculous" victory over Austria at Wagram and the Peace of Vienna.

From 1810 to 1813 Napoleon grew increasingly angry and disappointed with his elder brother Joseph, whom he had made king of Spain, as well as with his younger brother Louis, whom he had made king of the Netherlands. Napoleon felt that Joseph had utterly failed him—militarily, politically, and financially—and that both Joseph and Louis were "too soft" on their subjects.[61] *Did Napoleon unconsciously fear his own softness? Did he have to be hard on his subjects in order to allay his fear that his penis was not hard enough, that he was not man enough? Did he unconsciously externalized his own dissociated softness, sexual or otherwise, upon his brothers?* Louis did not see things Napoleon's way. He secretly traded with

Great Britain, defying Napoleon's irrational "Continental System."[62] The furious Napoleon wished to annex Holland to France. On March 16, 1810, under the threat of a French invasion, Louis was forced to sign a treaty with Napoleon, ceding the Dutch provinces south of the River Rhine—Brabant, Zeeland, and parts of Gelderland—to France. Holland also had to pay the salaries and upkeep of the French soldiers and customs agents who oversaw the blockade of England.

The narcissistic Napoleon had little empathy for other people's feelings. Whenever his grandiose self-esteem was threatened by failure or defeat, he humiliated people, which made him feel powerful and superior. In 1810 Napoleon visited the newly "French" provinces that he had just taken from Louis with his newly wedded Austrian wife Marie-Louise. He forced his younger brother Louis to pay court to him in the very provinces Napoleon had just torn away from Louis. The newly French Flemish merchants were happy about their improved commerce. When Louis complained, the emperor wrote him arrogantly, "Everyone knows that, without me, you are nothing!"[63]

Furious with his "soft" brother, the "hard" Napoleon finally sent his French troops to Holland, where they seized large chunks of Louis' kingdom. Finally, on July 1, an enraged, fearful and depressed Louis, who also had serious marital troubles, broke down. He abdicated his throne of the Netherlands in favor of his eldest son, Napoléon-Louis-Charles Bonaparte. During the night of July 1–2 Louis fled Holland for Austria in a panic.[64] His wife, Queen Hortense, whose relations with Louis had never been very good, took advantage of her freedom to become pregnant by Napoleon's twenty-five-year-old aide-de-camp, the handsome French nobleman Auguste-Charles-Joseph de Flahaut de la Billarderie,[65] son of Adelaïde Filleul, the marquise of Souza-Botelho. Her husband, the *maréchal de camp* Count Charles-François de Flahaut de la Billarderie, had been guillotined at Arras during the Terror of 1794, when his son was nine-years-old. Castelot called Flahaut "the natural son of Talleyrand," but other scholars believed him to be the son of the British statesman William Windham, who had sanctimoniously denounced France in Parliament as "one universal brothel."[66] On July 8 the seventy-one-year-old French archtreasurer Charles-François Lebrun was named lieutenant-general of the emperor and left for the Netherlands. On July 9 Napoleon issued an imperial decree removing Louis from the throne of Holland and annexing the entire Netherlands to France.

While waging fratricidal war on his younger brother Louis in the Netherlands, Napoleon was busy censoring the press in his own country. On August 3, 1810, he issued an imperial decree allowing only one newspaper to be published in each *département* of France. Only a few literary and scientific journals were exempt from this restriction.[67] On August 7 the depressed and defeated Louis wrote his mother, Letizia from the hot springs at Töplitz, outside Berlin, where he was recovering from his trauma: "I am as well as possible, and out of [political] affairs for good, I assure you."[68] Louis later went to Rome, where he joined his exiled brother Lucien.

Already in the summer of 1810, Napoleon was contemplating war with Russia. The chief cause was not political or military, but his personal feeling of narcissistic injury at the hands of the tsar, who had refused Napoleon his sister in marriage. On August 15 the entire French empire celebrated Napoleon's forty-first birthday. On August 21 his former spurned fiancée Désirée Clary became a future queen of Sweden: the Swedish Riksdag had met at Örebro and elected her husband, the forty-seven-year-old French nobleman Jean-Baptiste-Jules Bernadotte, the heir to the Swedish throne.

Bernadotte was Napoleon's former marshal and Prince of Ponte-Corvo. Napoleon did not oppose this move, hoping to have a solid ally in northern Europe. Jean Tulard called it a "heavy error."[69]

Bernadotte, who had been repeatedly humiliated by Napoleon, and whose wife had been abandoned by him, would play a key role in Napoleon's downfall. Bernadotte took charge of Sweden, reorienting its foreign policy against France. Napoleon at first demanded that Sweden declare war on his enemy, Great Britain. Mindful of France's great military power, Bernadotte formally complied, but engaged in no actual hostilities against Britain. In 1812 Sweden took Russia's side in its war with France, and in 1813 Sweden joined to the anti-French coalition and beat the French forces in Germany.

The United Kingdom of Great Britain and Ireland, which Napoleon called *l'Angleterre*, never ceased fighting Napoleon's France and running his blockade. In September 1810, defying Napoleon's "Continental System," an enormous convoy of twelve hundred British merchantmen sailed under a neutral flag for the Danish strait of Øresund in the Baltic Sea, escorted by twenty British Royal Navy men-of-war, seeking a continental port to unload their merchandise. France being Europe's mightiest power, Denmark, Prussia, and Sweden feared to defy Napoleon openly by permitting the British ships to dock in their ports. On October 23 Napoleon wrote Tsar Aleksandr of Russia asking him to seize the British ships in the Baltic Sea and confiscate their wares. As he had done with Napoleon's request to marry his sister, the tsar refused, inflicting yet another narcissistic injury on the proud emperor. On November 11 an angry and vengeful Napoleon annexed large areas of northern Germany, including the Hanseatic cities and the Duchy of Oldenburg, between Bremen and the North Sea, to the French Empire, pushing the French border with Prussia eastward to the Elbe.[70]

Emperor Napoleon of France became increasingly angry with Tsar Aleksandr of Russia. As Napoleon saw it, if Aleksandr violated the Treaty of Tilsit by making peace with England and refusing to enforce Napoleon's Continental System, Napoleon would have no choice but to make war on Aleksandr: "he could not retreat without jeopardizing the security of his policies and his imperial position."[71] On December 2, 1810, Napoleon sent an ominous message to his foreign minister, Jean-Baptiste de Nompère de Champagny, a fervent supporter of Napoleon's blockade of England and of his annexation of Holland, for transmission to the fifty-eight-year-old Russian ambassador to France, Prince Fyodor Aleksandr Kurakin: "If Alexander opened his ports to neutral ships carrying colonial and English merchandise, and if effect made peace with England, Napoleon warned, war would come."[72] On December 5 a furious Napoleon sent a similar message to Champagny for transmission to his ambassador to Russia, General Caulaincourt. In response, on December 31 a defiant Tsar Aleksandr issued a decree withdrawing Russia from Napoleon's Continental System and severing its military alliance with France.[73] Napoleon's self-righteous and self-destructive invasion of Russia was now a matter of time.

30

Fathering a Legitimate Son and Entering Russia

On February 17, 1811, the servile French Senate, not knowing whether Empress Marie-Louise's child would be a boy or a girl, issued a *sénatus-consulte* conferring the title of *Roi de Rome* on Emperor Napoleon's as-yet-unborn son. This was a political act directed personally against Pope Pius VII, the Bishop of Rome and Napoleon's prisoner. On March 20 the nineteen-year-old Empress Marie-Louise bore her husband Napoleon a son and heir, Napoleon II, the future Duke of Reichstadt, who was later baptized Napoléon-François-Charles-Joseph. Napoleon II would become the tragic King of Rome. His Christian names included those of his father, paternal grandfather, paternal uncle, and paternal great uncle. He would die in 1832. There were two physicians in attendance: Jean-Nicolas Corvisart, first physician to the emperor and Antoine Dubois, first obstetrician to the empress. It was the young mother's first childbirth, she was scared, and the birth was difficult. Marie-Louise screamed in pain, and Napoleon told the doctors that if they had to choose between the mother's life and the child's the mother came first. Dubois had to use a forceps to deliver the neonate. At one point he fainted, but his colleague, Corvisart, came to his aid.

The birth of Napoleon II was traumatic for all concerned—except for his father. Napoleon was ecstatic at the 101-gun salute announcing the birth of his son. It gave the Emperor the illusion of immortality.[1] On March 22, 1811, Napoleon wrote Josephine, "My son is big ands well. I hope that he will have good fortune. He has my chest, my mouth and my eyes."[2] As if realizing that the news would pain his former wife, he added that he was very happy with her son Eugène. This newborn baby, however, was his only legitimate son. Rome was part of his empire, and his son was its king. Three days later he sent the delivering physician, Dubois, one hundred thousand francs, a vast amount of money at that time. Frau Schwarzenberg, the wife of the Austrian ambassador to Paris who had mediated Napoleon's marriage to Marie-Louise, came over to congratulate Napoleon on the birth of his son. Napoleon gave her a talisman he had worn since his Egyptian campaign of 1798–1799, a stone scarab from the tomb of one of the Pharaohs of ancient Egypt, saying, "I have always worn it as a talisman. Take it. I have no need of it now!"[3] There were endless rumors, however, about the paternity of the *roi de Rome*, intimating that Napoleon was not the real father. [4]

Many Napoleon scholars believed that in 1811, because of his marriage and paternity, Emperor Napoleon of France made fewer wars and spent more time at home with his wife and child. In fact, the birth of his child did not distract Napoleon from his warmaking, nor from his attempts to control and censor the press. His conflict with Tsar Aleksandr of Russia was inexorable. Napoleon's marriage to Marie-Louise marked a turning point in his life. He was temporarily less eager for war, overate, and grew fat. Europe enjoyed peace for a while. Owen Connelly thought that "the Austrian marriage killed the General Bonaparte that lived within the emperor of the French and thus made a contribution to killing his empire."[5] Napoleon later recalled that in 1811 he had felt "out of sorts."[6] In fact, he was obsessed with the impossible task of conquering Russia. The psychoanalyst Pierce Clark thought that Napoleon at first tried to win over Aleksandr by "cajolery, diplomacy and easy promises" until he realized "that he must fight as never before."[7] Jacques Castelot thought that "it looked as if Napoleon wanted to shatter his own edifice."[8]

On June 9, 1811, Napoleon's son, the king of Rome and future Duke of Reichstadt, was baptized at Notre-Dame cathedral in Paris in what was called "the dynastic enthronement." His given names were Napoléon-François-Charles-Joseph—those of some of Napoleon's dearest emotional objects: himself, his step uncle Cardinal Fesch, his dead father Carlo, and his elder brother Joseph. The *roi de Rome*, whom Napoleon also called *l'aiglon* (the eaglet), was later known as Napoleon II, the Duke of Reichstadt, and the Prince of Parma, Piacenza, and Guastalla. Napoleon would lose him less than three years later, when Marie-Louise abducted her son and fled to Vienna upon Napoleon's defeat by the Allies.

Napoleon's son would die of tuberculosis or pneumonia in 1832, eleven years after Napoleon's own early death on Saint Helena.

The conflict between Pope Pius VII and Emperor Napoleon intensified. It had all the earmarks of a father-son conflict. Pius himself had some affection for Napoleon. He reportedly said, "The son is somewhat mutinous, but he remains the son."[9] Pius, imprisoned by Napoleon at Savona, sent Emperor Napoleon a delegation of six cardinals, eight archbishops and 81 bishops asking him to recognize the supremacy of the Holy Church of Rome and swear obedience to the pope. The threat to his power made Napoleon feel righteous rage. He answered the pope sharply that he was Charlemagne, vowing to annul his Concordat with the papacy. Napoleon's step-uncle, Joseph Cardinal Fesch, wishing to remain in the good graces of both Napoleon and the Holy See, tried in vain to mediate the conflict, but neither Napoleon nor Pius would give in.

On June 17, 1811, Emperor Napoleon convened a national council of bishops from all the French sees and the Italian bishoprics annexed to the French empire. It was presided over by his step uncle, Joseph Cardinal Fesch. Ninety-five bishops showed up. The German Church also joined the deliberations. For six weeks the ecclesiastical council deliberated how to end the impasse between the emperor and the pope. The council split into pro-Napoleon and anti-Napoleon camps.[10] To avoid feeling powerless, Napoleon needed absolute control. He could not abide any challenge to his authority. In the midst of the council's lengthy deliberations, Napoleon's anxiety and rage overwhelmed him. He had the leaders of the opposition—Maurice-Jean-Madeleine de Broglie, the bishop of Ghent, Etienne-François de Boulogne, the bishop of Troyes, and François-Joseph Hirn, the bishop of Tournai—whom Napoleon called the "renegade" bishops—arrested during the night, cast into the dungeons of the castle of Vincennes, and stripped of their posts. Only the seventy-five-year-old Charles-François d'Aviau du Bois de Sanzay, the archbishop of Bordeaux, escaped punishment. A furious Napoleon suspended the council's deliberations. On August 2 they resumed —after the pope's terrified delegates had signed a decree giving Napoleon's metropolitans the right to name his bishops to every vacant seat in his empire. Pope Pius VII refused to abdicate at Napoleon's demand, and the Emperor of the French abrogated their Concordat. Finally the assembled churchmen made their pro-Napoleon decrees conditional on their acceptance by the Pope—a blow to the emperor.[11]

On April 24, 1812, Tsar Aleksandr of Russia, angered by Napoleon's expansion of the Grand Duchy of Warsaw, incited by Talleyrand and by his own family, court and nobles, and emboldened by having signed a treaty of alliance with King Carl XIII of Sweden and by Napoleon's defeats in Iberia, delivered an ultimatum to Emperor Napoleon of the French: evacuate Oldenburg, Prussia, Pomerania, the Grand Duchy of Warsaw, and all the German lands east of the Elbe, or face war with Russia. The date on the document was April 8, the old-style date of the Julian calendar employed in Russia. The furious Napoleon could not possibly have accepted Aleksandr's ultimatum, without severe damage to his self-esteem. He decided to invade Russia.

Napoleon's decision to invade Russia was one of the most self-destructive acts of his entire political and military career. Harold Parker thought that no less than seven key aides of the Emperor had "gravely warned Napoleon against an invasion of Russia."[12] Incredibly, Napoleon turned a deaf ear to their pleas and proceeded to destroy himself and his army in Russia. The psychoanalyst Pierce Clark thought that "the clarification and realization come too late; he has beguiled others too long. The pattern of his inner plan has become too set and unalterable. He is too slow in renouncing this infantile dream of world domination."[13]

For Napoleon, it was time to say adieu to his ex-wife Josephine. On April 30, 1812, before leaving Paris for Russia, he saw Josephine for the last time at her castle of Malmaison. Josephine was not well: Napoleon would never see her again. She died two years later. Napoleon had seen Josephine two years earlier, and rarely saw her since. Raoul Brice thought that Napoleon "would have gone to see her often but for the jealousy of Marie Louise, which obliged him to limit his visits."[14] Napoleon's own sense of relief after his fifteen years with Josephine and his emotional involvement with his second wife and son may also have played their part in making his visit to his ex-wife rarer. On May 5, the day after the second birthday of Alexandre Walewski, his son by Maria Walewska, who was now living in Paris, Emperor Napoleon signed an imperial decree at Saint-Cloud conferring on the little boy the title of *comte de l'Empire* and giving him real estate in the Kingdom of Naples, with an annual revenue of one hundred seventy thousand francs. Napoleon had been moved by the sight of his former lover and of her son the day before.[15]

To invade Russia, Napoleon had raised a new *Grande Armée* of more than six hundred thousand men. The army of 1812 had less French than non-French soldiers. Owen Connelly thought that by June 1812 Napoleon's army had 611,000 men—three hundred thousand Frenchmen and 311,000 non-French Europeans speaking at least ten different languages—with two thousand guns and two hundred fifty thousand horses.[16] In May 1812 this vast army was encamped on the banks of the River Vistula in the puppet Polish "Grand Duchy of Warsaw." Napoleon planned to take charge of his army there. "The first wave was 490,000 strong; 121,000 more would follow."[17]

On May 9, 1812, nine days after he said adieu to Josephine, Emperor Napoleon and Empress Marie-Louise left Paris for the "Grand Duchy of Warsaw." A week later, on May 16, they reached the Saxon frontier, where Napoleon's sixty-one-year-old ally—or vassal—King Friedrich August of Saxony and his queen Maria Amelia Augusta welcomed them personally. They proceeded to the Saxon capital of Dresden, where Austrian emperor Franz and his wife Maria Ludovica joined them. On May 18, Napoleon and Marie-Louise made a grand appearance at the Dresden opera, in front of all the crowned heads of Central Europe. The psychoanalyst Pierce Clark called it "one of the most spectacular moments of history . . . Napoleon, one-time Corsican exile, stands supreme within the focus of monarchical splendour."[18]

After the opera, there was a reception at the Saxon king's palace. With his unconscious narcissistic defenses in full force, Napoleon treated the assembled royalty haughtily. As he saw it, he was their superior. They had to defer to him. Napoleon's fifty-seven-year-old aide-de-camp and confidant, General Louis de Narbonne-Lara, was with him. The biographer André Castelot marveled at the scene:

> Inside the palace, it was difficult to get anywhere near the master. "I got into a crowd of kings," said Narbonne to Napoleon, "and had a hard time getting through it." Sovereigns intermingled with high dignitaries elbowed one another aside so as to be present at he levee. [Emperor] Francis of Austria, astonished, saw Napoleon take precedence over him, go to the table first, keep the sovereigns at a respectful distance, and preside at table still wearing his hat, while he, Francis—a Hapsburg!—was uncovered. "*Das ist ein ganzer Kerl!*"—That's quite a fellow!—he exclaimed.[19]

Napoleon's ill-fated invasion of Russia was inaugurated at the Dresden conference between Napoleon and his European allies—or vassals—which opened on May 18, 1812, and lasted twelve days. Napoleon's narcissism was augmented by his political needs and physical fatigue. As Owen Connelly put it, "He wanted a demonstration that his allies were behind him and wanted to impress the Russians with that fact. *And personally, no doubt, he needed adulation and reassurance.* He was already tired from the journey, and the campaign had not even started."[20]

Emperor Franz of Austria and his foreign minister, Count Metternich, were caught between Russia and France. Allying Austria squarely with either adversary was out of the question, while neutrality was difficult and dangerous to sustain. Believing that Napoleon, whose military force was superior, would defeat Aleksandr, Metternich negotiated a treaty of alliance with Napoleon. They agreed that Austria would send a thirty thousand-man "auxiliary army corps" under Prince Carl Philipp zu Schwarzenberg—with the status of an "independent contingent"—to join Napoleon's *Grande Armée* and help France fight Russia.[21] In return, Napoleon gave Austria back the Polish province of Galicia (now in the western Ukraine)—breaking his promise to his Polish lover Maria Walewska to restore the freedom of her beloved motherland. The psychoanalyst Pierce Clark saw this concession as a betrayal: "Napoleon moves on, betraying his trust as liberator of the Poles by bartering away their fair Galicia to Austria for her support of the Russian venture."[22]

On June 23, 1812, the main body of Napoleon's huge army reached the River Niemen at Kaunas (Kovno), in Russian Lithuania, on the border between the "Grand Duchy of Warsaw" and Russia. On June 24–25, Napoleon's "French" army crossed the River Niemen into Russia. This was the beginning of Napoleon's most self-destructive act of his entire career, and the prelude to his downfall two years later.

31

A Suicidal Invasion

Napoleon's disastrous Russian campaign of 1812 and the horrific carnage that accompanied it have been described in great detail by many historians and writers. Hundreds of thousands were lost on both sides. At first, Napoleon was moderately victorious. In mid-August, on his forty-third birthday, he defeated the uncoordinated Russians at the western Russian city of Smolensk on the Dniepr River, and on September 7 Emperor Napoleon of France won an ambiguous victory over the sixty-seven-year-old Russian commander, Marshal Prince Mikhail Ilarionovich Golenishchev Kutuzov, at the village of Borodino, which the French called the Battle of the Moskova after the nearby river. Though the Russians had forty-five thousand casualties, Napoleon had some thirty thousand himself, including forty-seven generals, and Kutuzov, who withdrew eastward, also claimed victory. Nonetheless this initial though ambiguous "victory" reinforced Napoleon's tragic sense of invincibility.

On September 13, 1812, the French were within sight of Moscow. On September 14, when Napoleon ascended the Poklonnaya Gora overlooking Moscow, he was "ecstatic with joy."[1] That evening, the ninety-five thousand surviving Frenchmen of Napoleon's *Grande Armée* occupied Moscow, most of whose people had fled. The rest of Napoleon's army was spread far and wide in Germany, Austria and Poland. At the request of his staff officers, Napoleon spent that night at a foul-smelling inn in the village of Dorogomilov, west of Moscow.

Unbeknownst to Napoleon, the Russians had planned a fiery welcome for him. Most of Moscow's buildings were made of wood. The forty-nine-year-old military governor of Moscow, General Count Fyodor Vassilievich

Rostopchin, a conservative, nationalist former foreign minister under Aleksandr's father Pavel, had ordered the city set on fire, and Moscow's three hundred thousand residents had fled the city. The paranoid Rostopchin believed that Moscow was riddled with pro-French secret societies that would help Napoleon against the Tsar. To boost morale, he had repeatedly issued false statements to his townspeople proclaiming Russian victories on the battlefield. When the French had defeated the Russians at Smolensk and Borodino and were advancing on Moscow, Rostopchin assured the Muscovites that he had a foolproof defense plan.

That night fires broke out in Moscow's old German Quarter, and by the following day two thirds of Moscow was on fire. On September 15, 1812, Napoleon left Dorogomilov for the deserted and burning Moscow. Most of the city was on fire. Napoleon nevertheless headed for the Kremlin fortress. But his euphoria had collapsed. Napoleon's former ambassador to Russia, General Caulaincourt, later recalled that Napoleon became depressed at seeing the burning, empty city and had a "changed expression" on his face.[2]

As he had done in Berlin and Vienna, Napoleon now installed himself at the Tsar's palace in the Kremlin. The remaining Russians burned down their city around him; the Kremlin alone, which was made of stone, withstood the fire. Finally the Moscow fires engulfed the Kremlin, and Napoleon's valet, Constant Wairy, awakened the sleeping Napoleon. When he awoke amid the blaze, he was like the ancient Roman emperor Nero in burning Rome. Napoleon climbed the Kremlin bell tower accompanied by General Caulaincourt and Grand Chamberlain Montesquiou-Fezensac. The Moscow flames echoed his inner fire. Napoleon was both horrified and ecstatic. The perceptive poet-psychoanalyst Pierce Clark understood his state of mind:

> Napoleon is agitated, consumed with fury and passion as the flames that now begin to envelop the inner citadel threaten, yes, even the Kremlin, his own quarters. He paces to and fro, then abruptly sits down. For the moment he is moved to see in it not only his own destruction but a heroic gesture on the part of the enemy. Both moods struggle for mastery. "What a tremendous spectacle! It is their own work! So many palaces! What extraordinary resolution! What men! These are Scythians indeed!"[3]

In fact, Napoleon could not stop exclaiming his indignation: "This is unbelievable! Those barbarians, those savages! To burn down their own city! What worse could an enemy do? They draw upon themselves the curse of posterity."[4] Was he unconsciously projecting his own barbarity in invading Russia and denying his humiliation by Tsar Aleksandr? While Napoleon thought of the Russians as "Tartar barbarians," the Russians thought of the French in exactly the same terms. To the Russians, the invading Frenchmen were like the "Tatars" or Mongols who had invaded Russia in the late middle ages.

Two thirds of Moscow burned down in the fire. On September 15, 1812, a depressed Napoleon moved into the Kremlin's Petrovsky Palace, where he spent five dreary and unhappy weeks amid the ashes of Moscow, unable to decide what to do next. Denying reality, he believed that his occupation of Moscow would force Tsar Aleksandr of Russia to make peace with him. Incredibly, On September 20 Napoleon wrote Aleksandr a "fraternal" letter:

> *To my brother, the emperor Alexandre.* The beautiful and superb city of Moscow no longer exists. [The military governor] Rostopchin has caused it to be burned down. Four hundred arsonists have been arrested in the act: all have admitted that they had acted on orders of this governor and of the chief of police: they were executed by a firing squad. The fire seems to have died down finally . . . This deed is loathsome, and to no purpose. Did you wish to rob me of my means of support? . . . How could you consign to destruction the loveliest city in the world, a city it has taken hundreds of years to build; how could you lay it waste for so little gain! Out of kindness and in the interests of Your Majesty, I have now taken charge of the town which the Russian Army had sacrificed. At least the municipal authorities and the militia should have been left in the city, as was the case in Vienna, on two occasions, and in Berlin and Madrid; Milan, likewise, acted thus when [the Russian general Aleksandr Vassilyevich] Suvaroff [Suvorov] entered [it] at the head of his army [in 1799] . . . The arson sanctions the pillage to which the soldier gives himself up to save the debris from the flames. Had I thought that such things were done on the order of Your Majesty, I would not have written Him this letter: but I hold it impossible that, with his principles, his heart, the justice of his ideas, he would have authorized such excesses, unworthy of a great sovereign and of

a great nation . . . I have warred against Your Majesty without bitterness: a little note from him, before or after the last battle, would have stayed my forward march, and I would even have been willing to forego the advantage of my entry into Moscow. If Your Majesty still has any of his old sentiments for me, he will take this letter in good spirit. In any case, he cannot but be grateful to me for informing you of the recent occurrences.[5]

It may be psychologically significant that the French *Votre Majesté* (Your Majesty) is feminine, and that throughout this letter Napoleon addressed Aleksandr in the feminine third person singular. Was Aleksandr unconsciously a mother as well as a brother to him? Did Napoleon really believe that Aleksandr still loved him, after he had invaded the Tsar's Mother Russia? If so, he was deluding himself.

The Russian tsar, however, was waiting in his capital of Saint Petersburg for the Russian winter to arrive, cut Napoleon's supply lines and freeze Napoleon's army out of Russia. Aleksandr had assured his sister Yekaterina, Duchess of Oldenburg, that he was "more firmly resolved than ever to fight the monster who has brought misfortune over the entire world."[6] Napoleon, for his part, was convinced that he had brought nothing but happiness to the world.

Owen Connelly thought that Napoleon now had very few options: "If he withdrew to the west, it would signal weakness and make his bargaining position worse. Winter was too near for a march on St. Petersburg, where the czar resided. And it was too late to renew the pursuit of Kutuzov. Moreover, if he withdrew, his fickle European allies might defect—especially Austria and Prussia. His whole alliance system might collapse. His enemies had been cheered too much already by the news from Spain, where Wellington had taken Madrid. Napoleon also feared the reaction at home to a setback. There was always the danger of a coup [d'état] in Paris while he was away."[7] Indeed, by invading Russia, the self-destructive Napoleon had placed himself in an untenable situation as soon as he had taken Moscow.

Napoleon spent most of October 1812 in Moscow, living more in fantasy than in reality. One of his first acts was to order his men to remove the huge golden cross from the Kremlin tower of the fifteenth-century tsar Ivan Vasilyevich or Ivan the Great, who had expanded Russia by conquering its neighboring lands or winning the allegiance of their princes, retaken parts of the Ukraine from Poland-Lithuania and thrown of the yoke of the Tartars. Removing the great cross did not help. Napoleon's hungry and cold soldiers died of malnutrition and disease, his horses died from lack of forage, and he was losing his means of transport, his artillery and his cavalry. During the day, the depressed and anxious Napoleon paced about the Kremlin palace halls, awaiting Tsar Aleksandr's reply to his peace offer of September 20. To lift his own spirits, and that of his men, he held daily reviews of his Imperial Guard, handing out medals and promotions with great fanfare. This was an unconscious defense against his deepening feeling of helpless despair. His reality testing seriously impaired, Napoleon issued bizarre and impossible orders to his army:

> *He sent out strange orders from the Kremlin*; for example, one was for the local purchase of 10,000 horses, a total impossibility. (More realistically, he sent orders to Hugues Bernard Maret, his foreign minister, in Vilna [the Lithuanian capital of Vilnius], to procure 14,000 [horses] in Germany and Poland, authorizing 4,000,000 francs for the purchase. But there was not time for the horses to arrive before the snows.) Napoleon also decreed that the [Russian] markets be opened and that peasants who brought foodstuffs to sell be protected absolutely. He gave orders to find materials and make clothes and shoes. None of this could be done.[8]

Encouraged by his sister, his courtiers, and his generals, Tsar Aleksandr of Russia was not in a negotiating mood. He ignored Napoleon's peace overture. On Friday, October 16, 1812, with most of Moscow burned down, his army greatly diminished, and no answer from the tsar, Napoleon finally came to his senses. His unconscious denial of reality broke down. "Finally, however, the French emperor no longer could ignore the approach of winter and the deterioration of his army."[9]

Napoleon decided to withdraw his army toward Poland via the western Russian city of Smolensk, on the road from Moscow to Warsaw, where he had won his first victory over the Russians two months earlier. By Saturday, October 17, the French retreat from Moscow was in full swing. But the month Napoleon had lost in Moscow trying to make up his mind would cause vast and horrible losses to his men.

Unbeknownst to him, while Napoleon was in Russia, he had serious trouble back home in Paris. With his narcissistic high-handedness, Napoleon had hurt, humiliated and alienated many statesmen and generals. One of them was Brigadier General Claude-François de Malet, a disgraced, embittered fifty-eight-year-old republican nobleman. In 1801 Malet had been dismissed from the army by War Minister Louis-Alexandre Berthier, now a marshal and the chief of staff of Napoleon's army. In 1808 he had been arrested by Police Prefect Louis-Nicolas Dubois and imprisoned at Vincennes for a previous plot with General Moreau. In 1810 Malet had been transferred to Claude-Henri Jacquelin-Dubuisson's *maison de santé* in Paris, where he was kept under house arrest and police surveillance, and where he met several like-minded reactionaries. Seething with vengeance, Malet used Napoleon's absence to stage a *coup d'état* against his emperor. Fortunately for Napoleon, his loyal aides in Paris put down the revolt and arrested Malet. When the presiding judge at his court-martial asked Malet to name his accomplices, Malet replied: "All of France and you yourself, had I succeeded!" Malet was found guilty of treason, sentence to death and executed by firing squad on October 29. Napoleon received the news by special courier on November 9.[10] It could not have made him very happy to learn that he had nearly lost his throne.

Napoleon's decision to retreat from Russia came at a heavy cost to his self-esteem, which his grandiose self and superego interpreted as a deep humiliation. His depression deepened and he thought of killing himself. During the retreat from Moscow, in his suicidal depression, Napoleon reportedly asked his personal physician, the 47-year-old Dr. Alexandre-Urbain Yvan, for poison, to use if he ever decided to end his life. Yvan gave him what he said was a poison capsule, which Napoleon reportedly carried with him ever since. But Dr. Yvan's "poison" could not kill Napoleon. It was a nonlethal mixture of opium, strychnine, belladonna and hellebore that had been made by Dr. Pierre-Jean-Georges Cabanis, one of Napoleon's best-known physicians.[11]

By early November 1812 it was snowing heavily in western Russia. Napoleon's army constantly trudged through ice and snow. The temperature dropped rapidly. Thousands of French soldiers died of cold, exposure and starvation; so did thousands of their horses. As he had done with the *pestiférés* at Jaffa in 1799, Napoleon left his wounded, sick and dying men to die where they fell. As the biographer André Castelot put it, "Those poor, useless human bundles had been piled on wagons or gun carriages, and some of the drivers intentionally drove the horses into deep ruts in the road. The unfortunate wounded men—most of them amputees—who fell from the vehicles were left behind."[12] It was a great tragedy. Of the 100,000 Frenchmen who had left Moscow, about half died on their way out of Russia. Only 50,000 had reached Smolensk, of whom only 30,000 were still capable of fighting. "[Napoleon's] army had disintegrated astoundingly in just nine days."[13]

By November 9, 1812, the unhappy Napoleon was more preoccupied with General Malet's plot back home in Paris, of which he had just learned, than with his dying men. Malet was not the first plotter who had tried to topple Napoleon. Who else was preparing a *coup d'état* against him? Should he remain in Russia or return to France? Napoleon ordered his army to leave Smolensk and head for Vilnius, the Russian Lithuanian capital. But the Russians kept harassing the retreating Frenchmen from behind. Owen Connelly thought that "Napoleon's [military] reputation alone saved the *Grande Armée* from total destruction before it reached the [Byelorussian river of] Berezina. The Russian generals were loath to attack him. Furthermore, they could not be sure, with visibility reduced by snow and fog, just how many fighting men were in the French column, which stretched for miles."[14]

The psychoanalyst Pierce Clark believed that Napoleon faced an excruciating choice at the Berezina River: to save his army or to save himself. Clark thought that when Napoleon ordered his army to cross the frozen Berezina, he was acting rationally, if selfishly: "And now comes the supreme test. Napoleon has made a monstrous decision, one warranted politically and strategically, but not personally. It is the so-called first law of nature—self-preservation—but at the deliberate instigation of cool calculation. He determines if need be to sacrifice his army bit by bit that he may save its head. He now becomes strong; his narcism thus fully protected, the personal Napoleon is courageous, keen and resourceful. He must move swiftly if his army is to cross the Beresina [sic] in safety."[15]

On November 27–28, 1812, Napoleon's malignant narcissism took its final deadly toll in Russia at the horrific Battle of the Berezina, where one hundred twenty thousand frenzied Russian soldiers badly battered the surviving Frenchmen and inflicted enormous losses on them. Horror scenes multiplied at the Berezina, as they always do in war. A surviving French Imperial Guard sergeant recalled that "many of the survivors were walking barefoot, using pieces of wood as canes, but their feet were frozen so hard that the sound they made on the road was like that of wooden clogs."[16] Thousands of French soldiers froze to death. To survive, the desperate men set upon their dying comrades, stripping them of their clothes and making them freeze to death in seconds. Dying horses were eaten alive. The Battle of the Berezina was a sheer catastrophe for Napoleon. What was left of his army was saved by the brave Marshal Michel Ney, "the fiery redhead" who galloped to the front lines and rallied his men.[17]

For Napoleon it was the last straw. On November 29, 1812, a defeated, traumatized and humiliated Napoleon left the Berezina River for the Russian Lithuanian capital of Vilnius with the remnants of his disintegrating army. During the end of November and the beginning of December 1812, the Russian winter decimated the retreating Frenchmen, many of whom froze to death. It is impossible to determine Napoleon's catastrophic losses with precision. Since entering Russia, anywhere from four hundred thousand to five hundred seventy thousand of his six hundred thousand men had been killed, captured or deserted.[18] Napoleon became depressed. Pierce Clark believed that while the relentless Russian winter raged outside, Napoleon's inner gloom was even more terrible.[19]

On December 2, 1812, Napoleon instructed General Caulaincourt to send Grand Chamberlain Elisabeth-Pierre de Montesquiou-Fezensac to Paris with the text of his "famous and terrifying" 29th Bulletin of the *Grande Armée*, dated December 3, which admitted his defeat, to be published in the official *Le Moniteur*. "I will tell all. It is better for them to know the details from me than from private letters." In fact, Napoleon's bulletin was an exercise in unconscious denial and rationalization. Napoleon minimized his losses, blamed his calamity on the marauding Russian Cossacks and on the cold weather, and exalted his men's heroism.[20] The unconscious defenses were vital to his psychological survival. Pierce Clark thought that Napoleon's "ego-ideal had been fearfully wounded. Only a Napoleonic mind can endure such punishment and live."[21]

On December 3, 1812, Napoleon reached the Byelorussian town of Molodechno, northwest of Minsk, on the road to Vilnius. Napoleon now came to his senses, or panicked, depending on one's point of view. As he had done in Egypt thirteen years earlier, Napoleon abandoned his army, reversing and *reenacting his own early abandonment by his mother and wet nurse*. He secretly informed two men—his secretary-of-state, Pierre-Antoine-Noël-Bruno Daru, and his closest aide and confidant, General Géraud-Christophe-Michel Duroc—that he was leaving for France at once, and placing Marshal Murat at the head of the debris of his army. Everybody else was kept in the dark. To prepare his desertion, in early December 1812 Napoleon dictated the 29th Bulletin of the *Grande Armée*, admitting his defeat but praising the "good humor" and "gaiety" of his soldiers. This "famous and terrifying" document[22] was sent by special courier to Paris and printed in *Le Moniteur* on December 16, two days before Napoleon himself arrived in Paris. It included the following lines:

> Until November 6 the weather was perfect, and the army's movements were executed with the greatest success. The cold wave set in on the 7th. From then on, every night, we lost several hundred horses which died in the encampment . . . This army, which had been so splendid on the 6th, was in very different condition by the 14th: without artillery, without a supply train, and almost without cavalry . . . This difficulty, together with a sudden and severe cold wave, made our position very trying. Those men whom Nature had not molded strongly enough to remain unaffected by the hazards of fate and fortune seemed to be shaken: they lost their lively spirits and good humor; their thoughts dwelled only upon misfortunes and catastrophes . . . The enemy, having observed along the roadsides the traces of this frightful calamity which had overwhelmed the French army, tried to take advantage of it.[23]

Marshal Charles-Nicolas-Victor Oudinot said that Napoleon's 29th Bulletin "confounded France."[24] Napoleon's marshals and generals knew that his own tragic and self-destructive decisions had led the French army into this horrible predicament. Had he not invaded Russia, had he spent the winter waiting in Smolensk, had he left Moscow in September, his army would not have been devastated by the Russian winter. The 29th Bulletin of the *Grande Armée* was not an acceptance of reality but its denial, an unconscious attempt to alleviate Napoleon's unbearable feelings of guilt and worthlessness. [25]

How did Napoleon's surviving troops, starving and freezing in Lithuania, feel about their abandonment by their emperor? The psychoanalyst Pierce Clark believed that Napoleon had played the role of benevolent father to his soldiers, who loved him and identified with him.[26] Following Freud's notions of group psychology, but totally ignoring Clark's work, the American psychiatrist Franklin Klaf also believed that Napoleon was "a good father" to the *Grande Armée* of 1812.[27] He served as an ego ideal and a good role model, and his men thought him to be infallibly guided by fate. When telling his marshals his decision to leave, he treated all of them like equal sons and siblings, appointing his brother-in-law Joachim Murat, the king of Naples, as his successor, to continue the army's identification with himself. Klaf thought that "Napoleon was such a skilled practitioner of an effective variety of mass paternalism that he might almost be termed an artificer. He epitomized the great father, caring equally (or seeming to care equally) for all of the 'children' of his army."[28] This enabled him to bind together soldiers of many nations into a cohesive army.

Did Clark and Klaf seriously think that Napoleon's freezing and dying men in 1812 loved their "good father" Napoleon, and that the handful of survivors did not resent their abandonment by their emperor? Connelly thought the idea "ludicrous." Napoleon, Connelly observed, removed his youngest brother Jérôme, the King of Westphalia, his only blood relative on the Russian campaign, from the command of the right wing of the *Grande Armée*, sent him home to Paris for "alleged incompetence" and replaced him with Marshal Davout, the commander of the French army of Germany, whom Napoleon "did not like but depended on."[29] Connelly's statement was inaccurate, however. Napoleon did not dismiss Jérôme from his post: he gave Davout, who had already snubbed Jérôme in his own kingdom, precedence over him, which made Jérôme furious. Besides, many scholars thought that Jérôme was indeed militarily incompetent: he had failed to pursue the retreating Russian army corps of General Prince Bagration, giving them time to escape. And Napoleon did not send Jérôme back to Paris: Jérôme left the army without authorization and returned to his palace at Cassel in Westphalia. [30]

On December 30, 1812, after twelve days of secret negotiations, the fifty-three-year-old Prussian general Count Johann David Ludwig Yorck von Wartenburg, who commanded the two Prussian divisions in Marshal Macdonald's 10th Corps of Napoleon's *Grande Armée*, formally capitulated to the Russians at the East Prussian town of Tauroggen (now the Lithuanian town of Taurage), taking his two divisions out of the *Grande Armée* and making them "neutral." In effect, by signing the Tauroggen Convention, Yorck had defected to Napoleon's enemy, falsely claiming to have his king's consent for this capitulation. The Tauroggen Convention that Yorck signed with the Russians stipulated that Prussia would reoccupy its former eastern territories between Memel (now the Lithuanian town of Klaipeda), Tilsit (now the Russian city of Sovyetsk), and the Baltic

Sea coast. Yorck's troops at once evacuated Königsberg (now the Russian city of Kaliningrad). Yorck's defection marked the beginning of Prussia's abandonment of France. The Prussian public's outrage at his defection forced a reluctant King Friedrich Wilhelm to briefly suspend Yorck of his command and to replace him with the fifty-year-old Prussian general Count Friedrich Kleist von Nollendorf.

By early 1813, Napoleon's catastrophic defeat in Russia had consequences in central and southern Europe. His European "allies" and vassals began to plan their attack on France. Prince Eugène, Napoleon's stepson, led the pitiful remnants of Napoleon's army from Russia to Germany. Despite his staggering defeat in Russia, despite the tragic and useless death of hundreds of thousands of his men, Napoleon still believed that he could defeat Russia if he set out in the spring with a new army, and his legislature once more helped Napoleon act out his dangerous delusions. While his marshals and generals were disillusioned, the French people continued to idealize their Emperor. Rather than die of a broken heart, Napoleon's love affair with Mother France intensified. Pierce Clark thought that "France, the coquette, is not merely enthusiastic; she is fascinated and adoring."[31]

Marshal Joachim Murat, the King of Naples, whom Napoleon had placed at the head of his army in Russia, had wavered between loyalty to Napoleon and negotiation with his enemies. Like Napoleon's other marshals, Murat was disillusioned with his emperor. Like Napoleon himself, he had abandoned the traumatized remnants of the *Grande Armée* in Russia to take care of his own kingdom, leaving them in the hands of Napoleon's stepson, Prince Eugène, the commander of the 4th Corps, who led them back to France. On January 11, 1813, the French senate, though "shocked beyond measure" by the catastrophe in Russia, [32] issued a *sénatus consulte* giving Emperor Napoleon's a new army of three hundred fifty thousand men, of which one hundred fifty thousand were of the following year's class, under the age of military service.[33] This reinforced Napoleon's illusion that he could rescue victory from the jaws of defeat and restore his tottering self-esteem.

Napoleon never gave up. Doing so would have meant the collapse of his grandiose omnipotent self and his emotional undoing, if not his suicide. Napoleon's ambivalent quest for peace in 1813 did not last very long. He denied the reality of his ignominious defeat in Russia and once more felt grandiose, omnipotent and invincible. Within a short time he was eager to go to war on Russia again. Napoleon appealed to his marshal and brother-in-law, King Joachim Murat of Naples, who had abandoned the remnants of Napoleon's army in Prussia and returned to his kingdom of Naples, to come to Paris and take over his cavalry. While Napoleon needed Murat, he was furious with Murat for having abandoned his army in Russia. Unconsciously projecting his own guilt feelings on Murat, he saw his action as a desertion, if not a defection. On January 1, 1813, King Joachim Murat returned to France, and on January 26 Emperor Napoleon received him at the Tuileries Palace and reproached him for the very thing that Napoleon himself had done not long before—abandoning his army.[34]

Prince Eugène, Napoleon's stepson and viceroy of Italy, who had replaced Murat as the commander of Napoleon's *Grande Armée* in Russia, retreated with the dismal remnants of that army from the East Prussian town of Posen (now the Polish city of Poznan) to Berlin, which Marshal Augereau's 11th Corps had been occupying since January 1813. On February 10 King Friedrich Wilhelm of Prussia, emboldened by Napoleon's defeat in Russia, ordered a mass conscription in his whole kingdom. Eugène and Augereau met in mid-February and joined their two armies. In late February they abandoned Berlin, which King Friedrich Wilhelm re-occupied in early March; masses of Prussians enlisted in their army to fight Napoleon. Nonetheless, Napoleon still thought he could raise a fresh new army and defeat both Prussia and Russia.

The British field marshal and military historian Garnet Joseph Wolseley, who called Napoleon "the greatest of the great,"[35] believed that by 1813 Napoleon's physical and mental "powers" had declined, and that this was the beginning of his fall.[36] This thesis has been hotly debated by scholars. In fact, Napoleon's "powers" had much to do with his emotional state. When things went his way, when he won his battles and succeeded in his projects, he felt omnipotent and could do most anything. When he failed, he felt gloomy and his "powers" declined.

On January 19, 1813, Napoleon went to Fontainebleau, where Pope Pius VII, who had excommunicated Napoleon, had been his prisoner for the past eight months, after a three-year detention at Savona. Napoleon desperately wished to mend his oedipal quarrel with the Holy Father and to get the pope to crown his infant son, the king of Rome, as Emperor Napoleon II, his successor to the French throne. Napoleon embraced Pius and spent five days at Fontainebleau arguing with him. The Emperor of the French wanted the Holy Father to reside at Avignon, the medieval seat of the popes who had been exiled from Rome, and to renounce the papal states. Finally, on January 25, a new Concordat was signed between the pope and the emperor. The pope agreed to let the French metropolitans invest new French bishops, including those in the former Papal States which had been annexed to France, if he had not done so himself six months after they were nominated by the French government. Satisfied with his victory, Napoleon returned to Paris; Pius remained his prisoner at Fontainebleau. The captive old pope however, was deeply ambivalent about what he had signed. Three days later, on January 28, he signed a secret declaration annulling his signature on the agreement with France. On February 13 Napoleon promulgated his new pact with the Pope as French Imperial law, but Pius VII formally retracted it on March 24. The son and the father were back at war. [37]

Buoyed by Napoleon's calamitous defeat in Russia, the vengeful allies quickly sprang to action. On February 28, 1813, King Friedrich Wilhelm of Prussia, eager to heal his narcissistic injuries by wreaking vengeance upon Napoleon, signed a secret Treaty at the East Prussian city of Kalisch with Tsar Aleksandr of Russia. Kalisch was the former and present Polish city of Kalisz, which had become Prussian after the partition of Poland in 1793. Prussia's action began the Sixth Coalition against France, initiated by Prussia and Russia and later joined by Great Britain and Austria.[38] The Allies wished to break Napoleon's Continental System, which had hurt Europe no less than it did England, once and for all. Pierce Clark observed that "this malignant concept is to die with Napoleon's decline. Gone is the Grand Army and all the painted fabric of a hideous nightmare from Napoleon's mind; yet the principle is not dead. No, it will not die, for it is born of the deepest unconscious strivings of his mind; it is knit in the very fibre of his being and will only cease to be when he too is destroyed."[39]

Political and military events now followed in quick succession. On March 16, 1813, Prussia abrogated its alliance with France. The next day King Friedrich Wilhelm of Prussia declared war on France and called upon "his people" to unite against the enemy.[40] That same day the dismal remnants of Napoleon's army, under Prince Eugène, evacuated the Saxon capital of Dresden and headed for France. On March 19 the Prussian general Count Johann David Ludwig Yorck von Wartenburg, who had signed the Tauroggen Convention with Russia, and who had then been briefly and reluctantly suspended by his king, entered the Prussian capital of Berlin, and on March 22 King Friedrich Wilhelm himself also returned to

Berlin. The Prussians were ecstatic. Their revenge on Napoleon was at hand. Married Prussian ladies gave their gold wedding rings ro their Crown, wearing iron rings inscribed "I have given gold for iron."[41]

In the spring of 1813 Napoleon's armies fought bitter battles against the allies. Then, while the allies publicly negotiated with Napoleon at Prague, they secretly conferred among themselves at the Lower Silesian town of Trachenburg (now the Polish town of Zmigród) and at the East Prussian town of Reichenbach (now the Polish town of Dzierzoniów) on how to defeat him on the battlefield. As if all this was not bad enough for Napoleon, his war in Spain went worse for him. On June 21, 1813, his army was badly defeated by the forces of Great Britain and the Spanish rebels at the Basque city of Vitoria-Gasteiz, southeast of Bilbao. After five years of humiliating off-and-on reign in Spain, Napoleon's elder brother Joseph, whom the Spaniards called "the intruder king" was forced to leave his kingdom for France—another humiliating defeat not only for Joseph but also for Napoleon himself.

On June 24, 1813, ten days after the start of the Prague peace talks and twenty days after signing the brief Pläswitz armistice, Prussia, Russia and Austria signed a secret treaty of military alliance against France at Reichenbach. The dramatic news of Napoleon's defeat in Spain reached Vienna on June 26, emboldening Emperor Franz and his foreign minister Metternich to defy Napoleon. To buy time for the allies to prepare for their decisive battle against France, they decided that Count Metternich would travel to the Saxon capital of Dresden and seek a meeting with Napoleon on the pretext of "mediating" a peace treaty.

In mid-August 1813, Napoleon's war against the allies in Germany resumed. Napoleon now faced four armies numbering over half a million fighting men led by some of his former allies, such as the Austrian prince Carl Philipp zu Schwarzenberg:

> Soon arrayed against him were four great armies, the strength of which would grow, not diminish, as the campaign progressed: the [Austrian] Army of Bohemia (240,000), under Austrian Prince Schwarzenberg; the [Swedish] Army of the North (120,000), under Swedish Crown Prince Bernadotte; the [Prussian[Army of Silesia under Prussian Prince Blücher; and the [Russian] Army of Poland

(60,000), under Russian Marshal Bennigsen. These totaled 515,000 but soon would exceed 600,000.[42]

Napoleon's forces, on the other hand, totaled only three hundred seventy thousand men. His main army never exceeded two hundred fifty thousand, less than half the size of the combined allied armies. Most of these, moreover, were "green French troops and uncertain allied and foreign contingents."[43] The four allies—Russia, Austria, Prussia and Great Britain—named the Austrian field-marshal Prince Carl Philipp zu Schwarzenberg—the commander of the Austrian Army of Bohemia and the former Austrian ambassador to Paris who had arranged Napoleon's marriage to Marie-Louise—the supreme commander of their Allied armies against France. Schwarzenberg knew Napoleon well, feared his surprise tactics, and was prudent in his moves. Fortunately for Napoleon, the generals under Schwarzenberg's command bickered among themselves, and the four allied armies were very different from each other.[44]

On August 26, 1813 Napoleon's French forces suffered a bad blow at the hands of the Austrians and Prussians. The twenty thousand men of General Gouvion Saint-Cyr's French corps in Dresden were attacked and decimated by Prince Schwarzenberg's Austrian Army of Bohemia, numbering from one hundred fifty thousand to two hundred thousand men. Field-Marshal Blücher, commanding the Prussian Army of Silesia, who had been pursued by the French army of Marshal Macdonald, then turned around, attacked, and defeated Macdonald's army at the Silesian town of Wahlstatt, near Liegnitz (now the Polish town of Legnica) on the River Katzbach (now the Kaczawa). The Prussians called it "the massacre of the Katzbach." With Blücher was the Prussian 1st Corps, commanded by General Yorck von Wartenburg. The victorious Blücher was made the Duke of Wahlstatt.

In May 1813 Napoleon's *Grande Armée* had fought the allied forces at the Saxon towns of Lützen and Bautzen, as a prelude to the great battle of Leipzig. Napoleon lost numerous men, including his grand marshal of the palace, friend and confidant, General Géraud-Christophe-Michel Duroc. Though mortally wounded, Duroc survived long enough to receive Napoleon's visit before dying. Vincent Cronin believed that Napoleon wept when Duroc died: "As he left the farmhouse, tears streamed down his cheeks, on to his uniform. An aide-de-camp had to support him as he walked in silence back to his tent."[45] Napoleon's former secretary Bourrienne claimed that Duroc himself had told him that Napoleon could not feel true grief: "What distresses me most, I confess [Duroc said], is how little he feels sorry for his old comrades in arms. He says in solemn tones, 'Such a one has died a hero's death.' Then, the next moment, he does not give it another thought."[46] Bourrienne also claimed that the dying Duroc, "who was in severe pain, seeing that the visit was dragging on, turned over painfully to rest on his side and with the right hand gestured to [Napoleon] to go away. [saying] 'Ah, Sire, at least let me die in peace!'"[47]

We should keep in mind the unreliability of Bourrienne's memoirs. Duroc's death was a severe emotional blow to Napoleon. His blood brother, his best friend, perhaps his only true friend, had abandoned him. Napoleon could not mourn his loss. He felt guilty for Duroc's death in his battle. On May 24, 1813, the day after Duroc died, Napoleon dictated a *Bulletin de la Grande Armée* with a romanticized version of Duroc's death.[48] Napoleon was inconsolable. In his unconscious mind, Duroc played the role of Napoleon's alter ego as well as his stern mother.

Duroc's death was a terrible abandonment to Napoleon, throwing him back to his early abandonment by his nursemaid and mother. On June 7, 1813, the emperor wrote the Countess of Montesquiou, "The death of the duke of Frioul has grieved me. In twenty years, this was the only time that he had not known how to please me."[49] Two years later, a prisoner of the British on Saint Helena, Napoleon proposed to change his name to Colonel Duroc.[50] By identifying with Duroc and assuming his identity, Napoleon unconsciously wished to restore his unbearable loss, just as he had done with his abandoning mother. Why he wished to demote himself by choosing Colonel Duroc rather than Général Duroc remains a psychological riddle. Was it due to his greater love for Duroc when the latter was a colonel, or to Napoleon's youthful memories of being a colonel of the Corsican *Garde nationale*? Vincent Cronin believed that Napoleon's love for Duroc was described in the Gospel of Saint John: "Greater love hath no man than this, that a man may lay down his life for his friends."[51]

Unable to mourn his losses, Napoleon built monuments to his dead friends: he had named the frigate that took him home from Egypt *La Muiron*, after Colonel Muiron, who had sacrificed his life to save Napoleon's at Arcola in 1796;[52] he had the heart of General Max Caffarelli, who had been killed at Acre in 1799, embalmed and kept in a reliquary at the *palais des Tuileries*, "one of Napoleon's treasured belongings."[53] Napoleon now bought the Saxon farmhouse where Duroc had died and erected a monument there saying: "Here General Duroc, Duke of Friuli, Grand Marshal of the Palace of the Emperor Napoleon, wounded by a cannon-ball, died in the arms of his Emperor and friend."[54] If Duroc had died in his arms, Napoleon presumably would not need to feel guilty for his death. But Napoleon did feel guilty, and he unconsciously sought to punish himself for it.

Napoleon's old rival, General Jean-Victor-Marie Moreau, had returned from America to fight Napoleon but was killed in battle. Despite his past military successes, Napoleon was neither omnipotent nor invincible. His defeat by the superior allied forces was now a matter of time. On October 16–19, 1813, Napoleon's diminished army finally fought the combined armies of Prussia, Austria, Russia and Sweden near the Saxon city of Leipzig. Because several nations were involved, the French called this terrible battle *la Bataille des Nations* and the Germans *die Völkerschlacht*. As usual, military historians have given wildly varying figures for the combating forces—which kept changing during the battle when fresh reinforcements came in. Napoleon's forces were greatly outnumbered. The battle of Leipzig was one of the bloodiest, and most terrible of Napoleon's wars. The French casualties were staggering: anywhere from thirty-eight thousand to fifty thousand French soldiers were killed or wounded, and another thirty thousand were taken prisoner. The allies also lost anywhere from fifty-five thousand to sixty thousand men. Napoleon's empire east of the Rhine was destroyed.

After the Leipzig disaster, a defeated and humiliated Napoleon retreated to the Saxon capital of Dresden. Napoleon's puppet states in central Europe began to fall like so many dominoes, and the one hundred thousand survivors of his army retreated to the Thuringian capital of Erfurt, where Napoleon had held his glittering summit with Tsar Aleksandr five years earlier. What a fall he had taken since then! Napoleon and his army then proceeded to Frankfurt on the Main, capital of the Confederation of the Rhine, on their way back to France. Prince Schwarzenberg sought to cut Napoleon's retreat toward Frankfurt and France. Bavaria, an erstwhile ally of France, had joined Napoleon's enemies.

On November 8, 1813, at Frankfurt, the victorious allies made a new peace proposal to Napoleon: they would offer to let him rule France "within its natural boundaries" of 1792 (the Alps and the Rhine) in return for a peace treaty.[55] The rest of Napoleon's empire would revert to its former rulers. The following year, at the Congress of Châtillon, which was held between the invading Allies and Napoleon's France in February-March 1814, these terms were called "the Frankfurt bases." While the angry Tsar Aleksandr of Russia wanted Napoleon dethroned, the rulers of Austria, Prussia and the German states "would have been satisfied just to have France relinquish control over Germany and Italy."[56]

The desperate Napoleon received the allied peace proposal with its "Frankfurt bases"—the "natural" 1792 borders of France. Accepting the allied offer would have saved Napoleon from losing his throne. He could have cut his losses and kept France. Tragically for himself, a proud Napoleon rejected the allied offer. Owen Connelly thought that he did so, "apparently in the belief that he somehow was being hoodwinked."[57] In fact, it was Napoleon's narcissistic grandiose self that would not let him accept what he would have experienced as an unbearable humiliation. Napoleon would have preferred a "glorious" battlefield death to a compromise that would have destroyed the delicate, fragile, elaborate, and shaky psychological edifice on which his self-esteem depended.

After he had rejected the allied peace proposal in 1813, Napoleon's fate was sealed. From now on it was one disaster after another. Emboldened by Napoleon's defeat by the allies, his Dutch subjects rebelled against French rule. On November 18 Napoleon named the loyal general Henri-Gatien Bertrand his Grand Marshal of the Palace, and on November 20, in a desperate effort to set his house in order, he replaced Hugues Bernard Maret, his foreign minister, with General Caulaincourt, his former ambassador to Russia, perhaps hoping that Caulaincourt could turn the heart and mind of Tsar Aleksandr in his favor. On November 22 Russian troops entered Amsterdam. Napoleon was ruined. He had lost the Netherlands, and by the end of November most of his *Grande Armée* had left Germany. Napoleon still had small garrisons at Glogau, Erfurt, Würzburg, Wesel and Mainz. Marshal Davout's 13th Corps held Hamburg, General Lemarois held Magdeburg, and General Cornu de Lapoype held Wittenberg.[58]

Napoleon's self-destructive invasion of Russia and his rejection of the allied peace offer led to their inevitable outcome. On December 1, 1813, the allies decided to invade France and to topple Napoleon from his throne. On December 2 the Allied armies crossed the River Rhine into France. War broke out again. On December 10 British naval forces landed on the coast of French-held Tuscany in Italy, near their former naval base of Leghorn (Livorno). The vengeful Emperor Franz of Austria, who had been repeatedly humiliated by Napoleon and had lost many territories — as well as his daughter—to him, promised to restore Tuscany to his brother, Archduke Ferdinand. Napoleon's undoing was near.

By late 1813 the Spanish rebels had defeated Napoleon's troops and removed his elder brother Joseph from his throne. Just before his defeat at

Leipzig, Napoleon had sent Antoine-René-Charles-Mathurin de La Forest, his fifty-seven-year-old aide and former ambassador to Joseph's court in Madrid, to the castle of Valençay in France, where the deposed King Fernando VII of Spain was Napoleon's prisoner. La Forest negotiated a peace treaty with Fernando. On December 11 Emperor Napoleon of the French and King Fernando VII of Spain signed the Treaty of Valençay, which won the freedom of the French prisoners of war in Spain, liberated Fernando VII from his captivity and recognized him as King of Spain and the Indies.[59] This was a big political coup for Fernando, who had been Napoleon's unwilling guest since 1808.

At the end of 1813 the popular unrest and fear of the approaching enemy in France grew into a panic. The allies called this war the Campaign of France. On December 21, Prince Schwarzenberg's Austrian Army of Bohemia began to cross the Rhine into northern Switzerland, from Basel to Schaffhausen, invading the French-ruled Helvetic Republic. The Allied invasion of France was now a *fait accompli*. On December 29 Field-Marshal Gebhard Leberecht von Blücher's Prussian Army of Silesia, numbering one hundred ten thousand men, began crossing the River Rhine into France, while Prince Schwarzenberg's Austrian Army of Bohemia, numbering two hundred ten thousand troops, marched through French Switzerland. Bernadotte's Swedish Army of the North marched through Holland on the French Low Countries. Napoleon had no more than one hundred twenty thousand men left to defend France against the massive Allied invasion.[60]

On December 29, 1813, with the Allies already occupying parts of eastern France, the French legislators defied their emperor for the first time. An anxious and rebellious Legislative Corps voted 229 to 31 to invite the Emperor to declare that he would not continue the war except for the independence of the French people and the integrity of France.[61] Napoleon took his legislature's resolution as a personal affront. As in his childhood, when he was humiliated by his mother, he reacted with uncontrollable narcissistic rage. He at once issued an imperial decree dissolving the Legislative Corps. On New Year's Eve, December 31, a deputation of the Legislative Corps came to confront their Emperor with their resolution. Napoleon spoke to this deputation in the presence of his thirty-five-year-old secretary-archivist, Baron Agathon-Jean-François Fain. Echoing Louis XIV's *l'état c'est moi*, Napoleon announced to the stunned legislators that he had just dissolved their Legislative Corps, assuming dictatorial powers, and that they no longer had any say in anything:

> Do you not know that, in a monarchy, the throne and the person of the monarch are inseparable? What is a throne? A piece of lumber covered with a velvet rug. But in the language of monarchy, *le trône c'est moi!* Supposing even that I am at fault, you should not have reproached me in public. Dirty linen should be washed in private. Besides, France needs me more than I need France.[62]

Embarrassed by the seeming arrogance of Napoleon's statement, some scholars have denied that he had uttered this last sentence, yet Christopher Herold observed that Napoleon himself confirmed having said it.[63] In reality, Napoleon never needed Mother France more than he did at that point in time. He felt like a lost child, and France was the good mother he looked to for succor.

Behind Napoleon's back, King Joachim Murat of Naples had been secretly negotiating with the allies, who were threatening his kingdom, yet the ambivalent Murat secretly hoped that Emperor Napoleon would recover from his defeats and that he and Napoleon would once more have supremacy. One of Murat's main motives was "sibling rivalry" and jealousy. The king of Naples was bitterly jealous of Napoleon's stepson, Prince Eugène, the viceroy of Italy, whom, Murat felt, Napoleon favored over him. Murat had wanted the whole of Italy as his realm, but Napoleon had kept central and northern Italy for his adopted son. Napoleon's kings and viceroy were like jealous siblings vying for the love of their father. The ambivalent Murat had written Napoleon several letters, which Napoleon did not answer. Instead, Napoleon had dispatched the double-dealing Fouché to deal with Murat; the former police minister played the double agent, deceiving both Napoleon and Murat.

On January 11, 1814, after days of agonizing over his decision, Murat signed his treaty of alliance with Austria and decided to occupy central Italy with his Neapolitan army, betraying his emperor and brother-in-law and declaring war on Napoleon.[64] It was fateful decision that would lead to Murat's tragic death the following year. When Napoleon learned of Murat's "treason," he suspected that the "real" culprit was his own sister Caroline, Murat's wife, who had plotted against him with Talleyrand and

Fouché while he was in Spain: "Murat! Murat! My brother-in-law in full treason . . . It's his wife who is the cause of his defection."[65] Caroline had indeed helped realize her ambivalent husband's wish to avenge himself on Napoleon for his love of Eugène, but Murat was also supported in his "treason" by the Italian party in Naples and by the *carbonari*, a secret society advocating liberal and patriotic ideas, a precursor of the *risorgimento*. Tragically, Caroline's "treason" brought about her widowhood and her loss of her throne, let alone her brother's downfall.

32

Downfall and Exile

In early 1814, after eighteen years of almost constant warfare on their soil, the Sixth Coalition allies—Great Britain, Russia, Austria, Prussia and Sweden, finally fought Napoleon on his own turf: they invaded France. Their onslaught forced Napoleon to take precautionary and defensive millitary measures. On January 21, fearing a defeat on his own soil, Napoleon transferred his most important prisoner, Pope Pius VII, from Fontainebleau back to Savona in Italy, where the pope had been imprisoned before. On January 24 Napoleon named his elder brother, Joseph, lieutenant general of the emperor, with the mission of defending Paris. But Joseph was not a great military leader: Napoleon himself had considered him militarily incompetent in Spain. Why then did he place Joseph in charge of his capital?

Military historians have divided the Campaign of France from January to April 1814 into six "great phases": (1) Napoleon's first offensive against the Prussian Field-Marshal Gebhard Leberecht von Blücher's Army of Silesia and Napoleon's defeat at La Rothire (January 27–February 1); (2) Napoleon's second offensive against Blücher's Army of Silesia and the five-day battle (February 8–12); (3) Napoleon's first operations against the Austrian Prince Schwarzenberg's Army of Bohemia and the battle of Montereau (February 15–25); (4) Napoleon's final operations against Blücher's Army of Silesia at Soissons and Laon (February 27–March 10); (5) Napoleon's final operations against Schwarzenberg's Army of Bohemia at Arcis-sur-Aube (March 13–20); (6) The failure of Napoleon's operations against the enemy's communication lines at Saint-Dizier and Paris

(March 25–31) that led to Napoleon's first abdication on April 11 under the pressures of his marshals.[1] It is beyond the scope of this volume to give detailed accounts of these military operations, which the reader can find in every military history of Napoleon. While this division may be militarily neat, it is not psychologically meaningful. The entire campaign was Napoleon's desperate attempt to save himself from the disaster that he had unconsciously brought upon himself.

On March 29, 1814, Napoleon's elder brother Joseph Bonaparte, the former king of Spain and now the lieutenant general of the emperor and military commander of Paris, published a fateful proclamation to the citizens of Paris:

> An enemy column has moved on Meaux; it is advancing on the road from Germany; but the Emperor is following it up close, at the head of a victorious army. The Council of the Regency has provided for the safety of the Empress and of the King of Rome. I remain with you. Let us arm ourselves to defend this city, her monuments, her wealth, our wives, our children, all that is dear to us. Let this vast city become a camp for a few moments, and let the enemy find his shame under her walls which he hopes to breach in triumph. The Emperor is marching to our rescue; support him by a short and lively resistance, and let us save French honor.[2]

It was a valiant but desperate and useless appeal. Two days later, Marshal Marmont signed the capitulation of Paris to the allied armies, and Tsar Aleksandr of Russia published his own proclamation to the French people, declaring that the allies would no longer deal with "Napoleon Bonaparte" nor with any member of his family.[3]

Napoleon's self-inflicted and predictable defeats in March 1814 shattered his narcissistic illusion of omnipotence and his lifelong denial of his feelings of helplessness and forced him to deal with the reality of his powerlessness in the face of his enemies. On March 31 he moved his imperial court to Fontainebleau, south of Paris. On Friday, April 1, All Fools' Day, desperate to save their country from foreign occupation, France's remaining political institutions voted the end of Napoleon's empire. On April 2, egged on by Talleyrand, the French senate, "a rump Senate of 64 members appointed by Napoleon,"[4] voted to dethrone the emperor who had appointed them, electing a new provisional government. Ten years after electing him Emperor, the senate declared that as a "foreigner" Napoleon could not be the Emperor of the French. The sixty-one-year-old liberal senator Count Jean-Denis Lanjuinais, who had plotted against Napoleon five years earlier, signed the dethronement motion. Two months later Lanjuinais was created a Peer of France by its new king, Louis XVIII.[5]

Everyone hurt by Napoleon now sought to take revenge on him. The general council of the *département* of the Seine published its own proclamation denouncing "Bonaparte" and listing his crimes. Napoleon, it said, had decimated the French people by conscripting them into his armies. He had imposed unbearable taxation. He had closed the seas of the Two Worlds to France and won her the enmity of the world. He had imprisoned the Holy Father, betrayed his ally the king of Spain, devastated the friendly Spanish nation, ruined France herself, refused the honorable peace offered by the Allies, gave the "patricidal" order of exposing the National Guard to defend the capital, and sacrificed France to his own ambition and vengeance. Finally, the council formally renounced all obedience to Napoleon.[6]

Narcissistic injuries kept raining upon Napoleon's head. Savoring his vengeance against the emperor, his former foreign minister, Talleyrand, talked Tsar Aleksandr of Russia, the leader of the occupying allies, into restoring the Bourbon monarchy and setting up a provisional French government headed by himself. On April 2, 1814, after being deposed by his own Senate, a defeated and desperate Napoleon reviewed his Imperial Guard at Fontainebleau prior to taking leave from them. His foreign minister and Grand Equerry, General Caulaincourt, informed him that Tsar Aleksandr had refused to negotiate with him.

The Bourbons, led by Louis XVIII, were preparing their *coup de grâce* against Napoleon. Their secret agent was the thirty-nine-year-old Count Eugène-François-Auguste d'Arnaud de Vitrolles, a royalist statesman from Provence who had emigrated to Germany twenty years earlier to escape the Revolution. The Count of Vitrolles had returned to Paris under Emperor Napoleon's amnesty and had served as the Emperor's Inspector of the Imperial Sheepfolds. In March 1814 the Count of Vitrolles met in Paris with the seventy-one-year-old Carl Theodor von Dalberg, the Prince Primate of the Rhenish Confederation. Both men were in Talleyrand's pay. Dalberg asked Vitrolles to cross the French lines and to plead the Bourbon cause at the congress of Châtillon, where the Allies and Napoleon were negotiating France's future. Vitrolles accepted, but achieved nothing at Châtillon. Later, at Troyes, he met the Austrian foreign minister, Prince Metternich, but could not persuade him to take the side of the French

Bourbons. On the night of April 2–3, 1814, the Count of Vitrolles reached Paris, where he contacted Talleyrand and the Paris royalists.

On April 4 came "the 18 Brumaire in reverse." Five of Napoleon's marshals—Lefebvre, Moncey, Macdonald, Oudinot, and Ney—burst into his Fontainebleau study and in their agitation demanded his abdication.[7] Napoleon had promoted these men to their lofty ranks, yet they now felt that only Napoleon's abdication could save France from foreign occupation and despoilment. Like all other turning points in Napoleon's life, his dramatic confrontation with his rebellious marshals had its bizarre and irrational aspects. Even though their emperor had been deposed by the senate, Napoleon's troops were still eager to fight for him. Napoleon rightly told the rebellious marshals that his army would obey him, at which the hotheaded Ney cried, "The army will obey its generals!"

As Vincent Cronin correctly observed, this was untrue, and Napoleon knew it. The army was loyal first and foremost to its emperor, to whom it had sworn its allegiance, and Napoleon could easily have replaced his rebellious marshals.[8] Nevertheless, Napoleon yielded to them and agreed to abdicate in favor of his son the next day. Why did Napoleon submit to his rebellious marshals? Cronin thought that "these men were his comrades, with whom he had shared glory and suffering. Of all Frenchmen, they were closest to him." This is hardly an adequate psychological explanation. Napoleon had dismissed men who were closer to him when they betrayed him or rebelled against him, and now it was either he or his five marshals who had to go. There were many able French generals who were eager to replace them, and the other marshals had not mutinied. Yet the most powerful man in France chose to lose his throne, his career, and his country and yield to his rebellious underlings. A better explanation can be found in what Napoleon told his rebellious marshals when he accepted their demand to abdicate: "*I have tried to bring happiness to France and have not succeeded. I do not wish to increase our sufferings.*"[9] In his unconscious mind, France was his idealized and beloved mother. He had tried to make her happy but had failed. There was nothing left for him but to pay the price for failing her.

Trying to save what was left of his self-esteem as well as take care of his wife and son, the badly defeated Napoleon gave his rebellious marshals an abdication document that he had signed, making his abdication conditional upon the Allies recognizing his son as his successor as Emperor of the French:

> The foreign Powers having declared that the Emperor Napoleon was an obstacle to the restoration of peace and the integrity of the French territory, the Emperor Napoleon, faithful to his principles and to his oaths to do all possible for the happiness and glory of the French people, declares that he is ready to abdicate in favor of his son, and to submit the Act to the Senate in due form by a message *as soon as Napoleon II has been recognized by the Powers, together with the recognition of the constitutional regency of the Empress.* If these conditions are met, the Emperor will immediately withdraw to a place which shall be agreed upon. Done at our palace of Fontainebleau this fourth day of April, 1814.[10]

To Napoleon, his son was an extension of his own self, yet, as always, he thought of his narcissism as altruism. The phrase he would add in his second, unconditional abdication, "to give up France and life itself," indicated how fused Napoleon was with his adoptive motherland: to give up Mother France was to die.

On the evening of March 29, 1814, Empress Marie-Louise, who had been sent away from Paris by Joseph Bonaparte when the allies were about to take the city, arrived in Blois with her three-year-old son, Napoleon II, where she awaited in vain for eight days her husband's orders to join him. "He sent none, perversely waiting to see if she would come to him, now that he had fallen. Probably, she wanted to go and, until about 10 April, she could have made the journey. But then Allied troops appeared [in Blois] and she and the boy were delivered to her father, the emperor of Austria. Napoleon never saw them again."[11] By not sending for her, out of his narcissistic pride, Napoleon himself caused his loss of his second wife, who still loved him and wanted to go back to him.[12]

Napoleon had deluded himself about his conditional abdication. Thanks to Talleyrand's intrigues, the Allies would not accept his conditions. Talleyrand persuaded Marshal Marmont that he could save France by abandoning Napoleon. The Allies decided to restore the Bourbons to the French throne and make Louis XVIII France's king. On April 5, 1814, in the middle of his talks with Napoleon's four envoys—Foreign Minister Caulaincourt and Marshals Ney, Marmont and Macdonald—Tsar Aleksandr of Russia was informed that the 6th Corps of Napoleon's army—under orders from Marmont's deputy General Joseph Souham—had defected to the Allies the previous night. The Allies now demanded Napoleon's immediate and unconditional abdication. Marmont hotly denied that he had authorized his deputy's defection, but the deed had been done and Napoleon had been undone.[13]

On April 6, 1814, at two o'clock in the morning, Napoleon's envoys Caulaincourt, Ney, Marmont, and Macdonald returned to their emperor in Fontainebleau. Faced with the Tsar's implacable demand for his unconditional abdication, a humiliated, desperate, and helpless Napoleon became enraged and cried that he was issuing a call to his army and going back to war. When he calmed down and realized the hopelessness of his situation, however, the defeated Napoleon dictated and signed his second, unconditional abdication:

> The Powers having declared that the Emperor Napoleon was the sole obstacle to the restoration of peace in Europe, the Emperor Napoleon, faithful to his oath, declares that he renounces, for himself and his children, the thrones of France and Italy, and that there is no sacrifice, not even that of his life, which he is not ready to make for the interests of France.[14]

Indeed, at this point Napoleon was deeply depressed and thought of taking his own life. His twenty-eight-year-old Polish mistress, Maria Walewska, the mother of Napoleon's illegitimate four-year-old son, Alexander Walewski, had rushed from Paris to Fontainebleau to try to comfort her lover. The narcissistically-injured and deeply depressed Napoleon, however, was too ashamed to see anyone, not even her. Having lost his self-esteem, feeling helpless and worthless, he was contemplating suicide. Barred from his presence, Maria wrote Napoleon an affectionate note, which he only received after she had left town. He at once wrote her back: "Marie! . . . The feelings which animate you touch me profoundly. They are worthy of your lovely soul and the goodness of your heart . . . Think affectionately of me! Never doubt me!"[15] Was Napoleon aware how deeply he doubted himself?

After signing his unconditional abdication on April 6, the unhappy Napoleon had second thoughts. He was deeply ambivalent about abdicating. Despite Marmont's surrender, which exposed them to the enemy, Napoleon's elite Imperial Guard was still eager to fight for him. Napoleon deluded himself that he could spring a surprise on the Allies and drive them out of France. On April 7 Marshals Ney and Macdonald—whom Foreign Minister Caulaincourt called "the commissioners of pity"[16]—brought Napoleon's unconditional abdication to Tsar Aleksandr. Not surprisingly, the Russian emperor was milder this time: "[Tsar Aleksandr] spoke of Napoleon sadly—even compassionately . . . [Aleksandr] proved to be the strongest supporter of the wounded eagle . . . [he] suggested the overlordship of the island of Elba for his friend from the days of Tilsit . . . [Aleksandr] set the figure of two million francs for the stipend that [King] Louis XVIII [of France] was to pay to 'the King of the Island of Elba.'"[17] Apparently, Tsar Aleksandr felt magnanimous in victory.

While Napoleon's marshals, generals and servants fled Fontainebleau in a panic, his imperial guards roamed the streets of Fontainebleau carrying torches and crying "Down with the traitors! To Paris! To Paris!" [18] But the Imperial Guard was minuscule compared with the vast Allied armies. Napoleon tried to reverse himself, but it was too late. "Everything was collapsing around the conquered master."[19] The Allies had taken Paris. He had abdicated. His minions had fled. Napoleon was lost. With his irrational invasion of Russia, he had brought about his own destruction.

The "commissioners of pity," Marshals Ney and Macdonald, brought Napoleon the deed they had signed with Tsar Aleksandr. Napoleon understood that this was the end of his career. He felt helpless and worthless. His depression grew deeper and his suicidal ideation increased. The prefect of the Seine-et-Oise *département*, Count Adrien de Plancy, found Napolen "all alone, and sadly leaning against the embrasure of a window."[20] General Jean-Martin Petit, the commander of Napoleon's troops at Fontainebleau, felt that "it was as though His Majesty were already buried." [21] Napoleon reportedly told his assembled troops at Fontainebleau, "I cannot embrace you all, but I embrace your general. Come, General Petit, that I may press you to my heart." In fact, by this time Napoleon was deeply depressed. Louis-Constant Wairy, Napoleon's valet, recalled that his master "fell into a kind of apathy—to the point where he did not even see things that were near him" and did not answer when spoken to.[22] Constant was one of the aides and servants who panicked and deserted Napoleon after his abdication at Fontainebleau—and took with him some of Napoleon's jewels and money, though he later denied it in his memoirs. Another was the Mameluke Roustam.[23]

As we have seen, the depressed and self-destructive Napoleon caused himself to lose his loving wife and his only legitimate son. The anxious Empress Marie-Louise had fled to Blois, whence she wrote Napoleon several times that she wanted to join him, and that she awaited his instructions. Marie-Louise badly wanted to join her husband at Fontainebleau, yet he would not tell her to come. Being the daughter of the Austrian emperor, she might have moved her father to make peace with Napoleon and give his throne to his son rather than to the Bourbons. Marie-Louise deluded herself that she could get her father to let her and Napoleon have Tuscany as well as Elba. André Castelot believed that if Marie-Louise and her son had been at Fontainebleau, the three-year-old Napoleon II could have been enthroned as Emperor of the French, and Foreign Minister Caulaincourt would have had a stronger hand in his dealing with the Allies.[24] But the depressed, suicidal, and ambivalent Napoleon urged his wife to wait, or to go to her father, and left the decision up to her. Unwittingly, he drove his loving wife away from him and into the arms of her father and those of her future lover and husband, Count Adam Adalbert Adrian von Neipperg.

When the Austrian foreign minister, Metternich, met General Caulaincourt, Napoleon's foreign minister, on April 12, 1814, he insisted that Marie-Louise be considered an Austrian archduchess or a princess—not the Empress of the French—and that her son was an Austrian prince—not the king of Rome. Emperor Franz of Austria, Napoleon's father-in-law, was behind this view. There was no way he was going to give back to Napoleon, who had repeatedly humiliated him and dissolved his Holy Roman Empire, his throne, or even Tuscany. Caulaincourt, who was still in Paris negotiating with the Allies, was stupefied by Napoleon's self-destructiveness in pushing his wife away from him: "I could never understand how the Emperor could have abused himself to this point."[25] André Castelot, too, was most amazed "that Napoleon, too, seemed to believe in the urgent necessity for a meeting between the father, the daughter, and the grandson. How could he have failed to realize that Francis would not let them join the exile?"[26] In fact, Napoleon was unconsciously repeating his life-and-death struggle with his mother. Having failed his idealized mother, France, he had to punish—if not kill—himself.

The "generous" Allied offer to make Napoleon king of the island of Elba was a poisoned chalice. Napoleon knew that he would be in mortal danger on Elba, because of its proximity to Corsica, where many people hated him as a traitor ever since his expulsion by Paoli's *consulta* in 1793, yet he accepted Elba as his residence after he abdicated.[27] Why did Napoleon agree to accept Elba? After all, he could simply have chosen exile in some place far away from Corsica. In his unconscious mind, Elba may have replaced Corsica, which in turn stood for his mother. His defeat caused him to regress to his fusional relationship with his mother. Elba symbolized Napoleon's ambivalent fusion with his mother. On Elba, he was at once near Mother Corsica and removed from her.

The Allies savored their vengeance on Napoleon, who had repeatedly humiliated them. The Treaty of Fontainebleau that they imposed on him was signed on April 11–12, 1814, by "His Majesty the Emperor Napoleon of the one part, and their Majesties the Emperor of Austria, the King of Prussia and the Emperor of all the Russias . . . of the other part." It gave Napoleon the little island of Elba in the Tyrrhenian Sea, east of northern Corsica, as a sovereign principality, with an annual income of two million francs—to be paid by France —"of which one million shall revert to the Empress." The treaty also gave Napoleon four hundred volunteer guards and let him retain his title of Emperor. Empress Marie-Louise received the Austrian-Italian duchies of Parma, Piacenza, and Guastalla with full sovereignty. Napoleon's adopted stepson and viceroy of Italy, Prince Eugène, was promised "a suitable establishment outside France." The defeated and depressed Napoleon signed his final abdication at Fontainebleau. His self-esteem was in tatters. What was a tiny Mediterranean island compared with Napoleon's vast former empire?

Caulaincourt took the treaty signed by Napoleon to the Allied sovereigns, who would sign it later that day or the next day. Incredibly, Great Britain's bitterest enemy, Napoleon, instructed his ambassador to the congress of Châtillon, General Caulaincourt, to sound out the British on the possibility of receiving him in their country: "I request that in your conversations with the English minister for foreign affairs you will sound him as to whether his government would see any objection to giving me an asylum in England with the privileges enjoyed by any citizen of England and with my full and absolute liberty."[28] It was the wishful fantasy of an unwanted child who wants to force his rejecting mother to love him. The British foreign secretary, Robert Stewart Viscount Castlereagh, who had led the Allied effort against Napoleon, demurred. A desperate and furious Napoleon threatened to abduct his wife Marie-Louise, while writing her to proceed to Vienna before being re-united with him.

On April 11, 1814, the day he signed his final abdication and the humiliating Treaty of Fontainebleau, Napoleon wavered between his suicidal feelings and his delusions of regaining his throne by force. He temporarily convinced himself that it would be morally wrong to commit suicide. Napoleon's Prefect of the Palace, General Philippe-Paul de Ségur, later recalled that Napoleon had said to him, "A violent death is cowardice.

I can see no greatness in shirking responsibility in that manner, like one who has gambled away his fortune . . . Suicide is incompatible with my principles and with the position I have occupied in the world. Between ourselves, a living drummer is better than a dead emperor . . . To kill myself would be a gambler's death. I am condemned to live. Besides, only the dead do not return."[29] The psychoanalyst Pierce Clark thought that "not always is the Emperor so clear-headedly opposed to suicide. He often regretted that he did not fall on his sword in the first occupation of the Kremlin."[30] Indeed, the following night Napoleon would take poison—although whether he had really intended to die remains uncertain.

April 12, 1814, was one of the worst days of Napoleon's life. He had lost his throne and his country. His foreign minister, General Caulaincourt, brought him the treaty of Fontainebleau, signed by the Allied sovereigns, with the humiliating terms of his abdication, which had become reality. Tuscany would not be his, and his wife would only get some minor Italian principalities. General Pierre-Jacques-Etienne de Cambronne, whom Napoleon had finally sent to Orléans to fetch his wife Marie-Louise to Fontainebleau, returned with the devastating news that she had left for Vienna. [31] Napoleon had acted too late: he had lost his wife and son forever. In fact, he had lost everything.

During the night of April 12–13, 1814, Napoleon's narcissistic injury, depression, anxiety, and rage became unbearable. Unable to kill those who had injured and humiliated him, he wanted to kill himself. He felt worthless, helpless, a total failure, deserted and abandoned by all the people he loved and cared about. He had failed Mother France and now she had rejected him. During that night he apparently tried to kill himself by taking the poison capsule that he had received from his personal physician, Dr. Alexandre-Urbain Yvan, in Russia, eighteen months earlier. This poison was a mixture of opium and of strychnine-containing *nux vomica* concocted by Cabanis under the Terror and used by Condorcet. But the poison was too old, weak and ineffective. Its only result was spasms, nausea, and vomiting. Napoleon survived.

Did Napoleon really want—and try—to kill himself when he took the old poison capsule that night? The psychoanalyst Pierce Clark thought that the narcissistic Napoleon would not have done so unless he was psychotically depressed: "Good evidence is advanced to prove that he actually attempted self-destruction before the abdication at Fontainebleau. But for all this the narcist rarely takes his own life except in outspoken melancholia; suicide is often on his lips but seldom in his heart. The dissolution of the ego into nothingness is hardly conceivable, and voluntary annihilation is rarely thought of."[32] The psychiatrist Frank Richardson did not consider Napoleon "a suicidal type":

> It is a known fact that from about 1812 he was always prepared for suicide, being provided with poison by Doctors Yvan, Cabanis, and Corvisart. It was the duty of his premier valet-de-chambre to see that the poison in a small leather sachet was always about his person. But many people who could not be called suicidal types have taken similar precautions against capture in wartime, and Napoleon . . . knew what to expect from his enemies . . . he was not a man to contemplate humiliation . . . He did not need to stage a half-hearted attempt at suicide to attract sympathy, and if in a moment of depression he did make a serious attempt it seems that he soon regretted it and did not care to speak of it. *It revealed a crack in his armour of self-sufficiency.*[33]

That armor of self-sufficiency was Napoleon's narcissism. The problem was between Napoleon and himself. The vast gap between what he thought he was and had to be and what he had become was too painful. By abdicating he had lost the props that sustained his self-esteem. His narcissistic injury was as devastating as his self-image was grandiose and omnipotent. The helpless humiliation of his downfall threw him back to his unbearable feelings of abandonment and helpless rage in his early life. At the same time, his wish to live was still powerful, so that his suicide attempt may have been half-hearted.

With Napoleon's consent—in the British case, at his request—the victorious Allies sent high-ranking "military commissioners" to escort the fallen Napoleon from Fontainebleau to Elba and watch over him on the way to make sure he did not escape. Russia sent the forty-year-old general Count Pavel Andreyevich Shuvalov, an aide-de-camp to Tsar Aleksandr. Austria dispatched two commissioners: Field-Marshal Franz von Koller and the Czech general Count Clam-Martinic—perhaps so that each could check up on the other and prevent him from cutting a deal with Napoleon. Prussia sent General Friedrich Ludwig Truchsess von Waldburg, scion of a noble Swabian family. Before signing the treaty of Fontainebleau, Napoleon had insisted that Great Britain guarantee the treaty. Lord Castlereagh, the British foreign secretary, deriding "Boney," sent a lower-ranking thirty-eight-year-old Scottish Highland officer, Colonel Sir Neil Campbell, who had fought Napoleon at Bautzen. Campbell arrived in Fontainebleau on April 16 and noted Napoleon's depressed, shabby, pathetic, and ridiculous appearance.[34]

The other commissioners arrived at Fontainebleau on April 17–19, 1814. On April 20 the fallen Napoleon took a heartbreaking leave of his remaining soldiers at Fontainebleau and left for Elba with a convoy of 14 carriages escorted by sixty-two Polish lancers.[35] He was accompanied by General Henri-Gatien Bertrand, his Grand Marshal of the Palace. General Antoine Drouot later led six hundred Imperial Guards to join Napoleon on Elba, where Drouot would become the governor and "war minister" of Napoleon's make-believe kingdom. In another self-destructive if not suicidal act, Napoleon chose to travel to Elba through fanatically royalist territory, which posed a grave danger to his life. In fact, as we shall see, he would be physically attacked and almost lynched on the way.[36]

On the first leg of Napoleon's journey to Elba, from April 20 to April 23, General Charles Lefebvre-Desnouettes, a forty-one-year-old former Grand Equerry to King Jérôme Bonaparte of Westphalia who had been wounded by the allies at the battle of Brienne on January 29, commanded the Polish escort which accompanied the fallen emperor to Roanne, on the River Loire, along with the Allied commissioners appointed by Russia, Austria, and Prussia to watch over him along the way. On the second leg of the trip, from Roanne to Lyon to Elba, Napoleon was escorted by the Allied commissioners. They traveled south through central France, retracing his journey of 1790 as a poor second lieutenant of the royal artillery. Wherever Napoleon went, he was greeted by angry mobs.

On April 24, 1814, Napoleon reached Provence, where royalist sentiment was high and where people hated him. It was a horrifying journey. Napoleon was in Bourbon-royalist territory, and some of the local people wanted his blood. At La Calade, a "wretched wagoners' tavern" in Aix-en-Provence,[37] Napoleon, fearing for his life, presented himself to the female innkeeper as "Colonel Campbell, an English officer from Napoleon's escort," and asked her to prepare dinner quickly for the former emperor and his suite. She replied angrily "that she would be much put out preparing dinner for such a monster," and that she would gladly lend her sharp knife to whoever wanted to stab Bonaparte, who had killed her son, her nephew and so many other young men in his wars.[38]

The night of April 25–26, 1814, was one of the worst in Napoleon's life. He was agitated, depressed, and terrified of being killed. But it was he who had chosen this route through enemy territory. General Truchsess von Waldburg, the Prussian military commissioner who escorted Napoleon from Fontainebleau to Fréjus, later claimed that Napoleon had sobbed bitterly and was in a psychotic state:

> At first I did not recognize him, and I came up to him. Hearing footsteps, he started and jumped up, enabling me to see his tear-stained face. He signaled to me to keep quiet and take a seat next to him. As long as the proprietress was in the room, he talked only of trivial things . . . We sat down at the dinner table; but since the dinner had not been prepared by his own cooks, he was afraid of being poisoned and was unwilling to eat anything. However, when he saw us eating with a good appetite, he felt ashamed to let us see how terrified he was, and took everything that was offered to him. He made a pretense at nibbling at it, but he sent the dishes away without really eating anything. Sometimes, after taking a dish of something, hc would throw it under the table to make us believe he had eaten it. His dinner consisted of a bit of bread and a flask of wine which he had brought from his carriage, and which he even shared with us.[39]

When a crowd gathered in front of La Calade, Napoleon panicked and decided to leave the inn at midnight. Unconsciously identifying with the aggressor, the deeply-traumatized Napoleon, his self-esteem in tatters, assumed his humiliator's identity. Frank Richardson thought that Napoleon "plumbed the depths of degradation" by disguising himself in a "grotesque mixture" of his allied escorts' uniforms—the Austrian uniform of Field-Marshal Koller, the Prussian uniform of General Truchsess von Waldburg, and the Russian uniform of General Shuvalov.[40] As with the Biblical David, however, who feigned madness to escape his enemy King Saul, this quasi-psychotic reaction helped Napoleon survive.[41]

On the evening of April 28, 1814, Napoleon and his escort went to the Mediterranean seaport of Saint-Raphaël, where he had landed in 1799 upon his return from Egypt. By previous arrangement with Lord Castlereagh, and by an irony of fate, a British frigate, the *Undaunted*, was awaiting him. When Napoleon boarded the British man-of-war its sailors gave him the honors due to a sovereign. On April 29 the *Undaunted* set sail for the isle of Elba. The Austrian commissioner, Field-Marshal Koller, was on board to watch over Napoleon. Two days later, on May 1, 1814, the *Undaunted* reached Corsica and sailed past Napoleon's home town of Ajaccio. On May 2 it sailed past Calvi, whence he had escaped to France in 1793. One can only imagine Napoleon's memories and feelings when he saw his native island.

In mid-April 1814 Napoleon's wife Marie-Louise and her son, the King of Rome, had left France for Vienna, escorted by the dashing one-eyed thirty-nine-year-old Austrian diplomat Count Adam Adalbert Adrian von Neipperg and his horsemen. Marie-Louise still wanted to join her fallen husband. On May 2, she crossed the French border into Germany. When she learned of Napoleon's humiliation by the mob in Provence, she wrote in her diary, "How cruelly his soul must have been affected! I blame myself for not having followed him. Am I, too, abandoning him? Oh, my God! What will he think of me? But I will go to be with him, even though it means being eternally unhappy."[42] Marie-Louise's ambivalence was obvious. Soon she opted for her father's palace in Vienna. In the fall she would have an affair with Count Adam Adalbert Adrian von Neipperg and abandon Napoleon for good. In 1821, after Napoleon's death, the widowed Marie-Louise married Count Neipperg.

On May 2, 1814, the day after Marie-Louise left France, the Bourbon king Louis XVIII returned to Paris in triumph after twenty-three years in exile. This was the Bourbon restoration that the royalists were pining for. Soon after this, on May 29, Napoleon's first wife, Josephine Bonaparte, died at Malmaison. Napoleon, who had lost his adopted motherland and his empire, now lost one of the most important women in his life.

33

A Desperate Comeback

With his 600 Imperial guards, Napoleon, the former ruler of Europe, now reigned over a tiny Mediterranean island off the Italian coast as "the Emperor of Elba." With Napoleon's consent, Colonel Sir Neil Campbell, the thirty-eight-year-old British military commissioner who had accompanied him from Fontainebleau, remained on Elba as his "guardian."[1] André Castelot thought that Napoleon had accepted this arrangement because "Campbell would have all the appearance of an accredited [British] ambassador whose presence alone would demonstrate the Emperor's sovereignty; and besides, he might prove useful in a possible resumption of the dialogue with the Allies."[2] In fact, Campbell was the unofficial British spy. Lord Castlereagh, the British foreign minister, had warmly endorsed the arrangement, which allowed him to keep an eye on "General Bonaparte."

Since his late thirties, Napoleon had been growing fat. His depression following his fall made him eat even more, as if to fill the void within himself. Now, at the age of forty-four, he was obese. He regressed to the oral-incorporative mode of dealing with the world. Like a baby, Napoleon fought his painful feeling of emptiness by overeating. Napoleon's favorite physician, Jean-Nicolas Corvisart, had opted to remain in Paris, and Napoleon's physician on Elba, Louis Foureau de Beauregard, reportedly tried to tell his patient not to eat so much and so fast. Napoleon replied that "he knew his 'draught' . . . and that if he passed it his stomach rejected the surplus, so he seldom needed a doctor."[3] To escape the bad feelings inside him—his bad introjects—Napoleon reportedly scratched his skin "to open a vent for the bad humors," which James Kemble diagnosed as "neurodermatitis."[4] This illness was self-inflicted: Napoleon reportedly told Foureau de Beauregard that he scratched certain places on his skin until they bled.[5]

On August 2, 1814, *Madame Mère* Letizia joined Napoleon on Elba. After twenty-one years of apparently separate existence, mother and son resumed their ambivalent fusional relationship. The deeply religious and highly superstitious Letizia brought with her to Elba her own chaplain, the sixty-two-year-old Corsican abbé Antonio Buonavita, who would later serve Napoleon himself as his chaplain on Saint Helena. On August 6, Fanny Bertrand, the pregnant wife of General Henri-Gatien Bertrand, arrived in the Elban capital of Porto Ferraio to join her husband, Napoleon's grand marshal of the palace. In her memoirs, Fanny claimed that she was the first one to tell Napoleon about Josephine's death over two months earlier. Napoleon made Fanny get into his carriage to tell him the latest news from Paris. When she told him that Josephine had died, he exclaimed "Ah, she is happy now!"[6]

Napoleon's adoring sister, Pauline Borghese, also joined him on Elba for a few days, but she later returned to Elba for good. Pauline gave Napoleon her jewels, which allowed him to buy an "ostentatious" property in the San Martino valley, including several small houses.[7] Napoleon alternately stayed at his official residence in Porto Ferraio and in several other Elba residences. In August he invited his mother Letizia to join him at his country residence in Marciana Alta, owned by its mayor, Cerbona Vadi. Down below, on the beach, was Marciana Marina. The marble plaque affixed to the mayor's house in Marciana Alta says "Napoleon the Great was a guest in this house from August 21 to August 23, 1814 and his August Mother from August 25 to September 5, 1814" implying that the two never actually met there.

In fact, Napoleon's invitation to Letizia was "the cover-up for a romantic little plot: the Emperor was looking for a discreet place where his impending meeting with Marie Walewska could be kept private."[8] On August 23, 1814, Napoleon moved down to a house in Marciana Marina, and two days later his mother occupied the house in Marciana Alta. Maria Walewska, the Polish mother of Napoleon's illegitimate four-year-old son, Alexandre Walewski, was in Naples, where she had gone to assure her son's pension. On September 1 Maria Walewska arrived from Naples with her brother, sister and son in the seaport of San Giovanni, near Marciana Marina, aboard a British vessel. They were met by General Bertrand, the grand marshal of the palace, and Captain Bernotti, an aide-de-camp to Napoleon recruited on Elba, who escorted them to Marciana Marina. That morning the corpulent Napoleon had climbed up with great difficulty to the secluded hermitage of Madonna del Monte, above Marciana Alta, where he would receive his lover.[9] They spent the night together. When Maria complained that her lover had refused to see her at Fonatinebleau the previous April, Napoleon reportedly answered that he had "had so much on his mind, then."[10] He did not tell her that he had been deeply depressed and had attempted suicide.

Maria Walewska stayed only two days with her lover Napoleon: on September 3, 1814, she was gone. Pierce Clark had a simple explanation for Walewska's departure: "The Emperor would like to keep Walewska by his side, but he does not wish to provide the Empress [Marie-Louise] with an excuse for not coming to live with him, and he sacrifices on the altar of the Hapsburg princess the phantom of his happiness."[11] André Castelot agreed with this view.[12] It may also be that Napoleon was no longer attractive to Maria, that he had lost his sexual potency along with his political power and self-esteem, or that the two lovers had fallen out and were disappointed with one another. Clark added, "In truth Napoleon is forsaken by wife and child. This loss cuts him no less than the loss of power."[13] To ward off the pain of that thought, he denied his painful reality, telling himself that his letters to Marie-Louise had been intercepted, and that she still longed to join him. Napoleon wrote to Marie-Louise's uncle, Grand Duke Ferdinand of Tuscany—whom Napoleon had deposed in 1801—asking for news of her, but received no reply from the vengeful Ferdinand.[14]

Elba's proximity to Corsica was dangerous to Napoleon. Raoul Brice thought that "the whole of Corsica was jubilant over Napoleon's fall."[15] Soon after he arrived in Elba, his police chiefs informed him that the sixty-two-year-old chevalier Louis-Guérin de Bruslart, a former *chouan* and royalist Bourbon agent who had been seething with vengeance ever since Napoleon executed his friend and colleague Louis de Frotté in 1800, was appointed the military governor of Corsica with the secret mission of assassinating Napoleon.[16] No proof has been found for this accusation[17] yet Napoleon himself believed it and feared being assassinated.

After some time on Elba, Napoleon could no longer bear his life on the island. His suspicions and fears grew worse in late 1814, when he received the French newspaper *Le Journal des débats* of November 19. It reported "that several agents or emissaries of Bonaparte have been arrested in Italy, and that as a result he will be transferred to the island of Saint Helena."[18] A furious Napoleon invoked Great Britain's guarantee of the Treaty of Fontainebleau: "I cannot believe that Europe wants to take up arms against me! In any case, I would not advise anyone to come and attack me here. He might pay dearly for it. I have provisions for six months, good artillery, and brave soldiers to defend me. The overlordship of Elba was guaranteed to me. This is my castle, and I would not advise anyone to come here and disturb me."[19] The bravura was unconsciously meant to calm himself. He was like a fearful child whistling in the dark.

In early 1815 Napoleon learned that the allies, worried about his possible escape from Elba and his return to France, were planning to deport him from Elba to the remote South Atlantic island of Saint Helena, and that King Louis XVIII of France would refuse to honor his commitment to pay Napoleon his annual French government pension of two million francs. This was the straw that broke the camel's back. Napoleon spent the first two months of 1815 on the Isle of Elba plotting his return to France. His plots were aided by the fact that his British guardian, Colonel Sir Neil Campbell, had fallen madly in love with a "ravishing" noblewoman "who spoke three languages, Italian, English, and French—all of them poorly."[20] Campbell and his lover met several times in Livorno, Florence, or Lucca, leaving Napoleon free and unguarded on Elba.

Napoleon's die was cast in February 1815. The Congress of Vienna, where the allies had been deliberating under Metternich's guidance for many months, secretly decided to deport Napoleon from Elba to Saint Helena. Napoleon received a visit from a thirty-five-year-old French nobleman, Pierre-Alexandre-Edouard Fleury de Chaboulon, a former sub-prefect of Rheims under the Emperor, who told Napoleon of great dissension among the allies—France, Austria and Great Britain were uniting against Prussia and Russia—and "huge levels of discontent in France"—as well as in Russia and Prussia—with King Louis XVIII.[21] An excited Napoleon made up his mind to leave Elba and try to make his desperate comeback in France. On February 16, with Colonel Campbell's British frigate, the *Partridge*, on its way to Campbell's medical consultation in Florence and to his lover in Livorno, Napoleon ordered his Governor of Elba and "war minister," General Count Antoine Drouot, to have his imperial brig, *l'Inconstant*, refitted, disguised as a British ship, and provisioned for three months for one hundred twenty men.

On the evening of February 25, 1815, Napoleon announced his fateful decision to leave Elba to his mother in the garden of her Porto Ferraio residence. Napoleonic legend has Letizia reply: "My son, it has not been God's will that you should die in an idleness unworthy of you, and if you must die now, I hope it is God's will that it not be by poison but with sword in hand."[22] This story rings true. Letizia made no attempt to stop her son from his desperate misadventure, nor expressed any maternal concern for his safety. Letizia could not think of any other outcome for Napoleon's decision than her son's death—which she had unconsciously wished ever since his birth. Little did she realize that, in her son's deepest feelings, France was an idealized image of herself; nor was Napoleon aware of this. Much of his emotional life had been spent trying to repair his damaged mother introject.

Napoleon left Elba for France on February 26, 1815, in a hypomanic state. He drafted no less than three imperial proclamations to the French people and army and four imperial decrees. The first proclamation was addressed to the French people; the second to the French army; the third proclamation, purporting to come from the Imperial Guard, was addressed to the generals, officers and soldiers of the army; the four decrees concerned Corsica. The proclamation to the French people put Mother France above all else: "Frenchmen! In my exile I heard your laments and your prayers. You demand that government of your choosing which alone is legitimate. You were objecting to my prolonged idleness. You were reproaching me with having sacrificed the great interests of the nation to my own leisure. I have crossed the sea amid all kinds of perils. I come to you to reassert my rights, which are also yours."[23]

Napoleon's "imperial fleet" on his voyage from Elba to France consisted of five ships: the single-masted, flat-bottomed *l'Inconstant*, commanded by Captain Chautard, the frigate *Caroline*, two xebecs, *l'Etoile* and *Saint-Joseph*, and the ninety-ton *Saint-Esprit* which Napoleon had requisitioned from its owner. Napoleon's flotilla took three days to reach France, landing in the Golfe Juan on March 1, 1815. The day before Napoleon's British "guardian," Colonel Sir Neil Campbell, had returned to Elba aboard the British frigate *Partridge* from his assignation with his lover in Livorno, only to find Napoleon gone.

The French people were ambivalent about their emperor's return. They did not like the reactionary rule of their new king, Louis XVIII, yet many of them had lost their husbands, fathers, or sons in Napoleon's wars. They feared more conscription, war, bloodshed, and taxes. They were caught between the devil and the deep blue sea. Rather than fight the "usurper" Napoleon on the battlefield, King Louis XVIII fought him in the press. On March 6, 1815, the French *Journal des débats* denounced "that man besmeared with the blood of generations . . . God grant that the cowardly warrior of Fontainebleau die the death of a traitor!" It was almost as if Louis XVIII and Napoleon's mother were on the same side: Letizia had also predicted Napoleon's death by the sword.[24] While the former emperor Napoleon and his tiny army from Elba rode north from the Golfe Juan to Paris via Grenoble, Lyon, Castellane, Digne, Sisteron and Gap, King Louis XVIII vied with the former emperor for the hearts and minds of his marshals and countrymen.

The inevitable and dramatic confrontation between Louis XVIII's troops and Napoleon's occurred at the village of Laffrey, near Grenoble, where Napoleon's party encountered a detachment of Louis XVIII's troops. The fifty-year-old general Jean-Gabriel Marchand had become the military commander of Grenoble. The war minister, Marshal Soult, had ordered Marchand to hold Grenoble against "Buonaparte's brigands." General Marchand's Fifth Battalion of the Line was commanded by a royalist major named Delessart. On the evening of March 7, 1815, Major Delessart's troops paraded at Laffrey, on the shore of a triple lake. The twenty-seven-year-old Colonel Nicolas-Louis Raoul, one of Napoleon's Imperial Guard officers, rode off toward Major Delessart, warning him that the emperor will soon be advancing toward him, and that if he opened fire, he would answer to France for it.

As Napoleonic legend would have it, Major Delessart stood firm, but when his men saw their emperor, his Polish lancers and his Imperial Guard, they trembled with fear and inner conflict. Delessart's deputy cried "There he is! Open fire!" but his soldiers did not obey him. There was a dead silence. Napoleon stood before the soldiers, bared his chest dramatically, and cried, "Soldiers of the Fifth! I am your Emperor. If there is one among you who would kill his Emperor, here I am!" Again there was silence. Then suddenly cries of "Long Live the Emperor!" rang out, as Delessart's soldiers broke ranks, fell to their knees before Napoleon, and went over to him.[25] The old magic was still working. The showdown at Laffrey was the turning point in Napoleon's comeback from Elba. Within two weeks King Louis XVIII would flee France and Napoleon would be back at the Tuileries Palace.

General Jean-Gabriel Marchand, the royalist commander at Grenoble, ordered his 7th and 11th regiments at Chambéry to join him. The two colonels commanding these regiments obeyed, but when General Marchand placed the two regiments on the Grenoble ramparts facing the road south to La Mure, the commander of the 7th Regiment had a change of heart and ordered his men to follow him and join the Emperor. This was the twenty-nine-year-old colonel Charles-Angélique-François Huchet de la Bédoyère, a former aide-de-camp to Marshal Lannes who had fought under Napoleon. When he joined Napoleon at this critical juncture, La Bédoyère reportedly warned him, "Sire, the more ambition, the more despotism. Your Majesty must abjure the system of conquests and extreme power which has caused France's misfortune and your own."[26] La Bédoyère's men obeyed him. They marched south toward Vizille, joined Napoleon, and marched back with him toward Grenoble. A grateful Napoleon quickly made La Bédoyère a brigadier general and his personal aide-de-camp, and later also made him a peer of France. Before the year was out, however, Napoleon would be toppled again by the allies and the young La Bédoyère would pay for his treason to the Bourbons with his life.

On the evening of March 7, 1815, General Marchand fled Grenoble for Paris with his few hundred remaining troops. That day Napoleon's return to France became known in Vienna. The pace of events became dramatic. On March 8, Napoleon reviewed his troops at Grenoble. He moved on to Bourgoin, and marched on Lyon, where the Count of Artois (the king's brother and future King Charles X) and the Duke of Orléans (the future King Louis-Philippe) had rallied three regiments and one thousand five hundred national guardsmen. Louis XVIII's war minister, Marshal Soult, had promised to send them thirty thousand men, who never arrived. On March 11 King Louis XVIII finally dismissed his disloyal war minister, Marshal Soult, who had done next to nothing to stop Napoleon, replacing him with his more effective forty-year-old secretary of state, Baron Eugène-François-Auguste d'Arnaud de Vitrolles. Two weeks later, when Napoleon had regained his throne, Soult rallied back to Napoleon, who conveniently "forgot" that Soult had proclaimed him "a usurper and an adventurer, the lowest of the low,"[27] naming Soult a Peer of France and chief of staff of the imperial army.

Europe was dumbfounded and incensed at Napoleon's return to France in violation of the treaty of Fontainebleau that he had signed. On March 13, 1815, the Congress of Vienna, led by the Austrian foreign minister, Prince Metternich, issued a formal proclamation declaring Napoleon an outlaw and an enemy of humanity. Its venomous language was drafted by the vengeful Talleyrand, who had never forgotten his humiliation by Napoleon:

> Napoleon Bonaparte's escape from Elba is an attack on the social order . . . By returning to France with plans for causing disturbance and upheaval, he has forfeited the protection of the law and demonstrated to the whole universe that with him there can be neither peace nor a truce . . . By thus breaking the treaty which had established him on the isle of Elba, Bonaparte destroys the only legal title to which his existence had been attached . . . Consequently, the Powers declare that Napoleon Bonaparte has placed himself outside civil and social relations and, as an enemy and disturber of the peace of the world, he is delivered to the public vengeance.[28]

When Napoleon's brother-in-law King Joachim Murat of Naples, who had rallied to the allies the year before, learned of Napoleon's return to France, he had another change of heart, due to his guilt feelings or to his wish for revenge on his wife Caroline, who had incited him to rebel against her brother. Murat offered to rally back to Napoleon, who, at this point, needed every ally he could get. On March 18, 1815, Murat impulsively—and unwisely—declared war on Austria and issued a grandiose proclamation: "A cry is making itself heard from the Alps to the Strait of Scylla, and this cry is the independence of Italy."[29] On March 19, without consulting Napoleon, Murat marched his army north to attack the Austrian armies in northern Italy. "When Napoleon heard [this], he was outraged; he still had some hope for negotiations with the Allies, but Murat had confirmed their worst fears. Napoleon knew, moreover, that Murat was not really fighting for him; he was out to become ruler of all Italy."[30] Few volunteers turned up to join Murat. Owen Connelly thought that "the Italian intelligentsia had grossly overestimated the interest of the common man in Italian unity—much less his willingness to die for it."[31]

Was Napoleon's charisma so great? Had the French people forgotten the disasters that he had inflicted on them? Did they hate Louis XVIII so much? As Napoleon approached Paris, Louis XVIII's soldiers defected to him *en masse*. While Louis XVIII left Paris in a panic, Napoleon spent the night of March 19–20, 1815 at Pont-sur-Yonne, about one hundred kilometers south of Paris. Antoine-Marie Chamans de Lavalette, Napoleon's adventurous aide-de-camp and postmaster general, later recalled Napoleon's triumphant return to Paris:

> Fallen from the throne, erased from the list of sovereigns, banished to the rock of Elba, he is a thing of the past; now he returns almost alone. Scarcely had he set foot on the French shore, when the people everywhere rose. All France repeated enthusiastically: "No more royalty. No more Bourbons. It is Napoleon alone that France desires." But within eight days I became aware that a deep gulf was yawning under our feet. The Emperor soon perceives this, for he no longer finds the submission, the deep respect, and the imperial etiquette to which he has been accustomed . . . He was galled to find that those whom he had raised to wealth and title had deserted him.[32]

Napoleon had not forgotten his dead first wife and great love, Josephine. On March 21, 1815, the day after he returned to Paris, he went to Malmaison to see the place where Josephine had died. At Malmaison he met his daughter-in-law, Hortense de Beauharnois Bonaparte, the former queen of Holland, then went alone to the first floor to see Josephine's last room. Napoleon's second wife, Marie-Louise, had fallen for the dashing one-eyed Count Adam Adalbert Adrian von Neipperg, who accompanied her on a trip to Aix-les-Bains in France in September 1814. Frank McLynn thought that Marie-Louise had still been hoping to rejoin her husband, but that she succumbed to Neipperg's "subtle charms" because her "appetite for sex was not far short of Josephine's or Pauline's."[33] Having lost his living wife to Count Neipperg, Napoleon was acting out a fantasy of fusion with his early mother, unconsciously symbolized by the dead Josephine. This gave him strength. He left Malmaison and returned to the Tuileries, vainly hoping to regain his former glory as *Empereur des Français*.

One of the first Frenchmen to see Napoleon at the Tuileries Palace after March 20 was Marshal Louis-Nicolas Davout, the only one of Napoleon's marshals who had not taken the oath of loyalty to Louis XVIII, who had rebuffed him. Davout's memo to the king had remained unanswered. He was furious with Louis XVII and sought our his previous "father," Napoleon, who at once offered Davout the job of war minister. When Davout demurred, Napoleon reportedly exclaimed: "I am facing Europe alone—and you want to abandon me?!" Davout at once accepted, and without delay set about organizing Napoleon's new army from the mobilized units and demobilized soldiers, freed prisoners of war, conscripts, national guards, and everyone else who could be drafted or mobilized. Within a short time Davout succeeded in raising a sizable military force for Napoleon.

The allies, however, as Napoleon might have known, were determined to punish the "enemy and disturber of the tranquillity of the world" who had broken all his treaties with them.[34] On March 25, 1815 Great Britain, Austria, Russia and Prussia "pledged to keep 150,000 troops each in the field until Napoleon was defeated, a total of 600,000. Minor powers in Germany would furnish another 100,000. War, then, became Napoleon's only hope of survival as emperor."[35] Napoleon's army, however, could not match the size and power of the allied armies determined to remove him once and for all.

Incredibly, then, Napoleon had returned to France and made his astonishing comeback as emperor. For 136 days, from March to June 1815, he reorganized France under his rule, while most of the high-ranking officials of Louis XVIII's regime fled France. The psychoanalyst Pierce Clark believed that Napoleon functioned better now than he had before: "His narcism is the more flexible as the egoistic projects are less sure and certain. Failures make the narcist more human. After the terrible disaster in Russia, as now on his return from Elba, he regresses . . . to the simpler and earlier pattern of sanity as in the consulate days."[36] But Napoleon needed complete control, and the French people no longer gave him absolute power. He had to share power with the legislature. There would be new and more serious clashes.

In yet another act of unconscious self-destruction, on March 21, 1815, Napoleon renamed the treacherous Joseph Fouché, who had repeatedly double-crossed him, to high office as his police minister. Fouché was an incorrigible double-dealer. While pretending to serve Napoleon, he wrote secret letters to Napoleon's enemies, the Bourbons and the British, referring to his master as "this raving madman."[37] *Why did Napoleon not have Fouché tried for treason and executed?* Some scholars think that Napoleon believed that Fouché held incriminating documents about his private life and feared his police minister.[38] Later, a prisoner of the British on Saint Helena, Napoleon himself declared that he had been waiting for his first battlefield victory before arresting Fouché; otherwise Fouché would have shaken his own government.

These explanations were unconscious rationalizations. If he had really wanted to rid himself of the traitor, Napoleon could have arrested Fouché and extracted the incriminating documents from him by pressure or even torture. He could have pre-empted Fouché by trying him for treachery and executing him without giving Fouché the opportunity to reveal anything damaging about him. *Napoleon unconsciously used Fouché to destroy himself.* By the time of his return to France from Elba, he was an old man who had lost his former *joie de vivre*. The psychoanalyst Pierce Clark thought that by this time "Napoleon's ego is blocked; the very essence of his narcism has become depleted, bankrupt . . . a strange wooden lethargy settled upon him. The emotional energy is now fixed upon an inner pattern that is no longer mobile."[39]

Napoleon's enemies, Great Britain, Prussia, Austria, and Russia, had joined together in a final Seventh Coalition to remove him from the throne once and for all. On April 15, 1815, the fifty-nine-year-old fugitive Bourbon king, Louis XVIII, published a declaration in the Belgian city of Ghent, vowing to "wipe out to the traces of abuses which could have distanced from us some Frenchmen." The king remained in Ghent, weakened, until June 22, four days after Napoleon was defeated by the Seventh Coalition Allies at Waterloo. And indeed, at that battle, as we shall see, the self-destructive Napoleon made three major "blunders" that cost him the loss of his throne and of France for good.[40]

34

Self-Destruction at Waterloo

Ever since March 13, 1815, when the Congress of Vienna had proclaimed Napoleon an enemy of humanity and declared war on him, his fate seemed to be sealed. Nevertheless, as the brilliant military commander that he had been, he might still have been able to save his throne and keep the powers out of France. But his self-destructive streak and his unconscious death wish came into play dramatically during the decisive battles in mid-June 1815. On June 9 the Congress of Vienna signed the final treaty that fixed the borders of the new Europe. France was deprived of all its territories east of the Rhine and pushed back to its "natural" 1792 boundaries. Two days later, on June 11, when the "atheist" Emperor Napoleon attended mass in the chapel of the Tuileries Palace, he was a badly-changed man: "His glance, which in the old days was so formidable because of its penetration, had lost its power and even its fixity . . . his tight-lipped mouth had none of its former magic; even the way he held his head no longer suggested the ruler of the world . . . Everything about him seemed disfigured and distorted; his complexion, ordinarily pale, was now distinctly greenish."[1]

Napoleon used to defeat his enemies by launching surprise preemptive strikes. By June 1815 his forces in France were vastly outnumbered by his enemies. He did have an army of three hundred thousand regular troops as well as one hundred seventy thousand national guardsmen for interior duty in France, but "his field army numbered only 125,000. Napoleon had to allot troops to defend the frontiers and hold down rebels in the royalist Vendée and Rhône areas. The Allies had 400,000 men under arms and a potential of 700,000. Napoleon's only hope was to take on the enemy armies one at a time."[2]

On June 12, 1815, Napoleon himself took charge of his army and led it north against the Allies, who were now in Belgium, a formerly French territory. Field-Marshal Gebhard Leberecht von Blücher, the commander in chief of the Prussian army, who had the byname of "Marshal Forward," had one hundred twenty thousand men under him. The British commander, the Duke of Wellington, had one hundred ten thousand men near Brussels. Neither Blücher nor Wellington had suspected that Napoleon was about to attack them. On June 13 Blücher wrote his wife: "We shall soon enter France, although it would be perfectly possible to stay right here for another year, because Bonaparte will not attack us."[3] On June 14 Wellington wrote Tsar Aleksandr that he would attack Napoleon's armies at the end of that month.

On June 15, Napoleon and his one hundred twenty-five thousand soldiers crossed the River Sambre into the southern Belgian city of Charleroi. Napoleon received his deputy, Marshal Ney—the man who had forced him to abdicate the year before—and gave him command of forty-five thousand men—the 1st and 2nd French army corps and of the light cavalry of the Imperial Guard.[4] Napoleon ordered Ney to push the British back toward the Brussels Road and to occupy Les Quatre Bras, a strategic position in the battlefield. But Ney, who had grown old, and who harbored deeply ambivalent feelings about Napoleon, vacillated and procrastinated, playing a decisive role in Napoleon's ultimate defeat at Waterloo. Which begs the question, why did Napoleon choose Ney, of all his marshals, to be his second in command?

Early in the morning of June 16, an anxious Napoleon sent another message to Marshal Ney reiterating his orders of the previous day: throw the British to the Brussels road and hold on to Les Quatre Bras. "Such a prompt and rapid movement would isolate the British army from Mons and Ostend, and . . . upon receiving the first order, your eight divisions can march rapidly and unimpeded on Brussels."[5] But the ambivalent and hesitatnt Ney was too slow in setting out, giving the Duke of Wellington time to have Les Quatre Bras occupied by the Dutch Prince of Orange.

While Marshal Ney's French forces fought the duke of Wellington's Britons at Les Quatre Bras, Napoleon's own troops fought Field-Marshal Blücher's Prussians at nearby Ligny, in the plain of Fleurus, where the French had defeated the Austrians 21 years earlier. The battle of Ligny and Fleurus was a savage butchery.[6] Napoleon won the battle that day after committing his elite Imperial Guard to the battle. But at the same time he robbed Ney of his victory at Les Quatre Bras—and mitigated his own ultimate victory—by failing to tell Ney that he had ordered General Jean-Baptiste Drouet d'Erlon, the commander of Napoleon's Imperial Guard, to march with his corps to Ligny.

Tragically for both, Napoleon and Ney now played a calamitous unconscious game in which both wished to cause the other to fail—and unintentionally caused themselves to fail as well. Both of them made bad decisions which ultimately made them lose the final battle at Waterloo. At the height of the battle of Ligny, Marshal Soult, Louis XVIII's former war minister, and now Napoleon's chief of staff, sent a courier to Marshal Ney with an ominous message: "At this moment the fighting is very intense. His Majesty has instructed me to tell you that you should maneuver on the field of battle so as to envelop the enemy's right wing and fall upon his rear with all available forces. If you act vigorously, his army will be routed. The fate of France is in your hands."[7]

At Waterloo, Marshal Michel Ney was the tragic victim of his own guilt feelings, his impotent and ambivalent rage and his wish for revenge on Napoleon, his shattered self-esteem, and his wish for self-destruction. Incredibly, when he received Soult's message, Ney, who had been "the bravest of the brave," the most impetuous and daring of Napoleon's marshals, was "stricken with paralysis."[8] Ney unconsciously took revenge on Napoleon with his indecision, procrastination and inaction, which prevented Napoleon from "mopping up" the defeated Prussians after the Ligny victory; they retreated in good order to Wavre without being pursued by the French.

The outcome of the battle of Ligny and Fleurus on June 16, 1815, was inconclusive. Despite Marshal Ney's inaction, Napoleon might have won, were it not for Nature's intervention. During the night of June 16–17 it rained heavily in southern Belgium. The roads became muddy and nearly impassable. General Drouot d'Erlon, the commander of Napoleon's elite Imperial Guard, complained about the wetness of the soil.[9] Napoleon spent a sleepless night at Fleurus, trying to decide what to do. Later, he rued his "mistake." Had he pursued the retreating Prussians with his entire force, he later said, a prisoner of the British on Saint Helena, the battle of Waterloo would have been fought a day earlier, and the British and Prussians would never have had the time to link up and defeat him. Napoleon blamed the indecisive Marshal Ney for his troubles.

In fact, Napoleon unconsciously caused his own defeat at Waterloo. His blunders—underestimating Field-Marshal Blücher's Austrian forces, wasting time, and attacking Wellington frontally—were fatal self-destructive errors. Further, he had also made the mistake of naming Marshal Ney as his deputy instead of Marshal Murat and naming Marshal Soult as his chief of staff instead of Marshal Davout, even though Ney had caused Napoleon's abdication the year before, and both Ney and Soult had served Louis XVIII. Vincent Cronin pointed out the major blunders Napoleon made on June 17, 1815, that brought about his defeat:

> [His first blunder was that] on the morning of the 17th Napoleon had a unique opportunity to crush Wellington with overwhelming odds, while the Prussians were in full retreat. Instead of seizing it, *he wasted the morning visiting the wounded and, through muddled staff work for which Napoleon must bear the blame, failed to give Ney orders to attack.* That morning Napoleon behaved not as a great general, but as a retired soldier who has just been recalled to the colours and is still adjusting to war. In so doing he "lost the favourable moment which in war decides everything."[10]

Napoleon then committed another self-destructive blunder that compounded the gravity of his situation: "Napoleon's second blunder was that he misjudged the English: not only the ordinary soldiers, who to his surprise remained cool and quick-witted under fire, but also Wellington. Napoleon's tactics had remained the same, but Wellington had now learned to foil them, particularly by the use of reverse slopes."[11] This was not the first time Napoleon had committed such blunders. In 1806, at the battle of Jena and Auerstädt, he had badly misjudged the location of the Prussian army, giving his whole attention to the action at Jena and none to that at Auerstädt, where the Prussians launched their main attack. He had also misjudged the time at which they would launch their offensive. In 1807, after the terrible battle of Eylau, Napoleon had badly misjudged the Russian enemy's plans to attack at Friedland. In 1812 he had fatally misjudged the Russian Tsar's willingness to stand up to his invasion. In fact, Napoleon had misjudged his enemies' forces and intentions so many times that the military historian Owen Connelly titled his book about Napoleon's military campaigns, *Blundering to Glory*.[12]

Finally, on June 18, 1815, Napoleon was undone by his own narcissism, grandiosity, and belief in his own invincibility. Incredibly, and disastrously, Napoleon ordered Marshal Emmanuel Grouchy (who had earned his marshal's baton under Louis XVIII) to engage and push back a Prussian force of one hundred thosuand men, whose whereabouts were unknown, with a much smaller corps of only thirty thousand men—an impossible mission. The rigid Grouchy stuck to the letter of his orders and only succeeded in holding back one Prussian division, while all of Blücher's other divisions reached Mont Saint-Jean:

> Napoleon's third blunder was overconfidence. Early on the 18th he should have acted on Jerome's information about the Prussians. He should either have postponed the battle, or at least cautiously ordered Grouchy to head for Wahain; then only a single corps of Blücher's army at most would have been able to intervene at Waterloo. But Napoleon felt confident [that the battle of] Ligny had knocked all fight out of the Prussians. That confidence—which, when successful, is called daring, and, when unsuccessful, overconfidence—had always been a mark of the man. It had been there in 1793 when he bombarded Ajaccio citadel from the sea, believing his fellow-townsmen would rally to the French. It had been there in Elba: sowing 500 sacks of wheat on land that ordinarily yielded 100; expecting, month after month, Marie Louise and the King of Rome. It had been strengthened by the stupendous "flight of the eagle." And on the morning of 18 June it led to [Napoleon's] military downfall.[13]

After his numerous self-destructive blunders, Napoleon's ultimate and inevitable defeat came on June 18, 1815, south of Waterloo, a small village in the Plain of Fleurus, fifteen kilometers south of Brussels. While the psychoanalyst Pierce Clark believed that Napoleon's strategy and tactics at Waterloo were faultless, Clark thought that what lost Napoleon the battle was his indecision and his poor timing. Napoleon made two more fatal errors that day: waiting until noon before attacking, rather than ordering the charge at six in the morning; and overlooking the deep ravine that separated his forces from those of the enemy. Napoleon's cavalry fell into the ravine, and the battle was lost. Napoleon had asked a peasant on the road whether there were any obstacles, the peasant had shaken his head, and Napoleon assumed there were none. This was yet another self-destructive act. A good commander sends his scouts out to obtain such vital information; he does not rely on a peasant's shake of the head.[14]

As Clark put it, "Napoleon's enemy would have suffered the defeat, had it not been for the morning delay and the sunken ditch. We can only add that the immobility of Napoleon's mind explains both. It is set and patterned and cannot cope with change, even in the sacred precinct of his own soul. He has from that moment lost control of the wheel of his good fortune. He is no longer the Napoleon of facile genius and inventiveness; he already tastes the inner dregs of his narcissm and henceforth will but fabricate external excuses for his own internal defects so long as he lives."[15] It was no accident that Clark titled his book *Napoleon Self-Destroyed*.[16]

Nicolas-Louis Raoul, a twenty-seven-year-old battalion commander in Napoleon's Imperial Guard artillery who was gravely wounded at Waterloo and taken prisoner by the Allies, believed that Napoleon had caused his own defeat: "Even this battle might have been retrieved, had Napoleon not charged with the guard. We were mown down like grape—we wavered—turned our backs, and the rout was complete. A general disorganization of the army ensued, and Napoleon, relapsing into the stupor which he had shaken off, was cold as stone."[17] That stupor was nearly catatonic. After being defeated, Napoleon's traumatized self was overwhelmed, and he was nearly paralyzed by inner conflict and anxiety.

During the night of June 18–19, 1815 a deeply traumatized Napoleon withdrew his remaining army from the Waterloo battlefield toward Paris. His Imperial Guard had been beaten, his men had fled, and Marshal Ney had tried to get himself killed:

> Ney tried to rally the center, shouting, "Come see how a Marshal of France dies!" but he ended up inside the square of Guards in the valley along with Soult, stray guards and officers by the hundreds—and the emperor. At about 9:00 [the duke of Wellington], waving his hat, galloped forward and motioned his army into a general advance that carried all before it . . . Napoleon, on his little Arabian mare, Marengo, rode rapidly from the protection of the slowly disintegrating Guard battalion at La Haye Sainte, and under cavalry and grenadier escort made it to his carriage within the square of Guards at Maison-du-Roi. Thence he went by carriage to Genappe, half-way to the French border, where he mounted a horse and, accompanied by Ney, Soult, and others, rode for Paris. Behind him, at La Belle Alliance, Wellington and Blücher met and, to the duke's

> astonishment, although both were on horseback, Blücher embraced him, exclaiming "*Kamerad!*" and "*Quelle affaire!*" At the end, Napoleon had been outnumbered 2 to 1. He was beaten for the last time. His military career was over; his political career had only four days to run.[18]

Despite his bitter defeat at Waterloo, Napoleon could still have fought the Allies from Paris. He still had an army of one hundred twenty thousand men under Marshal Davout near Paris. Marshal Grouchy's corps and the survivors of Waterloo were on their way back to Paris from Belgium, and the National Guard and frontier forces were available. Napoleon, however, needed and wanted absolute power, reducing the legislature to a rubber stamp, while Marshal Davout, Napoleon's last war minister, warned him that he would not support another *coup d'état* against the legislature like the one that had brought him to power in 1799.

For Napoleon, this was the last straw. He gave up. On June 22, 1815, at the urging of his ministers and of the *Chambre des représentants* under Lafayette, who, through Napoleon's younger brother Lucien, who had returned to France, threatened to dethrone him, Napoleon abdicated again in favor of his legitimate son, the King of Rome. Napoleon felt as a child sacrificing itself for its mother. Attempting to salvage his self-esteem, he dictated the following declaration to Lucien:

> I am offering myself as a sacrifice to the hatred of the enemies of France. Let it be hoped that they are sincere in their declarations, and that their resentment is confined to my person . . . My political life is over, and I proclaim my son Emperor of the French, under the name of Napoleon II.[19]

Napoleon added this last sentence at the insistence of Prince Lucien and Lazare Carnot, the interior minister under Louis XVIII and Napoleon's former rival. It was a delusion to hope that the allies would agree to put his son on the throne of France. After all they had gone through with him, their only intention was to restore Louis XVIII and the Bourbon dynasty. Napoleon would go to his final exile on Saint Helena deluding himself that he was still Emperor of the French, while the British would treat him as a mere General Bonaparte.

35

Imprisonment, Illness, and Death

After Napoleon's final abdication, the French legislature set up a new provisional government commission headed by the "traitor" Joseph Fouché. On June 25, 1815, with Fouché's "permission," Napoleon left Paris for the castle of Malmaison, the former home of his dead first wife, Josephine. Her daughter Hortense, Napoleon's stepdaughter and daughter-in-law, the former queen of Holland, who had inherited the castle, was willing to receive him there. Fouché falsely promised Napoleon French passports which would enable him to leave for the United States rather than to be captured by the British, who were trying to seize him. But the double-dealing Fouché secretly planned to arrest Napoleon and hand him over to the British.

Having lost everything, feeling desperate, enraged, helpless, and worthless, a traumatized and depressed Napoleon spent five melancholy days (June 25–29, 1815) at Malmaison with the memories of his dead first wife, where he once more contemplated suicide. On June 29, his last day at Malmaison, Napoleon learned that the Prussians had made an incautious military advance into France and placed a vanguard on the Lower Seine river. In his despair, Napoleon suddenly imagined that he could "hew the Prussians to pieces"if given command of the French army.[1] He impulsively donned his Imperial Guard uniform, boots, spurs and all, and immediately summoned the forty-five-year-old general Nicolas-Léonard Becker, who had been appointed by Fouché's provisional government commission to watch over Napoleon at Malmaison.

Napoleon gave General Becker the following message to the provisional government commission: "Let them appoint me general, and I will command the army. Go to Paris: a carriage is ready for you. Explain to the Provisional Government that I have no intention of taking power again. I want to defeat the enemy, to crush him, and compel him by means of a victory to give a favorable turn to the negotiations . . . Then I shall leave."[2] As might have been expected, Fouché's Government Commission rejected Napoleon's offer out of hand. For Fouché, Napoleon, not the Prussians, was the most dangerous enemy.

Napoleon vainly hoped to escape the British with Fouché's passports. On July 1, 1815, the thirty-eight-old British ship captain Frederick Lewis Maitland, a future rear-admiral, learned from the captain of a ship leaving the Atlantic port of Rochefort that French civilians had arrived on the nearby island of Aix, that two French ships, the *Saâle* and the *Méduse*, were preparing to set sail from Rochefort, and that Napoleon planned to set sail for the United States aboard one of these two frigates. Ironically, Napoleon, the youthful author of the horror story *Nouvelle Corse* with its island of Gorgona, was considering sailing for America aboard a ship called *Medusa*. He later chose the *Saâle*, perhaps because of his horror of the Medusa.

On July 3, 1815, Napoleon's party arrived at Rochefort, planning to board a Danish ship and sail for the United States. Its captain had offered to take him there. Irrationally, and self-destructively, however, Napoleon wanted to force England—the idealized Great Good Mother of his youth and the hated Great Bad Mother of his adulthood, on which he had made war for so long—to love him despite everything, or else to destroy him utterly. He wished to give himself up to Great Britain. Although he could have evaded the British blockade and broken away aboard the Danish ship, he did not sail for America.

Using the unconscious rationalization that the British Royal Navy was preventing any vessel from leaving port, Napoleon did not board the Danish ship, staying on shore at Rochefort, still hoping to be embraced by the British as their imperial guest. In reality the British had no intention of inviting him to London. Like a child trying to force his rejecting and hated mother to love him, Napoleon was courting the hospitality of a nation that he had sought to destroy. The only response he could rationally expect was humiliation, imprisonment and exile, yet he irrationally expected hospitality, refuge and asylum.

Napoleon spent a full week (July 3–9, 1815) with his aides at Rochefort unable to decide what to do: escape to the United States or give himself up to the British. It was an unconscious revival of his early-life dilemma:

break away from his bad mother or stick to her and try to force her to love him. The naval prefect at Rochefort advised Napoleon to board a French corvette skippered by the thirty-one-year-old Captain Charles Baudin, who had fought for Napoleon at Toulon the year before. Baudin was ready to spirit Napoleon off to America; but Napoleon's endless hesitations killed the project. Napoleon also turned down a proposal by the thirty-four-year-old Jean-Victor Besson, the captain of a sloop at Rochefort, who had served in Napoleon's Imperial Guard in Russia. Besson had offered to hide Napoleon in a big barrel on his ship, "well padded and provided with air holes." But Napoleon secretly wished to be taken prisoner by the British, impossibly hoping that they would embrace him as their guest. André Castelot thought that Napoleon wanted comfort, luxury, pomp and ceremony: "Imagine leaving the country with only his valet when he could go to the English with a retinue of some fifteeen officers in dress uniform, plus sixty servants—not to mention his sumptuous plate dishes and his vast amount of luggage."[3] The deeper reason for Napoleon's wish to go to the British was his unconscious need to punish himself and to repeat his early rejection by his mother.

Joseph Fouché, the head of the French Provisional Government Commission, had secretly asked the British to prevent Napoleon from leaving France for America. The British had a naval base at the French port of Quiberon Bay, and many warships patrolling the French Atlantic coast. On of them, the HMS *Bellerophon*, was commanded by the 38-old captain Frederick Lewis Maitland, a future rear-admiral. Captain Maitland was descended from a well-known Scottish military family. He was a seasoned sailor who had taken part in the British Egyptian expedition. Captain Maitland had been ordered to the French Atlantic coast a month earlier to serve under Admiral Sir Henry Hotham, whose job was to prevent Napoleon from escaping and conduct him to permanent exile on Saint Helena.[4]

On July 7, 1815, Captain Maitland received word from Admiral Hotham that Napoleon was on his way to Rochefort, planning to embark for America. Maitland already knew that Napoleon had been at Rochefort since July 3. Hotham told Maitland that the British government would refuse to give Napoleon the safe-conduct that he had asked for, and ordered Maitland "to do his utmost to prevent Bonaparte from escaping."[5] In another dispatch, Admiral Hotham ordered Captain Maitland "to employ all means to intercept the fugitive, upon whose capture the repose of Europe would appear to depend."[6] Napoleon had a snowball's chance in hell of eluding the British navy.

On July 8, 1815, while Napoleon was still at Rochefort, King Louis XVIII returned to the Tuileries Palace in Paris. The Bourbon monarchy had again been restored. Napoleon would never again return to the throne of France. Fouché's provisional government commission had required Napoleon to leave Rochefort. To appear to comply, to gain time, and to win the confidence of the British Royal Navy, Napoleon disembarked from the *Saâle* onto the Isle of Aix. He spent four days on the island, the last appendage of France that he still clung to, before he let go of his adopted motherland for good. Each night he went back to the *Saâle* and spent the night on it, in case he decided to sail away on short notice. On July 10, when Napoleon sent his emissaries to Maitland to negotiate his safe conduct to America, the thin, pallid and wily Scotsman misled them into believing that he would cooperate, while knowing full well that he planned to intercept and capture Napoleon as soon as he could.

On July 13, 1815, Napoleon dictated a pathetic letter addressed to the Prince Regent of Great Britain and Ireland, the future King George IV, pleading for asylum and hospitality in England. In this letter the unhappy and regressed Napoleon compared himself to the ancient Athenian hero Themistocles, the great Greek who created the Athenian navy and empire and was nevertheless rejected by his own people:

> Your Royal Highness, exposed to the factions which divide my country, and to the enmity of the greatest Powers of Europe, I have ended my political career. I come, like Themistocles, to sit at the hearth of the British people; I put myself under the protection of its laws, which I claim from Your Royal Highness, as that of the most powerful, the most constant, the most generous of my enemies. [7]

Napoleon's choice of Themistocles was hardly accidental. Napoleon, who had previously seen himself as a new Alexander the Great, now identified with the tragic Greek hero. Like Napoleon's, Themistocles' life was very tragic. Thirty years earlier, Napoleon had learned at the military school of Brienne that during the Greek-Persian wars, Themistocles had persuaded the ruling council of Athens to build a new fleet with revenue from their newly-discovered silver mines. This fleet and Themistocles' brilliant naval strategies helped the Athenians crush the vastly-superior Persian fleet at the Battle of Salamis in 480 BCE. Persuading the

Peloponnesians to join the Athenian fleet, Themistocles had beguiled King Xerxes of Persia into ordering an all-out attack on the Greeks by sending him a false message, suggesting that he himself was ready to change sides. The Greeks enveloped the head of the Phoenician column as it emerged from the narrowest part of the strait and destroyed it; and though most of the other Asian contingents in the rear escaped, Xerxes had lost for good the command of the sea. Athens became the dominant power in the new Delian League of Greek city-states.[8]

Unhappily for Themistocles, however, he failed to persuade his fellow Athenians to transfer their capital to nearby Piraeus and to curb the power of their ruling council. Athens' chief rival in the Delian League, Sparta, accused Themistocles of plotting with the Persians against the Greeks. There was no proof of this false charge, but the envious Athenian ruling council banished Themistocles on this suspicion alone. Taking refuge at Argos, the hurt and vengeful Athenian hero instigated trouble for Sparta, which he regarded as the natural foe of Athens. This and his alleged association with the discredited Spartan regent led to a charge of treason against Themistocles in Athens. He was found guilty and condemned to death. A mortified Themistocles escaped to the Persian court. After learning Persian, he met the Persian king Artaxerxes, who granted Themistocles large fiefs and titles in exchange for his loyalty. By Greek myth, however, Themistocles committed suicide rather than take part in a new Persian naval war against the Athenians.[9]

Not only did Napoleon tragically identify with the unhappy ancient hero who had been unjustly rejected by his own ungrateful people, and who had killed himself for them, there was also not the slightest chance of Great Britain accepting his request for asylum. He gave his letter, addressed to Great Britain's Prince Regent, to his aide-de-camp, General Gourgaud, to carry it post-haste to England. Before dawn, Napoleon sent his two envoys, Count Emmanuel de Las Cases and General François-Antoine Lallemand, to Captain Maitland on the British vessel *Bellerophon*. Maitland told his guests that he had received no answer from his boss, Admiral Hotham, but nonetheless offered Napoleon asylum in England if he boarded his ship:

> If the Emperor wants to embark for England immediately, I have the authority to receive him on board and take him there. In my private opinion, there is no doubt that England would accord to Napoleon all the respect and hospitality to which he can lay claim.

> In my country, the Prince and the ministers do not exercise the kind of arbitrary authority that is exercised on the Continent. The English people possess a generosity of sentiment and a liberality of opinion superior to sovereignty itself. [10]

Even if Maitland was honest—which is far from certain—his private opinion did not matter, and he had no authority to make the offer he did. Maitland's government did not consider Napoleon "the Emperor," only "General Bonaparte." Las Cases and Lallemand brought Maitland's response back to Napoleon. Tragically deluding himself that Maitland's offer was genuine, and that he had the authority to make it, Napoleon decided to accept Maitland's "generous offer" to sail for Britain. In a final act of self-destruction, Napoleon made himself the victim of his British captors by giving himself up to them.

On July 14, 1815, just before Napoleon made up his mind to board the HMS *Bellerophon*, his elder brother, Joseph Bonaparte, the former king of Spain, visited Napoleon secretly on the Isle of Aix. Joseph made a fantastic proposal to save Napoleon:

> Joseph, plagued with doubt about the move, risked a last visit. Let me take your place, Joseph pleaded. You are ill; I can remain in bed a few days. The English captain, even if he comes ashore, would not know that I am not the Emperor. We look alike; he has never seen either of us. You can get away to the United States on the ship that I have chartered. Napoleon refused; he considered the ruse beneath his dignity. And he would not have history record that *Joseph saved him.* [11]

Thus did Napoleon's self-destructive narcissism make him miss the last chance of being saved from exile and early death on Saint Helena. His elder brother stayed on the Isle of Aix until midnight on July 14–15, 1815, when he bade farewell to his fallen younger brother, Napoleon. They would never see each other again.

Captain Maitland at first did take his prisoner to England, where, as ordered by his boss, Admiral Hotham, he docked his HMS *Bellerophon* first at Torbay, then at Plymouth. Napoleon, however, was never allowed ashore, to prevent a writ of *habeas corpus* issued by a British judge requiring his presence in court as a witness against a British admiral from being served on him.[12] On July 31, 1815, Lord Keith, the commander of the British fleet in the English Channel, handed Napoleon a letter from His Britannic Majesty's Government. This poignant letter, addressed to "General Buonaparte" rather than to "Emperor Napoleon," read as follows:

> It would hardly be compatible with our duties toward our country and the Allies of His Majesty if General Buonaparte were left with the means or occasion to disturb the peace of Europe. For this reason it becomes absolutely necessary that he be restrained in his physical freedom, to whatever extent may be necessary for securing that first and paramount object. The island of St. Helena has been chosen for his future residence. Its climate is healthful, and its geographic situation is such that he can be treated with more indulgence there than would be possible elsewhere, in view of the indispensable precautions that would have to be taken to restrain him. General Buonaparte will be permitted to choose, from among those persons who have accompanied him to England—with the exceptions of Generals Savary and Lallemand—three officers, who together with his surgeon will have permission to accompany him to St. Helena but may not leave the island without the sanction of the British government.[13]

When the British government's message was translated into French by Lord Keith and by General Bertrand, Napoleon's Grand Marshal of the Palace, and read to Napoleon, he was filled with terrible narcissistic rage. Acting as if he were still Emperor of the French, quivering with fury, his teeth clenched, his brow knit, his face contorted with fury, Napoleon launched into a tirade against the "perfidious" British. As he had done on the ride back home to Paris from Russia in late 1812, the unhappy Napoleon compared himself to the medieval Mongol ruler Tamerlane, whom legend had placed in an iron cage:

> To St. Helena! The very thought of it horrifies me! To be confined for life on a tropical island at an immense distance from any continent, deprived of all communication with the world and all it holds dear to me! . . . It's worse than Tamerlane's cage of iron! I'd rather

be handed over to the Bourbons! And among other insults—*but it's only a trifle, a very secondary thing*—they call me "general."[14]

In fact, this "trifle" was a deep narcissistic injury to Napoleon: he, the Emperor of the French, the Conqueror of Europe, a mere general! His grandiose yet shaky self-esteem, which he had struggled to maintain all his life in the face of countless early rejections, defeats, humiliations and failures, was mortally wounded. Napoleon once again thought of killing himself. However, "with astounding self-control," Napoleon calmed down and asked his valet Louis-Joseph-Narcisse Marchand, who would accompany him to his exile, to read him out from the biographies of great men.[15] Five days later, on August 5, 1815, when the HMS *Northumberland* arrived in Plymouth harbor and rendezvoused with the HMS *Bellerophon* to carry Napoleon to Saint Helena, his "astounding" ego strength allowed him to resign himself to his cruel fate, which he could no longer change, and use his leisure to write his memoirs. [16]

During his five years on Saint Helena (1815–1821), Napoleon's physical condition and appearance quickly deteriorated. Saint Helena abounded with tropical and other diseases. Napoleon's self-destructiveness never ceased. He neglected his health and overate. He was obese; his immune system became run down; he caught diseases quickly. In 1816, Napoleon apparently caught rheumatic fever or osteoarthritis. He suffered from crippling pain, fever and dizzy spells. Amoebic dysentery was endemic on Saint Helena, and Napoleon caught it in 1817. Napoleon's suffering grew. He felt martyred, comparing himself to Jesus Christ.

Paranoid conspiracy theorists cannot give up their absurd belief that Napoleon was poisoned to death. They cite "scholars" who thought that Napoleon was slowly murdered by arsenic poisoning at the hands of Count Charles-François-Tristan de Montholon—one of Napoleon's most devoted servants who accompanied him to the miseries of Saint Helena—under the secret orders of the French Bourbons. These "scholars" keep propounding the arsenic-poisoning theory.[17] Some of the world's most prominent medical scholars, however, think that there were no obvious motives for such a "murder," nor any proof that Napoleon ever had symptoms of arsenic poisoning.[18]

The key argument of the conspiracy theorists who believe that Napoleon died of arsenic poisoning rather than cancer is that Napoleon died fat and even "obese"[19] whereas cancer is a wasting disease that emaciates the body. Another "proof" is the high quantity of arsenic in hairs purported to be Napoleon's. The erroneous notion that Napoleon died fat, however, comes from an autopsy by an unreliable British naval surgeon, Walter Henry, which said, "The whole surface of the body was deeply covered in fat. Over the sternum where generally the bone is very superficial the fat was upwards of an inch deep, and an inch and a half or two inches on the abdomen."[20] In fact, as at least two British biographers have shown, Henry was highly unreliable. [21]

Even if it were true that there was much fat on Napoleon's sternum at his death, that fat does not mean that Napoleon was overweight. In fact, he was thin and emaciated. Napoleon's Corsican physician, Francesco Antommarchi, who arrived in Saint Helena in 1819, two years before Napoleon's death, recalled that Napoleon had become extremely thin: "The Emperor had grown considerably thinner since my arrival at Saint Helena; his bulk was not one fourth of what it had been."[22] It is hard to believe that Antommarchi would have written this if it had been untrue. As two of Napoleon's best medical scholars have put it, "The bright star of the truth has always been clouded by violent passions and prejudices both political and partisan regarding the death of Napoleon."[23]

In 1818 Napoleon lost his two British naval physicians, Barry Edward O'Meara and John Stokoe, both of whom had been sympathetic and helpful to him, when they left the inhospitable isle of Saint Helena. In 1819 two Corsican Roman Catholic priests, one old, the other young, arrived in Saint Helena "to administer to Napoleon's soul" as his chaplains. One was the sixty-seven-year-old abbot Antonio Buonavita, who had been Napoleon's mother's chaplain on the Isle of Elba and had suffered a stroke that left him aphasic. The other priest was the thirty-year-old abbot Angelo Vignali, whom Raoul Brice called "a young peasant of no education who could afford the prisoner no spiritual succor whatever"[24] and André Castelot "an ignorant priest sent to St. Helena by Madame Mère and [her half-brother Joseph Cardinal] Fesch."[25]

As Buonavita was ill, Letizia had asked Fesch to recruit a younger priest to assist him. The young Vignali had left Corsica for Rome to complete his religious training and had been recruited by the cardinal. The older priest served as Napoleon's titular chaplain until his departure from Saint Helena in mid-March 1821, less than two months before Napoleon's death, leaving the ignorant Father Vignali to administer Napoleon's last rites and bury him.

In his last year of life, when he was quite ill with stomach cancer—the disease that had killed his father—Napoleon wrote several last wills and testaments. On April 15, 1821, three weeks before his death, he willed his earthly belongings to his son, the King of Rome, whom he had already lost, and whom he hoped would continue his great deeds:

> My arms; to wit, the sword that I wore at Austerlitz, my dagger, my glaive, my hunting knife, and my two braces of pistols from Versailles. My golden dressing case that I used on the mornings of Ulm, Austerlitz, Jena, Eylau, Friedland, Lobau, La Moskowa, and Montmirail, they are to be given to my son when he is sixteen years old . . . My field glass, the French one, my orders, my camp beds, my uniforms, the great necklace of the Legion of Honor, my spurs, my Consul's glaive, the gold chain of the Order of the Golden Fleece, the three silver brandy flasks carried by my chasseurs in the field, the "alarm clock" belonging to Frederick the Great that I took at Potsdam, Sobieski's saber, they are to be given to my son when he is sixteen years old . . . Four boxes found on the table of Louis XVIII in the Tuileries on March 20, 1815, they are to be given to my son when he is sixteen years old.[26]

Napoleon himself had lost his own father when he was not quite sixteen years old. Now he was dying and his son was only ten years old. Did Napoleon not know, or was he unconsciously denying, that the Austrians would not allow his son to receive all these relics?

Until his very last days, Napoleon's ambivalent feelings about his will kept vacillating. On the night of April 24–25, 1821—ten days before he died—he dictated a "secret codicil" to his will. In that codicil he rewarded all his friends, going all the way back to his childhood, and offered justifications for the controversial actions of his career. In true Corsican fashion, he left one hundred thousand francs to a French nobleman who had tried to murder the Duke of Wellington during the English occupation of Paris.[27] Raoul Brice pointed out that in that "secret" codicil Napoleon had sought reunion with his idealized Corsica by asking to be buried there with his ancestors.[28] Seventeen years after the fact, Napoleon still felt guilty about his execution of the Duke of Enghien. He made his aides add the following lines to his will:

"I had the Duc d'Enghien arrested and tried because it was necessary for the security, the interest, and the honor of the French people at a time when the Comte d'Artois [brother of Louis XVI and Louis XVIII and the future King Charles X], as he himself acknowledged, had sixty assassins in his pay in Paris [planning to murder me]. Under similar circumstances, I would still do the same thing."[29]

In his will, Napoleon also left very generous sums of money and large properties to many of the people who had been kind to him. For example, he left the "ignorant" thirty-two-year-old Corsican priest Angelo Vignali, his last chaplain, one hundred thousand francs, writing, "I desire that he build his house near Ponte Nuovo di Rostino." Napoleon also specified the religious ceremony that Father Vignali was to observe at his funeral: "When I am dead, you will place the altar at my head and you will continue to celebrate the mass before all the usual ceremonies. You will not stop before I am in the earth." After Napoleon's death, Father Vignali did indeed go back to Corsica and built his house at Ponte Nuovo di Rostino, only to be killed in a local vendetta a few years later.[30]

On the night of April 28, 1821 the dying Napoleon summoned his valet, Louis-Joseph-Narcisse Marchand, to take down a second and final codicil to his will. Marchand could find no paper in the humble room, so he picked up a playing card and wrote the codicil on it. In this final codicil, Napoleon bequeathed to his only legitimate son, the King of Rome, the Casa Bonaparte at Ajaccio, with its outbuildings, the two houses near Les Salines, with their gardens, and all his possessions in the territory of Ajaccio, capable of providing his son with an annual income of fifty thousand livres. Napoleon had Marchand make copies of his will and its two codicils and deliver them to his Corsican chaplain, Father Angelo Vignali, "under the seal of confession."[31] Tragically, however, Napoleon no longer owned all this property.[32] Raoul Brice thought that by that time Napoleon's "thought flickered in the socket" and that "his imagination had restored [this property] to him and added to it in the supreme mirage—Corsica."[33] This "supreme mirage" was the idealized image of his early mother which had unconsciously been displaced from France back to Corsica.

By now the unhappy Napoleon, dying of stomach cancer, like his father before him, had only one week more left to live. On May 2, 1821, Napoleon unconsciously regressed to his infancy, becoming "a docile, gentle child."[34] Indeed, in these last days before his death on May 5, 1821, the England Napoleon so hated, the split-off and denigrated Bad Mother that he sought to destroy most of his life, had once again become the admired, idealized Good Mother of his youth. The senior British military physician on Saint Helena, Archibald Arnott, examined him and fed him some wine with sugar. After each swallow, the dying Napoleon reportedly said—in English—"Good. Very good."[35] After life's fitful fever, he would sleep well.

Acknowledgments

I wish to express my gratitude to the late Dorothy Carrington, whose *Napoleon and His Parents* is a masterpiece of wise scholarship, and who gave me invaluable insights in her personal communications; to the late Harold T. Parker, whose studies of Napoleon's personality preceded my own work, and who graciously and meticulously read my manuscript at an early stage of its development and gave me his most valuable comments and suggestions; to Vamık D. Volkan, my friend, colleague, mentor, and editor, for the inspiration, encouragement, and guidance he has given me over the past twenty-two years; to his son, Kurt Volkan, my publisher; to my colleague Paul Elovitz, who introduced me to Leon Pierce Clark's little-known *Napoleon Self-Destroyed*; to Jean Tulard, whose *Dictionnaire Napoléon* and other scholarly works on Napoleon are indispensable to any serious scholar; to Owen Connelly, whose works on Joseph Bonaparte and on Napoleon's military campaigns were most helpful and who clarified several important points for me; to Dominique Bourel, the former director of the *Centre de recherche français de Jérusalem*, who provided me with a French republican calendar and drew my attention to several recent works on Napoleon; to my old friend, mentor, and teacher Claude Vigée, who has always supported me; to Catherine Grandguillotte of the *Bibliothèque nationale de France* and to Sylvie Clair of the *Archives municipales de la Ville de Marseille* for helping me find Désirée Clary's baptismal act; and, last but not least, to Jean-François Fiévet, the former director of the *Alliance Française de Jérusalem*, who invited me to speak on this study at an early stage in my work and encouraged me in this daunting endeavor.

Notes

Introduction

1. Voltaire 1767, Ch. 10.

2. Kurosawa 1952.

3. It is generally believed that there have been more books published on Napoleon than any other historical character except Jesus Christ and Alexander the Great. Estimates range from fifty thousand to two hundred thousand works.

4. Thiry, 1935–1948.

5. Masson 1897–1919, vol. 12, préface.

6. Brice 1937, 79; Tomiche-Dagher 1952, p. 323; Richardson 1972, p. 39.

7. Jones 1953–57, vol. 3, p. 191.

8. McLynn 1997, pp. 11–12, quoting Brill 1921, 1949. McLynn thought this "not so very strange when we consider the backward and primitive nature of eighteenth-century Corsican life."

9. Milton 1671, Book IV, line 220–221.

10. Brice 1937, p. 81.

11. Ibid., p. 93.

12. Clark 1929, p. xviii.

13. Previous generations were much less obsessive than we are about consistency and accuracy in name spelling. The spelling of surnames in eighteen-century Corsica was far from standardized. This was true of Christian names as well. For example, the middle name of Napoleon's mother, Maria Letizia Ramolino Bonaparte, was also spelled Laetizia or Laetitia. The name Paravisino was also given as Paravisini, Paravicini, Paraviccini, Paravicino, Pallavicino, and Pallavicini. Napoleon's first name was written at various times as Nabulio, Nabulion, Nabulione, Napulione, Napolione, Napoleone, and Napoléon, while his last name was "indistinctly" spelled as Buonaparte, Bonaparte, de Bonaparte, de' Buonaparte, and della Buonaparte. Moreover, many noblemen and aristocrats were executed during the bloody French Revolution, especially during the Terror of 1793–94. It was dangerous to bear a noble name in France. To conceal their

nobility and to "join the people," noble political and military leaders changed their family names, incorporating the noble-sounding de, du, de la, or des into their last names: des Mazis became Desmazis, des Aix became Desaix, la Fayette became Lafayette, du Gommier became Dugommier, d'Avoust became Davoust and, later, Davout, du Teil became Duteil, and la Grange became Lagrange. After Emperor Napoleon created his *noblesse d'Empire* (imperial nobility) in 1808, some noblemen reverted to their old names. As a result, during the Napoleonic era, not only were many names spelled in various different ways, but many names had two or more different forms. The reader would do well to assume an eighteenth-century attitude toward name spelling and other matters in this study (cf. Las Cases 1823, entry of August 16–21 1815; Carrington, 1988, p. xi).

Chapter 1

1. Carrington 1994–1998.
2. Carrington 1988, pp. 71–72, 232, n.16, based on Colonna de Cesari Rocca 1890–92.
3. Tulard 1989, pp. 517–520, quoting Boswell 1768.
4. Defranceschi 1991, p. 56.
5. Carrington 1988, pp. 67–70; Tulard 1989, p. 519.
6. Carrington 1988, pp. 49, 85.
7. Bainville 1933, p. 5; Carrington 1988, pp. 38–39, 68–69; Tulard 1989, p. 520; McLynn 1997, p. 10.
8. Anonymous 1889, pp. 52–53, 75–83; Las Cases 1823, entry of August 16–21, 1815; Carrington 1988, p. 93.
9. Tulard 1989, p. 522.
10. Carrington 1988, pp. 67–68.

Chapter 2

1. Cf. Richardson 1972, p. 72, p. 230, n. 4.
2. Las Cases 1823, entry of August 16–21, 1815; Lumbroso 1933; Richardson 1972, pp. 72, 230, n. 4.
3. Cronin 1971, p. 15.
4. Godechot 1969, p. 81; Cronin 1971, p. 15; Carrington 1988, pp. 16–17.
5. Carrington 1994–1998.
6. Brice 1937, p. 177.
7. Curiously enough, the baptismal records for the years 1741–1760, which include Carlo's and his wife Letizia's, are missing from the Ajaccio municipal register, as are the burial records for 1739–1759. See Carrington 1988, p. 214, n. 12.
8. Valynseele 1954, pp. 26–27; Carrington 1988, p. 16, pp. 213–214, n. 11.

9. Léonce de Brotonne thought that Carlo's first child, who was born and died in 1765, had been a boy named Napoleone (Brotonnne 1893, p. 13). This idea was picked up by numerous biographers. In fact, Carlo's first child had been a daughter, who was born and died in 1765, and was probably named Maria Anna or Marianna (Carrington 1988, p. 31, p. 217, n.37). Another daughter of the same name was born and died in 1771. A third daughter named Maria Anna (Marianna, Marianne, or Marie-Anne) was born in 1777 and survived. She later changed her name to Elisa, short for Elisabeth, perhaps to escape the fate of her dead namesake sisters. To Carlo, each of these daughters was a "replacement child" for her dead predecessors (Anisfeld & Richards 2000). He treated his daughters as "linking objects" to his grandmother (Volkan 1981); cf. Valynseele 1954; Tulard 1989, p. 245; McLynn 1997, pp. 4, 13.

10. The Corsicans compared Geltruda Buonaparte to the fierce "Saracen" princess Clorinda in the epic poem *La Gerusalemme liberata* by the "divine" but emotionally troubled sixteenth-century Italian poet Torquato Tasso (1544–95), who occasionally suffered from psychotic episodes. In that poem Clorinda disguises herself as a male warrior, fights her lover, the crusader Prince Tancredi, who thinks she is a man, and is killed by him. In 1624 the great composer Claudio Monteverdi (1567–1643) wrote a beautiful secular oratorio, *Il Combattimento di Tancredi and Clorinda*, based on Tasso's poem. This poem of Crusader times was loved by the Corsican freedom fighters, who sang many cantos from it, and by Carlo's eldest son, Joseph (Cronin 1971, pp. 33, 261; Carrington 1988, pp. 15, 32, 33, 37, 43, 211, n. 5; Tulard 1989, p. 244). Geltruda's difficult character—or personality disorder—gives us a clue to Carlo's family background. Serious personality disorders usually do not develop in normal, happy families (Akhtar 1992).

11. Carlo Maria di Buonaparte 1780; Carrington 1988, pp. 14, 202–203; Carrington 2002.

12. Carrington 1988, p. 14.

13. Ibid., pp. 16–17. Many scholars were fooled by the Ramolinos's fake documents (Larrey 1892, Tschudi 1900, Shaw 1928, Peretti 1932, Duhourçau 1933, Wilson 1933; Augustin-Thierry 1939, Arrighi de Casanova 1954, Stirling 1961; Decaux 1962, Martineau 1978, Le Nabour 2003). One even believed that "the Ramolinos had been the ruling clan in Lombardy [*sic*] in the fourteenth century and had emigrated to Corsica in the fifteenth" (Richardson 1972, p. 202).

14. Volkan 1981.

15. Carrington 1988, p. 214, n. 12.

16. After Letizia's father died in 1755, her bereaved mother, the Roman Catholic widow Angela Maria Pietrasanta Ramolino, wore black for two years before marrying a young Protestant Swiss-German naval captain serving in the French forces in Ajaccio, Franz or François Fesch, the son of a Basel banker. Fesch must have loved Angela Maria very much, for he gave up his religion, his fortune, and his officer's commission to marry her. Fesch's father disinherited him when

he converted to Catholicism, and the young man resigned from the French army to avoid strife with his wife's family (Carrington 1988, p. 58).

17. Laure-Adélaide-Constance Saint-Martin Permon Junot, duchesse d'Abrantès (1784–1838), one of Letizia's ladies-in-waiting when she was Madame, Mère de l'Empereur, flatteringly described the young Letizia as "ravishing, graceful, charming, one of the prettiest girls in Corsica" (Junot 1823, vol. 1, t. 2, p. 76, my translation from the French). The comte de Las Cases, Napoleon's memorialist, called Letizia "the most agreeable and beautiful woman in town, one of the most beautiful women of her time, her beauty was celebrated in the island" (Las Cases 1823, entry of August 16–21 1815, my translation from the French). However, Laure Junot's memoirs are unreliable. The French writer Théophile Gautier (1811–1872) called her *la duchesse d'Abracadabrantès* and the prominent Napoleon scholar Jean Tulard urged scholars to use her memoirs with caution (Tulard 1971; Tulard 1989, pp. 25–27). Carrington called Laure Junot's memoirs "lively fictitious accounts of blood relationship with Napoleon and his intimacy with her family . . . but her descriptions of Letizia . . . ring true" (Carrington 1988, p. 279). In any event, neither Laure Junot not Las Cases knew Letizia when she was young. Their flattering observations were made when she was old. Clark believed that "Letizia preserved her good looks and youthful appearance until old age," yet he also thought that Napoleon's early portraits were "replicas in miniature of Letitia's stern, lean and dark countenance" (Clark 1929, pp. 3–4, 226; cf. Carrington 1988, pp. 17–18, 66–67).

18. McLynn 1997, pp. 3–4

19. Most of Letizia's biographers described her as simple, frugal, austere, taciturn, cold and devout (Larrey 1892, Tschudi 1900, Shaw 1928, Peretti 1932, Duhourçau 1933, Wilson 1933; Augustin-Thierry 1939, Arrighi de Casanova 1954, Stirling 1961; Decaux 1962, Martineau 1978, Le Nabour 2003). One of them thought that Letizia was pathologically stingy: "Letizia was above all of a sordid avarice of which she never managed to rid herself—she would still be so when opulence had come." She told Napoleon, "You will be poor, but it is better to have a pretty living room, handsome clothes, a pretty horse and appear outside —and then eat bread at home" (Castelot 1967, p. 24, my translation from the French). She reproached her son sternly for the "enormity" of demanding money from his father (Richardson 1972, p. 66). Napoleon rationalized his mother's anal-retentive stinginess as far-sighted economic wisdom: "She gave me pride and preached reason to me. She was much too parsimonious, it was ridiculous; I went as far as to offer her considerable sums each month if she wanted to distribute them. She accepted—provided, she said, that she could keep them. At bottom, all this was but an excess of foresightedness on her part; her greatest fear was to find herself one day without anything. She had known want; and these terrible moments never left her thoughts" (Castelot 1967, p. 24, my translation from the French).

20. On the many unconscious meanings of money as love, blood, mother's milk, and even feces see Bergler 1959; Borneman 1976; Faber 1981, pp. 104–124

21. Napoleon reportedly told his valet on St. Helena that when he was a seventeen-year-old officer, his mother had spanked him for imitating her mother's rheumatic gai (Marchand 1952–55, vol. 1, p. 67). Many authors have repeated the story. (Antommarchi 1825, vol. 1, p. 276; Bertrand 1949–59, vol. 2, p. 137; Richardson 1972, p. 65). Carrington, however, demonstrated that this incident could only have happened when Napoleon was a child. (Carrington 1988, pp. 58–59, pp. 227–228, n. 28).

22. Some scholars believed that Carlo was planning to betray and abandon his wife. Carrington thought that Carlo had always intended to return to Letizia: "In the eyes of Corsican society [Carlo Maria Buonaparte] was married; he could only hope to recover his freedom by going abroad, for good, leaving the two families [the Bonapartes and the Ramolinos] to fight over the dowry. Was this what he planned when he went to Rome, having got Letizia with child? Personally I find this hard to believe: had he been capable of so Machiavellian a scheme, he surely would have carried it through. At all events [Carlo's uncle] Luciano must have sponsored the journey, for he held the purse-strings. To me, Carlo's behaviour seems rather that of a wilful, capricious young man, whose education at the Jesuits' college in Ajaccio had left him with the Voltairian scorn of the Church that became apparent in his later years" (Carrington 1988, pp. 22–23).

23. Brotonne 1893, p. 13.

24. Valynseele 1954; Carrington 1988, p. 31, pp. 217–218, n. 37; Tulard 1989, p. 245; McLynn 1997, p. 13.

25. Carrington 1988, pp. 30–31, pp. 217–218, n. 37; cf. Carlo Maria di Buonaparte 1780 1977, 2002; Tulard 1989, p. 245; McLynn 1997, p. 13.

26. Carrington 1988, p. 28.

27. Carlo Maria di Buonaparte 1766; Carrington 1988, pp. 28–29; Carrington 2002, p. 30. Carrington wryly observed that "Carlo never lost sight of his upper-class origin" (Carrington 1988, p. 30).

28. Carrington 1988, pp. 35–36; Carrington 2002, pp. 21–44.

29. Carrington 1988, pp. 31–32.

30. The eight surviving children were Giuseppe (Joseph 1768–1844), Napoleone (Napoléon 1769 1821), Luciano (Lucien 1775–1840), Maria Anna (Marianne 1777–1820), who later changed her name to Elisa; Luigi (Louis 1778–1846), Maria Paola (Marie-Paule or Pauline 1780–1825), Maria Annunziata Carolina (Marie-Annonciade-Caroline 1782–1839), and Geronimo (Jérôme 1784–1860). Thanks to Emperor Napoleon, all of them became kings, queens, or princes (Valynseele 1954; Carrington 1988, p. 31; Tulard 1989, p. 245).

31. Frugier 1985, p. 31, my translation from the French; Carrington 1988, pp. 31–32; Tulard 1989, p. 259.

32. Carrington 1988, pp. 42–44; Carrington 1997, p. 42

33. Dorothy Carrington first discovered this document in 1969 at a Napoleon exhibition in Paris, and she was deeply shocked. "But how could it be that this austere, heroic woman, mother of Joseph and already six months pregnant with

Napoleon, should indulge in clothes at such a time? . . . The letter was altogether contrary to the image of Letizia handed down by historians. But was that image correct?" (Carrington 1997, p. 42). Carrington confessed that this document changed her life, making her into a Napoleon scholar. In fact, Letizia did not write this letter herself. Carlo wrote his wife's letter in his own hand, Letizia's handwriting being "barely legible" (Carrington 1988, pp. 43–44). Under stress, Letizia regressed to the state of a "spoilt" child. The pregnant Letizia, who had lost two infant daughters and had to take care of a year-old baby son, felt abandoned and unloved. She sought compensation for her "anxieties and privations" by buying "smart clothes."

34. Carrington 1988, pp. 49–50.

35. Frugier 1985, pp. 31–32.

Chapter 3

1. Carrington 1988, p. 12, p. 210, n.21; Larrey 1892, vol. 2, p. 425; Connelly 1968, p. 6; McLynn 1997, p. 6.

2. Antommarchi 1825, vol. 1, pp. 251, 275; Héreau 1829, pp. 27–28; Lee 1834, pp. 5–6; Carrington 1988, pp. 12, 46; p. 210, n. 21.

3. Brice 1937, pp. 106, 141; cf. Larrey 1892; Wilson 1933, p. 4; Connelly 1968, p. xiii; Parker 1971–72, pp. 7–8.

4. Las Cases 1823, entry of August 8 1816; Brice 1937, pp. 106–107; Parker 1971–72, pp. 7–8; Carrington 1988, pp. 56–57.

5. "I was spoiled, one must admit," Napoleon told his memorialist. "I have always commanded; from my entry into life, I found myself endowed with power, and circumstances and my strength were such that as soon as I had command, I no longer recognized masters nor laws " (Las Cases 1823, entry of October 31 1816, my translation from the French; cf. Clark 1929, p. 150; Herold 1955, p. 278).

6. Carrington 1988, p. 57; Connelly 1968, p. 6; Brice 1937, pp. 106–107.

7. Connelly 1968, p. 6; Parker 1971–72, p. 8; Carrington 1988, p. 57.

8. When Napoleon became Empereur des François, he gave Camilla Ilari much money and real estate. Over his mother's objections, Napoleon forced his mother's cousin and his brother-in-law, Andrea Ramolino, to give up his Ajaccio house to Camilla in exchange for the Casa Bonaparte (Antommarchi 1825, vol. 1, p. 349; Larrey 1892, vol. 1, pp. 416–417; Carrington 1988, pp. 56–57).

9. Grief and mourning are painful, but they are essential for liberation from the past and for emotional growth (Pollock 1989; Volkan & Zintl 1993). Unable to grieve and mourn her losses, Letizia kept bearing new children to replace those she had lost. Of the thirteen children she bore, five died in infancy and eight survived. Were all of these children wanted? Parker believed that Joseph was very much wanted, that Letizia nursed him, that he slept in Carlo and Letizia's room and that he was put out of his parents' room at the age of three and a half years,

when his sister Maria Anna was born. Napoleon was quite another story (Parker 1971–72; Tulard 1989, p. 259).

10. Masson 1969, pp. 38–39; Marchand 1952–55, vol. 1, p. 67; Richardson 1972, p. 65; Carrington 1988, p. 92.

11. Larrey 1892; Bartel 1954, p. 33.

12. Carrington 1988, p. 234, n. 20.

13. Ibid., p. 75

14. Castelot 1967, p. 25; Versini 1977, pp. 193–195; Carrington 1988, pp. 63, 73, p. 232, n. 18.

15. Connelly 1968, p. xiii; Parker 1971–1972, p. 7; Frugier 1985, p. 33; Carrington 1988, p. 56. Joseph was the chief object of Napoleon's rage—and love—not only in his childhood but also in his adulthood, even when he was king of Spain.

16. Frugier 1985, p. 33.

17. Larrey 1892; Antommarchi 1825, vol. 1, p. 180; Connelly 1968, p. 7; Richardson 1972, p. 165; Tulard 1989, p. 245.

18. Carrington 1988, p. 90.

19. Ibid.

20. Connelly 1968, p. 8.

21. Joseph Bonaparte 1853–1854, cited in Connelly 1968, p. 8; Carrington 1988, pp. 100–101.

22. Flori 1975; Carrington 1988, pp. 85–86.

23. When they grew up, Lucien helped Napoleon gain power in France, but later they quarreled bitterly, and a furious Emperor Napoleon banished his younger brother Lucien from France. Richardson thought that the boy Napoleon hated Lucien for displacing him in their mother's affections: "Displacement by a younger child often leads children to be aggressive, disobedient and domineering, and to adopt unconscious devices to regain the affection of their parents of which they feel deprived. 'Napoleone' was displaced as the baby of the family by Lucciano [*sic*], later to be called Lucien, at the rather awkward age of six—too old to accept the new arrival naturally, and too young to be encouraged to take it philosophically. It could have been another stimulus to his aggressiveness" (Richardson 1972, p. 64).

24. Clark 1929, p. 6; cf. Gallo 1997, vol. 1, p. 24.

25. Montbas 1952, pp. 329–330; Roux 1984, pp. 201–206. One biographer thought it "highly likely" that Louis Bonaparte was Marbeuf's son: "The calendar favours Marbeuf as father far more than Carlo; additionally Louis was quite unlike his siblings in looks, character and temperament, and shared Marbeuf's brusque irascibility" (McLynn 1997, p. 10).

26. Carrington 1988, pp. 96–97, 102–103, 111–121.

27. Ibid., p. 102

28. The psychoanalyst Ludwig Jekels (1867–1954) thought that Napoleon's conversion from fiery Corsican nationalist to fervent French republican was his

unconscious resolution of an oedipal conflict in which Marbeuf played a pivotal paternal part (Jekels 1914, 1952).

29. Bertrand 1949–1959, vol. 3, p. 69.

30. Carrington 1988, p. 107.

Chapter 4

1. Carrington 1988, p. 122.

2. Idealized by Napoleon from a distance, Paoli was a "great father figure" to the young boy. Some of the early scholars of Napoleon's childhood and youth can no longer be relied upon. Among them were Baron François-Gilbert Coston, a nineteenth-century scholar of Napoleon's early life whose work "can be faulted today, but the seriousness of this work is not in question," and General Henri-François-Théodore Iung, whom Carrington considered "incautious, inexperienced and untrustworthy." Their work, like that of Masson, Chuquet, and Marcaggi, was "flawed to some degree by partiality, preconceptions, uncritical use of sources and insufficient study of archival material" (See Coston 1840, Iung 1880–81 1882–83; Carrington 1988, pp. 34, 219, 278, 281–282). Coston and Iung thought that the boy Napoleon was lonely and unhappy at Autun. Coston notes that even at school in Autun, Napoleon was morose and absorbed, spoke to nobody, and took solitary walks. The psychoanalyst Ludwig Jekels thought that Napoleon had developed a "neurosis" at Autun due to the "immense burden [that] weighed upon his soul," his "mother fixation" and his ambivalence about his father (Jekels 1952, pp. 4, 53–54). Carrington thought that "the shock of being transplanted to France must have crystallized diffuse emotions generated by family fireside talk: tales of the Father of the Nation and the patriots' heroic resistance, aided by the gallant deeds of the Bonaparte" (Carrington 1988, p. 123). Jekels wrote that Jung [sic] gave the following portrait of him at this time: "What a child! A savage, ruled solely by instinct. With his pallid complexion, bristling hair, small size, piercing gaze, and 'sickly' appearance." After which he adds: "Solitary he was, solitary he is, solitary he will remain" (Jekels 1952, p. 54).

3. Brice 1937, p. 4.

4. Clark 1929, p. 7.

5. Ibid.; Carrington 1988, pp. 18, 112, 113; Gallo 1997, vol. 1, p. 24.

6. Carrington 1988, pp. xxii, 98, 119, pp. 238–239, n. 14, p. 244, n. 19.

7. Carrington 1988, p. 123; cf. Jekels 1952, p. 37; Castelot 1967, p. 29, n. 1; Carrington 1988, pp. 144–145.

8. Jekels 1952, p. 37 (this was an error: Joseph Cardinal Fesch was Napoleon's step-uncle, not his half-brother).

9. Carrington 1988, p. 144. The letter of March 28, 1779, from the French war minister, the prince de Montbarey, to Carlo de Buonaparte had said, "the King has consented to place your son, Napoleone de Buonaparte, as a student in one of His

military schools. His Majesty has just decreed that he should be admitted to the school at Brienne" (Castelot 1971, p. 5; McLynn 1997, p. 16).

10. Richardson 1972, p. 165.

11. Ibid., p. 166

12. Carrington 1988, p. 143. Chuquet thought that Napoleon "was very homesick . . . heartsick for his homeland. . . . it pained him to think that not for six years, at least, would he again see his dear Corsica, so deeply graven on his heart." He gave his name as Napoleone; his schoolmates derided him as *la paille au nez* (Straw in the Nose). Napoleon became the laughing-stock of his fellow pupils, who derided him and his native land. "His very self-assurance and self-assertiveness may have provoked the older French boys to torment him." Napoleon felt isolated, regarding the whole world as his enemy (Chuquet 1897–99, quoted in Jekels 1952, p. 4; cf. Parker 1971–72, p. 11).

13. Pauline had a reputation for sexual promiscuity and was called *la paganetta* (the little pagan woman). One of her lovers claimed that Pauline had told him that she had twice committed incest with Napoleon (Castelot 1971, p. 201). Whether this was the truth, the incestuous fantasy of a disturbed woman or the vengeful calumny of a jilted lover is hard to say. Pauline's affair with this lover was brief, as were her other *coups de foudre*. She fell in love as quickly as she fell out of it, her idealizations followed by disillusionment. The rumors of Pauline's incestuous relationship with Napoleon spread outside France. Richardson indignantly rejected "the various allegations of sexual perversions which were made against Napoleon, just as I reject the allegations, much more widely repeated and believed, that he committed incest with his three sisters and with his step-daughter" (Richardson 1972, pp. 46, 178). Nonetheless, Napoleon's tormented relationships with his sisters were *emotionally* fusional and incestuous (Tulard 1989, p. 1314).

14. Marguerite was a substitute mother for Napoleon. Many years later, in 1805, when Napoleon was Empereur des François, he stopped at Brienne on his way to Milan to assume the crown of Italy, and went to see the old la mère Marguerite, seeking love, acceptance, food, and adoration from her. La mère Marguerite satisfied his needs, and the grateful Napoleon sent her a purse full of gold napoléons (Castelot 1971, pp. 254–255).

15. Carrington thought that this was a reference to the homosexual "nymphs" at the school "for no other form of dissipation was possible" (Carrington 1988, p. 154).

16. Castelot 1967, p. 36; Richardson 1972, p. 168. Carrington 1988, p. 154, p. 253, n. 24.

17. Cronin 1971, p. 31

18. Cronin, Ibid.

19. Carrington 1988, p. 146. During the French Revolution Berton was reduced to penury. Napoleon rescued him by making him an educational administrator, only to see him fail, lose his job, and become psychotic (Carrington, Ibid.; Cronin 1971, p. 31, Tulard 1989, p. 207; Gallo 1997, vol. 1, pp. 27–28).

20. Letizia told Napoleon's interior minister, Jean-Antoine-Claude Chaptal de Chanteloup (1756–1832), that Father Patrault had told her that he had nothing left to teach her son, and that she should remove Napoleon from Brienne. Letizia may have been unconsciously projecting her own grandiose self upon her son (Bourrienne 1830; Bourrienne 1885, vol. 1, p. 4; Chaptal de Chanteloup 1893, pp. 175–176; Carrington 1988, pp. 138, 141).

21. Bainville 1933, p. 10.

22. On the psychology of shame and humiliation see Wurmser 1981, Nathanson 1987, and Steinberg 1996.

23. The term "injustice collector" for the emotional (rather than sexual) masochist was coined by the psychoanalyst Edmund Bergler (Bergler & Meerloo 1963).

24. Hennet 1889; Vaublanc 1838, vol. 1, pp. 31–32.

25. Carrington 1988, p. 145.

26. Las Cases 1851, vol. 1, p. 92; Petit 1839, p. 23; Jekels 1952, p. 54; Cronin 1971, p. 33; Carrington 1988, p. 145; Gallo 1997, vol. 1, pp. 30–31.

27. In Ludwig Jekels's words, "Condemned one day to a punishment he must have keenly resented—that of eating his dinner, kneeling, in sack-cloth, at the refectory door—he evaded the ordeal, when the moment came, by a fit of vomiting and violent hysterics" (Jekels 1952, p. 54). Another psychoanalyst, Pierce Clark, thought that "the wounding of [Napoleon's] narcistic self-respect due to his failure to pass certain examinations manifests itself in an acute attack of nausea. As soon as he is reassured of a good standing in his class his nausea at once disappears. Not even his ordinarily astute mind perceives his deep unconscious desire for revenge against his masters and against his conscious mind, though he often falls ill at the threat of injury to his pride and self-respect" (Clark 1929, p. 12).

28. Cronin 1971, p. 36.

29. When she grew up, Caroline married General Joachim Murat (1767–1815), whom Napoleon later made king of Naples.

30. Chuquet 1897–99, vol. 1, pp. 113–114, 204, and vol. 2, pp. 25–26; Parker 1971–72, p. 13; Carrington 1988, p. 147.

31. Bourrienne 1885, vol. 1, p. 4.

32. Chaptal de Chanteloup 1893, pp. 175–176. The aging Napoleon told Montholon on Saint Helena that his sickly looks were "the result of overwork. . . . he [had] studied all through the recreation periods and even at night, because he could never bear the idea of not being top of his class" (Montholon 1847–49, vol. 2, p. 17). Carrington thought that "Napoleon was boasting. He was not good at all subjects, only at history and geography and, above all, mathematics" (Carrington 1988, p. 141). In fact, when Napoleon told Montholon this story, he had been deposed as Empereur des François, a profound injury to his narcissism. He may have tried to shore up his sagging self-esteem by glorifying his past (Bourrienne 1885, vol. 1, p. 4).

33. Campbell 1869, p. 277; Pichot 1873, p. 131; Carrington 1988, p. 162, p. 256, n. 4.

34. Carrington 1988, p. 137.

35. Bertrand 1949–1959, vol. 2, p. 136.

36. Bainville 1933, p. 135.

37. Cronin 1971, p. 211.

Chapter 5

1. Carrington 1988, p. 165.

2. Young 1910, p. 104; Carrington 1988, p. 142.

3. Count Bragelonne himself was a Marbeuf protégée. Napoleon had hated him and humiliated him in public. Carrington believed that Bragelonne's story was fabricated: "Did Balathier de Bragelonne perhaps revenge himself [for his humiliation by Napoleon] by repeating Corsican gossip? After all, he had been brought up in the entourage of Marbeuf and Madame Varese; he may have known that Marbeuf had dropped her in favour of Letizia" (Carrington 1988, p. 156; cf. D'Oguerau 1822, pp. 19, 30–38; Petit 1839, pp. 32–33; Coston 1840, vol. 1, p. 52; Iung 1880–1881, vol. 1, p. 92; Carrington 1988, p. 142).

4. Carrington 1988, p. 167; cf. Jekels 1952, p. 39.

5. Carrington 1988, pp. 164, 171 185–186.

6. Coston 1840, vol. 1, p. 44; Nasica 1852, p. 72; Iung 1880–81, vol. 1, pp. 105–107; Napoleon Bonaparte 1961, p. 14; Masson 1969, pp. 86–87; Carrington 1988, p. 174, p. 260, n. 27; Gallo 1997, vol. 1, pp. 35–37.

7. Ibid.

8. Ibid.

9. Ibid.

10. Ibid.

11. Carrington admired the teenage Napoleon's "maturity" in his letter to his father of September 1784: "The lucidity, authority and sense of responsibility in the letter of this fifteen year-old schoolboy are once again surprising." Carrington observed that "Napoleon's mind and feelings are still fixed on his homeland." She thought that Napoleon's "detached manner of announcing the news and his carefully laid plans for himself and Joseph hardly suggest that he was hoping for anything from the inspector's visit, in spite of the efforts Carlo had been making on his behalf in Paris" (Carrington 1988, p. 174). In fact, Napoleon had pinned his most ardent hopes on the inspector's visit; his "detached" manner was a mask, an unconscious defense against powerful feelings of violent ambition and fear of failure and disappointment (cf. Gallo 1997, vol. 1, pp. 35–37).

12. Castelot 1967, pp. 46–47; Carrington 1988, p. 175; Gallo 1997, vol. 1, p. 37

13. Napoleon Bonaparte 1969, p. 17; Castelot 1971, p. 10; Cronin 1971, p. 39; Carrington 1988, pp. 175–176, 260, n. 29; Gallo 1997, vol. 1, pp. 37–38.

14. Le Sage 1715–1735.

15. Cronin 1971, p. 40.

16. Cronin 1971, pp. 40–41; cf. Castelot 1967, p. 37; Gallo 1997, vol. 1, p. 42.

17. Vincent Cronin thought that Napoleon had drafted his memo to the war minister because "as he later told a friend, Napoleon quite often felt physical attraction for men; it was because he had personal experience of homosexual urges that he was so eager to see them damped down" (Cronin 1971, p. 41). Cronin did not name that "friend." He thought that Napoleon was "sensing a national malaise" that broke out the following year in the Affair of the Queen's Diamond Necklace and in the painting *The Oath of the Horatii* by Jacques-Louis David (Nanteuil 1985). In fact, Napoleon's reaction to the "nymph" Laugier de Bellecour and his memo to the minister had deep personal roots (Cronin 1971, p. 41). Years later the adult Laugier de Bellecour, still enraged with Napoleon, told a friend that Napoleon had invited him to his room to have sexual intercourse with him; the anonymous classmate, however, refuted this slander. "The author of the 1802 Leipsic pamphlet sets out to refute false stories about [Napoleon] told by Laugier to a friend, especially about [Napoleon] inviting Laugier to visit his room at night. He points out that they were all locked into the dormitories, each in his little cell, with servants watching the corridors all night. He described Napoleon as reserved, lonely and slow to make friends, nicknamed the Spartan, hardly the sort of boy for nightly snuggles with a 'nymph'" (Richardson 1972, pp. 235–236, n. 12).

18. In 1954 the French scholar Paul Bartel published Des Mazis' memoirs. (Bartel 1954). Several other scholars had serious doubts about their reliability. Cronin considered Des Mazis' memoirs "an important source," (Cronin 1971, p. 42) while Carrington called them "unconvincing" (Carrington 1988, p. 282). In one dramatic incident related by Des Mazis, the French aéronaute Jean-Pierre Blanchard, who invented the parachute and was the first man to cross the English Channel by balloon in 1785, was preparing painstakingly to ascend in a hot-air balloon when an impatient and angry Napoleon cut the retaining cords of Blanchard's balloon, which was pierced and collapsed. Napoleon was severely punished (Cronin 1971, p. 453; Carrington 1988, p. 179). It is hard to assess the truth of these memoirs. Carrington thought that "No more is needed to throw discredit on the journal. An incident of this kind did take place, but on 2 March 1784, eight months before Napoleon entered the school. . . . No balloons were sent up during Napoleon's stay at the École Militaire" (Carrington 1988, pp. 179–180).

19. Richardson 1972, pp. 166–169; Carrington 1988, pp. 178–179.

20. Gallo 1997, p. 41, my translation from the French; cf. Brice 1937, p. 8; Bainville 1933, p. 12.

21. Carrington called it "no more than schoolboy ragging" (Carrington 1988, p. 178). In his classic silent film *Napoléon*, Abel Gance, using poetic license, freely transposed this dramatic scene from Paris to Brienne (Gance 1927; Gance 1990).

22. The Aix physician was "the eminent doctor Turnatori" (Carrington 1988, p. 186), perhaps a Corsican. His Montpellier colleagues were Drs. de la Mure, de Sabatier, and Barthez (Gallo 1997, vol. 1, p. 48). None of them could save Carlo.

23. Gallo 1997, vol. 1, p. 44.

24. Years later, on St. Helena, poking fun at his dead father, the aging Napoleon reportedly told his Corsican physician Antommarchi that his father "had no sooner seen the coffin open than he was seized with a passion for priests; there were not enough for him in all Montpellier" (Antommarchi 1825, vol. 1, p. 259; Carrington 1988, p. 187). Napoleon reportedly told General Gaspard Gourgaud on St. Helena that Carlo "ended his life so pious that everyone in Montpellier thought him a saint" (Gourgaud 1889–99, vol. 1, p. 473; Carrington, Ibid.). Was this Napoleon's sarcastic way of getting back at his dead father?

25. The funeral costs were paid by Jean Bimar, the Montpellier coaching service owner, and by Joseph Fesch, Carlo's brother-in-law. (Carrington 1988, p. 189). In 1802 First Consul Napoleon Bonaparte refused the Montpellier city council's proposal to erect a monument to his dead father "on the pretext, which seems heartless, that his father's death had occurred too long ago to be worth commemorating" (Carrington 1988,p. 190). In fact, rather than being "heartless," Napoleon's refusal to erect a monument to his father may have expressed his unconscious oedipal triumph. Fearing First Consul Bonaparte, his brothers Louis and Joseph acted secretly to give their dead father the honor they felt he deserved. In 1803 they had Jean Bimar of Montpellier secretly disinter Carlo Buonaparte's corpse and dispatch it to Louis in a box declared to contain a clock. Louis re-interred his father's remains under a monument in the park of Saint-Leu-la-Forêt, in the Val d'Oise département, where Louis's wife Hortense owned a château. In 1819 Carlo's remains were ejected from their tomb by the new owner of the property, who was none other than the father of the Duc d'Enghien, whom Napoleon had executed in 1804. Carlo's remains were hidden in a cellar. In 1840, when Napoleon's own remains were placed in the Invalides in Paris, his father's were placed in the crypt of the church of Saint-Leu. In 1951, Carlo's remains found their final resting place in the Chapelle Impériale of his native town of Ajaccio (Carrington 1988, p. 191, p. 264, n. 58; Gallo 1997, vol. 1, p. 49).

26. Gallo 1997, vol. 1, p. 48, my translation from the French; cf. Castelot 1971, p. 13.

27. Jekels 1952, p. 48.

28. Napoleon Bonaparte 1961, p. 15; Gallo 1997, vol. 1, p. 50, my translation from the French.

29. Carrington 1988, p. 191, p. 264, n. 59.

30. Napoleon Bonaparte 1961, p. 15; Gallo 1997, vol. 1, pp. 50–51, my translation from the French.

31. The French neuropsychiatrist Jean-Raymond Frugier idealized Napoleon's relationship to his mother. Frugier thought that Napoleon's mother "had a weakness for him, but tried not to show it, taking him to task when necessary, equally with his

brothers and sisters. Later, after his father died, she became his confidante . . . Napoleon always kept in mind his mother's devotion, the indefatigable labor that she supplied to raise, in half-destitution, her numerous offspring, to please an extravagant husband, always living above his means, and also the dignity without pomposity with which she knew how to act in all the circumstances of her life" (Frugier 1985, p. 33, my translation from the French). In fact, the mother-son relationship was highly conflicted and tormented. Napoleon forever tried to break away from his mother while at the same time craving fusion with her. Arthur Chuquet thought that "Napoleon's grief was immense when he learned of his father's death," but that nonetheless "it is not expressed in his letters as naturally and spontaneously as might be expected. The tone is dignified but rather frigid, ceremonious, solemn. They are too careful, too affected, these lines by a sixteen-year-old child" (Chuquet 1897–99, translated in Jekels 1952, p. 48). In fact, Napoleon was not yet sixteen—and certainly not a child. Some scholars have thought that his letters to his great-uncle and mother after his father's death were cold, unfeeling and "stilted in the extreme" (Masson 1969, pp. 126–127; Carrington 1988, p. 191). Vincent Cronin believed that Napoleon "certainly experienced a deep sense of loss" but that his letters were "re-styled by an officer, and ended up a formal, rather stilted exercise in filial consolation" (Cronin 1971, p. 42).

32. Carrington did not find a sorrowful Napoleon mourning his father's death: "Historians have assumed that Napoleon was deeply distressed by his father's death. But this view is not supported by the available evidence. Des Mazis relates that when the news reached the École [royale] Militaire [in Paris], a priest, as was the custom, proposed to offer Napoleon consolation in the quiet of the infirmary, but that he refused, saying he had sufficient strength of spirit to do without being consoled. Was this reaction, which his friend took for stoicism, not rather indifference, or even relief? Certainly the letters Napoleon wrote to Luciano and Letizia after the event are stilted in the extreme. . . . In later years Napoleon spoke of Carlo's death as a liberation. It was even one of the lucky chances of life, he told Las Cases" (Carrington 1988, p. 191). In fact, Napoleon told Las Cases, had his father not died before the Revolution, "that would have meant the upsetting and ruin of my whole career" (Bainville 1933, p. 13).

33. Bainville 1933, pp. 13–14.

34. Cronin 1971, pp. 42–43.

Chapter 6

1. Las Cases 1823, entry of August 27–31 1815; cf. Cronin 1971, p. 454; Bainville 1933, pp. 15–26. In Napoleon's unconscious mind, the French *armée* (a feminine word in French), and France herself, may have been a mother figure to him. Napoleon unconsciously acted out with Corsica, with the French army, and with France, his deepest conflict between his deep yearning for fusion and his profound need for separation and individuation.(Mahlet & al. 1975).

2. Among the titles given by biographers and scholars to Napoleon's literary works are *Lettres sur la Corse* (Letters on Corsica), *Sur le Suicide* (On Suicide), *Lettre à Matteo Buttafuoco, député de la Corse à l'Assemblée nationale* (Letter to Matteo Buttafuoco, Deputy of Corsica to the National Assembly), *Discours de Lyon or Discours sur le bonheur* (Lyons Address or Address on Happiness), *Dissertation sur l'Autorité* (Dissertation on Authority), *Sur l'Amour de la Patrie* (On Love of the Fatherland), *Le comte d'Essex* (The Count of Essex), *Le Masque prophète* (The Prophetic Mask), *Nouvelle corse* (Corsican Novel), *Dialogue sur l'Amour* (Dialogue on Love), and *Rencontre au Palais-Royal* (Meeting at the Royal Palace), *Clisson et Eugénie* (Clisson and Eugenia), and *Souper de Beaucaire* (Supper at Beaucaire). All of these were written before Napoleon was twenty-four-years-old. See Napoleon Bonaparte 1822; Healey 1959.

3. Cronin 1971, p. 44.

4. Cronin 1971, p. 46. Years later, when he became Emperor of the French, Napoleon abolished the ancient practice of castrating promising young boy singers, such as the famous Farinelli, to preserve the special quality of their voices (Cronin 1971, p. 260).

5. Guns are unconscious phallic symbols. In Napoleon's unconscious mind, the big and powerful guns may have symbolized the big penis that he wished to have. Firing cannon gave him a sense of omnipotence, an antidote to his early and chronic feelings of helplessness.

6. Napoleon did not know it, but Madame de Warens had not written her own memoirs: they had been ghost-written by the Savoyard general François-Amédée Doppet, who was eleven-years-old when Madame de Warens died, and who sought to clear her reputation and to tarnish Rousseau's. See Warens 1786; Rousseau 1782–89 1995; Bainville 1933, pp. 16–17; Gallo 1997, vol. 1, p. 62.

7. Napoleon Bonaparte 1925; Cronin 1971, pp. 89, 455; Richardson 1972, p. 107; Gallo 1997, vol. 1, p. 63.

8. Napoleon Bonaparte 1907, pp. 5–6; Clark 1929, p. 17; Jekels 1952, p. 39; Herold 1955, p. 35; Napoleon Bonaparte 1961, vol.1, p. 16; Castelot 1971, p. 18; Gallo 1997, vol.1, p. 65.

9. Napoleon Bonaparte 1961, p. 17; Gallo 1997, vol. 1, p. 62.

10. After Marbeuf's death, Corsica was administered directly from Paris by the *contrôleur général*, Charles-Alexandre de Calonne (Masson 1969, pp. 17, 153; Jekels 1952, p. 38; Carrington 1988, pp. xxv 194, pp. 227–228, n. 28; Gallo 1997, vol. 1, p. 68).

11. Napoleon Bonaparte 1961, p. 17; Gallo 1997, vol. 1, p. 62.

12. See Masson 1893; Hopkins 1909; Aretz 1927; Richardson 1972, p. 49; Gallo 1997, vol. 1, p. 73; Castelot 1998.

13. Napoleon Bonaparte 1961, pp. 18–19.

14. Cronin 1971, p. 91.

15. Carrington 1988, pp. 193–194, italics added.

16. Gallo 1997, vol. 1, pp. 87–88, based on Bartel 1954.

17. Bainville 1933, p. 22; Gallo 1997, vol. 1, p. 90; based on Bartel 1954.
18. Napoleon Bonaparte 1961, vol. 1, p. 23.
19. Carrington 1988, pp. 86–87.
20. Ibid., p. 87.
21. Clark 1929, p. 16.
22. Carrington 1988, p. 188.
23. Bertrand 1949–59, vol. 2, p. 316; Cronin 1971, pp. 59–60; Gallo 1997, vol. 1, pp. 71, 127–128.
24. McLynn 1997, pp. 53–54.
25. Napoleon Bonaparte 1961, p. 28; cf. Gallo 1997, vol. 1., p. 130.
26. Ibid., pp. 28–29; Ibid.
27. Bainville 1933, p. 27; Castelot 1967, p. 98; Gallo 1997, vol. 1, p. 132; McLynn 1997, p. 51.
28. Bainville 1933, p. 27; Castelot 1967, p. 99; Cronin 1971, p. 61; Tulard 1987, p. 53; Gallo 1997, vol. 1, pp. 132–133.
29. Cronin 1971, p. 61.
30. Bainville 1933, p. 27; Godechot 1969, p. 20; Cronin 1971, p. 61; Gallo 1997, vol. 1, p. 133; McLynn 1997, p. 51.
31. Connelly 1968, pp. 21–22.
32. McLynn 1997, p. 52.
33. Ibid.; cf. Bainville 1933, p. 28; Cronin 1971, p. 62.
34. Bainville 1933, p. 28; Connelly 1987, p. 14; McLynn 1997, p. 54

Chapter 7

1. Castelot 1967, pp. 97, 101, 105; Cronin 1971, p. 63; Tulard 1989, pp. 583–584, 1011, 1022, 1570; McLynn 1997, p. 54.
2. Carrington 1988, p. 276, citing Bourrienne 1830 and Belliard & al. 1830.
3. Owen Connelly believed that Napoleon "was contemptuous of the king, who, he wrote Joseph, could have saved his throne if he had 'mounted his horse' and taken command of the Swiss [guards]" (Connelly 1987, p. 14). In fact, on the evening of August 10 1792, the day of the riot at the royal palace, Napoleon wrote his elder brother, Joseph, "The King came out of it well . . . but an incident like this is unconstitutional and a very dangerous example" (Cronin 1971, p. 63; Gallo 1997, vol. 1, p. 145). Connelly thought that on that very day Napoleon became a republican and a Jacobin, renouncing his king (Connelly 1987, p. 14). In fact, Napoleon had joined the Jacobin club at Auxonne the year before.
4. Bainville 1933, p. 29.
5. Ibid.; Tulard 1989, pp. 656, 1382; Gallo 1997, vol. 1, pp. 148–152; McLynn 1997, p. 57.
6. McLynn 1997, pp. 57–58; cf. Gallo 1997, vol. 1, pp.148–152.

7. Jekels 1952, p. 61; Gallo 1997, vol. 1, p. 153; based on Pasquier 1893–1895, cf. Pasquier 1967.

8. Jekels 1952, p. 16.

9. Ibid., p. 11.

10. Ibid., p. 18.

11. McLynn 1997, p. 61.

12. Ibid., p. 62.

13. Gallo 1997, vol. 1, p. 156.

14. McLynn 1997, p. 62.

15. Bainville 1933, p. 31; Jekels 1952, p. 38; Gallo 1997, vol. 1, p. 156.

16. Gallo 1997, vol. 1, pp. 157, my translation from the French.

17. Castelot 1971, p. 30.

18. Hudson 1914, p. 41; Bainville 1933, p. 31; Cronin 1971, p. 69; Tulard 1989, p. 1227; McLynn 1997, p. 63.

19. Castelot 1971, p. 30.

Chapter 8

1. Jekels 1914, 1952.

2. Coston 1840, vol. 2, pp. 87–88; Masson 1969, p. 202; Clark 1929, p. 19, Brice 1937, p. 5; Napoleon Bonaparte 1961, pp. 23–24; Castelot 1967, pp. 85–86; Tulard 1989, p. 517; Carrington 1988, p. 47.

3. Brice 1937, p. 141; Carrington 1988, p. 64–66.

4. Grotstein 1981.

5. Connelly 1968, p. xiii.

6. Carrington 1988, p. 57.

7. Hudson 1914, p. 14.

8. Las Cases 1823, entry of October 31, 1816; Clark 1929, p. 150; Herold 1955, p. 278.

9. Clark 1929, p. xxii.

10. Arnault 1833, cited in Cronin 1971, p. 158.

11. Clark 1929, p. xxiii.

12. Bartel 1954, p. 31; Parker 1971–72, p. 8.

13. Piers & Singer 1953; Lynd 1958; Wurmser 1981; Broucek 1982; Miller 1985; Nathanson 1987 1992; Morrison 1989; Lewis 1992; Steinberg 1996; Tangney & Dearing 2002.

14. Kohut 1972.

15. Wurmser 1987, p. 76.

16. Steinberg 1996.

17. Parker 1971–72, pp. 8–9, and p. 9, n. 13.

18. Carrington 1994–98, letter of 4 September 1996.

19. Ibid.

20. Lasswell 1948, pp. 39–41.
21. Loewenberg 1995, p. 11.
22. Carrington 1988, pp. 40, 130–131.
23. Parker 1971–72, p. 10.
24. McLynn 1997, p. 13.
25. Las Cases 1823, entry of September 23 1816; Herold 1955, p. 26.
26. Freud 1961, Freud & Zweig 1970, p. 97.
27. McLynn 1997, pp. 12–14.
28. Reich 1945, quoted in McLynn 1997, p. 13.
29. Ibid.
30. Coston 1840, Montbas 1952, Roux 1984, Carrington 1988, pp. 102–103.
31. Carrington 1988, pp. 103–104. The younger and more prejudiced Count Roux de Laric was the son of an obscure Provençal nobleman, unwillingly sent to Corsica. Roux de Laric was an embittered, unpaid officer on Marbeuf's staff, a secret enemy of Marbeuf, disdainful of the Corsicans. He was a secret protégé of Marbeuf's rival, Jean-François de Narbonne-Pelet-Fritzlar, and of his ally, Colla de Pradine, the intendant of Corsica. Roux de Laric defamed Carlo Buonaparte as Marbeuf's "base and servile spy" (Roux 1984, pp. 163–209). The more objective Count Colchen was the secretary to Pradine's successor, Bertrand de Boucheporn, from 1780 to 1785, but his account is based on speculation and hearsay (Montbas 1952; Carrington 1988, pp. 96, 102–104).
32. Jekels 1952, p. 38.
33. Bourrienne 1829–31, vol. 1, pp. 7, 32; Jekels 1952, p. 28.
34. Belliard & al. 1830, p. 238; Carrington 1988, p. 143.
35. Carrington 1988, p. 144.
36. Jekels 1952, p. 28, based on Coston 1840.
37. Clark 1929, p. 77.
38. Cronin 1971, p. 272.
39. Roederer 1909, pp. 244–252; Herold 1955, p. 260.
40. Frugier 1985, p. 19.
41. Pérès 1827. His absurd and pathetic attempt to "prove the non-existence of Napoleon" had been preceded by that of the Anglican archbishop Richard Whately (Whately 1819).
42. Marmont 1857, quoted in Richardson 1972, p. 16.
43. Iung 1880–81, quoted in Richardson, 1972, p. 16.
44. Richardson1972, p. 16.
45. Clark 1929, p. 217.
46. Bainville 1933, p. 189.
47. Las Cases 1823, entry of September 23, 1816; Herold 1955, p. 26.
48. Manceron 1969, quoted in Richardson 1972, p. 66.
49. Carrington 1988, p. 91.
50. Jekels 1952, p. 61. Frank McLynn used Jekels's theories extensively without giving any credit to his source (McLynn 1997, pp. 63–67).

51. Bainville 1933, p. 32; cf. Gallo 1997, vol. 1, pp. 162–163.
52. Bainville 1933, p. 27.
53. Carrington 1988, p. 194.
54. Cf. Clark 1929; Gay 1964.

Chapter 9

1. Bainville 1933, p. 31; Cronin 1971, pp. 70, 108; Tulard 1989, p. 1096.

2. The fiery Lucien Bonaparte signed his letter to the *Convention nationale* in Paris "Brutus Bonaparte, *citoyen sans-culotte*." His greatest achievement at that time was to get the convention to change the name of the Provençal village of Saint-Maximin to Marathon—site of the ancient battle in which the Athenians repulsed the first Persian invasion of Greece (Tulard 1989, p. 1096; Gallo 1997, vol.1, p. 180).

3. McLynn 1997, p. 70.
4. Gallo 1997, vol. 1, p. 178.
5. Jekels 1952, p. 17; Tulard 1989, p. 526.
6. Gallo 1997, vol. 1, pp. 162–163; cf. Bainville 1933, p. 32.
7. Gallo 1997, vol. 1, p. 163.
8. Tulard 1989, p. 526.
9. Castelot 1967, p. 137.
10. Ibid., pp. 117–118, my translation from the French.
11. Bainville 1933, p. 34.
12. Castelot 1971, p. 32.
13. Ibid.
14. Bainville 1933, p. 34.
15. Richardson 1972, pp. 68–69.
16. Cronin 1971, p. 179.
17. Antommarchi 1825, 1826; Meynell 1911; Cronin 1971, p. 179.

18. Masséna 1848–50, quoted in Fisher 1912, p. 36; Becker 1931, p. 261; Phipps 1926–39, vol. 4, pp. 11–12; Parker 1971–72, p. 20, n. 54; Richardson 1972, p. 69.

19. Bainville 1933, p. 36.
20. Cronin 1971, p. 71.
21. Gallo 1997, vol. 1, p. 163.
22. Cronin, 1971, p. 71.
23. Ibid.; cf. Castelot 1967, p. 118; Gallo 1997, vol. 1, p. 164.
24. Castelot 1967, p. 118.
25. Napoleon Bonaparte 1793, 1822, 1887–88, 1967–68, 1979.
26. Castelot 1967, p. 118.
27. Napoleon Bonaparte 1793, cited in Gallo 1997, vol. 1, p. 165.
28. Napoleon Bonaparte 1793, cited in Castelot 1967, pp. 118–119.

29. Napoleon Bonaparte 1793; Bainville 1933, p. 35; Castelot 1967, p. 118; Cronin 1971, p. 71.

30. Clark 1929, p. 27.
31. Bainville 1933, p. 34.
32. Parker 1993–1999, letter of November 29, 1995, p. 6.
33. Herold 1955, p. 83; Carrington 1988, p. 109.
34. Las Cases 1823, entry of September 1–6, 1815.
35. Castelot 1971, pp. 32–33; Tulard 1989, p. 376.
36. Connelly 1987, p. 15.
37. Bainville 1933, p. 36.
38. Gallo 1997, vol. 1, p. 172, my translation from the French
39. Ibid., p. 173.
40. Ibid.
41. Clark 1929, p. 41.
42. Las Cases 1823, entry of September 1–6, 1815; cf. Brice 1937, p. 139; Richardson 1972, p. 49; Gallo 1997, vol. 1, p. 172. For the rest of his life Napoleon suffered from persistent itches and chronic headaches (Gourgaud 1889–1899, quoted in Richardson 1972, pp. 49–50). When Napoleon was Emperor of the French, his personal physician, Alexandre-Urbain Yvan, who was in close proximity to Napoleon for eighteen years, correctly diagnosed Napoleon's itch as psychosomatic, although he did not use this term (Richardson 1972, p. 49; McLynn 1997, p. 285). Napoleon's St. Helena physician, Francesco Antommarchi, and Napoleon's valet, Constant Wairy, both reported that when Napoleon's skin itched he tore savagely at his own flesh until he drew blood (Antommarchi 1825, Wairy 1895, quoted in Richardson 1972, p. 50). Raoul Brice thought that Napoleon's itch was "an affection, parasitic undoubtedly, which is only contracted at night from sheets or clothing infected by the acarus (itch-mite)," that is, scabies (Brice 1937, p. 139). Reuben Friedman called the story of Napoleon's "scabies" infection an unfounded legend (Friedman 1940). Frank Richardson thought that Napoleon "had some kind of sinus on his thigh, probably resulting from a wound at the siege of Toulon, at which he would tear in moments of stress, and when the blood flowed he felt physical and mental relief" (Richardson 1972, p. 50). Could his chronic itch have expressed Napoleon's trauma of being splashed by his gunner's blood, as well as his rage at people who "got under his skin"?
43. Tulard 1989, p. 1642.
44. Marmont 1857, vol. 1, p. 45; cf. Castelot 1971, p. 34.
45. Cronin 1971, p. 77, based on Chuquet 1897–1899.
46. Castelot 1971, p. 35 and Gallo 1997, pp. 175–176.
47. Bécat 1969, p. 31, n. 1.
48. Richardson 1972, p. 22.
49. McLynn 1997, p. 76.
50. Clark 1929, p. 29; cf. McLynn 1997, p. 76.
51. Connelly 1987, p. 18.

Chapter 10

1. Bruun 1932.
2. Moffet 1962; cf. Lewis & Lucas 1983.
3. Du Teil 1896, pp. 205–222; Carrington 1988, p. 192.
4. Castelot 1967, pp. 132–133.
5. Cronin 1971, p. 79.
6. Ibid.
7. Bainville 1933, p. 38; Castelot 1967, p. 133; Cronin 1971, p. 79.
8. Bainville 1933, p. 31.
9. Cronin 1971, p. 91.
10. Gallo 1997, vol. 1, p. 195.
11. Tulard 1989, p. 424. Bainville 1933, p. 31; Jekels 1952, p. 35; Cronin 1971, p. 91; Tulard 1987, p. 72, Tulard 1989, 424; Gallo 1997, vol. 1, p. 195.
12. Connelly 1968, p. 27.
13. Cronin 1971, p. 91.
14. During the year 1793 an anxious *Convention nationale* sent—and recalled —no less than nine "representatives on mission" to control its armies in southern France and execute the "enemies of the revolution." These fiery executioners were all in their thirties: Stanislas-Louis-Marie Fréron, Don Juan de la Terreur; Paul-François-Jean-Nicolas de Barras, a republican nobleman and one of the five future rulers of France in the *Directoire*; Antoine-Chrisophe Saliceti, the French-Corsican leader who had fought Paoli in Corsica; Augustin de Robespierre, Maximilien's younger brother; Thomas-Augustin Gasparin, who apparently had some military experience; Antoine-Louis Albitte, the Jacobin who executed the rebels in Marseille; Jean-François Ricord, who guillotined "rebels" and "traitors"; Philibert Simond; and a man named Escudier. These *députés-en-mission* were very powerful. Owen Connelly thought that they "had life-or-death authority, wherever sent, over both generals and civil officials" (Connelly 1987, p. 16). Saliceti, Gasparin, and Ricord were at Marseille in August 1793; Fréron and Barras arrived in Toulon during the last phase of its siege by the republican army. After the defeat of Toulon at the end of that year, Barras merged the *armée du Var* with the *armée d'Italie* (Bainville 1933, pp. 35–40; Tulard 1987, p. 63; Tulard 1989, p. 165; Gallo 1997, vol. 1, p. 171).
15. Connelly 1968, p. 26, based on Girod de l'Ain 1959; cf. Cronin 1971, p. 91.
16. Cronin 1971, p. 91.
17. Gallo 1997, vol. 1, p. 195.
18. Castelot 1967, p. 133; Cronin 1971, p. 91.
19. Castelot 1971, p. 37; cf. Gallo 1997, vol. 1, p. 181.
20. The chief "Thermidorian" leaders were the nobleman Paul-François-Jean-Nicolas de Barras de Fox d'Amphoux, the firebrand rebel-killer Joseph Fouché, and their colleague Jean-Lambert Tallien. Barras would become the head of the

ruling *Directoire exécutif* from 1795 to 1799 and Fouché would be Napoleon's infamous police minister, while Tallien would have a much less successful career and was best known for his wife Theresa, nicknamed *Notre Dame de Thermidor*.

21. Gallo 1997, vol. 1, p. 187.

22. Castelot 1967, p. 176; Gallo 1997, vol. 1, p. 192.

23. Tulard 1989, p. 1096.

24. Bonaparte's plan was a two-pronged French offensive on the army of Piedmont-Savoy-Sardinia. One part of the French army would push the Piedmontese to Saorgio (Saorge), an Alpes Maritimes village on the River Roya (Roia), west of the Piedmont border. The French armée d'Italie would push the enemy further north to the Tenda Pass (Col de Tende), in the Maritime Alps between France and Italy, on the road to the Piedmontese capital of Turin. At the same time another part of the armée d'Italie would push the Piedmontese eastward toward the Ligurian town of Oneglia (Oneille), east of San Remo on the Mediterranean coast.

25. Horward 1997, p. 8.

26. Bainville 1933, p. 41; Jekels 1952, p. 39; Horward 1997, pp. 7–8.

27. Défossé 1986.

28. Tulard 1989, p. 425, based on Girod de l'Ain 1959, my translation from the French; Cronin 1971, p. 92; Castelot 1971, p. 36.

29. Frank McLynn dismissed out of hand "the wild story that Joseph really wanted to marry Désirée until Napoleon 'leaned on' him by pointing out that stable should marry flighty and flighty stable" (McLynn 1997, p. 83).

30. Castelot 1971, p. 36. McLynn, however, found no sign of any objection to Napoleon's marriage to Désirée on Madame Clary's part at that stage "nor of Joseph's supposed objection on the grounds that one Bonaparte in the family was enough" (McLynn 1997, p. 84).

31. McLynn 1997, pp. 84–85; cf. Napoleon Bonaparte 1887–1888.

32. Aretz 1927, pp. 44–49; Jekels 1952, pp. 39–40; Gallo 1997, vol. 1, p. 193.

33. Richardson 1972, p. 127.

34. Las Cases 1823, entry of September 1–6, 1815; Aretz 1927, p. 46; Jekels 1952, pp. 39–40.

35. Jekels, Ibid.; McLynn 1997, p. 81.

36. Manceron 1969, quoted in Richardson 1972, p. 131.

37. In 1817 Napoleon reportedly told General Gaspard Gourgaud on Saint Helena: "I can more easily conceive of incest between father and daughter than between son and mother. In the one case, it is the man who commands; in the other, he must obey his mother" (Gourgaud 1889–1899, vol. 2, p. 231; Herold 1955, p. 16; Richardson 1972, p. 131). Napoleon would never obey his mother—nor any other woman. Throughout his life, he led a subtle but interminable life-and-death power struggle with his mother—who survived him.

38. Chabot 1900.

39. Napoleon Bonaparte 1961, p. 52.

40. Ibid.

41. Cronin 1971, p. 81; cf. McLynn 1997, p. 85; Las Cases 1823, entry of September 1–6, 1815; Marmont 1857, vol. 1, p. 61; Castelot 1971, p. 43; Cronin 1971, p. 81; and Gallo 1997, vol. 1, p. 200.

42. Castelot 1971, p. 44.

43. Las Cases 1823, entry of September 1–6, 1815; Marmont 1857, vol. 1, p. 61; Castelot 1971, p. 43; Cronin 1971, p. 81; Gallo 1997, vol. 1, p. 200; McLynn 1997, p. 86.

44. Castelot 1967, pp. 154–156.

45. Castelot 1971, p. 41, based on Bertrand 1949–59.

46. Napoleon Bonaparte 1961, pp. 52–53; Gallo 1997, vol. 1, p. 201.

47. Castelot 1971, p. 44, based on Girod de l'Ain 1959.

48. Carrington 1988, p. 179.

49. Ibid.

50. Castelot 1971, p. 45.

51. Clark 1929, pp. 183–184.

52. Richardson 1972, p. 29. Frank McLynn was certain that "in these dark days in Paris in the summer of 1795 Napoleon contemplated suicide" but pointed out that at other times he thought of joining the Ottoman Turkish army (McLynn 1997, p. 87).

53. Bainville 1933, pp. 42–43.

54. Napoleon Bonaparte 1961, vol. 1, pp. 57–58.

55. Las Cases 1823, entry of September 1–6 1815; Las Cases 1961, vol. 1, p. 112; Bainville 1933, p. 43; Brice 1937, p. ix; Castelot 1967, p. 166; Cronin 1971, p. 83; Tulard 1989, pp. 334, 373; Gallo 1997, vol. 1, pp. 204, 209–212; McLynn 1997, p. 93. Bonaparte was not the only general sacked in this manner: seventy-four other French generals, suspect like him of robespierriste sympathies, were dismissed from the French army in September 1795.

56. Tulard 1989, p. 334

57. .Ibid., my translation from the French.

58. .Ibid.

59. Clark 1929, p. 34.

60. Castelot 1967, p. 176; Cronin 1971, p. 87; Gallo 1997, vol. 1, p. 223.

61. Bainville 1933, p. 50.

62. .Ibid., based on Fain 1828

Chapter 11

1. Las Cases 1823, entry of May 19 1816; Wilson 1934, p. 99; Castelot 1964, p. 113; Richardson 1972, p. 122; Tulard 1989, pp. 976, 1227.

2. Bainville 1933, pp. 50–51. This dramatic and well-known scene was a romanticized in Abel Gance's classic film *Napoléon* (Gance 1927, 1990) and in

other films. As the poetic psychoanalyst Pierce Clark described it, "The boy weeps at sight of his father's sword; as he kneels to kiss its hilt, Bonaparte is touched at the simple emotion of the youth, and he grants permission for him to keep it. On the boy's return home his mother is so grateful at the general's kindness that she hastens to call on him in person to express her thanks" (Clark 1929, p. 35). Freud believed that swords were unconscious phallic symbols. In Napoleon's unconscious mind, "Josephine" may have been the phallic mother of his early life, as well as a stand-in for his elder brother Joseph.

3. Bainville 1933, p. 51.

4. Castelot 1964, p. 113, my translation from the French.

5. Cronin 1971, p. 103.

6. Richardson 1972, p. 112.

7. Freud 1961, Freud & Zweig 1970, p. 97.

8. Josephine's parents had been married two years before her birth, in 1761, when her father was twenty-six-years-old and her mother twenty-five. Like many men in other places and times, Tascher wanted a son and heir rather than a daughter, but his wife bore him three daughters in a row, of whom Marie-Josèphe-Rose was the first. Her disappointed husband neglected her and spent his time womanizing at Fort-Royal (now Fort-Napoléon) rather than at home with his wife and daughter. Marie-Josèphe-Rose was only baptized when she was five weeks old (Castelot 1964, pp. 15–18; Tulard 1989, p. 976). The delay in her baptism may have expressed her parents' ambivalence about her.

9. Tulard 1989, p. 976.

10. Bainville 1933, p. 51.

11. Castelot 1971, pp. 53–55.

12. McLynn 1997, pp. 80, 84.

13. Castelot 1964, pp. 113–114; Castelot 1971, p. 54; Cronin 1971, p. 105; Tulard 1977, new edition 1987, pp. 78–79; Gallo 1997, vol. 1, p. 226; based on Napoleon Bonaparte 1833, 1931.

14. Tulard 1989, pp. 166, 1227. The five members of the *Directoite exécutif* elected on 9 Brumaire Year IV of the French Republic (October 31, 1795) by the new French legislature were Paul-François-Jean-Nicolas de Barras, Jean-François Reubell, Louis-Marie de la Revellière-Lépeaux, Lazare-Nicolas-Marguerite Carnot, and Charles-Louis-François-Honoré Letourneur. All five were in their forties. These five former *conventionnels* became the all-powerful rulers of France for the next four years. Reubell was an Alsatian Jew-hater. Letourneur was a former head of military personnel and a moderate member of the *conseil des Anciens*. Révellière-Lépeaux came from the formerly-rebellious Vendée. Carnot was the "organizer of the victory" at Fleurus. Barras, the only member of the *Directoire* who lasted until its end, was the former member of the *comité de Salut public* who had toppled Robespierre and had crushed the royalist revolt against the *Convention nationale*.

15. Cronin 1971, p. 106.

16. Richardson 1972, p. 103.

17. Connelly 1987, p. 22.

18. Gear & al. 1981.

19. Castelot 1964, pp. 122, 140.

20. Clark 1929, p. 35.

21. Cronin 1971, p. 107; Castelot 1964, p. 123; Napoleon Bonaparte 1981.

22. Tulard 1989, p. 1227. Was it Barras or Carnot who gave Bonaparte this command? Barras told Josephine that he had given Bonaparte the *armée d'Italie*, but Napoleon believed that it was Carnot who had given him this appointment because "he appreciated my great ability" (Castelot 1971, p. 56). Carnot may have initiated Napoleon's appointment in the *Directoire exécutif*, but Barras had supported it, or Carnot and Barras may have joined forces in order to convince their three colleagues and pass the appointment (ibid.). If the appointment was Napoleon's wedding gift from Barras, this may well have embarrassed Napoleon, so he may have mistakenly attributed it to Carnot (Cronin 1971, pp. 107–108). But Barras could not have given Napoleon the command of the *armée d'Italie* without Carnot's consent, since Carnot was the director in charge of the French armies (Castelot 1964, p. 122; Tulard 1989, p. 1321; Gallo 1997, vol. 1, pp. 227–228).

23. Cronin 1971, p. 107.

24. Ibid., pp. 107–108; Castelot 1971, p. 56; Gallo 1997, vol. 1, p. 226.

25. Castelot 1964, pp. 115–124; Castelot 1967, p. 184; Gallo 1997, vol. 1, p. 228.

26. Cronin 1971, p. 108; cf. Castelot 1964, pp. 115–124; Castelot 1971, pp. 56–57;; Gallo 1997, vol. 1, p. 228.

27. Cronin 1971, p. 109.

28. Castelot 1964, pp. 115–124; Castelot 1971, p. 56; Cronin 1971, pp. 108–109; Gallo 1997, vol. 1, p. 228.

29. Castelot 1964, p. 116; Tulard 1989, p. 977.

30. Ibid.

31. Cronin 1971, p. 108.

32. Castelot 1964, pp. 17–19; Tulard 1989, p. 976; Gallo 1997, vol. 1, p. 228.

33. Carrington 1988, p. 219.

34. Clark 1929, p. 36.

35. Ibid., p. 78

36. Aretz 1927, p. 54; Castelot 1967, pp. 185–186, based on Girod de l'Ain 1959; Castelot 1971, p. 57; Richardson 1972, p. 109.

37. Although Désirée was not happy in Sweden, and often returned to Paris, she had been saved from marrying a man who could not truly love anyone but himself. Bernadotte's Norway had been torn off the Kingdom of Denmark and annexed to Sweden. In 1813 Bernadotte allied himself with Napoleon's enemies and helped bring about his downfall. In 1818, while Napoleon was a prisoner of the British on Saint Helena, Bernadotte became King Carl Johan of Sweden and Norway and Désirée became Queen Desideria, though she remained in France.

38. Gallo 1997, vol. 1, p. 233.
39. Richardson 1972, p. 230, n. 4.
40. Castelot 1967, p. 189; Castelot 1971, p. 59; Gallo 1997, vol. 1, p. 234; based on Napoleon Bonaparte 1833, 1931.
41. Castelot 1971, p. 59.
42. Ibid., p. 60; Gallo 1997, vol. 1, p. 235.
43. Connelly 1987, p. 22, based on Napoleon Bonaparte 1833, 1931.
44. Richardson 1972, p. 113, based on Masson 1893, 1894.
45. Turquan 1909, 1912; Masson 1893, 1894; Belloc 1932; Bainville 1933, p. 56; Castelot 1964, p. 147.
46. Castelot 1964, p. 147, based on Napoleon Bonaparte 1833, 1931.
47. Bainville 1933, p. 56.

Chapter 12

1. Connelly 1987, p. 8; Gallo 1997, vol. 1, p. 242.
2. Bainville, 1932, p. 55; Herold 1955, p. 214; Godechot 1969, p. 22; Tulard 1989, p. 954; Gallo 1997, vol. 1, p. 241. By some accounts this proclamation was issued on April 10, the day before the battle of Montenotte. See Napoleon Bonaparte 1887–88, vol. III, p. 33 and Herold 1955, p. 214.
3. Connelly 1987, p. 25, based on Las Cases 1823, entry of January 1816, "Bataille de Montenotte"; cf. Las Cases 1961, p. 368.
4. Castelot 1971, p. 62, based on Napoleon Bonaparte 1833, 1931.
5. Castelot 1967, p. 193; Gallo 1997, vol. 1, p. 240; based on Napoleon Bonaparte 1833, my translation from the French; Napoleon Bonaparte 1931, pp. 25–26.
6. Gallo 1997, vol. 1, p. 257, based on Napoleon Bonaparte 1981.
7. Castelot 1971, p. 62.
8. Napoleon Bonaparte 1964.
9. Herold 1955, p. 211, based on Napoleon Bonaparte 1854–1869 and 1858–1870, vol. VI, p. 39.
10. Connelly 1968, p. 30.
11. Ibid.
12. Bainville 1933, p. 57.
13. Cronin 1971, p. 116.
14. Connelly 1987, p. 22.
15. Hastier 1955.
16. Richardson 1972, p. 114.
17. Tulard 1989, p. 404.
18. Castelot 1964, p. 129.
19. Tulard 1989, p. 955.
20. Napoleon Bonaparte 1961, p. 103.

21. Napoleon Bonaparte 1833, 1931; Napoleon Bonaparte1961, pp. 103–104; Castelot 1964, p. 134; Castelot 1967, p. 202; Castelot 1971, p. 66; Connelly 1987, p. 22; Gallo 1997, vol. 1, p. 255.

22. Bainville 1933, pp. 54–55.

23. Cronin 1971, p. 114.

24. Castelot 1967, pp. 197–198; Godechot 1969, p. 22; Castelot 1971, pp. 63–64; Gallo 1997, vol. 1, p. 248.

25. Castelot 1967, p. 198.

26. Tulard 1989, p. 1523; Cronin 1971, p. 117; Gallo 1997, vol. 1, pp. 248, 251

27. Connelly 1968, p. 30; Cronin 1971, p. 130.

28. Castelot 1964, p. 131; Castelot 1967, pp. 202–203; Napoleon Bonaparte 1833, 1931, 1981; Gallo 1997, vol. 1, p. 254.

29. Clark 1929, p. 40; Castelot 1967, p. 203; Cronin 1971, p. 131; Gallo 1997, vol. 1, p. 256.

30. Connelly 1987, p. 29.

31. Clark 1929, p. 225; cf. Cronin 1971, p. 120; Horward 1997, p. 9, n. 18.

32. Bainville 1933, p. 58; Tulard 1989, p. 1085.

33. Twenty years later, an aging prisoner of the British on Saint Helena, Napoleon recalled that it was only after Lodi that he conceived the first ideas of high ambition. He told Count Las Cases, "after Lodi, I regarded myself no longer as a mere general but as a man destined to influence the fate of people. It occurred to me that I could become a decisive actor on the political stage" (Las Cases 1823, entry of September 18, 1816). Napoleon also told Gourgaud, "I already saw the earth in flight beneath me, as if I were being lifted up into the air and carried to the sky" (Gourgaud 1889–99, vol. 2, pp. 55–56; Bainville 1933, p. 58). Napoleon saw Lodi as the place that made him feel omnipotent; after Lodi, he could do anything (Herold 1955, p. 47; Castelot 1971, p. 68).

34. Castelot 1964, p. 135; Castelot 1967, p. 204; Cronin 1971, p. 130; Connelly 1987, p. 30.

35. Connelly 1987, p. 30.

36. Napoleon Bonaparte 1931, 1981; Castelot 1964, p. 131.

37. Napoleon Bonaparte 1931, 1981; Castelot 1964, p. 136.

38. Napoleon Bonaparte 1833, 1931, 1981; Castelot 1964, pp. 135–136; Castelot 1967, p. 204; Cronin 1971, p. 130; Connelly 1987, p. 30.

39. Broers 2004.

40. Castelot 1964, p. 142, my translation from the French.

41. Ibid.

42. Ibid.

43. Ibid., pp. 141–142, my translation from the French.

44. Ibid., p. 142, my translation from the French.

45. Castelot 1967, p. 215, my translation from the French.

46. Castelot 1964, p. 143; Castelot 1967, p. 216; Gallo 1997, vol. 1, p. 254, my translation from the French.

47. Castelot 1964, p. 144, my translation from the French.
48. Hamelin 1911; Cronin 1971, p. 135.
49. Castelot 1964, p. 146; my translation from the French .
50. Castelot 1964, pp. 146–147.
51. Ibid., pp. 148–149; Cronin 1971, p. 132.
52. Cronin 1971, p. 132.
53. Margerand 1931; Tulard 1989, pp. 49–53.
54. Cronin 1971, p. 121.
55. Ibid., p. 132
56. Castelot 1971, p. 73. Napoleon denied the affair and took no action against Hippolyte Charles until three years later, when he was in Egypt and "the veil was lifted" from his eyes. In Napoleon's unconscious mind, Josephine was his mother and Charles was his father. The drama of his early life was reenacted.
57. Herold 1955, p. 16; Castelot 1964, p. 151; Castelot 1967, p. 219; Castelot 1971, p. 73; Gallo 1997, vol. 1, p. 257, my translation from the French.
58. Castelot 1964, p. 152, my translation from the French.
59. Castelot 1964, p. 152; Castelot 1967, p. 219; Gallo 1997, vol. 1, p. 259, my translation from the French.
60. Castelot 1964, pp. 153–154; Gallo 1997, vol. 1, p. 259, my translation from the French.

Chapter 13

1. Parker 1993–99, letter of December 29, 1995.
2. Connelly 1987, pp. 1–2.
3. Connelly 1987, p. 37.
4. Castelot 1964, p. 160; Gallo 1997, vol. 1, p. 262, my translation from the French.
5. Castelot 1971, pp. 79–82.
6. The British decision to withdraw from Corsica in the fall of 1796 had a complicated history. In the summer General Bonaparte had decided to infiltrate Corsica with small parties of armed Corsicans refugees and ordered General Claude-Henri Vaubois, commanding the French forces at Leghorn (Livorno), to be ready to receive some nine hundred Corsicans, including Generals Casalta, Cervoni, Casabianca, and Gentili, who would be in overall command. By September the British admiral Nelson reported that a large French naval force was embarked at Leghorn and ready to sail. One of the principal reasons for Britain's union with Corsica had been to use the island as a base to support Austria and Piedmont-Sardinia in northern Italy, and to exert influence over the Italian states. By the end of August 1796, following Bonaparte's successful campaign in Northern Italy, this was no longer possible. In addition, Spain's defection (on August 18) meant that troops were needed elsewhere, particularly to

strengthen Gibraltar's defenses. The British decided to evacuate Corsica and with it the nearby island of Elba. On October 26 the British viceroy Sir Gilbert Elliot wrote from San Fiorenzo Bay to inform the Duke of Portland that the last British garrison (from Calvi) had been taken off safely, before sailing for Porto Ferrajo (he formally relinquished command as Viceroy on 15 November). Also taken off were the remaining three hundred royalist refugees, nearly all men from Dillon's Regiment, together with seventy Corsicans, who had been closely associated with the British occupation, including Napoleon's rival Pozzo di Borgo.

7. Castelot 1964, p. 163; Castelot 1967, pp. 235–236; Castelot 1971, pp. 80–81.

8. Castelot 1964, pp. 163–164; Gallo 1997, vol. 1, pp. 262–263.

9. Napoleon Bonaparte 1931, letters of November 1796.

10. Castelot 1964, p. 164, n. 1, my translation from the French.

11. Bainville 1933, p. 60.

12. Ibid.

13. Cronin 1971, p. 225.

14. Castelot 1964, p. 169, my translation from the French; Cronin 1971, p. 123, based on Dry 1906; McLynn 1997, p. 127.

15. Fornari 1974.

16. Bainville 1933, p. 66.

17. Ibid., p. 64.

18. Cronin 1971, p. 125.

19. Clark 1929, p. 42.

20. Connelly 1987, p. 48.

21. Castelot 1967, p. 259.

22. Clark 1929, p. 45.

23. Gallo 1997, vol. 1, p. 236, my translation from the French.

24. Clark 1929, p. 45.

25. Napoleon Bonaparte 1858–1870, vol. II, pp. 472–473; Herold 1955, p. 179.

26. Brice 1937, p. 109.

27. Tulard 1989, p. 1618.

Chapter 14

1. Cronin 1971, pp. 142–143; Castelot 1971, pp. 94–95.

2. Tulard 1989, p. 1620.

3. Castelot 1971, p. 92.

4. Bainville 1933, p. 94; Cronin 1971, p. 173.

5. Bainville 1933, pp. 94–95.

6. Napoleon Bonaparte 1858–1870, vol. III, Letter No. 2189, last paragraph; Napoleon Bonaparte 1884; Napoleon Bonaparte 1934a.

7. Bainville 1933, p. 46.

8. Brice 1937, p. 117.

9. Bainville 1933, pp. 71–72.

10. Godechot 1969, p. 29.

11. Bainville 1933, p. 71, based on Miot de Melito 1881.

12. McLynn 1997, p. 165.

13. Ibid., p. 165.

14. Ibid., p. 170.

15. Tulard 1989, p. 643; McLynn 1997, p. 173.

16. Castelot 1967, p. 292, my translation from the French.

17. Ibid., p. 293, my translation from the French.

18. Ibid., pp. 293–294, my translation from the French.

19. Connelly 1987, p. 52.

20. Clark 1929, p. 51.

21. Over one hundred fifty members of the *Institut Français* accepted General Bonaparte's invitation. They included the fifty-two-year-old scientist Gaspard Monge, a well-known mathematician, physicist, and statesman; the fifty-one-year-old engraver and diplomat Dominique-Vivant Denon; the forty-nine-year-old chemist Claude-Louis Berthollet, who had discovered dyes and bleaches; the forty-eight-year-old geologist Dieudonné-Sylvain Dolomieu (Déodat de Gratet de Dolomieu), who had killed a fellow Maltese monk in a duel when he was eighteen and later described the mineral dolomite and gave his name to the Dolomites; the forty-three-year-old chemist and mechanic Nicolas-Jacques Conté, who invented graphite mining; the thirty-nine-year-old painter, poet, and translator François-Auguste Parseval-Grandmaison, whose job would be "to sing Napoleon's exploits"; the thirty-nine-year-old Belgian-French painter and engraver Pierre-Joseph Redouté, nicknamed *le Raphaël des Fleurs*; the thirty-year-old mathematician-physicist Jean-Baptiste-Joseph Fourier, who discovered the mathematical series that bears his name; the twenty-six-year-old naturalist Etienne Geoffroy Saint-Hilaire, who created the menagerie at the Jardin des Plantes in Paris; and the twenty-two-year-old diplomat Matthieu-Maximilien-Prosper de Lesseps, whose son would build the Suez Canal (Clark 1929, p. 52; Bainville 1933, pp. 77–79; Cronin 1971, pp. 145–146; McLynn 1997, p. 171).

22. Cronin 1971, p. 146.

23. Among the French artists and scientists who turned down Napoleon's invitation to Egypt were the sixty-year-old abbé Jacques Delillle, a poet who had translated Virgil's Latin into French and wrote *les Jardins*, and who "regretted that at sixty he was too old"; the thirty-five-year-old operatic composer Etienne-Nicolas Méhul, author of *Joseph*, *L'Irato* and *le Chant du Départ*, who "did not want to leave France"; a singer named Loys, who "was afraid of catching a chill: like many, he probably believed Napoleon's destination to be Flushing" (the Dutch port city of Vlissingen); and the twenty-seven-year-old poet Louis-Jean-Népomucène Lemercier, a gifted dramatist with a withered right arm, author of *Méléagre*, *Le Tartuffe révolutionnaire*, (which had been banned by the Directoire

exécutif) and *Agamemnon*, who simply refused without stating his reasons (Cronin 1971, p. 146).

24. McLynn 1997, p. 173.

25. Clark 1929, p. 52.

26. Hastier 1955.

27. Bainville 1933, p. 78.

28. Ibid.

29. Brice 1937, pp. ix–x.

30. Wallach 2003.

31. Cezzâr 1962; Husayn Afandi 1964. In Arabic, the word *malik* means king, malaka means to reign or to own, and *mamluk* means slave. The Mamelukes had ruled Egypt and Syria in the late Middle Ages.

32. Connelly 1987, pp. 51–55.

33. Bainville 1933, p. 80; Castelot 1967, p. 312; Castelot 1971, pp. 107–108; Cronin 1971, p. 158; McLynn 1997, p. 181.

34. Clark 1929, pp. 56–57; Bainville 1933, p. 80; Castelot 1964, p. 209; Castelot 1967, pp. 314–315; Cronin 1971, p. 159; Richardson 1972, pp. 115, 127; McLynn 1997, p. 182, based on Napoleon Bonaparte 1961.

35. Cronin 1971, p. 158.

36. Clark 1929, p. 121; Rothstein 1980; Gear & al. 1981.

37. Budge 1982.

38. Las Cases 1823, entry of November 11, 1816; Herold 1955, p. 76.

39. Cronin 1971, pp. 159–160.

40. Tulard 1989, pp. 939–940.

41. Cezzâr 1962.

42. Cronin 1971, p. 159; McLynn 1997, p. 186.

43. Bainville 1933, p. 80.

44. Castelot 1971, p. 112.

45. Richardson 1972, p. 85.

46. McLynn 1997, p. 186.

47. Aretz 1927, p. 140.

48. McLynn 1997, pp. 186–187.

49. Ibid., p. 187.

50. Richardson 1972, p. 128.

51. Pauline Fourès remained with Napoleon until he left for France in 1799, and then became the mistress of his successor, Kléber. After the latter was killed in 1800, Pauline returned to France. Back in France, First Consul Bonaparte gave her a rich dowry and, true to his compulsive matchmaking, arranged for her to marry Henri, comte de Ranchoup, whom he made the French consul in Hamburg (Régis 1946).

52. Wilson 1802; Cronin 1971, pp. 160, 229–230; Connelly 1989, pp. 57–58; Tulard 1989, p. 1752; McLynn 1997, pp. 189–190.

53. Cronin 1971, p. 161.

54. Tulard 1989, p. 1574.
55. Wilson 1802; Marmont 1857, vol. 2, pp. 12–14; Cronin 1971, p. 162; Richardson 1972, p. 23; Tulard 1989, p. 596.
56. Connelly 1987, p. 58.
57. McLynn 1997, p. 195.
58. Marmont 1857, vol. 2, p. 27; Connelly 1987, p. 58.
59. Connelly 1987, p. 59.
60. Cronin 1971, p. 163.
61. Marmont 1857, vol. 2, p. 31.
62. Bainville 1933, p. 82.
63. Connelly 1987, p. 59.
64. Cronin 1971, p. 164.
65. Connelly 1987, pp. 59–60, n. 4.
66. Bainville 1933, p. 82.
67. Brice 1937, p. 118.
68. Connelly 1987, p. 51.
69. Godechot 1969, p. 35.
70. Ibid.
71. Clark 1929, pp. 59–60.
72. Richardson 1972, p. 115.
73. McLynn 1997, pp. 198–199.

Chapter 15

1. Bainville 1933, p. 87.
2. Castelot 1964, p. 208.
3. Bainville 1933, p. 89.
4. Ibid., p. 90
5. Ibid.
6. Ibid.; cf. Schiffer 1973.
7. Schiffer 1973.
8. Castelot 1971, p. 127.
9. Cronin 1971, p. 166.
10. Castelot 1971, p. 127.
11. Ibid., p. 129.
12. McLynn 1997, p. 210.
13. Castelot 1971, p. 129.
14. McLynn 1997, p. 205.
15. Bainville 1933, p. 92.
16. Brice 1937, p. 254.
17. Connelly 1987, p. 56.
18. Tulard 1989, pp. 1129–1130, 1481–1482.

19. Goldsmith 1806; Fleischmann 1910; Richardson 1972, pp. 174–175.
20. Tulard 1989, p. 64.
21. Cronin 1971, p. 271.
22. Richardson 1972, pp. 175–176.
23. See Fleischmann 1910 and Roustam 1911. The novels began to appear during the consulate, after Bonaparte became first consul of France. In 1801 Pierre-Nicolas Rougeron published *Viscellina ou le mamelouk français* and in 1803 Joseph Lavallée published *Lettres d'un mameluck*. In 1804 Roustam was rumored to have strangled Napoleon's forty-three-year-old would-be assassin, General Jean-Charles Pichegru, to death in his jail cell, and in 1806 Roustam was said to have assassinated the forty-three-year-old admiral Pierre-Charles de Villeneuve, who, in reality, had almost certainly killed himself. In 1814, after Emperor Napoleon was toppled by the Sixth Coalition allies, he made a half-hearted attempt to poison himself at Fontainebleau. Failing, he asked Roustam for his pistols so he could shoot himself. Roustam fled, claiming that he had to go to Paris and kiss his wife goodbye before leaving with Napoleon for the Isle of Elba. Roustam never returned. He died in 1845, when he was sixty-three-years-old, "as famous as he was mediocre" (Tulard 1989, p. 1482).
24. Bainville 1933, pp. 93–94.
25. Castelot 1971, p. 135.
26. Cronin 1971, p. 214.
27. Castelot 1971, p. 136.
28. Castelot 1967, p. 407, my translation from the French.
29. Ibid., p. 406, my translation from the French; Castelot 1971, p. 131.
30. Castelot 1971, p. 139; Tulard 1987, p. 23.
31. Castelot, 1971, p. 139.
32. Hudson 1914, p. 103.
33. Cronin 1971, p. 170.
34. Bainville 1933, p. 105.
35. Ollivier 1959; Tulard 1999.
36. Cronin 1971, p. 174.
37. Tulard 1989, p. 623.
38. McLynn 1997, p. 222.
39. Tulard 1989, p. 1175.
40. McLynn 1997, p. 223.
41. Clark 1929, p. 72.
42. Bainville 1933, p. 113.
43. Godechot 1969, p. 36, my translation from the French.
44. Bainville 1933, p. 105.

Chapter 16

1. Tulard 1989, p. 475.
2. Bainville 1933, p. 123; McLynn 1997, p. 225.
3. Bainville 1933, p. 110.
4. Ibid., pp. 111–112.
5. Castelot 1967, p. 454.
6. Bainville 1933, p. 111.
7. Castelot 1967, p. 457, my translation from the French.
8. Bainville 1933, p. 110.
9. Clark 1929, p. 98; Cronin 1971, p. 225.
10. Cronin 1971, pp. 225–226.
11. Cronin 1971, p. 226.
12. Clark 1929, p. 74.
13. Connelly 1987, p. 63; Tulard 1989, p. 1151.
14. Tulard 1989, p. 1005.
15. Castelot 1971, p. 166.
16. Ibid., p. 173.
17. Ibid., p. 176.
18. Ibid.
19. Clark 1929, p. 101.
20. Connelly 1987, p. 68.
21. Ibid.; Chandler 1991
22. Connelly, 1987, p. 68; Chandler 1991.
23. Connelly 1987, pp. 68–70; Chandler 1991.
24. Connelly 1987, p. 70; Chandler 1991.
25. Richardson 1972, p. 37, quoting Campbell 1869; Chandler 1991.
26. Las Cases 1823, entry of August 29, 1816.
27. Godechot 1969, pp. 37–38, my translation from the French.
28. Castelot 1967, p. 527, my translation from the French.
29. Godechot 1969, p. 38, my translation from the French.
30. Bainville 1933, p. 121.
31. On Napoleon's self-destructiveness see Clark 1929; Jekels 1952; Bergler 1933; McLynn 1997, pp. 66–67.
32. Shakespeare, *King Henry the Fourth Part II*, Act III, scene 1, line 31.
33. Bainville 1933, p. 122.
34. Ibid., p. 121.
35. Ibid., p. 123.
36. Cronin 1971, p. 298; Tulard 1987, p. 319.
37. Cronin 1971, p. 197. Later, as emperor, Napoleon legislated by decree. Being the second-born son, he deeply envied his elder firstborn brother Joseph. As emperor, he abolished primogeniture, the right of the firstborn son to inherit from his father.

38. Ibid.
39. Tulard 1989, p. 699.
40. McLynn 1997, p. 239.

Chapter 17

1. Castelot 1971, p. 186.
2. Ibid.
3. Garnier 1872, vol. 1, p. 476; Freud 1953, vol. 4, pp. 26, 233; Cronin 1971, p. 239.
4. Freud 1953, vol. 4, p. 233, vol. 5, pp. 497–498.
5. Freud 1953, vol. 5, p. 554.
6. Cronin 1971, p. 239.
7. Freud 1953, vol. 4, p. 233.
8. Castelot 1967, pp. 543–544.
9. Freud 1953, vol. 4, p. 234.
10. Ibid., note 1.
11. Castelot 1971, p. 187.
12. Ibid., p. 187.
13. Cronin 1971, p. 239.
14. Tulard 1989, p. 1107.
15. McLynn 1997, p. 243.
16. Cronin 1971, p. 239.
17. Ibid.
18. Ibid.
19. Ibid., pp. 239–240.
20. Bainville 1933, p. 128.
21. Ibid.; cf. McLynn 1997, p. 244.
22. Tulard 1989, pp. 498–499, 1175.
23. Cronin 1971, p. 240.
24. Tulard 1989, pp. 370, 1077, 1510.
25. Cronin 1971, p. 243, based on Roederer 1909.
26. Ibid.
27. Connelly 1987, p. 71, note 3.
28. Bainville 1933, p. 132.
29. Cronin 1971, pp. 226–227.
30. Usher 2000, p. 65.
31. Ibid.
32. Richardson 1972, p. 163.
33. Clark 1929, p. 118.
34. Cronin 1971, pp. 214–215.
35. Connelly 1987, p. 71, note 3; Hoiberg et al. 2005.

36. Tulard 1989, p. 1840; Dalisson 2004.
37. Richardson 1972, p. 18.
38. Brice 1937, p. 111.
39. Cronin 1971, p. 228.
40. Brice 1937, p. 118.
41. Cronin 1971, p. 186.
42. Ibid.
43. Ibid., p. 191
44. Ibid., p. 245
45. Ibid., pp. 206–207
46. Ibid., p. 207
47. Carrington 1988, p. 179. The first loan occurred at Valence in 1786 and the second one in 1795, when Napoleon was destitute and desperate in Paris and his mother asked him for money. Napoleon made Des Mazis the administrator of the French national lottery. In 1814 Des Mazis commanded a national guard battery defending Napoleon's Paris from the allied onslaught.
48. Tulard 1989, pp. 660–662.
49. Ibid.
50. Ibid., pp. 498–501.
51. Ibid., p. 1097.
52. Castelot 1971, p. 198.
53. Godechot 1969, p. 42; Castelot, 1971, p. 198.
54. Bainville 1933, p. 32.
55. Ibid., p. 140.
56. Ibid., p. 141.
57. Ibid.
58. Napoleon Bonaparte 1854–1869, vol. VII, p. 460; Herold 1955, p. 35.
59. McLynn 1997, pp. 243–244.
60. Tulard 1989, p. 1577.
61. Bainville 1933, pp. 137–138.
62. Guillon 1894; Tulard 1989, p. 1577.
63. Bainville 1933, p. 146.
64. Ibid.
65. Ibid.; cf. Tulard 1989, pp. 943, 1261, 1608.
66. Tulard 1989, pp. 749, 1472. The formal decree in the *Moniteur*, however, said that Fouché's police ministry would be reestablished "if other circumstances demanded it" and that Fouché himself would then be reappointed to his job, "the government being unable to find anyone more worthy of its trust." The "disgraced" Fouché kept Bonaparte's ear and trust and continued to play a key role in Napoleon's government, retaining his access to the Tuileries Palace, receiving politicians, and taking part in key meetings. It was yet another self-destructive act on Napoleon's part. Deep in his heart, Fouché never forgot the narcissistic injury inflicted on him by Bonaparte. Twelve years later he was instrumental in Emperor Napoleon's downfall.

Chapter 18

1. Aretz 1927, p. 160.
2. Ibid., pp. 158–172.
3. Cronin 1971, p. 278.
4. Castelot 1971, p. 203.
5. Richardson 1972, p. 131.
6. Castelot 1971, p. 204; Richardson 1972, p. 131.
7. Castelot 1971, p. 204, based on Weymer 1909.
8. Ibid.
9. Richardson 1972, p. 131.
10. Castelot 1971, p. 204, based on Weymer 1909.
11. Cronin 1971, p. 278.
12. Ibid.
13. McLynn 1997, p. 275.
14. Richardson 1972, pp. 47–48; McLynn 1997, pp. 275–276, 284–285.
15. McLynn 1997, p. 276.
16. Ibid.
17. Richardson 1972, p. 48. By 1808 the greedy and voracious Mademoiselle George had borrowed heavily and was deeply in debt. She left France for Russia, where she hoped to marry into money. She returned to France unmarried in 1813 and rejoined the *Comédie-Française*. In 1817 she left again. By 1830 she had become so big and fat that she was called *la baleine* (the whale). Napoleon had several other actresses as mistresses, but Mademoiselle George was "the only one of his actresses to touch his heart" (Richardson 1972, p. 131). She remained his mistress for at least two years (1802–1804).
18. Wilson 1802; Cronin 1971, pp. 229–230.
19. Cronin 1971, p. 231.
20. Castelot 1971, p. 206.
21. Cronin 1971, p. 233.
22. Brice 1937, pp. 120–121.
23. Castelot 1971, p. 206.
24. Whitworth 1887; Bainville 1933, p. 148; Brice 1937, pp. 120–121; Cronin 1971, pp. 232–233; Castelot 1971, pp. 206–207; McLynn 1997, p. 264.
25. Richardson 1972, p. 40.
26. Cronin 1971, p. 232, based on Whitworth 1887.
27. Bainville 1933, p. 147.
28. Cronin 1971, p. 233.
29. Bainville 1933, p. 148.
30. Cronin, Ibid., based on Whitworth 1887.
31. Godechot 1969, p. 44; Tulard 1989, pp. 578–579.

32. Castelot 1971, p. 207.
33. Ibid.
34. Bainville 1933, pp. 146–147.
35. Castelot 1967, p. 616; Castelot 1971, pp. 207–208.
36. Godechot 1969, p. 44.
37. Cronin 1971, p. 236.
38. Godechot 1969, p. 45, my translation from the French.
39. Ibid.
40. Brice 1937, p. 121.
41. Parker 1993–1999, letter of December 29, 1995.
42. Godechot 1969, p. 45.
43. Tulard 1989, p. 1314.
44. Ibid., my translation from the French.
45. Ibid., my translation from the French.
46. Cronin 1971, p. 269.
47. Richardson 1972, p. 209.
48. Cronin 1971, p. 299.
49. Ibid.
50. Ibid., pp. 298–299.

Chapter 19

1. Castelot 1967, p. 625.
2. Tulard 1989, pp. 322, 663. The health officer's name was Courson, but his first name is not given, and Castelot thought that the man who revealed Cadoudal's identity was not Courson but a captured *chouan* named Quérelle (Castelot 1971, p. 211).
3. Tulard 1989, p. 322, my translation from the French.
4. McLynn 1997, p. 293.
5. Tulard 1989, p. 663.
6. Castelot 1967, pp. 698–702; Tulard 1989, p. 664.
7. Cronin 1971, p. 242.
8. Tulard 1989, p. 664.
9. Ibid., p. 1071.
10. Carrington 1994–1998, letter of May 9, 1994.
11. Tulard 1989, pp. 663–665.
12. Connelly 1968, pp. 52–53, based on Joseph Bonaparte 1853–1854.
13. Herold 1955, pp. 258–259, based on Roederer 1909.
14. Bainville 1933, p. 159.
15. Castelot 1971, p. 220.

Chapter 20

1. Bainville 1933, p. 163–164; Cronin 1971, pp. 245–246.
2. Cronin 1971, p. 245.
3. Ibid., p. 246.
4. Ibid.
5. Bainville 1933, p. 164; Godechot 1969, p. 48; Castelot 1967, p. 671; Castelot 1971, p. 222; Cronin 1971, p. 246; Tulard 1989, p. 562.
6. Castelot 1971, p. 222.
7. Ibid.
8. Castelot 1967, p. 672; Castelot 1971, p. 222.
9. Ibid.
10. Castelot 1971, p. 224.
11. *Gazette nationale ou le Moniteur universel*, May 19, 1804, my translation from the French; cf. Castelot 1971, p. 224.
12. The fourteen imperial marshals named by Napoleon in 1804 were, by order of descending age, Louis-Alexandre Berthier (51), Bon-Adrien Jeannot de Moncey (50), Pierre-François-Charles Augereau (47), André Masséna (46), Jean-Baptiste Jourdan (42), Jean-Baptiste-Jules Bernadotte (41), Guillaume-Marie-Anne Brune (41), Joachim Murat (37), Adolphe-Edouard-Casimir-Joseph Mortier (36), Jean-Baptiste Bessières (36), Jean de Dieu Soult (35), Jean Lannes (35), Michel Ney (35), and Louis-Nicolas Davout (34).
13. Tulard 1989, p. 635.
14. Tulard 1989, p. 1199, my translation from the French.
15. Ibid.
16. Connelly 1968, p. 54.
17. Ibid., based on Miot de Melito 1881.
18. Connelly 1968, pp. 54–55.
19. Tulard 1989, p. 706.
20. Cronin 1971, p. 276, based on Roederer 1909.
21. Roederer 1909, pp. 212–213; Herold 1955, p. 257.
22. Cronin 1971, p. 276.
23. Castelot 1971, p. 225, based on Rémusat 1888–1889.
24. Richardson 1972, p. 95, based on Rémusat 1888–1889.
25. Castelot 1971, p. 225.
26. Ibid.; Cronin 1971, p. 249 and Richardson 1972, p. 31.
27. Bainville 1933, p. 166.
28. Ibid, based on Las Cases 1823.
29. Ibid.
30. Teneo 2000, pp. 35–36.
31. Ibid. p. 36
32. Castelot 1967, pp. 711–713; Richardson 1972, pp. 228–229; based on Wairy 1895. Tulard did not mention this incident in his article on Bruix.

33. Napoleon Bonaparte 1931, p. 92; Castelot 1964, p. 352.
34. Tulard 1989, pp. 288, 402.
35. Napoleon Bonaparte 1931, p. 93.
36. Castelot 1967, p. 714.
37. Aretz 1927, p. 182.
38. Castelot 1971, p. 302.
39. Richardson 1972, p. 135.
40. Castelot 1971, p. 302.
41. Cronin 1971, p. 278.
42. Aretz 1927, pp. 186–187.
43. Brice 1937, p. 280.
44. Cronin 1971, p. 248.
45. Ibid.
46. Ibid.
47. Ibid., p. 247.
48. Dundes 1993.
49. Cronin 1971, p. 247.
50. Ibid.
51. Falk 1996, p. 360.
52. Cronin 1971, p. 247.
53. Ibid., p. 201.
54. Carrington 2002.
55. Bainville 1933, p. 170.
56. Cronin 1971, p. 250, 461, based on Masson 1908 and Consalvi 1950.
57. Bainville 1933, pp. 169, 266.
58. Ibid., p 171; Cronin 1971, p. 251.
59. Connelly 1968, p. xiii.
60. Cronin 1971, p. 252.
61. Ibid.
62. Connelly 1987, p. 77.
63. Cronin 1971, p. 252.
64. McLynn 1997, p. 304; Cronin 1971, pp. 252–253, Castelot 1971, p. 252. The territory of the French Republic at that time included France, Belgium, the Savoy, the left bank of the River Rhine in Germany, and the Piedmont in Italy.
65. Clark 1929, p. 109.
66. McLynn 1997, p. 304.
67. Tulard 1989, p. 1071.
68. Stirling 1961, pp. 140–144; Nanteuil 1985.
69. Carrington 1994–1998, letter of May 9, 1994.
70. Marmont 1857, vol. 2, pp. 242–243; Napoleon Bonaparte 1887–1888, vol. III, pp. 3–4; Clark 1929, p. 152; Herold 1955, p. 49.
71. Tulard 1989, pp. 1071–1072.

Chapter 21

1. Tulard 1989, p. 1726.
2. Connelly 1987, p. 84.
3. Bainville 1933, p. 179. To face the mortal threat from France, Great Britain had allied itself in an anti-French "coalition" with Russia, which made Napoleon's task that much more difficult, if not impossible.
4. Tulard 1989, p. 569.
5. Bainville 1933, p. 182.
6. Ibid.
7. Ibid.
8. Ibid., pp. 182–183.
9. Napoleon Bonaparte 1931, p. 99.
10. Cronin 1971, p. 302.
11. Hoiberg et al. 2005.
12. Tulard 1989, p. 1726.
13. Bainville 1933, p. 183.
14. Castelot 1971, p. 256; Tulard 1989, p. 969.
15. Castelot 1971, p. 256.
16. Cronin 1971, p. 265; Castelot 1971, p. 257.
17. Cronin 1971, p. 265.
18. Castelot 1971, p. 257.
19. Clark 1929, p. 109.
20. Connelly 1987, p. 78.
21. Bainville 1933, pp. 176–177.
22. Tulard 1989, p. 1072.
23. Connelly 1987, p. 88.
24. Napoleon Bonaparte 1854–1869, vol. XI, pp. 448–453; Bainville 1933, p. 185; Herold 1955, pp. 126–129.
25. Ibid.
26. Ibid.; Bainvillc 1933, p. 186.
27. Kircheisen 1911–1934, vol. VI, pp. 502–503; Herold 1955, p. 129, n. 4.
28. Herold 1955, p. 129, note 4.
29. Carrington 1994–1998, letter of May 9, 1994.
30. Bainville 1933, pp. 186–187.
31. Cronin 1971, p. 258.
32. Tulard 1989, p. 458. In effect, without intending it, Napoleon launched the process of German unification, which Bismarck completed in 1870–1871, when he conquered Alsace and Lorraine from France and united all Germany under Prussia in the Second *Reich*.
33. Tulard 1989, p. 383.
34. Clark 1929, pp. 110–111.

Chapter 22

1. Falk 1996, pp. 368–370.
2. Geyl 1949, p. 317 and Dixon 1967, p. 330, citing Leroux 1850.
3. Geyl 1949, p. 9 and Dixon 1967, p. 330.
4. Carrington 1994–1998, letter of May 9, 1994.
5. Dixon 1967, p. 330.
6. Weider 1998.
7. Napoleon Bonaparte 1897, vol. 1, p. 159.
8. Schwarzfuchs 1974, p. 27.
9. Potok 1978, pp. 309–311.
10. Schwarzfuchs 1974, p. 27.
11. Falk 1996, p. 596.
12. Herold 1955, p. 111.
13. Tulard 1989, p. 1182.
14. Napoleon Bonaparte 1854–1869, vol. XII, letter no. 411; Herold 1955, pp. 111–112.
15. Tulard 1989, p. 988.
16. Falk 1996, p. 596.
17. Margolis & Marx 1985, p. 614.
18. Ibid., p. 615
19. Schwarzfuchs 1989, p. 187; Tulard 1989, p. 988.
20. Piétri 1965, p. 101, Tulard, Ibid. Some of the members of the Great Sanhedrin of the French Jews were members of the Assembly of Jewish Notables.
21. Piétri 1965, p. 101. When Napoleon liberated Poland from Prussia and Austria in 1807, the long-suffering Polish Jews welcomed him as a redeemer. Two Polish-Jewish Hassidic leaders, Rabbi Jakob Izak, the Seer of Lublin, and Rabbi Israel of Kozienice, proclaimed Napoleon's wars *havlay mashiah* (the throes of the Messiah, wars of Gog and Magog, or Armageddon). They believed they could accelerate the Messiah's arrival by magic. Napoleon had become their Messiah.
22. Ibid.
23. Barruel 1798–1799.
24. McLynn 1997, p. 436.
25. Ben-Sasson 1976, p. 762.
26. Tulard 1989, p. 989.
27. Margolis & Marx 1985, p. 615.
28. Ben-Sasson 1976, p. 762.
29. Tulard 1989, p. 989.

Chapter 23

1. McLynn 1997, p. 354.
2. Godechot 1969, p. 53.
3. Bainville 1933, p. 195.
4. Napoleon Bonaparte 1854–1869, vol. XIII, p. 170; Herold 1955, p. 206; Castelot 1971, p. 294.
5. Connelly 1987, p. 98.
6. Pingaud 1901; Bainville 1933, p. 196; Tulard 1989, p. 201.
7. Connelly 1987, pp. 101–102.
8. Ibid., pp. 102–103.
9. Ibid., p. 102.
10. Tulard 1989, p. 1421.
11. Castelot 1971, p. 297.
12. Ibid., p. 346
13. Bainville 1933, p. 197; Castelot 1971, p. 297; Tulard 1989, p. 345.
14. Castelot 1971, pp. 297–298.
15. Bainville 1933, p. 197.
16. Klein 1946, pp. 103–104. "Projective identification" is an unconscious process combining projection and "introjection," the latter being the psychoanalytic term for unconscious identification or the incorporation of an emotional "object" into the self. Melanie Klein defined "projective identification" as an unconscious splitting-off [of unbearable] parts of the self and projecting them on to another person.
17. Bainville 1933, p. 198.
18. Godechot 1969, p. 54.
19. Brice 1937, p. 260.
20. Tulard 1989, p. 1430.
21. Castelot 1971, p. 301.
22. Revel 1815; Aretz 1927, pp. 202–203.
23. Cronin 1971, p. 279.
24. Castelot 1971, pp. 307–308.
25. Cronin, 1971, p. 279.
26. Castelot 1971, p. 308.
27. Cronin 1971, p. 279.
28. Castelot 1971, p. 308.
29. Cronin 1971, p. 279; Castelot 1971, p. 308; Tulard 1989, p. 1739.
30. Ibid.
31. Castelot 1971, p. 307; Cronin 1971, p. 279.
32. Cronin 1971, p. 280.
33. Clark 1929, p. 78.
34. Ibid.
35. Castelot 1971, p. 310, quoting D'Ornano 1934; Cronin 1971, p. 279; McLynn 1997, p. 364.

36. Castelot 1971, p. 311, quoting D'Ornano 1934.
37. Ibid., quoting D'Ornano 1934.
38. Ibid., p. 312, quoting D'Ornano 1934.
39. Ibid., p. 315, quoting D'Ornano 1934.
40. Ibid., p. 316, quoting D'Ornano 1934.
41. Ibid., quoting D'Ornano 1934.
42. Ibid., quoting D'Ornano 1934.
43. Ibid., quoting D'Ornano 1934.
44. Cronin 1971, p. 280, quoting D'Ornano 1934.
45. Castelot 1971, pp. 316–317, quoting D'Ornano 1934.
46. Ibid., p. 31, quoting D'Ornano 1934.
47. Ibid., quoting D'Ornano 1934.
48. Ibid., quoting D'Ornano 1934.
49. Ibid., quoting D'Ornano 1934.
50. Connelly 1987, p. 110.
51. Bainville 1933, pp. 204–205.
52. Connelly 1987, p. 105.
53. Castelot 1971, p. 327.
54. Clark 1929, pp. 78–79.
55. Castelot 1971, p. 334.
56. Bainville 1933, p. 209.
57. Ibid., pp. 209–210.
58. Frank Richardson thought that Napoleon's attraction to Aleksandr may also have been homosexual (Richardson 1972, p. 163), but the narcissistic aspect of this love seems more important psychologically.
59. Hoiberg et al. 2005.
60. Clark 1929, p. 121.
61. Ibid.
62. Bainville 1933, p. 220.
63. Tulard 1989, p. 1619.

Chapter 24

1. Launay 1968, pp. 9–15.
2. Marmont 1857, vol. 6, pp. 274–276, 285, my translation from the French. Raoul Brice found that Napoleon's portraits at different times in his life "reveal astonishing contrasts. One might suppose that they portrayed different men altogether—the lean general and the corpulent Emperor" (Brice 1937, p. 140). Marmont's description rings true and accords with Lazare Carnot's observations on Napoleon (Carnot 1824). Marmont, however, was not objective, as Napoleon had made him wait five years for his promotion from general to marshal, and he had also turned against Napoleon in 1814, when the allies invaded France and

toppled the emperor, while Carnot had had severe conflicts with Napoleon. Brice believed that "Marmont was incapable—like many another—of impartiality towards a benefactor. His criticisms were made with the object of excusing his treason in 1814. But, allowing for exaggeration, his portrait of Napoleon the corpulent emphasizes as it ought the contrast with the meager Bonaparte" (Brice 1937, p. 140).

3. Richardson 1972, p. 56.
4. Ibid.
5. Brice 1937, p. 145.
6. Clark 1929, pp. 104–106 (italics added).
7. Ibid., p. 122.
8. Ibid., pp. 122–123.
9. Guthrie 1913; Brice 1937, p. 172; Richardson 1972, pp. 55–56.
10. Brice 1937, pp. 138–173.
11. Sokoloff 1937, quoted in Richardson 1972, p. 57.

Chapter 25

1. Connelly 1987, p. 117.
2. Ibid.; cf. Tulard 1989, pp. 674, 991.
3. Connelly 1987, p. 118.
4. Tulard 1989, p. 210.
5. Ibid., p. 676.
6. Bainville 1933, p. 223.
7. Connelly 1987, p. 119.
8. Cronin 1971, p. 262.
9. McLynn 1997, p. 392.
10. Bainville 1933, p. 228; Castelot 1971, pp. 352–353.
11. Castelot 1971, p. 353, quoting Chateaubriand 1814.
12. Bainville 1933, p. 229.
13. Ibid.
14. Ibid.
15. Ibid.
16. Connelly 1968, p. 97.
17. Ibid.
18. Ibid., footnote.
19. Bainville 1933, p. 232.
20. Bainville, Ibid.
21. Cronin 1971, p. 221.
22. Napoleon Bonaparte 1858–1870, vol. XI, p. 528 and D'Haussonville 1968–1969, vol. II, pp. 78, 101 (my translations from the French); McLynn 1997, p. 352. Napoleon wrote Fesch on January 7, 1806, and again on February 22, 1806,

"tell people [in Rome] that I am Charlemagne, the sword of the church, their emperor; that I must be treated the same; that they should not know that there was a Russian empire . . . if the Pope does not accept my conditions, I shall reduce him to the condition he was in before Charlemagne."

23. Tulard 1989, p. 1331.
24. Castelot 1968, p. 224, quoting Napoleon Bonaparte 1858–1870, my translation from the French.
25. Tulard 1989, p. 1331.
26. Castelot 1968, p. 220, my translation from the French.
27. Ibid., p. 224, quoting Napoleon Bonaparte 1858–1870, my translation from the French.
28. Tulard 1989, p. 1331.
29. Castelot 1971, p. 202.
30. Ibid.; Tulard 1989, pp. 288–289, 402; McLynn 1997, p. 276.
31. Castelot 1971, p. 202.
32. Ibid.
33. Tulard 1989, pp. 1547–1551.
34. Castelot 1971, p. 234, based on Bausset-Roquefort 1828.
35. Ibid, quoting Grétry 1919–1922.
36. Cronin 1971, p. 282.
37. Brice 1937, pp. 228–229.

Chapter 26

1. Connelly 1968, p. 103.
2. Ibid., pp. 103–104.
3. Richardson 1972, p. 139, based on Avrillion 1833.
4. Bainville 1933, p. 231.
5. Connelly 1968, p. 108.
6. Ibid., p. 109.
7. Ibid., p. 112.
8. Bainville 1933, p. 234; cf. Connelly 1987, p. 123.
9. Connelly 1987, p. 132.
10. Castelot 1971, p. 355.
11. Bainville 1933, pp. 234–235.
12. Ibid., p. 235.
13. Castelot 1971, p. 355.
14. Connelly 1968, p. 114.
15. William Shakespeare, *Henry IV, Part I*, Act V, scene iv, line 119.
16. Castelot 1971, p. 356.
17. Tulard 1989, p. 317, based on Fain 1908, my translation from the French.
18. Bainville 1933, p. 237.

19. Tulard 1989, p. 671, my translation from the French; Castelot 1971, pp. 356–357.
20. Bainville 1933, p. 239.
21. Ibid.
22. Castelot 1971, p. 357.
23. Castelot, Ibid.; Tulard 1987, p. 303; Tulard 1989, pp. 671–672, my translation from the French.
24. Bainville 1933, p. 239.
25. Castelot 1971, p. 357.
26. Clark 1929, p. 126.
27. Ibid.
28. Castelot 1971, p. 358.
29. Ibid.
30. Napoleon Bonaparte 1931, p. 179; Castelot 1971, p. 359.
31. Ibid.
32. McLynn 1997, p. 404.
33. Connelly 1968, p. 123; McLynn 1997, p. 405.
34. Bainville 1933, p. 241.
35. Ibid.
36. Castelot 1971, p. 360.

Chapter 27

1. Napoleon Bonaparte 1931, p. 185.
2. Jacques Bainville thought that this occurred during the night of January 12, 1809 (Bainville 1933, p. 242), but it was more likely during the night of January 1–2 (Godechot 1969, p. 59; Castelot 1971, p. 361).
3. Bainville 1933, p. 242.
4. Ibid., pp. 242–243.
5. Napoleon Bonaparte 1931, p. 186.
6. Godechot 1969, pp. 59–60.
7. Napoleon Bonaparte 1931, pp. 187–188.
8. General Legendre's humiliation by Emperor Napoleon on January 13, 1809, was reported many decades later in the posthumous memoirs of General Thiébault (Thiébault 1896; Savant 1958). Thiébault, however, was "the worst tongue of the army" (Tulard 1989, p. 1636). Jacques Bainville explained Napoleon's outburst of rage against Legendre: "*During a review at Valladolid he happened to be near General Legendre, who had been one of those who surrendered with Dupont at Baylen* [italics added], and there was a terrible scene in front of the troops when Napoleon, *in a voice of thunder, hurled reproaches at one of those responsible for the catastrophe* [italics added]. Baylen, like Trafalgar, was a red-hot brand that seared him; and without thinking that every soldier of his guard could

hear, he relieved his feelings and his nerves on the man before him, detailing the consequences of the disaster—Madrid evacuated, the insurrection raised to fever pitch, the English in the Peninsula, the course of events altered, and the 'destiny of the world' perhaps altered too!" (Bainville 1933, p. 243). Napoleon first arrested Legendre, later released him, and then suspended him (Tulard 1989, p. 1819). Frank Richardson thought that Napoleon often abused his senior officers in front of their troops, as had done Admiral Bruix in 1804, and thought that "some of [these] scenes were well-nigh incredible" (Richardson, 1972, p. 38). The incident with General Legendre, if it occurred, is especially puzzling, however. Why did Napoleon wait six months to confront Legendre and punish him? Legendre, after all, was not just "one of those who surrendered with Dupont at Baylen" as Bainville put it, but the general who personally signed the surrender. In Napoleon's unconscious mind Legendre may have symbolized the part of himself that he most hated. To Napoleon, England unconsciously symbolized his bad mother. His life's struggle was against her. Surrendering to England was the worst possible personal disaster to him. Legendre was the unconscious hook on which Napoleon hung his feelings. He unconsciously projected his feelings of failure, shame and humiliation and externalized his bad self-esteem upon Legendre.

9. Tulard 1989, p. 1636.

10. Connelly 1968, pp. 131–132, based on Thiébault 1896.

11. Connelly 1987, p. 133.

12. Castelot 1971, p. 362.

13. Ibid.

14. For the full text of Napoleon's outburst at Talleyrand see Bergler 1935, p. 48; Castelot 1968, p. 277; Godechot 1969, p. 60; Castelot 1971, pp. 362–363.

15. Bainville 1933, p. 246.

16. Ibid.

17. Ibid.

18. Ibid.

19. Ibid.

20. Castelot 1971, p. 362.

21. Bainville 1933, p. 246.

22. Clark 1929, p. 139.

23. Bergler 1933, 1935.

24. Castelot 1971, p. 363; Tulard 1989, p. 1621; McLynn 1997, p. 409.

25. Connelly 1968, p. 148.

26. Napoleon Bonaparte 1854–1869, vol. XVIII, pp. 253–254, 292–293; Godechot 1969, p. 60.

27. Ibid.

28. Connelly 1968, pp. 148–149.

29. Ibid., p. 149.

Chapter 28

1. McLynn 1997, p. 412.
2. Castelot 1971, p. 367.
3. Ibid.
4. Ibid.
5. Connelly 1987, pp. 133–134.
6. Bainville 1933, p. 248.
7. Tulard 1989, p. 1170.
8. Cronin 1971, p. 305.
9. Ibid., based on Vandal 1891–96.
10. Connelly 1987, p. 144.
11. Tulard 1989, p. 1737.
12. Connelly 1987, p. 144, based on Rothenberg 1982.
13. Castelot 1971, p. 375, based on Tascher 1932.
14. Bainville 1933, p. 252.
15. Richardson 1972, p. 16.
16. Bainville 1933, p. 253.

Chapter 29

1. Bainville 1933, p. 255.
2. Tulard 1989, p. 750.
3. Bainville 1933, p. 255.
4. Brice 1937, p. 59; italics added.
5. McLynn 1997, pp. 422–423, based on Wairy 1895.
6. Ibid., p. 423.
7. Brice 1937, p. 260, based on Roederer 1909.
8. McLynn 1997, p. 446.
9. Castelot 1971, p. 382, based on Cambacérès 1963.
10. Bainville 1933, p. 262.
11. Castelot 1971, p. 385.
12. Ibid., p. 384.
13. Cronin 1971, p. 306.
14. Castelot 1971, p. 384, based on Bausset-Roquefort 1828.
15. Bainville 1933, p. 263.
16. McLynn 1997, p. 465.
17. Bainville 1933, p. 263.
18. Ibid.
19. Castelot 1964, pp. 485–536.
20. Brice 1937, p. 260; Castelot 1964, p. 509, my translation from the French.
21. Brice 1937, p. 260.

22. McLynn 1997, pp. 465–466.
23. Hudson 1914, pp. 135–136, based on Mollien 1898.
24. Brice 1937, p. 260.
25. Hudson 1914, p. 137.
26. Ibid.
27. Cronin 1971, p. 307.
28. Bainville 1933, p. 264.
29. Ibid., pp. 264–265.
30. Ibid., p. 265.
31. Ibid., p. 266.
32. Ibid.
33. Ibid., pp. 266–267.
34. Ibid., p. 267.
35. Ibid.
36. Ibid.
37. Brice 1937, p. 237.
38. Richardson 1972, p. 123.
39. Brice 1937, pp. 28–29.
40. Bainville 1933, p. 265.
41. Brice 1937, p. 29.
42. Ibid., p. 237.
43. Tulard 1989, pp. 1140–1141.
44. Connelly 1987, p. 151.
45. Connelly 1968, p. 168; Tulard 1989, p. 680. Connelly gave the date erroneously as February 8, 1808, and the name of the fourth province as Biscay.
46. Tulard 1989, p. 680.
47. Ibid.
48. Connelly, pp. 168–171; Tulard 1989, p. 680.
49. Cronin 1971, p. 263.
50. Connelly 1968, p. 175.
51. Castelot 1971, p. 391.
52. Cronin 1971, p. 308, based on Marie-Louise Bonaparte 1922.
53. Tulard 1989, p. 447, my translation from the French.
54. Bainville 1933, p. 268.
55. Ibid.
56. Tulard 1989, p. 750, my translation from the French.
57. Ibid.
58. Connelly 1987, p. 132.
59. Connelly 1987, p. 131.
60. Connelly 1987, pp. 131–132.
61. Herold 1955, p. 163; Castelot 1967, pp. 698–702; Cronin 1971, p. 264.
62. Bainville 1933, pp. 274–275.
63. Tulard 1989, p. 1091.

64. After his abdication and his panic flight from Holland, the traumatized Louis Bonaparte received political asylum from the Austrian *Kaiser*, Franz. He later lived in Prussia and in Russia, but was rejected by their rulers and left for Rome.

65. Castelot 1971, p. 400.

66. Tulard 1989, p. 736.

67. Tulard 1987, p. 319.

68. Tulard 1989, p. 1091. At the time of Napoleon's troubles in early 1814, Louis was in Rome. He returned to France, but was received coolly by his elder brother and wife. In 1815, during the "100 days" of Napoleon's comeback from Elba, he refused Louis a seat in the French Chamber of Peers. After Napoleon's exile to Saint Helena, Louis tried to rejoin his wife, Hortense, who rebuffed him. He became a mediocre writer who styled himself the Count of Saint-Leu, after the town of Saint-Leu-la-Forêt in the Val d'Oise *département*, north of Paris, where his wife Hortense owned a castle, where Louis finally settled, and where Napoleon's grand marshal of the palace, General Henri-Gatien Bertrand, had married Fanny Dillon. When he died in 1846, King Louis of Holland was buried in the local church of Saint-Leu.

69. Tulard 1989, p. 201.

70. Connelly 1987, p. 156.

71. Parker 1991, pp. 95–96.

72. Ibid., p. 96, based on Napoleon Bonaparte 1854–1869, vol. XXI, no. 17179, pp. 297–299.

73. Connelly 1987, p. 155.

Chapter 30

1. The French novelist and poet Victor-Marie Hugo (1802–1885) made Napoleon cry at the birth of his son, "The future, the future, the future is mine!" but answered him, "No, the future is no man's, it is God's" (Hugo 1835, Napoléon II, *Poésie* 1, p. 706; Castelot 1968, p. 386; my translation from the French).

2. Napoleon Bonaparte 1931, p. 231; cf. Cronin 1971, p. 308.

3. Brice 1937, p. 276.

4. Richardson 1972, pp. 187–201.

5. Connelly 1987, p. 155.

6. Castelot 1971, p. 404.

7. Clark 1929, p. 153.

8. Castelot 1071, p. 405.

9. Cronin 1971, p. 222.

10. Tulard 1989, pp. 449–451.

11. Ibid., p. 1331

12. Parker 1991, pp. 86–87.
13. Clark 1929, pp. 153–154.
14. Brice 1937, p. 261.
15. Tulard 1989, p. 1740.
16. Connelly 1987, p. 159.
17. Ibid.
18. Clark 1929, pp. 156–157.
19. Castelot 1971, p. 411.
20. Connelly 1987, p. 159; italics added.
21. Hoiberg et al. 2005.
22. Clark 1929, p. 157.

Chapter 31

1. Castelot 1971, p. 426.
2. Castelot 1971, p. 428, based on Caulaincourt 1935–1936.
3. Clark 1929, p. 166.
4. Castelot 1971, p. 428.
5. Castelot 1968, pp. 456–457, my translation from the French; Clark 1929, p. 171; Connelly 1987, p. 172.
6. Castelot 1971, pp. 429–430.
7. Connelly 1987, p. 172.
8. Connelly 1987, pp. 173–174; italics added.
9. Ibid., p. 174.
10. Tulard 1989, pp. 1120–1121.
11. Eighteen months later, in April 1814, when a fallen and suicidally depressed Napoleon tried to kill himself with Dr. Yvan's "poison," it failed to do the job (Castelot 1971, pp. 492–493; Cronin 1971, p. 370; Tulard 1989, p. 1756; McLynn 1997, pp. 594–595; based on Yvan 1846, Wairy 1895, Caulaincourt 1935–1936 and other memoirs).
12. Castelot 1971, p. 436.
13. Connelly 1987, p. 175.
14. Ibid., p. 177.
15. Clark 1929, p. 175.
16. Castelot 1971, p. 446.
17. Connelly 1987, p. 179, based on Montesquiou-Fezensac 1852.
18. Chandler 1966, p. 853; Connelly 1987, p. 181, note 4.
19. Clark 1929, p. 174.
20. Clark 1929, p. 176; Connelly 1987, p. 180.
21. Clark 1929, p. 178.
22. Castelot 1971, p. 447.
23. Ibid.

24. Ibid., based on Oudinot 1896.
25. Connelly 1987, p. 180.
26. Clark 1929, p. 147.
27. Klaf 1960.
28. Ibid., p. 71.
29. Connelly 1994–1995, letter of 20 January 1994.
30. Tulard 1989, p. 971.
31. Clark 1929, p. 179.
32. Ibid., p. 178.
33. Godechot 1969, p. 67.
34. Ibid.
35. Jekels 1952, p. 72, quoting Wolseley 1895.
36. Wolseley 1895.
37. Tulard 1989, p. 1331.
38. Connelly 1987, pp. 181–183.
39. Clark 1929, p. 179.
40. Connelly 1987, p. 181.
41. Castelot 1971, p. 455.
42. Connelly 1987, p. 189.
43. Ibid.
44. Tulard 1989, p. 1547.
45. Cronin 1971, p. 273, based on La Tour 1913.
46. Herold 1955, pp. 26–27, based on Bourrienne 1829–1831, vol. 5, p. 121.
47. Ibid., p. 27, based on Bourrienne 1837–39, vol. 5, p. 153.
48. Ibid., p. 27, based on Napoleon Bonaparte 1854–1869, vol. XXV, pp. 321–322.
49. Ibid., p. 27, based on Napoleon Bonaparte 1854–1869, vol. XXV, p. 368.
50. Castelot 1971, p. 584.
51. Cronin 1971, p. 273, quoting John 15:13.
52. Bainville 1933, p. 83.
53. Cronin 1971, p. 161.
54. Ibid., p. 273.
55. Connelly 1987, p. 194.
56. Ibid.
57. Ibid.
58. Ibid.
59. Tulard 1989, pp. 1697–1698. The "Indies" were the European colonies in Latin America.
60. Connelly 1987, p. 195.
61. Godechot 1969, p. 69.
62. Herold 1955, p. 83, based on Fain 1823, pp. 22–23 and Napoleon Bonaparte 1887–1888, vol. II, p. 463.
63. Herold 1955, p. 83.

64. Tulard 1989, p. 1208.
65. Ibid., p. 375, my translation from the French.

Chapter 32

1. Tulard 1989, pp. 360–361.
2. Godechot 1969, p. 70; my translation from the French.
3. Ibid., p. 71.
4. Castelot 1971, p. 483.
5. Tulard 1989, p. 1031.
6. Godechot 1989, pp. 71–74.
7. Castelot 1971, p. 484; Connelly 1987, p. 198.
8. Cronin 1971, p. 365.
9. Ibid.; italics added.
10. Castelot 1971, p. 484; italics added. The psychoanalyst Pierce Clark gave a more poetic version of this abdication document: "Since the allied powers have declared that Emperor Napoleon is the only obstacle to the peace of Europe, Emperor Napoleon, faithful to his oath, declares himself ready, for the welfare of his country, which is inseparable from the rights of his son, from those of the regency of the empress, and from the maintenance of the laws of the Empire, to descend from the throne, to give up France and even life itself" (Clark 1929, p. 181). Clark may have confused Napoleon's first, conditional abdication of April 4, 1814, with his second, unconditional one of April 6.
11. Connelly 1987, p. 199. Napoleon's mother Letizia left Paris on March 29, 1814, the same day as Marie-Louise. Letizia's magnificent château at Pont-sur-Seine, in the Aube, had been burned down by the Allied enemy. Letizia went to Tours with a French passport for Italy. She joined her half-brother, Joseph Cardinal Fesch, at Lyon, and the two left for Rome, where they lived at the opulent Palazzo Falconieri. Letizia remained in Rome until July 1814, when she received permission to visit her son on the Isle of Elba (Tulard 1989, p. 1072).
12. McLynn 1997, pp. 588–589.
13. Castelot 1971, pp. 486–487.
14.Clark 1929, p. 182; Castelot 1971, p. 488.
15.Clark 1929, p. 183.
16. Castelot 1971, p. 489.
17. Ibid.
18. Ibid.
19. Ibid.
20. Ibid., based on Plancy 1904.
21. Ibid.

22. Ibid., based on Wairy 1895.
23. Tulard 1989, p. 493; Wairy 1895.
24. Castelot 1971, p. 490; cf. McLynn 1997, pp. 588–589.
25. Castelot 1968, p. 619, my translation from the French.
26. Castelot 1971, p. 490.
27. Brice 1937, p. 86.
28. Ibid., p. 136.
29. Clark 1929, p. 183, based on Ségur 1895; Herold 1955, p. 36.
30. Clark 1929, p. 183.
31. Cronin 1971, pp. 368–369.
32. Clark 1929, pp. 183–184.
33. Richardson 1972, p. 29; italics added.
34. Castelot 1971, p. 495; McLynn 1997, p. 595, based on Campbell 1869.
35. McLynn 1997, pp. 595–596.
36. Ibid., p. 596.
37. Castelot 1971, p. 498, based on Waldburg-Truchsess 1816.
38. Ibid., based on Waldburg-Truchsess 1816.
39. Ibid., pp. 498–499, based on Waldburg-Truchsess 1816.
40. Richardson 1972, p. 28.
41. I Samuel 21:11–16.
42. Castelot 1971, p. 501, based on Marie-Louise Bonaparte 1922.

Chapter 33

1. Castelot 1971, pp. 515–516.
2. Ibid., p. 516.
3. Richardson 1972, p. 42, probably based on Marchand 1952–1955.
4. Ibid., p. 50, based on Kemble 1959.
5. Ibid., based on Marchand 1952–1955
6. Clark 1929, pp. 185–186.
7. Castelot 1971, p. 509, based on Christophe 1964.
8. Ibid., p. 510, based on Christophe 1964.
9. Ibid., pp. 510–511, based on Christophe 1964.
10. Ibid., p. 511, based on Christophe 1964.
11. Clark 1929, p. 186.
12. Castelot 1971, p. 512.
13. Clark 1929, p. 186.
14. Ibid.
15. Brice 1937, p. 86.
16. Ibid.
17. Tulard 1989, p. 311.
18. Castelot 1971, p. 518.

19. Ibid.
20. Castelot 1971, p. 515, based on Hyde de Neuville 1913.
21. McLynn 1997, pp. 602–603.
22. Castelot 1971, p. 519.
23. Ibid., p. 522.
24. Ibid., p. 526.
25. Bainville 1933, p. 363; Connelly 1987, p. 203.
26. Tulard 1989, p. 1010.
27. Ibid., p. 1586.
28. Godechot 1969, p. 75; Castelot 1971, p. 531, based on Nicolson 1946; Tulard 1989, p. 1719, my translation from the French.
29. Tulard 1989, p. 1208.
30. Connelly 1987, p. 204.
31. Ibid.
32. Clark 1929, pp. 188–189, based on Lavalette 1831.
33. McLynn 1997, p. 602.
34. Connelly 1987, p. 204.
35. Ibid.
36. Clark 1929, p. 189.
37. Tulard 1989, p. 750.
38. Ibid.
39. Clark 1929, p. 189.
40. Cronin 1971, p. 403.

Chapter 34

1. Castelot 1971, p. 542, based on Thiébault 1896.
2. Connelly 1987, p. 205.
3. Castelot 1971, p. 543, based on Blücher von Wahlstatt 1876.
4. Ibid.
5. Ibid., p, 544.
6. Ibid., based on Coignet 1897and François 1906.
7. Ibid.
8. Ibid.
9. Tulard 1989, p. 620.
10. Cronin 1971, p. 403.
11. Ibid.
12. Connelly 1987, title page.
13. Cronin 1971, p. 403.
14. Clark 1929, pp. 195–196.
15. Ibid., p. 199.
16. Ibid., title page.

17. Ibid., pp. 200–201, quoting Raoul's memoirs.
18. Connelly 1987, p. 217.
19. Castelot 1971, p. 557; Connelly 1987, p. 219.

Chapter 35

1. Castelot 1971, p. 559, based on Maitland 1904.
2. Ibid., p. 562, based on Maitland 1904.
3. Ibid., based on Maitland 1904.
4. Ibid., p. 563, based on Maitland 1904.
5. Ibid., p. 564, based on Maitland 1904.
6. Ibid.
7. This heart-rending letter, which had no chance of being answered, certainly not in the affirmative, has been quoted by every Napoleon biographer and scholar. See Las Cases 1823, entry of July 14, 1815; Brice 1937, p. 45; Castelot 1971, p. 566; Connelly 1987, p. 220; McLynn 1997, p. 634.
8. Hoiberg & al. 2005.
9. Ibid.
10. Castelot 1971, p. 565, based on Las Cases 1823 and Maitland 1904.
11. Connelly 1968, p. 245.
12. McLynn 1997, pp. 635–636.
13. Castelot 1971, p. 572; McLynn 1997, p. 636.
14. Castelot 1971, p. 572, based on Marchand 1952–1955; italics added.
15. Ibid., pp. 572–573, based on Marchand 1952–1955.
16. Tulard 1989,pp. 1513–1521.
17. Forshufvud & Weider 1978; Weider & Forshufvud 1995.
18. Corso and Hindmarsh 1996; Hindmarsh & Corso 1998; Bourdial 2002.
19. Antommarchi 1826, vol. 2, pp. 161–163; Richardson 1972, pp. 53–54; McLynn 1997, pp. 656–662; Hindmarsh & Corso 1998; Bourdial 2002.
20. Richardson 1972, p. 53, quoting Henry 1823, 1839.
21. Cronin 1971, pp. 467–468; McLynn 1997, pp. 657–658.
22. Antommarchi 1826, vol. 2, pp. 161–163.
23. Corso and Hindmarsh 1996, p. 93.
24. Brice 1937, p. 92.
25. Castelot 1971, p. 604.
26. Ibid., p. 603, based on Napoleon Bonaparte 1977.
27. Napoleon Bonaparte 1977.
28. Brice 1937, p. 92.
29. Castelot 1971, p. 220.
30. Tulard 1989, pp. 1723–1724.
31. Ibid., p. 1723.
32. Brice 1937, p. 93.

33. Ibid.
34. Castelot 1971, p. 605.
35. Castelot, Ibid.

References

Abse, David Wilfred & Jessner, Lucie (1962) The Psychodynamic Aspects of Leadership. In Graubard, Stephen R. & Holton, Gerald (Eds.) *Excellence and Leadership in a Democracy*, pp. 76-93. New York: Columbia University Press.

Abse, David Wilfred & Ulman, Richard B. (1977) Charismatic Political Leadership and Collective Regression. In Robins, Robert S. (Ed.) *Psychopathology and Political Leadership*, pp. 35-52. New Orleans: Tulane University.

Akhtar, Salman (1992) *Broken Structures: Severe Personality Disorders and Their Treatment*. Northvale, New Jersey and London: Jason Aronson.

Anisfeld, Leon & Richards, Arnold K. (2000) The Replacement Child: Variations on a Theme in History and Psychoanalysis. *The Psychoanalytic Study of the Child*, vol. 55, pp. 301–318.

Anonymous (1889) *Mémoires historiques sur la Corse par un officier du régiment de Picardie, 1774-1777, publiés par M. V. de Caraffa*. Published in three issues of the *Bulletin de la Société des Sciences historiques et naturelles de la Corse*, vol. 19, nos. 100-102. Ed. Philippe Caraffa. Bastia: Veuve Eugène Ollagnier. New edition (1978) *Mémoires historiques sur la Corse par un officier du régiment de Picardie, 1774–1777, publiés par M. V. de Caraffa*. Marseille: Laffitte. [French].

Antommarchi, Francesco [François] (1825) *Mémoires du docteur F. Antommarchi, ou les derniers momens [sic] de Napoléon*. Two volumes and an Atlas. Paris: Barrois l'ainé. Numerous other editions from 1840 to 1969.

——— (1826) *The Last Days of Napoleon: Memoirs of the Last Two Years of Napoleon's Exile, by F. Antommarchi, Forming a Sequel to the Journals of Dr. O'Meara and Count Las Cases*. Second edition. London: Henry Colburn.

Aretz, Gertrude (1927) *Napoleon and His Women Friends*. Tr. Eden and Cedar Paul. London: George Allen & Unwin. Philadelphia: J. B. Lippincott Co.

Arnault, Antoine-Vincent (1833) *Souvenirs d'un sexagénaire*. Four volumes. Paris: Dufèy. New edition (1908) Ed. Auguste Dietrich. Paris: Garnier frères. [French].

Arrighi de Casanova, Marthe (1954) *Letizia mère de Napoléon a été calomniée*. Intr. B. de Moro-Giafferri. Brussels: Office international de Librairie. [French].

Augustin-Thierry, Amédée [Gilbert-Jules-Augustin Thierry] (1939) *Madame*

Mère. Paris: Albin Michel. New edition (1951) Paris: Albin Michel. [French].
Avrillion, Marie-Jeanne-Pierrette (1833) *Mémoires de Mlle Avrillion, première femme de chambre de l'impératrice, sur la vie privée de Joséphine, sa famille et sa cour*. Two volumes. Actual writer Charles-Maxime Catherinet de Villemarest. Paris: Ladvocat. New edition (1986) Nouvelle édition augmentée d'un index onomastique. Ed. Maurice Dernelle. Paris: Mercure de France. [French].
Bainville, Jacques (1933) *Napoleon*. Tr. Hamish Miles. Boston: Little, Brown, and Co.
Barruel, Augustin (1798-1799) *Mémoires pour servir à l'histoire du jacobinisme, par M. l'abbé Barruel*. Five volumes. Hamburg: P. Fauche. Abridged edition (1911) by E. Perrenet. Paris: La Renaissance française. [French].
Bartel, Paul (1954) *La jeunesse inédite de Napoléon, d'après de nombreux documents*. Paris: Amiot-Dumont. [French].
Bausset-Roquefort, Louis-François-Joseph de (1828) *Private Memoirs of the Court of Napoleon and of Some Publick Events of the Imperial Reign, from 1805 to the First of May 1814, to Serve as a Contribution to the History of Napoleon*. Philadelphia: Carey & Lea.
Bécat, Pierre (1969) *Napoléon et le destin de l'Europe*. Brussels: Éditions Arts et voyages. Paris: Dargaud. [French].
Becker, Carl Lotus (1931) *Modern History: The Rise of a Democratic, Scientific, and Industralized Civilization*. New York and Newark, New Jersey: Silver, Burdett and Co. Numerous other editions from 1933 to 1974.
Belliard, Augustin-Daniel & al. (1830) *Bourrienne et ses erreurs volontaires et involontaires, ou observations sur ses "Mémoires" par MM. le général Belliard, le général Gourgaud, le comte d'Aure, le comte de Survilliers* [Joseph Bonaparte], *le baron Meneval, le comte Bonacossi, le prince d'Eckmuhl, le baron Massias, le comte Boulay de la Meurthe, le ministre de Stein, Cambacérès, recueillies par A. B.* Two volumes. Paris and Leipzig: Charles Heideloff and Urbain Chanel. [French].
Belloc, Hilaire (1932) *Napoleon*. London: Cassell. Second edition (1934) London: Cassell.
Ben-Sasson, Haim Hillel (Ed. 1976) *A History of the Jewish People*. London: George Weidenfeld and Nicolson. Cambridge, Massachusetts: Harvard University Press.
Bergler, Edmund (1933) Unbewusste Motive im Verhalten Napoleons zu Talleyrand. *Die Psychoanalytische Bewegung*, vol. 5, pp. 319-369.
——— (1935) *Talleyrand • Napoleon • Stendhal • Grabbe: psychoanalytisch-biographische Essays*. Vienna: Internationaler Psychoanalytischer Verlag. [German].
——— (1959) *Money and Emotional Conflicts*. New York: International Universities Press. New edition (1985) New York: International Universities Press.

Bergler, Edmund & Meerloo, Joost A. M. (1963) *Justice and Injustice: The Origin of the Sense of Justice and its Relation to Everyday Life, the Law, and the Problems of Juvenile Deliquency and Crime*. New York and London: Grune and Stratton.

Bertrand, Henri-Gratien (1949–1959) *Cahiers de Sainte-Hélène: journal du général Bertrand, grand maréchal du Palais de l'Empereur Napoléon à Sainte-Hélène*. Three volumes. Ed. Paul Fleuriot de Langle. Paris: Sulliver & Albin Michel. [French].

Bloy, Léon (1912) *L'Âme de Napoléon*. Paris: Mercure de France. New edition (1983) Paris: Gallimard. [French].

Blücher von Wahlstatt, Gebhard Leberecht (1876) *Blücher in Briefen aus den Feldzügen, 1813–1815*. Ed. E. von Colomb. Stuttgart: J. G. Cotta. [German].

Bonaparte, Charles-Marie: see Buonaparte, Carlo Maria.

Bonaparte, Joseph (1853–1854) *Mémoires et correspondance politique et militaire du roi Joseph, publiés, annotés et mis en ordre par A. Ducasse*. Ten volumes. Paris: Perrotin. [French].

Bonaparte, Louis (1815) *Maria, or the Hollanders*. Two volumes. Boston: John Eliot, and Cummings and Hilliard.

Bonaparte, Lucien (1835–1836) *The Memoirs of Lucien Bonaparte (Prince De Canino), Written by Himself, Translated from the Original Manuscript, under the Immediate Superintendence of the Author*. Two volumes. London: Henry Colburn. New York : Harper and Brothers.

Bonaparte, Marie-Louise-Léopoldine-Françoise-Thérèse-Joséphine-Lucie (1922) *The Private Diaries of the Empress Marie Louise, Wife of Napoleon I*. Ed. & Intr. Frédéric Masson. London: John Murray.

Bonaparte, Napoleon (1793) *Le Souper de Beaucaire*. Avignon: Sabin Tournal. [French].

——— (1822) *Œuvres littéraires et politiques de Napoléon*. Six volumes. Paris: Charles-Louis-Fleury Panckoucke. New edition (1840) Paris: H.-L. Delloye.

——— (1833) Lettres à Joséphine. In Salvage de Faverolles (Ed.) *Lettres de Napoléon à Joséphine pendant la première campagne d'Italie, le Consulat et l'Empire; et lettres de Joséphine à Napoléon et à sa fille*. Two volumes. Paris: Firmin Didot frères. [French].

——— (1854–1869) and (1858–1870) *Correspondance de Napoléon Ier, publiée par ordre de l'Empereur Napoléon III, suivie des Œuvres de Napoléon Ier à Sainte-Hélène*. Thirty-two volumes. Paris: L'Imprimerie Impériale. Paris: Henri Plon & J. Dumaine. Reprinted (1974) New York: AMS Press. [French].

——— (1884) *A Selection from the Letters and Despatches of the First Napoleon, with Explanatory Notes By Captain the Hon. D. A. Bingham*. Ed. Denis Arthur Bingham. Three volumes. London: Chapman and Hall.

——— (1887–1888) *Napoléon Bonaparte: Œuvres littéraires*. Four volumes. Ed. Tancrède Martel. Paris: Nouvelle Librairie Parisienne. [French].

——— (1897) *Lettres inédites de Napoléon Ier (an VIII–1815), publiées par Léon*

Lecestre. Two volumes. Paris: E. Plon, Nourrit et Cie. [French].

——— (1897a) *New Letters of Napoleon I, Omitted from the Edition Published under the Auspices of Napoleon III; from the French by Lady Mary Loyd*. New York: D. Appleton. Reprinted (1898) London: W. Heinemann.

——— (1907) *Napoléon: manuscrits inédits, 1786-1791, publiés, d'après les originaux autographes, par Frédéric Masson et Guido Biagi*. Paris: Paul Ollendorff. [French].

——— (1911) *Œuvres amoureuses de Napoléon, d'après ses lettres d'amour à Joséphine, avec une introduction et des notes du bibliophile Pol André*. Paris: Albin Michel. [French].

——— (1929) *Clisson et Eugénie*. [fragments]. In Askenazy, S. (Ed.) *Rekopisy Napoleona (1793–1795) w Polsce; Manuscrits de Napoléon en Pologne (1793–1795)*. Warsaw: J. Wilder [Polish and French]. Complete version in Napoleon Bonaparte (1967-68) *Œuvres littéraires et écrits militaires*, ed. Jean Tulard, vol. 2, pp. 440–553. Paris: Société Encyclopédique Française. [French].

——— (1931) *Letters of Napoleon to Josephine: Complete Collection, with Preface by Dr. Léon Cerf*. Ed. Léon Cerf. Tr. Henry W. Bunn. New York: Brentano's.

——— (1931a) *Napoleon's Autobiography: The Personal Memoirs of Bonaparte, Compiled from His Own Letters and Diaries by Professor F. M. Kircheisen*. Tr. Frederick Collins. Intr. Henry Irving Brock. New York: Duffield & Co.

——— (1934) *Letters of Napoleon, Selected, Translated, and Edited by J. M. Thompson*. Oxford: Basil Blackwell. Reprinted (1934) as Napoleon Self-revealed, in Three Hundred Selected Letters. Boston and New York: Houghton Mifflin Co. New edition (1954) London: Dent. New York: Dutton.

———(1934a) Lettres de Napoléon à Talleyrand. *Revue des Deux Mondes*, January 1. [French].

——— (1935) *The Letters of Napoleon to Marie-Louise*. London: Hutchinson & Co. New York: Farrar & Rinehart.

——— (1961) *Letters and Documents of Napoleon, Selected and translated by John Eldred Howard. Vol. 1: The Rise to Power*. [No other volumes published.] London: Cresset Press. New York: Oxford University Press.

——— (1964) *Proclamations, ordres du jour, et bulletins de la Grande Armée par Napoléon Bonaparte*. Ed. & Intr. Jean Tulard. Paris: Union générale d'éditions. [French].

——— (1967–1968) *Œuvres littéraires et écrits militaires de Napoléon. Three volumes*. Ed. Jean Tulard. Paris: Société Encyclopédique Française. [French].

——— (1977) *Napoleon's Last Will and Testament: Commentaries by Jean-Pierre Babelon and Suzanne d'Huart*. A Facsimile Edition of the Original Document, Together with its Codicils, Appended Inventories, Letters, and Instructions, Preserved in the French National Archives. Tr. & Intr. Alex de Jonge. New York: Paddington Press.

——— (1979) *Œuvres littéraires*. Édition établie, annotée et présentée par Alain Coelho. Nantes: Temps singulier. [French].

——— (1981) *Lettres d'amour à Joséphine*. Première édition intégrale établie par Chantal de Tourtier-Bonazzi. Présentation de Jean Tulard. Paris: Librairie Arthème Fayard. [French].

Borneman, Ernest (1976) *The Psychoanalysis of Money*. New York: Urizen Books.

Boswell, James (1768) *An Account of Corsica, the Journal of a Tour to that Island; and Memoirs of Pascal Paoli*. London: E. & C. Dilly. Reprinted in Boswell, James (1923) *The Journal of a Tour to Corsica, & Memoirs of Pascal Paoli*. Ed. & intr. S.C. Roberts. Cambridge: Cambridge University Press. New edition (1977) Ed. Morchard Bishop. Norwood, Pennsylvania: Norwood Editions.

Bouhler, Philipp (1941) *Napoleon: Kometenbahn eines Genies*. Munich: Georg D. W. Callwey. Second edition (1942) Georg D. W. Callwey. [German].

Bourdial, Isabelle (2002) Napoléon n'a pas été assassiné! *Science & Vie*, no. 1022, November, pp. 81–93. [French].

Bourrienne, Louis-Antoine Fauvelet de (1829–1831) *Mémoires de M. de Bourrienne, secrétaire intime du Premier consul, ministre d'État, sur Napoléon, le Directoire, le Consulat, l'Empire et la Restauration*. Ten volumes. Ghostwritten by Charles-Maxime Caterinet de Villemarest. Paris: Ladvocat. Numerous later editions. [French].

——— (1830) *Private Memoirs of Napoleon Bonaparte, during the Periods of the Directory, the Consulate, and the Empire, by M. de Bourrienne, Private Secretary to the Emperor*. Four volumes. London: Henry Colburn and Richard Bentley. Edinburgh: Constable and Co. Numerous editions from 1832 to 1906.

——— (1837–1839) *Mémoires de M. de Bourrienne, ministre d'Etat, sur Napoléon, le Directoire, le Consulat, l'Empire et la Restauration*. Edition nouvelle, refondue et annotée par Désiré Lacroix. Five volumes. Paris: A. Savine. [French].

——— (1885) *Memoirs of Napoleon Bonaparte, by Louis Antoine Fauvelet de Bourrienne His Private Secretary, to Which Are Added an Account of the Important Events of the Hundred Days of Napoleon's Surrender to the English, and of His Residence and Death at St Helena, with Anecdotes and Illustrative Extracts from All the Most Authentic Sources*. Four volumes. Ed. Ramsay Weston Phipps. London: Richard Bentley & Son. Boston: Estes. Reprinted (1895) Paris and Boston: The Napoleon Society.

Breton, Guy (1965) *Napoleon and His Ladies*. Tr. Frederick Holt. London: Robert Hale. Reprinted (1966) New York: Coward-McCann.

Brice, Léon-Raoul-Marie (1937) *The Riddle of Napoleon*. Tr. Basil Creighton. London: Putnam. New York: G. P. Putnam's Sons.

Brill, Abraham Arden (1921) *Fundamental Conceptions of Psychoanalysis*. New York: Harcourt, Brace. Reprinted (1922) London: George Allen & Unwin. New edition (1973) New York: Arno Press.

——— (1949) *Basic Principles of Psychoanalysis*. Ed. & Intr. Philip R. Lehrman. Garden City, New York: Doubleday & Co. New edition (1976) Westport, Connecticut: Greenwood Press. Reprinted (1985) Lanham, Maryland: University Press of America.

Broers, Michael (2004) *The Napoleonic Empire in Italy, 1796–1814.* New York: Palgrave Macmillan.

Brotonne, Léonce de (1893) *Les Bonaparte et leurs alliances.* Paris: E. Charavay. Second edition (1901) Paris: H. Champion. [French].

Broucek, Francis J. (1982) *Shame and the Self.* New York & London: Guilford Press.

Bruun, Geoffrey (1932) *Saint-Just: Apostle of the Terror.* Boston, New York, Houghton Mifflin Co. New edition (1966) Hamden, Connecticut: Archon Books.

Budge, Ernest Alfred Wallis (1982) *The Gods of the Egyptians; or, Studies in Egyptian Mythology.* London: P. Lowe. Reprinted (1983) New York: Schocken Books. Vancouver: Douglas & McIntyre. Reprinted (1996) New York: Dover Publications.

Buonaparte, Carlo Maria di (1766) *Exercitationes accademicæ in secundam partem: Ethicæ de jur., nat., et gent. ... de Carolus Bonaparte patritius adjacensis.* Corte: Carolus Bonaparte. [Latin]. Reprinted in Carrington, Dorothy (2002) *Portrait de Charles Bonaparte, d'après ses écrits de jeunesse et ses mémoires.* Ajaccio: A. Piazzola. [French].

——— (1780) *Raggionamento istorico, o siano memorie domestiche della famiglia di Buonaparte di Ajaccio in Corsica scritte da me Carlo di Buonaparte quondam Giuseppe l'anno mille e settecento ottanta.* Manuscript. Paris: Archives Nationales, Fonds Braccini, 400 AP, no. 115. [Italian].

——— (1977) Livre de Raison. In Versini, Xavier (1977) *M. de Buonaparte ou le Livre inachevé.* Paris: Albatros. [French].

——— (1980) *Libro di prattico criminale: transcription du cours de procédure criminelle pris par un étudiant de l'Université de Corse, 1768.* Bastia: Association Franciscorsa. [Italian and French].

——— (2002) Exposé historique ou Mémoires domestiques de la famille Buonaparte d'Ajaccio en Corse ... In Carrington, Dorothy *Portrait de Charles Bonaparte, d'après ses écrits de jeunesse et ses mémoires.* Ajaccio: Alain Piazzola. [French].

Byron, George Gordon (1973–94) *Byron's Letters and Journals.* Thirteen volumes. Ed. Leslie A. Marchand. London: John Murray.

Cambacérès, Jean-Jacques-Régis de (1963) *Cambacérès: autographes, documents, manuscrits.* Paris: Librairie de l'Abbaye. [French].

——— (1976) *Cambacérès and the Bonapartes: Unpublished Papers of Jean-Jacques-Régis Cambacérès, Second Consul and Later Arch-Chancellor, Relating to the Emperor Napoleon and His Circle; A Calendar.* Ed. Richard Boulind. New York: H. P. Kraus.

Campbell, Neil (1869) *Napoleon at Fontainebleau and Elba, Being a Journal of Occurrences in 1814–1815, with Notes of Conversations by the late Major General Sir Neil Campbell, Followed by the Journal of Sir Neil Campbell from April 9, 1814 to April 1, 1815 ... with a Memoir of the Life and Services of That Officer.* Ed. Archibald Neil Campbell MacLachlan. London: John Murray.

Carnot, Lazare-Nicolas-Marguerite (1824) *Mémoires historiques et militaires sur Carnot, rédigés d'après ses manuscrits, sa correspondance et ses écrits*, précédés d'une notice par P.-F. Tissot. Paris: Baudouin frères. New edition (1861-1864) *Mémoires sur Carnot, par son fils ....* Two volumes. Ed. Lazare-Hippolyte Carnot. Paris: Pagnerre. New edition (1893) Paris: Charavay, Mantoux, Martin. [French].

Carrington, Dorothy (1988) *Napoleon and His Parents: On the Threshold of History*. London: Viking Press. Reprinted (1990) New York: E. P. Dutton & Co.

——— (1994-1998) Personal communications.

——— (1997) Corsica and Napoleon: How Dorothy Carrington discovered Corsican culture and history and became a Napoleanic scholar. *Napoleon: His Life, His Wars, His World*, vol. 1, no. 9, pp. 36–44.

——— (2002) *Portrait de Charles Bonaparte, d'après ses écrits de jeunesse et ses mémoires*. Ajaccio: Alain Piazzola. [French].

Castelot, André (1964) *Joséphine*. Paris: Librairie académique Perrin. [French].

——— (1967) *Bonaparte*. Paris: Librairie académique Perrin. [French].

——— (1968) *Napoléon*. Paris: Librairie académique Perrin. [French].

——— (1971) *Napoleon*. Tr. Guy Daniels. New York: Harper & Row.

Caulaincourt, Armand-Augustin-Louis de (1935–1936) *With Napoleon in Russia* and *No Peace With Napoleon! Together Being The Complete Memoirs of Napoleon's Grand Equerry, the Duke of Vicenza*. Two volumes. Tr. H. Miles & George Libaire. Ed. George Libaire. New York: William Morrow & Co. Inc. Reprinted (1976) Westport, Connecticut: Greenwood Press.

Cezzâr, Ahmet (1962) *Ottoman Egypt in the Eighteenth Century: The Nizâmnâme-i Misir of Cezzâr Ahmed Pasha*. Ed. & Tr. Stanford J. Shaw. Cambridge, Massachusetts: Harvard University Center for Middle Eastern Studies.

Chabot, Paul de (1900) *Les Chevaliers du Saint-Esprit de la province du Poitou de 1578 à 1700: notices extraites d'un manuscrit conservé à la Bibliothèque nationale et publiées avec des notes par le vicomte Paul de Chabot*. Vannes: Imprimerie de Lafolye. [French].

Chandler, David G. (1966) *The Campaigns of Napoleon*. New York: Macmillan Publishing Co. Reprinted (1967) London: Weidenfeld & Nicolson. Reprinted (1973) New York: Simon & Schuster. Reprinted (1974) as *The Campaigns of Napoleon: The Mind and the Method of History's Greatest Soldier* New York: Macmillan Publishing Co. Reprinted (1978) New York: Macmillan. Reprinted (1993) London: Weidenfeld & Nicolson. Reprinted (1995) Reading: Osprey Publishing Co. New York: Hippocrene Books.

Chandler, David G. (1991) To Lie Like a Bulletin: An Examination of Napoleon's Rewriting of the History of the Battle of Marengo. *Proceedings of the Annual Meeting of the Western Society for French History*, vol. 18, pp. 33-43.

Chaptal de Chanteloup, Jean-Antoine-Claude (1893) *Mes souvenirs sur Napoléon, par le comte Chaptal, publiés par son arrière-petit-fils, le vicomte A. Chaptal*. Ed.

Antoine Chaptal. Paris: Plon & Nourrit. New edition (2002) Villiers-sur-Marne: Phénix éditions. [French].
Chateaubriand, François-Auguste-René de (1814) *Portrait of Bonaparte, Being a View of His Administration. By F. A. de Chateaubriand. Together with an ode to Napoleon.* New York: Eastburn, Kirk & Co.
Christophe, Robert (1964) *Napoleon on Elba.* Tr. Len Ortzen. London: Macdonald & Co.
Chuquet, Arthur (1897–1899) *La jeunesse de Napoléon.* Three volumes. Vol. I. *Brienne.* Vol. II. *La Révolution.* Vol. III. *Toulon.* Paris: Armand Collin. [French].
Clark, Leon Pierce (1929) *Napoleon Self-Destroyed.* Foreword by James Harvey Robinson. New York: Jonathan Cape and Harrison Smith.
Coignet, Jean-Roche (1897) *The Narrative of Captain Coignet, Soldier of the Empire, 1776–1850.* Tr. M. Carey. Ed. Lorédan Larchey. London: Chatto & Windus. Reprinted (1890) New York. New edition (1928) *The Note-books of Captain Coignet ...* Intr. John Fortescue. London: P. Davies. Reprinted (1985) London: Greenhill Books. Reprinted (1996) East Felling, Tyne and Wear: Worley Publications. Reprinted (1998) London: Greenhill Books.
Colonna de Cesari Rocca, Pierre-Paul-Raoul (1890) *Histoire de la Corse.* Paris: C. Bayle. New edition (1938) Ed. Louis Villat. Paris: Boivin & Cie. [French].
Colonna de Cesari Rocca, Pierre-Paul-Raoul(1892) *L'Armorial Corse.* Paris: H. Jouve. New edition (1975) Marseille: Laffitte. [French].
Connelly, Owen (1968) *The Gentle Bonaparte: A Biography of Joseph, Napoleon's Elder Brother.* New York: Macmillan Publishing Co. London: Collier-Macmillan Publishing Co.
——— (1987) *Blundering to Glory: Napoleon's Military Campaigns.* Wilmington, Delaware: Scholarly Resources.
——— (1994–1995) Personal communications.
Consalvi, Ercole (1950) *Memorie: A cura di Mario Nasalli Rocca di Corneliano.* Rome: A. Signorelli. [Italian].
Corso, Philip F. & Hindmarsh, J. Thomas (1996) Further Scientific Evidence of the Non-poisonous Death of Napoleon. *Science Progress*, vol. 79, pp. 89-96.
Coston, François-Gilbert de (1840) *Biographie des premières années de Napoléon Bonaparte, c'est-à- dire depuis sa naissance jusqu'à l'époque de son commandement en chef de l'armée d'Italie, avec un appendice renfermant des documents ou inédits ou peu connus.* Two volumes. Paris and Valence: Marc-Aurel frères. [French].
Cronin, Vincent (1971) *Napoleon.* London: William Collins. Reprinted (1972) Newton Abbott: Readers Union. Reprinted (1972) as *Napoleon Bonaparte: An Intimate Biography.* New York: William Morrow. New Edition (1973) Harmondsworth: Penguin Books. Reprinted (1987) Pleasantville, New York: Reader's Digest Association. New edition (1990) London: Fontana. Reprinted (1994) London and New York: HarperCollins.
D'Haussonville, Joseph Othenin Bernard de Cléron (1868–69) *L'Église romaine et*

le Premier Empire, 1800–1814, avec notes, correspondances diplomatiques et pièces justificatives entièrement inédites, par M. le comte d'Haussonville. Five volumes. Paris: Michel Lévy frères. [French].

D'Oguerau, Charles Dangeais (1822) *Mémoires historiques et inédits sur la vie politique et privée de l'Empereur Napoléon, depuis son entrée à l'école de Brienne jusqu'à son départ pour l'Egypte, par le comte Charles d'Og ... élève de l'école de Brienne.* Paris: Corréard. [French].

D'Ornano, Antoine-Philippe-Rodolphe (1934) *The Life and Loves of Marie Walewska by Count d'Ornano.* Montreal: L. Carrier. Reprinted (1935) London: Hutchinson & Co. New York: Antoine-Philippe-Rodolphe d'Ornano.

Dalisson, Rémi (2004) *Les Trois couleurs, Marianne et l'Empereur: Fêtes libérales et politiques symboliques en France, 1815–1870.* Paris: La Boutique de l'histoire. [French].

Decaux, Alain (1962) *Napoleon's Mother.* With a foreword by His Imperial Highness Prince Napoléon. Tr. Len Ortzen. London: Cresset Press.

Défossé, Gabriel (1986) *Montenotte: la première victoire de Napoléon Bonaparte, général en chef, commandant l'Armée d'Italie, 12 avril 1796 (23 germinal an IV).* Cagnes-sur-Mer: EDICA. [French].

Defranceschi, Jean (1991) *La Corse et la Révolution française.* Ajaccio: Éditions Cyrnos et Méditérranée. [French].

——— (2001) *La jeunesse de Napoléon: les dessous de l'histoire.* Paris: Lettrage. [French].

Delderfield, Ronald Frederick (1959) *Napoleon in Love.* London: Hodder & Stoughton. Reprinted (1960) Boston: Little, Brown & Co. Reprinted (1979) New York: Simon and Schuster.

Dixon, Norman F. (1967) *On the Psychology of Military Incompetence.* London: Jonathan Cape.

Dry, A. [William-Aimable-Emile-Adrien Fleury] (1906) *Soldats et ambassadeurs sous le Directoire, an IV–an VIII.* Paris: Plon-Nourrit. [French].

Du Teil, Joseph (1896) *Une Famille militaire au XVIIIe siècle: documents inédits sur le régiment Royal-Artillerie, la bataille d'Hastenbeck, les campagnes des Indes, l'école d'artillerie d'Auxonne et le siège de Toulon.* Paris: A. Picard et fils. [French].

Duhourçau, François (1933) *La mère de Napoléon: Letizia Bonaparte.* Avec cinq portraits. Paris: Editions Excelsior. [French].

Dundes, Alan (1993) Gallus as Phallus: A Psychoanalytic Cross-Cultural Consideration of the Cockfight as Fowl Play. *The Psychoanalytic Study of Society*, vol. 18, pp. 23–65. Reprinted (1994) in Dundes, Alan (Ed.) *The Cockfight: A Casebook.* Madison, Wisconsin: University of Wisconsin Press.

Ebers, Georg Moritz (1887) *The Bride of the Nile: A Romance.* Two volumes. Tr. Clara Bell. New York: George Munro. New York: William S. Gottsberger. Abridged edition (1887) New York: Harper & Bros. New edition (1915) New York: Daniel Appleton.

Faber, Melvin D. (1981) *Culture and Consciousness: The Social Meaning of Altered Awareness.* New York: Human Sciences Press.

Fain, Agathon-Jean-François (1823) *Manuscrit de mil huit cent quatorze [1814], trouvé dans les voitures impériales prises à Waterloo, contenant l'histoire des six derniers mois du règne de Napoléon ... Vol. 2 of Mémoires des contemporains, pour servir à l'histoire de la République et de l'Empire.* Seven volumes. Paris: Bossange frères. [French].

——— (1828) *Manuscrit de l'an III (1794–95), contenant les premières transactions des puissances de l'Europe avec la république française, et le tableau des derniers événements du régime conventionnel, pour servir à l'histoire du cabinet de cette époque, par le baron Fain, alors secrétaire au comité militaire de la Convention nationale.* Paris: Ambroise Dupont. [French].

——— (1908) *Mémoires du baron Fain, premier secrétaire du cabinet de l'empereur, publiés par ses arrière-petits-fils.* Ed. Paul Fain. Paris: Plon-Nourrit & Cie. New edition (2001) *Mémoires du baron Agathon-Jean-François Fain, présentés par Christophe Bourachot.* Paris: Arléa. [French].

——— (1998) *Napoleon: How He Did It. The Memoirs of Baron Fain, First Secretary of the Emperor's Cabinet.* Ed. Proctor P. Jones. San Francisco: Proctor Jones Publishing Co.

Falk, Avner (1996) *A Psychoanalytic History of the Jews.* Madison, New Jersey: Fairleigh Dickinson University Press. Cranbury, London and Mississauga: Associated University Presses.

Fisher, Herbert Albert Laurens (1912) *Napoleon.* London: Williams and Norgate. London: Thornton Butterworth. Reprinted (1913) New York: Henry Holt & Co. Numerous other editions from 1913 to 1937.

Fleischmann, Hector (1910) *Roustam, Mameluck de Napoléon, d'après des memoires et des documents inédits.* Paris: Albert Méricant Éditeur. [French].

Flori, François (1975) *Le Procès des Niolins, 1774.* Bastia: Société d'Etudes du Niolu [French]

Fornari, Franco (1974) *The Psychoanalysis of War.* Garden City: Doubleday. Reprinted (1975) Bloomington: Indiana University Press.

Forshufvud, Sten & Weider, Ben (1978) *Assassination at St. Helena: The Poisoning of Napoleon Bonaparte.* Ed. H. T. Mitchell. Foreword David G. Chandler. Vancouver: Mitchell Press.

François, Charles (1906) *From Valmy to Waterloo: Extracts from the Diary of Captain Charles François, a Soldier of the Revolution and the Empire.* Tr. & Ed. Robert Bruce Douglas. Preface by Julie Claretie. London: Everett & Co.

Freud, Sigmund (1953) *The Interpretation of Dreams.* In Strachey, James & al. (Trs. & Eds. 1953-1974) *The Standard Edition of the Complete Psychological Works of Sigmund Freud*, vols. 4–5. London: The Hogarth Press and the Institute of Psycho-Analysis.

——— (1955) *Group Psychology and the Analysis of the Ego.* In Strachey, James et al. (Trs. & Eds. 1953-1974) *The Standard Edition of the Complete Psychological*

Works of Sigmund Freud, vol. 18, pp. 65–143. London: The Hogarth Press and the Institute of Psycho-Analysis.

——— (1957) A Special Type of Choice of Object Made by Men (Contributions to the Psychology of Love I). In Strachey, James et al. (Trs. & Eds. 1953-1974) *The Standard Edition of the Complete Psychological Works of Sigmund Freud*, vol. 11, pp. 163-175. London: The Hogarth Press and the Institute of Psycho-Analysis.

——— (1961) Draft of a Letter to Thomas Mann, November 29, 1936. In *Letters of Sigmund Freud, 1873–1939*. Ed. Ernst L. Freud. Tr. Tania and James Stern. London: The Hogarth Press. New York: Basic Books.

Freud, Sigmund & Zweig, Arnold (1970) *The Letters of Sigmund Freud and Arnold Zweig*. Ed. Ernst L. Freud. Tr. Elaine and William Robson-Scott. London: The Hogarth Press and the Institute of Psycho-Analysis. New York: Harcourt Brace Jovanovich. Reprinted (1987) New York: New York University Press.

Friedman, Reuben (1940) *The Emperor's Itch: The Legend Concerning Napoleon's Napoleon's Affliction with Scabies*. New York: Froben Press.

Frugier, Jean-Raymond (1985) *Napoléon: essai médico-psychologique*. Paris: Albatros. [French].

Gallo, Max (1997) *Napoléon*. Four volumes. Paris: Robert Laffont. [French].

Gance, Abel (1927) *Napoléon: épopée cinégraphique en cinq époques*. [motion picture]. New edition (1986) Ed. Francis Ford Coppola. New York: Zoetrope Studios. [French].

Gance, Abel (1990) *Napoleon as Seen by Abel Gance*. Ed. Bambi Ballard & Moya Hassan. Intr. Kevin Brownlow. London and New York: Faber & Faber.

Garnier, Adolphe (1872) *Traité des facultés de l'âme, comprenant l'histoire des principales théories psychologiques*. Second edition. Three volumes. Ed. Paul Janet. Paris: Hachette. [French].

Gay, Peter (1964) Napoleon Against Himself: Review of Felix Markham's *Napoleon. The New York Review of Books*, vol. 2, no. 10.

Gear, María Carmen & al. (1981) *Working Through Narcissism: Treating its Sadomasochistic Structure*. By María Carmen Gear, Melvyn A. Hill & Ernesto Cesar Liendo. New York : Jason Aronson.

Geyl, Pieter Catharinus Aric (1949) *Napoleon: For and Against*. Tr. Olive Renier. London: Jonathan Cape. New Haven, Connecticut: Yale University Press. Revised edition (1976) Harmondsworth: Penguin Books.

Girod de l'Ain, Gabriel (1959) *Désirée Clary, d'après sa correspondance inédite avec Bonaparte, Bernadotte et sa famille*. Paris: Hachette. [French].

Godechot, Jacques-Léon (Ed. 1969) *Napoléon par Jacques Godechot: Textes de Metternich, Walter Scott, Channing, Godoy, Rostopchine, Hudson Lowe*. Paris: Albin Michel. [French]

Goldsmith, Lewis [Stewarton] (1806) *The Secret History of the Court and Cabinet of St. Cloud, in a Series of Letters from a Resident in Paris to a Nobleman in London Written During the Months of August, September, and October, 1805*. Philadelphia: J. Watts. Reprinted (1807) New York: Brisban & Brannan. New edition (1810) *The Secret History of the Cabinet of Bonaparte, including His Private Life, Character, Domestic Administration, and His Conduct to Foreign Powers ... with Two Appendices Consisting of State Papers, and of Biographical Sketches of the Persons Composing the Court of St. Cloud*. London: J. M. Richardson. New edition (1900) Boston: L. C. Page & Co.

Gourgaud, Gaspard (1889–1899) *Sainte-Hélène: journal inédit de 1815 à 1818, avec préface et notes de MM. le vicomte de Grouchy et Antoine Guillois. Two volumes. Ed. Emmanuel-Henri de Gouchy & Antoine Guillois*. Paris: Flammarion. New edition (1944-1947) *Journal de Sainte-Hélène, 1815-1818, édition augmentée d'après le texte original*. Two volumes. Ed. Octave Aubry. Paris: Flammarion. [French].

——— (1932) *The St. Helena Journal of General Baron Gourgaud, 1815-1818, being a Diary written at St. Helena during a part of Napoleon's captivity, now translated into English for the first time by Sydney Gillard, and edited with and introduction and notes by Norman Edwards. With a preface by Hilaire Belloc and five illustrations*. London: John Lane & The Bodley Head.

Grétry, André-Ernest-Modeste (1919–1922) *Réflexions d'un solitaire ... manuscrit inédit, publié par les soins de la Commission pour la publication des oeuvres des anciens musiciens belges; avec une introduction et des notes, par Lucien Solvay et Ernest Closson*. Four volumes. Brussels and Paris: G. van Oest. Reprinted (1978) New York: AMS Press. [French].

Grotstein, James S. (1981) *Splitting and Projective Identification*. York: Jason Aronson. New edition (1985) New York: Jason Aronson.

Guillon, Edouard (1894) *Les complots militaires sous le Consulat et l'Empire*. Paris: Plon, Nourrit et Cie.[French].

Guthrie, Leonard George (1913) Did Napoleon Bonaparte Suffer from Hypopituitarism (dystrophia adiposo-genitalis) at the Close of His Life? *The Lancet*, vol. 182, no. 4698, pp. 823-826.

Hamelin, Fortunée (1911) *Une ancienne muscadine: Fortunée Hamelin, lettres inédites, 1839–1851*. Ed. André Gayot. Préface de M. Émile Faguet. Paris: É. Paul. [French].

Hastier, Louis (1955) *Le Grand amour de Joséphine*. Paris: Corrêa. [French].

Healey, Frank George (1959) *The Literary Culture of Napoleon*. Geneva: Librairie E. Droz.

Hennet, Léon-Clément (1889) *Les Compagnies de cadets-gentilshommes et les écoles militaires*. Paris: L. Baudoin. [French].

Henry, Walter (1823) *Report to Governor Sir Hudson Lowe on the Autopsy of Napoleon Bonaparte*. British Museum, Add. MS. 20,214 ff. 200–201.

——— (1839) *Trifles from my Portfolio, or, Recollections of Scenes and Small Adventures, During Twenty-nine Years' Military Service in the Peninsular War and Invasion of France, the East Indies, Campaign in Nepaul [sic], St. Helena During the Detention and until the Death of Napoleon, and Upper and Lower Canada, by a Staff Surgeon*. Two volumes. Quebec: William Neilson. New edition (1843) *Events of a Military Life Events of a Military Life; being recollections after service in the Peninsular War, Invasion of France, the East Indies, St. Helena, Canada, and elsewhere.* Two volumes. London: William Pickering. New edition (1970) *Surgeon Henry's Trifles: Events of a Military Life.* Ed. & Intr. Pat Hayward. London: Chatto & Windus.

Héreau, Joachim (1829) *Napoléon à Sainte-Hélène: opinion d'un médecin sur la maladie de l'empereur Napoléon et sur la cause de sa mort, offerte à son fils au jour de sa majorité, par J. Héreau.* Paris: F. Louis. [French].

Herold, J. Christopher (Ed. 1955) *The Mind of Napoleon: A Selection from His Written and Spoken Words.* New York: Columbia University Press. Reprinted (1961) New York: Columbia University Press.

Hindmarsh, J. Thomas & Corso, Philip F. (1998) The Death of Napoleon Bonaparte: A Critical Review of the Cause. *Journal of the History of Medicine,* vol. 53, pp. 201-218.

Hobsbawm, Eric John (1962) *The Age of Revolution: Europe 1789–1848.* London: Weidenfeld & Nicolson. Cleveland: World Publishing Co. Reprinted (1964) New York: New American Library. Reprinted (1969) New York: Praeger. Reprinted (1978) London: Abacus. Reprinted (1996) New York: Vintage Books.

Hoiberg, Dale H. & al. (Eds. 2005) *Encyclopædia Britannica 2005 Ultimate Reference Suite DVD.* Chicago: Encyclopædia Britannica, Inc.

Horward,Donald D. (1997) André Masséna, Prince D'Essling, in the Age of Revolution (1789–1815). *Napoleonic Scholarship: The Journal of the International Napoleonic Society,* vol. 1, no. 1, pp. 5-21.

Hudson, William Henry (1914) *The Man Napoleon.* New York: Thomas Y. Crowell Co. Reprinted (1915) London: G. G. Harrap & Co.

Hugo, Victor-Marie [Marcel Barthe] (1835) *Les Chants du Crépuscule.* Paris. Brussels and Leipzig: Allgemeine niederlandische Buchhandlung. Reprinted (1836–1837) in *Ouevres complètes de Victor Hugo,* twenty volumes. Brussels: A. Wahlen. [French].

Husayn Afandi [Hussein Effendi] (1964) *Ottoman Egypt in the Age of the French Revolution.* Tr. & Ed. Stanford J. Shaw. Cambridge, Massachusetts: Harvard University Center for Middle Eastern Studies.

Hyde de Neuville, Jean-Guillaume (1913) *Memoirs of Baron Hyde de Neuville: Outlaw, Exile, Ambassador.* Two volumes. Tr. Frances Jackson. London: Sands.

Iung, Henri-François-Théodore (1880–1881) *Bonaparte et son temps, 1769–1799, d'après des documents inédits.* Three volumes. Paris: Charpentier. [French].

——— (1882–1883) *Lucien Bonaparte et ses mémoires, 1775–1840, d'après les papiers déposés aux archives étrangères et d'autres documnets inédits.* Three volumes. Paris: Charpentier. [French].

Jekels, Ludwig (1914) Der Wendepunkt im Leben Napoleons I. *Imago,* vol. 3, pp. 313–381. [German].

——— (1952) The Turning Point in the Life of Napoleon I. In Jekels, Ludwig &

Bergler, Edmund, *Selected Papers by Ludwig Jekels, including two papers written in collaboration with Edmund Bergler*, pp. 1–73. London: Imago Publishing Co. Reprinted (1953) New York: International Universities Press. Reprinted (1970) Freeport, New York: Books for Libraries Press.

Jones, Ernest (1953–57) *The Life of Sigmund Freud*. Three volumes. New York: Basic Books.

Jung, Carl Gutav (1953–92) *The Collected Works of C. G. Jung*. Eds. Herbert Read, Michael Fordham, Gerhard Adler. Twenty-two volumes. Princeton: Princeton University Press. New edition (1966) London: Routledge and Kegan Paul. New edition (1992) New York Pantheon Books.

Junot, Laure-Adelaïde-Constance Saint-Martin Permon, duchesse d'Abrantès (1823) *Mémoires, ou Souvenirs historiques de Madame Laure Junot, duchesse d'Abrantès, sur Napoléon, sa cour et sa famille*. Eighteen volumes. Paris: Ladvocat. Many editions from 1831 to 1929. New edition (1967–68) *Mémoires complets et authentiques de Laure Junot, duchesse d'Abrantès: Souvenirs historiques sur Napoléon, la Révolution, le Directoire, le Consulat, l'Empire, la Restauration, la révolution de 1830 et les premières années du règne de Louis-Philippe*. Thirteen volumes. Paris: Jean de Bonnot. [French].

Kemble, James (1959) *Napoleon Immortal: The Medical History and Private Life of Napoleon Bonaparte*. London: John Murray.

Kircheisen, Friedrich M. (1911–1934) *Napoleon I.: Sein Leben und seine Zeit*. Nine volumes. Munich and Leipzig: Georg Müller. [German].

Klaf, Franklin S. (1960) Napoleon and the Grand Army of 1812: A Study of Group Psychology. *Psychoanalysis and the Psychoanalytic Review*, vol. 47, no. 3, pp. 69–76.

Klein, Melanie (1946) Notes on Some Schizoid Mechanisms. *International Journal of Psycho-Analysis*, vol. 27, pp. 99-110.

Kohut, Heinz (1971) *The Analysis of the Self: A Systematic Approach to the Psychoanalytic Treatment of Narcissistic Personality Disorders*. New York: International Universities Press.

——— (1972) Thoughts on Narcissism and Narcissistic Rage. *The Psychoanalytic Study of the Child*, vol. 27, pp. 360–400. Reprinted (1978) in Kohut, Heinz *The Search for the Self. Selected Writings of Heinz Kohut: 1950–1978*, two volumes, ed. P. H. Ornstein, pp. 615–658. New York: International Universities Press.

——— (1976) Creativeness, Charisma, Group Psychology: Reflections on the Self-Analysis of Freud. In Gedo, John E. & Pollock, George H. (Eds.) *Freud: The Fusion of Science and Humanism*, pp. 379–425. New York: International Universities Press. Reprinted (1978) in Kohut, Heinz *The Search for the Self. Selected Writings of Heinz Kohut: 1950–1978*, Ed. Paul H. Ornstein, vol. 2, pp. 793–843. New York: International Universities Press.

——— (1978) *The Search for the Self. Selected Writings of Heinz Kohut: 1950–1978*. Ed. Paul H. Ornstein. Two volumes. New York: International Universities Press.

Kurosawa, Akira (1952) *Rashomon*. [motion picture]. Tokyo: Daiei Co. New York: RKO Radio Pictures. [Japanese].
La Tour, Jean-Charles-Gabriel Lacombe de (1913) *Duroc: duc de Frioul, grand maréchal du Palais impérial, 1772–1813*. Paris: M. Imhaus and Libraririe militaire R. Chapelot. Reprinted (2004) Paris: Nouveau monde édition and Fondation Napoléon. [French].
Larrey, Félix-Hippolyte (1892) *Madame Mère (Napoleonis mater): essai historique par le baron Larrey*. Two volumes. Paris: E. Dentu. [French].
Las Cases, Emmanuel-Auguste-Dieudonné-Marius-Joseph de (1823) *Mémorial de Sainte-Hélène, ou Journal où se trouve consigné, jour par jour, tout ce qu'a dit et fait Napoléon pendant dix-huit mois, du 20 juin 1815 au 25 novembre 1816, par le comte de Las Cases*. Eight volumes. Paris: Lebègue.
——— (1961) *Mémorial de Sainte-Hélène: Texte établi avec introduction, bibliographie et notes par André Fugier*. Two volumes. Paris: Garnier Frères. [French].
Lasswell, Harold Dwight (1948) *Power and Personality*. New York: W. W. Norton.
Launay, Jacques de (1968) *Napoléon: un portrait psychopolitique*. Brussels: Pierre de Méyère. [French].
Lavalette, Antoine-Marie Chamans de (1831) *Memoirs of Count Lavalette, Written by Himself*. London: Henry Colburn and Richard Bentley. Reprinted (1832) Philadelphia: T. T. Ash. New edition (1936–37) *The Adventurous Life of Count Lavalette, Bonaparte's Aide-de-camp and Napoleon's Postmaster-general, by Himself*. Two volumes. Tr. & Ed. L. Aldersey White. London: Lovat Dickson.
Le Nabour, Eric (2003) *Letizia Bonaparte: la mère exemplaire de Napoléon 1er*. Paris: Pygmalion, Corps 16. [French].
Le Sage, Alain-René. (1715–1735) *Histoire de Gil Blas de Santillane*. Four volumes. Paris: Les Libraires associés. New edition (1962-1966) Two volumes. Paris: Garnier frères. [French].
Lee, Henry (1834) *The Life of the Emperor Napoleon, with an appendix, containing an examination of Sir W. Scott's Life of Napoleon Bonaparte; and a notice of the principal errors of other writers respecting his character and conduct*. London. Reprinted (1835) New York: Charles de Behr.
Leroux, Pierre (1850) *Œuvres de Pierre Leroux, 1825–1850*. Paris: L. Nétré. New edition (1978) Geneva: Slatkine Reprints. [French].
Lewis, Gwynne & Lucas, Colin (Eds. 1983) *Beyond the Terror: Essays in French Regional and Social History, 1794–1815*. Cambridge and New York: Cambridge University Press.
Lewis, Helen Block (1992) *Shame: The Exposed Self*. New York & Toronto: The Free Press.
Loewenberg, Peter (1995) *Fantasy and Reality in History*. Oxford: The Clarendon Press. London and New York: Oxford University Press.
Lumbroso, Alberto (1933) I Bonaparte dell'isola e i Buonaparte del continente. *Archivio storico di Corsica*, vol. 9, January-March. [Italian].
Lynd, Helen Merrell (1958) *On Shame and the Search for Identity*. New York:

Harcourt, Brace & World Publishing Co.

Mahler, Margaret S., Pine, Fred & Bergman, Annie (1975) *The Psychological Birth of the Human Infant: Symbiosis and Individuation*. New York: Basic Books.

Maitland, Frederick Lewis (1904) *The Surrender of Napoleon: Being the Narrative of the Surrender of Buonaparte and His Residence on Board the H. M. S. Bellerophon, with a Detail of the Principal Events that Occurred on that Ship between the 24th of May and the 8th of August 1815*. New edition. Ed. William Kirk Dickson. Edinburgh and London: William Blackwood and sons.

Manceron, Claude (1969) *Le citoyen Bonaparte: la jeunesse de Napoléon, 1769–1796*. Paris: Robert Laffont. [French].

Marchand, Louis-Joseph-Narcisse (1952–1955) *Mémoires de Marchand, premier valet de chambre et exécuteur testamentaire de l'empereur sur l'île d'Elbe et Sainte-Hélène, publiés d'après le manuscrit original*. Two volumes. Ed. Jean Bourguignon & Henri Lachouque. Paris: Librairie Plon. New edition (1985) Paris: Jules Tallandier. [French].

Margerand, Joseph (1931) *Les Aides de camp de Bonaparte, 1793–1804*. Paris: Pierre Bossuet. [French].

Margolis, Max L. & Marx, Alexander (1985) *A History of the Jewish People*. New York: Atheneum Publishers.

Markham, Felix (1964) *Napoleon*. New York: New American Library.

——— (1975) *The Bonapartes*. New York: Taplinger.

Marmont, Auguste-Frédéric-Louis Viesse de (1857) *Mémoires du maréchal Marmont, duc de Raguse, de 1792 à 1841, imprimés sur le manuscrit original de l'auteur*. Nine volumes. Paris: Perrotin. [French].

Martineau, Gilbert (1978) *Madame Mère: Napoleon's Mother*. Tr. F. Partridge. London: John Murray.

Masséna, André (1848–50) *Mémoires de Masséna, rédigés d'après les documents qu'il a laissés et sur ceux du dépôt de la guerre et du dépôt des fortifications, par le général Koch; avec un atlas*. Seven volumes. Ed. Frédéric Koch. Paris: Paulin et Lechevalier. New Edition (1966) *Mémoires d'André Masséna, duc de Rivoli, prince d'Essling, maréchal d'Empire, rédigés d'après les documents qu'il a laissés et sur ceux du dépôt de la guerre et du dépôt des fortifications, recueillis par le général Koch*. Paris: Jean de Bonnot. [French]

Masson, Frédéric (1893) *Napoléon et les femmes. I. L'amour*. Paris: Paul Ollendorff. New edition (1898) Paris: Borel. New edition (1906) Paris: Manzi, Joyant et Cie. Reprinted (1910) Paris: Paul Ollendorff. [French].

——— (1894) *Napoleon: Lover and Husband*. Tr. J. M. Howell. New York: The Merriam Co. New edition (1899) New York and Chicago: The Werner Co. Reprinted (1907) Akron, Ohio: Saalfield Publishing Co.

——— (1897–1819) *Napoléon et sa famille (1769–1821)*. Thirteen volumes. Paris: Paul Ollendorff. New edition (1930) Paris: Albin Michel. [French].

——— (1908) *Le sacre et le couronnement de Napoléon*. Paris: Librairie Jules Tallandier. [French].

——— (1969) *Napoléon dans sa jeunesse (1769–1793)*. New edition. Paris: Albin Michel. [French].

McLynn, Frank (1997) *Napoleon: A Biography*. London: Jonathan Cape. Reprinted (1998) London: Pimlico. Reprinted (2002) New York: Arcade Publications.

Merezhkovsky, Dmitri Sergeyevich (1929) *Napoleon: A Study*. Tr. Catherine Zvegintzov. London and Toronto: J. M. Dent & Sons. Reprinted (1929) as *The Life of Napoleon*. London and Toronto: J. M. Dent & Sons. New York: E. P. Dutton & Co.

Meynell, Henry (1911) *Conversations with Napoleon at St. Helena*. London: A. L. Humphreys.

Michaud, Louis-Gabriel (1855) Duroc. In Michaud, Louis-Gabriel (Ed.) (1854–65) *Biographie universelle (Michaud) ancienne et moderne ... Nouvelle édition, publiée sous la direction de M. Michaud, revue, corrigée, et considérablement augmentée d'articles omis ou nouveaux; ouvrage rédigé par une societé de gens de lettres et de savants*. Forty-five volumes. Paris: Madame C. Desplaces. Leipzig : F. A. Brockhaus. [French].

Michelet, Jules (1872–75) *Histoire du XIXe siècle*. Three volumes. Vol. 1. *Directoire; Origine des Bonaparte*. Vol. 2. *Jusqu'au 18 brumaire*. Vol. 3. *Jusqu'à Waterloo*. Paris: G. Baillière and Michel Lévy frères. [French].

Miller, Susan Beth (1985) *The Shame Experience*. Hillsdale, New Jersey: The Analytic Press.

Milton, John (1671) *Paradise Regained*. London. Reprinted (1931–38) in Patterson, Frank A. (Ed.) *The Works of John Milton*. 18 volumes. New York: Columbia University Press. Reprinted (1950) in *Complete Poetry and Selected Prose of John Milton*. Intr. Cleanth Brooks. New York: Random House Modern Library.

Miot de Melito, André-François (1881) *Memoirs of Count Miot de Melito, Minister, Ambassador, Councillor of State, and member of the Institute of France, between the years 1788 and 1815. By General Fleischmann*. Two volumes. Ed. Wilhelm August von Fleischmann. Tr. Frances Sarah Johnston Cashel Hoey and John Lillie. London: Sampson Low, Marston, Searle, & Rivington. New York: Charles Scribner's Sons.

Moffett, Cleveland (1962) *The Reign of Terror in the French Revolution*. New York: Ballantine Books.

Mollien, François-Nicholas (1898) *Mémoires d'un ministre du trésor public, 1780–1815*. Three volumes. Ed. Charles Gomel. Paris: Guillaumin. [French].

Montbas, Hugues de (1952) *Robespierre et les Bonaparte vus par le comte Colchen. Revue des Deux Mondes*, vol. 122, September 15. [French].

Montesquiou-Fezensac, Raymond-Aimery-Philippe-Joseph de (1852) *A Journal of the Russian Campaign of 1812*. Tr. & Intr. William Thomas Knollys. London: Parker, Furnivall, and Parker. New edition (1970) *The Russian Campaign, 1812*. Tr. Lee B. Kennett. Athens, Georgia: University of Georgia Press.

Montholon, Charles-Jean-François-Tristan de & al. (1847–1849) *Récit de la captivité de l'Empereur Napoléon à Sainte-Hélène*. Four volumes. Paris: Paulin. [French].
Morrison, Andrew P. (1989) *Shame: The Underside of Narcissism*. Hillsdale, New Jersey: The Analytic Press.
Nanteuil, Luc de (1985) *Jacques-Louis David*. New York: Abrams Art Books. New edition (1990) New York: H. N. Abrams. London: Thames & Hudson.
Nasica, Tommaso (Ed. 1850–1852) *Mémoires sur l'enfance et la jeunesse de Napoléon jusqu'à l'âge de vingt-trois ans, précédés d'une notice historique sur son père, par T. Nasica, conseiller à la cour d'appel de Bastia ... dédiés à S. A. I. le prince président, par l'abbé Nasica*. Paris: Ledoyen. [French].
Nathanson, Donald L. (1992) *Shame and Pride: Affect, Sex, and the Birth of the Self*. New York: W. W. Norton.
Nathanson, Donald L. (Ed. 1987) *The Many Faces of Shame*. New York and London: Guilford Press
Nicolson, Harold George (1946) The Congress of Vienna: A Study in Allied Unity, 1812–1822. London: Archibald Constable & Co. New York: Harcourt, Brace & Co. New edition (2000) New York: Grove Press.
Ollivier, Albert (1959) *Le dix-huit brumaire, 9 novembre 1799*. Paris: Éditions Gallimard. New edition (1967) Paris: Éditions Gallimard. [French].
Oudinot, Nicolas-Charles-Victor (1896) *Memoirs of Marshal Oudinot, duc de Reggio*. Compiled from the unpublished memoirs of Marie-Charlotte-Eugénie-Julienne de Coucy Oudinot, Duchess of Reggio. Ed. Gaston Steigler. Tr. Alexander Teixera de Mattos. London: H. Henry & Co. Reprinted (1897) New York: Daniel Appleton & Co.
Parker, Harold T. (1971–1972) The Formation of Napoleon's Personality: An Exploratory Essay. *French Historical Studies*, vol. 7, pp. 6-26. Reprinted (1989) in Kafker, Frank A. & Laux, James M. (Eds.) *Napoleon and His Times: Selected Interpretations*. Malibar, Florida: Robert E. Krieger Publishing Co.
——— (1985) Napoleon's Changing Self-Image to 1812: A Sketch. In *The Consortium on Revolutionary Europe, 1750–1850: Proceedings 1984*. Athens, Georgia: Consortium on Revolutionary Europe.
——— (1991) Why did Napoleon Invade Russia? A Study in Motivation, Personality, & Social Structure. In *The Consortium on Revolutionary Europe, 1750–1850: Proceedings 1990*, pp. 86–96. Tallahassee, Florida: Institute on Napoleon and the French Revolution, Florida State University.
——— (1993–1999) Personal communications.
——— (1997) Toward Understanding Napoleon, Or, Did Napoleon Have a Conscience? In *The Consortium on Revolutionary Europe, 1750–1850: Selected Papers, 1997*, Eds. Kyle O. Eidahl, Donald D. Horward & June Severn, pp. 201-208. Tallahassee, Florida: Institute on Napoleon and the French Revolution, Florida State University.
Pasquier, Etienne-Denis (1893–1895) *Histoire de mon temps: mémoires du chan-*

celier duc de Pasquier, publiés par M. le duc d'Audiffret-Pasquier. Six volumes. Paris: Plon, Nourrit & Cie. One-volume abridgement (1964) *Souvenirs du chancelier Pasquier, 1767–1815. Introduction et notes de Robert Lacour-Gayet*. Paris: Hachette. [French].

——— (1967) *The Memoirs of Chancellor Pasquier, 1767–1815*. Tr. Douglas Garman. Ed. Robert Lacour-Gayet. London: Elek. Reprinted (1968) Rutherford, New Jersey: Fairleigh Dickinson University Press.

Pérès, Jean-Baptiste (1827) *Comme quoi Napoléon n'a jamais existé, ou, Grand erratum source d'un nombre infini d'errata à noter dans l'histoire du XIXe siècle, par feu M. J.-B. Pérès*. Notes bio-bibliographiques par Gustave Davois. Paris: L'Édition bibliographique. Reprinted (1983) in Louis Geoffroy, *Napoléon et la conquête du monde, 1812-1832: histoire de la monarchie universelle (Napoléon apocryphe), suivi de Comme quoi Napoléon n'a jamais existé, par J.-B. Pérès*. Paris: Tallandier. [French].

Peretti, Lydie (1932) *Letizia Bonaparte*. Préface de Pierre Bonardi. Paris: Plon. [French].

Petit, A.-N. (1839) *Napoléon à Brienne*. Troyes: Bouquot. [French].

Phipps, Ramsay Weston (1926–39) *The Armies of the First French Republic and the Rise of the Marshals of Napoleon I*. Five volumes. Oxford: Oxford University Press. London: Humphrey Milford. Reprinted (1980) Westport, Connecticut: Greenwood Press.

Pichot, Amédée (Ed. 1873) *Napoléon à l'île d'Elbe: chronique des événements de 1814–1815, d'après le Journal du colonel sir Neil Campbell, le "Journal d'un détenu", et autres documents inédits ou peu connus, pour servir à l'histoire du Premier Empire et de la Restauration ... recueillis par M. Amédée Pichot*. Paris: E. Dentu. [French].

Piers, Gerhart & Singer, Milton B. (1953) *Shame and Guilt: A Psychoanalytic and Cultural Study*. Springfield, Illinois: Charles Thomas. Reprinted (1971) New York: W. W. Norton.

Piétri, François (1965) *Napoléon et les israélites*. Paris: Editions Berger-Levrault. [French].

Pingaud, Léonce [Pierre Philibert] (1901) *Bernadotte, Napoléon et les Bourbons (1797–1814)*. Paris: Plon-Nourrit. New edition (1933) *Bernadotte et Napoléon (1797–1814)*. Paris: Plon. [French].

Plancy, Adrien de (1904) *Souvenirs du comte de Plancy (1798–1816), publiés par son petit-fils, le baron de Plancy*. Intr. Frédéric Masson. Paris: Paul Ollendorff. [French].

Pollock, George H. (1989) *The Mourning-Liberation Process*. Two volumes. Madison, Connecticut: International Universities Press.

Potok, Chaim (1978) *Wanderings: Chaim Potok's History of the Jews*. New York: Alfred A. Knopf.

Régis, Roger (1946) *Pauline Fourès, dite Bellilote: maîtresse de Bonaparte en Egypte*. Paris: les Éditions de Paris. [French].

Reich, Wilhelm (1945) *Character Analysis: Principles and Technique for Psychoanalysts in Practice and Training.* Tr. Theodore P. Wolfe. New York: Orgone Institute Press. Reprinted (1949) New York: Orgone Institute Press. Reprinted (1950) London: Vision Press. New edition (1972) Tr. Vincent R. Carfagno. New York: Farrar, Straus and Giroux.

Rémusat, Claire-Elisabeth-Jeanne Gravier de Vergennes de (1880) and (1888–1889) *Memoirs of Madame de Rémusat, 1802-1808.* Preface by Paul de Rémusat. One volume and three volumes. Tr. Frances Sarah Johnston Cashel Hoey and John Lillie. London: Sampson, Low, Marston, Searle and Rivington. New York: Daniel Appleton & Co.

Rétif de la Bretonne, Georges (1969) *Anglais, rendez-nous Napoléon.* Paris: J. Martineau. [French].

Revel, Jean-Honoré-François (1815) *Buonaparte et Murat, ravisseurs d'une jeune femme, et quelques-uns de leurs agents, complices de ce rapt, devant le tribunal de première instance du département de la Seine. Mémoire historique, écrit par le mari outragé, J.-H.-F. Revel, capitaine pensionné.* Paris: Imprimerie de L.-G. Michaud. [French].

Richardson, Frank McLean (1972) *Napoleon: Bisexual Emperor.* London: William Kimber & Co. Reprinted (1973) New York: Horizon Press.

Roederer, Pierre-Louis (1909) *Autour de Bonaparte: journal du comte P.-L. Roederer, ministre et conseiller d'état, notes intimes et politiques d'un familier des Tuileries.* Introduction et notes par Maurice Vitrac. Paris: H. Daragon. [French].

Rosebery, Archibald Philip Primrose, Fifth Earl of (1900) *Napoleon: The Last Phase.* London: Thomas Nelson & Sons. New York: Harper & Brothers. Reprinted (1928) London: Jonathan Cape.

Rothenberg, Gunther Erich (1982) *Napoleon's Great Adversaries: The Archduke Charles and the Austrian Army, 1792–1814.* London: B. T. Batsford. Bloomington: Indiana University Press. Reprinted (1995) Staplehurst, England: Spellmount Publishers.

Rothstein, Arnold (1980) *The Narcissistic Pursuit of Perfection.* New York: International Universities Press. Second Revised Edition (1984) New York: International Universities Press. New Edition (1999) New York: International Universities Press.

Rousseau, Jean-Jacques (1782–89) *Les Confessions de J.-J. Rousseau, suivies des Rêveries du promeneur solitaire.* Four volumes. Geneva, Lausanne and London. New edition (1789) Four volumes. Paris: Poinçot. [French].

——— (1995) *The Confessions, and, Correspondence, Including the Letters to Malesherbes.* Tr. Christopher Kelly. Ed. Christopher Kelly, Roger D. Masters, & Peter G. Stillman. Hanover, New Hampshire: University Press of New England.

Roustam, Raza (1911) *Souvenirs de Roustam, mamelouck de Napoleon 1er.* Ed. Paul Cottin. Preface by Frédéric Masson. Paris: Paul Ollendorff. [French].

Roux, Christine (Ed. 1984) *Les Makis de la résistance corse, 1772–1778.* Paris: Editions France-Empire. [French].

Sauzay, Alexandre (1856) Duroc. In Hoefer, Jean-Chrétien-Ferdinand (Ed.) (1853–66) *Nouvelle Biographie générale depuis les temps les plus reculés jusqu'à nos jours, avec les renseignements bibliographiques et l'indication des sources à consulter.* Forty-six volumes. Paris: Firmin Didot frères. [French].

Savant, Jean [Jean-Victor Savant-Aleina] (Ed.) (1958) *Napoleon in His Time.* Tr. Katherine John. London: Thomas Nelson. New York: G. P. Putnam's Sons.

Schiffer, Irvine (1973) *Charisma: A Psychoanalytic Look at Mass Society.* Toronto and Buffalo: University of Toronto Press. Reprinted (1974) New York: The Free Press.

Schwarzfuchs, Simon (1974) *Napoleon, the Jews, and the Sanhedrin.* London, Boston and Henley-on-Thames: Routledge & Kegan Paul. Reprinted (1979) London: The Littman Library of Jewish Civilization.

——— (1989) *Du Juif à l'Israélite: histoire d'une mutation, 1770–1870.* Paris: Librairie Arthème Fayard. [French].

Ségur, Paul-Philippe de (1895) *An Aide-de-Camp of Napoleon: Memoirs of General Count de Ségur of the French Academy ...* Tr. H. A. Patchett-Martin. London: Hutchinson. New York: David Appleton & Co.

Shaw, Clement (1928) *Letizia Bonaparte (Madame Mère).* London: G. Howe. New York: Vikingh Press.

Sokoloff, Boris Fyodorovich (1937) *Napoleon: A Doctor's Biography.* New York: Prentice-Hall. Reprinted (1938) as *Napoleon: A Medical Approach.* London: Selwyn & Blount.

Steinberg, Blema S. (1996) *Shame and Humiliation: Presidential Decision Making on Vietnam.* Montreal: McGill-Queen's University Press. Pittsburgh: University of Pittsburgh Press.

Stendhal [Marie-Henry Beyle] (1876) *Vie de Napoléon: fragments.* Intr. R. Colomb. Paris: Calmann-Lévy. Reprinted (1929) in Stendhal (1913–1934) *Oeuvres complètes de Stendhal, publiées sous la direction d'Edouard Champion.* Eds. Paul Arbelet & Édouard Champion. Seventy- five volums. Paris: H. & E. Champion. Reprinted (1930) in Stendhal (1927–36) *Oeuvres complètes.* Thirty-two volumes. Paris : le Divan. Reprinted (1998) in Stendhal, *Napoléon.* Ed. Catherine Mariette. Paris: Stock. [French].

Stendhal [Marie-Henry Beyle] (1956) *A Life of Napoleon.* Intr. R. Gant. London: The Rodale Press. Reprinted (1977) New York: H. Fertig.

Stirling, Monica (1961) *A Pride of Lions: A Portrait of Napoleon's Mother, Letizia Bonaparte.* London: William Collins Publications. Reprinted (1962) as *Madame Letizia: A Portrait of Napoleon's Mother.* New York: Harper & Row.

Tangney, June Price & Dearing, Rhonda L. (2002) *Shame and Guilt.* New York: Guilford Press.

Tascher, Charles-Marie-Maurice de (1932) *Notes de campagne. Maurice de Tascher, sous-lieutenant au 8e régiment de hussards, puis capitaine au 12e régiment de chasseurs, mort à l'âge de vingt-sept ans, lors de la retraite de Moscou (1806–1813).* Eds. Ferdinand de Tascher & Robert Balsan. Châteauroux:

Société d'imprimerie, d'édition et de journaux du Berry. New edition (1933) Le *journal de campagne d'un cousin de l'Impératrice (1806–1813)*. Avertissement du Comte Ferdinand de Tascher. Paris: Librairie Plon. [French].

Teneo, Martial (2000) Napoleon as an Operatic Dictator. *Member's Bulletin of the Napoleonic Society of America*, No. 67, Winter/Spring, pp. 35-36.

Thiébault, Paul-Charles-François-Adrien-Henri-Dieudonné (1896) *The Memoirs of Baron Thiébault (Late Lieutenant-General in the French Army)*. Two volumes. Tr. and condensed by Arthur John Butler. London: Smith, Elder & Co. New York: The Macmillan Co. Reprinted (1994) Felling, Tyne and Wear, England: Worley Publications.

Thiry, Jean (1935-1948) *Napoléon Bonaparte*. Twenty-eight volumes. Tournai & Paris: Casterman. New edition (1975-1976) Paris: Éditions Berger-Levrault. [French].

Tomiche-Dagher, Nada (1952) *Napoléon écrivain*. Paris: Armand Colin. [French].

Tschudi, Clara (1900) *Napoleon's Mother*. Tr. E. M. Cope. London: Svan Sonnenschein & Co.

Tulard, Jean (1971) *Bibliographie critique des mémoires sur le Consulat et l'Empire, écrits ou traduits en français*. Geneva: Librairie E. Droz. [French].

——— (1987) *Napoléon, ou le mythe du sauveur*. Nouvelle édition, revue et complétée, avec une chronologie, une filmographie et des tableaux annexes. Paris: Librairie Arthème Fayard. [French].

——— (1989) *Dictionnaire Napoléon, publié avec le concours du Centre national des Lettres: Nouvelle édition, revue et augmentée*. Paris: Librairie Arthème Fayard. New edition (2000) Two volumes. Paris: Librairie Arthème Fayard. [French].

——— (1999) *Le 18 brumaire: comment terminer une révolution*. Paris: Perrin. [French].

Turquan, Joseph (1909) *The Love Affairs of Napoleon*. Tr. James Lewis May. London: John Lane. Reprinted (1914) London: John Lane.

——— (1912) *The Wife of General Bonaparte*. Tr. Violette Montagu. London: John Lane.

Usher, Rod (2000) Ivan the Ill. *Time Europe*, vol. 155, no. 7, February 21, pp. 64–65.

Valynseele, Joseph (1954) Le *Sang des Bonaparte: Avec une préface de Raoul de Warren et une étude sur l'héraldique napoléonienne, par Hervé Pinoteau*. Paris: Joseph Valynseele [French].

Vandal, Albert (1891–96) *Napoléon et Alexandre Ier: l'alliance russe sous le premier Empire*. Three volumes. Paris: Plon, Nourrit et Cie. [French].

Vaublanc, Vincent-Marie Viénot de (1838) *Souvenirs, par le Comte de Vaublanc, ancien ministre de l'Intérieur*. Two volumes. Paris: F. Ponce Lebas. [French].

Versini, Xavier (1977) *M. de Buonaparte ou le Livre inachevé*. Paris: Albatros. [French].

Volkan, Vamık D. (1981) *Linking Objects and Linking Phenomena: A Study of the Forms, Symptoms, Metapsychology, and Therapy of Complicated Mourning*. New York: International Universities Press.

Volkan, Vamık D. & Zintl, Elizabeth (1993) *Life After Loss: The Lessons of Grief.* New York: Charles Scribner's Sons. New edition (1994) New York: Maxwell Macmillan Collier Books.

Voltaire, François-Marie Arouet de (1758) *Le Huron, ou l'Ingénu ... par M. de V***.* Lausanne: The Author. New edition (1767) Paris: Lacombe. Reprinted in all editions of Voltaire's complete works.

——— (1759) *Candide, ou l'optimisme, traduit de l'allemand par Mr. Le Docteur Ralph.* Paris. Reprinted in Voltaire, François-Marie Arouet de (1785-1789) *Oeuvres completes de Voltaire.* Seventy volumes. Kehl: Imprimerie de la Société littéraire-typographique. New edition (1995) *Candide.* Ed. & Intr. Sylviane Léoni. Paris: Hachette, Librairie générale française, Le Livre de Poche. [French].

Wairy, Louis-Constant (1895) *Memoirs of Constant, First Valet de Chambre of the Emperor, on the Private Life of Napoleon, His Family and His Court.* Four volumes. Tr. Elizabeth Gilbert Martin. Pref. Imbert de Saint-Amand. New York: Charles Scribner's Sons. New edition (1992) in *Napoleon: An Intimate Account of the Years of Supremacy, 1800–1814.* Intr. Jean Tulard. Ed. Proctor P. Jones. San Francisco: Proctor Jones Publishing Co.

Waldburg-Truchsess, Friedrich Ludwig von (1816) *A Narrative of Napoleon Bonaparte's Journey from Fontainebleau to Fréjus in April 1814.* London: John Murray.

Wallach, Janet (2003) *Seraglio.* New York: Nan A. Talese.

Warden, William (1816) *Letters written on Board His Majesty's Ship, the Northumberland, and at Saint Helena, in which the conduct and conversations of Napoleon Buonaparte and his Suite, during the voyage, and the first months of his residence in that Island are faithfully ... related.* London: R. Ackermann.

Warens, Françoise-Louise-Éléonore de La Tour de (1786) *Mémoires de Madame de Warens, suivis de ceux de Claude Anet, publiés par un C. D. M. D. P. pour servir d'apologie aux Confessions de J.-J. Rousseau.* Chambéry. [French].

Weber, Max (1947) *The Theory of Social and Economic Organization*, Being Part I of *Wirtschaft und Gesellschaft.* Tr. A. M. Henderson and Talcott Parsons. Ed. & Intr. Talcott Parsons. London: W. Hodge. New York: Oxford University Press. New edition (1957) Glencoe, Illinois: The Free Press.

Weider, Ben (1998) Napoleon and the Jews. *Napoleon: His Life, His Wars, His World*, no. 12, July, pp. 34-39. Revised version (1998) in *Napoleonic Scholarship*, vol. 1, no. 2, December, pp. 41-45. Reprinted (1999) in *The Consortium on Revolutionary Europe: Proceedings 1998.* Tallahassee, Florida: Florida State University Press.

Weider, Ben & Forshufvud, Sten (1995) *Assassination at St. Helena Revisited.* Forewords by David G. Chandler and David C. Hamilton-Williams. New York: John Wiley & Sons.

Weymer, Marguerite-Josephine (1909) *A Favourite of Napoleon: Memoirs of Mademoiselle George.* Edited, from the original manuscript, by P. Cheramy.

London: Eveleigh Nash. New York: The John McBride Co.
Whately, Richard (1819) *Historic Doubts Relative to Napoleon Buonaparte*. London: Printed at Oxford. New edition (1985) Edited and with a critical introduction by Ralph S. Pomeroy. Berkeley, California: Scholar Press.
Wheeler, Thomas Gerald (1974) *Who Lies Here? A New Inquiry into Napoleon's Last Years*. New York: G. P. Putnam's Sons.
Whitworth, Charles & al. (1887) *England and Napoleon in 1803; Being the Despatches of Lord Whitworth and Others, Now First Printed from the Originals in the Record Office*. Edited for the Royal Historical Society by Oscar Browning London: Longmans, Green & Co.
Wilson, Robert McNair (1933) *Napoleon's Mother*. London: Eyre & Spottiswoode. Philadelphia: J. B. Lippincott.
——— (1934) *The Mind of Napoleon: A Study of Napoleon, Mr. Roosevelt, and the Money Power*. London: Routledge.
Wilson, Robert Thomas (1802) *History of the British Expedition to Egypt; to which is subjoined, a sketch of the present state of that country and its means of defence*. Illustrated by Ralph Abercromby. London: C. Roworth and T. Egerton. Reprinted (1803) Philadelphia: Conrad & Co.
Wolseley, Garnet Joseph (1895) *The Decline and Fall of Napoleon*. With Plans and Illustrations. London: Pall Mall Magazine Library. Reprinted (1895) Boston: Roberts Brothers.
Wurmser, Leon (1981) *The Mask of Shame*. Baltimore: Johns Hopkins University Press.
——— (1987) Shame, the Veiled Companion of Narcissism. In Nathanson, Donald L. (Ed.) *The Many Faces of Shame*, pp. 64–92. New York: Guilford Press.
Young, Norwood (1910) *The Growth of Napoleon: A Study in Environment*. London: John Murray.
Yvan, Napoléon-Alexandre (Ed.) (1846) *Le docteur Alexandre-Urbain Yvan*. Paris. [French].

Index

About the Author

Avner Falk is an internationally known scholar in the fields of psychohistory, psychobiography, and political psychology. He holds a Ph.D. in Clinical Psychology from Washington University, served in the Israel Defense Forces as a Mental Health Officer, and was appointed Clinical Lecturer in Psychiatry at the Hebrew University Medical School. He has been an independent scholar in applied psychoanalysis since 1983. His previous books include *Herzl, King of the Jews: A Psychoanalytic Biography of Theodor Herzl*, *A Psychoanalytic History of the Jews*, and *Fratricide in the Holy Land: A Psychoanalytic View of the Arab-Israeli Conflict.*